Culture, Courtiers, and Competition

The Ming Court (1368–1644)

———

Harvard East Asian Monographs 301

The Harvard University Asia Center gratefully acknowledges a generous grant from the James P. Geiss Foundation of Princeton, NJ, to subsidize publication of this work. The James P. Geiss Foundation was established in honor of the late James P. Geiss (1950–2000) and sponsors research on the Ming dynasty.

Culture, Courtiers, and Competition

The Ming Court (1368–1644)

Edited by David M. Robinson

Published by the Harvard University Asia Center and
Distributed by Harvard University Press
Cambridge (Massachusetts) and London 2008

Printed in the United States of America

The Harvard University Asia Center publishes a monograph series and, in coordination with the Fairbank Center for East Asian Research, the Korea Institute, the Reischauer Institute of Japanese Studies, and other faculties and institutes, administers research projects designed to further scholarly understanding of China, Japan, Vietnam, Korea, and other Asian countries. The Center also sponsors projects addressing multidisciplinary and regional issues in Asia.

Library of Congress Cataloging-in-Publication Data

Culture, courtiers, and competition : the Ming court (1368–1644) / edited by David M. Robinson.

    p. cm. -- (Harvard East Asian monographs ; 301)

   Includes index.

   ISBN-13: 978-0-674-02823-4 (cl : alk. paper)

   1. China--Court and courtiers. I. Robinson, David M., 1965– II. Title: Ming court (1368–1644).

DS753.2.C85 2008

951'.026--dc22

2008009022

Index by Eileen M. Doherty-Sil

♾ Printed on acid-free paper

Last figure below indicates year of this printing

17 16 15 14 13 12 11 10 09 08

Acknowledgments

The essays in this volume were first presented at the Ming Court Culture conference, held at Princeton University on June 12–13, 2003. The topic of the conference was inspired by the work of the late James P. Geiss, whose meticulous, often revisionist, scholarship set daunting standards in the field and whose keen interest in court politics, material culture, and personal dynamics is reflected in many of the essays collected here. In addition to the studies included in this volume, Ellen Soullière presented a paper on Ming imperial women and literacy; John Wills shared his work on the place of foreign envoys at the Ming court; Peter Ditmanson discussed the place of Confucian ideologues at the court of the Ming founder; and Nicholas Standaert prepared an essay on ritual dances and their visual representations at the Ming and Qing courts.[1] These papers and the observations offered by their authors contributed significantly to our understanding of the Ming court.

It is a pleasure to acknowledge our collective debt to those who made the conference such a stimulating experience and to those who contributed so much to the completion of the conference proceedings. The East Asian Studies Program at Princeton University and the James P. Geiss Foundation provided generous financial support. We are much indebted to the program's Martin Collcutt, Richard Chafey, and Hue Su for their unflagging help with logistics and the Geiss Foundation's Margaret Hsu for her

---

1. The paper titles are as follows: Ellen Soullière, "How to Be a Woman: Imperially Sponsored Chinese Texts of the 14th to 16th Centuries"; Nicolas Standaert, "Ritual Dances and Their Visual Representations in Ming and Qing," which appeared in *The East Asian Library Journal* 12, no. 1 (Spring 2006) under the same title; John Wills, "Foreign Tributaries at the Ming Court"; and Peter Ditmanson, "Shifting Moral Politics at the Hongwu Court (1368–98)."

enthusiasm and sense of purpose. A generous subvention from the Geiss Foundation made possible this volume's publication. Professors Susan Naquin, Evelyn Rawski, Thomas Nimick, Benjamin Elman, and Willard Peterson graciously agreed to serve as commentators. Their perspectives, informed by deep knowledge of both the Ming and the succeeding Qing dynasties, provided stimulating points of comparison. I would also like to express gratitude to others in attendance at the conference who offered insightful comments and suggestions about specific papers and the larger issues that emerged from them, especially Cary Liu, Wen Fang, Marsha Haufler, and Martin Hcijdra.

DMR

Contents

Figures

Ming Emperors

Hongwu 洪武 emperor
Zhu Yuanzhang 朱元璋 (r. 1368–98, temple name Taizu 太祖)

Jianwen 建文 emperor
Zhu Yunwen 朱允炆 (r. 1399–1402, temple name Huidi 惠帝)

Yongle 永樂 emperor
Zhu Di 朱棣 (r. 1403–24, temple names Chengzu 成祖, Taizong 太宗)

Hongxi 洪熙 emperor
Zhu Gaochi 朱高熾 (r. 1425, temple name Renzong 仁宗)

Xuande 宣德 emperor
Zhu Zhanji 朱瞻基 (r. 1426–35, temple name Xuanzong 宣宗)

Zhengtong 正統 emperor (also reigns as Tianshun 天順 emperor)
Zhu Qichen 朱祁鎮 (r. 1436–49, 1457–64, temple name Yingzong 英宗)

Jingtai 景泰 emperor
Zhu Qiyu 朱祁鈺 (r. 1450–56, temple names Daizong 代宗 and
　　Jingdi 景帝)

Chenghua 成化 emperor
Zhu Jianshen 朱見深 (r. 1465–87, temple name Xianzong 憲宗)

Hongzhi 弘治 emperor
Zhu Youcheng 朱祐樘 (r. 1488–1505, temple name Xiaozong 孝宗)

Zhengde 正德 emperor
Zhu Houzhao 朱厚照 (r. 1506–21, temple name Wuzong 武宗)

Jiajing 嘉靖 emperor
Zhu Houcong 朱厚熜 (r. 1522–66, temple name Shizong 世宗)

Longqing 隆慶 emperor
Zhu Zaihou 朱載垕 (r. 1567–72, temple name Muzong 穆宗)

Wanli 萬曆 emperor
Zhu Yijun 朱翊鈞 (r. 1573–1620, temple name Shenzong 神宗)

Taichang 泰昌 emperor
Zhu Changluo 朱常洛 (r. 1620, temple name Guangzong 光宗)

Tianqi 天啟 emperor
Zhu Youjiao 朱由校 (r. 1621–27, temple name Xizong 熹宗)

Chongzhen 崇禎 emperor
Zhu Youjian 朱由檢 (r. 1628–44, temple name Sizong 思宗)

Culture, Courtiers, and Competition

The Ming Court (1368–1644)

Introduction

David M. Robinson

Drawing from a variety of disciplines and incorporating a wide range of Chinese documentary sources, material artifacts, and contemporaneous foreign accounts, the chapters in this volume offer a multifaceted portrait of the Ming dynasty court (1368–1644). They demonstrate that the court was an arena of competition and negotiation. In this arena, a large cast of actors pursued individual and corporate ends, personal agency deeply shaped protocol and style, and people, goods, and tastes from all corners of the empire (and beyond) converged. Rather than a monolithic and immutable set of traditions, Ming court culture underwent frequent reinterpretation and rearticulation, processes often driven by immediate and keenly felt personal imperatives, mediated through social, political, and cultural interaction, and producing sometimes unexpected results.

The chapters in this volume address several common themes. First, they contribute to recent scholarship that rethinks previous notions about imperial isolation; instead, they stress the court's myriad ties both to local Beijing society and to the empire as a whole. Forms of interaction examined here include personnel, religious patronage, material objects, musical tastes, and the flow of information. Second, the contributors reveal the court as an arena of competing interests and perspectives. Palace women, Tibetan monks, imperial craftsmen, court painters, Confucian educators, moralists, Mongol warriors, palace eunuchs, foreign envoys, musical performers, and others all strove to advance their interests and forge advantageous relations with the emperor himself and among themselves. The court was far from monolithic or static.

Finally, the case studies in this volume illustrate the importance of individual agency. In the evocative classic, *1587, A Year of No Significance*, Ray Huang offered a vision of the Ming court, indeed the entire Ming government, as largely in thrall to the founding emperor, Hongwu (1328–98, r. 1368–98). A prolific writer, the founder penned scores of admonitions, demanding that his descendents and their courts follow his will in everything from hair ornaments, styles of gowns, and the frequency of audiences with officials to diplomatic relations with neighboring countries, the role of eunuchs in the palace, and investiture titles for imperial clansmen. More recent scholarship has done much to illumine the adaptability of local and central governments to shifting social and economic conditions during the Ming period.[1] The chapters in this volume show that the founder's legacy may have formed the warp in the dense tapestry of Ming court practices and tastes, but the weft varied considerably according to the specific personalities, ambitions, and circumstances of each reign.

Hongwu and his descendents enjoyed greater wealth than perhaps any previous imperial family.[2] For the most part managed by palace eunuch bureaus, imperial workshops at their height employed approximately 15,000 men. These craftsmen produced a stunning variety of goods, from exquisitely wrought armor, finely woven brocade textiles, and jewel-encrusted golden headpieces for court women to ivory paperweights, scissors, paper, and fans used in the palaces.[3] The holdings of art collections around the world today testify further to the enormous concentration of wealth and talent available to the Ming court.

To circumvent the limitations of written accounts, which are so often infused with the perspectives and interests of the literati, many of the contributors to this volume turned to such material objects as imperial portraits, picturebook illustrations, books, funerary statues, religious objects, and clothing. These material objects lend insight into artistic exchanges,

---

1. Heijdra, "The Socio-economic Development of Rural China During the Ming." On the increasing autonomy of local administration, see Brook, *Confusions of Pleasure*, pp. 89–93. For discussion of informal changes in personnel administration at the central government, see Nimick, "The Placement of Local Magistrates in Ming China."

2. See the chapter by Scarlett Jang in this volume, pp. 116–85. One scholar estimates that the court's budget was approximately one million ounces of silver late in the fifteenth century and about six million during the late sixteenth century; see He Benfang, "Mingdai gongzhong caizheng shulüe," p. 77. He provides an overview of the Ming court's expenditures and sources of revenue.

3. Wang Yuquan et al., *Zhongguo jingji tongshi*, pp. 418–23. For examples of jewelry excavated in Nanjing, see Nanjingshi bowuguan, *Mingchao shoushi guanfu*.

the growing importance of visual culture, and imperial self-perceptions at the Ming court. Not directly subject to the political and cultural agendas of civil officials and literati historians, these material objects offer valuable alternatives to the written record.

Even discarded objects tell a tale of how the desire for court goods and market demand undermined state efforts to regulate sociopolitical status. During the fifteenth century, porcelains manufactured at Jingdezhen for imperial use that fell short of its strict standards were intentionally broken and buried to prevent their use outside the Forbidden City.[4] An early seventeenth-century guidebook to Beijing, however, shows that by late in the dynasty such efforts were not completely successful. In a discussion of items for sale in the City God Market of the capital, the editors of the guidebook note: "Today that which [people] compete to purchase on the market are usually things that were at the time not adopted for imperial use. There are dragon patterns with five talons [an exclusive prerogative of the imperial family]. [In order that] they did not fall into use among the people, sometimes one talon was effaced and then [the item was] sold."[5]

As the preceding anecdote shows, examination of the Ming court raises wider questions about late imperial (or early modern) China, such as the production, transmission, consumption, and perception of culture. To some, the phrase "court culture" suggests a set of cultural practices unique to the court. Studies of the sixteenth-century English Stuart court, for example, are sometimes framed in terms of a "court-country dichotomy," highlighting the contrast between cultural values of a privileged, isolated few at the court and the more broadly held views of the country as a whole.[6] A variation of this binary vision is to posit the court as the principal site of cultural production, from whence patterns and objects of cultural consumption diffuse through the rest of society. This view often stresses a unilateral flow of influence; court culture influenced a wider swath of subordinate territory yet retained its distinctiveness. More recently, scholars working in a variety of periods and cultures have downplayed courtly isolation and stressed the interplay of the court and wider spheres of tastes, materials, and personnel. Most authors in this volume

---

4. See the catalogue compiled by the Jingdezhen Institute of Ceramic Archeology and the Tsui Museum of Art, *A Legacy of Chenghua*.

5. See Liu Tong and Yu Yizheng, *Dijing jingwu lüe*, *juan* 4, "Chenghuang miao shi" 城隍廟市, p. 164.

6. For a critique of such scholarship, see Smuts, *Court Culture and the Origins of a Royalist Tradition*, pp. 2–5.

adopt this position, arguing against the court's isolation and documenting its myriad ties to the rest of the empire. Although such an interpretive framework better captures the shifting, negotiated, and multivalent dimensions of cultural production, it does beg the question what, if anything, should be considered court culture, that is, something readily distinguishable from culture writ large.

The authors in this volume offer a number of answers to this question. All note that the Ming court was embedded in larger social, intellectual, cultural, and economic structures, that people, goods, and tastes flowed in and out of the court, and that the court commanded enormous prestige and wealth readily acknowledged by those beyond the court. However, the contributors reach divergent conclusions on the degree of friction involved in these interactions. Scarlett Jang in her discussion of palace eunuch publishing and Julia K. Murray in her chapter on the compilation of educational picturebooks intended for the heir apparent and young emperors see a high degree of consonance between the court and wider developments in Ming culture. Their studies indicate that the court and educated men shared many fundamental attitudes regarding the importance of the written word, the didactic function of the Confucian canon, the critical role of education and its ties to political power, and even particular aesthetic preferences in book production such as layout and illustrations.

Despite this considerable common ground, the court and the literati disagreed over who was to dictate the terms of interaction. The emperor and his close attendants rejected various literati efforts to determine who could produce what kinds of books for the throne; the emperor resisted literati attempts to exceed well-established precedents regarding their role as imperial educators. Yet even these tensions reflect common assumptions; both sides contested these issues because they considered them important. In his study of the Jiajing emperor's (r. 1522–66) relations with officials who presented lectures on the classical texts and thought, Hung-lam Chu draws a similar conclusion. Both emperor and lecturers took for granted that intense study of the Confucian classics was essential for the ruler's morality and ability to govern wisely. The central tension arose over who was to dictate the terms of study and who was to play the role of educator.

If most chapters in this volume suggest considerable congruence between court culture and the beliefs and attitudes held by educated society, the chapters by Dora C. Y. Ching and David M. Robinson throw into relief dissonant elements of court culture such as Tibetan Buddhist rituals, artifacts, and personnel or imagery drawn from Mongol models of rulership. The imperial harem, eunuch and military personnel, and formal interactions with foreign envoys also distinguished the court from the rest of society. Literati cast these facets of court culture as alien (in the case of Tibetan or Mongol influence) or inimical to proper order (for instance, overly powerful imperial females, affines, or military men).

Although such a characterization might seem to confirm a court-society dichotomy, scattered documentary evidence dissolves any absolute bifurcation. Small statues of Tibetan Buddhist deities were sold in Beijing's markets; Mongolian fur hats and Korean silk gowns enjoyed popularity in the capital; interest in martial arts and military exploits was widespread and sustained. Thus, although Ming court culture was distinctive, it was neither isolated nor without points of resonance with the broader society. The same characterization holds true for the Ming court's relation with other courts in the world.

Most chapters in this collection hew closely to the particulars of late imperial / early modern China; however, the Ming court can also be understood in a wider comparative context. Wherever they existed, most princely, royal, and imperial courts articulated and sought to impose visions of order. This order often began with efforts to ensure proper relations and attitudes among those physically present at the court. Acknowledging the centrality of personnel, Jonathan Shepard has defined a court as "an entourage of notables revolving around an overlord, of variegated and fluctuating composition but observing ritual deference towards him."[7] Sometimes powerful magnates or aristocrats, who commanded nearly equal (or occasionally superior) political, ritual, or military resources, constituted the principal members of the court. In other cases, court members depended on ties to the chieftain, prince, king, or emperor for their livelihoods or privileged status in the greater polity or community. Ambitious courts attempted to order these various groups through titles, offices, clothing, access to the ruler, and participation in ritual and spectacle.[8]

---

7. See Shepard, "Courts in East and West," p. 14.

8. On the use of courts, ranks, and titles to transform an aristocratic elite to one defined through its relation to the imperial government during the seventh to tenth centuries, see Peter Bol, *"This Culture of Ours,"* pp. 32–75 and the scholarship cited therein. On similar efforts, often inspired by Chinese models, in classical Japan, see Piggott, *The Emergence of Japanese Kingship.* The consequences of these reforms differed dramatically. The use of court ranks, ceremony, and etiquette to tame competing elites was, of course, not unique to China. For a slightly dated but still influential study based on the

The great courts of the world often understood the proper regulation of the imperial family, notables, officials, warriors, and others at the court as one facet of an overarching order. Members of the court and those scholars and thinkers who articulated this more expansive order commonly integrated the realm of human action and morality into larger cosmic processes. Social hierarchies on earth reflected, represented, or derived from hierarchies inherent in the natural world. Rulers, in an effort to consolidate their power and legitimacy, also attempted to conflate the human realm with that of the divine. Discussing developments in early modern Europe, John Adamson has noted a trend "to express the elevated status of the prince in gestures and symbols that resemble, and were often derived from, religious liturgical practice." He cites examples from courts in Madrid and Portugal, which used the cult of Corpus Christi to draw parallels between the sacred person of the king and Christ.[9] In his *Akba-namah*, a "masterpiece of historiographical propaganda," Abu al-Fazl articulated a new conception of rulership for his lord, the Mughal sultan Akbar (1542–1605, r. 1556–1605), that similarly effaced any bifurcation between the sacred and the profane. "Kingship," he wrote, "is a refulgence from the Incomparable Distributor of justice . . . a ray from the sun, the illuminator of the universe and the receptacle of all virtues."[10] Akbar's promulgation of a solar calendar and his worship of the sun reflected this understanding of Akbar as "the maturation of the light of sovereignty."[11]

In all cases, the creation and maintenance of a court was an exercise in power, persuasion, and negotiation. In recent decades, historians of early modern Europe have done much to dismantle past notions of absolutist kings who tamed the aristocratic nobility and enjoyed unchallenged authority at their courts. "Rather than being a centralized institution in which power 'radiated' from the person of the prince," Adamson writes of the court, "influence and, in some cases, formal authority as well, emanated from a variety of subsidiary sources: entrenched office-holders, noble magnates, senior prelates, major army commanders, not to mention the

---

particulars of the reign of Louis XIV, see Elias, *The Court Society*. In the case of China, the court also claimed the right to decide the ranks and titles of gods and spirits, which in turn decided the kinds of sacrifices to which they were entitled. For the example of Confucius, see Wilson, "Sacrifices and the Imperial Cult of Confucius." Wilson's essay also includes citations to other cults and the ranks of their tutelary spirits.

9. Adamson, "The Making of the *Ancien-Régime* Court, 1500–1700," p. 28.

10. Cited in Streusand, *The Formation of the Mughal Empire*, p. 130.

11. Ibid., pp. 132–36; the quotation appears on p. 132.

satellite courts of the royal apanages."[12] No ruler could afford to assume that relatives, nobles, officials, the military, or the world at large would unquestioningly accept his view of the world.

Even in the most autocratic cases, the court often proved a corrosive environment. Although perhaps formally acknowledged in the abstract, rulers' power and status provided opportunities for negotiation or challenge whenever they took concrete form. Princes faced a variation of the "graying of politics" confronted by many twentieth-century socialist regimes. Once all elements of life are saturated with greater meaning, even such otherwise innocuous choices as clothing or music become powerful political statements. The preservation of an imperial vision of order required constant adjustment to shifting realities, negotiation with a variety of actors, and an occasional willingness to turn a blind eye to challenges too large or too small to permit effective resolution.

The Chapters

David Robinson and Dora Ching recast the Ming court by considering it in the wider context of Eurasia. Viewing the Ming dynasty as a successor-state to the Mongol empire, Robinson traces the Ming imperial family's engagement with Mongol rulers, most especially Khubilai (1215–94), the founder of the Great Yuan Nation. This facet of Ming imperial identity violated the ethos and interests of many literati officials, who, as compilers of most extant documentary records, glossed over this strand of imperial rulership. In addition to reconsidering contemporary state chronicles and private writings in the context of post–Mongol empire Eurasia, Robinson draws on materials beyond the control of literati officials. These include imperial portraits that represent Ming emperors as Mongol *khaghan*s (khan of khans), often on the hunt or on horseback beyond the walls of the imperial palace; imperially produced porcelains and religious statues that reflect the Ming imperial family's ongoing engagement with Tibetan Buddhism; and funerary figures dressed in Mongolian garb excavated from princely tombs. In doing so, Robinson decenters the literati and offers a more complex and cosmopolitan picture of the Ming court. Finally, he shows that this association with Khubilai, like most other elements of court culture, was subject to transformation and re-evaluation. He identifies the accession of the Jiajing emperor in the 1520s as a turning point in

---

12. Adamson, "The Making of the *Ancien-Régime* Court, 1500–1700," p. 17.

the identity of the Ming imperial family. Raised far from the Ming court and its complex body of customs and protocols, Jiajing was an outsider less wedded to court traditions, who felt freer to challenge the literati and eunuch bureaucracies and to change established court ritual, practice, and culture.

Ching, too, combines documentary and material evidence to rethink the Ming court by exploring a dramatic transformation in imperial portraiture. To explain the change from a more three-dimensional and naturalistic rendering of the early Ming emperors to a pose of rigid frontality and iconic representation by late in the fifteenth century, Ching turns to the Ming court's engagement with Tibetan religious figures. Motivated by both political and religious goals, early in the fifteenth century, the third Ming emperor, Yongle (r. 1403–24), greatly increased exchanges between his court and Tibetan Buddhist hierarchs, resulting in a steady stream of gifts, religious objects, and personnel from Tibet to the Chinese court. Through a detailed analysis of style, composition, and medium, Ching argues that during the mid- and late fifteenth century, Tibetan Buddhist traditions of representing religious figures as icons influenced Ming imperial portraiture. The result was the "icon of rulership," which became the standard imperial portraiture for the remainder of the dynasty. In addition to reviewing the ritual uses of imperial portraiture, Ching also traces the divergent ways different Ming emperors interacted with court painters and artisans. Like several other essays in this volume, Ching's chapter illustrates the importance of contingency, exchange, and interaction in the formation and evolution of culture at the Ming court. Ching's analysis of imperial portraiture also makes clear that the Ming court existed in a wider Eurasian context.

Scarlett Jang and Joseph S. C. Lam investigate two important institutions that spanned the course of the Ming dynasty. Jang's exploration of the structure and function of inner court publishing activities shows the importance of eunuchs, another critical but poorly understood group at the Ming court, even in areas usually more associated with scholar-officials. The inner court produced exquisitely crafted books on a surprisingly broad range of subjects: Confucian classics such as the *Analects*, *Mencius*, and famous twelfth-century thinker and educator Zhu Xi's commentaries on the *Four Books*; moral primers by empresses on proper behavior for imperial women; works on mathematics, medicine, and geography; even vernacular novels such as *The Romance of the Three Kingdoms*. Ming emperors composed the largest number of titles produced by the inner court press. In these imperially sponsored works, emperors instructed family members on rulership, the proper place of affines, and the correct role of civil officials. Many of the eunuchs who oversaw the production and storage of books at the Depository of Chinese Classics, the Depository of Buddhist Sutras, and the Depository of Daoist Texts and Scriptures were graduates of the dynasty's eunuch academy, which at any one time might enroll as many as a thousand eunuch students.

Jang provides a powerful corrective to common characterizations of eunuchs as ill-educated, venal men who lacked legitimacy within the imperial system. Elite palace eunuchs received a well-rounded education in the classics, history, administrative precedents, and calligraphy. She shows that eunuchs figured in the education of the emperor, the crown prince, and palace women. They also produced such important works as compilations of administrative precedents, compendiums of rites, and even the dynastic calendar.

Joseph Lam's essay highlights the interactions of patrons, audiences, and performers in the evolution of musical culture at the Ming court. Music and religion at the court drew deeply on local traditions beyond the walls of the Imperial City. Civil bureaucrats, eunuchs, and networks of religious patronage brought renowned musicians from around the empire to the court. Once employed at the court, these master performers joined the emperor and other patrons in a subtle process of instruction, accommodation, and elaboration.

Depending on the tastes and political needs of individual emperors, musical culture at the Ming court varied widely. Grand, relatively stable traditions of music for major state rituals, formal banquets, and annual celebrations drew heavily from Confucian theories and were housed in the eunuch-run State Sacrificial Music Office. This variety of music was, however, not static; emperors periodically ordered changes. Jiajing's wide-ranging changes in the mid-sixteenth century were directly tied to larger revisions of ceremony that hinged on the major political and ritual controversies of his court. Music was not just background noise. The emperor, the imperial family, eunuchs, and civil officials considered music an integral part of court life that had consequences for the health of the dynasty.

As Lam demonstrates, music at the Ming court also had a more personal dimension. Southern arias, northern melodies, Uighur songs, *qin* music, Kun operas, and *pipa* performances variously enjoyed times of popularity with the emperor and his intimates. Imperial women figured in the musical culture of the court both as performers and as patrons. As was true in the realm of religious patronage, court women (from the empress

and concubines to palace servants and entertainers) formed a key link between court tastes and practices and those beyond the palace walls.

The eunuchs' ubiquitous presence often challenged what scholar-
officials considered their proper role at the court and their relationship
with the emperor. Scholar-officials felt it their responsibility and their privilege to educate the Ming imperial family. As several contributors demonstrate, however, no one at the court took for granted the scholar-officials'
ability to monopolize the role of imperial educators. Through a detailed
study of the daily and classics-mat lectures, Hung-lam Chu evokes the
shifting relationship between the Jiajing emperor and his aspiring teachers.
Designed to deepen the ruler's understanding and appreciation of Confucian statecraft, the lectures were also intended to perfect the emperor's
morality. The emperor, however, dominated the sessions, often intimidating less experienced lecturers unnerved by close physical proximity to the
Son of Heaven. Lecturers who wished to gain the ear of the emperor in the
hope of influencing his views had to adapt to his tastes in delivery, intona-
tion, dress, and subject matter.

The emperor periodically turned the tables on his instructors, taking the
opportunity to lecture them on proper Confucian morality and correct rulership.[13] As Scarlett Jang and Julia Murray (see below) note, during the first
century of the dynasty, Ming emperors compiled guides for the proper behavior of both imperial family members and officials. In doing so, the emperor was acting as teacher. Thus, Jiajing's actions formed part of an on-
again off-again family tradition. Eventually, the emperor lost interest in the
lectures and devoted his time to Daoist regimes for fertility and longevity.
As Chu notes, at least a few Confucian-minded scholars from the Hanlin
Academy were not above turning their literary skills to writing Daoist
prayers as a way to maintain some influence or favor with the emperor.
Chu argues that Confucian civil officials' inability to put aside personal
agendas and to present a united front to the errant Jiajing ultimately ended
their influence over the ruler's behavior and thought.

Julia Murray, too, examines efforts to shape rulers and their successors
through education. Through a finely textured study of picture books compiled as educational texts for various heirs apparent and one emperor,

---

13. One might understand the numerous collections on rulership compiled by order
of the emperor as reminders to civil officials of who was actually in charge. For an early
and somewhat flawed catalogue of many of these titles and the dates of their compilation, see Li Jinhua, *Mingdai chizhuanshu kao.*

Murray explores the complex interplay of competing agendas, publishing markets, and visual culture. As she notes, during the first seventy years of the dynasty at least four emperors issued instructions for future rulers and members of the imperial family. Murray shows that during the late fifteenth and early sixteenth centuries when civil officials turned their hands to the task, the reception was generally cool. One Nanjing official whose duties had nothing to do with the education of the crown prince submitted a lavishly executed picturebook with more than 100 illustrations of moral exemplars. Fellow bureaucrats assumed that his motivation was to secure a post at the court in Beijing. The emperor rejected out of hand a second and simpler album as slanderous and inappropriate. Emperors did not lightly grant civil officials the opportunity to shape crown princes.

In 1572, the domineering prime minister Zhang Juzheng 張居正 (1525–82) succeeded where others had failed. Consisting of 117 exemplary and cautionary tales in two volumes, the *Emperor's Mirror, Illustrated and Discussed* (*Dijian tushuo* 帝鑒圖説; compiled at Zhang's behest) was immediately incorporated into the education of the nine-year-old Wanli (r. 1573–1620) emperor. Zhang circulated a smaller woodblock version of the same title to capital officials. As Murray observes, Zhang thereby assumed the role of earlier rulers who had educated the imperial family and the bureaucracy.

The considerable commercial success of the *Emperor's Mirror* and another later picturebook, *Cultivating Rectitude, Illustrated and Explained* (*Yangzheng tujie* 養正圖解), owed much to the appealing combination of pictures and stories, the entertainment value of historical figures (especially the depraved ones), and glimpses into the normally inaccessible world of the palace. Although an imperial tutor had rejected *Cultivating Rectitude*, a palace eunuch chanced on a deluxe printed version of the work in the southern metropolis of Nanjing and promptly recommended it to the throne. The episode neatly brings together personal ambition, publishing, the influence of eunuchs, and the Ming court's many ties to the rest of the empire.

Taken together, the studies by Robinson, Jang, Chu, and Murray suggest that the composition of the court challenged many scholar-officials' sense of identity. The need to reconcile deeply held beliefs about their proper role at the court with daily frustrations and compromises probably sharpened the rhetorical edge of scholar-officials' memorials and other writings. Neither the emperor nor the civil bureaucracy itself assumed that efforts to educate or influence the throne were selfless acts of pure-minded Confucians. This skepticism and constant competition from others at court (e.g., palace eunuchs, military men, palace women, religious figures, and fellow officials) encouraged officials to adopt a moralistic rhetoric. These more inclusive studies of the court offer a more accurate and nuanced understanding of the writings and self-perceptions of literati.

The battles between the Wanli emperor and his civil bureaucracy have often been seen as evidence of imperial intransigence that contributed to the dynasty's ultimate collapse.[14] Kenneth M. Swope offers a different perspective on this controversial emperor, exploring Wanli's response to a series of military crises during the sixteenth century. Rejecting previous characterizations of the Wanli as an apathetic ruler whose lack of attention to state matters precipitated dynastic decline, Swope argues that the emperor was keenly interested in the great military campaigns of the day. He shows that the emperor cultivated relations with leading military families in the empire, families that much of the civil bureaucracy considered dangerous and untrustworthy. In order to meet the challenges of a major military mutiny in the northwest, the large-scale Japanese invasions of Korea during the 1590s, and a stubborn rebellion in the southwest, the emperor overrode his bureaucracy's objections and directed these far-flung military campaigns to a successful conclusion.

Swope's work throws light on the continuing importance of the military at the Ming court and throughout the empire. Several scholars have commented on the resurgence of military concerns in China during the seventeenth century; some term it the militarization of Ming society. It is more accurate to say the military and the martial never disappeared from either the court or society in general.[15] Swope's case study also illustrates the need to understand emperors as individuals with agency. As a boy, Wanli had learned the importance of military affairs to the empire from his tutor, the powerful minister Zhang Juzheng. Although Wanli would later grow disillusioned with the memory of his intimidating tutor, he retained a deep interest in military preparedness and in the powerful military families that guarded his borders. Swope's revisionist perspective serves as a useful historiographical reminder about the dangers of generalizations based exclusively on the perspectives and concerns of the civil bureaucracy. Wanli's

---

14. Writing during the early decades of the twentieth century, the noted historian of the Ming and Qing dynasties, Meng Sen (*Mingdai shi*, p. 275), opined: "The decline of the Ming began after the Zhengde [1506–21] and Jiajing [1522–66] reigns. It became more severe with the Wanli court. Portents of the Ming's collapse were fixed, once the Wanli reign began."

15. In *Bandits, Eunuchs, and the Son of Heaven*, I make this point based on the particulars of the fifteenth and early sixteenth centuries.

alienation from the majority of his civil officials did not mean alienation from all officialdom. In the nomenclature of the Ming dynasty, military officers were no less "officials" (*guan* 官) than were their civil counterparts.

Remaining Questions

Given the size, complexity, and duration of the Ming court, this collection of essays makes no pretense of being comprehensive. The number of important questions, themes, perspectives, and materials not examined in this volume, of course, far outnumber those we do consider. In the spirit of *paozhuan yinyu* 抛磚引玉 (casting a brick and receiving a piece of jade), we hope that these studies will encourage others to deepen and broaden our understanding of the Ming court. Here I would like to note two larger questions that grow out of this collection of essays: princely courts and the place of the Ming court in a wider historical context.

The chapters in this volume focus mainly on the court in Beijing.[16] However, as several authors note, the Ming imperial family went to considerable lengths to preserve a strong sense of corporate identity and unity. After the first decades of the dynasty, princely courts were denied political and military control over the areas where they were invested.[17] In exchange, they enjoyed privileges that marked them off from the rest of the local population.[18] They received generous (at least during the early decades of the dynasty) subsidies.[19] Sumptuary laws permitted them to maintain princely palaces constructed of materials and in styles prohibited to the rest of the

---

16. The Nanjing court, both during the earliest decades of the dynasty and later, when it became a secondary capital, remains a promising topic of research. For a primarily political account, see Farmer, *Early Ming Government*.

17. Some aspired to more. For a discussion of the 1425 revolt by the Prince of Han, see Chan, "The Chien-wen, Yung-lo, Hung-hsi, and Hsüan-te Reigns," 7: 288–89. On the Prince of Anhua's 1510 revolt and the Prince of Ning's 1519 revolt, see Geiss, "The Cheng-te Reign," 7: 409–12, 423–30. For the imperial princes' changing role in the polity during the first three reigns of the dynasty, see Gu Cheng, "Mingdai de zongshi," pp. 89–95.

18. For discussion of the princes of Henan, see Des Forges, *Cultural Centrality and Political Change in Chinese History*, pp. 15–21.

19. Craig Clunas (*Superfluous Things*, p. 161) has noted that sixteenth-century western European visitors to China were struck by the wealth of the Ming provincial imperial aristocracy. However, such observations applied only to the upper ranks of provincial aristocracy. By the late sixteenth century, if not earlier, enormous discrepancies in income emerged within the ever-growing ranks of imperial clansmen; see Gu Cheng, "Mingdai de zongshi," pp. 103–7.

population. They maintained staffs of eunuchs, military honor guards, and administrative advisors denied to commoners. Imperial princes of the first rank were expected to visit the emperor annually. Government statutes enjoined princes to ensure that their processions to and from the capital were awe-inspiring sights that would impress officials and commoners.[20] If generationally senior to the emperor, princes might sit and receive bows from the Son of Heaven.[21] They also received from the Beijing court a wide range of gifts: exquisitely printed inner court books, finely woven silk textiles, intricately wrought jewelry of gold and silver, as well as valuable paintings, calligraphy, playbooks, and porcelains from the imperial collection.[22] When they died, members of princely families were dressed in clothing designated for the imperial family, buried in elaborate underground palaces complete with wooden or porcelain tomb figurines including honor guards and entertainers and gifts from the court in Beijing, and honored with ceremonial archways and stone tomb statuary.[23]

Thus, although the central node of the Ming court was in Beijing, the secondary court in Nanjing and princely establishments in the provinces meant that the greater court extended throughout much of the empire.[24] Material goods, ritual, protocol, personnel, and social markers tied together this extended court system. Certain imperially commissioned books on protocol and ceremony that circulated between the imperial family in Beijing and the princes seem to have been only dimly known to even the capital bureaucracy.[25] More research is needed on the links between the pro-

---

20. Shen Shixing, *Da Ming huidian* (hereafter cited as *DMHD*), 56.22a.

21. *DMHD*, 56.19a–21a.

22. For instance, wedding gifts made of silver were frequently produced by the Directorate of Ceremonial in Beijing; see Wang Jichao, "Mingdai qinwang zangzhi de jige wenti," p. 65. The flow of goods crafted in Beijing court workshops ensured at least a minimum of ritual and material consistency throughout the imperial family. On the perception that during the Hongwu reign (1368–98), imperial princes received the libretti for large numbers of plays from the court upon departing Beijing for their assigned feoffs, see Idema, "State and Court in China," p. 178*n*11.

23. For a brief description and black-and-white photographs of the princely archways and statuary, see Paludan, *The Chinese Spirit Road*, pp. 181–86.

24. Su Jinyu ("Henan fanfu jia tianxia," p. 41) estimates that Ming princes of various ranks were resident in "nearly a hundred" cities.

25. Huang Zhangjian, "Du *Huang Ming dian li*." Copies of the *Huang Ming dian li* 皇明典禮 did exist within the capital bureaucracy, but the fact that the emperor specially granted copies to the Grand Secretariat and the Ministry of Rites suggests that they were not common; see the memorial of gratitude from Zhu Geng, "Xie ci *Huang Ming dian li* jie."

vincial courts and the Beijing court as well as among princely establishments.[26] Recent archeological studies suggest considerable diversity in the construction materials and layout of princely mausoleums.[27] Evidence also indicates growing interaction between princely establishments and local cultural traditions.[28] The same might be said of the imperial court. In everything from accent and linguistic usage to a preference for noodles and open-oven baked breads, the court in Beijing was deeply shaped by the regional customs of North China.[29] Lam shows the interplay of local musical traditions with the princely courts. Princely courts often acted as important sources of cultural patronage.[30] Further work on princely establishments will no doubt force us to rethink our notions of the boundaries of the Ming court(s) and its engagement with Chinese society and culture as a whole.[31]

A second overarching question is the place of the Ming court in the larger span of late imperial / early modern history. When one considers the Ming court's ongoing engagement with Tibetan Buddhism, the legacy of the Mongol Yuan dynasty, and the incorporation of Mongols, Jurchens, Koreans, Tibetans, and others into the emperor's bodyguard and the ruling family's religious life, one begins to perceive important links with the preceding Yuan and succeeding Qing dynasties. For much of the postwar period, Chinese and Japanese scholars, whose interests often focused on

-----

26. The Beijing court was concerned that princely establishments might develop dangerously wide political and economic networks; see *DMHD*, 56.31a–b.

27. Dong Xinlin, "Mingdai zhuhou wanglingmu chubu yanjiu"; Wang Jichao, "Mingdai qinwang zangzhi de jige wenti." The most substantial account to date on Ming princely tombs is Liu Yi, *Mingdai diwang lingmu zhidu yanjiu*; see esp. pp. 153–325 for the considerable variation among princely tombs according to time and region.

28. The few extant records of food consumption at several princely courts suggest a measure of conformity during the early Ming; see Qiu Zhonglin, "Huangdi de canzhuo," p. 29.

29. On the "northernization" of imperial cuisine, see Qiu Zhonglin, "Huangdi de canzhuo." This northernization is reflected in the fact that by the late Ming, nearly 80 percent of palace eunuchs hailed from North China, most especially the Northern Metropolitan Area (Qiu Zhonglin, "Mingdai zigong qiuyong xianxiang zailun," p. 139).

30. For a preliminary study that stresses princely courts as sites of cultural production, largely in the literati tradition, see Su Derong, "Mingdai zongshi wenhua jiqi shehui yingxiang." Su's essay is intended as a partial rebuttal of Gu Cheng's characterization of Ming imperial clansmen as a "gargantuan parasitic group" ("Mingdai de zongshi," p. 89). Especially early in the dynasty, many imperial princes were important cultural figures; see Idema, *The Dramatic Oeuvre of Chu Yu-tun*.

31. I explore this question in my forthcoming *Ming Court in Eurasia*.

socioeconomic developments, tended to view the Ming and Qing as a single period that exhibited considerable continuity.[32] Over the past decade, landmark studies by such scholars as Mark Elliott, Pamela Crossley, Evelyn Rawski, Nicola di Cosmo, Patricia Berger, and others have significantly advanced our understanding of the Qing dynasty, clarifying many of its distinctively Manchu facets, often through contextualization in a larger Eurasian setting.[33] Their work has opened the way to a more nuanced and informed consideration of the court, ideologies of rulership, and relations with surrounding countries and peoples from the thirteenth to the early twentieth centuries.

The practices and tenor of the Ming court were deeply shaped by both previous Chinese dynasties and its immediate predecessor, the Mongol empire. Facile dismissals of the Ming court as recidivist, xenophobic, or reactionary clearly miss the depth of the court's engagement with such groups as the Mongols, Tibetans, and Koreans. One has the sneaking feeling that extensive historical rewriting commissioned by the Qing government has shaped our views of the Ming in ways that are still not fully appreciated. Qing rulers were quick to criticize the Ming and to distance themselves from what they labeled a flawed and fallen regime.[34] As several scholars have shown, the Qing court derived many of its institutional practices and ideological postures from the Great Yuan Nation.[35] The Qing also freely drew on Ming institutional practices. Knowing more about the

———

32. On the question of periodization, see von Glahn, "Imagining Pre-modern China"; and Brook, *Confusions of Pleasure*, p. 264*nn*15–16.

33. Elliott, *The Manchu Way*; Crossley, *A Translucent Mirror*; Rawski, *The Last Emperors*; Berger, *Empire of Emptiness*; Hostetler, *Qing Colonial Enterprise*; di Cosmo, "Qing Colonial Administration in Inner Asia"; idem, "Kirghiz Nomads on the Qing Frontier."

34. For instance, in 1709, the Kangxi emperor opined, "The Ming dynasty's expenditure was extremely profligate. Its construction projects, too, were vast. Its daily expenditure corresponds to what [we] now use in a year. The money spent on cosmetics for the palace women was 400,000 taels of silver. The silver spent on supplies was one million taels. It was not until Shizu (Fulin [i.e., the Qing Shunzhi emperor, r. 1644–61]) took the throne that all this was eliminated" (cited in Qiu Zhonglin, "Huangdi de canzhuo," p. 29). As Qiu notes, such remarks should be taken with a grain of salt.

35. Farquhar, "Mongolian Versus Chinese Elements in the Early Manchu State"; idem, "Emperor as Bodhisattva in the Governance of the Ch'ing Empire." This theme runs through much of Berger's elegant *Empire of Emptiness*. At one point, she terms the Qing the "New Mongols." James Millward ("The Qing Formation," p. 113) has recently observed: "The Qing looks almost like a project to restore an empire along Mongol lines" and stresses the importance of "the Mongol imperial legacy" for understanding the Qing in a wider Eurasian context.

Ming court will improve our understanding of the Qing court as well. For instance, did the Ming court contribute anything to Qing's Inner Eurasian face? In any case, it seems clear that the Qing ruling family was far more successful than its Ming counterpart in enforcing its view of the world. This was especially true in the imperial family's clashes with the civil bureaucracy and other contending interests.[36] Perhaps the Qing rulers learned from the Ming imperial family's failure to keep family interests at the center of things.

---

36. Even at the height of Qing power, the throne encountered repeated challenges to efforts to impose its will on officialdom. For an evocative case study, see Kuhn, *Soulstealers*.

Works Cited

Adamson, John. "The Making of the *Ancien-Régime* Court, 1500–1700." In idem, *The Princely Courts of Europe: Ritual, Politics, and Culture Under the* Ancien-Régime, *1500–1750.* London: Weidenfeld and Nicolson, 1999, pp. 24–30.

Berger, Patricia. *Empire of Emptiness.* Honolulu: University of Hawai'i Press, 2003.

Bol, Peter. *"This Culture of Ours": Intellectual Transitions in T'ang and Sung China.* Stanford: Stanford University Press, 1992.

Brook, Timothy. *Confusions of Pleasure.* Berkeley: University of California Press, 1999.

Chan, Hok-lam. "The Chien-wen, Yung-lo, Hung-hsi, and Hsüan-te Reigns." In *CHC,* 7: 182–304.

CHC, 7, see Mote and Twitchett, *Cambridge History of China*

CHC, 8, see Twitchett and Mote, *Cambridge History of China*

Clunas, Craig. *Superfluous Things: Material Culture and Social Status in Early Modern China.* Urbana: University of Illinois Press, 1991.

Crossley, Pamela. *A Translucent Mirror: History and Identity in Qing Imperial Ideology.* Berkeley: University of California, 1999.

Des Forges, Roger. *Cultural Centrality and Political Change in Chinese History: Northeast Henan in the Fall of the Ming.* Stanford: Stanford University Press, 2003.

di Cosmo, Nicola. "Kirghiz Nomads on the Qing Frontier: Tribute, Trade, or Gift Exchange?" In *Political Frontiers, Ethnic Boundaries, and Human Geographies in Chinese History,* ed. idem and Don J. Wyatt. London and New York: Routledge Curzon, 2003, pp. 351–72.

———. "Qing Colonial Administration in Inner Asia." *International History Review* 20, no. 2 (June 1998): 287–309.

DMHD, see Shen Shixing et al., *Da Ming huidian*

Dong Xinlin 董新林. "Mingdai zhuhou wanglingmu chubu yanjiu" 明代諸侯王陵墓初步研究. *Zhongguo lishi wenwu* 中國歷史文物, no. 45 (2003, no. 4): 4–13.

Elias, Norbert. *The Court Society.* Trans. Edmund Jephcott. New York: Pantheon Books, 1969.

Elliott, Mark. *The Manchu Way: The Eight Banners and Ethnic Identity in Late Imperial China.* Stanford: University of Stanford Press, 2001.

Farmer, Edward. *Early Ming Government: The Evolution of Dual Capitals.* Cambridge: Harvard East Asia Research Center, 1976.

Farquhar, David. "Emperor as Bodhisattva in the Governance of the Ch'ing Empire." *Harvard Journal of Asiatic Studies* 38, no. 1 (1978): 5–35.

———. "Mongolian Versus Chinese Elements in the Early Manchu State." *Ch'ing-shih wen-t'i* 1, no. 6 (1971): 11–23.

Geiss, James. "The Cheng-te Reign." In *CHC,* 7: 403–39.

Gu Cheng 顧誠. "Mingdai de zongshi" 明代的宗室. In *Ming Qing shi guoji xueshu taolunhui lunwenji* 明清史國際學術討論會論文集, ed. Ming Qing shi guoji xueshu taolunhui, Lunwenji mishuchu, Lunwenzu 明清史國際學術討論會論文集秘書處論文組. Tianjin: Tianjin renmin chubanshe, 1982, pp. 89–111.

He Benfang 何本方. "Mingdai gongzhong caizheng shulüe" 明代宮中財政述略. *Gugong bowuyuan yuekan* 故宮博物院月刊 4 (1992): 70–77.

Heijdra, Martin. "The Socio-economic Development of Rural China During the Ming." In *CHC*, 8: 417–578.

Hostetler, Laura. *Qing Colonial Enterprise: Ethnography and Cartography in Early Modern China*. Chicago: University of Chicago Press, 2001.

Huang, Ray. *1587, A Year of No Significance: The Ming Dynasty in Decline*. New Haven: Yale University Press, 1981.

Huang Zhangjian 黃彰健. "Du *Huang Ming dian li*" 讀皇明典禮. *Zhongyang yanjiuyuan Lishi yuyan yanjiusuo jikan* 中央研究院歷史語言研究所集刊 29, *xia* (1958): 669–76.

Idema, Wilt Lukas. *The Dramatic Oeuvre of Chu Yu-tun, 1379–1439*. Leiden: E. J. Brill, 1985.

———. "State and Court in China: The Case of Hung-wu's Imperial Theatre." *Oriens Extremus* 23, no. 2 (1976): 175–89.

Jingdezhen Institute of Ceramic Archeology and the Tsui Museum of Art. *A Legacy of Chenghua*. Hong Kong: Tsui Museum of Art, 1993.

Kuhn, Philip. *Soulstealers: The Chinese Sorcery Scare of 1768*. Cambridge: Harvard University Press, 1990.

Li Jinhua 李晉華. *Mingdai chizhuanshu kao* 明代敕撰書攷. Beiping: Yanjing daxue tushuguan, 1932.

Liu Tong 劉侗 and Yu Yizheng 于奕正, comps. *Dijing jingwu lüe* 帝京景物略. 1635. Reprinted—Beijing: Beijing guji chubanshe, 2001.

Liu Yi 劉毅. *Mingdai diwang lingmu zhidu yanjiu* 明代帝王陵墓制度研究. Beijing: Renmin chubanshe, 2006.

Meng Sen 孟森. *Mingdai shi* 明代史. 1957. Reprinted—Taibei: Huaxiangyuan chubanshe, 1993.

Mote, Frederick W., and Denis Twitchett, eds. *The Cambridge History of China*, vol. 7, *The Ming Dynasty, Part I*. Cambridge: Cambridge University Press, 1988.

Millward, James. "The Qing Formation, the Mongol Legacy, and the 'End of History' in Early Modern Central Eurasia." In *The Qing Formation in World-Historical Time*, ed. Lynn A. Struve. Cambridge: Harvard University Asia Center, 2004, pp. 92–120.

Nanjingshi bowuguan 南京市博物館, ed. *Mingchao shoushi guanfu* 明朝首飾冠服. Beijing: Kexue chubanshe, 2000.

Nimick, Thomas. "The Placement of Local Magistrates in Ming China." *Late Imperial China* 20, no. 2 (1999): 35–60.

Paludan, Ann. *The Chinese Spirit Road: The Classical Tradition of Stone Tomb Statuary*. New Haven: Yale University Press, 1991.

Piggott, Joan. *The Emergence of Japanese Kingship*. Stanford: Stanford University Press, 1997.

Qiu Zhonglin 邱仲麟. "Mingdai zigong qiuyong xianxiang zailun" 明代自宮求用現象再論. *Danjiang shixue* 淡江史學, no. 6 (1994): 125–46.

———. "Huangdi de canzhuo: Mingdai de gongshan zhidu jiqi xiangguan wenti" 皇帝的餐桌: 明代的宮膳制度及其相關問題. *Taida lishi xuebao* 臺大歷史學報 34 (2004): 1–42.

Rawski, Evelyn. *The Last Emperors: A Social History of Qing Imperial Institutions*. Berkeley: University of California Press, 1998.

Robinson, David. *Bandits, Eunuchs, and the Son of Heaven: Rebellion and the Economy of Violence in Mid-Ming China*. Honolulu: University of Hawai'i Press, 2001.

Shen Shixing 申時行 et al. *Da Ming huidian* 大明會典. 1587. Reprinted—Taibei: Dong-
    nan shubaoshe, 1964.

Shepard, Jonathan. "Courts in East and West." In *The Medieval World*, ed. Peter Linehan
    and Janet Nelson. London: Routledge, 2001, pp. 14–36.

Smuts, R. Malcolm. *Court Culture and the Origins of a Royalist Tradition in Early Stuart En-
    gland.* Philadelphia: University of Pennsylvania Press, 1987.

Streusand, Douglas. *The Formation of the Mughal Empire.* Dehli: Oxford University Press,
    1989.

Su Derong 蘇德榮. "Mingdai zongshi wenhua jiqi shehui yingxiang" 明代宗室文化及
    其社會影響. *Henan shifan daxue xuebao* 河南師範大學學報 23, no. 4 (1996): 21–24.

Su Jinyu 蘇晉予. "Henan fanfu jia tianxia" 河南藩府甲天下. *Shixue yuekan* 史學月刊
    1991, no. 5: 40–45.

Twitchett, Denis, and Frederick W. Mote, eds. *The Cambridge History of China*, vol. 8, *The
    Ming Dynasty, 1368–1644, Part II.* Cambridge: Cambridge University Press, 1998.

von Glahn, Richard. "Imagining Pre-modern China." In *The Song-Yuan-Ming Transition in
    Chinese History*, ed. Paul Jakov Smith and Richard von Glahn. Cambridge: Harvard
    University Asia Center, 2003, pp. 35–70.

Wang Jichao 王紀潮. "Mingdai qinwang zangzhi de jige wenti" 明代親王葬制的幾個
    問題. *Wenwu*, no. 561 (2003, no. 2): 63–65, 81.

Wang Yuquan 王毓銓, Liu Chongri 劉重日, and Zhang Xianqing 張顯清, eds. *Zhong-
    guo jingji tongshi: Mingdai jingji juan* 中國經濟通史明代經濟卷, vol. 1. Beijing: Jingji
    ribao chubanshe, 2000.

Wilson, Thomas. "Sacrifices and the Imperial Cult of Confucius." *History of Religions* 41,
    no. 3 (2002): 258–87.

Zhu Geng 朱賡 (1535–1608). "Xie ci *Huang Ming dian li* jie" 謝賜皇明典禮揭. In *Zhu
    Wenyi ji* 朱文懿集, 1.13b–14a; reprinted in *Jingshi wenbian* 經世文編, ed. Chen Zilong
    陳子龍, 1638. Facsimile reprint of Pinglutang ed., Beijing: Zhonghua shuju, 1962,
    juan 436, 6: 4777.

ONE

The Ming Court
David M. Robinson

This chapter is intended to provide background information for the more focused discussions that follow by situating the Ming court in historical terms and in the scholarly literature. It begins with a sketch of the Ming court as it developed in Beijing and treats, among other matters, the composition and physical size of the court, the rhetoric of the emperor's role, his relations with scholar-officials, tensions over courtly order, and outside observers' insatiable interest in the court. The second half briefly reviews some influential characterizations of the Ming court, primarily in English-language scholarship, with special attention to the questions of imperial isolation and oriental despotism.

Composition and Setting of the Ming Court

In physical scale, population, and vision of order, the court of the Ming dynasty (1368–1644), like those of most other Chinese dynasties, ranked among the world's greatest and most ambitious. The emperor constituted the formal center of the Ming court and, in terms of ritual significance, political power, and economic resources, commanded a dominant position.[1] Occasionally, the reins of power might be held by senior imperial women, eunuchs, or favored civil officials. Such times, however, were the exception.

---

1. The emperor's position vis-à-vis his political and social rivals varied greatly over the course of Chinese history, and the trend toward concentration of greater power in the hands of the ruler was not an unbroken march toward "despotism." For a wide-ranging discussion of the question, see Zhou Liangxia (a well-known historian of the Yuan period), *Huangdi yu huangquan*.

Arrayed around the emperor were his preteen male offspring, his daughters, his empress and consorts, palace women, imperial in-laws,[2] and palace eunuchs. Contemporary usage termed these groups the "inner court."

The size of each group fluctuated significantly over the course of the dynasty, and reliable numbers are scarce. By late in the sixteenth century, palace eunuchs numbered perhaps twenty thousand; palace serving women varied anywhere between three and twelve thousand.[3] In contrast to the Song (960–1279) and Qing (1636–1911) periods, the emperor's sons other than the heir apparent resided in their "kingdoms" after achieving their majority, and hence the bulk of the imperial clan lived outside Beijing.[4] Over time, the imperial Zhu clan reached prodigious size.[5] By late in the dynasty, as many as "100,000 imperial kinsmen were on the state payroll."[6] An ever-diminishing proportion of its members enjoyed the wealth and prestige of the score or two of princes of the first and second ranks, however. Ties between the court and the lower ranks of the imperial clan seem to have grown increasingly attenuated, especially from the sixteenth century on.

Deceased members of the imperial family also figured prominently at the court. Ming emperors made daily visits to the Hall of Venerating the

2. With the exception of the opening decades of the dynasty, imperial consorts were drawn not from elite civil or military families but from middle- and lower-level military households, most especially those garrisoned in and around the capital. Although imperial affines might wield considerable power, they never challenged either the emperor's pedigree or power as they had during the earlier Han or Tang dynasties. See Soullière, "The Imperial Marriages of the Ming Dynasty."

3. Geiss, "Peking Under the Ming (1368–1644)," p. 29; Naquin, *Peking*, p. 126.

4. For the imperial clan during the Song dynasty, see Chaffee, *Branches of Heaven*. For a discussion of the Qing imperial family and the large numbers of male clansmen resident in the capital, see Rawski, *The Last Emperors*, pp. 72–126.

5. Some scholars adduce very high numbers indeed. Chen Baoliang (*Mingdai shehui shenghuo shi*, p. 68) estimates that by 1626 the number of imperial clansmen had reached nearly 630,000. The Ming period lacks the careful demographic studies that have shed light on the imperial clan during the Song and Qing periods. For brief comments of the difficulties of historical demographics and reference to much of the relevant scholarship for the Ming period, see Heijdra, "The Ming—Rural Socio-economic Development," pp. 428–39. Support of the imperial clansmen constituted a considerable financial drain; see Gu Cheng, "Mingdai de zongshi," pp. 95–105; and Zhao Yi, "Mingdai zongshi renkou yu zonglu wenti."

6. Hucker, "Ming Government," p. 25. See also Des Forges, *Cultural Centrality*, p. 18. Des Forges notes that by the turn of the seventeenth century, there were approximately 20,000 descendents of the Zhu family in the single locality of Kaifeng.

Ancestors (Fengxiandian 奉先殿), located within the Forbidden City,[7] where they viewed hanging scroll portraits of deceased emperors and made private offerings to their ancestors. Just beyond the palace walls was the Ancestral Temple (Taimiao 太廟), where more formal or public rites were conducted.[8] Located outside the imperial city, the Ming imperial tombs, whose grounds were tended by palace eunuchs and guarded by special military garrison forces, linked the court to its dynastic forefathers.[9]

Members of the "outer court," senior civil and military officials interacted with the emperor through audiences, private meetings, scholarly assemblies, banquets, outings, and various celebrations, both formal and informal. During the dynasty's early decades, hereditary nobles from outside the imperial clan often enjoyed the throne's special favor and were frequent participants in court events.[10] Despite considerable variation according to reign and personality, members of the Grand Secretariat and the Hanlin Academy often enjoyed privileged access to the throne.[11] Nominally tutors to the heir apparent but in fact more like confidential councilors to the emperor, grand secretaries held a multivalent position at the court. As elite scholars drawn from the ranks of the literati, they seldom enjoyed the emperor's unquestioned confidence, but as the emperor's men, the grand secretaries could not count on the allegiance of civil officials in the bureaucracy.[12] Young, comely men who demonstrated outstanding erudition and writing skills on the civil service examination were appointed to the prestigious Hanlin Academy. Burdened with only minimal administrative duties, the Hanlin bachelors were to further develop their talents,

---

7. For the physical lay-out of the Hall for Venerating the Ancestors and changes in it during the Ming and Qing periods, see Xu Yilin, "Fengxiandian."

8. On these temples and the imperial ancestral cult during the Ming, see Taylor, "Official Religion in the Ming," pp. 861–72. For the use of portraits in imperial family rituals, see the chapter by Dora Ching in this volume, pp. 321–64.

9. Thirteen of the sixteen Ming emperors are buried northwest of Beijing. The founder is buried near Nanjing. For a description of Ming tomb statuary, see Paludan, *The Chinese Spirit Road*, pp. 156–92.

10. For the position of military elites at early Ming courts, see Dreyer, *Early Ming China*.

11. Early sixteenth-century Korean observers were aware of the link between physical proximity to the heir apparent and the Hanlin bachelors' prestige. The academy was located within the Forbidden City 禁中. See *Chungjong taewang sillok*, 十五年七月戊子, in Wu Han, *Chaoxian Lichao shilu*, 3: 932.

12. Hucker, *The Ming Dynasty*, pp. 43, 89–91.

which when mature would be available to the emperor.[13] Supported by the state, allowed access to imperial libraries, and wrapped in the mantle of scholars of the realm, Hanlin academicians enjoyed great prestige and were often fast-tracked to posts within the Grand Secretariat. The system was intended to make administrative and literary expertise available to the imperial family without putting it in thrall to the civil bureaucracy as a whole. In private meetings with the emperor on matters of state and less regularly through lectures, banquets, and outings, the Hanlin scholars were expected to display insight into pressing administrative, economic, or military issues, deep erudition in history and the classics, or virtuoso skill in extemporaneous poetry. Despite their status as the "emperor's men," individual Hanlin scholars, like individual grand secretaries, strove for greater autonomy from the throne and identified with the wider literati bureaucracy.

As individuals, foreign envoys seldom counted as key figures at the Ming court, but as a category they held considerable significance. Thoroughly interwoven into imperial regulations governing court protocol, they played an essential role in accentuating the emperor's unique position as ruler of all under Heaven and buttressing the status of the court in Eurasia.[14] Foreign envoys also brought goods, information, and new fashions to the Ming court. As physical emblems of their participation in the Ming court, heads of foreign polities received letters patent, seals of office, imperial calendars, cash, silks, and robes. These heads of foreign polities varied from Jurchen tribal leaders in the northeast and headmen of aboriginal groups such as the Yi, Zhuang, and Luoluo in the southwest to Chosŏn

---

13. The eminent Chinese historian Qian Mu (*Guoshi dagang*, pp. 684–89) identified the Hanlin Academy as one of the praiseworthy features of the Ming dynasty. Qian stressed the many benefits that a Ming emperor might gain from close association with such outstanding scholars. This outlook is, of course, premised on the notion that Confucian scholars would naturally act as teachers to Ming rulers. As several chapters in this volume show, Ming emperors seldom shared this view.

14. In an often criticized but still influential essay, John Fairbank ("Preliminary Framework," p. 3) observed long ago, "China's external order was so closely related to her internal order that one could not long survive without the other; when the barbarians were not submissive abroad, rebels might more easily arise within." Danjō Hiroshi ("Minsho no tai-Nichi gaikō") has argued that the Ming founder considered Japanese acceptance of the Ming "tributary" framework so critical to his fledgling dynasty that when his overtures were rejected, he fabricated a domestic political incident to explain the Ming's lack of formal relations with the Muromachi *bakufu*. For an examination of the founder's difficulties in implementing his new international order vis-à-vis Korea and the links to domestic order, see idem, "Chōsen ōchō hen *Ribun*," pp. 1–15.

kings, Muromachi *shōgun*s, Tibetan prelates, and Vietnamese emperors. Foreign leaders valued these imperial artifacts; their wide circulation throughout Asia ensured that the Ming court in an extended sense was international, especially since the reception of these tokens of imperial inclusion often entailed the local leader's performance of rituals of gratitude to and respect for the Ming court, and that official communications generally used the Ming calendar to mark time.

Finally, Buddhist, Daoist, and Muslim religious figures, adepts in the occult, singers, dancers, musicians, acrobats, painters, and craftsmen were also members of the court. Their prominence varied considerably from reign to reign, even from year to year, and their presence in the historical record is often shadowy, the details of their activities frustratingly oblique, and descriptions of their influence on the court nearly always negative (the vitriol indirectly reflects their importance, since the records were written by rivals—civil officials).

Although the emperor may have been the center of the court, nearly all the other groups noted above interacted, with or without the emperor's mediation. The result was a complex social and political environment that required constant negotiation, jockeying, and observation. It was a "cockpit of competition."[15] The varied cast of actors also produced a rich cultural milieu that provided ample opportunity for the transmission, adaptation, and interpenetration of sartorial, religious, linguistic, gastronomic, and artistic traditions.

If personnel and personal dynamics constituted one fundamental component of the Ming court, physical setting was another.[16] Even today, the sheer enormity of the Forbidden City in Beijing strikes nearly all visitors. Massive walls flank the main entrance at the Meridian Gate (today's Tiananmen Square). The northern half of the Forbidden City contained the myriad courtyards, twisting lanes, and gardens reserved largely for the imperial family's use; to the south the banks of offices lining the great open

———

15. The phrase is from Adamson, "The Making of the *Ancien-Régime* Court, 1500–1700," p. 17.

16. For useful descriptions of the physical plant of the Imperial City and the Forbidden City, see Geiss, "Peking Under the Ming"; and Naquin, *Peking*, pp. 128–37. For a concise description of many of the features common to Chinese imperial cities, see Steinhardt, *Chinese Imperial City Planning*, pp. 1–28. As Steinhardt ("Why Were Chang'an and Beijing So Different," p. 339) has pointed out, the ideal of a perfectly aligned imperial city was so closely tied to imperial legitimacy that rulers "had their actual city schemes amended for the historical record through publication of fictitious city plans."

squares between the three great halls boldly announced an empire of redoubtable power and size. During the Ming period, it was the world's largest walled complex, occupying an area of one-half square mile.[17] One can
imagine the wonder and fear of those who made their way toward the Son
of Heaven in an age before skyscrapers and cavernous suburban malls.
Along the central north-south axis of the Forbidden City towered a series
of imposing halls, where dynastic business was conducted. Across the
stone-paved squares in front of the great halls stood row upon row of imperial honor guards dressed in body armor and helmets, who in the words
of a Timurid envoy visiting Yongle's court, "held halberts [sic], clubs, steel
javelins, battle axes, spears, swords, and maces."[18] Hundreds of civil officials dressed in silk gowns and positioned in ranks according to their official grades (nine full and nine half grades) stood at attendance before the
emperor. This was the home of the Ming imperial court, the empire's political and ritual center.

Ming Courtly Order

Chinese political philosophy accorded central place to the imperial court in
general and the person of the emperor in particular. Imperial rhetoric
maintained that the emperor and the people around him held a pivotal role
in the cosmos.[19] If the Son of Heaven erred, then all under Heaven fell
into disequilibrium. As one fifteenth-century writer put the matter, "Order
and chaos in the realm originate in the single heart/mind of the ruler."[20]
When the emperor and those close to him misused their great powers,
people throughout the empire suffered.

---

17. Geiss, "Peking Under the Ming," p. 29.

18. Naqqash, "Report to Mirza Baysunghur," p. 287. For pictorial representation of
the imperial bodyguard, probably during the sixteenth century, see the two court-
commissioned scrolls examined in Na and Kohler, *The Emperor's Procession*. See Figs. 1.1
and 8.8 of the present volume. For an argument that the painting is a 1581 portrait of
Wanli, see Zhu Hong, "*Mingren chujing rubi tu* benshi zhi yanjiu."

19. In fact, this concept predates the imperial period. Robin Yates ("Cosmos and
Central Authority in the Early Chinese Empire," p. 367) observes of the 239 B.C. *Spring
and Autumn Annals of Lü Buwei* and an earlier Yin Yang text, "the macrocosm and the
microcosm—humans, the state, and the natural order—were bound together in a single,
complex, organic whole through the medium of the body of the ruler."

20. Zhang Lun 章綸 (1413–83), "Yangsheng gongqin lunzheng dunxiaoyi shu" 養聖
躬勤論政惇孝義疏, *Zhang gong yi mei shu* 張恭毅美疏, in Chen Zilong, *Jingshi wenbian*,
47.1b; reprint ed., 1: 656.

This rhetorical position laid nearly all aspects of the emperor's life open to the potential scrutiny and comment of officialdom.[21] Each year, officials submitted thousands of memorials that discussed the behavior of the emperor, the heir apparent, imperial affines, eunuchs, and imperial favorites. Reading habits, lectures, sexual behavior, religious practices, consumption of food and wine, leisure activities, travel, construction expenses, clothing, titles, companions, and a hundred other facets of imperial life were the concerns of the emperor's ministers and officials. Officials were fully aware of the potential for controlling the emperor's behavior inherent in this articulation of the relationship between Heaven and the ruler.[22]

The emperor's unique position took concrete form through his interactions with others at court and beyond. Rituals within the palace or in the suburbs often called for large casts, usually accompanied by music, dance, and the manipulation of sacred objects. The ruler's supreme status was highlighted through the use of ritual space in palace halls and the physical postures imposed on his courtiers and attendants. Dynastic regulations prescribed in great detail the clothing styles, titles, and physical proximity to the emperor permitted various members of the imperial family, palace eunuchs, military guards, civil officials, and foreign dignitaries. How and when each group offered ritual salutations to the emperor were matters of great import to the state and court. Even when officials or foreign envoys thought otherwise (or perhaps precisely because they thought otherwise), ritual and protocol drove home the principle that the Son of Heaven was the lodestar and central reference point of the court and of the empire as a whole.

Another, more prosaic way to accentuate the emperor's unique status was through regulation of access to the Forbidden City in general and to his person in particular. Imperial regulations required on-duty civil officials, military personnel, and palace eunuchs to wear small "waist-badges" 腰牌 and other forms of identification made of ivory, bronze, or wood,

---

21. As many fine studies have shown, Chinese emperors also drew on other sources to legitimate their rule, including popular religious beliefs and notions of destiny. For a recent discussion of the incorporation of these elements into official dynastic accounts of the Ming founder and their relation to historical rewriting under Zhu Di, see Hok-lam Chan, "Xie Jin (1369–1415) as Imperial Propagandist." His essay includes citations to previous scholarship on the question.

22. The tensions inherent in this formulation of the emperor's role in the realm and cosmos dated back at least to Dong Zhongshu 董仲舒 (179–104 B.C.) of the Former Han and in a less fully articulated form to the early Zhou dynasty (1046–256 B.C.).

which authorized their presence in normally restricted parts of the Forbidden City.[23]

Each of the myriad rituals and customs at the Ming court was an occasion to confirm the emperor's unique status and power. In this sense, the Ming court resembled many other courts throughout history; it functioned as what the cultural anthropologist Clifford Geertz has called an "exemplary center." In Geertz's words, "By the mere act of providing a model, a paragon, a faultless image of civilized existence, the court shapes the world around it into at least a rough approximation of its own excellence. The ritual of the court, and in fact the life of the court, is thus paradigmatic, not merely reflective, of social order."[24] Apropos of court feasts at the Ming court, the late Frederick Mote similarly observed, "The proper order of human society, as well as the cosmic relationships, were [sic] symbolized in all the regulations and alluded to in all the words spoken at these occasions."[25] Although Geertz highlighted the court's production of order, while Mote here cast regulations and words as symbols of cosmic patterns, both drew attention to the court's link to more encompassing visions of order.[26]

The Emperor and the Literati

Officials, scholars, and writers were deeply invested in the imperial state and its rhetoric. Officials owed much of their social, economic, and political standing to mastery of a state-approved curriculum, successful navigation of the state-run civil service examinations, and adroit use of resources to be gained through government service. Members of this same elite community commonly exploited their state-bestowed position to defy government challenges to their interests, whether at the capital or in their home regions. A similar tension characterized officials' views of the emperor and imperial rhetoric.

23. Shen Defu (1578–1642) wrote that all badges were made of ivory; see Shen, "Yapai" 牙牌, in Wanli yehuo bian (hereafter cited as YHB), juan 13, 2: 347–48. However, examples of bronze waist badges survive in the Capital Museum and the Military Museum in Beijing.

24. Geertz, Negara, p. 13.

25. Mote, "Yüan and Ming," p. 219. Elsewhere in this volume, Joseph Lam notes the cosmological connotations of banquet music; see pp. 269–320.

26. For a characterization of the first Chinese "empire," the Qin, as "cosmographic and cosmological" for its attempts to align territory, administrative structures, and subjects with its understanding of the cosmos, see Yates, "Cosmos and Central Authority in the Early Chinese Empire."

Since emperors constituted a vital source of prestige, power, and patronage, high-ranking officials treasured their access to the ruler. Their collected writings nearly always include written evidence of their interactions with the Son of Heaven: policy statements addressed to the throne, answers to the emperor's questions on the classics, the highly formulaic letters to the throne humbly accepting or declining office, and poems commemorating various events at the court.[27] Senior civil court ministers could serve as important cultural and political patrons in their own right, although as Kathlyn Liscomb notes, "These government officials presented their special relationship with emperor as fundamental to their identity in all spheres of activity."[28] This cooperation between ruler and servitor could also take the form of literati officials' participation in such efforts to buttress the legitimacy and prestige of the court as the compilation of dynastic histories, imperial genealogies, and large-scale literary projects.[29]

Although lauded as evidence of loyalty to the throne and commitment to principle, remonstrance against the emperor entailed considerable risk; irate rulers were quick to register displeasure through public tongue-lashings, administrative penalties, corporal punishments, or worse. Men might voice criticism as a cynical way to "purchase fame" and establish a reputation for principled bravery. Given the depth of the officials' investment in the imperial system, however, one could argue that officials' complaints of emperors' many and manifest failings as sages and rulers more often grew out of a faith in the imperial vision of order. If they could right the emperor's errant behavior, they could restore balance to the court, the realm, and the cosmos. Such an understanding was simultaneously empowering and optimistic.

———

27. These sources often provide insights into the personal dynamics of the court not available in such imperially compiled sources as the Veritable Records. For examples, see Hung-lam Chu's chapter in this volume, pp. 186–230. *The Eight Views of Beijing* 北京八景圖, an early fifteenth-century amalgam of paintings, poems, and essays, was "conceived in part as an elegant way to express [the] gratitude of this group of officials for being chosen to join the emperor in imperial retinues that twice visited Beijing in 1409 and 1413" (Liscomb, "The Role of Leading Court Officials as Patrons," p. 39). High-ranking civil officials at court were far from alone in advertising links to the throne. Local gazetteers, temple gazetteers, and even mountain and river gazetteers commonly included texts from imperially commissioned steles, the emperor's orders, and snippets roughly comparable to "Washington slept here."

28. Liscomb, "Foregrounding the Symbiosis of Power," p. 135. Liscomb's essay develops themes first discussed in her "Role of Leading Court Officials as Patrons."

29. For a recent study on rewriting history to legitimate the rule of Zhu Di, see Hok-lam Chan, "Xie Jin (1369–1415) as Imperial Propagandist."

By the same logic, however, imperial rejection of their sage counsel was not merely a political rebuff but a threat to the larger political and cosmic order.[30] Truculent rulers prompted some officials and thinkers to develop political and ideological supplements to ensure just and effective governance regardless of the virtue or ability of any particular emperor. During the Southern Song and the Yuan periods (twelfth to fourteenth centuries), important alternatives included personal moral cultivation, a renewed commitment to local community, and a reconceptualization of law codes as a check against government abuses. Driven in part by ideological concerns and in part by bureaucratic imperatives, civil officials during the fifteenth, sixteenth, and seventeenth centuries again redefined the role of the Son of Heaven by confirming his ritual centrality but diminishing his importance in day-to-day governance and policy formation. The issue was never fully resolved, and Ming rulers' efforts to realize their own vision of imperial rule periodically sparked paralyzing conflicts at the court.

Castles in the Sand

In fact, whether considered synchronically or diachronically, the entire Ming court is best understood as an arena of unresolved tensions and ongoing negotiation. A cursory reading of the detailed descriptions of court ritual and protocol found in such state compendium as the *Collected Administrative Statutes of the Great Ming Dynasty* (*Da Ming huidian* 大明會典) or the *Draft Treatise of the Ministry of Rites* (*Libu zhigao* 禮部志稿) suggests close imperial control of even the most minute facets of court life. These same compilations, however, record such a staggering number of infractions that one can only conclude that contemporaries keenly sensed the imperial order's fragility.

As illustrative examples, let us return to a few aspects of the court order limned above. Although some foreign dignitaries may have found Ming court audiences a marvel of dignity and control (in 1516 Seid Ali Akbar

---

30. This formulation created the potential for grave difficulties, "when 'sage kings' did not occupy the throne of the Son of Heaven and when the persuasive relevance of rhetorical models of sage emperors was extremely curtailed owing to the fact of rule by persons other than Han Chinese" (Langlois, "Political Thought in Chin-hua Under Mongol Rule," p. 137). The productive irritant of how to resolve this predicament lay behind much of Daoxue 道學 thought. For evolving notions of rulership in China, see Bol, "Whither the Emperor?" Bol argues that Huizong (r. 1101–25), the last ruler of the Northern Song, represented "the last gasp of the ancient model of kingship," by which Bol means "an emperor and sage who orchestrated heaven and man" (p. 134). Rhetoric that granted the emperor's centrality, however, survived long after Huizong.

Khatai wrote, "several thousand people stood in front of the emperor, no one daring to make a sound"),[31] Chinese accounts note palace eunuchs' struggles to rein in unruly civil officials, whose pushing, spitting, and shouting added nothing to the desired decorum of this daily court ritual.[32] In 1429 an exasperated emperor complained with asperity to his minister of rites that even at imperial audiences, protocol related to clothing, titles, and positions within prescribed ranks was violated. "There are those," he continued, "within the private quarter of the court (*neifu* 内府), who perform ritual prostration without authorization" 私行禮拜. This ritual prostration should have been reserved for the emperor.[33] State banquets, intended to symbolize "the proper order of human society, as well as the cosmic relationships," often reflected a more raucous court reality. In 1500, complaints reached the throne about those who flouted proper etiquette by leaving banquets before their formal conclusion and those who "crashed" feasts.[34] If these examples suggest a measure of disregard for imperial order, other instances indicate an acceptance of court order that did not preclude attempts to manipulate that order to enhance status, when for instance, hereditary nobles jockeyed for more prestigious seats at state banquets. The emperor himself was not above rearranging seating charts to display his particular favor.[35]

Finally, the control of access to the Forbidden City and the emperor himself was not always rigorous. The court's periodic reminders to officials and others that borrowing or lending identification passes was prohibited and subject to prosecution suggests the prevalence of such violations.[36] Officials regularly inveighed against the calamitous results of allowing unauthorized or, perhaps more accurately, undesirable people access to the emperor and the imperial family. In one particularly egregious instance, palace eunuchs allowed some thuggish friends to watch the Son of Heaven play kickball in his private quarters.[37]

---

31. Seid Ali Akbar Khatai, *Khataynama*, p. 74.

32. See Yu Ruji, "Fan jiuju shiyi" 凡糾舉失儀, in idem, *Libu zhigao* (hereafter cited as *LBZG*), 10.7a–8b (*Wenyuange Siku quanshu* ed., 597.130).

33. *Ming Xuanzong shilu*, 51.7a; Yu Ruji, "Lizhi zhi xun" 禮制之訓, in *LBZG*, 3.21a (*Wenyuange siku quanshu* ed., 597.59).

34. *Ming Xiaozong shilu*, 158.1b–2a; Yu Ruji, "Ding qingcheng yu yan baiguan yi" 定慶成與宴百官儀, in *LBZG*, 93.13b–14a (*Wenyuange siku quanshu* ed., 598.694–95).

35. For a mid-sixteenth-century example, see *Ming Shizong shilu*, 130.4b.

36. Yu Ruji, "Ruchao menjin" 入朝門禁, in *LBZG*, 10.31a–b (*Wenyuange Siku quanshu* ed., 597.142).

37. For discussion of the incident and its imagery, see Robinson, *Bandits, Eunuchs, and the Son of Heaven*, pp. 99–120.

Over the Walls and Through the Gate

As for the court's relation with a wider swathe of society, the exclusive nature of the larger court community (which included imperial family members, palace eunuchs, high-ranking military and civil officials, religious specialists, palace women, and servants) had several consequences. First, if much of Ming court life was devoted to confirming the emperor's unique importance, it also conferred special status and privilege on all participants. Subordination to the emperor and other exalted figures at the court often translated into superior status vis-à-vis those beyond the court. To boost their prestige, literati officials commissioned paintings of themselves dressed in official court gowns standing in front of the Forbidden City, its walls and halls obscured by auspicious clouds. Some of these paintings suggest privileged access to the court by adopting a perspective that allowed the viewer to peer over the towering walls. Direct access to the court and its members was a rare mark of distinction carrying enormous social, political, and economic capital that was not restricted to elite men. As one knowledgeable observer from late in the sixteenth century wrote, "Women outside the palace tended to have special confidence in the palace midwives and thereby employ them more than the common run of midwife, because of their status in the palace."[38]

The court's exclusivity led to an insatiable curiosity about its inner workings. Painters offered tantalizing (even erotically charged) glimpses into the highly restricted realm of court women and their activities. Such works could safely be set only in the historical past.[39] Guidebooks like the 1635 *Brief Account of the Sites and Things of the Capital* (*Dijing jingwu lüe* 帝京景物略) lovingly enumerated items from the Forbidden City available in Beijing's markets.

Surrounding countries, too, evinced great interest in the Ming court. Through its diplomatic ties, the Ming court hosted envoys and missions from scores of countries. Although still inadequately studied, these foreign observers left accounts written from a variety of perspectives.[40] These ac-

---

38. Shen Bang 沈榜 (1550–96), *Wan shu za ji* 宛署雜記, cited in Cass, "Female Healers in the Ming," p. 39.

39. Vinograd, "Palace and Court in the Later Ming Dynasty Public Imagination." See also Naquin, *Peking*, pp. 141–43. For observations of the links between erotica and the imperial court, see Clunas, *Pictures and Visuality in Early Modern China*, pp. 150–58.

40. For one of the few that has been translated into English and studied at some length, see Meskill, *Ch'oe P'u's Diary*. For preliminary discussion of accounts by Korean

counts and less formal reports supplied political and cultural elites from Japan, Korea, the Ryūkyūs, Vietnam, Manchuria, Mongolia, Tibet, Central Asia, Persia, and beyond with information about the ceremonies, foods, clothes, dances, material wealth, and gossip of the Ming court. Impressed by the Ming imperial palace complex, with its paved courtyards, latticed arcades, magnificent columns, and floors of fine cut stones, an early fifteenth-century Persian envoy effused, "All master craftsmen of every art would be astonished to look at them."[41] Throughout the fifteenth and sixteenth centuries, Mongolians saw the Ming court as a center of Tibetan Buddhism, the lavish patron of Tibetan monks, and the repository of exquisitely produced Tibetan sutras written in gilt script.[42]

These foreign delegations brought a staggering wealth of goods to the court: the Ryūkyū king sent horses, ivory, agate, sandalwood, and spices; Korean courts supplied horses, high-quality paper, inks, ramie and cotton fabrics, and ginseng; the "king of Japan" offered samurai swords, folding fans, sulfur, silver, and tea-bowls; Vietnam brought southeastern Asian spices, medicines, and precious metals; Mongol and Jurchen envoys arrived with steppe horses, furs, leathers, and hunting falcons; Tibetans brought Buddhist icons, pennants, horses, and relics; missions from western Asia contributed lions, jade, and textiles.[43] Later, European visitors including Matteo Ricci (1552–1610) would submit religious paintings, maps of the world, prisms, hourglasses, and a small harpsichord.[44] The perception, impact, and circulation of these goods have not yet received serious consideration, nor have contemporaneous conceptions of gift-sharing networks among the courts of Asia.[45] At the emperor's behest, court artists

---

envoy missions, see Ledyard, "Korean Travelers in China." For a relatively comprehensive list of accounts from Korean envoy missions to the Ming court, see Im Kijung, "Yŏnhaengnok kwa Han'gukhak yŏn'gu," pp. 8–20.

41. Geiss, "Peking Under the Ming," p. 69.

42. Serruys, "Early Lamaism in Mongolia." China had long been a "Central Buddhist Realm" (Sen, *Buddhism, Diplomacy, and Trade*, pp. 55–101).

43. These are far from exhaustive lists. For an official contemporaneous list of "tribute offerings" from various countries, see Shen Shixing, *Da Ming huidian* (hereafter cited as *DMHD*), *juan* 105–8, 5: 1586–626.

44. Spence, *The Memory Palace of Matteo Ricci*, pp. 194–95.

45. Thomas Allsen's meticulous studies of the Mongol empire provide an example of the insights to be gained from such analysis; see his *Commodity and Exchange in the Mongol Empire* and *Culture and Conquest in Mongol Eurasia*. For a classic work on foreign exotica during the Tang period, see Schafer, *The Golden Peaches of Samarkand: A Study of T'ang Exotics*. For the impact on imperial portraiture of exchanges with Tibetans at the

produced imposing paintings of tribute animals, and even of legation heads, for display in the palace. Both these artists and others produced simplified copies of such paintings to satisfy the curiosity of people outside the court.[46] Through these products, images of court spectacle and power spread beyond the walls of the Forbidden City.

Study of the Ming Court

For all its scale and splendor, until recently the Ming court has eluded systematic study. We know surprisingly little about life within the walls of the Forbidden City during the Ming. In part because the religious practices of the imperial family, especially the emperor, often became a matter of political contention, they have been studied in some detail.[47] Several scholars have shed light on facets of entertainment, especially theater, at the earliest Ming courts.[48] Joseph Lam's examination of the ritual music of the Ming dynasty gives some sense of the function, organization, and variety of music used at the many ritual events at the court.[49] Palace women, whether imperial consorts, members of the harem, wet nurses, or menial servants, constituted a critical element of the court that remains only partially understood.[50] Another promising line of inquiry is the "emperor's table," as Qiu

Ming court, see Dora Ching's chapter in this volume, pp. 321–64. On the popularity of imported Japanese crafts among literati elites, see Clunas, *Superfluous Things*, pp. 58–59.

46. Whitfield, "Rugong."

47. Yang Qiqiao, *Ming Qing shi jueao*, pp. 1–151; also available in a recently published illustrated version entitled *Ming Qing huangshi yu fangshu*, pp. 1–134. Geiss, "The Chia-ching Reign," 7: 479–82; Naquin, *Peking*, pp. 143–70. See also Fisher, *The Chosen One*. For citations to scholarship on links between the Ming court and Tibetan Buddhism, see the bibliographies included in chapters in this volume by Dora Ching (pp. 321–64) and David Robinson (pp. 365–421).

48. Iwaki Hideo, "Min no kyūtei to engeki." Iwaki argues persuasively for the influence of "commoner" traditions on musical tastes at the Ming court. His analysis of the relation between eunuchs (one main medium through which "commoner" music was transmitted to the court) and civil officials, however, is less compelling. See also Idema, "Stage and Court in China." In later studies, Idema argued that the founding emperor's taste and agendas resulted in an extensive rewriting of Yuan theater. For a recent expansion on this theme and a discussion of how efforts to produce authoritative texts could serve "to domesticate its content and to rein in dangerous social or cultural energies that were destabilizing to the Ming court or to the ideological world of the literati," see West, "Text and Ideology" (quotation on p. 329).

49. Lam, *State Sacrifices and Music in Ming China*.

50. The most important work on this vast subject is Soullière, "Palace Women in the Ming Dynasty." For a concise summation of many of Soullière's arguments, see her

Zhonglin has recently put it.[51] Political histories of the Ming period often include coverage of the court, but generally only so far as its practices and members had obvious political ramifications.

Art historians and archeologists have produced perhaps the richest body of scholarship on the Ming court. They have examined imperial portraiture,[52] court painting styles,[53] books and book illustrations,[54] porcelains,[55] and architecture. Art historians from the People's Republic of China often analyze in detail individual objects or groups of objects or trace particular stylistic influences. Chinese archeology tends toward physical description of sites and excavated objects.[56] Other scholars such as Marsha Weidner, Wang Cheng-hua, and Patricia Berger have engaged broader questions of political ideology, religious belief, and the interplay of

---

"Imperial Marriages in the Ming Dynasty." See also Cass, "Female Healers in the Ming."

51. Qiu Zhonglin, "Huangdi de canzhuo." On the ritual uses of food at the court and the bureaucratic administrations responsible for its procurement and preparation, see Mote, "Yüan and Ming," pp. 210–20. Ray Huang ("Fiscal Administration During the Ming Dynasty," p. 90) remarked on the enormous scale of operations of the Ming imperial kitchens, describing them "as the world's largest grocery store and dining hall," which "served from 10,000 to 15,000 persons daily."

52. Fong, "Imperial Portraiture of the Ming Dynasty," pp. 327–33. For more detailed consideration and relevant scholarship, see Dora Ching's chapter in this volume, pp. 321–64.

53. Barnhart, *Painters of the Great Ming.*

54. For meticulous studies by Julia K. Murray, see the literature cited in her chapter (pp. 231–68) in this volume. For examples of books and illustrations produced by the Directorate of Ceremonial publishers during the early Ming, see Zhou Shaoliang, "Ming Yongle nianjian neifu kanben fojiao jingji." For an extended discussion of the Directorate of Ceremonial's publishing activities, see Scarlett Jang's chapter in this volume (pp. 116–85). For several examples, of varying quality, of Buddhist and Daoist texts commissioned by the emperor and imperial women during the Wanli period for distribution as a way to accumulate good merit, see Zhou Shaoliang, "Mingdai huangdi, guifei, gongzhu yinshi de jiben fojing." Zhou's explanation of the specific motivations for publishing the texts is not persuasive.

55. The scholarship on Ming porcelains is far too voluminous to cite in its entirety. For a useful introduction, see Cort and Stuart, *Joined Colors.*

56. This in no way diminishes the importance of their invaluable work. During the past several decades, archeologists have uncovered an enormously rich body of physical objects, tombs, and architectural remains that have yet to be integrated by historians and others into understandings of the Ming period. For recent comments about the need to combine archeological and documentary materials in the context of court culture, see the useful study by Liu Yi, *Ming Qing gongting shenghuo,* p. 376.

court and society.[57] Taken as a whole, art historians and archeologists have shed light on several facets of the Ming court—from rulership, artistic patronage, and religious devotion to aesthetics, ties between popular religion and the throne, and the composition of the court.[58]

These stimulating studies offer important insights into the dynamics of the Ming court; their methodologies and ambitious scope suggest how much remains to be known about the tone and tenor of court life and practices—how these men and women lived their lives, interacted, advanced their interests, and sought spiritual solace. What did they eat, how did they dress, how were they educated? How did they worship, play, care for the ill, and bury their dead? Despite the rhetorical emphasis on the court's centrality, the Ming court itself has remained something of a black box to modern historians. There is no Ming counterpart to Evelyn Rawski's wonderfully detailed *The Last Emperors: A Social History of Qing Imperial Institutions*, which examines religious practices, palace women, servants, state rituals, and family relations at the Qing court.[59] Historians of the Qing have at their disposal a qualitatively different source base for their reconstruction of the Qing period. Far more official documents, private chronicles, and material objects survive; historians may also mine far richer accounts by foreign envoys, travelers, merchants, and missionaries. The contrast with the many detailed studies of European courts during the fourteenth to seventeenth centuries is also striking. Much has to do with the relatively open and fluid nature of European courts—more personal accounts, diaries, letters, readier access to the person of the ruler and his courtiers, and more public display.

Intellectual fashion also explains the paucity of research on the Ming court. From the 1950s to 1980s, scholars from Japan and the People's Republic of China expended much energy on the study of what were perceived as the real engines of history—socioeconomics and "the people" (especially "peasant rebels"). China's rulers and members of the elite were

—

57. Marsha Weidner, "Buddhist Pictorial Art in the Ming Dynasty"; idem, "Imperial Engagements with Buddhist Art and Architecture"; Berger, "Miracles in Nanjing"; Wang Cheng-hua, "Material Culture and Emperorship."

58. For an overview of the cultural activities of Ming emperors, see Chen Baoliang, "Mingdai huangdi yu Mingdai wenhua." Despite the title of his article, Chen does not address the issue of the relation between the emperors' cultural activities and Ming culture as a whole. For a slightly different coverage of the same question, see idem, *Mingdai shehui shenghuo shi*, pp. 56–67.

59. Rawski, *The Last Emperors*.

consciously denigrated as parasitic, self-serving, and not particularly important.[60] In many places around the globe during the nineteenth and twentieth centuries, the court was perceived as the epitome of all that was backward, corrupt, effete, and debased about the *ancien régime*.[61] Its study seemed to border on nostalgic antiquarianism. In the United States, Taiwan, and elsewhere, the humanistic tradition, most especially the tastes of literati in thought, art, literature, and religion, proved more appealing than developments at court. In recent years, study of the Ming period has grown more diverse, but the court has seldom been the central focus.

Images of the Ming Court

The Ming dynasty is frequently characterized as a turning point in China's relations with the rest of the world. Viewing the past in light of developments during the nineteenth and twentieth centuries, contemporary Chinese scholars and pundits have often rued the Ming government's failure to pursue the technological, logistical, and economic advantages so prominently displayed during Zheng He's storied state-sponsored naval voyages of the early fifteenth century to as far away as East Africa.[62] The influential Chinese television documentary *Heshang* (1988) argued that in the fifteenth century China turned inward from the azure seas to the yellow lands of Asia, with disastrous consequences for modern China. Several scholarly studies of world history have held that Ming China turned its back not only on the rapidly expanding maritime world but also on the world as a whole. They point to China's loss of interest in Central Asia, the steppe, Southeast Asia, and the Indian Ocean.[63] In this view, the complacent

---

60. There are important exceptions. For a recent review of Japanese scholarship on the Ming to the early 1980s, see Fuma Susumu, "Ming Studies in Japan."

61. For brief comments on the Indian case, see Ali, *Courtly Culture and Political Life in Early Medieval India*, pp. 1–3.

62. This view often informs popular accounts of contemporary China. In *The Coming Collapse of China*, Gordon Chang writes: "Long before the advent of the Internet, China shut itself off from the rest of the world." After Zheng He's voyages, "his fleet, the mightiest in the world, was disbanded and China retreated into itself. Contentment and an antimercantilist outlook ensured centuries of isolation, and that eventually led to decline" (p. 85).

63. André Wink ("From the Mediterranean to the Indian Ocean," p. 437) has noted, "The Chinese were still present on the Malabar coast in the fifteenth century, but here they would soon disappear, as they did from all parts of the Indian Ocean to the west of Malacca. . . . The Chinese ceased to be a major power in the Indian Ocean alto-

Chinese turned inward just as Western Europe began its march to world domination.[64]

This stress on an inward-looking Ming state sometimes carries over into descriptions of the Ming court. In her magisterial *Peking: Temples and City Life, 1400–1900*, Susan Naquin often highlights the Ming court's isolation. She notes the "isolated, feminized palace world" of the Ming court.[65] In her discussion of visual portrayals of the Ming court, Naquin remarks on the impression of "detached isolation" and the "imperial isolation" that the paintings evoke.[66]

If much of court life was intended to seem distantly august, privy only to a select few, it was never an island unto itself. Naquin's meticulous scholarship clearly demonstrates the importance of the court's religious patronage to the local economy of Beijing and surrounding counties through massive infusions of capital for construction, periodic refurbishing, support of religious orders, and special donations for ceremonies.[67] Building on the pioneering work of Chinese scholar Xu Daling, the late James Geiss made this argument in a broader way.[68] He argued that the directions, tastes, and demands of the Ming court were the most important determi-

---

gether." Here Wink fails to distinguish between the actions of the central government and private Chinese traders. Even leading authorities in the China field sometimes make such claims. Richard Barnhart (*Painters of the Great Ming*, p. 103) has observed that by the end of the fifteenth-century changes, "China had withdrawn from the rest of the world." Noted cultural historian of the Qing period, Richard Smith (*Chinese Maps*, p. 12) has written, "The termination of Zheng's expeditions in 1433 . . . signaled a precipitous decline in Chinese interest in people overseas. Ming China increasingly turned inward, preoccupied with the threat of barbarian invasion from the north." Richard von Glahn ("Foreword," p. xii) notes a tendency to contrast "the self-imposed cultural parochialism and isolation of the Ming" with the "consciously polyethnic and colonial empire" of the Qing.

64. For evidence of Chinese overseas commerce, see Wills, "Maritime China from Wang Chih to Shih Lang"; idem, "Relations with Maritime Europeans, 1514–1662"; Atwell, "International Bullion Flows and the Chinese Economy"; idem, "Notes on Silver, Foreign Trade, and the Late Ming Economy"; idem, "A Seventeenth-Century 'General Crisis' in East Asia"; idem, "Ming China and the Emerging World Economy"; and Wang Gungwu, "Ming Foreign Relations: Southeast Asia"; idem, "Early Ming Relations with Southeast Asia"; idem, "Merchants Without Empire."

65. Naquin, *Peking*, p. 124.

66. Ibid., p. 138.

67. Ibid., pp. 144–70. Naquin (ibid., pp. 123, 130, 131, 143) notes periodically the variety of links between the court and the surrounding city.

68. Xu Daling, "Mingdai Beijing de jingji shenghuo."

nants of Beijing's development. "The history of Peking," he wrote, "and its environs was largely shaped by the peculiar interests of emperors and their courtiers."[69] From the towering city walls, the concentration of military and political elites, and the prominence of palace eunuchs to the flow of tax silver, exquisite goods, and the lavishly sponsored religious temples, the Ming court exercised a profound influence over the capital and surrounding counties.

Scholarship from the People's Republic of China has tended to focus on the deleterious impact of the imperial family and affines on Beijing's economy and society. The proliferation of estates held by the imperial family, imperial-in-laws, eunuchs, and favored ministers has been offered as evidence of imperial abuse.[70] Others like Han Dacheng have described how those with access to imperial power gained unfair market advantages for stores, warehouses, and transportation services that enjoyed considerable tax exemptions. More important, he contends, those with connections to imperial power always triumphed in legal battles.[71]

Producers throughout the empire labored to satisfy the court's voracious appetite for goods. The imperial porcelain kilns in Jingdezhen, Jiangxi province, produced, among other things, rice bowls, fruit dishes, teacups, wine bowls, decanters, tableware, ritual ware for ancestral offerings, and enormous fish bowls. In 1600 alone, these kilns produced a total of 235,000 pieces of porcelain for the court at the cost of 200,000 taels of silver.[72] Tens of thousands of valuable hardwood trees from distant Sichuan, Huguang, Jiangxi, and Zhejiang provinces were used in palace construction and repair. In fact, palace construction and fuel consumption in the capital had an observable and baneful influence on the forests of neighboring counties.[73] The imperial span extended to the emperor's table. The palace

---

69. Geiss, "Peking Under the Ming," p. iii.

70. See the classic studies by Wang Yuquan in *Laiwuji*. For an argument that farmers on these imperial estates paid less in rent than they would have paid in taxes on regular lands, see Ray Huang, *Taxation and Governmental Finance in Sixteenth Century China*, p. 107.

71. Han Dacheng, "Mingdai quangui jingying de gongshangye" 明代權貴經營的工商業, in idem, *Mingdai shehui jingji chutan*, pp. 356–94.

72. For a detailed discussion of the variety and costs of imperial ware produced at Jingdezhen, see Iida Atsuko, "Minchō Keitokuchin gokishō no keihi." The figure for 1600 is on p. 37; charts listing the numbers and varieties of goods appear on pp. 39–40.

73. Du Xin, "Mingdai Beijing diqu de senlin gaikuang"; Qiu Zhonglin, "Renkou zengchang." Qiu notes that the court's demand for lumber peaked in the mid-fifteenth century at 57,000 tons per annum, largely for heating and cooking fuel. The court's voracious appetite for firewood and charcoal helped drive up prices for wood, which

eunuch Liu Ruoyu 劉若愚 (1584–1642) compiled a list of the ingredients used each month in the imperial kitchens. A sampling from the first lunar month includes: ground squirrels from beyond the Great Wall, Manchurian pine nuts, Shanxi apples, Jiangxi sugar, Zhangzhou oranges and *ganlan* (*Burseracea carnarium album*), Mount Wutai mushrooms, Jiangnan black mushrooms, Beijing potatoes, Nanjing "hawk-beak bamboo sprouts" 鷹嘴筍 from Mount Wudang, *huang jing* 黃精 (a medicinal plant noted in the *Materia Medica* 本草綱目), and Lu'an tea 六安茶.[74] Incense burners, fans, paintings, books, ceramics, tapestries, jewels, furs, and statues produced for the Ming imperial family drew on materials from every province in the empire and inspired emulation outside the court.

Goods, services, wealth, and people flowed relatively freely during the Ming period, especially during the dynasty's last century.[75] Seldom, however, could any individual or family hope to rival the imperial court's ability to mobilize material and artisanal resources. For instance, imperial table settings could include as many as twenty-seven items. As Jan Stuart writes, "The ability to set a vast number of tables with decorated porcelains provided an unparalleled opportunity to disseminate images of power or good fortune that were the themes of the porcelain designs."[76] This was one way the Ming court distinguished itself from all other centers of power within China and on the broader stage of Asia.

Whether this strong imperial presence in the economic realm and material culture led to developmental stagnation that derailed China's march toward world domination is open to debate. It does demonstrate the steady stream of manpower, material, and revenue into the Imperial City. It was not, however, a one-way street. By no later than the mid-fifteenth century, those products and skills were available for sale in the markets of Beijing. At the "Inner Market" (or Court Market) 內市 located outside Xuanwu Gate, the northern gate of the Forbidden City, connoisseurs with deep

---

eventually contributed to the growth of coal as the primary fuel among Beijing's other residents.

74. Liu Ruoyu 劉若愚, "Yinshi haoshang jilüe" 飲食好尚紀略, in *Zhuozhongzhi* 酌中志, pp. 178–79; cited in Qiu Zhonglin, "Huangdi de canzhuo," p. 15.

75. For useful discussions, see Heijdra, "The Ming—Rural Socio-economic Development"; and Brook, "Communications and Commerce." As Brook (pp. 705–7) notes, some established elite families found this flow of wealth and products a disturbing challenge. For perceptions of these challenges and how established cultural elites sought to overcome them, see Clunas, *Superfluous Things*.

76. See Stuart, "Layers of Meaning," in Cort and Stuart, *Joined Colors*, p. 34.

pockets could purchase "Xuande reign bronzes, Chenghua reign ceramics, Yongle reign lacquerware from the imperial orchards, and Jingtai reign cloisonné from imperial workshops. Their exquisiteness far surpasses those of antiquity."[77] Curio shops in the capital sold smaller versions of Tantric Buddhist statues housed in imperially sponsored temples. During the late Ming, illustrated educational materials originally compiled for a young emperor and an heir apparent enjoyed considerable popularity in editions customized for both high-end and more popular markets. Sumptuous Inner Palace editions with gold satin cases and imperial seals were surreptitiously removed from the Forbidden City and sold in the capital. The quality and prestige associated with the imperial court ensured a steady demand for its goods.[78]

Far more than physical objects flowed out of the Forbidden City. Fashion and sensibilities at the court left their mark on the tone and style of the capital as a whole. The well-informed observer Shen Defu (1578–1642) noted the small ways the court's eating habits shaped the capital's diet and market stalls. Imperial affines and eunuchs followed the court's taste for out-of-season vegetables. Responding to this market demand, farmers and peddlers offered cucumbers and "white string beans" 白扁苣 even in the dead of Beijing's winter.[79] In a series of richly documented studies,

---

77. See Sun Chengze (1592–1676), *Chun ming meng yu lu, juan* 6, "Hou shi" 後市, p. 100.

78. The examples of the Tibetan statue, picturebooks, and Inner Palace books come from the chapters in this volume by David Robinson (pp. 365–421), Julia K. Murray (pp. 231–68), and Scarlett Jang (pp. 116–85). For a contemporaneous comment by a member of Jiangnan's cultural elite that suggests mild derision for certain kinds of imperial porcelains, see Clunas, *Superfluous Things*, p. 102. Some Jiangnan literati also frowned on the food served in the Forbidden City; it lacked the delicate flavor they esteemed (Qiu Zhonglin, "Huangdi de canzhuo," p. 17). As Qiu notes, the imperial kitchens produced great delicacies, but in general they favored the more strongly flavored cuisine of North China.

79. Shen Defu, "Suichao mudan" 歲朝牡丹, "Jixiang" 機祥, in *YHB, juan* 29, 3: 733. Inexpensive peonies were also available in the capital at New Year's. For a discussion of the changes in agriculture, fertilizer use, and heat-forced cultivation in the capital's suburbs, see Geiss, "Peking Under the Ming," pp. 79–87. In an example of the interplay among Jiangnan literati tastes, imperial fashion, and market prices in Beijing, Shen Defu stressed the role of Suzhou elites in dictating fashion. Explaining a spike in prices for Xuande incense burners, Shen noted, "It is all due to the leaders of fashion from Suzhou making these things the subject of their 'elegant discussion,' which the imperial relatives who buy from merchants blindly and frivolously imitate" (cited in Clunas, *Superfluous Things*, p. 137). Paul Smith ("Impressions," p. 108) notes that by late in the fifteenth century, the "vitality and ebullience that had been bottled up in Jiangnan began

Qiu Zhonglin has argued that court preferences in textiles, clothing, banquet foods, and morality had an observable impact on the social tone and values of the entire capital.[80] Court rituals, too, spread far beyond the walls of the Forbidden City. During the sixteenth and early seventeenth centuries, both local officials and lineage leaders employed the Five Bows and Three Kowtows ritual, which began as an act of respect by court officials for the Ming emperor, in local community pact rituals. As material objects, tastes, and rituals traveled, they acquired new meanings and were used in new contexts.[81]

The Ming imperial family sought to harness all the resources of the empire. Like preceding Chinese and foreign dynasties that ruled the Central Plains, the Ming court attempted to bring under its control not only tax revenues and manpower but also the power of deities. At least a portion of nearly every day of the year was devoted to ritual activities at the court. Offerings to Confucian, Daoist, Buddhist, and folk worthies were important events in the life of the court and demanded special clothing, fasting, music, incense, processions, sacrifices, and banquets. Ritual engagement with dozens of local temples and cults meant that court personnel, most commonly eunuchs but also high-ranking civil and military officials, traveled regularly from the court to sites throughout the empire. The court's representatives brought legitimacy, wealth, and influence to major temple complexes with empire-wide followings, such as those devoted to Guangong, Dongyue, and Guanyin.[82] On behalf of the emperor, palace eunuchs also traveled semiannually to such distant locales as the temple dedicated to the spirit of the Yiwulü Mountains 醫巫閭山, located in the northeast corner of the Ming empire (present-day Beining, Liaoning prov-

---

spreading to all regions of China." Thus, the tastes of court elites, influenced by Jiangnan fashions, shaped Beijing's economy.

80. Qiu Zhonglin, "Cong jinli lüshen kan Mingdai Beijing"; idem, "Mingdai Beijing de shehui fengqi bianqian"; idem, "Mingdai Beijing dushi shenghuo."

81. McDermott, "Emperor, Elites, and Commoners."

82. On state religion during the Ming, see Taylor, "Official Religion in the Ming," and literature cited therein. For an analysis of the Ming court's patronage of Guangong 關公 (Guan Yu 關羽), see Cai Dongzhou and Wen Tinghai, *Guan Yu chongbai yanjiu*, pp. 155–71. For an argument that the Ming imperial household's patronage (largely by the empresses dowager and palace eunuchs) constituted the "decisive factor" in the revival of the pilgrimage to Putuoshan, the sacred island of Guanyin, during the sixteenth century, see Ishino, "Mindai Banreki nenkan ni okeru Futazan no fukkyō."

ince).[83] Each trip added another strand to the web of connections that bound the court and its personnel to the rest of China. In more prosaic terms, such trips ensured the flow of gifts, foods, musical traditions, and local knowledge to and from the court.

Art historians have also explored the complex strands that linked the Ming court, its imperial collections, and its patronage to a wide variety of painters, both professional and amateur (the line between the two was often a function of social discourse and posture). Kathlyn Liscomb has drawn attention to the early Ming court's role as a magnet for aspiring painters throughout the realm, who were attracted by the prestige and patronage of the imperial family, imperial-in-laws, and high ministers. At the same time, she observes, "artistic talent and ideas did not flow in one direction . . . but circulated freely from the capital back to many regional centers."[84] In this sense, the Ming court (like many other courts) offered an arena in which painters from a variety of traditions converged and interacted. Marsha Weidner has shown that the use of palace-style architecture in Buddhist and Daoist complexes, the fusion of images of emperors and empresses with Buddhist deities, and patronage by princely courts, the throne, and others members of the imperial clan mean that it is misleading to draw any absolute lines between "court culture" and developments outside the Forbidden City.[85]

Ming emperors clearly traveled far less than did their Mongol and Manchu counterparts during the preceding Yuan and succeeding Qing periods. Throughout the first half of the dynasty, however, most Ming rulers spent time outside the Forbidden City. The Ming founder had a rough-scrabble upbringing far from the capital. His son Yongle spent considerable time on

---

83. For the texts of the prayers offered at Beizhen Temple on behalf of the throne, see Sonoda, *Manshū kinseki shikō*, vol. 1; and Zhao Jie and Zhou Hongshan, *Beiningshi wenwuzhi*, pp. 243–62.

84. Liscomb, "Shen Zhou's Collection of Early Modern Painting," p. 216. Elsewhere, Liscomb ("The Role of Leading Court Officials as Patrons," p. 46) has used the simile of a stream to describe the interaction between the capitals and regional centers of art. "For a time, the court was fed by the influx of many regional tributaries, joining to form the dominant artistic stream, which then revitalized and broadened regional schools of painting. This stimulated change in such local centers as Suzhou, which then rose to challenge the preeminence of the capitals."

85. See Weidner, "Imperial Engagements with Buddhist Art and Architecture." For the ties between Yongle and popular religion, see Chan Hok-lam, "'Zhenwushen Yonglexiang' chuanshuo suyuan," pp. 87–127.

military expeditions into the steppe. As a young man, the fifth emperor, Xuande (r. 1426–35), had repeatedly campaigned with his grandfather Yongle on the Mongolian steppe, and he toured the northern border as emperor. During the mid-fifteenth century, Zhengtong (r. 1436–49, 1457–64) spent a year on the steppe as an involuntary guest of the Oirat Mongol leader Esen (d. 1455). Early in the sixteenth century, Zhengde (r. 1506–21) sojourned along the northern border for several months, experiencing frontier military culture. Later in his reign, he left Beijing for more than a year to sample the delights of Jiangnan. The heirless Zhengde was succeeded by Jiajing (r. 1522–66), who was born and raised in a province distant from the capital. Experiences gained outside Beijing influenced each emperor's views, expectations, and style of rulership. These experiences further undermined any absolute demarcation between the court and the rest of the empire. Perhaps the characterization of imperial isolation springs from generalizations based on the lives of the last few Ming emperors who seldom ventured beyond the capital. In any case, greater attention to individual variation and changes in the Ming court over time are in order.[86]

Repopulating the Ming Court

Again and again, the art historian Craig Clunas has demonstrated that some of our most cherished assumptions regarding the nature of Chinese aesthetics and painting are flawed. He often traces the problem back to a retrospective rewriting of history, in which certain sensibilities and tastes, which eventually grew dominant (at least in art theory circles, both Chinese and later Western), would so overshadow other contemporaneous styles and perspectives that the latter gradually evaporated from historical accounts and present collections.[87] The resultant understanding of the past is inevitably myopic and misleading.

A similar problem confronts those interested in the Ming court. Civil officials have long loomed deceptively large in our understanding of the Ming court, in large part, because they wrote the records available to us

---

86. Critical to this are more English-language biographies of Ming emperors. Despite its critics, Ray Huang's finely drawn portrait of Wanli remains essential reading for the student of the Ming; see *1587*, pp. 1–41. Henry Tsai's *Perpetual Happiness: The Ming Emperor Yongle* is another welcome step in this direction. The Liaoning jiaoyu chubanshe has published a series of biographies (of varying quality) on each of the Ming emperors. Additional biographies in Chinese and Japanese are available for several emperors.

87. Clunas, *Superfluous Things*; idem, *Pictures and Visuality in Early Modern China*.

today. The chapters in this volume show that scholar-officials played a more humble role. One group among many, they were seldom united in their interests. As the place of scholar-officials diminishes to a more realistic scale, the importance of a wide variety of other actors becomes clearer. Military men, eunuchs, religious specialists, palace women, and entertainers also contended for influence and power at the court, often far more effectively than scholar-officials.

Although literati accounts pass over them lightly, military personnel were ubiquitous at the Ming court. Early in the fifteenth century, the capital began as a military outpost and for the remainder of the dynasty, as much as a quarter of the country's military garrisons were stationed in and around Beijing. Early sixteenth-century records show at least 140,000 soldiers in the capital garrisons; as many as another 100,000 were rotated into these garrisons each year from border units.[88] Government regulations required members of the Brocade Guard and other units in the capital garrisons to attend nearly every ceremony, procession, and state banquet in the Forbidden City.[89] Scores of mounted military officers served as outriders for the many imperial processions each year to the Ming imperial tombs north of Beijing and to the suburbs south of the city (see Fig. 1.1). Hundreds of foot soldiers marched as an honor guard for the emperor when he ventured outside the walls of the Forbidden City. Rows of warriors in armor and hefting weapons arrayed themselves around the emperor's throne during the daily morning court audiences. As set forth in such official compendiums of rites as the *Collected Rites of the Great Ming Dynasty* (*Da Ming jili* 大明集禮), investiture rituals, funerals, offerings at the Ancestral Temple, sacrifices in the hope of good harvest, and dozens of other ceremonies required the presence of military guards. Numerous rituals devoted to military matters were also conducted at the court. Military dances and music constituted a major category of court performances.

These military men and martial displays were visible symbols not only of the empire's power but also of the emperor's role as supreme military leader. The imposing military display was calculated to impress foreign

---

88. See Robinson, *Bandits, Eunuchs, and the Son of Heaven*, for figures and relevant scholarship. The most complete study of the Ming troop rotation system is Peng Yong, *Mingdai banjun zhidu yanjiu*. As Peng and others have noted, the number of rotation troops dropped sharply during the last decades of the fifteenth century.
89. See, e.g., *DMHD*, 142.1a–11a.

Fig. 1.1 Anonymous. *Emperor's Return to the Capital* 入蹕圖. Sixteenth century. Scroll 92.1 ×
30003.6 cm. Portion. National Palace Museum, Taipei, Taiwan, Republic of China.

envoys.[90] It also reminded civil officials and others of the imperial family's
puissance.

This martial dimension found expression in the physical layout of the imperial grounds. Early during the Yongle reign (1403–24), the Ming expanded
the Yuan dynasty's hunting grounds south of the capital, increasing their size
and elaborating on the bridges and lodges on the grounds. There, emperors
from Yongle to Zhengde rode, hunted, and honed their military skills alongside military officers. Civil officials were not excluded, nor were less martial
pastimes. To judge from their many complaints of abuses associated with
the Southern Lakes Park hunting grounds, however, civil officials never felt
at ease with this facet of court life. Rulers after Zhengde paid scant attention
to the park, with the notable exception of Wanli (r. 1573–1620), who began
repairs to its crumbling walls and dilapidated buildings.[91]

Recent scholarship has thrown much needed light on the pervasive influence of another often-maligned group at the court, palace eunuchs.[92]

90. If the experiences of the early fifteenth-century Timurid envoy Ghiyathuddin
Naqqash are indicative, the strategy succeeded. He repeatedly refers to the presence of
the imperial bodyguard at court, carefully enumerating the warriors' various weapons;
see his "Report to Mirza Baysunghur," pp. 287, 288, 290.

91. Chen Yuhe, "Nanhaizi yu Mingdai zhengzhi." For further discussion of Wanli's
military interests, see the chapter by Kenneth M. Swope in this volume (pp. 61–115).

92. Tsai, *The Eunuchs in the Ming Dynasty*; Wei Jinlin, *Mingdai huanguan zhengzhi*; Wen
Gongyi, *Mingdai de huanguan he gongting.*

Often castrated as children, by the mid-fifteenth century, most eunuchs hailed from poor families in the counties surrounding Beijing, who saw palace service as an opportunity for social and economic advancement. A few well-known exceptions of adult males also became eunuchs in order to gain employment at the court. Palace eunuchs, whose numbers ranged in the thousands, cared for the personal needs of the imperial family. In the process, they often became trusted and influential members of the inner court, and their patronage extended far beyond the walls of the Forbidden City.[93] Their support was essential to civil officials, who nonetheless cast them as bitter foes. Overturning long-standing stereotypes about eunuchs' avarice, moral turpitude, and pernicious influence on generations of emperors, newer studies reveal their importance to nearly every facet of Ming court life.[94] Some of the most informative studies of eunuchs are based not on official histories or court annals but on stele inscriptions recounting patronage of temple construction and the lives of influential eunuchs. Less encumbered by scholar-official pretensions, these accounts relate in detail the eunuchs' vital economic, social, and religious roles in Beijing and its environs.[95]

Eunuchs constituted perhaps the most important pillar of the court's institutional memory. They transmitted myriad details of everyday life from one generation to the next. They oversaw the niceties of seating order at banquets, maintained proper protocol at the daily morning audiences, supervised the court's sexual life, and saw to the imperial family's medical needs. Palace eunuchs taught young members of the imperial clan how to appreciate calligraphy and painting. They helped determine the imperial palate. They figured prominently in the imperial family's religious beliefs and practices. Eunuchs, not civil officials, oversaw sacrifices to imperial ancestors in the Ancestral Temple.[96] Through their daily stewardship, eunuchs taught boys from the imperial family how to be first heirs apparent and then emperors. The chapters by Scarlett Jang, Joseph Lam, Julia

---

93. For a brief discussion of eunuchism in the capital region, patronage ties to local society, and relevant scholarship, see Robinson, "Notes on Hebei Eunuchs During the Mid-Ming"; and idem, *Bandits, Eunuchs, and the Son of Heaven*, pp. 34–36, 99–117.

94. See the chapters in this volume by Scarlett Jang (pp. 116–85), Julia K. Murray (pp. 231–68), and David Robinson (pp. 365–421).

95. Naquin, *Peking*; Chen Yunü, *Mingdai ershisi yamen huanguan yu Beijing fojiao*; Dong Yiran, "Cong shike tuoben cailiao kan Mingdai jingcheng huanguan de chong fo zhi feng."

96. Sun Chengze, *Chun ming meng yu lu, juan* 6, "Neiguanjian" 内官監, p. 95.

Murray, and David Robinson in this volume illustrate how tightly eunuchs were woven into the tapestry of Ming court life. Jang demonstrates that eunuchs used both oral *and written* sources to preserve court precedents and drew on both to guide the throne on important ritual matters.

Ming Despotism and Individual Agency

Two widely divergent images regarding the power of the Ming emperors coexist uneasily. Many scholars since the seventeenth century have argued that Ming emperors wielded greater power and faced fewer effective checks on their rule than did rulers in previous periods. The late Frederick Mote held that this despotism had begun during the Song dynasty but reached its culmination with the Ming founder Hongwu, "the harshest and the most unreasonable tyrant in all of Chinese history."[97] Scholars from China, Japan, and Korea frequently use such terms as "autocratic," "totalitarian," or "autocratic totalitarianism" to describe dynastic governments from roughly the tenth to early twentieth centuries. The basic reasoning is that from the tenth century on, aristocratic families with exalted pedigrees, who often played critical roles in government and culture, lost their privileged political, economic, and cultural status. These studies are generally interested more in the state writ large than in the court or even the emperor, yet the question is relevant to understanding the Ming court.[98] Mote observed that Hongwu's massive purges and calculated use of torture "terrorized the whole world of officialdom."[99] In an effort to bolster his status vis-à-vis civil officials, Hongwu placed "the imperial throne on a much-elevated dais to keep it above and away from" officials, appointed eunuchs to oversee civil officials' decorum at daily audiences, and subjected even high officials to humiliating beatings at court. All these measures influenced the tone of the early Ming court.[100]

———

97. Mote, "The Growth of Chinese Despotism," p. 20. Hongwu and his reign are considered from a variety of perspectives in two recent collections: Schneewind, *Long Live the Emperor*; and Chu Hung-lam, *Ming Taizu de zhiguo linian yu shijian*.

98. For a study of Hongwu, tracing his "increased imperial autocratic control" to the "patriarchal despotic system of feudal autocracy," see Wang Hongjiang, "On the Strengthening of Imperial Autocracy at the Beginning of the Ming."

99. Mote, "The Growth of Chinese Despotism," p. 28.

100. Mote (ibid., p. 31) maintains that Hongwu "established a reign of terror that more or less persisted throughout the 277 years of the Ming dynasty." Mote's notions of the reign of terror were almost certainly shaped by Wu Han's classic 1949 biography of Hongwu, *Zhu Yuanzhang zhuan*, in which Wu coined the term "terror politics"

As noted in the Introduction, Ray Huang offered a fundamentally different interpretation of the Ming emperor, a man bound by convention and precedent, dependent on his civil bureaucracy, a "prisoner of the Forbidden City." In his 1961 review of Karl Wittfogel's *Oriental Despotism*, Mote had already stressed that total power "did not mean totalitarian power, omnipresent and omnicompetent." In addition to the practical limitations posed by distance, numbers, and the flow of information, "Chinese humanism" constituted the greatest check on the emperor's power. Mote reasoned that "legitimacy of the dynasty had to be established and maintained in Confucian terms" and that "the emperor and his people had certain collective goals which had to be justified in terms of the values of the society."[101]

Through his deeply evocative and nuanced portraits of the Wanli emperor and the principal officials of the day, Huang, in contrast, stressed the power of administrative precedent and the civil bureaucracy as brakes on the ruler's power. He offered example after example in which tradition or the founder's will stymied the wishes of the emperor (and often his officials, too). Ellen Soullière would later elaborate on this theme, noting, "under the mature Ming system, even strong emperors operated under severe limitations. Their role was to react and to arbitrate, almost never to initiate."[102] Although "the Ming was the most profoundly anti-aristocratic of all Chinese dynasties,"[103] the Ming emperor delegated many duties to his civil officials and his palace eunuch staff, thus forgoing what in principle should have been untrammeled power.

The chapters in this volume generally occupy the middle ground and are concerned more with exploring the shifting dynamics of imperial rulership and court culture than with the debate over oriental despotism or such questions as the reach of the state.[104] They make clear that Ming emperors (and others at their courts) enjoyed considerable agency. They were not slavishly bound to the will of the dynastic founder, nor were they helpless in the face of accumulated administrative and ritual precedent. Dora Ching

---

(*konghu zhengzhi* 恐怖政治), a phrase that would become widely adopted in the following decades. See also Ye Dingyi's similarly inspired *Mingdai tewu zhengzhi*.

101. Mote, "Growth of Chinese Despotism," pp. 33, 34.

102. Soullière, "Reflections on Chinese Despotism and the Power of the Inner Court," p. 136.

103. Ibid., p. 138.

104. Paul Smith ("Problematizing the Song-Yuan-Ming Transition," pp. 19–30) situates the Ming state in a long phase of relative passivity that stretched from the twelfth to the seventeenth century.

demonstrates how the individual religious beliefs, personalities, and political agendas of various emperors during the fourteenth and fifteenth centuries reshaped imperial portraiture. Late fifteenth-century portraits differ dramatically from those approved by the founder. Joseph Lam shows how musical tastes and ambitions varied greatly from emperor to emperor. He also makes clear that it was not merely a progression from a dominant founder to meek and nondescript later rulers. David Robinson argues that the early sixteenth century marked an important shift in the identity of the imperial family. The change hinged on the particulars of one emperor's upbringing. The personalities, ambitions, and experiences of individual emperors could reshape court practices and dynamics.

At the same time Ming emperors enjoyed considerable agency, they faced nearly constant challenge: most directly by imperial family members and civil officials, slightly less directly by local elites, and in the broadest sense by commoner subjects and surrounding countries. Sometimes these were grand political battles with grave and obvious consequences for the dynasty. During the tumultuous decades of the late sixteenth and early seventeenth century, rancorous debate surrounded the selection of Wanli's successor. The consequences of that debate outlived the dynasty, complicating efforts by Ming loyalists to resist the Qing after the fall of Beijing in 1644.[105]

At other times, the scale, if not ferocity, of the contests was more limited. For instance, in 1527, Jiajing announced that Buddhist nuns exercised a deleterious moral influence and ordered the destruction of an imperially sponsored nunnery in the capital. Within days, various female members of the imperial family, including the "sage mother" and "sage aunt" (the biological mother and aunt, respectively, of the deceased Zhengde) made clear their objections to the emperor's plans. After considerable debate within the imperial family, a senior civil official crafted a face-saving way for the emperor to withdraw (beaten) from the fray.[106] In this case, limitations on

---

105. See Ray Huang, "Lung-ch'ing and Wan-li reigns," p. 550; and Struve, "Southern Ming," p. 642.

106. Yu Ruji, "Chu nisengsi" 處尼僧寺 and "Sengdao beikao" 僧道備考, in *LBZG*, 89.33a–36b (*Wenyuange siku quanshu* ed., 598: 615–17). The Hongzhi emperor had established the temple in question, Huanggu si 皇姑寺. The account in the *Ming Shizong shilu* (83.8b–9a), in contrast, omits all mention of debate within the imperial family. In fact, it states that the temple was destroyed, "its members" scattered, and the registration of the clergy checked. Shen Defu notes the misleadingly brief *Shilu* entry and discusses in detail the negotiations between the emperor and the imperial women; see Shen, "Hui Huanggu si" 毀皇姑寺, in *YHB, juan* 27, 3: 685–86. For a discussion of the temple (also

the emperor's behavior had nothing to do with the founder's *Ancestral Injunctions*. Senior women in the imperial family simply would not brook interference in their religious and social practices. Most Ming emperors could no more achieve unchallenged power than Tantalus could slake his thirst.

Conflicts of interest and perspective between the emperor and his civil bureaucracy form a central theme in Ming political history and deeply influenced the tone and composition of the court.[107] During his decades in power, the Ming founder put to death tens of thousands of officials in sanguinary purges. Spilling far less blood, Zhengde clashed with his officials over his attempts to revive a tradition of personal rule and an active military posture. Zhengde donned military garb and ordered his officials to do the same. He avoided audiences with his ministers and largely rejected even the formal palaces of the Forbidden City. Instead, he traveled the streets of Beijing incognito at night, established an alternative site of governance in his Leopard Quarters, and eventually left the capital itself, first to Xuanfu in the north and then to Nanjing in the south.[108]

Jiajing's tensions with Beijing's political elite began before he even stepped foot in the city. After Zhengde died without an heir in 1521, senior court officials determined that according to dynastic precedent the throne should go to a cousin, the only son of the Hongzhi emperor's younger brother. Jiajing's unusual succession led to a long series of complicated questions regarding protocol, ritual, power, and legitimacy that bled into all facets of court life. Was he to be treated as the adopted son of the deceased Zhengde or as his cousin? What would be the ritual and political consequences for such treatment? These questions eventually culminated in the Great Rites Controversy, a decade-long political struggle that severely strained relations between the emperor and much of his civil bureaucracy. Inspired in large part by a desire to see his parents receive what he felt were proper honors and titles, Jiajing ordered the most far-ranging

---

known as Baoming Temple 保明寺) and its patronage, see Thomas Li and Susan Naquin, "The Baoming Temple," pp. 136–40.

107. This is not an argument for simple bifurcation. As noted above, the emperor and his civil bureaucracy were mutually dependent. Individual emperors did maintain genial relations with individual ministers. Confucian rhetoric held a special place for rulers and servitors who achieved a "salt and sour plum" relationship, that is, one mutually complementary and characterized by harmony. See the chapter by Hung-lam Chu in this volume (pp. 186–230). Yet the effusive praise lavished on such examples and the way that the early fifteenth-century Xuande emperor was lionized for his appreciation of civil officials suggests that such relations were the exception rather than the rule.

108. Geiss, "The Leopard Quarter During the Cheng-te Reign."

series of changes to Ming court rituals since the dynasty's founding a century and half earlier.[109] As the chapters in this collection show, the Great Rites Controversy would touch everything from music and rites to architecture, portraiture, and the emperor's ongoing education in the classical corpus of history and political philosophy.[110]

Now is a particularly propitious time for systematic examination of the Ming court. As the preceding pages have shown, scholars from various fields have already begun to consider the place of the Ming court, and their work provides a useful point of departure. Thus, this volume is less an effort to "bring the court back in" (since it is clear that it never really left) and more one of putting the court at the center of our consideration. Additionally, the amount of source material available for the Ming period has increased significantly in recent years. Many rare editions and archival materials have been reprinted in the People's Republic of China.[111] A smaller but not inconsiderable number of newly uncovered manuscripts have also become available.[112] Finally, over the past six decades, a series of archeological discoveries have provided new materials for a thoroughgoing consideration of the Ming court—its principal participants and their interactions, concerns, and activities. The chapters in this volume represent a preliminary effort at an integrative understanding of a long-neglected facet of late imperial–early modern Chinese history.

———

109. Zhao Kesheng, *Mingchao Jiajing shiqi guojia jili gaizhi*.

110. Several chapters in this volume offer synopses of the Great Rites Controversy from a variety of vantage points. Among the most detailed are the treatments by Hung-lam Chu (pp. 186–230) and Dora C. Y. Ching (pp. 321–64).

111. These include but are not limited to the various *Four Treasuries*–inspired reprint series. Siku jinhuishu congkan bianzuan weiyuanhui 四庫禁燬書叢刊編纂委員會, comp., *Siku jinhuishu congkan* 四庫禁燬書叢刊 (Beijing: Beijing chubanshe, 1997); Siku quanshu cunmu congkan bianzuan weiyuanhui 四庫全書存目叢刊編纂委員會, comp., *Siku quanshu cunmu congkan* 四庫全書存目叢刊 (Ji'nan: Qilu shushe, 1995–97); and *Xuxiu Siku quanshu* 續修四庫全書 (Shanghai: Shanghai guji chubanshe, 2002). The majority of Ming-period archival materials are now available in 101 volumes of reduced-size facsimile reproductions; see Zhongguo diyi lishi dang'anguan and Liaoningsheng dang'anguan, *Zhongguo Mingchao dang'an zonghui*. For introductory comments on this series, see Amari Hiroki, "Minchō tōan o riyō shita kenkyū no dōkō ni tsuite"; and idem, "Kichōna Mindai no tōan shiryōshū," pp. 46–50, 62. See also the 300 volumes (memorials, border affairs, and foreign relations) of the massive compilation of "basic materials on the Ming period" edited by Ren Mengqiang and Li Li, *Mingdai jiben shiliao congkan*.

112. For a recently available source about the many transgressions of Hongwu's sons, see Zhang Dexin, "Taizu huangdi qinlu"; and Hok-lam Chan, "Ming Taizu's Problem with His Sons: Prince Qin's Criminality and Early-Ming Politics."

Works Cited

Adamson, John. "The Making of the *Ancien-Régime* Court, 1500–1700." In *The Princely Courts of Europe: Ritual, Politics, and Culture Under the* Ancien-Régime, *1500–1750*, ed. idem. London: Weidenfeld and Nicolson, 1999, pp. 24–30.

Ali, Daud. *Courtly Culture and Political Life in Early Medieval India.* Cambridge: Cambridge University Press, 2004.

Allsen, Thomas. *Commodity and Exchange in the Mongol Empire.* Cambridge: Cambridge University Press, 1997.

———. *Culture and Conquest in Mongol Eurasia.* Cambridge: Cambridge University Press, 2001.

Amari Hiroki 甘利弘樹. "Kichōna Mindai no tōan shiryōshū" 貴重な明代の档案史料集. *Tōhō* 東方, no. 252 (2002): 26–29.

———. "Minchō tōan o riyō shita kenkyū no dōkō ni tsuite—*Chūgoku Minchō tōan sōkai* kankō ni yosete" 明朝档案を利用した研究の動向について——『中国明朝档案総匯』刊行によせて. *Manzokushi kenkyū* 満族史研究 1 (2002): 73–91.

Atwell, William. "International Bullion Flows and the Chinese Economy Circa 1530–1650." *Past and Present* 95 (1982): 68–90.

———. "Ming China and the Emerging World Economy, c. 1470–1650." In *CHC*, 8: 376–416.

———. "Notes on Silver, Foreign Trade, and the Late Ming Economy." *Ch'ing-shih wen-t'i* (1977): 1–33.

———. "A Seventeenth-Century 'General Crisis' in East Asia." *Modern Asia Studies* 24, no. 4 (1990): 661–82.

Barnhart, Richard. *Painters of the Great Ming.* Dallas: Dallas Museum of Art, 1993.

Berger, Patricia. *Empire of Emptiness.* Honolulu: University of Hawai'i Press, 2003.

———. "Miracles in Nanjing: An Imperial Record of the Fifth Karmapa's Visit to the Chinese Capital." In *Cultural Intersections in Later Chinese Buddhism*, ed. Marsha Weidner. Honolulu: University of Hawai'i Press, 2001, pp. 145–69.

Bol, Peter. *"This Culture of Ours": Intellectual Transitions in T'ang and Sung China.* Stanford: Stanford University Press, 1992.

———. "Whither the Emperor? Emperor Huizong, the New Policies, and the Tang-Song Transition." *Journal of Sung-Yuan Studies*, no. 31 (2001): 103–34.

Brook, Timothy. "Communications and Commerce." In *CHC*, 8: 579–707.

———. *Confusions of Pleasure.* Berkeley: University of California Press, 1999.

Cai Dongzhou 蔡東洲 and Wen Tinghai 文廷海. *Guan Yu chongbai yanjiu* 官羽崇拜研究. Chengdu: Bashu shushe, 2001.

Cass, Victoria. "Female Healers in the Ming and the Lodge of Ritual and Ceremony." *Journal of the American Oriental Society* 106, no. 1 (1986): 233–45.

Chaffee, John. *Branches of Heaven: A History of the Imperial Clan of Song China.* Cambridge: Harvard University Asia Center, 1999.

Chan, Hok-lam 陳學霖. "Ming Taizu's Problem with His Sons: Prince Qin's Criminality and Early-Ming Politics." *Asia Major*, 3d series 20, no. 1 (2007): 54–103.

———. "Xie Jin (1369–1415) as Imperial Propagandist: His Role in the Revisions of the *Ming Taizu shilu.*" *T'oung Pao* 91 (2005): 56–124.

————. "'Zhenwushen Yonglexiang' chuanshuo suyuan" 真武神・永樂像傳説溯源. In idem, *Mingdai renwu yu chuanshuo* 明代人物與傳説. Hong Kong: Zhongwen daxue chubanshe, 1997, pp. 87–127.

Chang, Gordon. *The Coming Collapse of China*. New York: Random House, 2001.

CHC, 7, see Mote and Twitchett, *Cambridge History of China*

CHC, 8, see Twitchett and Mote, *Cambridge History of China*

Chen Baoliang 陳寶良. "Mingdai huangdi yu Mingdai wenhua" 明代皇帝與明代文化. *Shixue jikan* 史學集刊 1992, no. 3: 20–27.

————. *Mingdai shehui shenghuo shi* 明代社會生活史. Beijing: Zhongguo shehui kexue chubanshe, 2004.

Chen Yuhe 陳宇赫. "Nanhaizi yu Mingdai zhengzhi" 南海子與明代政治. *Ming Qing luncong* 明清論叢 4 (2003): 105–13.

Chen Yunü 陳玉女. *Mingdai ershisi yamen huanguan yu Beijing fojiao* 明代二十四衙門宦官與北京佛教. Taibei: Ruwen chubanshe, 2001.

Chen Zilong 陳子龍, ed. *Jingshi wenbian* 經世文編. Pinglutang, 1638. Facsimile reprint— Beijing: Zhonghua shuju, 1962.

Chu Hung-lam (Zhu Honglin 朱鴻林), ed. *Ming Taizu de zhiguo linian yu shijian* 明太祖的治國理念與實踐. Hong Kong: Chinese University of Hong Kong, forthcoming.

Clunas, Craig. *Pictures and Visuality in Early Modern China*. Princeton: Princeton University Press, 1996.

————. *Superfluous Things: Material Culture and Social Status in Early Modern China*. Urbana: University of Illinois Press, 1991.

Cort, Louise Allison, and Jan Stuart, eds. *Joined Colors: Decoration and Meaning in Chinese Porcelain*. Washington, DC: Arthur M. Sackler Gallery, Smithsonian Institution, 1993.

Danjō Hiroshi 檀上寛. "Chōsen ōchō hen *Ribun* shūsai no 'Bōbun' ni miru Minsho no taigai seisaku" 朝鮮王朝編『吏文』收載の「傍文」に見る明初の対外政策. In *Chūgoku Min Shin chihō tōan no kenkyū* 中国明清地方档案の研究, ed. Fuma Susumu 夫馬進. Kyoto, 2000, pp. 1–15.

————. "Minsho no tai-Nichi gaikō to Rin Ken jiken" 明初の對日外交と林賢事件. *Shisō* 史窓, no. 57 (2000): 35–55.

Des Forges, Roger. *Cultural Centrality and Political Change in Chinese History: Northeast Henan in the Fall of the Ming*. Stanford: Stanford University Press, 2003.

DMHD, see Shen Shixing, *Da Ming huidian*

Dong Yiran 董毅然. "Cong shike tuoben cailiao kan Mingdai jingcheng huanguan de chong fo zhi feng" 從石刻拓本材料看明代京城宦官的崇佛之風. In *Gu Cheng xiansheng jinian ji Ming Qingshi yanjiu wenji* 顧誠先生紀年暨明清史研究文集, ed. Wenji bianweihui 文集編委會. Zhengzhou: Zhongzhou guji chubanshe, 2005, pp. 335–45.

Dreyer, Edward. *Early Ming China: A Political History, 1355–1435*. Stanford: Stanford University Press, 1982.

Du Xin 杜欣. "Mingdai Beijing diqu de senlin gaikuang" 明代北京地區的森林概況. *Shoudu bowuguan congkan* 首都博物館叢刊 8 (1993): 65–70.

Fairbank, John. "A Preliminary Framework." In *The Chinese World Order: Traditional China's Foreign Relations*, ed. idem. Cambridge: Harvard University Press, 1968.

Fisher, Carney. *The Chosen One: Succession and Adoption in the Court of Ming Shizong*. Sydney: Allen and Unwin, 1990.

Fong, Wen. "Imperial Portraiture of the Ming Dynasty." In *Possessing the Past: Treasures from the National Palace Museum, Taipei*, ed. idem and James Watt. New York: Metropolitan Museum of Art, 1996, pp. 327–33.

Fuma Susumu. "Ming Studies in Japan, Part One (Beginnings to 1980)." *Ming Studies*, no. 47 (2003): 21–61.

Geertz, Clifford. *Negara: The Theatre State in Nineteenth-Century Bali*. Princeton: Princeton University Press, 1980.

Geiss, James. "The Chia-ching Reign, 1522–1566." In *CHC*, 7: 440–510.

————. "The Leopard Quarter During the Cheng-te Reign." *Ming Studies*, no. 24 (Fall 1987): 1–38.

————. "Peking Under the Ming (1368–1644)." Ph.D. diss., Princeton University, 1979.

Gu Cheng 顧誠. "Mingdai de zongshi" 明代的宗室. In *Ming Qing shi guoji xueshu taolunhui lunwenji* 明清史國際學術討論會論文集, ed. Ming Qing shi guoji xueshu taolunhui, Lunwenji mishuchu, Lunwenzu 明清史國際學術討論會論文集秘書處論文組. Tianjin: Tianjin renmin chubanshe, 1982, pp. 89–111.

Han Dacheng 韓大成. *Mingdai shehui jingji chutan* 明代社會經濟初探. Beijing: Renmin chubanshe, 1986.

Heijdra, Martin. "The Ming—Rural Socio-economic Development." In *CHC*, 8: 417–578.

Huang, Ray. "Fiscal Administration During the Ming Dynasty." In *Chinese Government in Ming Times: Seven Studies*, ed. Charles Hucker. New York: Columbia University Press, 1969, pp. 73–128.

————. "Lung-ch'ing and Wan-li Reigns." In *CHC*, 7: 511–84.

————. *1587, A Year of No Significance: The Ming Dynasty in Decline*. New Haven: Yale University Press, 1981.

————. *Taxation and Governmental Finance in Sixteenth Century China*. Cambridge: Cambridge University Press, 1974.

Hucker, Charles. *The Ming Dynasty: Its Origins and Evolving Institutions*. Ann Arbor: Center for Chinese Studies, University of Michigan, 1978.

————. "Ming Government." In *CHC*, 8: 9–105.

Idema, W. L. "State and Court in China: The Case of Hung-wu's Imperial Theatre." *Oriens Extremus* 23, no. 2 (1976): 175–89.

Iida Atsuko 飯田敦子. "Minchō Keitokuchin gokishō no keihi ni kansuru ichi kōsatsu" 明朝景徳鎮御器廠の経費に関する一考察. In *Sakuma Shigeo sensei beiju kinen Mindaishi ronshū* 佐久間重男先生米寿記念明代史論集, ed. Sakuma Shigeo sensei beiju kinenkai 佐久間重男先生米寿記念会. Tokyo: Kyūko shoin, 2002, pp. 33–65.

Im Kijung 林基中. "Yŏnhaengnok kwa Han'gukhak yŏn'gu" 燕行錄과韓國學研究. In *Yŏnhaengnok kwa Tong Asea yŏn'gu* 燕行錄과東亞細亞研究. Seoul: Tong'guk taehakkyo, Han'guk munhak yŏn'guso, 2001.

Ishino Kazuharu 石野一晴. "Mindai Banreki nenkan ni okeru Futazan no fukkyō" 明代萬暦年間における普陀山の復興. *Tōyōshi kenkyū* 東洋史研究 64, no. 1 (2005): 1–36.

Iwaki Hideo 岩城秀夫. "Min no kyūtei to engeki" 明の宮廷と演劇. *Chūgoku bungakuhō* 中国文学報 1 (1954): 113–32.

Kuhn, Philip. *Soulstealers: The Chinese Sorcery Scare of 1768*. Cambridge: Harvard University Press, 1990.

Lam, Joseph. *State Sacrifices and Music in Ming China: Orthodoxy, Creativity, and Expressiveness*. Albany: State University of New York Press, 1998.

Langlois, John. "Political Thought in Chin-hua Under Mongol Rule." In *China Under Mongol Rule*, ed. idem. Princeton: Princeton University Press, 1981, pp. 137–85.

LBZG, see Yu Ruyi, *Libu zhigao*

Ledyard, Gari. "Korean Travelers in China over Four Hundred Years, 1488–1887." *Occasional Papers on Korea* 2 (1974): 1–42.

Li, Thomas, and Susan Naquin. "The Baoming Temple: Religion and the Throne in Ming and Qing China." *Harvard Journal of Asiatic Studies* 48 (1988): 131–88.

Liscomb, Kathlyn. "Foregrounding the Symbiosis of Power: A Rhetorical Strategy in Some Chinese Commemorative Art." *Art History* 25, no. 2 (2002): 135–61.

———. "The Role of Leading Court Officials as Patrons of Painting in the Fifteenth Century." *Ming Studies*, no. 27 (Spring 1989): 34–62.

———. "Shen Zhou's Collection of Early Modern Painting and the Origins of the Wu School's Eclectic Revivalism." *Artibus Asiae* 52, no. 3/4 (1992): 215–54.

Liu Tong 劉侗 and Yu Yizheng 于奕正, comps. *Dijing jingwu lüe* 帝京景物略. 1635. Reprinted—Beijing: Beijing guji chubanshe, 2001.

Liu Yi 劉毅. *Mingdai diwang lingmu zhidu yanjiu* 明代帝王陵墓制度研究. Beijing: Renmin chubanshe, 2006.

———. *Ming Qing gongting shenghuo* 明清宮廷生活. Tianjin: Tianjin guji chubanshe, 2000.

McDermott, Joseph. "Emperor, Elites, and Commoners: The Community Pact Ritual of the Late Ming." In *State and Court Ritual in China*, ed. idem. Cambridge: Cambridge University Press, 1999, pp. 299–351.

Meskill, John. *Ch'oe P'u's Diary: A Record of Drifting Across the Sea*. Tucson: University of Arizona Press, 1965.

Mote, Frederick. "The Growth of Chinese Despotism: A Critique of Wittfogel's Theory of Oriental Despotism as Applied to China." *Oriens Extremus* 8 (1961): 1–41.

———. "Yüan and Ming." In *Food in Chinese Culture*, ed. K. C. Chang. New Haven: Yale University Press, 1977, pp. 195–257.

Mote, Frederick W., and Denis Twitchett, eds. *The Cambridge History of China*, vol. 7, *The Ming Dynasty, 1368–1644, Part I*. Cambridge: Cambridge University Press, 1988.

Na Chih-liang and William Kohler. *The Emperor's Procession: Two Scrolls of the Ming Dynasty*. Taibei: National Palace Museum, 1970.

Naqqash, Ghiyathuddin. "Report to Mirza Baysunghur on the Timurid Legation to the Ming Court at Peking." Trans. in W. M. Thackston, *A Century of Princes: Sources of Timurid History and Art*. Cambridge, MA: Aga Khan Program for Islamic Architecture at Harvard University, 1989, pp. 279–97.

Naquin, Susan. *Peking: Temples and City Life, 1400–1900*. Berkeley: University of California Press, 2000.

Paludan, Ann. *The Chinese Spirit Road: The Classical Tradition of Stone Tomb Statuary*. New Haven: Yale University Press, 1991.

Peng Yong 彭勇. *Mingdai banjun zhidu yanjiu* 明代班軍制度研究. Beijing: Zhongyang minzu daxue chubanshe, 2006.

Qian Mu 錢穆. *Guoshi dagang* 國史大綱. Shanghai: Guoli bianyiguan, 1948; rev. ed., Beijing: Shangwu yinshuguan, 2002.

Qiu Zhonglin 邱仲麟. "Cong jinli lüshen kan Mingdai Beijing shehui fengqi de bian-qian guocheng" 從禁例屢申看明代北京社會風氣的變遷過程. *Danjiang shixue* 淡江史學 6 (1992): 67–88.

———. "Huangdi de canzhuo: Mingdai de gongshan zhidu jiqi xiangguan wenti" 皇帝的餐桌: 明代的宮膳制度及其相關問題. *Taida lishi xuebao* 臺大歷史學報 34 (2004): 1–42.

———. "Mingdai Beijing de shehui fengqi bianqian—lizhi yu jiazhiguan de gaibian" 明代北京的社會風氣變遷—禮制與價值觀的改變. *Dalu zazhi* 大陸雜誌 88, no. 3 (1994): 28–42.

———. "Mingdai Beijing dushi shenghuo yu zhian de zhuanbian" 明代北京都市生活與治安的轉變. *Jiuzhou xuekan* 九州學刊 5, no. 2 (Oct. 1992): 49–106.

———. "Renkou zengzhang, linsen kanfa yu Mingdai Beijing shenghuo ranliao de zhuanbian" 人口增長, 林森砍伐與明代北京生活燃料的轉變. *Zhongyang yanjiu-yuan, Lishi yuyan yanjiusuo jikan* 中央研究院歷史語言研究所集刊 74, no. 1 (2003): 141–86.

Rawski, Evelyn. *The Last Emperors: A Social History of Qing Imperial Institutions.* Berkeley: University of California Press, 1998.

Ren Mengqiang 任夢強 and Li Li 李莉. *Mingdai jiben shiliao congkan* 明代基本史料叢刊. Beijing: Beijing xianzhuang shuju, 2004.

Robinson, David. *Bandits, Eunuchs, and the Son of Heaven: Rebellion and the Economy of Violence in Mid-Ming China.* Honolulu: University of Hawai'i Press, 2001.

———. "Notes on Hebei Eunuchs During the Mid-Ming." *Ming Studies* 34 (1995): 1–16.

Schafer, Edward. *The Golden Peaches of Samarkand: A Study of T'ang Exotics.* Berkeley: University of California Press, 1963.

Schneewind, Sarah, ed. *Long Live the Emperor! Uses of the Ming Founder Across Six Centuries of East Asian History.* Minneapolis: Society for Ming Studies, 2008.

Sen, Tan. *Buddhism, Diplomacy, and Trade.* Honolulu: University of Hawai'i Press, 2003.

Seid Ali Akbar Khatai. *Khatayname.* Trans. Zhang Zhishan 張至善 as *Zhongguo jixing* 中國紀行. Beijing: Sanlian shudian, 1988.

Serruys, Henry. "Early Lamaism in Mongolia." *Oriens Extremus* 10 (1963): 181–216.

Shen Defu 沈德符. *Wanli yehuo bian* 萬曆野獲編. 1619. Reprinted—Beijing: Zhonghua shuju, 1997.

Shen Shixing 申時行, comp. *Da Ming huidian* 大明會典. 1587. Photographic reprint—Taibei: Dongnan shubaoshe, 1964.

Smith, Paul Jakov. "Impressions of the Song-Yuan-Ming Transition: The Evidence from *Biji* Memoirs." In idem and Richard von Glahn, eds., *The Song-Yuan-Ming Transition in Chinese History.* Cambridge: Harvard University Asia Center, 2003, pp. 71–110.

———. "Problematizing the Song-Yuan-Ming Transition." In idem and Richard von Glahn, eds., *The Song-Yuan-Ming Transition in Chinese History.* Cambridge: Harvard University Asia Center, 2003, pp. 1–34.

Smith, Richard. *Chinese Maps: Images of "All Under Heaven."* Oxford: Oxford University Press, 1996.

Sonoda Kazuki 園田一龜, comp. *Manshū kinseki shikō* 滿洲金石志稿. Dairen: Minami Manshū tetsudō kabushiki kaisha, 1939.

Soullière, Ellen. "The Imperial Marriages of the Ming Dynasty." *Papers on Far Eastern History*, no. 37 (1988): 15–42.

———. "Palace Women in the Ming Dynasty: 1368–1644." Ph.D. diss., Princeton University, 1987.

———. "Reflections on Chinese Despotism and the Power of the Inner Court." *Asian Profile* 12, no. 2 (1984): 129–44.

Spence, Jonathan. *The Memory Palace of Matteo Ricci.* New York: Penguin Books, 1984.

Steinhardt, Nancy. *Chinese Imperial City Planning.* Honolulu: University of Hawai'i Press, 1990.

———. "Why Were Chang'an and Beijing So Different." *Journal of the Society of Architectural Historians* 45, no. 4 (1986): 339–57.

Struve, Lynn. "Southern Ming." In *CHC*, 7: 641–725.

Sun Chengze 孫成澤. *Chun ming meng yu lu* 春明夢餘錄. 1761. Reprinted—Beijing: Beijing guji chubanshe, 1992.

Taylor, Romeyn. "Official Religion in the Ming." In *CHC*, 8: 840–92.

Tsai, Henry. *The Eunuchs in the Ming Dynasty.* Albany: State University of New York Press, 1996.

———. *Perpetual Happiness: The Ming Emperor Yongle.* Seattle: University of Washington Press, 2001.

Twitchett, Denis, and Frederick W. Mote, eds. *The Cambridge History of China*, vol. 8, *The Ming Dynasty, 1368–1644, Part II.* Cambridge: Cambridge University Press, 1998.

Vinograd, Richard. "Palace and Court in the Later Ming Dynasty Public Imagination." Presented at the Conference on Chinese Court Painting / Zhongguo gongting huihua xueshu yantaohui 中國宮廷繪畫學術研討會. Beijing, Palace Museum, Oct. 16, 2003.

von Glahn, Richard. "Foreword." In Lynn Struve, ed., *The Qing Formation in World-Historical Time.* Cambridge: Harvard University Asia Center, 2004, pp. xi–xiv.

Wang Cheng-hua 王正華. "Material Culture and Emperorship: The Shaping of Imperial Power at the Court of Xuanzong (r. 1425–1435)." Ph.D. diss., Yale University, 1998.

Wang Gungwu. "Early Ming Relations with Southeast Asia: A Background Essay." In *The Chinese World Order: Traditional China's Foreign Relations*, ed. John King Fairbank. Cambridge: Harvard University Press, 1968, pp. 34–62.

———. "Merchants Without Empire: The Hokkien Sojourning Communities." In *The Rise of Merchant Empires: Long-Distance Trade in the Early Modern World*, ed. James Tracey. Cambridge: Cambridge University Press, 1990, pp. 400–421.

———. "Ming Foreign Relations: Southeast Asia." In *CHC*, 8: 301–32.

Wang Hongjiang. "On the Strengthening of Imperial Autocracy at the Beginning of the Ming." *Chinese Studies in History* 33, no. 3 (2000): 12–27.

Wang Yuquan 王毓銓. *Laiwuji* 萊蕪集. Beijing: Zhonghua shuju, 1983.

Wei Jinlin 衛建林. *Mingdai huanguan zhengzhi* 明代宦官政治. Shijiazhuang: Huashan wenyi chubanshe, 1998.

Weidner, Marsha. "Buddhist Pictorial Art in the Ming Dynasty: Patronage, Regionalism, and Internationalism." In *Latter Days of the Law: Images of Chinese Buddhism, 870–1850*, ed. idem. Lawrence: Spencer Museum of Art, University of Kansas; Honolulu: University of Hawai'i Press, 1994, pp. 51–87.

————. "Imperial Engagements with Buddhist Art and Architecture." In *Cultural Intersections in Later Chinese Buddhism*, ed. idem. Honolulu: University of Hawai'i Press, 2001, pp. 117–44.

Wen Gongyi 溫功義. *Mingdai de huanguan he gongting* 明代的宦官和宮廷. Chongqing: Chongqing chubanshe, 2000.

West, Stephen. "Text and Ideology: Ming Editors and Northern Drama." In *The Song-Yuan-Ming Transition in Chinese History*, ed. Paul Jakov Smith and Richard von Glahn. Cambridge: Harvard University Asia Center, 2003, pp. 329–73.

Whitfield, Roderick. "Rugong: Ming yuanti junma shizitu" 入貢: 明院體駿馬獅子圖. Presented at the Conference on Chinese Court Painting / Zhongguo gongting huihua xueshu yantaohui 中國宮廷繪畫學術研討會. Beijing, Palace Museum, Oct. 16, 2003.

Wills, John. "Maritime China from Wang Chih to Shih Lang: Themes in Peripheral History." In *From Ming to Ch'ing: Conquest, Region, and Continuity in Seventeenth Century China*, ed. Jonathan Spence and John Wills. New Haven: Yale University Press, 1979, pp. 203–38.

————. "Relations with Maritime Europeans, 1514–1662." In *CHC*, 8: 333–75.

Wink, André. "From the Mediterranean to the Indian Ocean: Medieval History in Geographic Perspective." *Comparative Studies in Society and History* 44, no. 3 (July 2002): 416–45.

Wu Han 吳晗. *Chaoxian Lichao shilu zhong de Zhongguo shiliao* 朝鮮李朝實錄中的中國史料. Beijing: Zhonghua shuju, 1980.

————. *Zhu Yuanzhang zhuan* 朱元璋傳. Shanghai, 1949; rev. ed., 1965. Reprinted—Beijing: Shenghuo Dushu Xinzhi sanlian shudian, 1979.

Xu Daling 許大齡. "Mingdai Beijing de jingji shenghuo" 明代北京的經濟生活. *Beijing daxue xuebao* 北京大學學報 42 (1959): 185–207.

Xu Yilin 許以林. "Fengxiandian" 奉先殿. *Gugong bowuyuan yuankan* 故宮博物院院刊 1989, no. 1: 70–76, 48.

Yang Qiqiao 楊啟樵. *Ming Qing huangshi yu fangshu* 明清皇室與方術. Shanghai: Shanghai shudian chubanshe, 2004.

————. *Ming Qing shi jueao* 明清史抉奧. Hong Kong: Guangjiaojing chubanshe, 1984.

Yates, Robin D. S. "Cosmos and Central Authority in the Early Chinese Empire." In *Empire*, ed. Susan Alcock, Terence D'Altroy, et al. Cambridge: Cambridge University Press, 2001, pp. 351–68.

Ye Dingyi 葉丁易. *Mingdai tewu zhengzhi* 明代特務政治. Beijing: Zhongwai chubanshe, 1950.

YHB, see Shen Defu, *Wanli yehuo bian*

Yu Ruji 俞汝楫, comp. *Libu zhigao* 禮部志稿. 1620. Reprinted in *Wenyuange siku quanshu*.

Zhang Dexin 張德信. "Taizu huangdi qinlu jiqi faxian yu yanjiu jilu: jianji *Yuzhi jifei lu*" 太祖皇帝欽錄及其發現與研究輯錄: 兼及御制紀非錄. *Ming Qing luncong*, no. 6 (2005): 83–110.

Zhao Jie 趙杰 and Zhou Hongshan 周洪山, comps. *Beiningshi wenwuzhi* 北寧市文物志. Shenyang: Liaoning minzu chubanshe, 1996.

Zhao Kesheng 趙克生. *Mingchao Jiajing shiqi guojia jili gaizhi* 明朝嘉靖時期國家祭禮改制. Beijing: Shehui kexue xueyuan wenxian chubanshe, 2006.

Zhao Yi 趙毅. "Mingdai zongshi renkou yu zonglu wenti" 明代宗室人口與宗祿問題.
    Changchun shifan xuebao 長春師院學報 (*zhesheban* 哲社版) 1986, no 2: 13–19.

Zhongguo diyi lishi dang'anguan 中國第一歷史檔案館 and Liaoningsheng dang'an-
    guan 遼寧省檔案館, eds. *Zhongguo Mingchao dang'an zonghui* 中國明朝檔案總匯.
    Guilin: Guangxi shifan daxue chubanshe, 2001.

Zhou Liangxia 周良霄. *Huangdi yu huangquan* 皇帝與皇權. Shanghai: Shanghai guji
    chubanshe, 1999.

Zhou Shaoliang 周紹良. "Mingdai huangdi, guifei, gongzhu yinshi de jiben fojing" 明代
    皇帝, 貴妃, 公主印施的幾本佛經. *Wenwu* 文物 8 (1987): 8–11.

———. "Ming Yongle nianjian Neifu kanben fojiao jingji" 明永樂年間内府刊本佛
    教經籍. *Wenwu* 文物 4 (1985): 39–41.

Zhu Hong 朱鴻. "*Mingren chujing rubi tu* benshi zhi yanjiu" 「明人出警入蹕圖」本事
    之研究. *Gugong xueshu jikan* 故宮學術季刊 22, no. 1 (2004): 183–213.

TWO

Bestowing the Double-edged Sword: Wanli as Supreme Military Commander

Kenneth M. Swope

The Wanli emperor reigned for forty-seven years (1573–1620), the longest and one of the most controversial and tumultuous reigns of the Ming. The period has become synonymous with imperial lassitude and avarice, eunuch abuses, bureaucratic factionalism and infighting, military reverses, and general dynastic decline. Historians have tended to place much of the blame squarely on Wanli's shoulders. Indeed, his official biographers noted in the eighteenth-century *Official History of the Ming Dynasty*, "When discussing the fall of the Ming, in actuality its demise started with Wanli; certainly he cannot be excused from blame!"[1] Later historians have tended to follow this precedent; a recent Chinese biography, for example, has subheadings referring to Wanli's seclusion in the Forbidden City, the construction of his grand tomb complex, his indulgence in wine and sex, and his avarice.[2] Another historian calls Wanli "a muddleheaded emperor at the head of a rotten state."[3] Despite Wanli's faults, or perhaps because of them, a number of biographical studies of this enigmatic emperor have appeared in Chinese

---

1. See Zhang Tingyu et al., *Ming shi* (hereafter cited as *MS*), p. 295.
2. See He Baoshan et al., *Ming Shenzong yu Ming Dingling*. This 1998 work is essentially an abridged update of their 1990 biography, *Wanli huangdi*.
3. Cao Guoqing, *Wanli huangdi da zhuan*, p. 233.

in the past few years.[4] There is even a recent novel derived from a Chinese television series about his reign.[5] Unfortunately, with the exception of Fan Shuzhi's thorough and well-researched *Wanli zhuan,* most have remained wedded to traditional interpretations of Wanli and his reign.

Western scholars of Wanli have echoed these sentiments, most being content to perpetuate common stereotypes of Wanli as a selfish profligate, although such characterizations have been problematized somewhat by the enormously influential work of Ray Huang.[6] While attempting to discern the underlying reasons for Wanli's well-documented erratic behavior and poor governance, Huang perpetuates traditional stereotypes in these works. He goes so far as to say that Wanli "earned a reputation as the most venal and avaricious occupant of the imperial throne in history."[7] The influence of Huang's portrayal of Wanli on subsequent scholars in the West is undeniable. As one historian notes in a recent work, "It is almost superfluous to write at any length about the Wanli reign because it has been so effectively portrayed and analyzed in the writings of Ray Huang."[8]

These hardly sound like the qualities one would expect to find in a military leader; yet, in the rest of this chapter, I argue that Wanli, for all his faults, was in fact interested in and devoted to maintaining Ming military supremacy in East Asia and that he was also a fairly effective supreme commander of the armed forces, certainly superior to both his immediate predecessors (the Jiajing and Longqing emperors) and his successors. Furthermore, I suggest that Wanli, following the practice of his tutor and immensely powerful court minister, Zhang Juzheng 張居正 (1525–82; grand secretary, 1567–82), sought to curb the power of civil officials and restrain bureaucratic factions by turning to prominent military officials and their families to circumvent the normally cumbersome Ming bureaucratic pro-

---

4. In addition to the aforementioned works, see, e.g., Fan Shuzhi, *Wanli zhuan;* and Wang Tianyou and Xu Daling, *Mingchao shiliu di,* pp. 310–44.

5. See Hu Yuewei et al., *Wanli wangchao.*

6. See Charles Hucker's biography of Wanli (under Chu I-chün) in Goodrich and Fang, *Dictionary of Ming Biography* (hereafter cited as *DMB*), pp. 324–38. See also Huang, *1587,* and idem, "The Lung-ch'ing and Wan-li Reigns, 1567–1620," in *CHC,* 7: 511–84.

7. *CHC,* 7: 554.

8. See Mote, *Imperial China,* p. 1026*n*3. Mote adds that Wanli "grew into a most perverse ruler, addicted to alcohol and sex, infinitely avaricious, and petulantly defiant toward his courtiers" (ibid., pp. 733–34). For another recent example of the continuing influence of such interpretations of Wanli, see J. Zhao, "A Decade of Considerable Significance."

cess.[9] In other words, he viewed military affairs as one of the few areas in which he had some chance of asserting his will, and he did so fairly often, at least until the early seventeenth century when he became increasingly disgusted with the rampant factionalism of the late Ming and retreated from any involvement in governing. Yet even toward the end of his reign, he remained concerned about the growing Manchu threat and approved the release of funds and the dispatch of a Ming expeditionary force to meet the Manchus in Liaodong in 1619.[10] Although the expedition was a disaster, it included a number of military officials Wanli had grown quite fond of over the years. Even in the wake of defeat, he sought to protect the only surviving commander, Li Rubo 李如柏, the son of the renowned Li Chengliang 李成梁 (1526–1618).[11]

This interpretation serves to highlight important aspects of Ming emperorship and court culture that are often overlooked. The Ming, like all Chinese dynasties, was founded by virtue of military power, and the military remained the foundation of Ming authority. Although historians have long recognized the military roles and achievements of such monarchs as Hongwu and Yongle, far less attention has been devoted to most of the later Ming emperors (with the notable exception of Zhengde). This obscures the fact that Ming emperors themselves were cognizant of their military heritage and consistently strove to maintain the military primacy of

---

9. Surviving records of Wanli's reign are rife with accounts of his battles with his civil officials over everything from the naming of the heir apparent to disputes over promotions and determinations of assignments. For overviews of Wanli's running disputes with his officials, see, among other works, *MS*, pp. 261–92; Qian Yiben, *Wanli dichao* (hereafter cited as *WLDC*); and *Shenzong shilu* (hereafter cited as *HZSL*) in Yao Guangxiao et al., *Ming shilu*. Perhaps the most concise traditional treatment of the major struggles, including the "Trunk of State Controversy," the battles with the Donglin party, the disputes over eunuch tax collectors, and the notorious Three Cases of the Wanli-Taichang reigns, can be found in Gu Yingtai, *Ming shi jishi benmo* (hereafter cited as *JSBM*), pp. 2386–411. For a recent English-language summary and interpretation of these events, see Dardess, *Blood and History in China*, pp. 1–30.

10. For more on this campaign, see Huang, "The Liao-tung Campaign of 1619." For a contemporary view of the debacle, written around 1620, see Yu Yanfang, *Chaonu yicuo*.

11. For the official biographies of Li Chengliang and his sons, see *MS*, pp. 6183–204. In English, see also *DMB*, pp. 830–35, for a biography of Li Chengliang's eldest son, Li Rusong; and Hummel, *Eminent Chinese of the Ch'ing Period* (hereafter cited as *ECCP*), pp. 450–52, for a biography of Li Chengliang. For an overview of the entire Li family and their role as defenders of the northern frontier in the late Ming, see Swope, "A Few Good Men."

the Ming in Asia. One of the emperor's most important duties was to make broad decisions concerning military affairs in the everyday operations of the empire. Even a cursory examination of *The Veritable Records* testifies to the prevalence of military actions throughout the empire and the emperor's responsibility to find solutions to military problems. However, a persistent anti-military bias among both official and unofficial historians of the Ming, most of whom hailed from or were sympathetic to the values and interests of the literati class, has tended to obscure this facet of Ming emperorship. Consequently, an important dimension of Ming court culture has remained poorly understood and little studied until recently.[12]

Military officials in the field were frequently given a great deal of latitude by Ming emperors, and they often enjoyed unparalleled access to the throne because of their constant presence at ceremonial and diplomatic functions. Furthermore, the hereditary military system of the Ming appears to have worked to the advantage of at least some families in the Ming, since some imperial favorites retained influence over several generations. Additionally, given the well-documented factionalism of Ming politics in general, military officers perhaps seemed less tainted in the eyes of emperors, if only because they appeared to concern themselves with more concrete problems of government about which the monarch could actually do something.

Military decisions were one of the few arenas in which later Ming emperors could act "imperiously" and get away with it. Thus, the study of how emperors used their position to affect military decision-making and to fashion images of themselves as legitimate Sons of Heaven is integral to a better understanding of Ming court culture in all its dimensions. Unfortunately, in addition to the problem mentioned above of literati biases embedded in the sources, the tendency of surviving sources to ritualize and exalt the person of the emperor has made it difficult to get much sense of the personalities and predilections of most Ming emperors. Given the lack of the kind of personal writings we have for their Qing successors, Ming monarchs often come across as sterile, two-dimensional figures whose agency, if portrayed at all, often appears negative and counterproductive to the enlightened programs and policies of their civil officials. As a result, modern scholars are forced to rely on inferences and creative interpretations of both written and material culture sources, as can be seen in many of this volume's contributions.

---

12. In addition to the present study, see Robinson, *Bandits, Eunuchs, and the Son of Heaven.*

Within this framework, imperial consultation with officials and the process of decision-making as it pertained to the formulation of defense policy are vital components of court culture. Despite popular images of Ming monarchs after Yongle as having been for the most part circumscribed by ritual and precedent and therefore unable to exercise imperial prerogatives, debates over military affairs seem to have consistently provided open and lively forums for rulers and ministers alike. Careers were often made and broken on the individual's position on defense, and success or failure in the military realm could have a far greater impact on progress up or down the career ladder compared to achievements in other arenas, in part because the end result of one's policy suggestions were often so visible.[13]

In the case of Wanli, although the influential minister Zhang Juzheng was posthumously discredited, those who later followed his general policies, particularly in the realm of national defense, seem to have found favor with the monarch, and he consistently shielded them from charges of incompetence, corruption, or other malfeasance. Such actions, of course, belie the widely held notion that the Wanli court was a shadow organization in the hands of sycophants and eunuchs. Simply put, like any other rational ruler, Wanli patronized those officials whose policy recommendations proved both successful and in accord with his own grand strategic preferences. Viewed in this light, it is my contention that military operations can serve as a valuable "back door" into the inner workings of the Ming court and provide us with the opportunity to view court culture from a wider lens than can what was taking place within the confines of the Forbidden City.

Generals could, and often did, have greater influence at court than might be expected, despite their relative lack of direct access to the monarch, which itself has possibly been exaggerated. As David Robinson notes in Chapter 1 of this volume, military officers were in fact always present at major ceremonial gatherings, and they were particularly prominent in tributary displays and, of course, in the ceremonial executions of captured rebels and defeated enemies. Occasions such as these offered emperors the opportunity to bask in the military glory of their commanders and exult in the awesomeness of the Ming empire before their subjects. They also served as reminders of the potential of military power, in terms both of its

---

13. On the relationship between policy arguments and career paths in Ming times, see Waldron, *The Great Wall of China*, pp. 53–165; and Johnston, *Cultural Realism*, pp. 175–247.

importance in maintaining law and order within and without the empire and of the need to make sure that military commanders were competent and loyal. Peter Lorge has observed that generals "were the arbiters of dynastic fortune in ways that civil officials were not, since the only crises that threatened dynastic survival were military ones."[14] If one accepts this basic premise, then Wanli's interest in military affairs and his general disinclination to heed the shrill cries of his righteous literati critics become more understandable since they point to a different orientation in the focus of his particular reign (and court, for that matter).

Therefore, we must examine the direct and indirect relationships cultivated between Ming emperors and their military officials when considering the topic of Ming court culture. In this context, it is important to consider both actual military officials and civil officials entrusted with military affairs. The latter had a great deal of power in Ming decision-making and often forged networks with purely military officials to get things done in a more timely fashion. It seems obvious that Wanli took advantage of such networks, particularly in his handling of crises in Ningxia and Bozhou, where he delegated field authority to the ranking civil officials Mei Guozhen 梅國楨 (js. 1583) and Li Hualong 李化龍 (1554–1612), respectively. Wanli was also instrumental in advising and supporting their selections of specific military officers from favored families. In this way, Wanli could not only perpetuate the traditional Ming practice of putting civil officials in overall command of major military operations but also assure that his military favorites remained in key positions in the field.[15] And in some cases, such as the appointment of Li Rusong 李如松 (d. 1597) to the post of military superintendent (tidu 提督) in Ningxia and Korea, Wanli established new dynastic precedents.[16] One suspects that similar arrangements held true for other reigns.

My aim in this chapter is neither to act as an apologist for Wanli nor to gloss over his many faults as a ruler and a person. Instead, I will attempt to offer a more balanced interpretation and portrayal of Wanli as a monarch, one that, while acknowledging his many shortcomings, more fully evaluates his reign and its achievements, particularly in the area of military affairs. I

---

14. Lorge, *War, Politics, and Society in Early Modern China*, p. 178.

15. On the principle of civil oversight in Ming times, see Li Du, *Mingdai huangquan zhengzhi yanjiu*, pp. 168–74.

16. On the relationship of imperial authority to military authority in Ming times, particularly as it pertained to the creation of new positions, see ibid., pp. 152–226.

also want to draw attention to the importance of military policy debates as part of Ming court culture. For although we certainly need to know more about the education, daily activities, and personal lifestyles of the various members of the Ming court, it is important that we remember that the business of government was also conducted there, and that business often entailed defending the empire against internal and external threats, not to mention the occasional campaigns of conquest and expansion.

Wanli in the Context of Court and Military

Additionally, it must not be forgotten that all Ming emperors remained the supreme commanders of the dynasty's military forces. Despite later efforts by literati chroniclers to obscure this fact, many Ming monarchs took this role seriously.[17] Certainly this might be one area in which comparisons with the war-oriented monarchs of early modern Europe are particularly apt. Much has been made of the efforts of kings such as Philip II of Spain (r. 1556–98) and Gustavus Adolphus of Sweden (r. 1611–32) to bask in the glory of their military triumphs and direct the Grand Strategy of their respective states, but far less attention has been devoted to the activities of Ming emperors along these lines.[18] The insights of scholars concerning the machinations of monarchs, generals, and courtiers in these other contemporary contexts can suggest how we might profitably study the Ming court in this regard. They also suggest other entrées into court culture. For whereas scholars of early modern Europe take the intimate relationship between court politics and military affairs for granted, scholars of China have seemed somewhat disinclined to make this connection, perhaps because literati chroniclers generally devoted more attention to artistic, ritualistic, and aesthetic concerns when discussing court life.

---

17. This is not to say that all historians have obscured the military interests and achievements of the later Ming emperors. However, later historians have tended to discount sources that seem to exalt the dynasty's military prowess in favor of the standard portrayals of Ming decline favored by the Donglin and Fushe groups and their partisans. See, e.g., Ray Huang's discussion in *CHC*, 7: 563–64. On the links between factional affiliation and historical writing in the late Ming, see Miller, "Opposition to the Donglin Faction."

18. For an example, see Parker, *The Grand Strategy of Philip II*. Gustavus Adolphus was a warrior-king in every sense of the term, eventually dying on the field of battle after having survived numerous serious injuries earlier in his career. In contrast to Ming emperors, Qing monarchs have fared far better in this regard; see Perdue, "Culture, History, and Imperial Chinese Strategy"; and Waley-Cohen, *The Culture of War in China*.

Yet, helping create and pursue a Grand Strategy was one way that Ming emperors could make a difference and leave a positive legacy. In the words of Geoffrey Parker, Grand Strategy

encompasses the decisions of a given state about its overall security—the threats it perceives, the ways it confronts them, and the steps it takes to match ends and means—and each involves the integration of the state's overall political, economic, and military aims, both in peace and war, to preserve long-term interests, including the management of ends and means, diplomacy and national morale and political culture in both the military and civilian spheres.[19]

This definition touches on several issues germane to the present study. Although the hoary notion of a changeless imperial Chinese state continues to live in popular interpretations, scholars favor more dynamic and nuanced explanations. Within this conceptualization of the role of the state in the daily lives of its subjects, we should also reconsider the actions of the rulers at the head of the state itself. As one might expect, a wide range of "management styles," if you will, resulted in a number of different approaches to Grand Strategy during the Ming.[20] Furthermore, the monarch alone did not determine approaches to Grand Strategy. They were instead the products of the views of an often-dizzying array of political actors ranging from the grand secretaries to the nine ranking ministers to prominent generals to eunuchs to friends and associates of the imperial family. It is my contention that this decision-making process should be considered part of court culture because an individual's position on defense matters often had profound repercussions for his status within and without the court, not to mention access to the monarch.

It can also provide insights into how those in and around the Ming court viewed the problems confronting the empire and its subjects in times of crisis. In other words, military crises allow us to get a sense of the political culture of the Ming court and how that political culture responded to particular stimuli. To give a specific example, one thing that jumps out at the modern reader in the memorials submitted by officials at all levels of government concerning the threat of a Japanese invasion of China in the 1590s is the overarching concern for national morale. Both the Wanli

---

19. Parker, *The Grand Strategy of Philip II*, p. 1.

20. Parker (ibid., pp. 11–45), by the way, refers to Philip II as CEO of the Spanish Empire, an image with particular resonance for students of Ming history, considering the enormous burdens placed on Ming rulers by the actions of the founder.

emperor and his officials evince a strong desire to prevent a widespread panic. They stress the importance of the people and officials acting in concert and emphasize that the Japanese are the common enemy. It is clear that the emperor in particular wants petty local disputes and private interests put aside for the time being. Part of this can be attributed to the government's desire to maintain stability and national authority, but it also underscores the ways in which the Ming court highlighted its paternal oversight of its subjects, not to mention those of its tributary, Korea.

Did imperial leadership really matter when it came to deciding Grand Strategy and making important military decisions? Based on my study of Wanli, I would suggest that it did. Moreover, a closer examination of how Ming emperors approached military crises and how these conceptualizations shaped court culture in general can also help us understand other facets of Ming court life such as the type of tutoring received by heirs apparent, or even the musical tastes of particular monarchs. The Tianqi emperor (r. 1621–27), for example, is said to have been particularly fond of military drum dances.[21] Was this perhaps due to the fact that martial dances became increasingly popular in the late Ming as a way of edifying the populace at large about the rising threat of the Manchus? Or were these dances brought into the court by the young ruler's eunuch favorites? Perhaps they were no more than the continuation of traditional musical forms, revived in the late Ming to draw attention to the dynasty's eroding martial prowess, although it is worth noting that civil officials tended to regard the emperor's delight in such pastimes as unbecoming. In any event, this reinforces the centrality of military affairs in many aspects of Ming court culture.

Turning to the case of Wanli specifically, given the Ming's disastrous loss against the Jurchens in 1619 and its eventual defeat at the hands of both domestic rebels and Qing invaders, historians have been wont to assume that the Ming military along with its supreme commander(s) had sunk to a state of decay long before the early seventeenth century. In actuality such an interpretation is not grounded in the primary sources but seems either to come from sources written after the Qing conquest or to be derived from biased observers such as Matteo Ricci, who, as far as I can tell, had little experience with Ming armies in the field and was unduly

---

21. See Dardess, *Blood and History in China*, p. 44.

influenced by the opinions of the civil officials with whom he spent most of his time.[22]

In fact, the Ming witnessed a rather impressive military revival from 1570 to 1610. During that period, imperial armies managed to force the Mongols to sue for peace and then deter them, put down a number of significant internal rebellions and mutinies, and assisted the Koreans in defeating what might have been the most impressive military force on the globe in the late sixteenth century, the Japanese armies commanded by Toyotomi Hideyoshi (1536–98). Contrary to popular perceptions, the Ming state was also expanding and consolidating its frontiers at this time, fighting a series of border engagements with the Burmese and encouraging Han Chinese settlement into formerly aboriginal territories in the southwest and northwest. Scholars also often overlook the fact that the very circumstances that enabled Nurhaci (1559–1626) to rise to leadership of the Latter Jin were in large part created by aggressive Ming interventionist policies into Jurchen affairs. Although not all these endeavors were unqualified successes, they still point to both a rejuvenated military machine and a competent supreme commander.

The remainder of this chapter examines some of these engagements and discusses the pivotal role played by the Wanli emperor in making both general policy and strategic decisions. He was not always consistent, but the emperor did generally implement an aggressive policy toward both domestic rebels and foreign threats. If anything, he was more forceful when dealing with the latter, which suggests that he took his role as the supreme ruler of the East Asian world seriously and saw it as a stage where he could showcase his leadership abilities with the least opposition from his civil official detractors. That is to say, with respect to international affairs, most notably the Ming response to Hideyoshi's invasion of Korea, Wanli could truly behave like the one and only Son of Heaven. His resolute refusal to accept any of Hideyoshi's conditions for peace testifies to this conclusion. At the same time, the course of the Sino-Japanese peace talks and the reception of the Japanese ambassador in Beijing highlights the centrality of Ming China in arbitrating international disputes and accentuates yet another dimension of Ming court culture that is sometimes downplayed.

---

22. These issues are discussed at length in Swope, "Three Great Campaigns," chaps. 1–2.

Although Wanli himself never actually took the field, he did express an interest in doing so on at least one occasion. Furthermore, he took great care, following the example set by Zhang Juzheng, to appoint competent military officers to important posts and often defended or absolved them from charges of corruption leveled by jealous civil officials.[23] He also repeatedly bestowed the ceremonial double-edged sword (*bao jian* 寶劍) on commanders in the field, giving them full authorization to do as they saw fit without having to memorialize the throne first. In the Chinese rendering, this meant they could "kill first and report it later." Despite the potentially subversive power such a command might have imparted to certain commanders, it proved integral to Ming success in these campaigns, particularly in the suppression of the massive Miao revolt instigated by Yang Yinglong 楊應龍 (d. 1600) in Bozhou. Moreover, in doing this, Wanli was following the maxims set forth since ancient times by military thinkers, who repeatedly emphasized that commanders in the field should be invested with total command authority since they were better equipped to deal with any tactical difficulties which might arise. In theory they already held the full trust of the ruler.[24]

As explained below, Wanli himself made the final decision to send troops and supplies to Korea. Furthermore, in addressing the Korean king concerning his decision, Wanli was clearly positioning himself as the arbiter of the East Asian diplomatic and political order and the rightful head of the so-called Chinese tributary system of foreign and commercial relations that the Japanese hegemon Hideyoshi sought to supplant. In contrast to the standard portrayals of him as petty and tightfisted, Wanli repeatedly authorized the dispensation of funds from imperial coffers to provide extra

---

23. It was, of course, in any case not that common for Chinese emperors to lead their armies in person on the battlefield, especially in the late imperial period. For a discussion of institutional changes in the middle imperial period and how they affected the relationship of the throne to the military establishment, see Graff, *Medieval Chinese Warfare*, pp. 244–46. He also examines a number of emperors who did lead armies, most notably Li Shimin, Tang Taizong (r. 626–49). Given the track record of the Ming, with the capture of the Zhengtong emperor at Tumu in 1449 and the bizarre escapades of the Zhengde emperor in the early sixteenth century, it is understandable why Wanli's officials were so opposed to him taking the field himself. On the former event, see Frederick W. Mote, "The T'u-mu Incident of 1449," in Kierman and Fairbank, *Chinese Ways in Warfare*, pp. 243–72. On Zhengde, see Robinson, *Bandits, Eunuchs, and the Son of Heaven*, esp. pp. 99–120.

24. See, e.g., the discussion in *Tai Gong's Six Secret Teachings*, in Sawyer, *The Seven Military Classics of Ancient China*, pp. 33, 64–65.

rewards and supplies for troops in the field. He also appointed military officers to high posts formerly reserved solely for civil officials, over the protests of some of the most powerful civil officials in the empire. In conjunction with Wanli's later withdrawal from governmental affairs, this precedent-setting decision probably hastened the militarization of late Ming society described by Lynn Struve.[25] All these examples point to a monarch who was far more than an irresolute profligate and call for further investigation into the reign of this enigmatic and much-maligned emperor.

Wanli's interest in military affairs stemmed from his childhood tutelage under Zhang Juzheng.[26] After Zhang's death, many of his associates and protégés were discredited and cashiered, but a number of his military appointees continued to enjoy the emperor's patronage and protection. As a modern Chinese biographer notes, Zhang explicitly rejected not only the notion that civil matters were important and military matters unimportant but also the prevailing idea that civil officials should completely dominate their military counterparts.[27] He also eschewed the common practice whereby commanders bought their posts and instead selected talented leaders who were brave, skillful, and, most important, experienced, such as Qi Jiguang 戚繼光 (1528–88), Wang Chonggu 王崇古 (1515–89), Tan Lun 譚綸 (1520–77), Liang Menglong 梁夢龍 (1527–1602), and the previously mentioned Li Chengliang.[28] Zhang revived the old military field (*tuntian* 屯田) system, strengthened border defenses in general, and tried to establish, and even expand, a stable defense perimeter.[29] His programs included a mixture of offensive and defensive strategies along all the empire's frontiers and the selective opening of border markets, particularly in the northwest.

———

25. Struve, *The Southern Ming*, p. 7.

26. The childhood education of Ming emperors is treated in the chapter in this volume by Julia K. Murray (pp. 231–68).

27. See Zhang Haiying, *Zhang Juzheng gaige*, p. 151.

28. There are numerous biographies of Qi Jiguang in Chinese and in English. See, among others, Millinger, "Ch'i Chi-kuang"; Huang, *1587*, pp. 156–88; and *DMB*, pp. 220–24. For his official biography, see *MS*, pp. 5610–617. See also Fan Zhongyi, *Qi Jiguang zhuan*. For Wang Chonggu's biography, see *DMB*, pp. 1369–73; for Tan Lun's, *DMB*, pp. 1243–46; and for Liang Menglong's, *DMB*, pp. 898–902. Tan and Liang were both *jinshi* degree holders who also happened to be gifted military administrators and field commanders. They should not be considered strictly military officials.

29. On Zhang Juzheng's military reforms, see Zhang Haiying, *Zhang Juzheng gaige*, pp. 29–60.

Among other things, actions such as these improved Ming military morale to a level not witnessed since the mid-fifteenth century.[30] They also helped start a new era in Ming-Mongol relations, one in which the Ming was not always on the defensive. Finally, the atmosphere fostered by Zhang also may have led Wanli to adopt a hard-line approach toward a series of domestic and foreign military foes throughout his reign; if so, this suggests yet another linkage between what would generally be accepted as an aspect of court culture (the education of the monarch) and affairs in the empire beyond the court.

Matters were no doubt helped by the adoption early in Wanli's reign of a general policy of assigning all high posts in the Ministry of War only to officials with military experience.[31] This policy made a great deal of sense at the time. Zhang and his fellow officials had witnessed firsthand the panic caused by Altan Khan's (1507–82) raiding in the environs of the capital during the Jiajing reign.[32] Zhang wanted to restore Ming glory by increasing the power of the central government at the expense of the localities by improving administration as a whole and reviving the military. The modern Chinese scholar Zhang Haiying even suggests that Zhang Juzheng's desire to improve the military's effectiveness was at the heart of all his reforms.[33] A stronger military would be congruent with Zhang's aims of centralizing power in general and enhancing the role of the emperor.

Zhang's decision to close local academies and transfer the supervising censors to the Inner Cabinet were also part of this plan.[34] This distrust of local officials and of the nefarious influence of factional politics permeated Wanli's subsequent relations with his bureaucrats and probably bolstered his general suspicion of civil officials. Wanli may have seen military offi-

---

30. For a full discussion of Ming military operations during the Wanli reign, see Qu Jiusi, *Zuben Wanli wu gong lu* (hereafter cited as *WGL*). This work's preface offers an insightful look into the military climate of the late Ming as viewed from the perspective of the court. The work as a whole consists of biographies of enemies of the state, ranging from horse thieves and highwaymen to mutineers to serious rebels who commanded forces in the hundreds of thousands. Although Ray Huang has criticized this and other similar works, it does provide a fairly comprehensive picture of late Ming military operations and is evenhanded in its criticism of the problems of the Ming military.

31. See *CHC*, 7: 520.

32. On Altan Khan, see *DMB*, pp. 6–9; *WGL*, pp. 639a–784b; *JSBM*, pp. 2362–67; and Zhuge Yuansheng, *Liangchao ping rang lu* (hereafter cited as *PRL*), pp. 29–64.

33. Zhang Haiying, *Zhang Juzheng gaige*, pp. 29–32.

34. On the role of academies in championing local versus national interests, see Elman, "Imperial Politics and Confucian Societies," pp. 396–99.

cials as less prone to forming potentially destabilizing factional alliances because they spent so much time in the field and away from the capital. Although military officers created patronage networks as extensive as those of their civil counterparts, they tended to do so on the fringes of the empire. Moreover, from the perspective of the throne, they were extending the control of the state and spreading the fame and awe-inducing qualities of the monarch.[35] They were not pestering him to name an heir or urging him to attend to the tiresome business of court audiences.

To extend this admittedly conjectural line of thought even further, Wanli may even have favored military officials because he believed that their extension of Ming control within the empire and along the frontiers might help fill his government's rapidly emptying coffers. Indeed, contrary to standard representations of his deployment of eunuch tax collectors around the empire as proof of Wanli's unquenchable avarice, Harry Miller has recently argued persuasively that Wanli's strategy was in fact an adroit attempt to find desperately needed revenue by fleecing the rich, who had been dodging taxes for generations.[36] On the other hand, Wanli may have favored military officers simply because he was enamored with their free and rugged lifestyle, something he himself could scarcely experience. He would not have been the only Ming monarch to feel this way.[37] Stories of his drilling eunuch guard units in the Forbidden City lend credence to such an interpretation; reputedly, much to the dismay of his tutors and advisors, this was one of his favorite activities.[38]

Apparently some civil officials feared the young emperor might emulate some of his predecessors and lead units in the field, a veritable invitation for disaster in their eyes. Emperors were simply not supposed to behave in such a fashion; they were to be Confucian paragons and moral exemplars, not commanders in chief. Certainly by the time of Wanli, the prevailing culture of the Ming court prized civil over military accomplishments. By all accounts, Wanli was intelligent and a fast learner. His inclination for things martial must have been unsettling to many in positions of authority, particularly because such interests were congruent with those of Zhang Juzheng, who had many enemies.

---

35. Qu Jiusi says as much in his preface; see *WGL*, pp. 1a–3a.
36. Miller, "State Versus Society," pp. 255–343.
37. See Geiss, "The Leopard Quarter During the Cheng-te Reign."
38. See Huang, *1587*, pp. 121–23; and *HZSL*, pp. 2772–774, 2794.

It seems likely that Zhang Juzheng, because of his predilection for autocratic rule, envisioned a similar role for Wanli when the emperor reached
his maturity. Thus, Wanli became upset when his ministers sought to con-
strain him after Zhang's death. Reading between the lines of the surviving
records, Wanli, like Zhang Juzheng, advocated real solutions to real problems and disdained empty speech and the unproductive harping of rival
factions. This can be seen time and again in the emperor's discussions of
military operations with field officers and in his repeated dismissals of im-
peachments of his favored military officers. As Wanli put it during a court
audience in 1590:

The thing is, the governors and governors-general nowadays treat army officers
with nothing but disdain! Ordinarily they put them under restriction, will not permit them to do a thing. Only in a time of emergency would they push them forward. It happens in all defense areas. Whenever there is a victory, the civil officials
are rewarded and promoted; all the credit is theirs. In the case of defeat and failure,
some army officers are named as scapegoats. All excuses and empty words![39]

Later in this same audience, the emperor harangued his officials about
their belittling of military skills and their frequent attempts to keep the
truth of matters from him. In the seventh month of 1591, Wanli addressed
the court ministers and said the empire was divided because officials constantly fought with one another for personal gain.[40] Throughout the 1590s,
Wanli was constantly at odds with his officials over everything from merit
evaluations to military affairs to the touchiest issue of all, the naming of his
heir apparent.[41]

Border affairs seemed to be the one area in which Wanli could exert his
will to some degree, either because most civil officials were unsure of
themselves in these matters or because they deemed them to be less important than court politics. As the modern historian Fan Shuzhi notes, when
Wanli finally assumed power, he threw himself into border affairs and
sought to reverse the static border policies of his forebears and make the
army strong and formidable once again.[42] To a degree, he was able to indulge this ambition. As a result, the Ming pursued a much more aggressive
frontier policy, clashing with the Mongols in the northwest, the Jurchens in
the northeast, the Burmese in the southwest, and the Japanese in Korea, in

---

39. Cited in Huang, *1587*, p. 231.
40. *MS*, p. 274.
41. See He Baoshan et al., *Ming Shenzong yu Ming Dingling*.
42. Fan Shuzhi, *Wanli zhuan*, p. 227.

addition to a wide array of domestic foes, the vast majority of whom were successfully quelled. Blessed with an unusual coterie of talented military commanders, from about 1570 to 1610 the Ming military was probably at its strongest since the Yongle reign (1403–24), and it would never attain the same level of effectiveness again. For this reason, Fan Shuzhi calls the Three Great Campaigns of 1592–1600 the high point of Wanli's reign.[43]

During the Three Great Campaigns, Wanli made appointments, issued commands, overruled the recommendations of censors and civil officials, and even expressed a desire to go to the battlefront in Ningxia himself. This does not sound like the man the modern historian Cao Guoqing accuses of "resting on lofty pillows without any worries."[44] Cao's charge that Wanli never responded to memorials or never offered opinions on border affairs is likewise incorrect, as is his assertion that Wanli's negligence led directly to the rise of the Manchus and their victory over the Ming.[45] During the conflict with Japan in Korea, Wanli repeatedly sent scathing admonitions to King Sŏnjo of Korea urging him to rectify his personal behavior and rally the Korean populace to their national salvation. He solicited advice on both military and diplomatic matters from all quarters and was intimately involved in the peace negotiations, even though those charged with conducting the negotiations misled him about Hideyoshi's aims and demands. When made aware of the latter's intent to renew hostilities in Korea, Wanli wasted no time punishing those officials he believed had failed him and appointing men more amenable to his own vision.

This act, incidentally, reveals another unpleasant dimension of Ming court culture. Peter Lorge has commented on the dramatic increase in violence at court over the course of the last three imperial dynasties in China: "Officials could be flogged in front of the emperor, sometimes even tortured, and executions, imprisonment and exile to distant frontiers was [sic] not uncommon."[46] In the case mentioned above, the discredited minister

---

43. Fan Shuzhi, *Wanli zhuan*, p. 227. For a brief overview of Ming military actions along the frontiers in the 1580s and 1590s, see *MS*, pp. 267–71. The Three Great Campaigns of the Wanli Era (*Wanli san da zheng* 萬曆三大征) are discussed below. See also Swope, "Civil-Military Coordination in the Bozhou Campaign"; idem, "Deceit, Disguise, and Dependence"; and idem, "All Men Are Not Brothers."

44. Cao Guoqing, *Wanli huangdi da zhuan*, p. 233.

45. On the problems with suggesting that Wanli's negligence and incompetent leadership led to the rise of the Manchus, see Kye, "An Indirect Challenge to the Ming Order."

46. Lorge, *War, Politics, and Society in Early Modern China*, p. 179.

of war, Shi Xing 石星 (d. 1597), who had advocated a peaceful solution to the crisis in Korea, died in prison, possibly as a result of torture, and his family was exiled to the frontier. Wanli's actions in this case certainly are not defensible on moral grounds, but they also contradict charges that the emperor had no interest in matters of state. On the contrary, Wanli was incensed that what he had been led to believe was both a military and diplomatic triumph and a reassertion of the primacy of the Ming empire in East Asia was in fact essentially a sham orchestrated by Shi Xing and his lackeys. Although the errant minister of war was forced to suffer arbitrary imperial justice, Wanli was only acting in the manner of his imperial ancestors. The culture of the Ming court in this regard was akin more to those of the Mongol Yuan and Manchu Qing than to that of the Han Chinese Song dynasty.[47]

Even in the waning days of his reign, Wanli demonstrated an interest in the punitive expedition sent to battle the forces of Nurhaci in Liaodong and authorized extra funds. The commanders in charge of the Ming armies on that fateful campaign were among the most experienced and decorated commanders in the empire and had long enjoyed the support of the emperor. In short, the Wanli portrayed in the traditional sources on the Three Campaigns is an intelligent, concerned monarch, capable of leading the empire in a time of crisis even if sometimes prone to fits of anger and petulance. Although some might argue that the sources deliberately portray the monarch in a flattering light, given the number of extremely negative contemporary appraisals of Wanli, it seems unlikely that these authors would go out of their way to praise him.[48]

---

47. In a presentation at the Columbia University Seminar on Traditional China, David Robinson forcefully argued that Ming court culture was indeed strongly influenced by Mongol traditions and practices and that the Ming was as much a consciously multiethnic empire as both the Mongol Yuan and the Manchu Qing; see also the Introduction and Robinson's chapter in this volume, pp. 365–421. It is worth speculating that these steppe practices may have in fact contributed to an inherently more brutal court culture, although I am wary of perpetuating ethnic stereotypes or falling into the trap of blaming Ming court violence on pernicious Mongol influences as historians of Russia used to do in blaming the Mongol occupation for later tsarist excesses. See the discussion (and refutation) of such assertions in Halperin, *Russia and the Golden Horde*, pp. 116–17.

48. For more on sources pertaining to the Three Great Campaigns, see Swope, "Three Great Campaigns."

Wanli as Decision-maker

What, then, were Wanli's contributions to military decision-making and his role as supreme commander of the empire's military forces? Although this section focuses primarily on the Three Great Campaigns, it also briefly discusses his involvement in the Liaodong campaign of 1619 and examines the implications of Wanli's actions for the study of Ming court culture in general and for civil-military relations in the Ming. Clearly, military men and military culture were as much parts of court life as civil officials and civil culture, and perhaps exerted an even stronger influence in many reigns.[49] Moreover, one cannot simply posit a clear civil-military dichotomy; many civil officials had decidedly military orientations and connections.[50] As Allan Barr has noted, in the late Ming period in particular, there appears to have been a renewed interest in military affairs and in reviving the martial spirit of the Ming among the literati.[51]

Wanli's patronage of certain officials and policies should certainly be viewed within the larger political context of his reign, keeping in mind the point raised above that military affairs were often an arena for waging political battles at court. His distaste for many of his civil officials notwithstanding, Wanli could never have presided over the successful completion of the many military actions of his reign without the help of capable civil officials who worked with military commanders in the field. It is important to note that although these men were not partisans of the Donglin, they also were not lackeys of the eunuch faction at court. They constituted an alternative power bloc, one that Wanli trusted and relied on to pursue his own policy goals.

THE NINGXIA MUTINY OF 1592

Surveys of the late Ming period commonly note that the Longqing and Wanli reigns were important for the history of Ming-Mongol relations because, after the investiture of Altan Khan as *Shunyi wang* (Obedient and righteous prince) in 1571 and the establishment of regular trade fairs, the

---

49. See Robinson, *Bandits, Eunuchs, and the Son of Heaven.*

50. On the frequently close relationship between civil and military officials and their interdependence in late imperial China, see Lorge, *War, Politics, and Society in Early Modern China.*

51. Barr, "The Wanli Context of the 'Courtesan's Jewel Box' Story," pp. 110–15. See also Chen Baoliang, "Wan Ming de shangwu jingshen."

northwestern frontiers were generally calm and the Mongols ceased to be a military threat. Although this assertion is more or less true, it does obscure the continuing conflicts, sometimes involving tens of thousands of combatants on both sides, between the Ming and the various Mongol tribes of the steppe throughout the rest of the dynasty.[52] Moreover, it ignores the third side of the Ming "peace triangle," military force. Throughout the last decades of the sixteenth century and into the seventeenth century, the Ming launched what can best be described as the equivalent of destabilizing surgical strikes into Mongol (and Manchu) territory, burning settlements, killing threatening leaders, and capturing valuable livestock. Li Chengliang and his sons were prominent in these kinds of operations. Again, these actions were apparently the brainchild of Zhang Juzheng and similarly sanctioned by Wanli, who was eager to maintain Ming military prestige.

Zhang valued concrete results. He also promoted the worthy and allowed them to operate with as few administrative fetters as possible. To this end he afforded his frontier commanders great latitude in the completion of their duties and was willing to look the other way from time to time when charges were leveled by those jealous of their achievements. An example of this can be seen in the case of Pubei 哱拜 (d. 1592), a Chahar Mongol who submitted to the Ming late in the Jiajing reign (1522–66), after being forced from his tribal lands as the result of a dispute. The several hundred followers Pubei brought with him would become his core fighting force. Within a decade, Pubei rose to become regional military commissioner of Huamachi, near the strategically important garrison city of Ningxia.[53] After Pubei received further promotions and rewards from the court, some officials began to complain that he and his sons and associates were becoming unruly and difficult to control.[54] Zhang Juzheng brushed aside such objections, either because he trusted Pubei or perhaps because he feared upsetting him. Acting on Zhang's advice, Wanli refused to punish him. Cao Guoqing sees this as just another example of Wanli's incompetence and shortsightedness. Of course, Wanli was still a teenager at this time, and most major governmental decisions were still being vetted by Zhang Juzheng. However, the emperor's refusal to demote Pubei accords

---

52. On the peace settlement with Altan Khan, see Serruys, "Four Documents." On the fragmentation of the peace after the deaths of Altan Khan and Zhang Juzheng, see Okano, "Banreki nijū nen Neika heihen," pp. 587–88.

53. Mao Ruizheng, *Wanli san da zheng kao* (hereafter cited as *SDZK*), p. 13.

54. See Tan Qian, *Guoque* (hereafter cited as *GQ*), p. 4667.

well with his later preference for results over accusations, an attribute that he also appears to have learned during his tutelage under Zhang Juzheng.[55]

In 1589 Pubei was promoted to the post of regional vice commander of Ningxia, and his son, Bo Cheng'en 哱承恩 (d. 1592), inherited his father's post as regional military commissioner in the Ningxia guard because he was also "fierce and warlike."[56] By this point Pubei, who reportedly had some 2,000–3,000 personal retainers in his service, wanted to retire from active duty and pass his post to his son. However, the leading civil official in the region, Grand Coordinator Dang Xin 黨馨 (js. 1568), opposed such a transfer of power for fear that "the tail would grow too big to shake" and threaten the security of the frontier.[57] During the next three years, Dang Xin and Pubei clashed over a number of issues pertaining to military administration and military actions in the northwest. In the spring of 1592, Pubei found himself embroiled in a mutiny of the Ningxia garrison instigated by a Chinese officer (although the rebellion is usually attributed to Pubei and his sons, most likely because of their Mongol ancestry).[58] The mutineers killed Dang Xin and a subordinate, burned and looted government offices in the city of Ningxia, and quickly seized some forty-seven outlying frontier fortresses, throwing all of Shaanxi province into a panic.[59] They demanded the Ming government give them a free hand in the area or they would join forces with the Ordos Mongols and threaten the very existence of the dynasty.[60]

The rebellion was reported to the throne on April 19, 1592, by a surveillance official from Shaanxi. He informed the emperor that the entire province was in an uproar and only a single official was resisting the mutineers with any success. Recognizing the gravity of the situation, Wanli immediately called for a meeting with Shi Xing, the minister of war.[61] They decided that the affair needed to be settled quickly lest it engulf the entire northwest frontier in war. An edict was issued for the selection of 7,000 fearless men from Xuanda and Shanxi to go to the rescue. Wanli offered

---

55. See Cao Guoqing, *Wanli huangdi da zhuan*, p. 233.

56. *PRL*, p. 116.

57. See Okano, "Banreki nijū nen Neika heihen," p. 600; and Fan Shuzhi, *Wanli zhuan*, p. 228.

58. For details on the outbreak of the mutiny, see Swope, "All Men Are Not Brothers," pp. 91–96.

59. See *WLDC*, p. 648; *HZSL*, p. 4585; and *PRL*, p. 124.

60. See Xia Xie, *Ming tongjian* (hereafter cited as *MTJ*), p. 2719.

61. *WGL*, p. 100a.

his condolences to the families of notable officials who had perished at the hands of the mutineers and ordered that these families be treated with honor.[62] Wanli also made a number of civil and military appointments and invested these officials with great temporary authority.[63] The most notable appointment was that of Ma Gui 麻貴 (fl. 1580–1620), a prominent frontier general who commanded a sizable personal army and whose family's influence was likened to that of the Li family in the east.[64] Ma Gui would later serve with great distinction in Korea and in further actions in the northwest.

Wanli's forceful and decisive actions certainly belie his reputation for neglect of and lack of interest in affairs of state. Indeed, the emperor was heavily involved with both strategic and tactical discussions concerning the mutiny as soon as he was made aware of the situation. For several years, Wanli had frequently engaged in regular discussions with his grand secretaries about unrest along the northern frontier, and he does not appear to have been surprised by the rebellion in Ningxia because he had been concerned about maladministration in the region for some time. Had the emperor known of the gravity of Pubei's complaints earlier, Dang Xin might have been replaced with someone more flexible and the mutiny could have been averted. But now Wanli was vigorous in soliciting suggestions for suppressing the rebels quickly. The seriousness of the threat was readily apparent to the monarch. Soldiers had rebelled, imperial seals of authority had been stolen, and key border fortresses had capitulated or been captured. The emperor wanted to make a swift impression and contain the threat.

Wei Xueceng 魏學曾 (*js.* 1553), supreme commander of the three border regions of Xuanfu, Shaanxi, and Datong and a civil official with a proven track record of battling nomadic tribes outside Shanhaiguan, was invested with full authority by the emperor and told to follow the usual strategy of arresting the ringleaders and dispersing the rest of the rebels.[65] When Wei complained that he lacked the material and manpower resources to deal with the rebels and simply assumed a defensive posture, he was criticized by both the throne and more hawkish officials for not engaging the mutineers.[66] Although Wanli was apparently willing to compromise somewhat by not slaughtering all the mutineers, thereby demonstrating his Confucian restraint, he also disdained empty words and inaction. Addition-

---

62. Ibid.
63. *WGL*, p. 100b; *SDZK*, p. 18.
64. See *MS*, p. 6203.
65. For details on Wei's career, see *MS*, pp. 5975–77.
66. See Mei Guozhen, *Xi zheng ji* (hereafter cited as *XZJ*), 1.12a.

ally, despite Wei's record, many officials at court had no confidence in his ability to suppress the uprising.

At a court conference, the supervising secretaries and Wanli decided to use force before the situation grew more serious.[67] In this campaign, perhaps more than the others discussed here, the emperor took an active role in making strategic and tactical decisions and interacting with his officials. In addition to consulting with the supervising censors, who were generally of slightly lower rank than the six ministers, the emperor discussed affairs with the heads of the Six Ministries and various censors outside the capital so as to get a better sense of what was going on in the field. This management style would continue during the next two campaigns. The emperor was also not above accepting advice and appointing officials from outside the regular hierarchy provided that they had demonstrated some special skill or talent and could produce results. Nonetheless, the practice also bespeaks the emperor's distrust of his regular civil officials and his preference for circumventing the cumbersome Ming bureaucracy.

For his part, Wei Xueceng continued to press for a peaceful solution, citing the safety of the innocents trapped inside Ningxia as his primary concern. His most vocal critic was Mei Guozhen, a censor from Zhejiang.[68] Like many of his contemporaries, Mei, although a *jinshi* degree holder, admired martial deeds and qualities and is said to have excelled at mounted archery as a youth.[69] One cannot help but be struck by how often officials like Mei got the ear of Wanli over their more stodgy counterparts. Wanli apparently had a good working relationship with Mei Guozhen and invested him with tremendous authority in the field. This relationship is demonstrated in Mei's letters to the throne and his memorials to other of-

----

67. According to Charles Hucker (*Dictionary*, p. 133, s.v. *chi-shih-chüng*), supervising secretaries (*jishi zhong* 給事中) were "normally charged to monitor the flow of documents to and from the throne, to return for revision any documents considered improper in form or substance, to check on the implementation of imperial orders, to criticize and propose imperial policies, and sometimes to assist in keeping the Imperial Diary." In this case it appears that the secretaries were acting in their capacity to propose and criticize imperial policies.

68. Mei Guozhen was incidentally a friend and associate of the famous late Ming social critic Li Zhi 李贄 (1527–1602), a scathing critic of Wanli and Ming administration in general. Nevertheless, this association does not appear to have affected Wanli's relationship with Mei Guozhen. On Li Zhi, see *DMB*, pp. 807–17; and Huang, *1587*, pp. 189–221. On his ties to Mei Guozhen, see Jiang, "Heresy and Persecution in Late Ming Society," p. 6.

69. See *MS*, p. 5979.

ficials, which reveal a wonderfully frank appraisal of the Ming military's strengths and weaknesses as well as shed insight into the emperor's preference for a military solution to the crisis and his impatience with official dithering.

Over the next six weeks, government forces recaptured the outlying areas but were unable to dislodge the mutineers from their fortified bastion in Ningxia. Furious debates raged at court as to what exactly should be done and how the Ming should counter the possibility of large-scale Mongol involvement. Wanli listened to all sides and almost seems to have relished the opportunity to do something concrete as opposed to bickering with officials over the formal installation of his heir. Many officials continued to be critical of Wei Xueceng's handling of the mutiny and his perceived policy of appeasement. Again, Mei Guozhen took the lead: "If a renowned general assumes responsibility from Wei, then certainly his heroism will envelop the rebels like clouds and the garrisons can be defended [from further depredations], and they [the rebels] will only be able to retreat and shut themselves in [Ningxia]."[70] Mei added that the emperor needed to be decisive and had to use his best generals and troops if he wished to ensure the speedy pacification of the rebels, saying, "There can be no victory in this national emergency if everyone waits in fear of your majesty's orders to arrive."[71]

Mei Guozhen then suggested appointing Li Chengliang, by this time the Earl of Ningyuan, as military superintendent (*tidu*) of Ningxia.[72] Li was to proceed to Ningxia with troops raised from Shanxi, Datong, and Xuanfu. Mei recommended Li because of his experience in leading troops in battle, especially against the Mongols, and because of his reputation as a military disciplinarian. Moreover, his sons Li Rusong, Li Rubo, and Li Ruzhen 李如楨 (d. 1631) were talented generals in their own right. His younger sons, Li Ruzhang 李如樟 and Li Rumei 李如梅 (fl. 1585–1620), had already earned distinction in the military despite their tender years, as had their cousin, Li Ruwu 李如梧. The Li family was greatly feared and respected along the northern frontiers. Following the maxims of the military classics to overawe one's foes, Mei hoped that their reputation alone would help quell the mutiny.[73]

———

70. *XZJ* 1.6b.
71. *XZJ* 1.9b.
72. *HZSL*, p. 4593.
73. *XZJ* 1.3a.

Mei's recommendation immediately sparked controversy. The Li family had made quite a few enemies over the years, both because of its great power in northeast China and because of its disdain for traditional Confucian sensibilities.[74] Li Rusong and Li Rubo in particular had been accused of arrogance and high-handed behavior toward their civil counterparts, including the slapping of officials. Both had been censured on several occasions but had been cleared by Wanli. The Li family was also tainted by virtue of its association with the now-discredited Zhang Juzheng. Complicating matters further was the fact that the title of military superintendent had theretofore been reserved as a supplementary designation for civil grand coordinators, since it bestowed sweeping, albeit temporary, powers on the recipients to deal with grave military threats. Wang Dewan, the supervising secretary for the Office of Scrutiny in the Ministry of War, opposed Li Chengliang's appointment on the grounds that he was too distant (in Liaodong) and had already retired from active service. To give him a new post violated policy. Others argued that the Li themselves were like wolves in temperament and simply could not be trusted with such an important assignment.

Mei Guozhen countered these arguments by replying, "Sometimes in order to keep the tiger at bay, you have to send in the wolves." He added that it was just this kind of savagery that would enable the Li to prevail in this engagement.[75] Besides, he continued, their authority would only be temporary. Mei concluded his entreaty to Wanli: "If your majesty has any doubts, do not employ them, but if you employ them, do not have any doubts."[76] Other officials also vouched for the Li family, and after considering both sides, Wanli decided that the suppression of the mutiny was paramount. He appointed Li Chengliang military superintendent, with Mei Guozhen to accompany him as army inspecting censor for Ningxia.[77] After all this discussion, Li Chengliang did not leave Liaodong, both because of his advanced age (66) and because of rumors of an impending Japanese invasion of Korea. In his stead, his eldest son, Li Rusong, was appointed military superintendent of Ningxia and commander of Shaanxi in charge of suppressing the mutiny of Pubei.[78] Never before in the dynasty's history

---

74. See *MS*, p. 6192.
75. *XZJ* 1.6b.
76. *XZJ* 1.7b.
77. *WLDC*, pp. 661–62.
78. *HZSL*, p. 4602; *XZJ* 1.15a.

had a purely military officer been given such a title.[79] Once the precedent was established, it was much easier for later officials to receive temporary powers of this magnitude.

As significant as the decision to appoint Li may have been, even more revealing was Wanli's desire to don military garb, hoist a spear, and go to the front himself.[80] This may well have simply been an empty gesture on Wanli's part. In light of his obvious anger at the handling of the revolt, however, his desire may have been sincere. If so, this suggests that Wanli wanted a greater involvement in running the empire, or at least in the management of military affairs, but was consistently frustrated by his civil officials. Events over the next several years seem to bear this observation out, particularly Wanli's handling of the war with Korea and his berating of both his own officials and the Korean king.

Nonetheless, the incident may also speak to Wanli's overall weakness of character and lack of resolve. Truly vigorous and assertive monarchs could, and did, go on campaign themselves, at least until the Zhengde reign (1506–21), but Wanli was dissuaded from acting on this desire. Wanli did, however, continue to monitor the affair from afar and issued a new call for brave volunteers to do their part even as he urged his newly appointed superintendent to hasten to the front.[81] He also received regular updates and responded to memorials and policy suggestions, proffering his often-incisive commentary whenever he felt the occasion called for it.

Wanli and his advisors continued to stew over Wei Xueceng's refusal to act. Wei was told that if he refused the imperial command and did not attack immediately, he would be executed. Heeding the advice of Shi Xing, Wanli also bestowed the double-edged sword upon Wei, granting him full command authority in the field.[82] As noted above, in following this ancient practice, the emperor allowed Wei to act without waiting for permission from the court, a power considered crucial to the success of distant military campaigns. Wanli would bestow the same authority on commanders in Korea and Bozhou. At the same time, special rewards were conferred on those the court deemed worthy (including, oddly enough, Wei Xueceng),

---

79. See Zhang Jincheng, comp., *Qianlong Ningxia fuzhi* (1780), 2 vols. (Yinchuan: Ningxia renmin chubanshe, 1992), p. 410; *MS*, p. 6192; and *MTJ*, p. 2722.

80. *WGL*, p. 108a.

81. See Zhi Yingrui, *Ping xi guanjian*, pp. 89–90.

82. The symbolic bestowal of authority by the emperor through the use of ceremonial weapons dates back to ancient China and is mentioned recurrently in the military classics. See, e.g., Sawyer, *The Seven Military Classics of Ancient China*, p. 267.

and other local officials were impeached for their laxity. Troop buildups continued as small units from all over the empire were dispatched to Ningxia, a tactic seemingly born both because of necessity and because of its psychological impact on the defenders. The Ming would do the same thing several years later in quelling Miao revolts in southwest China.

The siege continued through June and July, with Li Rusong and Mei Guozhen arriving at the end of July. In the meantime, the Ming had learned of the Japanese invasion and occupation of most of the Korean peninsula. Still, both the emperor and the court considered quelling the mutiny to be paramount. Wei Xueceng continued to advocate a policy of buying the Mongols off with titles and avoiding a lengthy struggle, to the great dismay of Wanli, who said that to give into the mutineers' demands would be the most galling shame and humiliation for the Ming and, by implication, the monarch himself. The emperor continued to blast Wei, charging that he was always listening to the timid and the foolish and that his pacification plan was an incredible disgrace. Wanli believed that the end was near for the mutineers and even broached the idea of arresting and executing Wei Xueceng.[83]

Wanli subsequently approved a plan put forth by Shi Xing that called for the construction of a dike around the city to be used to flood it if the rebels refused to come forth and surrender. Once more, it was Wanli who made the final decision after consultation with his officials. Along the model of a CEO outlined above, the emperor listened to a variety of proposals carefully before finally deciding on a strategy that seems to have accorded with his own preferences. Significantly, he favored aggressive action even as he was considering how to deal with the looming threat on the eastern border. Indeed, it seems that the emperor favored quick military action precisely because he realized the need to free troops for the upcoming defense of Korea. Wanli also continued to respond to memorials sent from officials at the front and urged them to lead their troops bravely, showering them with gifts of cash, titles, and ceremonial clothing, thereby demonstrating the beneficence of the monarch and reinforcing the ties between the court and the frontier.[84]

It is not clear exactly who offered Wanli direct counsel at this time, but sources frequently refer to the "Nine Chief Ministers," who, during the Ming period, consisted of the heads of the Six Ministries, the censor in

---

83. See *WGL*, p. 112b; and *SDZK*, p. 23.
84. *WGL*, p. 115a.

chief of the Censorate, the chief minister of the Court of Judicial Review, and the transmission commissioner of the Office of Transmission.[85] Given the absence of a prime minister in the Ming governmental structure after 1380, these individuals can be likened to a Joint Chiefs of Staff for Ming emperors and were employed accordingly. One problem with the arrangement was that all the officials were essentially equals, and personality or imperial favor could play a role in the relative weight an individual voice carried. Additionally, there were jurisdictional overlaps, and the monarch had to take these into account when considering the counsel offered by various ministers (a problem common to any consultative bureaucracy). In the end, the emperor was theoretically the final and sole arbiter of policy, but, as might be expected, this was rarely the case in practice.

Wanli also communicated regularly with his civil officials in the field, as evidenced by the extensive records left by Mei Guozhen, Song Yingchang 宋應昌 (1530–1606), and Li Hualong for the Three Great Campaigns. The grand secretaries also attended at least some of these discussions, as did numerous lower-ranking censorial officials. In general Wanli seems to have placed a great deal of trust in Shi Xing, his minister of war, until Shi was discredited by the failure of his Korean policy. In terms of actual activity, Wanli seems to have read and responded to numerous proposals from the provinces. At the very least, he appointed officials to act on them in his name. Unfortunately Ming sources are not as explicit about this as those we have from the Qing, where surviving memorials are often covered with the emperor's vermilion rescripts.

By late August, the water assault plan was on the verge of succeeding, but Wanli had finally tired of Wei Xueceng, who continued to entertain thoughts of accepting the surrender of the mutineers. Wei found himself impeached by a supervising censor, and Wanli said that he was amazed at Wei's neglect of his duties after he had been so favored by the emperor himself. Wei was arrested by the Brocade Guard and brought back to Beijing.[86] According to the *Ming shi*, the main reason for Wei's arrest was because he had withheld information from the emperor.[87] Again, one wonders why Wanli would even care if he was as uninterested in governing as commonly charged. Clearly the emperor was frustrated that he was not being properly apprised of the situation in the field and found this unaccept-

———

85. See Hucker, *Dictionary*, p. 176.
86. *JSBM*, p. 2381; *WLDC*, p. 691.
87. *MS*, p. 5980.

able. Wanli's intolerance for bureaucratic obfuscation would be manifested repeatedly over the next several years. Wei Xueceng was replaced by another veteran censorial official, Ye Mengxiong 葉夢熊 (*js.* 1561), who was likewise invested with the authority of the double-edged sword. Wanli apparently still trusted in the policy of investing his commanders in the field with temporary authority, but it needed to be properly exercised.

The dismissal of Wei Xueceng was almost certainly tied to the situation in Korea. By late August, it was obvious that the Ming would have to intervene militarily in Korea to prevent a Japanese invasion of China, if nothing else. The initial Ming expeditionary force of about 3,000 had been annihilated in Pyŏngyang, and the Ming knew the unrest in Ningxia had to be quelled so that Li Rusong, who otherwise would have been stationed in Liaodong, could get back to the eastern border. As the Ming were constructing the dike around Ningxia, an official reported that the Japanese had crossed the Taedong River at Pyŏngyang in Korea and that the Korean king, Sŏnjo, was seeking permission to enter Liaodong with his court. The king had fled to the town of Ŭiju on the banks of the Yalu, and two of his sons had been captured by the Japanese.[88] Although the Ming did not necessarily want to deny Sŏnjo's plea for aid, it was put in a difficult position by his request. Wanli told the king to sit tight and hold out for the time being while the Chinese court decided exactly how much help to give. The Ming did appoint Song Yingchang, another veteran civil official with extensive experience in military affairs, as military commissioner (*jinglüe* 經略) of Korea in September.[89]

The mutiny in Ningxia was finally quelled in late October by a combination of external pressures and internal friction among the ringleaders. Many among the victorious forces were ordered to hasten to Korea, including Li Rusong, who was now appointed supreme commander of the expedition to chastise the Japanese. Wanli was understandably pleased. He even authorized the release of Wei Xueceng from prison after Mei Guozhen and Li Rusong interceded on Wei's behalf.

In assessing Wanli's role in this crisis, it is apparent that he took a keen interest in the insurrection from the beginning and that his appointment decisions, most notably those of Mei Guozhen and Li Rusong, were instrumental in bringing the mutiny to a successful conclusion. Wanli dem-

---

88. *GQ*, p. 4676.
89. *MS*, p. 275. For Song's orders and appointment directive, see Song Yingchang, *Jinglüe fuguo yaobian* (hereafter cited as *FGYB*), pp. 1–4.

onstrated a preference for actions over words and a predilection for the employment of dynamic, if at times controversial, military leaders. This is not to say he ignored the advice of all his civil officials, for the surviving documents indicate that he was in frequent contact with officials at court and in the field, in marked contrast to what many historians of the period might expect. Wanli was involved in the selection and dismissal of officials and freely vented his anger against those who failed to follow orders. Throughout the crisis, Wanli favored a hard-line approach toward the mutineers, an approach that would surface again during the war in Korea. With one foe bested, the court was now able to direct the bulk, but not all, of its attention toward the crisis in Korea.

THE RESCUE OF KOREA

The Japanese invasion of Korea, which lasted from 1592 to 1598, is without a doubt one of the most significant events of the sixteenth century, not just in East Asia but in the entire world. The war remains important for the study of international relations, diplomacy, and war in early modern East Asia. From the Ming perspective, the war represented a serious challenge to its authority as the major imperial power in East Asia and threatened to undermine the legitimacy of the international order the Ming inherited and perpetuated.[90]

The war offered Wanli another opportunity to flex his military muscles while exercising his sovereign authority as the Son of Heaven in international affairs. It also allowed him to regain some of the prestige he may have felt he had lost when forced to yield to his civil officials on the matter of naming his heir apparent. When dealing with the king of Korea, Wanli clearly was in the superior position and did not have to answer to criticisms that his actions violated dynastic precedents. Wanli realized that he *needed* to do something important. Judging from the exchanges that took place between Wanli and his bureaucrats throughout his reign, he felt that many officials would have preferred that he simply did what they told him and never think or act on his own. Yet their behavior in the deliberations concerning the war in Korea suggests that his officials were far from capable of running the show on their own. Once again, it was Wanli who made the difference, sending tens of thousands of Chinese troops to Korea on two separate occasions.

---

90. For a lengthy discussion of this aspect of the conflict, see Swope, "Deceit, Disguise, and Dependence."

The Japanese invasion began in late May 1592 as over 150,000 Japanese troops landed around the southeastern port city of Pusan. Although the Koreans were not caught completely unaware, factional rivalries caused Korea's envoys and primary intelligence gatherers to work at cross-purposes prior to the invasion. Consequently, defensive preparations were limited. Even the Chinese had some inkling of an impending attack, gleaned from the king of the Ryūkyūs and from Chinese traders in the summer of 1591.[91] Other sources confirmed these initial reports, and Wanli had ordered the Ministry of War to repair coastal defenses throughout the country toward the end of 1591.[92] In the first month of 1592, Song Ying-chang, then pacification commissioner of Shandong, memorialized the throne, asking for seasoned troops to meet the possible threat of a Japa-nese invasion. The Ministry of War promised to look into the matter.[93] In the second month of 1592, the Ministry of War reported that the Japanese were indeed planning to attack China, citing information from the Koreans and the king of the Ryūkyūs. Warning his officials that the Japanese were crafty, Wanli ordered again that coastal defenses be strengthened and that the situation in Korea be investigated.[94] Therefore, even before the mutiny in Ningxia, Wanli was directing his attentions toward Korea and a potential clash with the Japanese.

Korea's defenses crumbled faster than even Hideyoshi himself pre-dicted. The Japanese embarked on a *Blitzkrieg*, which brought them to Seoul within a couple of weeks as the king and his retinue fled under a rain of insults and garbage hurled by the citizens of Seoul.[95] Stores were looted, and government records were burned, most significantly the registers of slaves and criminals. The Korean court's flight would not stop until it reached the Chinese border and messengers were dispatched to beseech the Chinese for aid. Japanese progress might have been even faster had it not been for the rivalries between Hideyoshi's leading commanders, most

---

91. See Song Maocheng, *Jiuyue qianji* 4b; and *MS*, p. 8357. See also Li Guangtao, *Chaoxian Renchen Wohuo shiliao* (hereafter cited as *CXSL*), pp. 1904–5.

92. *MS*, p. 8291.

93. See *HZSL*, p. 4525; and He Baoshan et al., *Ming Shenzong yu Ming Dingling*, p. 100.

94. See Zheng Liangsheng, *Ming dai Wokou shilu* (hereafter cited as *WKSL*), p. 474. Volume 2 of this work, cited here, consists of excerpts taken from the *Ming shilu*. Since all citations contain the original *juan*, readers are referred to Zheng's work, which has the added benefits of being annotated and punctuated.

95. See Yu Sŏngnyong, *Chingbirok* (hereafter cited as *CBR*), p. 309.

notably Konishi Yukinaga 小西行長 (1558–1600) and Katō Kiyomasa 加藤清正 (1562–1611).

The invasion of Korea and the Ming response to this challenge can serve as a microcosm of court politics during the Wanli era. Much of the infamous bickering and petty turf wars that characterized the Ming political scene can be found here in abundance. Despite his legendary irascibility, Wanli consistently displayed an interest in what was taking place in Korea and sought to build a consensus among his officials for a course of action. But he was frustrated time and again by the differing recommendations of his officials, which ranged from appeasement and investiture (of Hideyoshi as king of Japan) to all-out war on the Korean peninsula. Although the war has a prominent place in the more general chronicles of the period such as the *Veritable Records* and the *Wanli dichao*, it is often no more than the backdrop for the increasingly rancorous political battles waged by various factions of Ming officialdom, most notably those who would later revive the Donglin Academy and their rivals. Charges and countercharges abound, and it becomes increasingly difficult to follow events. It is easier to see why Wanli became so frustrated with his officials that he simply refused to get involved in most matters. The records of the time frequently note Wanli's furor at his officials. Wanli also went out of his way to protect certain officials, most often military men or those who could be seen as having close ties to the military, such as the later commissioner for Korean affairs, Yang Hao 楊鎬 (d. 1629),[96] from charges leveled by censors or civil bureaucratic rivals. In this sense, Wanli performed the functions of a supreme commander as articulated in the military classics and as illustrated by his more forceful and illustrious ancestors.

In 1592, Wanli acted quickly upon hearing reports that the Japanese had crossed the Taedong River at Pyŏngyang and were advancing toward the Yalu. He ordered all the officials of the coastal areas of Liaodong and Shandong to begin training for battle and instructed them to heed his commands without delay.[97] Wanli was well aware of the military weakness of Korea, and he asked the Ministry of War to submit proposals and opinions regarding the situation there. Ironically, because Korean resistance had crumbled so fast, some on the Ming side actually suspected the Koreans of being in league with the Japanese. Wanli dispatched officials to

---

96. For his biography, see *ECCP*, pp. 885–86; and *MS*, pp. 6685–88.

97. The defense policies put forth by Ming officials are wonderfully detailed in memorials contained in *FGYB*, esp. pp. 46–84.

Korea to investigate these rumors. After meeting with King Sŏnjo, these officials became convinced of the king's sincerity and Korea's dire peril. They returned to Beijing to ask their government to send troops.[98] According to Fan Shuzhi, Wanli resolved at this point to send troops to Korea "without the least hesitation" but was in a difficult situation militarily because of the mutiny in Ningxia.[99] At this point all the emperor could do was to tell Sŏnjo to rally his own forces to resist with all their strength and assure him that Ming troops would arrive as soon as possible. In his letter to the king, Wanli said, "The Japanese have overrun Korea, and I sympathize with the king's desire to flee. Relief troops have already been dispatched. Thus I order you and the high ministers of your country to gather troops for a stout defense so you can come up with a plan for recovering your country. How, then, can you remain in fear of extermination?"[100]

Actions and statements such as these typified Wanli's behavior throughout the Korean War. Contrary to the charges of Ray Huang and others that he was being tightfisted and petty, the emperor repeatedly approved requests for funds, troops, and supplies and often released additional cash for rewards or to meet exigent circumstances. For example, in the sixth month of 1592, Wanli approved a request to ship 60,000–70,000 *dan* of grain to Tianjin to support military units preparing for a possible Japanese invasion. Touring censors were dispatched to Shandong later that month to quiet fears of a Japanese attack. The court also authorized the recruitment of mercenaries and the requisition of funds from the Court of the Imperial Stud for allocation for local defense needs. The Ministry of Revenue approved a request by the regional inspector of Shandong for 40,000 taels of silver for troop maintenance and defense.[101]

Although the Koreans had requested 100,000 troops, the initial Ming expeditionary force, under the command of a seasoned veteran named Zu Chengxun 祖承訓 (fl. 1570–1600), numbered about 3,000 troops.[102] The Ming believed it would need 100,000 soldiers in any case, but this first mission was to be no more than a probing attack. The court also sent the Koreans 20,000 *liang* of silver to help pay for troops and supplies.[103] Weapons, including firearms, which the Koreans were sorely lacking, were sent ahead to

---

98. *CXSL*, p. 13.
99. Fan Shuzhi, *Wanli zhuan*, p. 236.
100. *WKSL*, p. 478, excerpted from *juan* 250 of Yao Guangxiao et al., *Ming shilu*.
101. *WKSL*, pp. 476–77.
102. On Korea's request, see *FGYB*, pp. 5–11.
103. See *CXSL*, p. 28; and *PRL*, p. 248.

the Korean capital-in-exile at Ŭiju.[104] Crossing into Korea in late July, the Ming force advanced to Pyŏngyang in late August and was annihilated by a Japanese ambush, the Ming commander barely escaping with his life.[105]

News of the debacle shocked and alarmed Wanli and his court. Song Yingchang was immediately appointed military commissioner of Jizhen, Baoding, and Liaodong and ordered to begin making preparations for a massive punitive expedition to Korea.[106] Soon thereafter, Song requested another 200,000 *liang* of silver to buy mounts and issued production orders to factories in Tianjin, Yongping, and Liaodong for more transport carts, large mobile cannon, small cannon, reliable field pieces, crossbows, blankets and covers, crossbow bolts, bullets, and sundry other military supplies.[107] As was his style, Wanli invested Song with sweeping powers to do as he saw fit.[108]

In the meantime, Wanli issued a call for loyal and brave officials all over the empire to hasten to the assistance of Korea, promising them great rewards. They could contribute to the war cause in whatever way they saw fit by, among other actions, assuming posts in Korea, strengthening coastal defenses in China, or sending men, money, or materials to the front. Wanli also made sure that the most decorated commanders of the empire were mobilized for the campaign, no matter how distant they might be from the action in late 1592. The emperor chastised those he felt were lax in their duty. When one grand secretary asked to retire on account of his mother's illness, the emperor shot back, "With the Japanese troubles in the east and [Pubei] in the west, which require diligent effort day and night, how could a minister just sit by and watch?"[109] Most notably, when he felt they were the best men for the job, Wanli appointed commanders even if they had been previously impeached. For example, Chen Lin 陳璘 (d. 1607), a noted firearms expert, was brought to the capital from Guangdong to oversee the firearms division, despite having been impeached on charges of bribery and cruelty to his men earlier in his career.[110]

---

104. It is unclear if they did so at this time, but later the Chinese typically dispatched experts to train the Koreans in the use of Chinese weapons and in Chinese battle tactics. These experts remained in Korea even after the withdrawal of the Japanese in 1598.

105. *PRL*, p. 240.

106. *GQ*, p. 4682.

107. See *FGYB*, pp. 46–50; and Li Guangtao, *Renchen Wohuo yanjiu*, p. 22.

108. See *FGYB*, pp. 35–39; and *WLDC*, pp. 695–99.

109. *WKSL*, p. 483.

110. For Chen's biography, see *DMB*, pp. 167–74; and *MS*, pp. 6404–8.

In order to buy time, Wanli also authorized the appointment of a private trader named Shen Weijing 沈惟敬 (fl. 1540–97), who had connections to Shi Xing, to serve as Ming envoy to the Japanese.[111] Here we see court politics at work again. Because of his role in quelling the Ningxia mutiny, Shi Xing enjoyed the emperor's favor. This allowed him to serve as the patron of Shen Weijing, who was connected to Shi through the minister's wife's family. Shen allegedly had experience battling Japanese pirates decades earlier and could apparently speak Japanese with reasonable facility. And, as we have seen, Wanli liked men who could get things done. At the time this looked like serendipity, but in the long run it would prove an almost disastrous decision, particularly for the Koreans. But such was the fluid nature of the Ming court, not to mention Wanli's desire to act without fetters.

As soon as the Ningxia mutiny was put down, Li Rusong and other notable commanders of the campaign were sent to Korea. Li was made supreme commander of the Eastern Expedition to Chastise the Japanese and concurrently superintendent of military affairs for Jizhen, Liaodong, Baoding, and Shandong, thereby acquiring even more power than he already enjoyed in the suppression of the Ningxia mutiny.[112] Li requested extra funds and more supplies to help his men combat the bitter Korean cold.

Around the same time, Song Yingchang came under fire from an investigating censor who suggested he was acting too timidly. Song submitted his resignation in response to the charges. Wanli, for his part, forcefully rejected the request, reprimanding both officials in the process:

As for you, Song Yingchang, you have already accepted the order to become military commissioner [of Korea], but now on account of one word from Guo Shi, you think you can avoid your prior responsibilities. Who will then take responsibility for defending our coasts and borders? Are a few meaningless words enough to make you shirk your responsibilities to the Court? What will become of discipline under the state if no one takes his assignments seriously? The situation with the Japanese is paramount. You, Song Yingchang, must be ready to move today. The nine ministers and supervising secretaries here [in Beijing] have proven unable to reach an accord; from now on there is no need to debate this further. In selfishly harboring his own schemes, Guo Shi has unnecessarily hampered the affairs of state; so he is hereby demoted and sent to the frontier. Anyone else

---

111. For the full story of Shen Weijing, see Swope, "Deceit, Disguise, and Dependence."

112. *FGYB*, pp. 136–37.

who wishes to add another gratuitous remark to this confusion will be sent off with him.[113]

Here we see an example of just the kind of forceful leadership Wanli is often criticized for lacking as well as his loyalty toward his handpicked favorites. We also get a relatively rare public glimpse of the emperor's continual frustration over the incessant petty turf wars that characterized late Ming politics. Plus, Wanli acts imperiously to goad his officials into action as seen in his reference to the inability of the nine ministers and supervising secretaries to reach an accord. The emperor simply demotes and exiles the offending official, demonstrating the autocratic authority of the Ming monarch while also revealing a disturbing (at least from the perspective of the officials) aspect of Ming court culture: offend the emperor at your own risk! Finally, we also see the primacy of Korea and the importance of the Japanese threat in the eyes of the Ming court.

On the sixth day of the eleventh month of 1592, Shen Weijing returned to Korea with a directive from the Ministry of War ordering a complete Japanese withdrawal from the Korean peninsula.[114] Shen then spent several days in the Japanese camp as his Korean allies waited eagerly for word of concrete Ming assistance. Shen emphasized to the Japanese that Wanli himself had given the orders for mobilization. In doing so, Wanli was both fulfilling his role as the tributary father in his relationship with King Sŏnjo (and the Japanese for that matter) and asserting his military and political primacy in Asia. The emperor's threat to mobilize military aid from faraway Siam and other states, despite the fact that he would later reject such aid when it was offered, can be viewed as a pointed and direct rejoinder to Hideyoshi's own boasts that he had compelled the world to join his cause.[115]

These conclusions are borne out by Wanli's own words in an imperial decree to the Korean king concerning the Ming decision to send military aid:

For generations, you have been our Eastern neighbor, and you have always been docile and obedient. Your gentry take pleasure in learning and culture. I heard that your nearby land had been invaded and was being plundered by the rapacious Japanese villains and that your capital city had been looted and Pyŏngyang occu-

---

113. *WLDC*, p. 699. For a slightly different translation of this edict, see Miller, "State Versus Society," p. 235.

114. See Sin Kyŏng, *Chaejo pŏnbang chi* (hereafter cited as *CPC*), p. 237. This source is romanized as *Zaizao fanbang zhi* in Chinese.

115. On the promise of aid from other tributaries, see *CXSL*, p. 29.

pied, forcing your people to scatter near and far, and I was deeply disturbed. And now Your Highness has fled for the western coast and is seeking refuge among the rustics. You must now focus your attention on the task at hand and strengthen your resolve. For, as soon as I heard the news yesterday, I ordered the border officials to begin mobilizing troops to come to your aid. I will also dispatch a high civil and a high military official to act in concert. They will assemble 70,000 crack troops from the various defense commands around Liaoyang, which will be sent forth to assist you in chastising the [Japanese] bandits and in conjunction with your own country's men, they will catch the enemy in a vise and annihilate them. Furthermore, I have issued imperial commands to the tributary kings of the myriad states in all directions so that they, too, can assist in helping with this nasty business. I have also issued an order to the various coastal garrisons of the southeast and promulgated an edict to countries such as Siam and Ryūkyū to assemble an army of 100,000 to join us in attacking Japan and drive them from their nests. . . . Now Your Highness must focus on maintaining what your ancestors have bequeathed to you. How can you just lightly cast it all away? Now you must exert all your energy in the business of saving your state and restoring its prestige, and you should order all your civil and military officials and ordinary people to likewise exert themselves to the utmost. For if Your Highness's mind is open and you rectify your past transgressions, then you will be able to recover the territory that you have lost. The masses will face this calamity out of filiality to their father, and the ministers of your country, recognizing your righteousness, will certainly all look up to you. Your Highness will thereby regain the respect you once had.[116]

This passage is one of the clearest articulations of the Ming imperial perception of the Japanese invasion of the Asian mainland and its larger ramifications. It also provides much insight into Wanli's state of mind and personal agenda. One suspects that he relished the chance to go to war in Korea on some levels because it afforded him the opportunity to act as the Son of Heaven. He could put aside his family troubles and the meaningless squabbles that embroiled his officials in favor of what could certainly be seen as a noble cause, even if there was a great deal of self-interest involved. Additionally, other memorials and letters to King Sŏnjo find Wanli sermonizing on the debilitating evils of factionalism and royal corruption and laziness, the very things he himself was often charged with facilitating.

---

116. *CPC*, pp. 238–39. Ironically enough, the Ming later refused offers from the king of Siam to launch a naval assault on Japan's rear while the Japanese were preoccupied in Korea; see Wolters, "Ayudhya and the Rearward Part of the World," pp. 168–73.

But in Korea Wanli could easily be seen in the role of the savior, a role he may well have enjoyed.[117]

Finally, in order to further boost morale, Wanli announced that 100,000 *liang* of silver would be distributed for special rewards after the Japanese were defeated.[118] This is yet another action that contradicts his reputation as a miser and again illustrates the role of the court in the person of the emperor as the giver of beneficence to the masses. The kinds of rewards Ming soldiers could earn in Korea for a single battle dwarfed their annual salaries, and the emperor was undoubtedly aware of this fact. For the most part, these strategies bore fruit, and the Ming amassed a force of perhaps 44,000. In early February 1593 alongside the Koreans, they counterattacked the Japanese and dislodged them from Pyŏngyang.[119]

After the liberation of Pyŏngyang, the allies quickly advanced to re-capture Kaesŏng, just north of Seoul, and pressed on toward the capital. Although temporarily checked at Pyokchegwan, just north of the Korean capital, they nevertheless regained the initiative and forced the Japanese to abandon Seoul in the spring of 1593. After most of the Japanese forces either returned home or withdrew to what constituted a Pusan perimeter, the war settled into an uneasy period of bizarre and ultimately farcical negotiations. Representatives on both sides continually misrepresented not only the positions of their own governments but also the intentions of their adversaries. Wanli favored a fairly aggressive policy that made total Japanese withdrawal from Korea a prerequisite for any kind of peace arrangement, but he was stymied by Shen Weijing and Shi Xing, who adopted a more conciliatory approach. Eventually both men paid for it.[120]

---

117. Indeed, many later Korean accounts display a profound sense of gratitude toward Wanli. See, e.g., *CPC*, p. 2. Ceremonies honoring Wanli's spirit continue to be performed in Korea down to the present; see Mason, "The *Sam Hwangje Paehyang*."

118. Fan Shuzhi, *Wanli zhuan*, p. 238. Fan notes that, interestingly enough, after these actions Wanli retreated further into the Forbidden City, although he continued to display a keen interest in military affairs.

119. For a detailed discussion of this battle, see Swope, "Turning the Tide."

120. The matter of the peace talks and the investiture of Hideyoshi as king of Japan are treated in a number of places. The most detailed account, which includes lengthy excerpts from primary sources, is Li Guangtao, *Wanli ershisan nian feng Riben*. See also Swope, "Deceit, Disguise, and Dependence." For more information on the Japanese occupation of Korea from 1593 to 1596, see Swope, "Three Great Campaigns," chap. 5; Kitajima, *Hideyoshi no Chōsen shinryaku*, pp. 64–67; and Hawley, *The Imjin War*, pp. 299–400.

These discussions suggest that Wanli's reluctance to get too deeply involved with the day-to-day administration of his realm hurt his credibility
with Ming officialdom in general, particularly those already frustrated with
his truculence about naming an heir apparent. Wanli initially favored an
aggressive approach in Korea, but he largely deferred to the advice of Shi
Xing. Wanli left his officials to hash out the details of the peace agreement,
with the result that they tended to bicker back and forth without coming to
a decision.[121] In the end, it was the emperor himself who finally ordered
that a Japanese envoy be allowed to come to Beijing to request investiture
for Hideyoshi as a vassal of the Ming. Wanli's decision seems to have been
based on his assumption that the Ming was in fact victorious in the conflict,
which was not entirely true. Perhaps he also sought a reification of his own
position as the pre-eminent monarch in East Asia, a status that he may well
have believed was diminished by the perceived slights he suffered at the
hands of his own contentious bureaucracy. This conclusion is borne out by
communications between Wanli and Sŏnjo in which the Chinese emperor
chastised his Korean subordinate and exhorted him to set a better example
for his people![122] If he could not make his will felt in domestic affairs, then
Wanli would assert himself on the international stage.

In other words, it is entirely possible that Wanli pushed for the investiture of Hideyoshi as a tributary vassal in order to soothe his own wounded
ego and prove that *he*, not his officials, was the Son of Heaven. Unfortunately, the engrained culture of officialdom was such that this kind of imperial behavior was seen as distracting the monarch from his "real business" of naming an heir and listening to their sound advice. Coupled
with the literati's near-monopoly on the historical record, it is no wonder
that the voices and viewpoints of the emperor's literati foes prevailed during the ensuing centuries.

A Japanese envoy was eventually allowed to come to Beijing in the winter of 1595–96. After what amounted to a series of interrogation sessions in
which the emperor was at least tangentially involved, the Ming decided to
grant Hideyoshi investiture as a tributary vassal, which, of course, was not
what the Japanese commander wanted. Wanli and his officials prepared

---

121. For the full extent of the disagreements within Ming officialdom, see the documents contained in Li Guangtao, *Wanli ershisan nian feng Riben*, pp. 77–124. See also
WLDC, pp. 738–62, 847–48, for more on the Korean context of factional disputes
within Ming officialdom.

122. See *GQ*, p. 4711.

an edict that is full of the imperial rhetoric typical of such documents.[123] Wanli would also appoint another military officer as his special envoy to Japan. By this point he was committed to peace but continued to monitor the situation and prepare for other eventualities. The ultimate failure of the mission to Japan is well documented elsewhere, but it is important to note that, on hearing of its failure, Wanli again acted decisively, immediately authorizing the dispatch of troops to Korea for another punitive expedition and appointing high officials to reprise the roles played by Song Yingchang and Li Rusong in 1592. Wanli also authorized the appointment of many of his favorite commanders from earlier campaigns, including Li Rubo and Li Rumei, younger brothers of Li Rusong; and Chen Lin, who was appointed commander of the Chinese navy.[124]

The second Japanese invasion of Korea, which commenced in the spring of 1597 and involved almost as many troops as the first, was not nearly as successful for the invaders, although the level of savagery and brutality on the part of the Japanese was even greater according to contemporary accounts. This time, however, the allies were able to check the Japanese advance south of Seoul and for the last year of the war the Japanese were on the defensive, holed up in a ring of fortified strongholds that stretched from Ulsan in the southeast to Sunchŏn in the south. Again Wanli invested one of his field commanders, this time Xing Jie 形玠 (*js.* 1571), with the authority of the double-edged sword. Wanli would also defend his favored officials from charges raised by military censors, most prominently after the allies saw defeat snatched from the jaws of victory at the siege of Ulsan in early 1598.[125] Interestingly, Yang Hao, who would later be the Ming commander of the 1619 expedition against the Manchus in Liaodong, was the civil official in charge in the field. Although Wanli initially recommended Yang's arrest and execution, Yang would be cleared of all charges and later rehabilitated at the behest of the emperor. Yang was also close to the Li family, an association that contributed to

---

123. For excerpts, see Swope, "Deceit, Disguise, and Dependence," pp. 774–75. See also *GQ*, pp. 4745–46. The original document is in the collection of the Osaka City Museum. For the meetings at the Ming court, see *HZSL*, pp. 5172–209.

124. See *WKSL*, p. 620; and *MS*, p. 6405.

125. This incident is described in Kenneth M. Swope, "War and Remembrance: Yang Hao and the Siege of Ulsan, 1597–98," forthcoming in the *Journal of Asian History*. See also the treatment in Li Guangtao, "Ding Yingtai yu Yang Hao." For the Korean perspective on these events, see Ledyard, "Confucianism and War"; and *CXSL*, pp. 1286–96.

his original censure but also may well have carried considerable weight with the emperor.

Even after the defeat at Ulsan, the tide of the war did not turn in favor of the Japanese. In fact, Hideyoshi, after close consultation with his generals and with his own health failing, finally decided that the affair in Korea needed to be brought to a conclusion and ordered the gradual withdrawal of Japanese forces. At the same time in China, Wanli was coming under increasingly heavy fire from his own officials for his alleged neglect of government. In the spring of 1598, a group of officials gathered outside the Wenhua Gate of the Forbidden City and beseeched the monarch to invest his eldest son as heir apparent, but there was no response.[126]

In the fifth month of 1598, Lü Kun 呂坤 (1536–1618), the minister of justice, submitted a long memorial warning the emperor of signs of restiveness and danger all over the empire. Known as the "You wei shu" 憂危疏 (Memorial on impending disasters), the document seemed to place the blame on the failings of the emperor himself. Lü was especially concerned with mounting military costs and with deficiencies in training, supplies, and recruitment methods.[127] He also exhorted Wanli to reform and set a better example. Although the emperor definitely saw the memorial, he did not respond to its contents other than to permit Lü to retire after he was indicted on false charges. Wanli himself later admitted to ordering the investigation that led to Lü's removal from office.

This incident once again illuminates the connections between military policy, imperial conduct, and official expectations. It also demonstrates the dangers inherent in criticizing the throne within the context of Ming court culture. However, it is worth noting that Wanli did not have his detractor killed or exiled, merely removed from office. Perhaps he actually agreed with some of the recommendations but disliked the way in which they had been presented, not to mention the aspersions cast on his own character. Returning to the war itself, Wanli also ordered the demotion and retirement of Yang Hao.[128] The war would drag on for several more months until the Japanese navy was finally smashed at the Battle of Noryang Strait in December 1598.

---

126. *MS*, p. 280.

127. See *MTJ*, pp. 2783–84.

128. *WLDC*, p. 1139. Wan Shide 萬世德 (*js*. 1568) was appointed as his replacement.

THE BOZHOU CAMPAIGN

With the conflict in Korea finally over, Wanli could now deal with a threat to Ming security in the jungles of the southwest, the rebellion of the Miao chieftain Yang Yinglong.[129] This was a military problem that had vexed the Ming for some eleven years and it became the last, and the most successful from the Ming standpoint, of the Three Great Campaigns of the Wanli emperor. The Ming tolerated Yang's depredations for so long because it regarded Sichuan as being less strategically important than Ningxia or the Korean border and because Ming armies had been able to contain him in an area with relatively few Han settlers. But Yang's actions were always in the background. Accounts of the other two campaigns are peppered with references to Yang's actions in the territory known to the Ming as Bozhou, part of what is modern-day Sichuan, Guizhou, and Yunnan. By the late 1590s, however, Yang and his followers had become too great a threat to countenance.

Yang's family had held positions of authority in the region since the Tang dynasty, and the post of pacification commissioner of Bozhou was first bestowed on the clan during the reign of Khubilai Khan (1260–94). The Yangs were not originally from the area, but over the centuries and through continued intermarriage and interaction with the locals, they came to identify themselves with the Miao and their interests.[130] Throughout the Ming period, the territory of Bozhou was responsible for sending 2,500 *dan* of lumber and military supplies, including horses, to the Ming court every three years.[131] It is possible that these exactions became more onerous over time, and at least one scholar suggests that these burdens led to Yang's revolt.[132] Yang Yinglong inherited his father's post in the Longqing period, and he honored his obligations to the court by forwarding fine wood for public works and palace construction. He initially earned much distinction fighting various aboriginals and Tibetans on behalf of the Ming, and like

---

129. For a detailed discussion of the rebellion of Yang Yinglong, see Swope, "Civil-Military Coordination in the Bozhou Campaign"; and idem, "Three Great Campaigns," chap. 7. For a biography of Yang, see *DMB*, pp. 1553–56.

130. For the earlier history of the Yangs in Bozhou, see *WGL*, pp. 500a–507b; and *Zunyi fuzhi* (hereafter cited as *ZYFZ*), pp. 681–88.

131. See *ZYFZ*, p. 689. On the history of the Yangs in Bozhou during the Ming, see Swope, "Three Great Campaigns," pp. 387–94.

132. See Okano, "Minmatsu Hashū ni okeru Yō Ōryō no ran," pp. 63–66.

his counterpart Pubei in the north, continually displayed his military prowess, being in the forefront of every battle.[133]

Despite intimations that Yang was a potential threat, not to mention his run-ins with other local notables, the court stuck by its policy of rewarding frontier commanders who achieved concrete results. Accordingly Yang received rewards of gold and ceremonial clothing and was promoted to regional military commissioner (rank 3a).[134] Surviving sources, however, hold that these rewards were not enough to satisfy Yang's growing ambitions. They charge that Yang was of a fierce disposition from birth and that he delighted in killing.[135] He regarded most government troops as weak. Because the Ming always relied on locally recruited aboriginal forces to quell uprisings in the southwest, he became scornful of it and disrespectful of its laws.[136]

Within the context of Ming court culture, perhaps the most interesting aspects of Yang's behavior were his affronts to imperial prestige and dignity. Much like the cases of Pubei and Hideyoshi, Yang's actions threatened the legitimacy of Ming rule. Indeed, to prevent subsequent aboriginal insurrections after Yang's uprising was crushed in 1600, the Ming embarked on a systematic program of sinicizing the area, encouraging Han settlement, building schools, and incorporating former aboriginal districts into the regular administrative structure of the empire by making them prefectures (*zhou* 州) and counties (*xian* 縣).[137] The charges leveled against Yang maintained that he held regular feasts in his mountain stronghold and that he used dragon and phoenix emblems (traditional symbols of imperial authority and status) on his clothing. He also adorned himself with fabulous jewelry, and elephant tusks served as the frame for his bed.[138] Yang even employed eunuch servants and demanded other local chieftains send women to serve as his "palace ladies." Imperial sources note that Yang behaved in the manner of an aboriginal emperor and "came to regard all of Sichuan as a tiger would regard its den."[139] These points are mentioned time and again in various sources and were apparently galling to Ming au-

133. See *SDZK*, pp. 65–66.

134. *JSBM*, p. 2383; *SDZK*, p. 66.

135. *HZSL*, p. 6631.

136. *ZYFZ*, pp. 900–901.

137. For a recent discussion of the relationship between Ming imperial expansion and ethnicity, see Shin, *The Making of the Chinese State*.

138. *PRL*, p. 404.

139. *HZSL*, pp. 6631–32.

thorities, for eunuchs and palace ladies were the prerogative of the Son of Heaven alone and constituted a sort of imperial capital.[140] For Yang to arrogate such privileges was treason of the highest order.

It is unclear whether the court would have acted against Yang had he been accused only of arrogance and imperial pretensions, although it is certainly possible. It is also possible that these details were added to the sources later as further "evidence" of Yang's villainy. In any case, Yang also became entangled in a number of local power struggles and then threw his lot in with dissatisfied local Miao groups that resented Han intrusions into the area. The initial requests for assistance in quelling Yang's nascent rebellion were dismissed by the central authorities on the grounds that Bozhou was a distant corner of the empire and there were more pressing matters at hand. Even the regional inspector of Shandong, Li Hualong, who would later command the Ming expeditionary force that crushed Yang, complained that he did not have time to investigate the matter fully and argued that Yang should be given the opportunity to redeem himself through meritorious service.[141] Nonetheless, the court was already thinking about how to reorganize local administration and ordered the Ministry of War to investigate the matter and make recommendations. Some advocated incorporation of these areas into the regular administrative structure; others, including Li Hualong, opposed reorganization. The issue was shelved for the time being.

To the surprise of many, Yang surrendered to the authorities but unexpectedly was sentenced to death. He managed to get his sentence commuted by promising to pay a hefty fine and offering to lead 5,000 troops to the defense of Korea against the Japanese. But Yang's offer was not sincere, and once freed, he holed up in his mountain stronghold and rebelled again, looting and plundering isolated prefectures and districts. In 1595 Yang was again brought to justice and again bought his way out of the death penalty. His son Yang Chaodong 楊朝棟 was given his hereditary post, and another son was held in Chongqing as a guarantee of Yang Ying-

---

140. Imperial relatives were allowed to have eunuchs and to bestow them on their favorites, but this was a privilege specifically granted by the monarch. It seems, however, that nobles around the empire employed eunuch servants; see Tsai, *The Eunuchs in the Ming Dynasty*, p. 18.

141. See *MS*, p. 8045. For biographies of Li Hualong, see *DMB*, pp. 822–26; and *MS*, pp. 5982–87. His compilation of documents pertaining to the quelling of Yang's rebellion, *Ping Bo quan shu* (hereafter cited as *PBQS*) is the most complete source on the rebellion and its aftermath.

long's good behavior. Considering the matter settled, Wanli promoted and rewarded the officials responsible for Yang's capitulation and once again turned his attention to matters in Korea. Within a year, however, Yang was back to his old tricks, raiding into Huguang, Sichuan, and Guizhou, and claiming that he was the emperor of Bozhou.[142] Over the next three years Yang and approximately a hundred thousand Miao followers rampaged all over the area, settling old scores and sowing fear and panic among the locals. Preoccupied with the Japanese threat, Wanli did little at this time other than assure that Yang's rebellion was relatively contained until early 1599, when he vowed to stamp Yang's movement out.[143]

Eventually, the emperor authorized further appointments and approved a counteroffensive against Yang. The Ming troops fell for a feint and were annihilated by the rebel forces, prompting Wanli to appoint Guo Zizhang 郭子章 (1543–1618), one of the more notable officials of the era, to the post of pacification commissioner of Sichuan.[144] Former Censor in Chief Li Hualong was elevated to the post of vice minister of war and placed in charge of the military affairs of Sichuan, Huguang, and Guizhou.[145] Wanli then ordered several distinguished commanders of the Korean campaign to travel with all due haste to Sichuan.

Arriving on the scene in July 1599, Li Hualong solicited cash and troops from all over the empire.[146] The struggle between rebel and government forces continued the rest of the year, and at one point the rebels seemed to be gaining the upper hand and were even in position to strike at the important cities of Chongqing and Chengdu. The emperor intervened again, depriving some civil officers of their posts and demoting them to the status of commoners while bestowing the double-edged sword of authority on Li Hualong.[147] Li would perform the same role as Mei Guozhen had in Ningxia or Song Yingchang in Korea for the remainder of the Bozhou campaign, alternating between cajoling and consoling his fellow officials, while simultaneously keeping in contact with the emperor in distant Beijing. However, because of the distances involved and the time lag between communications, not to mention the fact that this rebellion, though serious, was no real threat to dynastic stability, Wanli's involvement in decision-

142. *PRL*, p. 419.
143. See Cao Guoqing, *Wanli huangdi da zhuan*, p. 241.
144. For a biography of Guo, see *DMB*, pp. 775–77.
145. For Li's letter of appointment, see *PBQS*, p. 1.
146. *WGL*, p. 522a.
147. *MS*, p. 5985.

making seems to have been somewhat less than had been the case with the Ningxia and Korean campaigns. And after the decision was finally made (by the emperor) to crush the Yangs once and for all, there was little debate at court, although that had not been the case over the previous twelve years.

Wanli's choice proved to be a fine appointment; Li was a veteran of many frontier wars and had a reputation as a fair-minded official who worked well with both civil and military colleagues, making him Wanli's kind of man. He had in fact worked closely with Li Rumei in Liaodong prior to his appointment in Sichuan. Together he and Guo Zizhang labored tirelessly, mobilizing Han and aboriginal troops and erecting defense works around lands claimed by Yang Yinglong. Li was a master planner, continually sending memorials to the Ministry of War asking for more troops and supplies and carefully calculating the costs of weapons, equipment, and provisions.[148] He was also eager to have more experienced commanders at the front, complaining: "Sichuan not only has no troops, it also lacks even one person versed in military affairs."[149] Using his viceregal powers, Li issued a number of commands to local authorities calling for the creation of *baojia* defense forces and demanding that the strictest discipline be observed by all troops in the region so as to not cause undue hardship to the local populace. Li begged the emperor to curtail his practice of sending out eunuch tax commissioners, arguing that their depredations may have led some people to rebel, a charge that may be rather dubious if one accepts the premise that the tax collectors primarily went after the rich.[150]

Although he ignored Li's plea concerning the eunuch tax collectors, Wanli told the Ministry of War to recruit troops from Shaanxi, Gansu, Yansui, and Zhejiang to quell the rebellion.[151] The distinguished commanders of the empire were ordered to rush to the rescue of Sichuan.

Wanli also issued a decree addressing Yang's revolts and his crimes. In this decree Yang was accused of violating the principles of Heaven and turning his back on the kindness of the Ming. All Yang's heinous deeds were recounted, and he was threatened with a force of 500,000 men. The emperor charged that Yang and his allies were responsible for the deaths of over 100,000 people. His atrocities were known throughout the empire, and he had cut himself off even from his ancestors. Wanli further warned

---

148. See *PBQS*, pp. 401, 413, 471–72.
149. *PBQS*, p. 650.
150. See *PBQS*, pp. 21–23, 99.
151. *WLDC*, p. 1177.

Yang's family and associates that they, too, would die with Yinglong for taking part in his dastardly deeds. Miao rebels were offered a chance to live if they killed Yang and his top lieutenants. Other allies were warned that Yang was untrustworthy, and he might turn on them at any time. After all, reasoned the emperor, Yang regarded all their lands as his own, and he would freely sacrifice any of them to save himself. Wanli reminded them that when one person rebelled, according to the law, all relatives within nine degrees of kinship were held responsible and subject to the same punishment. Wanli finished his proclamation by stating, "If you kill Yang and his associates, things can return to the way they were before. Heaven will bestow its riches on you and look on you as it did before. There can be good fortune, or there can be disaster. The choice is yours."[152]

Here is yet another example of the supposedly indifferent Wanli emperor directly involved in matters of defense and providing forceful imperial leadership in the face of a military crisis. The tone of this proclamation is strikingly similar to his letter to the king of Korea and reveals the emperor's exultation in his status as the Son of Heaven, the light of the Ming court thereby shining even into the darkest corners of the empire, the very den of the "Tiger of Sichuan." On a more prosaic level, the edict articulates the court's rightful position as the defender of the principles of Heaven and bestower of favors, positions even Wanli's officials could accept.

In the tenth month of 1599, the court ordered Li Hualong to Chongqing to begin mobilizing the forces from Sichuan, Huguang, and Guizhou. Wanli communicated with local aboriginal officials to secure their assistance in putting down the uprising. Upon his arrival from Korea, the redoubtable Liu Ting 劉綎 (1552–1619), a Han man whose family had a long relationship with the Yangs, was summoned to Li Hualong's office and lectured on the importance of loyalty to the state. Liu's presence was important to morale, since he and his father had served along the southwestern frontier for decades. As Li put it, "In the palaces and among the common people alike, there is no one who has not heard of Big Sword Liu."[153] Liu pledged to do his utmost for the Ming, vowing to "eat the flesh and sleep on the hide" of Yang Yinglong.[154]

The end of 1599 and the first month of 1600 were filled with skirmishes between the rebels and the government contingents, which continued to

---

152. For the full text, see *PBQS*, pp. 477–82.
153. *PBQS*, p. 703.
154. *PBQS*, pp. 96–97; *MTJ*, p. 2801.

arrive from all over the empire. Wanli's influence on the selection of officials and recruitment of troops is apparent even if his role in deciding
strategy was more limited than it had been in Ningxia and Korea. The emperor personally selected many of the civil and military officials and used
his influence to keep the latter in particular out of trouble when suspicion
was cast on their activities during the campaign (as in the charges of bribery leveled at Liu Ting). Renowned and colorful, the assembled commanders included many veterans of the first two Great Campaigns. The Ming
force was said to have eventually numbered some 240,000 men and included troops from Sichuan, Huguang, Guizhou, Yansui, Ningxia, Henan,
Shandong, Tianjin, Guangdong, Yunnan, Guangxi, Zhejiang, and even
some Japanese units that had surrendered in Korea.[155] Each commander
and each army inspecting censor received a ceremonial sword and full authority to act as he saw fit in the field from Li Hualong. Li recognized the
utility of replicating the level of trust the monarch had demonstrated in
him. The date for the expedition was fixed for March 26, 1600, and Li addressed the assembled civil and military officers in a stirring speech at
Chongqing in late February.[156]

The government forces embarked on an eight-pronged assault and bat-
tled the rebels in the jungles and ravines for nearly four month before en-
circling Yang at his isolated stronghold of Hailongtun. In the end, the rebels were crushed, and Yang immolated himself. Government records
indicate that the Ming killed 22,687 rebels, captured another 1,124 rebels
and their followers, took 5,539 noncombatant prisoners of war, obtained
the surrender of 126,211 Miao, freed 1,614 prisoners, captured 767 head of
livestock, and confiscated 4,444 weapons.[157] Wanli declared the victory the
verdict of Heaven, ordered a tax amnesty for the regions affected by the
rebellion, and would later attend the ritual dismemberment of the surviving
rebels in January 1601.[158] Rewards were showered on the victorious civil
and military officials. Li Hualong handed the double-edged sword back to
the emperor on April 30, 1601.[159]

In summarizing the campaign for posterity, Li Hualong emphasized that
its successful conclusion owed everything to the leadership of Wanli and,

---

155. *JSBM*, p. 2384.
156. For details of the speech, see Swope, "Three Great Campaigns," pp. 423–24.
157. *PBQS*, p. 287.
158. See *MTJ*, p. 2811; and *GQ*, p. 4866.
159. *PBQS*, p. 371.

most important, his willingness to bestow on Li the authority of the double-edged sword. Li said Wanli's trust allowed for the proper coordination of the efforts of civil, military, and censorial officials and the throne.[160] The success of the campaign also testifies to the considerable abilities of Li Hualong.

THE MING ENTERS THE SEVENTEENTH CENTURY

Despite the success of these military campaigns, it would be wrong to view them out of context. More often than not, particularly over the final century of its existence, the Ming empire was hamstrung by rampant factionalism and uninspired imperial leadership. Few men possessed the vision and forceful character to effect substantial changes in policy during the late Ming. Li Hualong and Mei Guozhen were among the few officials who managed to maintain a level of credibility with all branches of government, including the throne. This particular dynamic of Ming court culture is too often glossed over in favor of examinations of the relationships among various factions of civil officials. Military and censorial officers were often even more important in the eyes of the emperors than their civil counterparts; they, too, could influence policy decisions and determine the tenor of court culture.

In the wake of the government victory at Bozhou, it might have seemed as if the Ming was still in the midst of a renaissance. After all, had the Ming not just defeated three formidable enemies simultaneously on three geographically distant frontiers? For all his failures in other areas, Wanli had good reason to feel pride in his military accomplishments during the 1590s. Indeed, in the decade following Bozhou, the Ming continued to pursue military actions with a fair degree of success, especially in the southwest, where a series of minor uprisings caused in part by the disruptions of Yang Yinglong's revolt were successively quelled and the way paved for further Han settlement. Likewise, Ma Gui and others continued to keep order along the northwestern frontier. The Ming was also still in the prime of its life with respect to artistic and cultural achievements. But Ming government continued to wallow in decadence and factionalism.

For all his concern and leadership in the Three Campaigns, Wanli was still a capricious and neglectful ruler for the most part. Had he acted more forcefully earlier in his reign and named his second son heir, maybe he

---

160. *PBQS*, p. 291.

could have made all his wishes reality and forced his officials into line. But he did not and instead allowed his government to sink into a cesspit of intrigue, albeit not entirely of his own making, from which it never emerged. In addition to these problems, the Ming state was increasingly beset by natural disasters that seriously drained the resources of a state already operating in a mode of deficit spending.[161]

The emperor continued to patronize his favorite military officials. However, as they died off and military affairs, except for that of the Manchus, became less pressing, Wanli lost interest even in punishing those who angered him. He managed to rouse himself somewhat for the Liaodong campaign, since many of his old favorites, Yang Hao, Liu Ting, and Li Rubo, were involved in it. As things turned out, only Li Rubo survived the debacle, and he chose to commit suicide rather than suffer the indignity of a trial and execution. Yet Wanli demonstrated his loyalty to the Li clan by appointing his younger brother Li Ruzhen to the family post in Liaodong in 1619.[162] By this time it may have been clear that the military exploits of the late sixteenth century were a thing of the past. Rather than attempting cooperation to recreate these successes, Ming officialdom became even more divided, and no official capable of uniting the bickering factions ever emerged.[163] In some sense the deaths of Liu Ting and Li Rubo put a fitting cap on the Wanli era. As Liu Ting's official biographers put it, "[Liu] Ting was the bravest of the generals. In the campaigns to pacify the Burmese, the Lolo, the Japanese in Korea, the chieftain of Bozhou, and the Guo, he fought hundreds of major and minor battles, and his great name moved those all over the empire. When Ting died, the court was terrified, and the border situation became more perilous by the day."[164] Considering their ties to the emperor, when Liu Ting and Li Rubo died, perhaps part of Wanli died as well.

---

161. Contrary to what is often claimed, the Three Campaigns themselves were not to blame for the decline of the Ming. The total expenses of the campaigns ran to about 12 million *liang* of silver, spread over eight years. This sum constituted about one-third of a single year's revenue, high to be sure, but about equivalent to present-day North Korea's annual defense expenditures, and far below the 70–80 percent contemporary European monarchs were spending on their militaries in the sixteenth and seventeenth centuries.

162. See Swope, "A Few Good Men"; and *MS*, p. 6197.

163. For a recent reappraisal of factional politics in the Wanli era and their effects on historiography, see Miller, "Newly-Discovered Source Sheds Light on Late Ming Faction."

164. *MS*, p. 6396.

Concluding Comments

So what does all this tell us about Ming court culture? First and foremost, the insights gleaned from the study of Wanli's reign suggest that much more work should be done on imperial negotiation and manipulation of civil-military relations along the lines of Arthur Waldron's work on the Ordos recovery debate, cited above. Studies thus far have tended to focus only on those emperors who led armies in the field, namely Hongwu, Yongle, and Zhengde.[165] What about other monarchs? What role did they play in the turf wars between civil and military officials, and what kinds of concrete results, if any, did they realize from their machinations? Ming court life was influenced by a wide range of actors, including priests, mystics, eunuchs, and warriors. For all their seclusion and the enforced majestic solitude of their positions, Ming emperors were people with their own aims and ambitions like anyone else. Reading alternative sources and examining the actions of the throne from a perspective other than that presented by "orthodox" Confucian-minded official historians can add layers to this increasingly complex picture. The case of Wanli yields tantalizing glimpses of a man who was far more involved with his administration than has been commonly perceived. Careful re-evaluation of Wanli suggests the beginnings of an alternative, or at least parallel, vision of late Ming society and its problems. We also see what I believe are the roots of the militarization so decried by some late Ming social critics (and later historians) in the general circumstances created by Wanli's patronage of military officials over the objections of their civil counterparts.

Furthermore, the fact remains that many of the prominent civil officials discussed in this chapter were neither allies of those who became associated with the Donglin nor lackeys of court eunuchs. They were men of intelligence, integrity, and experience who managed to command the respect of both civil and military officials, as well as the emperor himself, who had little tolerance for the antics of self-interested officials. Furthermore, this study reopens the question of imperial authority and prestige, not only within China proper but also on the steppe and in the greater East Asian context. Wanli seemed keenly aware of his position as the Son of Heaven,

---

165. Philip de Heer's study of the Zhengtong and Jingtai reigns, *The Care-taker Emperor*, deals with the issue of the emperor's capture by Mongols while on campaign. More important, it examines in great detail court politics in light of civil-military relations.

and perhaps influenced by his early training under Zhang Juzheng, he was determined to exercise the rights conferred by his position and to contest challenges to his august authority.

The Ming empire and its rulers need to be examined in the same multi-ethnic and universalist light that many recent scholars have shone on the Mongols and the Manchus. In other words, to what degree did imperial ambitions contribute to Ming decisions to go to war or to expand Ming territory or authority? Finally, how did Ming emperors perceive and exercise their powers as supreme commanders of the army? Were they always content to delegate powers to their civil advisors? Or did at least some monarchs choose to use these powers to achieve specific political and/or military goals? And how did imperial decisions along these lines affect their portrayals by literati historians in subsequent periods? In the case of the Zhengde emperor, posthumously designated the Martial Ancestor (Wu-zong) with more than a hint of derision, the answer seems fairly obvious. Further exploration of these questions and issues could certainly go far toward enhancing our picture of Ming court culture and illuminating the relationship between events around the empire and conditions in the capital.

Works Cited

Barr, Allen H. "The Wanli Context of the 'Courtesan's Jewel Box' Story." *Harvard Journal of Asiatic Studies* 57, no. 1 (1997): 107–41.

Cao Guoqing 曹國慶. *Wanli huangdi da zhuan* 萬曆皇帝大傳. Shenyang: Liaoning jiaoyu chubanshe, 1994.

Chen Baoliang 陳寶良. "Wan Ming de shangwu jingshen" 晚明的尚武精神. *Mingshi yanjiu* 明史研究 1 (1991): 248–59.

CBR, see Yu Sŏngnyong, *Chingbirok*

CHC, see Mote and Twitchett, *Cambridge History of China*

CPC, see Sin Kyŏng, *Chaejo pŏbong chi*

CXSL, see Li Guangtao, *Chaoxian Renchen Wohuo shiliao*

Dardess, John W. *Blood and History in China: The Donglin Faction and Its Repression, 1620–1627*. Honolulu: University of Hawai'i Press, 2002.

de Heer, Philip. *The Care-taker Emperor: Aspects of the Imperial Institution in Fifteenth Century China as Reflected in the Reign of Chu Ch'i-yü*. Leiden: E. J. Brill, 1986.

Elman, Benjamin A. "Imperial Politics and Confucian Societies in Late Imperial China: The Hanlin and Donglin Academies." *Modern China* 15, no. 4 (Oct. 1989): 379–418.

Fan Shuzhi 樊樹志. *Wanli zhuan* 萬曆傳. Beijing: Renmin chubanshe, 1993.

Fan Zhongyi 范中義. *Qi Jiguang zhuan* 戚繼光傳. Beijing: Zhonghua shuju, 2003.

FGYB, see Song Yingchang, *Jinglüe fuguo yaobian*

Geiss, James. "The Leopard Quarter During the Cheng-te Reign." *Ming Studies* 24 (Fall 1987): 1–38.

Goodrich, L. C., and Fang Chao-ying, eds. *Dictionary of Ming Biography*. 2 vols. New York: Columbia University Press, 1976.

GQ, see Tan Qian, *Guoque*

Graff, David A. *Medieval Chinese Warfare, 300–900*. London: Routledge, 2002.

Gu Yingtai 谷應泰. *Ming shi jishi benmo* 明史紀事本末. 1658. Reprinted in *Lidai jishi benmo*. 2 vols. Beijing: Zhonghua shuju, 1997.

Halperin, Charles J. *Russia and the Golden Horde*. Bloomington: Indiana University Press, 1985.

Hawley, Samuel. *The Imjin War: Japan's Sixteenth-Century Invasion of Korea and Attempt to Conquer China*. Seoul: Royal Asiatic Society, Korea Branch; Berkeley: University of California, Institute of East Asian Studies, 2005.

He Baoshan 何寶善, Han Qihua 韓啓華, and He Dichen 何滌塵. *Ming Shenzong yu Ming Dingling* 明神宗與明定陵. Beijing: Beijing Yanshan chubanshe, 1998.

———. *Wanli huangdi—Zhu Yijun* 萬曆皇帝—朱翊鈞. Beijing: Beijing Yanshan chubanshe, 1990.

Hu Yuewei 胡月偉, Yao Bochu 姚博初, and Qian Facheng 錢法成. *Wanli wangchao* 萬曆王朝. Chengdu: Sichuan wenyi chubanshe, 2002.

Huang, Ray. *1587, A Year of No Significance: The Ming Dynasty in Decline*. New Haven: Yale University Press, 1981.

———. "The Liao-tung Campaign of 1619." *Oriens Extremus* 28, no. 1 (1981): 30–54.

Hucker, Charles O. *A Dictionary of Official Titles in Imperial China*. Stanford: Stanford University Press, 1985.

Hummel, Arthur O., ed. *Eminent Chinese of the Ch'ing Period.* 2 vols. Washington, DC: Government Printing Office, 1943.

HZSL, or *Shenzong shilu*, in Yao Guangxiao et al., *Ming shilu* (q.v.)

Jiang Jin. "Heresy and Persecution in Late Ming Society: Reinterpreting the Case of Li Zhi." *Late Imperial China* 22, no. 2 (Dec. 2001): 1–34.

Johnston, Alastair Iain. *Cultural Realism: Strategic Culture and Grand Strategy in Chinese History.* Princeton: Princeton University Press, 1995.

JSBM, see Gu Yingtai, *Ming shi jishi benmo*

Kierman, Frank A., Jr., and John K. Fairbank, eds. *Chinese Ways in Warfare.* Cambridge: Harvard University Press, 1974.

Kitajima Manji 北島万次. *Hideyoshi no Chōsen shinryaku* 秀吉の朝鮮侵略. Tokyo: Yamakawa shuppansha, 2002.

Kye, Seung B. "An Indirect Challenge to the Ming Order: Nurhaci's Approaches to Korea During the Imjin War, 1592–1598." In *A Transnational History of the Imjin Waeran: The East Asian Dimension.* Seoul: Sŏgang University, 2006, pp. 423–51.

Ledyard, Gari. "Confucianism and War: The Korean Security Crisis of 1598." *Journal of Korean Studies* 6 (1988–89): 81–120.

Li Du 李渡. *Mingdai huangquan zhengzhi yanjiu* 明代皇權政治研究. Beijing: Zhongguo shehui kexue chubanshe, 2004.

Li Guangtao 李光濤. "Ding Yingtai yu Yang Hao—Chaoxian renchen Wohuo luncong zhi yi" 丁應泰與楊鎬—朝鮮壬辰倭禍論叢之一. *Lishi yuyan yanjiusuo jikan* 歷史語言研究所季刊 53 (1982): 129–66.

Li Guangtao 李光濤. *Chaoxian Renchen Wohuo yanjiu* 朝鮮壬辰倭禍研究. Taibei: Lishi yuyan yanjiusuo, 1972.

———. *Wanli ershisan nian feng Riben guo wang Fengchen Xiuji kao* 萬曆二十三年封日本國王豐臣秀吉考. Taibei: Zhongyang yanjiuyuan, Lishi yuyan yanjiusuo, 1967.

Li Guangtao 李光濤, comp. *Chaoxian Renchen Wohuo shiliao* 朝鮮壬辰倭禍史料. 5 vols. Taibei: Zhongyang yanjiuyuan, Lishi yuyan yanjiusuo, 1970.

Li Hualong 李化龍. *Ping Bo quan shu* 平播全書. 1601. Reprinted in Congshu jicheng, nos. 3982–88. Changsha: Shangwu yinshuguan, 1937.

Lorge, Peter. "The Northern Song Military Aristocracy and the Royal Family." *War and Society* 18, no. 2 (Oct. 2000): 37–48.

———. "War and the Creation of the Northern Song." Ph.D. diss., University of Pennsylvania, 1996.

———. *War, Politics, and Society in Early Modern China, 900–1795.* London and New York: Routledge, 2005.

Mao Ruizheng 茅瑞徵. *Wanli san da zheng kao* 萬曆三大征考. 1621. Ming-Qing shiliao huibian, vol. 58. Taibei: Wenhai chubanshe, 1971.

Mason, David A. "The *Sam Hwangje Paehyang* (Sacrificial Ceremony for Three Emperors): Korea's Link to the Ming Dynasty." *Korea Journal* 31, no. 3 (Autumn 1991): 117–36.

Mei Guozhen 梅國楨. *Xi zheng ji* 西征集. 1592; preface dated 1638. Facsimile reprint in 2 vols. Tokyo: Tōkyō daigaku, 1973.

Miller, Harry S. "Opposition to the Donglin Faction in Late Ming China: The Case of Tang Binyin." *Late Imperial China* 27 no. 2 (Dec. 2006): 38–66.

———. "Newly-Discovered Source Sheds Light on Late Ming Faction: Reading Li Sancai's *Fu Huai Xiao Cao.*" *Ming Studies* 47 (Spring 2003): 126–40.

———. "State Versus Society in Late Imperial China, 1572–1644." Ph.D. diss., Columbia University, 2001.

Millinger, James F. "Ch'i Chi-kuang: Chinese Military Official: A Study of Civil-Military Roles and Relations in the Career of a Sixteenth Century Warrior, Reformer and Hero." Ph.D. diss., Yale University, 1968.

Mote, F. W. *Imperial China, 900–1800.* Cambridge: Harvard University Press, 1999.

Mote, Frederick, and Denis Twitchett, eds. *The Cambridge History of China*, vol. 7, *The Ming Dynasty, 1368–1644, Part I.* Cambridge: Cambridge University Press, 1988.

MTJ, see Xia Xie, *Ming tongjian*

Okano Masako 岡野昌子. "Banreki nijū nen Neika heihen" 万暦二十年寧夏兵変. In *Minmatsu Shinsho no shakai to bunka* 明末清初の社会と文化, ed. Ono Kazuko 小野和子. Kyoto: Kyōto daigaku jinbun kagaku kenkyūsho, 1996, pp. 587–623.

———. "Minmatsu Hashū ni okeru Yō Ōryō no ran ni tsuite" 明末播州における楊応竜の乱について. *Tōhōgaku* 東方学, no. 41 (Mar. 1971): 63–75.

Parker, Geoffrey. *The Grand Strategy of Philip II.* New Haven: Yale University Press, 1998.

PBQS, see Li Hualong, *Ping Bo quan shu*

Perdue, Peter C. "Culture, History and Imperial Chinese Strategy: Legacies of the Qing Conquests." In *Warfare in Chinese History*, ed. Hans van de Ven. Leiden: Brill, 2000, pp. 252–87.

PRL, see Zhiye Yuansheng, *Liangchao ping rang lu*

Qian Yiben 錢一本, comp. *Wanli dichao* 萬暦邸鈔. Ca. 1617. Reprinted in 3 vols. Taibei: Zhengzhong shuju, 1982.

Qu Jiusi 瞿九思. *Zuben Wanli wu gong lu* 足本萬暦武功錄. 1612. Reprinted in 5 vols. Taibei: Yiwen shuguan, 1980.

Robinson, David. *Bandits, Eunuchs, and the Son of Heaven: Rebellion and the Economy of Violence in Mid-Ming China.* Honolulu: University of Hawai'i Press, 2001.

Sawyer, Ralph D., trans. *The Seven Military Classics of Ancient China.* Boulder, CO: Westview Press, 1993.

SDZK, see Mao Ruizheng, *Wanli san da zheng kao*

Serruys, Henry. "Four Documents Relating to the Sino-Mongol Peace of 1570–1571." *Monumenta Serica* 19 (1960): 1–66.

Shin, Leo K. *The Making of the Chinese State: Ethnicity and Expansion on the Ming Borderlands.* Cambridge: Cambridge University Press, 2006.

Sin Kyŏng 申炅. *Zaizao fanbang zhi* [*Chaejo pŏnbang chi*] 再造藩邦志. Ca. 1693. Reprinted in 2 vols. Taibei: Guiting chubanshe, 1980.

Song Maocheng 宋懋澄. *Jiuyue qianji* 九籥前集. Ca. 1612. Facsimile reprint—Kyoto: Kyōto daigaku, 1973.

Song Yingchang 宋應昌. *Jinglüe fuguo yaobian* 經略復國要編. 1590s. Reprinted in 2 vols. Taibei: Taiwan xuesheng shuju, 1986.

Struve, Lynn A. *The Southern Ming: 1644–1662.* New Haven: Yale University Press, 1984.

Swope, Kenneth M. "All Men Are Not Brothers: Ethnic Identity and Dynastic Loyalty in the Ningxia Mutiny of 1592." *Late Imperial China* 24, no. 1 (June 2003): 79–129.

———. "Civil-Military Coordination in the Bozhou Campaign of the Wanli Era." *War and Society* 18, no. 2 (Oct. 2000): 49–70.

———. "Deceit, Disguise, and Dependence: China, Japan, and the Future of the Tributary System, 1592–1596." *International History Review* 24, no. 4 (Dec. 2002): 757–82.

———. "A Few Good Men: The Li Family and China's Northern Frontier in the Late Ming." *Ming Studies* 49 (2004): 34–81.

———. "The Three Great Campaigns of the Wanli Era, 1592–1600: Court, Military, and Society in Late Sixteenth-Century China." Ph.D. diss., University of Michigan, 2001.

———. "Turning the Tide: The Strategic and Psychological Significance of the Liberation of Pyongyang in 1593." *War and Society* 21, no. 2 (Oct. 2003): 1–22.

———. "War and Remembrance: Yang Hao and the Siege of Ulsan, 1597–1598." *Journal of Asian History*, forthcoming.

Tan Qian 談遷, ed. *Guoque* 國榷. 1653. Reprinted in 10 vols. Taibei: Dingwen shuju, 1978.

Tsai, Shih-shan Henry. *The Eunuchs in the Ming Dynasty*. Albany: State University of New York Press, 1996.

Turnbull, Stephen. *Samurai Invasion: Japan's Korean War, 1592–1598*. London: Cassell & Co., 2002.

Waldron, Arthur. *The Great Wall of China: From History to Myth*. Cambridge: Cambridge University Press, 1992.

Waley-Cohen, Joanna. *The Culture of War in China: Empire and the Military Under the Qing Dynasty*. London: I. B. Tauris, 2006.

Wang Tianyou 王天有 and Xu Daling 許大齡, eds. *Mingchao shiliu di* 明朝十六帝. Beijing: Zijincheng chubanshe, 1991.

WGL, see Qu Jiusi, *Zuben Wang wu gong lu*

WKSL, see Zheng Liangsheng, *Ming dai Wokou shilu*

WLDC, see Qian Yiben, *Wanli dichao*

Wolters, O. W. "Ayudhya and the Rearward Part of the World." *Journal of the Royal Asiatic Society of Great Britain and Ireland* 3–4 (1968): 166–78.

Xia Xie 夏燮. *Ming tongjian* 明通鑑. Ca. 1870. Reprinted 5 vols. Taibei: Xi'nan shuju, 1982.

Yao Guangxiao 姚廣孝, comp. *Ming shilu* 明實錄. 133 vols. + 21 vols. of appendixes. Taibei: Zhongyang yanjiuyuan, Lishi yuyan yanjiusuo, 1962–66.

Yu Sŏngnyong 柳成龍. *Chingbirok* 懲毖錄. Ca. 1600; published 1695. Reprinted in *Renchen zhi yi shiliao huiji* 壬辰之役史料匯輯, comp. Wu Fengpei 吳豐培 et al. Beijing: Quanguo tushuguan, Wenxian suowei fuzhi zhongxin chubanshe, 1990, 2: 257–470.

Yu Yanfang 于燕芳. *Chaonu yicuo* 剿奴議撮. Ca. 1620. Facsimile reprint—Nanjing: Nanjing daxue, 1928.

Zhang Haiying 張海瀛. *Zhang Juzheng gaige yu Shanxi Wanli qingzhang yanjiu* 張居正改革與山西萬曆清丈研究. Taiyuan: Shanxi renmin chubanshe, 1993.

Zhang Tingyu 張廷玉 et al., comps. *Ming shi* 明史. 1739. Reprinted in 12 vols. Taibei: Dingwen shuju, 1994.

Zhao, Jie. "A Decade of Considerable Significance: Late Ming Factionalism in the Making." *T'oung Pao* 87 (2002): 112–50.

Zheng Liangsheng 鄭樑生, ed. *Ming dai Wokou shiliao* 明代倭寇史料. 5 vols. Taibei: Wenshizhe chubanshe, 1987.

Zhi Yingrui 支應瑞. *Ping xi guanjian* 平西管見. 1592. Facsimile reprint of Naikaku bunko edition. Shan ben shu ying, vol. 70. Kyoto: Kyōto daigaku, 1970.

Zhuge Yuansheng 諸葛元聲. *Liang chao ping rang lu* 兩朝平攘錄. 1606. Reprinted—Taibei: Taiwan xuesheng shuju, 1969.

Zunyi fuzhi 遵義府志. 1841.

ZYFZ, see *Zunyi fuzhi*

THREE

The Eunuch Agency Directorate of Ceremonial and the Ming Imperial Publishing Enterprise

Scarlett Jang

Ever since the Chinese writing system first appeared on oracle bones and bronze vessels in the Shang dynasty (1767–1045 BCE), those who could read, write, recite, and interpret texts owned the past and thus became the cultural arbiters of their eras. They also owned or otherwise shared in political power. The text, or textuality, was therefore one of the most important cultural constructs of China's imperial past.[1]

This chapter is about books—more precisely, the woodblock-printed imperial publications produced by the Directorate of Ceremonial (Silijian 司禮監), the most powerful eunuch agency during the Ming dynasty. Woodblock-printed books were by their very nature public and highly mobile objects. They existed in multiple copies, often in the thousands, and once they were promulgated, they traveled far and wide, to be read,

I would like to thank David Robinson, the organizer of the Ming Court Culture Conference held in June 2003, from which this volume sprang; conference discussants Susan Naquin, Evelyn Rawski, Benjamin Elman, and Thomas Nimick; the anonymous readers; and Gary Smith for their invaluable editorial suggestions and critiques on various drafts of this essay. While they helped shape the direction of this essay, I take sole responsibility for any errors that this chapter might contain.

1. For a fine study of the text and authority in imperial China, see Connery, *The Empire of the Text.*

discussed, emulated, appropriated, and critiqued in the public arena. Not only were many of the Ming imperial publications used in the inner court[2] for the education of the emperor, crown prince, and selected palace women and eunuchs, but some of them were also given by the emperor to imperial clan members and affines and court officials as gifts, and sometimes as warnings. They were also found in public schools at all levels and in foreign courts, and they were used as master copies by other government offices as well as commercial publishers. Many were used to disseminate the imperially sanctioned Confucian ideology; others were used to fulfill specific political agendas, of which the issue of legitimacy was paramount. By delineating the patterns of this particular area of cultural production and its consumption, this chapter investigates issues of the readership, authorship, and functions of imperial publications, as well as their political ramifications. It also discusses the significance of the interaction between court and non-court culture represented by books and the politics surrounding the Directorate of Ceremonial as the sole overseer of the Ming imperial publishing enterprise.

Neifuben, Silijianben, *and* Jingchangben: *What's in a Name?*

Three types of book publishers existed during the Ming: official, private, and commercial. Official publishers occupied all levels of the government apparatus, from the National University (Guozijian 國子監) to the Six Ministries to all levels of provincial and prefectural government offices. They, including the Directorate of Ceremonial, published books under the imperial court's auspices.[3] Books published by the Directorate of Ceremonial are variously referred to as *neifuben* 內府本 (inner court editions), *Silijianben* 司禮監本 (Directorate of Ceremonial editions), or *Jingchangben* 經廠本 (Sutra and Classics Depository editions), because they were produced by

---

2. The term "inner court," or *neiting* 內廷, denotes a conglomeration of the imperial household and its numerous service agencies located inside the Forbidden City, as opposed to the "outer court," or *waiting* 外廷, represented by the vast civil and military bureaucracies.

3. Some scholars include all the royal clan members' publishing houses in the category of official publisher; see Li Zhizhong, *Zhongguo gudai shuji shi*, p. 108; and Zhou Xinhui, *Zhongguo gudai banke banhuashi lunji*, p. 246. Since the imperial clan members published books independently, without official sanction or interference, they should not be considered official publishers.

the Sutra and Classics Depository's workshops in the inner court, which
were supervised by the Directorate of Ceremonial.

During the reign of the founding Ming emperor, Hongwu, more than
seventy titles were published on his order by both government agencies
and the inner court.[4] Although 150 woodblock carvers, 312 artisans for book-
binding and mounting, and 58 printers are said to have worked for the inner court during the Hongwu reign,[5] it is not clear which inner court
agency or agencies oversaw the production.[6] It is clear, however, that the
Directorate of Ceremonial was placed in charge of inner court publications
in the early fifteenth century.

At some point during the Hongwu reign, the Directorate of Ceremonial,
one of the twelve major eunuch agencies, was a relatively minor office in
charge of court ceremonies with a low-ranking (7a) director.[7] By early in
the sixteenth century, it had evolved into the most powerful of the inner
court agencies. By then, its four top officers, customarily called great superintendents (*taijian* 太監), were ranked 4a.[8] Beginning in the Yongle
reign and throughout the dynasty, the Directorate of Ceremonial acted as
the emperor's personal secretariat. It handled incoming memorials and outgoing imperial edicts or pronouncements; it supervised the imperial household staff and the secret police units, the Eastern and Western Depots. It
also collaborated with the Imperial Embroidered Uniform Bodyguard,
which served as both the emperor's personal bodyguard and an intelligence
bureau.[9] Its middle- and high-level personnel were chosen from among the

---

4. The number is deduced from the list of publications ordered by the Hongwu
emperor provided in Li Jinhua, *Mingdai chizhuanshu kao fu yinde* (hereafter cited as
MDCZSK), pp. 1–26.

5. Cited in Zhao Qian, *Mingben*, in Ren Jiyu, *Zhongguo banben wenhua congshu*, p. 10.

6. During the Hongwu reign, the inner court eunuch agencies were frequently re-
organized, and their functions changed accordingly. Among them, the Directorate of
Palace Eunuchs (Neiguanjian 內官監) and the Directorate of the Palace Library (Bi-
shujian 祕書監) are said to have been involved in the inner court publishing matters at
some point. See Zhang Tingyu et al., *Mingshi* (hereafter cited as *MS*), *juan* 74, "Verification" (*huizheng* 會證), pp. 784–87; and Tsai, *The Eunuchs in the Ming Dynasty*, pp. 29–33.
See also Li Zhizhong, *Lidai keshu kaoshu*, p. 218.

7. In imperial China, civil and military officials were ranked from 1a to 9b in descending order. In the Ming, this ranking system was also applied to elite eunuchs.

8. The four great superintendents were commander (*tidu* 提都), keeper of imperial
seals (*zhangyin* 掌印), keeper of imperial brushes (*bingbi* 秉筆), and attendant to the
emperor (*suitang* 隨堂) (*MS*, 74.778).

9. Hucker, *Dictionary*, p. 451. For details of the organization of the Directorate of
Ceremonial and its personnel, see Tsai, *The Eunuchs in the Ming Dynasty*, pp. 39–44.

brightest and best-educated palace eunuchs. Probably for this reason, the Directorate of Ceremonial came to run the imperial publishing enterprise.

After the Yongle emperor ascended the throne in 1403, the Directorate of Ceremonial began to publish books regularly, starting with small quantities of limited titles of the classics and histories for the use of a few palace eunuchs, who would later become the emperor's eyes and ears in his surveillance of officials.[10] As the Directorate of Ceremonial's power increased, the volume of its publications grew steadily as well. Its publications not only comprised more titles but served more readers, including the imperial family members and palace women. One of the earliest titles specifically identified as a Directorate of Ceremonial publication is *The Heart-Mind Method in the Sage's Learning* (*Shengxue xinfa* 聖學心法), dated 1409, compiled by the Yongle emperor.[11] Another, identified as a Sutra and Classics Depository edition, is *Book of Poetry with Comprehensive Annotations and Commentaries* (*Shizhuan daquan* 詩傳大全), dated 1415.[12] We may thus assume that the Sutra and Classics Depository, which was under the Directorate of Ceremonial's supervision,[13] was founded prior to 1415 to accommodate the increasingly busy production of both secular and religious works under the Yongle emperor's auspices.[14]

Although the Sutra and Classics Depository is usually understood as being a sutra depository, it was actually an office with a staff of six or four eunuchs who oversaw three separate depositories: the Depository of Chinese Classics (Hanjingchang 漢經廠), the Depository of Foreign Sutras (Fanjingchang 番經廠),[15] and the Depository of Daoist Texts and Scriptures (Daojingchang 道經廠), each responsible for all matters related to the production of a specific type of book, from transcribing texts and carving woodblocks to printing and caring for the woodblocks and book collections. The Depository of Chinese Classics was responsible for the production of books in the four traditional Chinese bibliographic categories: classics (*jing*

———

10. Wei Yinru, *Zhongguo guji yinshua shi*, p. 95.

11. *MDCZSK*, p. 226.

12. A leaf from the Directorate of Ceremonial edition of this title is reproduced in Zhou Xinhui, *Mingdai banke tushi*, 1: 44.

13. Wei Yinru and Wang Jinyu, *Guji banben jianding congtan*, p. 38. K. T. Wu ("Ming Printing and Printers," p. 228) cites the Qing scholar Gao Shiqi (1645–1704) as writing that the Sutra and Classics Depository was established in 1444, which is incorrect.

14. For examples of inner court editions of religious works produced in the early Yongle era, see Zhou Xinhui, *Zhongguo gudai fojiao banhua ji*, 2: plates 21–25.

15. The term *fanjing* refers to Buddhist sutras written in foreign languages, especially the Tibetan language.

經), history (*shi* 史), philosophy (*zi* 子), and literature (*ji* 集); the Depository of Foreign Sutras and the Depository of Daoist Texts and Scriptures produced, respectively, Buddhist sutras and Daoist texts and scriptures.[16] Attached to the Sutra and Classics Depository were storage houses (*jingchang ku* 經廠庫), where books and woodblocks were kept. These storage houses also held paintings and examples of calligraphy collected by the Directorate of Ceremonial for the emperor.[17] In other words, the Sutra and Classics Depository oversaw the Ming emperors' private libraries, which were independent of the imperial library, the Pavilion of Literary Erudition (Wenyuange 文淵閣). The pavilion's collection of books, documents, paintings, and calligraphy belonged, theoretically speaking, to the Ming state.

The Sutra and Classics Depository continued to be an important part of the Directorate of Ceremonial's publishing operations until the late sixteenth century. During the Wanli reign (1573–1620), book production under its auspices started to dwindle. From that time on, the three depositories also assumed new responsibilities, including training young palace women and eunuch boys to tend temples inside the imperial compound and to perform religious rituals on various occasions and for festivals held in the Forbidden City, such as the emperor's birthday celebration, New Year's Day, and funerals.[18] For these occasions, the various eunuch agencies provided such items as tables, chairs, coal, firewood, banners, incense, incense burners, gongs, bells, and costumes necessary for the rituals, and the Directorate of Ceremonial prepared the necessary sutras or scriptures.[19]

A Visit to the Inner Court Publishing Facilities

From at least the second half of the sixteenth century, the Directorate of Ceremonial (Fig. 3.1a) was located in the northeastern corner of the inner court compound.[20] Both the Depository of Chinese Classics (Fig. 3.1c) and

---

16. Zhou Xinhui, *Mingdai banke tushi*, 1: 6.

17. Liu Ruoyu, *Zhuozhong zhi* (hereafter cited as ZZZ), 16.2003.

18. Ibid., pp. 2035, 2038, 2041.

19. Ibid., p. 2041.

20. Figure 3.1 is a portion of the *Ming Qing Beijingcheng tu* (The map of Ming and Qing Beijing city), published in 1986 and based on the *Jingcheng quantu* (The complete map of Beijing city) made during 1749 and 1760, and the *Qing Huangcheng gongdian yashu tu* (The map of the palaces and official buildings of the Qing imperial city), made in 1681. Some firsthand records of the city, dated variously between 1560 and 1774, were also consulted. See Xu Pingfang, *Ming Qing Beijingcheng tu*, pp. 1–2.

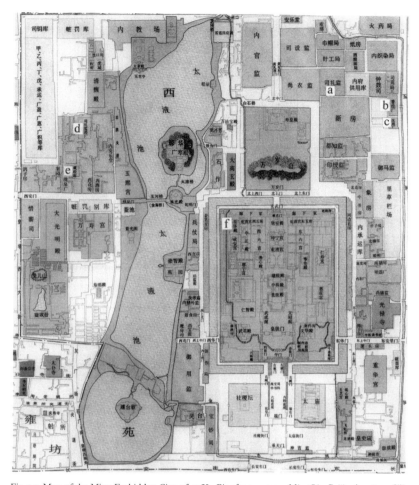

Fig. 3.1 Map of the Ming Forbidden City; after Xu Pingfang, comp., *Ming Qing Beijingcheng tu.* a. Silijian 司禮監; b. Fanjingchang 番經廠; c. Hanjingchang 漢經廠; d. Silijian jingchang 司禮監經廠; e. Jingchangku 經廠庫; f. Yinghuadian 英華殿.

Depository of Foreign Sutras (Fig. 3.1b) were located nearby.[21] The Office of the Sutra and Classics Depository (Fig. 3.1d) and its storage houses for books and their woodblocks (Fig. 3.1e) were located in the northwestern part of the compound. The court constructed additional storage houses in

---

21. According to the eunuch Liu Ruoyu 劉若愚 (1584–1642), at some point, the Depository of Foreign Sutras was located in (or near) the Yinghua Palace (Fig. 3.1f) (*ZZZ*, 16.2038). I have yet to discover the location of the Depository of Daoist Scriptures and Texts.

the inner court compound when space was needed.[22] The Office of Sutra
and Classics Depository Attendants (Jingchang zhifang 經廠直房) was located inside the innermost precinct of the inner court compound, which was
also the site of the imperial family's living quarters.[23] In the Office of the
Sutra and Classics Depository Attendants, eunuchs were on duty to re-
trieve books needed by the emperor. The office also kept a stock of paper
and brushes, among other things, for the emperor's use.[24]

The Logistics of the Directorate of Ceremonial's Publishing Operation

FUNDING

In addition to its annual budget, allocated by the Ministry of Revenues, the
Directorate of Ceremonial received funding from the imperial family's
seemingly inexhaustible discretionary funds. The Ming imperial family was
far richer than those of the previous dynasties. From the early sixteenth
century on, it not only owned vast amounts of land throughout the empire
but also established depots in provinces to collect surtaxes for its own coffers, bypassing the Ministry of Revenue.[25] As we will see, with rich funding,
the Directorate of Ceremonial was able to produce high-quality books in
terms of design and materials.

ARTISANS

During the Ming, various crafts were primarily family-run and hereditary,
and the Ming government carefully registered all kinds of artisans. Inner
court book production drew on artisans-in-residence (zhuzuo jiang 住作匠),
who came from the greater Beijing area and worked almost exclusively for
the inner court. They supplied the core of the manpower for the various
types of crafts needed in the inner court and were supervised by various

---

22. For instance, in 1447, on the Zhengtong emperor's order, about forty storage
rooms were built in the inner court compound to house the newly printed book *Wulun
shu* 五倫書 (Book on the five proper human relations) and its woodblocks; see Shen
Shixing, *Da Ming huidian* (hereafter cited as *DMHD*), 157.5a.

23. The Office of the Sutra and Classics Depository Attendants is not shown in
Fig. 3.1. For its location, see the map of the Ming Forbidden City in Zhu Xie, *Ming Qing
liangdai gongyuan jianzhi kao.*

24. *ZZZ*, 16.2065.

25. Xu Daling and Wang Tianyou, *Mingchao shiliudi*, p. 271. See also Ray Huang,
Taxation and Government Finance, p. 11.

palace eunuch agencies. When necessary, the inner court could also call on the rotating artisans (*lunbanjiang* 輪班匠), who were supervised by the Ministry of Works. Rotating artisans lived outside the greater Beijing area; they rendered their mandatory, unpaid services to all levels of government offices on a rotating basis, once in four years for most of the dynasty.[26] Owing in part to the unusual treatment and the hardships that the recruited artisans had to endure,[27] by the mid-fifteenth century the system began to deteriorate as they fled their corvée duties.[28] The exact locations of the woodblock carving and printing workshops are not clear, but some of the Jingchang storage houses were probably used for these purposes.

Records show that the number of artisans-in-residence employed by the Directorate of Ceremonial was second only to that of those working for the Directorate of the Imperial Domestic Services (Yuyongjian 御用監), a eunuch agency responsible for making all sorts of goods for imperial use, including palace screens, utensils, lamps and lanterns, furniture, ivory and jade objects, and papers and carpets.[29] The 1587 edition of the *Collected Administrative Statutes of the Great Ming (Da Ming huidian* 大明會典) reports that in 1531 the Directorate of Ceremonial alone employed 1,583 artisans. Among them, 1,275 were in book production: 62 paper makers, 81 paper cutters, 134 printers, 48 brush makers, 77 ink-cake makers, 315 woodblock carvers, 189 paper folders, 76 painters, and 293 bookbinders.[30] Records also indicate that the number of artisans working for the Directorate of Ceremonial fluctuated little from the mid-fifteenth century on. For instance, in

---

26. From the beginning of the Ming dynasty up to 1485, the rotating artisans served the civilian government branches once every one, two, three, or four years, depending on the type of craft. Military artisans (*junjiang* 軍匠) registered with and worked for the military on a permanent basis. See Chen Shiqi, *Mingdai guanshougongye de yanjiu*, pp. 71–74.

27. For example, artisans-in-residence were coerced into paying dues to their eunuch supervisors. Those who refused often received corporal punishment. Rotating artisans had to pay for their travel-related expenses, and many of them were forced to work beyond the prescribed time limits. For a detailed analysis of the pitfalls of the Ming artisan systems and measures taken by the Ming government to solve the related problems, see ibid., pp. 92–106.

28. Geiss, "Peking Under the Ming," p. 92.

29. *DMHD*, 189.276–89.

30. These numbers are cited in *DMHD*, which underwent two revisions, in 1529 and 1587, after its initial publication in 1502. The Directorate of Ceremonial also had a few carpenters, blacksmiths, goldsmiths, and other artisans. The edition of *DMHD* used in this chapter is the modern reprint of the 1587 Directorate of Ceremonial edition, whose head compiler was Grand Secretary Shen Shixing (1535–1614). See *DMHD*, 189.276.

1561, the Directorate of Ceremonial had 1,892 artisans; in 1567, the number was 1,816.[31] The numbers indicate that the Directorate of Ceremonial must have consistently maintained a busy publishing operation.

The Directorate of Ceremonial's ability to maintain a large number of artisans for book production may be explained by the fact that it was the most powerful among all eunuch agencies. However, other explanations for the consistently high number of artisans reported are possible. First, official Ming records tended to ignore changes in the number of things over time. For example, Ming official population reports, such as those in the *Veritable Records of the Ming* (*Ming shilu* 明實錄), remained largely static year after year despite the fact that the Ming population increased significantly over time; this owed much to the fact that local officials faced steep fines if they made errors in addition. It was safer for them to simply report the same figures given in the last successful report, sometimes with minor changes.[32] The minor fluctuations in the numbers of book-production artisans over time might be a reflection of this phenomenon. Second, after the late fifteenth century, many artisans working for the government simply bought their way out, hiring their own substitutes.[33] Even so, however, the number of artisans-in-residence working for the Directorate of Ceremonial in book production alone was the second largest group of artisans of any agency. Since the Directorate of Ceremonial's primary responsibility was not manufacturing objects, this single fact speaks of the tremendous power the Directorate of Ceremonial enjoyed.

CALLIGRAPHERS

Standard records do not explicitly identify calligraphers needed for transcribing texts for master copies, on which the wood-block carvings were based. Judging from the large number of Directorate of Ceremonial publications and given the time consumed by transcribing, the calligraphers were probably drawn from those working in various inner court agencies, such as the eunuch calligraphers serving in the Office of Documents (Wenshufang 文書房), a sort of palace secretariat supervised by the Direc-

---

31. *DMHD*, 189.288.

32. Ray Huang, *Taxation and Government Finance*, pp. 61–63. I am grateful to David Robinson for drawing my attention to this important point. A parallel can be seen in records of local administrative personnel; there were major changes in how clerks, runners, and laborers were recruited and paid for, but official numbers often remained static.

33. Geiss, "Peking Under the Ming," p. 103.

torate of Ceremonial that handled the emperor's paperwork,[34] and the imperial calligrapher-drafters (*zhongshu sheren* 中書舍人) serving at the emperor's informal palaces, the Literary Splendor (Wenhua 文華), Military Glory (Wuying 武英), and Benevolence and Wisdom (Renzhi 仁智) palaces. They should not be confused with the imperial calligrapher-drafters working at the Grand Secretariat. Those who served at the emperor's palaces were supervised by another eunuch agency, the Directorate of Imperial Domestic Services.[35] These inner-court calligraphers were all proficient in *kaishu* 楷書, the standard script, which was used exclusively in Directorate of Ceremonial publications because of its legibility.

Characteristics of Directorate of Ceremonial Publications

The finest Directorate of Ceremonial editions share several characteristics. First, their woodblock frames, larger than those of non–Directorate of Ceremonial publications, measure about 26.6 cm × 17.5 cm and above, compared to the dimensions of 19.6 cm × 12 cm and below commonly seen in non–inner court editions.[36] Second, their imprinted characters are large; they are thus often referred to as *dazi ben* 大字本, or large-character editions,[37] and they are elegantly done in the standard script, mimicking calligraphy done by the soft brush (Fig. 3.2), in contrast to the blocky, angular characters common in government and commercial imprints (Fig. 3.3). Third, inner court editions used high-quality wood and paper that facilitate fine carving and clear impressions.[38] Fourth, their page layout is

---

34. Zhang Shudong et al., *Zhongguo yinshua tongshi*, p. 213.

35. For a discussion of these two groups of imperial calligrapher-drafters, see Jang, "Issues of Public Service," pp. 102–4.

36. For example, the block frame of the 1447 inner court edition of *Book on the Five Human Relations* measures 30.3 × 18.6 cm. See Harvard-Yenching Library (Cambridge, MA), Rare Book T1667 6330.

37. Figure 3.2 shows characters in the preface by Empress Dowager Zhangshengciren 章聖慈仁 (d. 1538) to her *Lessons for Women* (*Nüxun* 女訓). Each measures approximately 1.6 × 1.8 cm. The characters of the text of the same book measure about 1.3 × 1.4 cm, whereas those in most non–Directorate of Ceremonial books measure less than 1 cm.

38. Space does not allow a detailed discussion of all the materials used for Directorate of Ceremonial publications and their quality. It suffices to note here that until the early sixteenth century, paper made of tree bark fibers was most often used for books. After the mid-sixteenth century, paper made from bamboo fibers was most common. Produced in Yongfeng 永豐, Jiangxi province, the best-quality paper used for printing

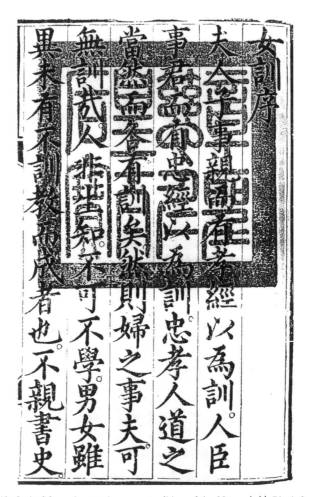

Fig. 3.2 Half of a leaf from the 1530 inner court edition of the *Nüxun* 女訓. Block frame 16.2 × 26.5 cm. Courtesy of the Harvard-Yenching Library (Rare Book T1682 0182).

———

books was *mianzhi* 綿紙 (cotton paper), which was white and durable; see Li Zhizhong, *Gushu banbenxue gailun*, p. 46. *Mianzhi* was actually made of tree fibers, not cotton. It is so called perhaps because the highest-quality *mianzhi* was as white as cotton. Ming official publications, including those by the Directorate of Ceremonial, typically used *mianzhi*. Commercial publications used paper made of bamboo fibers; see Wei Yinru and Wang Jinyu, *Guji banben jianding congtan*, p. 123. As far as woodblocks for printing books are concerned, the *limu* 梨木, or pear tree (*Pyrus sinensis*), and the *zaomu* 棗木 (*Zizyphus vulgaris*), commonly known as the date tree, were most desirable; both are known for their hardness, densely formed annual rings, and fine, smooth grain (Zhang Shudong et al., *Zhongguo yinshua tongshi*, p. 305).

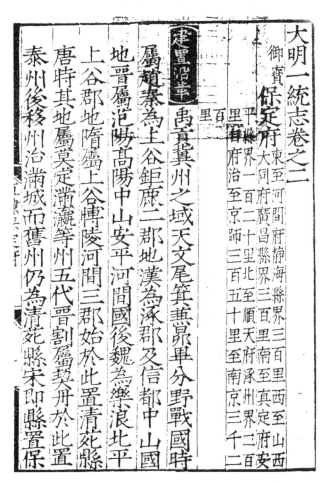

Fig. 3.3 Half of a leaf from the 1599 edition of the *Da Ming yitong zhi* 大明一統志 published by the commercial publisher Guirenzhai in Jianyang, Fujian. Block frame 12.3 × 19.3 cm. After Zhou Xinhui, *Mingdai banke tushi*, 1: 397.

elaborate, including double lines on all four borders (*sizhou shuanglan* 四周 雙欄; see Fig. 3.4a); thick black mouths (*cuheikou* 粗黑口; Fig. 3.4b) inside the elephants' trunks (*xiangbi* 象鼻; Fig. 3.4c), which themselves are verti- cal bars on the uppermost and lowermost segments of the block heart (Fig. 3.4d), the entire area of the center column of the page, along which the page is folded in the final form of a book; and a black fish tail (*yuwei* 魚尾; Fig. 3.4e), the blackened, fishtail-shaped area between the upper and lower elephant trunks. A white strip outlines both fishtails, with a circle be- tween the fins of the upper fish tail (Fig. 3.4f). Sometimes the white strips

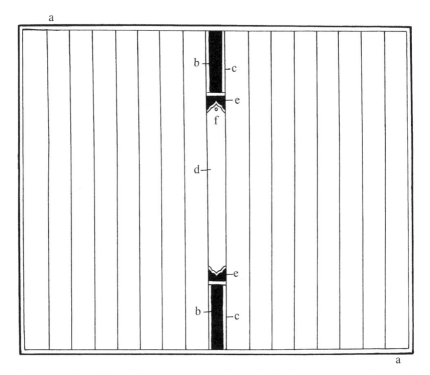

Fig. 3.4 Artist's rendering of the page layout typically seen in the finest inner court editions of secular titles. a. double lines on four borders; b. black mouth; c. elephant's trunk; d. block heart; e. black fish tail; f. circle

that outline the upper and lower fish tail are slightly scalloped.[39] All these features demonstrate the meticulous care taken to enhance the Directorate of Ceremonial books' overall aesthetic value. Other common characteristics of the finest inner court editions include exquisite packaging in satin brocade, and imperial seals stamped on some of the pages (see Fig. 3.2).[40] Thus one Ming writer, the Old Man of a Time of Peace (Taiping laoren 太平老人), ranked the Directorate of Ceremonial publications at the very

---

39. See Fig. 3.4e, for example. For a detailed discussion of the forms and terms of Chinese bookmaking, see Edgren, *Chinese Rare Books in American Collections*, pp. 10–15.

40. Other imperial seals that appear in Ming inner court editions include *Guangyun zhi bao* 廣運之寶 (Treasures of broadened fortunes); *Qinwen zhi xi* 欽文之璽 (Seal of imperial literature); *Zhangshengciren huangtaihou bao* 章聖慈仁皇太后寶 (Treasures of Empress Dowager Zhangshengciren); *Zhonggong zhi bao* 中宮之寶 (Treasures of the middle palace); and *Houzai zhi ji* 厚載之紀 (Seal of *houzai*), a seal made for the Hong-wu emperor's Empress Ma.

top of his list of the best things during the Ming empire; his list also in-cludes wine made at the inner court, ink stones from the Duan River (Duanxi 端溪) in Anhui, and silk brocades from Sichuan.[41]

Secular Titles Published
by the Directorate of Ceremonial

The Directorate of Ceremonial secular book publications[42] included titles from all four traditional Chinese bibliographic categories: classics, history, philosophy, and literature.[43] Among them, books authored by Ming em-perors and those compiled on their orders constitute the largest group, fol-lowed in descending order by reprints of titles created before the Ming, re-quired inner court school readers,[44] and religious works. Examples from the first three groups included the Four Books and the Five Classics; *Out-lines of the Comprehensive Mirror for Aid in Governance* (*Zizhi tongjian gangmu* 資治通鑑綱目); *The Hongwu Emperor's Poetic Anthology* (*Yuzhi shiji* 御製詩集); and primers on mathematics, linguistics, and calligraphy, such as *Detailed and Understandable Arithmetic* (*Xiangming suanfa* 詳明算法) and *One Hundred Family Names* (*Baijia xing* 百家姓). The Directorate also issued a small number of dictionaries and pharmaceutical reference books, such as *Chinese and Foreign Languages Translated* (*Huayi yiyu* 華夷譯語) and *A Comprehensive List of Medical Treatises* (*Yiyao jilan* 醫藥集覽). Fiction and musical plays constituted the smallest group among the Directorate of Ceremonial pub-lications. Available sources list only two titles, *Popular Explication of the His-tory of the Three Kingdoms* (*Sanguozhi tongsu yanyi* 三國志通俗演義) and *Poetic Songs of Yongxi* (*Yongxi yuefu* 雍熙樂府), a collection of musical plays

----

41. Taiping laoren, *Xiuzhong jin*, p. 259.

42. Discussions of the Directorate of Ceremonial's religious publications are beyond the scope of the present chapter. I will discuss this important topic in a further article.

43. The following observation on the Directorate of Ceremonial's publications is based on its publication inventory list made circa 1638 by the eunuch Liu Ruoyu and preserved in his *A Weighted and Unbiased Record* (*Zhuozhongzhi* 酌中志), a book about the inner court's customs, palaces, personnel, and the establishments. The list includes only books whose woodblocks were still present in the Directorate of Ceremonial's collec-tion. The number of the books in the Directorate of Ceremonial's collection would have been larger if handwritten editions and those whose woodblocks were no longer extant at the time were included; see ZZZ, 18.2081–87. For a more complete list of the Directorate of Ceremonial publications, see also Zhou Hongzu, *Gujin shuke*.

44. In the Ming, there was an inner court school for selected palace eunuchs and another for selected palace women; see below.

compiled by Guo Xun 郭勛 (1475–1541). The Directorate of Ceremonial also published a small number of books by Ming authors outside the imperial family (discussed below).

The Directorate of Ceremonial may have published more than 200 titles, second only to the 350 titles published by the National University in Nanjing and Beijing combined.[45] Since other government offices also published many of the titles published by the Directorate of Ceremonial, why did the imperial court need to have its own editions? Although the high quality of its publications corresponds with its unsurpassed wealth and prestige, Ming imperial publishing was not simply a matter of vanity. It was also a channel through which the imperial court displayed its independence from the outer court bureaucracy and expressed its own concerns. The Directorate of Ceremonial's monopoly of the imperial publishing enterprise also indicates the eunuch agency's prestige in the service of the Son of Heaven.

The Functions of the Directorate of Ceremonial's Secular Publications

THE EMPEROR AND THE IMPERIAL LECTURES

As Hung-lam Chu discusses in his chapter in this volume (pp. 186–230), during the Ming, as in the Tang, Song, and Yuan dynasties, designated Hanlin academicians known for their scholarly achievements gave two types of imperial lectures for the education of the emperor: the thrice-monthly series called the classics-mat lecture (*jingyan* 經筵) and the daily lecture (*rijiang* 日講). The Directorate of Ceremonial printed the books that the emperor's curriculum required. Although Ming emperors had studied the classics and histories since the time of the Hongwu emperor, the thrice-monthly lecture was not formalized until 1436. Each lecture involved two lecturers; one spoke on one of the Four Books, and the other, on one of the Five Classics.[46] After the chief grand secretary had chosen the subjects or topics for each lecture, the Hanlin lecturers were informed, and the lecturers would then select suitable chapters from the Four Books and from the Five Classics and write up their respective lecture essays. After the chief grand secretary approved them, calligrapher-drafters in the Grand Secretariat transcribed two copies of each of the lecture essays in standard

---

45. See Zhou Xinhui, *Mingdai banke tushi*, 1: 6, 8.

46. My discussion of the thrice-monthly lecture, daily lecture, and the rituals attached to them is based on *Ming neiting guizhi kao*, 2.42–45; Zhu Guozhen, *Yongchuang xiaopin* (hereafter cited as *YCXP*), 2.23–29; and *DMHD*, 52.338–39.

script. The copies were then transmitted to the Directorate of Ceremonial one day before the lecture. For easy reading, the lecture essays were punctuated with circles in red cinnabar made with a round ivory tube.[47] That evening, a eunuch clerk in the Directorate of Ceremonial would take the two lecture essays and two sets of the two books from its collection to the Palace of Literary Splendor.[48] One set was placed on the table used by the emperor, and the other on the table used by the lecturers.[49] Customarily, the audience of the thrice-monthly lecture also included the grand secretaries, the six ministers, selected nobles and court officials of rank 4 and above, and two of the highest-ranking eunuchs in the Directorate of Ceremonial, the keeper of imperial seals and the keeper of imperial brushes.[50]

For each daily lecture, there were also two Hanlin lecturers. Typically, the emperor, in the presence of some of the grand secretaries, first listened to the exposition on, for instance, *The Extended Meanings of the Great Learning* (*Daxue yanyi* 大學衍義), which was followed by another lecture on, say, *Major Achievements of the Zhenguan Era* (*Zhenguan zhengyao* 貞觀政要). For each lecture, one copy of each of the two selected books was placed on the emperor's table. Yellow slips indicating the beginning and the end of passages of the books selected for the lectures were sent to the Directorate of Ceremonial one day in advance. While the lecturer expounded on the passages in the chapter, a palace eunuch pointed with an ivory stick at these passages for the emperor, who listened in silence.[51]

No written copies were provided for the daily lecture, at least not until 1642.[52] The reason may be that the writing of lecture essays daily simply consumed too much time. We may also speculate that the daily lecture was shorter than the thrice-monthly lecture, and the content of the lecture was therefore easier to memorize. Even so, the Tianqi emperor (r. 1621–27)

---

47. *YCXP*, 2.24.

48. *Ming neiting guizhi kao*, p. 43. One of the readers of this volume wrote that the books used in imperial lectures were handwritten, not printed copies. The reader did not provide evidence to support this claim; the wording in my sources mentioned above is less than clear in this regard.

49. *DMHD*, 52.107; *YCXP*, 2.23–28.

50. *Ming neiting guizhi kao*, 2.42–43. For the questions of how the rituals associated with the thrice-monthly lectures were prepared and carried out, see Xie Mincong, *Ming Qing Beijing*, pp. 46, 49; and *DMHD*, 52.338.

51. *Ming neiting guizhi kao*, 2.43–44.

52. Ibid., p. 45.

ordered that written copies of the daily lectures be prepared, because a particular Hanlin lecturer was often unable to memorize his lectures.[53]

Ideally, a discussion among the participants followed each of the thrice-monthly and daily lectures.[54] As the chapters in this volume by Hung-lam Chu and Julia K. Murray demonstrate, many at court competed to shape the emperor and the heir apparent through education; everyone felt that written texts were critical to this project. Court officials hoped to mold the emperor, especially when he was still young, into a benevolent and able ruler. The Directorate of Ceremonial's monopoly of imperial publishing for the education of the Son of Heaven had profound political significance, at least on a symbolic level. Moreover, the presence of the two highest-ranking Directorate of Ceremonial eunuchs at the thrice-monthly lecture signified the elite eunuchs' prestigious status.

THE EDUCATION OF THE CROWN PRINCE

In imperial China, the education of the crown prince was no less important than that of the emperor. Although, as Julia Murray shows, other officials periodically compiled educational materials for the heir apparent on their own initiative, during the Ming the Office of the Overseer of Affairs (Zhanshifu 詹事府), a central government office in charge of the crown prince's public and private affairs, oversaw his education. It was staffed with seven to ten officials, including two Hanlin academicians who served as the crown prince's lecturers. The Bureau of Editorial Services (Sijingju 司經局) in this office was staffed with a head librarian, who made sure that there were always two or three copies of all the books that made up the entire curriculum necessary for the crown prince's education. Two editors, who assisted the head librarian, collated and edited texts and corrected the pronunciation of words when necessary. They also functioned as calligrapher-drafters for paperwork. These positions suggest that the Bureau of Editorial Services also published books for the crown prince's use.[55]

The Directorate of Ceremonial was, therefore, not specifically responsible for publishing books needed for the crown prince's education. Ming

———

53. *Ming neiting guizhi kao*, 2.45.

54. As Hung-lam Chu points out in his chapter in this volume (pp. 186–230), Ming emperors, unlike their Song counterparts, generally listened to the lectures passively.

55. *MS*, 73.762–63. Information about the scope and nature of the Bureau of Editorial Services publications is not available. For a discussion of the crown prince's education during the Ming, see Julia Murray's chapter in this volume (pp. 231–68).

emperors, however, often ordered the Directorate of Ceremonial to print works intended specifically for the crown prince. Compiled by Ming emperors, these books were instructions regarding how the crown prince should prepare himself to be an able and virtuous ruler. They included *Bright Mirror Records for the Crown Prince* (*Chujun zhaojian lu* 儲君昭鑑錄) by the founding emperor of the Ming dynasty, *Precious Mirror for the Palace of Literary Splendor* (*Wenhua baojian* 文華寶鑑), *Lessons for Attending to the Fundamentals* (*Wuben zhi xun* 務本之訓), *The Heart-Mind Method in the Sage's Learning* by the Yongle emperor, *Emperor's Instructions* (*Dixun* 帝訓) by the Xuande emperor, and *Great Lessons for the Palace of Literary Splendor* (*Wenhua daxun* 文華大訓) by the Chenghua emperor.[56] These titles were part of the crown prince's curriculum.[57]

In addition, the crown prince's library was full of other Directorate of Ceremonial publications regularly given to him by the emperor. Some, such as the Four Books and the Five Classics, were intended for use in the crown prince's daily lessons. The calligraphy primer *Yongzi bafa* 永字八法 (Eight basic stroke methods as shown in the character *yong*) in the Directorate of Ceremonial publication list could well have been used for calligraphy lessons.

THE EDUCATION OF PALACE EUNUCHS

The old chestnut that the Hongwu emperor prohibited palace eunuchs from learning how to read and write is demonstrably false.[58] Early in the Hongwu reign, select eunuch scribes helped the emperor and the crown prince handle paperwork. Moreover, the Hongwu emperor appointed many eunuchs to be in charge of such important state matters as taxation, diplomacy, and the acquisition of horses. All these positions required a certain degree of literacy.[59] However, he did deny them an education in the Confucian mode, which emphasized students' mastery of Confucian moral

---

56. Among these, only the first title was not published by the Directorate of Ceremonial. The term "Palace of Literary Splendor" is attached to many of these titles for the crown prince because that palace housed a study room where the crown prince was given lectures for his formal education.

57. On April 25, 1480, the Hanlin Academician Jiao Fang 焦芳 (*js.* 1464) expounded the "Jinxue bian" 進學編 chapter of the *Wenhua daxun* to the crown prince, the future Hongzhi emperor; see Ku and Goodrich, "A Study of Literary Persecution During the Ming," p. 298; see also *MS*, 306.3446.

58. *MS*, 304.3405.

59. Huang Zhangjian, "Lun *Zuxun lu* suoji Mingchu huanguan zhidu," esp. pp. 22–29.

philosophy, classical learning, and governing.[60] In 1403, his son, the Yongle emperor, informally appointed Hanlin academicians to teach a few select young palace eunuchs, who later became the emperor's eyes and ears in his surveillance of both military and civilian officials.[61]

Pressed by increasingly onerous paperwork, in 1429, the Xuande emperor established the Inner Court School (Neishutang 內書堂) to educate select young palace eunuchs to help relieve the burden. From this time on, palace eunuchs received a formal education in the Confucian mode, and many elite palace eunuchs were Inner Court School graduates. Their education enabled them to amass political power. They served as diplomats and regional military commanders, heard important court cases, and became the emperor's personal and political advisors, handling incoming memorials and outgoing imperial edicts. Not only did educated elite eunuchs change the traditional composition of officialdom, but they also compromised the literati's monopoly on scholarly texts and knowledge, a central pillar of literati identity.

Chen Yi 陳沂 (1469–1538), a Hanlin academician, reports that in his time as an Inner Court School lecturer, there were 400 to 500 eunuch students in the school.[62] These numbers seem to have remained more or less the same throughout the Ming. Writing in the mid-seventeenth century, the eunuch Liu Ruoyu reports that when each group of newly admitted eunuchs arrived at the inner court, some 200 to 300 of those aged ten or younger were selected and sent to the Inner Court School to study. They finished their basic education within three to five years.[63] The Ming court

---

60. These three areas of concern expressed in the *Analects* provided the basis on which the Song Neo-Confucian curriculum was designed, as seen in the contents of Zhu Xi's 朱熹 (1130–1200) curriculum, which included the Four Books, the Five Classics, and histories, such as *Zuo Commentary* (*Zuozhuan* 左傳), *Conversations from the States* (*Guoyu* 國語), *Records of the Grand Historian* (*Shiji* 史記), and dynastic histories. By the Ming dynasty, the Song Neo-Confucian curriculum had become the new orthodoxy, and it was, for the most part, designed for the selection of government officials through the civil service examinations. For an analysis of Zhu Xi and Neo-Confucian education, see "Part 2: Chu Hsi and Neo-Confucian Education," in de Bary and Chaffee, *Neo-Confucian Education*, pp. 106–276. For the contents of Zhu Xi's curriculum in particular, see Wm. Theodore de Bary, "Chu Hsi's Aim as an Educator," in ibid., p. 207. For an analysis of Ming Confucian education and curriculum, see Elman, "Changes in Confucian Civil Service Examinations."

61. Tsai, *Perpetual Happiness*, p. 76.

62. Cited in Li Xü, *Jiean laoren manbi*, 2.46

63. *ZZZ*, 16.2008–9.

did not admit eunuchs every year, and the intervals between admissions were highly irregular. If the imperial court accepted eunuchs in two consecutive years, in 1516 and 1517, for example,[64] some 400 to 600 young eunuchs would have started in these two years at the Inner Court School.[65]

According to Liu Ruoyu, the Inner Court School, located inside the Directorate of Ceremonial compound, was no more than a large hall. A rotation system for use of the hall may have accommodated the large number of students of varying seniority. In this hall, an altar with a sculpted portrait figure of Confucius faced south. Inscribed on the two columns flanking the altar was a couplet: "[Those of you who are] not yet able to enter the gate of the house of the sage Confucius must work hard and try to make the [last] few steps forward; [since you are] unable to fulfill your familial duties [of raising a family and continuing the family line], why not abandon them wholeheartedly?"[66] Adjacent to the Inner Court School, on the north side, was a lounge for the Inner Court School lecturers. Early in the Ming, before the establishment of the Inner Court School, emperors tended to appoint Hanlin academicians renowned for their literary achievements and skill in calligraphy to teach select palace eunuchs. From the 1420s, such appointments seem to have become the norm at the Inner Court School, although no written rule existed regarding this matter. [67]

The eunuch students had both required and optional readers. On the first day of school, every student received a copy of the "Inner Court Regulations" ("Neiling" 內令),[68] a chapter from *Ancestral Injunctions of the Brilliant Ming (Huangming zuxun* 皇明祖訓).[69] Other required readers, or official books (*guanshu* 官書), as they were called, included *Mirror Records of the Loyal (Zhongjianlu* 忠鑒錄), a collection of stories about loyal eunuchs of the past; a group of primers on foundational characters, poetry, and calligraphy, such as *One Hundred Family Names; One Thousand Masters' Poems (Qianjiashi* 千家詩), a collection of poems of the Tang and Song dynasties compiled by Liu Kezhuang 劉克莊 (1187–1269); *One Thousand Character Es-*

---

64. Tsai, *The Eunuchs of the Ming Dynasty*, p. 24.

65. If the imperial court had also admitted eunuchs in 1514 and 1515, however, the number of students in the Inner Court School by the end of 1517 could have been somewhere from 800 to 1,200.

66. *ZZZ*, 17.2058.

67. He Weizhi, *Mingchu de huanguan zhengzhi*, pp. 159–60.

68. Ibid.

69. Ibid. *Ancestral Injunctions of the Brilliant Ming*, edited by the Hongwu emperor, was published and given to Hongwu's sons in 1395; see *MDCZSK*, pp. 4–5.

say (*Qianziwen* 千字文), an essay written in different scripts as calligraphy models; and such Confucian classics as the *Book of Filial Piety, Great Learning, Doctrine of the Mean, Mencius,* and *Analects.*[70]

More advanced required readers included *Precious Gems in the Ancient Literary Styles* (*Guwen zhenbao* 古文珍寶), *Poems in Three Styles by Tang Masters* (*Tangxian santi shi* 唐賢三體詩), *Digest of Comprehensive Mirror for Aid in Governance* (*Tongjian jieyao* 通鑑節要), and *Comprehensive Collection of [the Studies] of Human Nature and Reason* (*Xingli daquan* 性理大全), collected works of 120 philosophers of the Neo-Confucian school. All these required subjects were taught systematically, according to their level of difficulty and individual students' progress.[71]

Only a handful of the brightest and most ambitious students could handle such difficult titles as *Extended Meanings of the Great Learning; Major Achievements of the Zhenguan Era; Garden of [Historical] Anecdotes* (*Shuoyuan* 説苑); *Complete Commentaries of the Five Classics* (*Wujing daquan* 五經大全); and *Comprehensive Study of Records and Documents* (*Wenxian tongkao* 文獻通考). Inner Court School Hanlin lecturers recommended some of these titles. Others were selected by elite Directorate of Ceremonial eunuchs with the emperor's approval,[72] although such approval might have been merely pro forma. The Directorate of Ceremonial printed all these books, which were loaned to students.

The students' daily activities included practicing calligraphy, memorizing texts, and reciting them aloud. Hanlin instructors monitored students' progress. Those who failed to memorize assigned texts, produced bad calligraphy, damaged books, or disobeyed school rules were reported to the Directorate of Ceremonial Commander, which determined appropriate punishments.[73] Students in the Inner Court School commonly needed three to five years to complete their basic education; within ten years or so, those who were motivated could be of great use for important tasks both inside and outside the court.[74]

A select group of aspiring eunuch students would also consume reference books on Ming laws, legal precedents, ritual protocol, and dictionaries of Chinese and foreign languages.[75] Looking at the rather extensive reading

———

70. *ZZZ*, 16.2008.
71. *ZZZ*, 18.2081.
72. Ibid.
73. *ZZZ*, 16.2008.
74. Ibid., p. 2009.
75. For a more complete list of the reference books, see *ZZZ*, 18.2083–84.

lists, one cannot help but be amazed at the comprehensive education of the Ming palace eunuchs, which was clearly based on the Confucian mode. All the required and optional titles for palace eunuchs also appeared on the required reading lists for serious office seekers who wished to pass all levels of the civil service examination during the Ming. They included the Four Books, the Five Classics, and readers on matters of law, precedents, and protocols in issuing laws and decrees.[76]

Perhaps the most surprising aspect of the eunuch students' education in the Inner Court School, and one with serious political consequences, was the inclusion of the so-called mock court decision (*panfang* 判仿) lessons,[77] in which students practiced writing responses to memorials in imitation of the emperor's manner of phrasing. Such lessons undoubtedly encouraged the abuse of imperial authority by the eunuchs.

During the early Ming, all the memorials from the outer court were submitted directly to the emperor through the Office of Transmission (Tongzhengsi 通政司), a central clearinghouse for imperial documents. The Hongwu and Yongle emperors personally wrote notations in cinnabar red on the memorials that required their decisions. Beginning in the 1420s, the Directorate of Ceremonial received all incoming memorials from all levels of government offices from the Office of Transmission via the Office of Documents, which was supervised by the Directorate of Ceremonial, before the memorial reached the emperor. It also processed the emperor's outgoing communications before they became imperial edicts or pronouncements.

Typically, the emperor consulted with the Grand Secretariat in order to arrive at decisions regarding cases presented in the memorials, which he then wrote on slips of paper. The eunuchs in the Office of Documents then transcribed the emperor's written decisions directly onto the memorials. The memorials would then be stamped with the imperial seals before they were dispatched to their offices of origin via the Office of Transmission.[78]

---

76. For the curricula and examination format of the civil service examinations, see Elman, "Changes in Confucian Civil Service Examinations," pp. 114–15.

77. *ZZZ*, 16.2008.

78. Regular memorials were first submitted to the Office of Transmission before they were transmitted to the Office of Documents; confidential ones were submitted by the memorialists at the Kuaiji Gate 會極門, where the Directorate of Ceremonial messenger received them (Silas Wu, "Transmission of Ming Memorials," p. 279). For an analysis of the Grand Secretariat as an important office in the Ming court's policy-

When the emperor rejected the Grand Secretariat's recommendations regarding memorials, he often turned to the elite Directorate of Ceremonial
eunuchs for alternatives.[79]

Beginning in the Zhengtong reign (1436–49), Directorate of Ceremonial
eunuchs are said to have personally composed and written imperial edicts
in cinnabar red on the outgoing memorials,[80] apparently because the emperor alone was unable to handle the volume of memorials. Liu Ruoyu reports that during his time, each day the Wanli emperor read and decided
on only a handful of the hundreds of memorials that poured in daily. The
keepers of imperial brushes and the keeper of Imperial Seals handled the
rest. Although they usually faithfully copied the Grand Secretariat's recommendations written on the paper slips attached to the memorials, they
occasionally changed the recommendations, especially those they suspected
the emperor would not like.[81] What the emperor liked or might not like
was, however, only their surmise, giving them great leeway to change the
recommendations at will.

Outer court officials thus had every reason to be antagonized by this
potentially dangerous practice. Under weak or irresponsible emperors, elite
eunuchs in the Directorate of Ceremonial could strongly influence the emperor's decisions. Worse, some eunuchs even intercepted the memorials
and wrote their own decisions on them, passing them off as the emperor's.
During the Zhengde reign (1506–21), the notorious Keeper of Imperial
Seals Liu Jin 劉瑾 (1451–1510), an Inner Court School graduate, reportedly
took memorials home, where he and his brother-in-law annotated them
without the emperor's knowledge.[82] These potentially nefarious practices
were made possible by the mock imperial decision lessons, through which
the eunuchs learned to imitate the emperor's style of wording.

Their well-rounded classical education transformed some palace
eunuchs from mere imperial servants with only functional literacy into men
possessing advanced abilities in reading and composition akin to those of

---

making process, see Zhang Zhian, *Mingdai zhengzhi yanjiu*, pp. 77–98; and Sun Chengze,
Chunming mengyu lu, 23.343–44.

79. Chan Hok-lam, "The Chien-wen, Yung-lo, Hung-hsi, and Hsüan-te Reigns,"
p. 287.

80. Ouyang Chen, "Ming neifu neishutang kaolüe," p. 59.

81. At the Directorate of Ceremonial, at any one point there was only one keeper of
imperial seals, but the number of keepers of imperial brushes could be four or five, and
sometimes eight or nine (ZZZ, 16.2003).

82. *MS*, 304.3413.

the literati.[83] Elite eunuchs, well educated and with administrative experience gained from the day-to-day services they rendered to the throne, became seasoned professional bureaucrats, not unlike their counterparts in the outer court. Moreover, they were able to amass political power by reading and deciding cases presented in the memorials from the outer court for the emperor—sometimes without the emperor's knowledge—acting as the emperor's delegates, by communicating with the outer court directly. The Hongwu emperor had prohibited such direct communications, but his order was ignored later in the dynasty. By the mid-fifteenth century, it was accepted that the Directorate of Ceremonial and the Grand Secretariat shared executive power equally.[84] In fact, the keeper of imperial seals was referred to as the inner court prime minister (*neixiang* 內相),[85] as opposed to the outer court prime minister (*waixiang* 外相), the chief grand secretary. In addition, educated elite eunuchs also oversaw other important judicial, military, economic, and diplomatic matters,[86] altering the traditional composition of officialdom.

The Hongwu emperor had striven to prevent palace eunuchs from receiving a Confucian education, because he feared that such an education would allow palace eunuchs to interfere in administrative matters. Paradoxically, the Yongle and Xuande emperors wanted palace eunuchs to be well educated, because educated elite eunuchs constituted a check against court officials, especially when the grand secretaries became increasingly powerful in the court's decision-making process.

The establishment of the Inner Court School also created two politically significant phenomena unique to the Ming. First, the Directorate of

---

83. Many of the elite eunuchs imitated the literati lifestyle. They composed poems and practiced calligraphy, which they gave to their eunuch friends and court officials; they played musical instruments; and they collected works of art.

84. Ouyang Chen, "Ming neifu neishutang kaolüe," p. 59. Shen Defu uses the term *duibing jiyao* 對柄機要 to describe the equal executive power of the Grand Secretariat and Directorate of Ceremonial; see Shen Defu, *Wanli yehuo bian* (hereafter cited as YHB), *buyi*, 1.814. The phrase meant standing on opposite sides and handling, or having the control of, confidential and other important matters. The term indicated that both offices functioned as a check and balance on each other.

85. Beginning in the Chenghua reign, court officials addressed the keeper of imperial seals as *neixiang* in their memorials to the emperor (see Ouyang Chen, "Ming neifu neishutang kaolüe," p. 61).

86. For a more detailed analysis of eunuchs' participation in these aspects of state affairs, see Tsai, *The Eunuchs in the Ming Dynasty*, pp. 159–82; and Wang and Du, *Mingchao huanguan*, pp. 4–18.

Ceremonial regularly selected young, bright, and intelligent Inner Court School graduates as the crown prince's informal tutors (*bandu* 伴讀) before and sometimes even after the crown prince received his formal education. Although *bandu* literally means "study companions," in the Ming they were the crown prince's private tutors. During the Hongwu and Yongle reigns, the crown prince's private tutors were selected from among the National University students, but beginning in the Xuande era, they were replaced by young educated eunuchs.[87] This is another instance in which palace eunuchs supplanted the traditional role of scholars in the education of the crown prince. The young eunuch tutors spent much time with their young imperial master, not only studying but also enjoying leisure time activities. They often made strong, lasting impressions on the young crown prince and eventually became trusted political advisors when the crown prince succeeded to the throne.

One such eunuch, whose influence on the imperial court's decision-making almost cost his emperor's life, was Wang Zhen 王振 (d. 1449), an Inner Court School graduate assigned as the Zhengtong emperor's (r. 1436–49) informal tutor before the emperor ascended the throne at age seven. Teacher Wang, as the young emperor addressed him, continued to be his trusted advisor and eventually became keeper of imperial seals. In 1449, Wang Zhen persuaded the emperor to personally lead a military campaign against the Mongol invaders led by Esen (d. 1455). The failed campaign resulted in the Zhengtong emperor's capture by the Mongols and Wang Zhen's execution at the hands of Ming military officers.[88] Even so, when the emperor was released and re-enthroned as the Tianshun emperor (r. 1457–64), he erected the Shrine of Uttermost Loyalty (Jingzhong ci 精忠祠) in Wang Zhen's honor.[89]

Another example was Wang An 王安 (d. 1621), also an Inner Court School graduate, the private tutor and personal advisor of the Taichang emperor (r. August 1–30, 1620), when the emperor was still heir apparent until the emperor's death. Wang An was instrumental in the Donglin parti-

---

87. He Weizhi, *Mingchu de huanguan zhengzhi*, p. 160.

88. For Wang Zhen's biography, see *MS*, 304.3407–8; and Wen Gongyi, *Mingdai de huanguan he gongting*, pp. 68–81, 133. For a detailed analysis of the 1449 military clash between the Chinese and Mongols, see Twitchett and Grimm, "The Cheng-t'ung, Ching-t'ai, and T'ien-shun Reigns," pp. 322–31.

89. Wang and Du, *Mingchao huanguan*, p. 151.

sans' return to power in the central government during the Taichang's brief reign and subsequently early in the Tianqi emperor's reign (1621–27).[90]

A second phenomenon brought about by the establishment of the Inner Court School was the cordial relationship that often developed between Inner Court School students and their Hanlin academician lecturers, which in many cases influenced the imperial appointments of grand secretaries. The selection of grand secretaries was no small matter, since they played an important role in the imperial court's decision-making process.

During the Ming, most Hanlin academicians had passed the highest level of the civil service examination and held the degree of *jinshi* of the first grade. The ultimate goal in their civil service career was usually to become a grand secretary, or chief grand secretary. Most grand secretaries were promoted from among the Hanlin academicians, and thus the contemporary expression, "Those who are not Hanlin academicians do not enter the Grand Secretariat" (*Fei hanlin bu ru nei ge* 非翰林不入內閣).[91]

Interestingly, the percentage of Inner Court School lecturers who later became grand secretaries was rather high. For instance, among the four Hanlin academicians appointed to teach at the Inner Court School in 1456, three became grand secretaries, as did all three Inner Court School lecturers appointed in 1601 and all six appointed in 1611.[92] Such scattered information is insufficient to conclude that most grand secretaries owed their positions to their former Inner Court School students, who later became keepers of imperial brushes or keepers of imperial seals. However, some correlation did exist. Some grand secretaries indeed owed their appointments to their former Inner Court School students.[93]

In traditional China, teachers were held in high regard. The fact that eunuchs helped their former teachers become grand secretaries may be seen in this light; they were simply grateful to their teachers for their successful careers in the inner court. Further, elite eunuchs' willingness to help their former teachers also stemmed from the fact that they needed allies at

---

90. For Wang An's biography, see *MS*, 305.3433. See also Dardess, *Blood and History in China*, pp. 32–35. For detailed studies of the Donglin faction in the political context of the sixteenth and seventeenth centuries, see also Wu Yingji, *Donglin shilüe*; Hucker, "The Tung-lin Movement of the Late Ming Period"; and Ono Kazuko, *Minki tōsha kō*.

91. *MS*, "Xuanjuzhi 2," 70.725.

92. Ouyang Chen, "Ming neifu neishutang kaolüe," p. 58.

93. For example, the appointments of Wang Yining 王一寧 (1397–1452) during the Jingtai reign (1450–56) and Yin Shidan 殷士儋 (*js.* 1547) in the Longqing era (1567–72) were made at the instigation of their former Inner Court School students (ibid.).

the Grand Secretariat in order to realize their own political agendas in the court's decision-making.

Moreover, elite eunuchs at the Directorate of Ceremonial were also instrumental in many other court officials' promotions. The promotions made possible by them, or by the emperor, without a formal evaluation process, were called *neiqian* 內遷, or promotions made by the inner court. Since elite eunuchs at the Directorate of Ceremonial had the power to appoint and promote officials, they also had the power to dismiss them. Records reveal plenty of such cases.[94] These practices enabled the Directorate of Ceremonial to infiltrate the central bureaucracy; they also contributed to the factionalism of both the outer court bureaucracy and the Directorate of Ceremonial.[95]

The systematic education of Ming palace eunuchs had no parallel in imperial Chinese history. The members of the Directorate of Ceremonial knew all too well that education was vital to their success, political and otherwise, and the Directorate of Ceremonial's publishing business was indeed also self-serving. As noted above, the Directorate of Ceremonial published both required and optional readers, as well as many reference books, for eunuch students at the Inner Court School. The most highly educated among the eunuchs were, with few exceptions, the ones who rose to the highest positions. In order to serve in the Directorate of Ceremonial, for example, one had to be a graduate of the Inner Court School.[96]

However, although elite eunuchs' ability to read and write as imperial proxies enabled them to play an important role in court politics, and even to usurp imperial authority in some instances, their political power existed only to the extent that the emperor allowed it. Individual eunuchs' power usually lasted no longer than their emperor's reign, because the new emperor often appointed his own trusted eunuchs to important positions. In

---

94. The Grand Secretaries Xu Youzhen 徐有貞 (1407–72) and Li Xian 李賢 (1408–66) were imprisoned by the Tianshun emperor (r. 1457–64) under the influence of Keeper of Imperial Seals Cao Jixiang 曹吉祥 (d. 1461). Grand Secretaries Liu Jian 劉健 (1433–1526) and Xie Qian 謝遷 (1449–1531) were forced to retire for criticizing Keeper of Imperial Seals Liu Jin (*MS*, 304.3408 and 3413, respectively).

95. See the account of the power struggle at the end of the Tianshun era (1457–64) between the court official Chen Wen 陳文 (d. 1468) and Grand Secretary Qian Pu 錢溥 and his collaborator Keeper of Imperial Seals Wang Lun 王綸 and its aftermath in Ouyang Chen, "Ming neifu neishutang kaolüe," pp. 58–59.

96. This is what Liu Ruoyu calls *zhengtu* 正途, or the "proper course" through which palace eunuchs obtained high positions (*ZZZ*, 16.2004).

other words, the eunuchs' political power depended more on their emperor's will and less on their own literacy.

The illiterate but most feared Keeper of Imperial Brushes Wei Zhongxian 魏忠賢 (1568–1627) in the Tianqi court is a case in point. His rise to power is complex, but the tremendous imperial favor that he enjoyed was a major factor. Yet as soon as the Chongzhen emperor (r. 1627–44) ascended the throne, Wei was condemned to death.[97] Moreover, although education enabled eunuchs to be effective and technically accomplished professional bureaucrats, it did not prepare them to become true literati or philosophers who could also interpret the texts. Although the political stature of literati scholars also relied on the emperor's will, they possessed power as interpreters of the texts and cultural arbiters that not even the Son of Heaven could take away from them.

THE EDUCATION OF PALACE WOMEN

Directorate of Ceremonial publications also served palace women, including the empress, imperial concubines, potential imperial consorts, and candidates for offices at the Six Bureaus (Liuju 六局), the six inner court agencies staffed with palace women who tended the affairs of the Six Palaces, or Liugong 六宮, a reference to the emperor's six principal consorts. During the Ming, potential imperial consorts and candidates for offices at the Six Bureaus were recruited as needed.[98] Usually unmarried young girls between the ages of thirteen and nineteen were recruited as potential imperial consorts, and unmarried older women between the ages of thirty and forty were recruited to fill the positions in the Six Bureaus.[99] In the early Ming when the Six Bureaus were first established, there were seventy-four such female officers, but the number increased manifold as time went by.[100] Although they had already received some basic schooling, these women were re-educated in the inner court. No equivalent of the Inner Court School is explicitly mentioned in Ming records. Scattered information

---

97. For Wei's biography, see, e.g., *MS*, 305.3433–37; Wang and Du, *Mingchao huanguan*, pp. 218–32. For detailed analyses of Wei's rise to power, see Miao Di, *Wei Zhongxian zhuanquan yanjiu*; and Mammitzsch, "Wei Chung-hsien."

98. Recruitment of palace women for different purposes could be done separately or simultaneously; see Hsieh, "From Charwoman to Empress Dowager," p. 33.

99. *YHB buyi*, 1.804–5.

100. Ibid., p. 805.

suggests that some of the recruited palace women were educated systematically and promoted according to their educational achievements. Educated palace eunuchs played an important role in both their education and promotion.

During the Hongwu reign, literate widows and unmarried women were recruited as teachers for palace women.[101] During the Yongle emperor's reign, some Confucian teachers volunteered, or were otherwise persuaded, to undergo castration in order to instruct palace ladies.[102] Later, the Directorate of Ceremonial selected old, educated palace eunuchs with good character, strong skills in calligraphy, and with little political influence for this purpose.[103] Palace maidens who passed strict academic evaluations filled high positions in the Six Bureaus, which, after the Yongle reign, were supervised by eunuchs selected from various eunuch agencies in the inner court.[104] Many of the positions in the Six Bureaus involved responsibilities that required literacy, such as the position of female scribe (*nüshi* 女史) in charge of paperwork, directress of the library (*siji* 司籍), and directress of the Registrar's Office (*sibu* 司簿). The two highest positions were chief of palace surveillance (*gongzhengsi* 宮正司) and seal keeper of the Six Bureaus (*Liuju zhangyin* 六局掌印).[105]

These palace women first studied such primers as *One Hundred Family Names* and *One Thousand Character Essay*, and they subsequently read some of the Confucian classics, including the *Book of Filial Piety*, *Book of Poetry*, *Great Learning*, *Doctrine of the Mean*, and *Analects*.[106] Their education also included poetry composition.[107] Their curriculum appears to have been less

----

101. Hsieh, "From Charwoman to Empress Dowager," p. 37; *YHB buyi*, 1.805.

102. Twitchett and Grimm, "The Cheng-t'ung, Ching-t'ai, and T'ien-shun Reigns," p. 306.

103. *ZZZ*, 16.2053.

104. *MS*, 74.783.

105. *ZZZ*, 16.2053. For the Six Bureaus and their duties, see *MS*, 74.782–83. The criteria for the final selection of imperial consorts are not clear, but those not selected might have been given positions at the Six Bureaus or assigned as chambermaids of the empress, empress dowager, or other high-ranking imperial consorts. They were also given to the feudal princes' households as chambermaids. Service women in the inner court could also be promoted as imperial consorts, especially if they bore the emperor's sons, although it was not always a guarantee. For a more detailed analysis of palace women's promotion and demotion, see Hsieh, "From Charwoman to Empress Dowager," pp. 46–48.

106. *ZZZ*, 16.2053.

107. Hsieh, "From Charwoman to Empress Dowager," p. 37.

extensive than that of the palace eunuchs, since their duties were far more limited than those of their male counterparts.

Among their required readings were also titles written exclusively for women, especially court women, including the ancient texts "Rules for the Inner Chambers" ("Neize" 內則), a chapter from *Book of Rites* (*Liji* 禮記); *Admonitions to Women* (*Nüjie* 女誡) by the renowned female scholar of antiquity Ban Zhao 班昭 (ca. 49–ca. 120); and the *Biographies of Exemplary Women* (*Lienü zhuan* 列女傳), said to have been authored by Liu Xiang 劉向 (77?–6? BCE).[108] Books for their moral guidance also included those by Ming empresses, such as *Lessons for the Inner Chambers* (*Neixun* 內訓) attributed to Empress Renxiao 仁孝皇后 (1362–1407); and *Lessons for Women* (*Nüxun* 女訓) by Empress Dowager Zhangshengciren 章聖慈仁太后, dated 1530. These books were intended to regulate young palace women's behavior, since they might one day be chosen as imperial consorts or even empresses. The Wanli emperor's birth mother, Empress Dowager Cisheng 慈聖太后 (d. 1614), was once a chambermaid in the household of Prince Yu 裕王, the future Longqing emperor. Her influence on the Wanli emperor is well known. If not for her intervention, the Wanli emperor's firstborn imperial son, Changluo 常洛 (d. 1620), might not have been invested as crown prince.[109] Owing to her example as a pious Buddhist, the Wanli emperor usually did not order the death penalty.[110]

The fact that the Directorate of Ceremonial was responsible for the schooling of palace ladies, many of whom would eventually become mothers of imperial sons or wives of the emperor, attests to the agency's importance to the imperial family's well-being, and also by extension, its importance to the future of the Ming empire.

———

108. It seems that palace ladies were required to be able to recite the *Biographies of Exemplary Women* (*MDCZSK*, p. 28).

109. It is reported that one day in 1601, amid the imperial succession controversy, Empress Dowager Cisheng asked the Wanli emperor why he had not installed Changluo as crown prince. The Wanli emperor answered without much thought that Changluo was only a son by a chambermaid. The Empress Dowager snapped back angrily, "I was once a chambermaid [in your father's household]." The frightened Wanli emperor immediately had Changluo invested as crown prince (*MS*, "Biography of Empress Dowager Cisheng," 114.1483). Although Changluo was the first-born imperial son and the rightful successor to the throne, the Wanli emperor purposefully delayed not only Changluo's formal education but also his installation as the crown prince, because he preferred the son by his favorite consort, Lady Zheng, to be his successor. For a discussion of the controversy, see Ray Huang, *1587*, pp. 80–86.

110. Ray Huang, "The Lung-ch'ing and Wan-li Reigns, 1567–1620," p. 514.

OTHER FUNCTIONS OF THE DIRECTORATE
OF CEREMONIAL'S PUBLICATIONS

Although the primary audience for the Directorate of Ceremonial's publications was the highly select few who lived inside the Forbidden City, the emperor on occasion ordered the Directorate to distribute its publications to imperial sons, court officials, various government offices, and foreign courts.[111] Some of these publications were gifts or warnings from the emperor; others were intended as master copies for reprints by other government offices for wider circulation.

For example, early in the sixteenth century, the Zhengde emperor ordered Hanlin academicians to edit the *Collected Administrative Statutes of the Great Ming* and commanded the Directorate of Ceremonial to print copies of the book. The emperor gave the printed copies to court officials.[112] In 1529, the Ministry of Rites requested permission to reproduce the *Collected Rites of the Great Ming* (*Da Ming jili* 大明集禮), which had been compiled under the Hongwu emperor, for nationwide circulation. The Jiajing emperor (r. 1522–66) ordered the Directorate of Ceremonial to carve and print the master copy of this title. The result was the 1530 Directorate of Ceremonial edition.[113]

In cooperation with the Directorate of Astronomy, the Directorate of Ceremonial also oversaw production of the master copies of both the state calendar (*datongli* 大統曆) and the calendar for the general population (*minli* 民曆) approved by the imperial court.[114] These master copies were then sent to the Ministry of Rites, which in turn distributed them to other major central government offices in Nanjing and Beijing. Each was responsible

---

111. The Ming imperial court regularly presented books and calendars to its neighboring tributary countries as gifts; see Zhang Lian, "Mingdai zhuanzhi wenhua zhengce," p. 364.

112. See the Zhengde emperor's preface, dated 1511, in *DMHD*, p. 2.

113. See the preface by the Jiajing emperor in Xu Yikui et al., *Da Ming jili*.

114. Officially, the Directorate of Astronomy oversaw the preparation and printing of these two calendars. In 1531, however, it had only one paper mounting artisan and twenty-eight printers, and it did not even have its own woodblock carvers. The Directorate of Astronomy had only two artisans who drew calendar charts (*cailijiang* 裁曆匠), whereas the Directorate of Ceremonial had eighty-three. Therefore some scholars suspect that the Directorate of Ceremonial shared many of the Directorate of Astronomy's responsibilities; see Luo Shubao, *Zhongguo gudai yinshua shi*, p. 305.

for printing further copies based on the master copy.[115] The Office of the Sacred Platform (Lingtai 靈台),[116] a eunuch agency supervised by the Directorate of Ceremonial, worked closely with the Directorate of Astronomy in producing both calendars. When a new group of eunuchs was admitted to the court, the Lingtai would usually select and train thirty or forty young eunuchs as astrologers.[117]

In the Confucian tradition, it was the duty of the ruler to regulate earthly affairs in accordance with heavenly ones. An accurate calendar was essential for this task. The publication of private calendars could be read as usurpation of the imperial power and cause social disorder.[118] Thus, the Directorate of Ceremonial's involvement in publishing the state calendar was no small matter. Indeed, the publication of the Ming state calendar was an international affair; its dates were used in much diplomatic correspondence in East Asia.[119] Foreign rulers considered the calendars important political symbols that reaffirmed ties to the Ming court. During the Xuande reign, the yearly production of calendars amounted to 509,000 copies;[120] many were intended for foreign courts such as Chosŏn Korea, Japan, and the Ryūkyū Kingdom.[121]

Authors of the Directorate of Ceremonial Publications and the Politics of Authorship

A seventeenth-century inventory of the Directorate of Ceremonial's publications shows that among the books by authors from the imperial family, those written or compiled by Ming emperors form the largest group. Titles by empresses and imperial concubines constitute the second-largest group.

---

115. Ibid., p. 306

116. *Lingtai* referred in ancient times to the sacred platform or terrace where rulers observed heavenly phenomena and tried to interpret their good and bad omens.

117. *ZZZ*, 16.2031.

118. In the Ming, commoners who studied astronomy were to be exiled to the frontiers as guards. Private publication of calendars was punishable by death. The law seems to have been relaxed, however, beginning in the Hongzhi reign (1506–21); see *YHB*, 20.524.

119. Chan Hok-lam, "Mingchu Chaoxian ruchao huanguan juyu—Hai Shou shiji tansuo," p. 61.

120. *YHB*, 20.525.

121. Zhang Lian, "Song Ming zhengfu zhi yuwai cishu," pp. 149, 150, 155. See also *YHB*, 20.525.

Their number is, however, far smaller than that of works by emperors. The Directorate of Ceremonial issued almost no titles by imperial princes or princesses; indeed, the list notes only three works by Ming princes: *The Emaciated Immortal's Manual of Remedies* (*Quxian zhouhou jing* 臞仙肘后經),[122] a book on astrology, divination, and magical calculations, and the *Broadened Discussion of the Comprehensive Mirror* [*for Aid in Governance*] (*Tongjian bolun* 通鑑博論), both by Prince Ning, Zhu Quan 朱權 (1378–1488), the sixteenth son of Hongwu; and the poetic anthology [*Hanchuntang*] *Enji shi* [含春堂] 恩紀詩, created by Prince Xing, Zhu Youyuan 朱佑杬 (d. 1519), the biological father of the Jiajing emperor. The first title was not particularly political in nature; the Hongwu emperor ordered Prince Ning to compile the second title.[123] The third title was issued only after the Jiajing emperor's enthronement.[124] The Directorate of Ceremonial did not publish politically charged books or works that lacked the emperor's imprimatur.

Although his father's poetic anthology had already been published elsewhere in 1502, Jiajing felt that the calligraphy and carving were insufficiently refined. He therefore ordered the Directorate of Ceremonial to recarve and publish it in 1526.[125] The reprinting of the book by the Directorate of Ceremonial also clearly indicates that Jiajing was acutely aware of the prestige of inner court editions, and he used this means to honor his father.

As noted above, woodblock-printed books were public in nature. The imperial court operated, as Chu Hong-lam observes, "mainly through ceremonial protocol and written communication." Woodblock-printed books were extremely powerful tools for disseminating imperial ideologies and fulfilling specific political agendas. As noted above, the inner court publications were intended largely for a select few in the Forbidden City. Some of them, however, circulated widely. More often than not, their conveyance from the Forbidden City to the outside world was done on impe-

---

122. *ZZZ*, 18.2084.

123. See Jiajing's preface to the anthology in Zhu Youyan, *Enji shiji*, p. 64.

124. The Palace Museum Library in Beijing has a copy of the 1526 inner court edition of this title. The title is rendered *Enji Hanchuntang shi* 恩紀含春堂詩 in Liu Ruoyu's inventory list (*ZZZ*, 18.2085).

125. In fact, the 1526 publication also included another book by Jiajing's birth father, the *Hanchuntang gao* 含春堂稿 (The Hanchuntang manuscript), a collection of miscellaneous notes originally dated 1500. Cited in *MDCZSK*, p. 55. See also Zhu Youyuan, *Hanchuntang gao*.

rial order, and more often than not, there was an important political agenda behind the order.

In what follows, we will look at a few inner court publications to elucidate these important issues: Who wrote the book and why? Who were its intended readers? Was it written by the person named as the author? If not, for what purpose, or purposes, was it reattributed? Under what circumstances was an inner court edition made accessible to Ming society at large? It is important to understand these issues because they reveal much about what mattered to members of the imperial court, what they thought about these matters, and how they dealt with them. These are crucial aspects of the Ming court culture and intellectual history.

THE EMPEROR AND EMPRESS

The compilation of many of the titles "authored" by Ming emperors and empresses involved court officials, especially Hanlin academicians. For example, Hongwu's secretariat was responsible for the compilation of his *Ancestral Injunctions of the Brilliant Ming*,[126] Hanlin academicians led by Hu Guang 胡廣 (1370–1418) compiled the Yongle emperor's *The Heart-Mind Method in the Sage's Learning*,[127] and Hu Guang and others assisted in the compilation of *Book of Exhortations* (*Quanshan shu* 勸善書), dated 1407, by Empress Renxiao (1362–1407), the Yongle emperor's consort.[128] At least two factors explain court officials' involvement in compiling books "authored" by Ming imperial writers. First, these projects were simply too large for a single imperial author, regardless of his or her erudition. Second, the education of imperial women authors was too limited to allow them to handle certain topics. There was no intent to falsify the books' authorship. As we will see, however, falsification and reattribution of authorship did occur. The questions, then, are under what circumstances and for what purposes.

The majority of books on Liu Ruoyu's inventory of Directorate of Ceremonial publications were intended as admonitions for the imperial family and its relatives. Forty-two of the ninety-eight titles (more than 40 percent) on Sakai Tadao's list of imperially sponsored books of exhortations were similarly intended as instructions to imperial clan members, rela-

---

126. Cited in Sakai, *Zōho Chūgoku zensho no kenkyū* (hereafter cited as *CGZS*), p. 26.
127. Ibid., p. 36.
128. Soullière, "Palace Women in the Ming Dynasty," p. 95.

tives, and consorts. The rest were for Ming officials and commoners.[129] Among these were *Ancestral Injunctions of the Brilliant Ming, Records as Perpetual Mirrors* (*Yongjianlu* 永鑑錄), dated 1392, by the Hongwu emperor and intended as warnings for feudal princes and imperial clan members; *True Stories of the Filial and Obedient* (*Xiaoshun shishi* 孝順事實), dated 1420, by the Yongle emperor; *The Mirror of the Deeds of Imperial Affines* (*Waiqi shijian* 外戚事鑑), published in 1426 on the Xuande emperor's order; and *Great Lessons for the Palace of Literary Splendor* (*Wenhua daxun* 文華大訓), dated 1482, edited by the Chenghua emperor for the crown prince.

Books by Ming empresses, intended as moral lessons for imperial women in particular, include *Lessons for the Inner Chambers* by Empress Renxiao; *Lessons for Women* by Empress Dowager Zhangshengciren, the Jiajing emperor's biological mother; and *Women's Mirror* (*Nüjian* 女鑒) by Empress Dowager Cisheng, the Wanli emperor's biological mother.[130]

These titles by Ming emperors and empresses are examples of the genre of household instructions (*jiaxun* 家訓). They reflect the Confucian teaching that in order to govern the country well, a ruler must first keep his family in order; and that to bring order to the universe, a ruler must first govern his country well. They also reflect the Ming imperial family's desire to ensure its longevity, or to "forever own the rivers and mountains" (*yongbao jiangshan* 永保江山).

The same desire to preserve imperial power inspired other titles compiled under Ming emperors' auspices, including the *Mirror for Ministers* (*Xiangjian* 相鑒), published in 1380 shortly after Prime Minister Hu Weiyong 胡惟庸 (d. 1380) was executed for treason on the Hongwu emperor's order,[131] and *The Mirror of Ministers Throughout the Ages* (*Lidai chen jian* 歷代臣鑑), dated 1426. These early Ming compilations reflected the imperial house's insecurity as the head of a newly founded and still precarious empire.

Some inner court editions were inextricably bound to the issue of imperial legitimacy. Early in his reign, the Yongle emperor enlisted the Directorate of Ceremonial in his campaign to legitimate his rule by ordering it to publish and distribute several titles to justify his usurpation of his nephew, the Jianwen emperor (r. 1399–1402).[132] One such book is the *Biographies of*

---

129. *CGZS*, p. 45.

130. *Nüjian* is no longer extant; it is recorded in *ZZZ*, 18.2083.

131. Cited in *CGZS*, p. 27. For the Hu Weiyong case, see Langlois, "The Hung-wu Reign, 1368–1398," pp. 137–39.

132. Ming imperial succession law dictated that the oldest imperial son, regardless of his birth mother's status in the hierarchy of imperial consorts, was the rightful succes-

Exemplary Women of the Past and Present (*Gujin lienü zhuan* 古今列女傳), a project likely initiated by Empress Ma, the Hongwu emperor's principal wife. For some reason the title was not printed during the Hongwu reign.[133] In the ninth month of 1403, the first year of his reign, Yongle ordered the book to be compiled, and in the twelfth month of the same year, it was ready for distribution among the Six Palaces and throughout the realm, or *banxing tianxi* 頒行天下, as it reads in Chinese.[134]

By honoring his parents' wish to publish the book, the Yongle emperor reminded his opponents that he was the son of the Hongwu emperor as well as Empress Ma's eldest surviving son, although he had in fact been born to a Mongolian consort of his father.[135] This was an attempt to minimize the charge of his usurpation. In 1405, the Directorate of Ceremonial published *Lessons for the Inner Chambers*, and in 1406, *The Biography of the Lofty Empress [Ma]* (*Gao huanghou zhun* 高皇后傳).[136] The name of Yongle's Empress Renxiao is attached to both, and both were bestowed on feudal princes and all court officials.

In fact, as Ellen Soullière has observed, Empress Ma had created *Lessons for the Inner Chambers*. Reattributing the book to Empress Renxiao was an attempt to claim that she was the rightful successor to and interpreter of Empress Ma's legacy and thus to further legitimize Yongle's own rule.[137] For the same reason, Yongle and his supporters rewrote history, producing, for example, *Records of Stabilizing Dangerous Situations Mandated by Heaven*

———

sor to his father's throne. If the oldest imperial son did not live long enough to occupy the Dragon Seat, then his oldest son was the legitimate successor. It was under this law that the Hongwu emperor's oldest grandson, the Jianwen emperor, inherited the throne, which was taken by force by his uncle, the Yongle emperor, in 1402. For the Yongle emperor's usurpation, see Chan Hok-lam, "The Chien-wen, Yung-lo, Hung-hsi, and Hsüan-te Reigns," pp. 193–205.

133. Cited in *CGZS*, p. 33.

134. *MDCZSK*, p. 28. Two chapters out of three of the 1403 inner court edition of this title are preserved in the Zhejiang Provincial Library. For a detailed study of the *Biographies of Exemplary Women of the Past and Present*, see Soullière, "Palace Women in the Ming Dynasty," pp. 26–75.

135. It has been recently confirmed that Yongle was born to Hongwu's Mongolian consort; see Chan Hok-lam, "Ming chu Chaoxian ruchao huanguan juyu—Hai Shou shiji tansuo," p. 66*n*7.

136. *CGZS*, pp. 34–35. In 1407 after the death of Empress Renxiao, these two titles were again promulgated for even wider circulation (ibid., p. 34).

137. Based on historical records and writing style, Soullière ("Palace Women in the Ming Dynasty," pp. 76–78) argues that Empress Ma, not Empress Renxiao, compiled *Lessons for the Inner Chambers*.

(*Fengtian jingnan zhi* 奉天靖難志), the Yongle emperor's official account of his campaign against the Jianwen emperor. They also extensively revised the Veritable Record of his father's reign and the imperial genealogy, *Jade Records of the Imperial Pedigree Originating in the Heavenly Pond* (*Tianhuang yudie* 天潢玉牒).[138]

Similarly, amid the furor of the Great Rites Controversy (*Daliyi* 大禮議), the Jiajing emperor ordered the compilation of the *Canon for the Clarification of Human Relations* (*Minglun dadian* 明倫大典), dated 1528, to assert his absolute imperial authority. Shortly after his enthronement and over the opposition of many in the court, Jiajing posthumously recognized his biological father, Prince Xing, as emperor and his biological mother as empress dowager. Jiajing inherited the throne from his uncle, the Zhengde emperor (r. 1506–21), not from his biological father, who had died as an invested feudal prince. His mother had already received the title "consort of invested prince." However, the real empress dowager was still alive.[139] Conferring these titles on Jiajing's birth parents was at odds with the imperial ritual protocols, causing a heated debate among court officials, which is referred to as the Great Rites Controversy.

Immediately after Jiajing's decision in the sixth month of 1528 to honor his parents, the Directorate of Ceremonial published the *Canon for the Clarification of Human Relations*. It chronicles in detail the Great Rites Controversy that occurred between March 1521, when the Zhengde emperor died, and March 1528, when the Jiajing emperor won the debate. In his preface to the book, Jiajing accuses the court officials who challenged his authority of destroying the three bonds in human relations—those between sovereign and officials, father and son, and husband and wife—and the five human relations.[140] In conjunction with the book's publication, Jiajing issued an imperial edict announcing that he had ordered the compilation of *Canon for the Clarification of Human Relations*, which contained both the worthy and the wicked memorials during the Great Rites Controversy. The edict also detailed the Heavenly mandated punishments against his opponents.

Jiajing made explicit the intended effect of the edict: "so that those in officialdom will examine and be vigilant about their own conduct." The

---

138. Chan Hok-lam, "The Chien-wen, Yung-le, Hung-hsi, and Hsüan-te Reigns," pp. 214–18.

139. For a detailed analysis of the Great Rites Controversy, see Fisher, *The Chosen One*, esp. chap. 2; Xu Daling and Wang Tianyou, *Mingchao shiliudi*, pp. 217–23. See also Geiss, "The Chia-ching Reign, 1522–1566," pp. 440–60.

140. See Jiajing's preface in Yang Yiqing et al., *Minglun dadian*.

edict, written in big characters, is said to have been hung over the Gate of Receiving Heaven's Mandate (Fengtian men 奉天門),[141] where the imperial audiences were usually held. The book and the edict must have sent a chill through all his imperial relatives and courtiers. The book symbolized Jiajing's absolute power and affirmed the legitimacy of his parents' new status.[142] It can also be said that the perceived need to publish the book reflected Jiajing's awareness that neither he nor his family had a legitimate claim to the throne.[143]

Titles written by empresses for women also arose from the tremendous pressure empresses felt by virtue of their status. They were surely well aware of those among their predecessors who had been seen as either "the agents of virtues" or "the agents of destruction,"[144] and their moral conduct was, or was seen as being, closely tied with the fortunes of the imperial family and, by extension, the dynasty. By the very act of writing or compiling books of moral instruction for women, Ming imperial women authors not only represented themselves as paragons of womanhood but also reinforced their status as paragons of imperial motherhood, who had the authority to instruct. The ideal of *muyi tianxia* 母儀天下, or "paragon of motherhood for the empire," was behind all these titles by Ming empresses.

During the Ming, the empresses wrote for the betterment of imperial women. The Hongwu and Yongle emperors may have encouraged this tradition. Three months after his enthronement in 1368, Hongwu ordered the *Admonitions to Women* by Ban Zhao of the Eastern Han dynasty (25–220 CE) to be edited and annotated; copies were made available to his imperial women. Hongwu expressed his intention to his Hanlin editors:

The way to maintain order in the family starts with carefully setting the boundaries between [the duties of] the husband and wife. Although the empress and imperial concubines should be paragons of motherhood for the empire, they should not be allowed to interfere in government matters. So far as other palace women are concerned, they are there only to take care of affairs in the inner chambers and attend to the daily needs [of the empress and imperial concubines]. If they are treated with too much affection, they become spoiled and act without any due regard to their positions. . . .

---

141. Cited in Xu Daling and Wang Tianyou, *Mingchao shiliudi*, pp. 222–23.

142. Ibid., pp. 225–26.

143. Geiss, "The Chia-ching Reign, 1522-1566," pp. 442–43.

144. Here, I borrow the terms "agents of virtues" and "agents of destruction" from Lisa Raphals's study of women in early China, *Sharing the Light*, p. 11.

I order you to compile and explain *Admonitions to Women* and stories of model imperial consorts of the past so that my descendents will know to what standards they should adhere.[145]

Empress Ma, Hongwu's empress, was widely admired for her virtue. Each time she listened to female inner court officers recite the *Biographies of Exemplary Women*, she thought that the book should be edited, annotated, and made the standard of behavior in the inner chambers. The result is the *Biographies of Exemplary Women of the Past and Present*, which was, as noted above, published in 1403 on the Yongle emperor's order.[146] Hongwu's stern teachings and the Yongle emperor's vigilance in keeping palace women in check prompted some imperial consorts to write books for palace women.

Ming empresses wrote and compiled books to legitimize their places in the lineage of Ming imperial motherhood. In 1530 the Jiajing emperor ordered the Directorate of Ceremonial to publish his mother's manuscript of *Lessons for Women* together with two earlier titles, *The Biography of the Lofty Empress [Ma]* and the *Lessons for the Inner Chambers*, attributed to Empress Renxiao. These three titles were published at the same time to illustrate Jiajing's intention to reaffirm his biological mother's newly acquired status as empress dowager. As mentioned above, Jiajing inherited the throne from his uncle, the late Zhengde emperor, and the real empress dowager, Zhengde's empress, was still alive. By placing his mother in the line of Ming empress-authors, Jiajing further attempted to legitimize his mother's position in the line of paragons of Ming imperial motherhood, as had been done for Empress Renxiao more than a century earlier. The large, imposing seal "Treasures of Empress Dowager Zhangshengciren" impressed on the *Lessons for Women* (see Fig. 3.2) belonged to its author, Jiajing's mother. With it, she proudly and emphatically asserted her new and unsurpassed status.

Affirmation of imperial women authors' position as paragons of imperial motherhood is most clearly expressed in the prefaces that they wrote for their books. In the preface to *Lessons for the Inner Chambers*, Empress Renxiao claimed that day and night, she had received teachings from her mother-in-law, Empress Ma, and that in 1404, based on those teachings, she compiled *Lessons for the Inner Chambers* for the purpose of teaching palace women. Empress Dowager Zhangshengciren likewise claimed that her *Lessons for Women* was based on teachings she had received from her husband's

---

145. Cited in *MDCZSK*, p. 2. The English translation is my own.
146. Ibid., p. 28.

mother and grandmother, the empress of the Hongzhi emperor (r. 1488–1505) and the empress of the Chenghua emperor, respectively. Empress Zhang (d. 1536), the author of the postscript to *Lessons for Women* and Jiajing's second empress, also acknowledges the teachings she received directly from Jiajing's birth mother, Empress Dowager Zhangshengciren, and from her book *Lessons for Women*. Empress Zhang traces the unbroken line of paragons of imperial motherhood from Empress Ma, Empress Renxiao, and those after them, including Empress Dowager Zhangshengciren, and finally to herself.[147]

No longer extant, *Mirror for Women* by the Wanli emperor's biological mother was in all likelihood published in connection with her new status as Empress Dowager Cisheng when the Wanli emperor ascended the throne in 1573. As mentioned above, Cisheng was once a chambermaid in the household of Prince Yu. Having borne the prince a son, she was given the title of "honorable consort" (*guifei* 貴妃) in 1567 when Prince Yu became the Longqing emperor. Empress Dowager Cisheng used her publication to emphasize the legitimacy of her newly acquired status as empress dowager when her son Wanli was enthroned,[148] especially in view of the fact that Longqing's empress, Empress Dowager Rensheng 仁聖 (d. 1596), was still alive.[149]

Later, the Honorable Imperial Consort Zheng (Zheng huangguifei 鄭皇貴妃; d. 1630), the Wanli emperor's favorite concubine, would try to position herself in the line of Ming empress-writers by compiling and publishing her own edition of the *Stories of Model Women for the Inner Chambers, Illustrated and Explained* (*Guifan tushuo* 閨範圖説), a book originally compiled and published by the official Lü Kun 呂坤 (1536–1618), famed for his writings on education and local governance.[150] In the midst of an imperial succession controversy that lasted almost two decades, Zheng huangguifei's publication caused an uproar among court officials. It was clear to them that Zheng huangguifei was attempting to elevate her status to that of empress by virtue of her own publication and to make her own son the rightful successor to the throne, instead of the first-born imperial son, Changluo, the future Taichang emperor.

---

147. The 1530 inner court editions of the *Lessons for the Inner Chambers* and *Lessons for Women* used here for discussion are copies held at Harvard-Yenching Library, Rare Book T1682 0182 (3–4) and T1682 0182, respectively.

148. Soullière, "Palace Women in the Ming Dynasty," p. 21.

149. *MS*, "The Biography of Empress Dowager Cisheng," 114.1483.

150. I discuss Lü Kun's book below.

Except for a handful of Ming emperors' literary anthologies, titles by Ming imperial authors reflect the Ming imperial house's desire to control its family members, those who served them, and their relatives. They were also used to fulfill its particular political agendas, especially those concerning legitimacy issues. The Directorate of Ceremonial helped achieve those goals by publishing these books.

COURT OFFICIALS AS AUTHORS

The Directorate of Ceremonial also published titles compiled by court of ficials under imperial auspices. These include annotated versions of the classics and history books, Ming history, Ming laws and rites, and Ming administrative geography. Liu Ruoyu's list of Directorate of Ceremonial publications contains a large number of such books, for example, *Book of Poetry with Comprehensive Annotations and Commentaries*; *Imperially Compiled Grand Pronouncements* (*Yuzhi dagao* 御製大誥); *Legal Precedents of the Great Ming Dynasty* (*Da Ming lü* [*li*] 大明律 [例]); *Memorials by Eminent Court Officials of Successive Dynasties* (*Lidai mingchen zouyi* 歷代名臣奏議); *Records of [the Administrative Geography of] the Great Ming Under One Rule* (*Da Ming yitong zhi* 大明一統志); and *Records of Rites and Ceremonies of the Brilliant Ming* (*Huang Ming dianli zhi* 皇明典禮誌).

These titles share one feature: they are large multiauthor productions intended to educate the emperor. Their chief compilers were usually senior grand secretaries, assisted by junior grand secretaries and Hanlin academicians. Many of the classics and history books were annotated in colloquial language for ease of comprehension and were intended for the instruction of the emperor, especially young emperors. They were "imperial readers" and reflect the widespread interest in influencing the minds of present and future rulers that Hung-lam Chu and Julia Murray explore in their chapters in this volume. The titles *Straightforward Explanation of the Comprehensive Mirror for Aid in Governance* (*Tongjian zhijie* 通鑑直解); *Straightforward Explanation of the Book of Documents* (*Shujing zhijie* 書經直解); and the *Emperor's Mirror, Illustrated and Discussed* (*Dijian tushuo* 帝鑑圖説), also cited by Liu Ruoyu in his list of Directorate of Ceremonial publications, were compiled and annotated by the Grand Secretary Zhang Juzheng 張居正 (1525–82) and his Hanlin subordinates in the early 1570s for the young Wanli emperor's education.[151]

---

151. For an analysis of imperial readers in general and the *Emperor's Mirror, Illustrated and Discussed* in particular, see Julia Murray's chapter in this volume, pp. 231–68.

Ming emperors and elite eunuchs used these works on Ming laws and precedents, rites, and history as reference tools, for instance, when writing the final versions of imperial pronouncements. During the preparations for the enthronement ceremonies of the early seventeenth-century Tianqi emperor, eunuchs in the Directorate of Ceremonial busily produced all the imperial announcements for that occasion. A request to confer the title "empress" upon the future Tianqi emperor's principal wife was approved by the keeper of imperial seals and was ready to be sent to the outer court officials. Some Directorate of Ceremonial eunuchs, however, raised a concern that since a proper title had not been chosen and conferred on the future emperor's deceased mother, the request might be seen as inappropriate. For relevant precedents, they immediately consulted the *Imperial Decrees of the Brilliant Ming* (*Huang Ming zhaozhi* 皇明詔制) published by the Directorate of Ceremonial.[152] This not only illustrates again the importance of the Directorate of Ceremonial publications but also makes clear that elite eunuchs challenged literati officials' monopoly over written records and ritual knowledge.

It is clear that the Directorate of Ceremonial's publications were sanctioned by the emperor and catered almost exclusively to him, his immediate family, and the inner court's elite male and female personnel. Although some works circulated outside the Forbidden City, the Directorate of Ceremonial was not a publishing house for general authors and readers. With the exception of the anonymous authors of many of the reference works, Liu Ruoyu's Directorate of Ceremonial publication inventory list includes only five titles by nonmembers of the imperial family written during the Ming period, such as *Selected Beauties from the Forest of Poetic Songs* (*Cilin zheyan* 詞林摘艷), a collection of musical pieces selected from popular dramas compiled by Zhang Lu 張祿 (fl. 1525); the aforementioned *Poetic Songs of Yongxi*, a collection of musical plays compiled by Guo Xun; and *The Four Essentials of Living in the Mountains* (*Shanju siyao* 山居四要), compiled by Wang Rumao 汪汝懋 (1308–69), a book about healthy living.

Like *Popular Explication of the History of the Three Kingdoms*, also reprinted by the Directorate of Ceremonial, the first two titles were probably seen primarily as entertainment pieces. The last is about personal hygiene. They were not intended to express the authors' political ideologies, and the imperial court therefore allowed the Directorate of Ceremonial to publish them. The fifth book is *The Eight Virtues, Illustrated and Discussed* (*Baxing*

---

152. ZZZ, 23.2139.

tushuo 八行圖説), a morality book compiled by Grand Secretary Shen Li 沈鯉 (1531–1615).[153] It probably made the Directorate of Ceremonial's publication list because of its moral didacticism, which the Ming imperial court supported.

The Directorate of Ceremonial seldom published works by palace eunuchs.[154] One rare exception is Yan Hong 晏宏 (fl. mid-fifteenth century), who participated in the publication of the *Comprehensive Annotations of the Outlined Mirror for Aid in Governance* (*Zizhi tongjian gangmu jishuo* 資治通鑑綱目集説).[155] According to Liu Ruoyu, palace eunuchs loved and admired this title, and the Directorate of Ceremonial printed it repeatedly. It was widely known in the inner court as Yan Hong's *Zizhi tongjian gangmu jishuo* 晏宏資治通鑑綱目集説.[156] Liu Ji's 劉璣 (1457–1532) preface to the book sheds light on the work's popularity among eunuchs. Liu indicates that Yan Hong supplements what is lacking in the *Abstract of the Comprehensive Mirror for Aid in Governance* edited by Zhu Xi by providing pronunciation notations and information on conferring posthumous titles, orthodoxies, and geographies. Yan's book also contains scholarship on *Abstract of the Comprehensive Mirror for Aid in Governance* by earlier historians. Obviously palace eunuchs found Yan's book useful because of its comprehensiveness. The popularity of Yan Hong's book among palace eunuchs is another indication of eunuchs' literacy and their aggressive pursuit of knowledge.

Some Observations on the Two-Way Mobility of Texts

"Two-way mobility" refers to the fact that just as some inner court editions traveled beyond the Forbidden City, books produced outside the City also flowed into the inner court. During the Hongwu reign, searching for good editions of books to enrich the new empire's collection of works in the imperial library, the Ming court ordered the Ministry of Rites to buy books

---

153. The eight virtues are loyalty, filial piety, benevolence, kindness, honesty, righteousness, harmoniousness, and peacefulness. The fifth title is the *Comprehensive Annotations of the Outlined Mirror for Aid in Governance* discussed below.

154. The eunuch Wang Ao 王翺 (b. 1529), a graduate of the Inner Court School, worked his way up to serve in the Directorate of Ceremonial. His anthologies of poetry and essays were published outside the court during the Wanli era; see *ZZZ*, 22.2129.

155. This title was compiled by Fu An 扶安 (1454–1525) and annotated by Yan Hong. It was first published in Shanxi province when Yan Hong was grand commander of the region; see the book's preface by Liu Ji 劉璣, dated 1529, copy held at Harvard-Yenching Library, Rare Book T2512 2532.5.

156. *ZZZ*, 22.2131.

throughout the empire and to have commercial publishing houses make impressions of all their printing blocks. The effort continued well into the Jiajing period.[157] The Ming court not only bought books and printing blocks from commercial publishers in Jianyang, Fujian,[158] a prosperous commercial printing center since the Song dynasty, but also had good editions in private collections hand-copied.[159] Lucille Chia suggests that the Ming government's book purchases included editions of the Four Books and the Five Classics that had relatively complete commentaries.[160] Although these early Ming Jianyang publications may have served as master copies for many imperial publications, late Ming Jianyang publications, particularly those that appeared in the reading lists for the civil service examinations, would become targets of government surveillance because of their poor textual integrity (see below).

The Wanli emperor is said to have been fond of reading popular books, including detective stories.[161] Several times a year, elite eunuchs at the Directorate of Ceremonial and the eunuch managers of his living quarters, the Hall of Imperial Tranquility (Qianqinggong 乾清宮), would venture out of the Forbidden City and purchase newly published books in the capital for the emperor's perusal. Each book-shopping spree yielded no less than a hundred titles, including morality and medical treatises; musical dramas; fiction; books on alchemy and divination; and Buddhist works, many of which were illustrated. For instance, the eunuch Chen Ju 陳矩 (d. 1607) acquired Lü Kun's *Stories of Model Women for the Inner Chambers, Illustrated and Expounded; Mirror for Conduct of Life from History* (Renjing yangqiu 人鏡陽秋), a finely illustrated imprint compiled and published by the renowned Huizhou bibliophile Wang Tingna 汪廷訥 (fl. first half of the seventeenth century); and *Extraordinary Traces of the Immortals and Buddhist Deities* (Xianfo qizong 仙佛奇蹤) by Hong Zicheng 洪自誠 (fl. 1596), also illustrated.[162]

Several other popular titles appear on Liu Ruoyu's Directorate of Ceremonial's publication inventory list: *Selected Beauties from the Forest of Poetic Songs; The Eight Virtues, Illustrated and Discussed; Stories of the Origin of Gautama Shakyamuni and His Manifestations* (Shishi yuanliu yinhua shiji 釋氏源流應化

---

157. Zhang Lian, "Mingdai zhuanzhi wenhua zhengce," pp. 358–59.

158. Ibid., p. 359; Chia, *Printing for Profit*, p. 175.

159. Zhang Lian, "Mingdai zhuanzhi wenhua zhengce," p. 359.

160. Chia, *Printing for Profit*, p. 175.

161. Ray Huang, *1587*, p. 31.

162. ZZZ, 1.1885.

事跡); *Popular Explication of the History of the Three Kingdoms*, and *Poetic Songs of Yongxi*. All these titles illustrate Wanli's wide and varied reading interests, giving us a glimpse of the diverse ingredients of inner court culture. Although space does not allow a full investigation of the interactions between the Ming court culture and non-court culture represented by books and the significance of these interactions, a few initial observations are possible.

THE FLOW OF MORALITY BOOKS

The Outward Movement and Its Impact.   One major category of publications by the imperial court was the exhortation book. To forestall the moral decay that he believed had characterized the late Yuan period, the Hongwu emperor ordered that books of exhortation written in easily understood colloquial language be disseminated among the general populace.[163] Two preeminent examples are the *Imperially Compiled Great Pronouncements* (*Yuzhi dagao* 御製大誥), and the *Public Bulletin for the Cultivation of People* (*Jiaomin bangwen* 教民榜文). First published in the inner court, the *Great Pronouncements* contains three separate compilations completed between 1385 and 1386;[164] the *Public Bulletin* was promulgated in 1398.[165] To encourage familiarity with the moral instructions in these compilations, Hongwu repeatedly ordered that they be taught at all levels of public schools, and that village youngsters and civil service candidates who could recite passages from them be rewarded.[166] These two titles emphasize the importance of all Confucian moral teachings, such as those on the five human relations, the four ethical principles (*siwei* 四維), and the eight cardinal virtues (*bade* 八德).[167]

It is not clear to what extent Hongwu's edicts were carried out during the long history of the Ming. The fact that he repeatedly issued similar edicts suggests that the imperial order was not being observed even during

———

163. *CGZS*, pp. 49–50.

164. The earliest of the three compilations was completed in October 1385; the second title, *Imperially Compiled Great Pronouncements, Sequel* (*Yuzhi dagao xubian* 御製大誥續編) was completed in March 1386, and the last, compiled in December 1386, was entitled *Imperially Compiled Great Pronouncements, Third Compilation* (*Yuzhi dagao sanbian* 御製大誥三編); see *CGZS*, p. 29.

165. *CGZS*, p. 56.

166. Such imperial edicts include those dated June 1387, 1390, and 1391; cited in *CGZS*, pp. 54–55.

167. The *Great Pronouncements* also contains regulations regarding government administration at all levels and for all judicial matters. The four ethical principles are propriety, justice, honesty, and a sense of shame.

his reign. As Sakai Tadao indicates, however, these two works were incorporated into many village covenants (*xiangyue* 鄉約), or rules of conduct for villagers, often compiled by retired or acting local government officials, National University students, and successful candidates in the local civil service examination.[168] The contents of the *Great Pronouncements* and *Public Bulletin* also seeped into popular works, such as the encyclopedic *Literary Forest of Collected Treasures and Ten Thousand Scrolls of Multitude Sorts of Stuff* (*Wenlin jubao wanjuan xingluo* 文林聚寶萬卷星羅).[169]

Popular works also consciously imitated and appropriated other morality books initially produced by the inner court. For example, the *Biographies of Exemplary Women of the Past and Present* was so popular that Ming commercial publishers created different editions, many of them illustrated for the general reading public's perusal.[170] Inspired by the Xuande emperor's *Book of the Five Human Relations* (*Wulun shu* 五倫書), which the imperial court promulgated in 1447, a certain Mr. Dong 董 published *The Five Human Relations, Illustrated and Discussed* (*Wulun tushuo* 五倫圖説) in 1588 after three years as a provincial chancellor of education.[171]

Popular morality books intended for female audiences in particular proliferated outside the imperial court. In addition to old titles that were appropriated and reprinted, private or family publications of biographies of contemporary female models also appeared in abundance; to name only a few, *Women's Mirror* (*Nüjing* 女鏡) by Xia Shufang 夏樹芳 (*juren* 1585); the illustrated *Models for Women* (*Nüfan* 女範) edited by Feng Ruzong 馮汝宗 (fl. early seventeenth century) in 1603; and *A Collection of Stories of Model Women* (*Nüfan bian* 女範編), also illustrated, edited by Huang Shangwen 黃尚文 in 1617. Both *Models for Women* and *Admonitions to Women* are included in the popular encyclopedia *A Required Book for a Household* (*Jüjia bibei* 居家必備) published during the late Ming period.

Lisa Raphals suggests that the boom in books for the moral guidance for women during the late Ming reflected a new social conservatism, manifested

---

168. For this and the organization of the village educational institutions, see *CGZS*, pp. 92–94.

169. Ibid., p. 58.

170. For a discussion of different editions and the appropriation of the *Biographies of Exemplary Women of the Past and Present*, see Raphals, *Sharing the Light*, pp. 113–38.

171. See Wan Guoqin's 萬國欽 (*js.* 1584) preface to Mr. Dong, *The Five Human Relations, Illustrated and Discussed* (reprinted—Haikoushi: Hainan chubanshe, 2001), p. 427. Standard bibliographies incorrectly identify Wan Guoqin as the book's author. For more titles inspired by the *Book on the Five Human Relationships*, see *CGZS*, p. 81.

by rituals and purity and female chastity cults.[172] Joanna Handlin Smith observes that during the late Ming, unprecedented numbers of women were active in the workforce, secret societies, and popular uprisings.[173] They therefore needed to be controlled. Extent records show that most readers for Ming palace women were written by women, but their popular counterparts were largely authored by men. Although the morality books by Ming empresses originated in the long tradition of imperial women authors writing for the betterment of palace women,[174] they were, after all, reflections of Ming emperors' desire to regulate their women. The rise of such morality books in Ming society at large reflected male anxiety over, or obsession with, the containment of women that was prevalent during the late Ming.[175] It is also true that the popularity of morality books for women outside the Forbidden City testifies to the imperial court's success in disseminating, through its own publications, the ideology that women, imperial or otherwise, needed to be regulated. That ideology was eagerly embraced by Confucian writers, male and female alike, outside the court.

The Ming imperial readers for women also had an international impact. A Chosŏn queen, Sohye wanghu Han ssi 昭惠王后韓氏 (1437–1504), compiled *Lessons for the Inner Chambers* (*Naehun* 內訓), published in 1475 and reprinted in 1621 in Korea. In 1408, the Ming imperial court gave the Korean court 50 copies of the *Biography of the Lofty Empress* [Ma] and 150 copies of the *Book of Exhortations*; both are attributed to Empress Renxiao.[176] The *Biography* contains a chapter on Empress Ma's lessons for imperial women. There is little doubt that Queen Sohye was inspired by it. She

---

172. Raphals, *Sharing the Light*, pp. 114–15.

173. Handlin, "Lü Kun's New Audience," pp. 26–28.

174. This tradition goes back at least to *Admonitions to Women* by Ban Zhao of the Eastern Han dynasty (25–220 CE), which was followed by, for instance, *Rules for Women* (*Nüze* 女則) by Empress Changsun 長孫, which was presented to Tang Emperor Taizong (r. 627–49) in 636; cited in Li Zhizhong, *Lidai keshe kaoshu*, pp. 1–2.

175. For this phenomenon, see also Ko, *Teachers of the Inner Chambers*.

176. The Ming court, like its Song counterpart, regularly gave books to its neighboring countries, including Siam, Korea, Japan, and Ryūkyū. Most of these books were the Ming state calendar, morality books, and Four Books and Five Classics and their commentaries. For example, in 1408, the Yongle court gave the Japanese court 100 copies each of the *Book of Exhortations* and *Lessons for the Inner Chambers*, compiled by Yongle's Empress Renxiao, *and* in 1589 the Wanli emperor bestowed on the Korean court a copy of the *Collected Administrative Statutes of the Great Ming*. For more complete lists of books given to the Korean and Japanese courts, see Zhang Lian, "Song Ming zhengfu zhi yuwai cishu," pp. 145–60.

also used the exact title of the work attributed to the Yongle emperor's Empress Renxiao.

Although the early Ming court's acquisition of Korean eunuchs and women as imperial consorts, chambermaids, cooks, singers, and dancers indicates the cosmopolitan nature of the Ming inner court personnel's composition during the fourteenth and fifteenth centuries,[177] Queen Sohye's *Lessons for the Inner Chambers* expressed the Chosŏn court's determination to "transform Korea into a normative Confucian society at the advent of the Chosŏn dynasty (1392–1910)."[178] Queen Sohye's book is written in classical Chinese, and her preface is dated the seventh year of the Chenghua reign (1475).[179] As noted above, the wide use of dates in the Ming state calendar in much diplomatic correspondence throughout East Asia clearly illustrates the Ming's suzerain status in relation to its neighboring countries.

The Inward Movement and Its Impact. During the Ming, popular readers for women found their way into the inner court. Examples include Lü Kun's *Stories of Model Women for the Inner Chambers, Illustrated and Expounded; Biographies of Exemplary Women; Book of Filial Piety for Women* (*Nü Xiaojing* 女孝經), a book said to have been authored by Madame Zheng of the Tang, which

---

177. For a discussion of the early Ming court's acquisition of Korean eunuchs, see Chan Hok-lam, "Ming chu Chaoxian ruchao huangguan juyu," pp. 57–93. For a discussion of the Ming and Qing imperial court's practice of acquiring Korean women and its impact, see Jiang Shunyuan, "Ming Qing gonggting Chaoxian cainü yanjiu."

178. Some Confucian ideologies were present in Korean histories as early as the twelfth century; see Haboush, "Filial Emotions and Filial Values," p. 129. Morality books for women continued to be popular in the Chosŏn dynasty well into the seventeenth century and beyond. Song Si-yŏl 宋時烈 (1607–89), a renowned Korean scholar of the Zhu Xi school of thought, would publish an anthology of women's readers, which included his own book *Admonitions to [My] Daughter* (*Kyenyosŏ* 戒女書), written on the occasion of his daughter's marriage, *Naehun*, and *Women's Four Books* (*Yosasŏ* 女四書) (ibid.). The last title is the Chinese book *Nü sishu* 女四書, popular during the late Ming and later in the Qing, which includes imperially sponsored titles as well as popular works: *Admonitions to Women; Lessons for the Inner Chambers* attributed to Empress Renxiao; *Women's Analects* (*Nü lunyu* 女論語) compiled by Song Ruoxin 宋若莘 of the Tang dynasty; and *Model Women: A Straightforward Record* (*Nüfan jielu* 女範捷錄), a book compiled by Wang Xiang's 王相 (17th c.) mother and edited by Wang, an official in the Wanli court.

179. See Empress Sohye wanghu Han ssi, *Naehun*, p. 11. This edition includes annotations in Korean by Yi Min-su.

was reprinted many times in the Ming;[180] and *Madame Cao's Admonitions to Women* (*Cao dagu Nüjie* 曹大家女誡).[181] With the exception of the first title, all were recarved and printed by the Directorate of Ceremonial.[182] These three titles were adopted into the curriculum for potential imperial consorts and candidates for offices at the Six Bureaus.

Lü Kun's *Stories of Model Women for the Inner Chambers, Illustrated and Expounded* was thrown into the spotlight during the highly contested imperial succession controversy during the Wanli period. As mentioned above, Zheng huangguifei used it as a basis to compile and publish her own edition of the book, in an attempt to elevate her status to that of empress in order to legitimize her own son's right to succeed to the throne. Although her edition of the book is no longer extant, Qing sources hold that a section of twelve stories of model empresses and imperial concubines, starting with the story of the Han Empress Ma and ending with her own story, was added to Lü Kun's original.[183] In autumn 1598, three years after the publication of Zheng huangguifei's book, printed pamphlets with an accusatory essay signed by one Zhu Dongji 朱東吉 flooded the capital.[184]

The essay was in fact created by Dai Shiheng 戴士衡 (*jinshi* 1589),[185] an outspoken scrutiny official in the Ministry of Personnel and a fervent defender of Changluo's right to be crown prince. It attacked Zheng huangguifei for drawing an outrageous parallel between her book and *Admonitions to Women* and *Lessons for Women* in her preface to her edition,[186] because empresses had compiled these two works. The essay also accused Zheng huangguifei and her family of trying to influence the emperor's decision regarding the imperial succession issue.[187] The Zheng family quickly circulated its own printed flyers accusing Dai of fabricating charges and pleaded with the Wanli emperor for a thorough investigation. In response to the Zheng family's request, the Wanli emperor issued this statement:

---

180. Among the extant Ming editions are the one published during the Jiajing period by the Gu family and the edition published by Mao Jin 毛晉 (1599–1659).

181. The word 家 in 曹大家 is pronounced as 姑 (*gu*). The author of *Nüjie*, Ban Zhao, is called 曹大家 because her husband's family name was Cao; see *Cihai*, 1: 1407.

182. *ZZZ*, 18.2085.

183. Gu Yingtai, *Mingshi jishi benmo* (hereafter cited as *JSBM*), 67.1067; *YCXP*, p. 217. See also *MS, juan* 226, "Biography of Lü Kun," p. 2608.

184. This essay is preserved in *ZZZ*, 1.1890–91.

185. Ibid., p. 1887.

186. The preface is preserved in ibid., p. 1889.

187. Ibid., p. 1890.

It was I who gave the *Guifan tushuo* to [Zheng] huangguifei. I thought it would be a good idea [for her] to read it whenever she had time, since its content and purpose are more or less similar to those of the *Nüjian* [by my birth mother Empress Dowager Cisheng]. For their personal grudges, Dai Shiheng and his party have many times banded together and fabricated charges. They have accused the inner court [of improper conduct] without any evidence. They have interfered with the imperial laws and statutes. They have brought false charges against the innocent and have misled people. How detestable they are indeed! I have already looked into the whole matter and understand it completely. There is no need for further investigation. This is the imperial order.[188]

Wanli stripped Dai of his official status and sent him to a border region for military service as punishment. Many of Dai's supporters who were implicated in connection with the essay were demoted.[189]

Imperial authors drew on other popular works collected by the imperial court. These include *Biographies of Exemplary Women of the Past and Present*, which is based on the *Biographies of Exemplary Women* attributed to Liu Xiang of the Han dynasty; and *Lessons for the Inner Chambers*, *Women's Mirror*, and *Lessons for Women*, all of which were inspired by the *Admonitions to Women* by Ban Zhao. By Ming times, both Han-dynasty works had become widely known and popular. The publication of Lü Kun's book, however, was a rare case that caused the imperial family much headache. It was also a rare case in which an imperial author's publication was under such close scrutiny that the Wanli emperor had to speak up on behalf of his favorite consort.[190] This may seem surprising, but then again the emperor himself was under constant scrutiny.

Although autocracy in imperial China reached its zenith in the Ming, as the Introduction to this volume notes, Ming emperors were not free to do whatever they wished. As Ray Huang observed nearly three decades ago, the Ming imperial court relied to an unprecedented degree on ideology to

---

188. The Wanli emperor's edict was attached to the Zheng family's printed flyers preserved in ibid., p. 1984.

189. *JSBM*, 67.1068.

190. This is a testimony to the fact mentioned earlier in this chapter that woodblock-printed books were circulated far and wide and subjected to public scrutiny. According to Zheng huangguifei's preface, she intended to promulgate her book throughout the realm. Although we do not know exactly how widely her book circulated, it was widely read in the capital city, Beijing. The sensational charges and counter charges between Dai and the Zheng family, and the Wanli emperor's public denunciation of Dai and his supporters had certainly helped the book draw attention.

govern, both in intensity and scope.[191] Not only did the officials of remonstrance, such as those in the Offices of Scrutiny in the Six Ministries, have
the right to admonish the emperor, all officials and Ming commoners were
in theory also obliged to do the same under Confucian precepts.[192] Although the emperor could refuse to listen and could even persecute those
who spoke up against his will, the burden was always his, because he had
to prove his virtue.

IMPERIAL CONTROL OF THE
TWO-WAY TRAFFIC IN BOOKS

The Ming imperial court desired total control of the two-way traffic in
books between the inner court and Ming society at large. As noted above,
the Wanli emperor entrusted elite eunuchs with the purchase of popular
books for the emperor's private collection. Presenting books to the throne
without imperial approval was an offense. As Julia Murray notes elsewhere
in this volume, Jiao Hong 焦竑 (1514–1620), the tutor to Heir Apparent
Changluo, was reprimanded when, without the required imperial request,
he tried to present the Wanli emperor a copy of his book *Cultivating Rectitude, Illustrated and Explained* (*Yangzheng tujie* 養正圖解) as part of Changluo's curriculum. Lü Kun was impeached for a similar offense. In 1595,
right after the publication of Zheng Huangguifei's augmented edition of
the book, Dai Shiheng accused Lü Kun of trying to establish a connection
with the inner court by presenting a copy of his book to Zheng Huangguifei's relative.[193] Lü Kun had to submit a memorial to the emperor to defend his innocence.[194] We already know that it was Chen Ju who brought
the copy of Lü Kun's book to the inner court. We also know that Dai Shi-
hong's impeachment of Lü Kun had more to do with factional politics
than with the book itself. The book was only a convenient excuse for Dai's
relentless criticisms of Lü Kun.[195] Dai's false accusation clearly illustrates

---

191. Ray Huang, *1587*, p. 88.
192. Lo Jung-pang, "Ming Policy Formulation," p. 50.
193. ZZZ, 1.1890.
194. *MS, juan* 226, "The Biography of Lü Kun," p. 2608, and *juan* 234, "The Biography of Dai Shiheng," pp. 2680–81.
195. In 1597, Dai again impeached Lü because Dai felt that things that Lü Kun had
discussed in his 1597 memorial to the emperor were not only improper but showed Lü's
flawed personal character. This time, Dai requested that Lü Kun be punished properly,

the impropriety and danger of presenting a book, or anything else for that matter, to the emperor and his family without imperial approval.

As part of the Ming court's control of imperial publications, the law prohibited private citizens from collecting and compiling proscribed books. *The Great Ming Code* states that a private householder who collected proscribed books such as those containing astronomical prophecies, based on which calendars were created, was to be punished by 100 strokes.[196] According to Liu Ruoyu, books on astronomical prophecy existed only in manuscript form for teaching eunuch students at the Office of the Sacred Platform. They were heavily guarded, apparently to prevent wide circulation.[197] As noted above, private publishers of calendars were subject to capital punishment. Before the Wanli reign, private Ming citizens were not allowed to collect works on Ming history.[198] Only scholar-officials who had been ordered to do so by the emperor could compile them, so as to ensure historical accuracy.[199]

The Ming court also prohibited private and commercial publishers from reprinting titles by imperial authors at will; this, too, was a crime punishable by death. Although the imperial court allowed government offices to reprint many imperially sponsored titles, they had to be exact reprints of the originals. No new interpretations or commentaries were to be included. In 1532, the administrative office of Jingzhou prefecture in the Southern Metropolitan region presented its own publication, *The Method of Reading the Great Ming Code* (*Da Ming lü dufa* 大明律讀法), to the imperial court. The angry Jiajing emperor responded, "*The Great Ming Code* was personally compiled by our founding father. How dare a later generation add supplements and commentaries to it and publish it at will!" He immediately had

———

but the Wanli emperor ignored his request, since Lü Kun had already retired (*MS*, 226.2608).

196. Jiang Yonglin, *The Great Ming Code*, p. 114.

197. *ZZZ*, 16.2031.

198. *MDCZSK*, p. 26. For instance, copies of the *Veritable Records of the Ming* were made available to the general public only after 1591; see Franke, "Historical Writing During the Ming," p. 89.

199. The Longqing emperor ordered the Ministry of Rites to burn the woodblocks of the *Comprehensive Chronicles of the Imperial Ming for Aid in Governance* (*Huang Ming zizhi tongji* 皇明資治通紀), a book dated 1555, by the provincial official Chen Jian 陳建 (1497–1567), which chronicled the history between the late Yuan period and the Zhengde reign (1506–21). The stated reason was that the book used nonofficial sources and hearsay, and its credibility was therefore compromised (*YHB*, 25.638).

the regional inspector prosecuted for negligence and the book's printing woodblocks burned.[200]

Plenty of evidence indicates, however, that the law had little effect on the book trade. For example, Hongwu's *Ancestral Injunctions* was recut and published in 1602 by the Jianyang commercial publishing house Dayoutang 大有堂.[201] During the late sixteenth and early seventeenth centuries, many commercial publishers reprinted several versions of the *Great Ming Code*, including some with commentaries.[202] Commentaries on *The Great Ming Code* were popular among commercial publishers because they fell into the category of the so-called *juyeshu* 舉業書, readers for the civil service examinations.[203]

The proliferation of commentaries on *The Great Ming Code* and other legal handbooks for magistrates also reflected the need to strengthen legal education among all levels of government officials. Many court ministers at the Hongzhi court attributed local officials' deficient legal knowledge to the outmoded nature of the book, originally compiled in 1367 by the first Ming emperor.[204] For these reasons, the imperial court might therefore have knowingly tolerated commercial reprints. Similarly, some Jianyang commercial publishers reprinted the *Records of the [Administrative Geography of] the Great Ming Under One Rule*, first published by the Directorate of Ceremonial in 1461.[205] Heavily guarded inner court manuscripts on astronomical prophecy were somehow transmitted to the outside world, however incomplete they may have been.[206] The imperial genealogy was also

---

200. Cited in Zhang Lian, "Mingdai zhuanzhi wenhua zhengce," p. 366.

201. A copy of this edition is in the collection of the Palace Museum Library, Beijing.

202. They include the 1599 *Lucid Commentaries on the Great Ming Code and Substatutes* (*Da Ming lüli zhushi xiangxing bingjian* 大明律例註釋詳刑冰鑑) and the *Newly Carved Precious Mirror for Governing the People: The Great Ming Code and Substatutes* (*Xinjuan da Ming lüli linmin baojing* 新鎸大明律例臨民寶鏡) published in 1632. For more titles related to *The Great Ming Code*, see Langlois and Morgan, "Ming Law," pp. 211–13.

203. In the Ming, provincial and metropolitan civil service examinations included a session on legal terms (Elman, "Changes in Confucian Civil Service Examinations," table 4.1, p. 114).

204. Langlois and Morgan, "Ming Law," pp. 202–4.

205. The reprints included the 1505 edition by Shenduzhai 慎獨齋 and the 1588 edition by Guirenzhai 歸仁齋.

206. *ZZZ*, 16.2031.

found on commercial publication lists,[207] perhaps reflecting its historical value and the public's fascination with royalty.

Although the circumstances under which these reprints were made are not clear, chances are that they were reprinted without imperial sanction. In fact, compared to the preceding Yuan and succeeding Qing dynasties, the Ming government had a rather lax attitude toward the book trade.[208] It abolished the Yuan government's practice of taxing book sales.[209] Further, government censorship of book publishing was largely limited to Confucian canonical titles, Ming history, and imperial publications. Even in these areas, government surveillance was not, as we have seen, carried out on a regular basis, and in 1591 the Ming court lifted the ban on the general public's collecting the *Veritable Records of the Ming*. Thereafter owning a copy of the *Veritable Records* became a status symbol among the rich.[210] The Ming state's lax attitude toward the book trade catalyzed the rapid growth of book publishing at all levels of government offices and among commercial publishing houses and private individuals, which reached its zenith in the late Ming period. It also facilitated the dissemination of scholarly knowledge, formerly monopolized by the educated elite, and helped ideologies regarded by the Ming ruling class as orthodox infiltrate the lives of the general populace.

---

207. See a copy of the edition published by Jiaqutang 嘉趣堂 in Wuxing, Jiangsu province, during the Jiajing era held at the Harvard-Yenching Library, Rare Book T9100 8415 (4).

208. In the Yuan, an author had first to present the manuscript to his local educational officials via a member of the gentry; it was then reviewed by higher levels of authority for approval; see Cai Cheng, *Jichuang conghua*, 19a. Official publications were reviewed by the Central Secretariat (Zhongshusheng 中書省), the core administrative unit of the Yuan central administration; see Lu Rong, *Shuyuan zaji*, 10.12a. In the Qing, a 1774 imperial edict announced that books containing antidynastic sentiments and heterodox opinions were to be burned together with their woodblocks; the subsequent literary inquisition lasted for the next fifteen years; see Brook, "Censorship in Eighteenth-Century China," p. 177. See also Guy, *The Emperor's Four Treasuries*, pp. 26–27.

209. The edict concerning the book trade was made in August 1638 (*MS*, 2.15).

210. Franke, "Historical Writing During the Ming," p. 752. The imperial court may have also lifted the ban on writing Ming history among individuals as well, such as the *Huang Ming zizhi tongji*, whose blocks were burned on the Longqing emperor's order (see note 199), but which reappeared in many different editions from the late sixteenth to the seventeenth century, including the 1630 supplemented edition by Dong Qichang 董其昌 (1555–1636), a renowned scholar-official, painter, calligrapher, and art theorist.

The Politics Surrounding the Directorate of Ceremonial
as the Imperial Publishing House

THE "DECLINE" OF THE DIRECTORATE
OF CEREMONIAL'S PUBLICATIONS

As discussed above, the finest Directorate of Ceremonial publications are characterized by elaborate page layouts, including the double fish tail, double lines in all four block borders, and black mouth designs. It is true that some non–Directorate of Ceremonial books published in the early Ming also show these features. They soon appeared less frequently, however. In fact, beginning in the Jiajing era, the black mouth design, a trademark of Yuan dynasty books, started to disappear from non–Directorate of Ceremonial books, and the white mouth design, a prominent feature of Song dynasty imprints, became the norm. The fish tail design all but disappeared (see Fig. 3.5),[211] thanks to many private literati publishers in the Suzhou area who preferred the Song style of imprints.[212] The preference for a simpler, less embellished, and more austere page layout might have had some connection with the Song literature movement (*Songwen yundong* 宋文運動) during the Jiajing period, in which the literary styles of Ouyang Xiu 歐陽 修 (1007–72) and Zeng Gong 曾鞏 (1019–83) of the Song dynasty were promoted. These two Song writers favored a flowing, simple, unembellished, and accessible language.[213]

Whereas literati publishers enjoyed the austere page layout, commercial publishers welcomed the new style because it cost less. The trend in page layout in the book trade outside the Forbidden City also made itself felt in

---

211. Mao Chunxiang, *Gushu banben changtan*, p. 64; and Li Zhizhong, *Zhongguo gudai shuji shi*, pp. 123–24. The book shown in Fig. 3.5 also features single lines on the four borders. An example of an inner court edition that has the white mouth design is the 1530 edition of the *Collection of Rites of the Great Ming*; see Fig. 3.6. Notice also that only one fish tail is featured.

212. Qu Yihua and Xun Changrong, *Zhongguo shuwenhua*, p. 61.

213. For an analysis of the Song literature movement and another movement that promoted the literary styles of Qin, Han, and Tang during the Ming, see Liu Dajie, *Zhongguo wenxue fada shi*, pp. 849–56. Li Zhizhong (*Zhongguo gudai shuji shi*, p. 124) also observes the connection between the literary movement and page layout design in woodblock printed books. However, Li does not differentiate between the two very different literary movements.

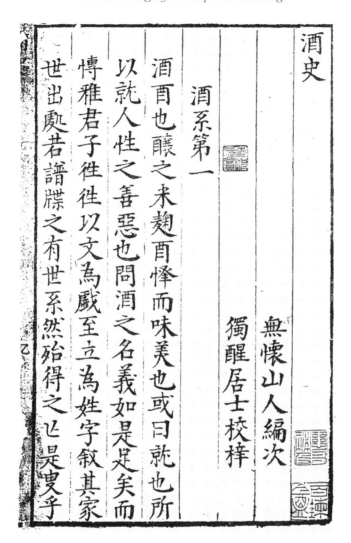

Fig. 3.5 Half of a leaf from *Jiushi* 酒史 published by Duxing jushi 獨醒居士 during the Longqing era (1567–72), showing the white mouth and single lines on the four borders designs. After Zhou Xinhui, *Mingdai banke tushi*, 1: 413.

the inner court publications. Many later Directorate of Ceremonial publications have a simple page layout featuring a single line on all four borders, a single fish tail, and white mouth designs. Thus, another element of non-court culture found its way into Ming court culture. The change may have been a deliberate aesthetic choice, reflecting the prevailing literati taste.

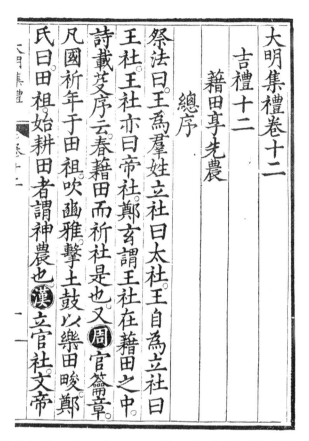

Fig. 3.6 Half of a leaf from the 1530 inner court edition of the *Da Ming jili* 大明集禮, showing the white mouth and single fish tail designs. Block frame 23.8 cm × 16.1 cm. After Zhou Xinhui, *Ming-dai banke tushi*, 1: 194.

However, it may instead have been that the late Ming emperors' lack of interest in imperial publishing caused eunuchs to invest less in the decorative excellence of imperial publications.[214]

—————

214. Compared to the three early Ming emperors, Hongwu, Yongle, and Xuande, later Ming emperors were far less personally involved in imperial publications, with the exception of the Jiajing emperor. Titles published on the imperial order during the last four reigns of the Ming include, in the Longqing reign (1567–72), only the 1570 edition of *Map of the Great Ming's Territory* (*Da Ming Yudi tu* 大明輿地圖); the 1587 edition of the *Collected Administrative Statutes of the Great Ming* and the 1579 *Essential Rules for the Feudal Princes* (*Zongfan yaoli* 宗藩要例) of the Wanli period; in the Tianqi reign, the 1624 edition of the *Supplement to the Elaboration of Meanings of the Great Learning* and the 1626 *Essential Records of the Three Reigns* (*Sanchao yaodian* 三朝要典); and in the Chongzhen era

The simpler page layout was also often accompanied by a decrease in the quality of paper and a smaller page size. For instance, the block frame of the 1613 inner court edition *Records of Rites and Ceremonies of the Brilliant Ming* measures only 21.1 × 14.6 cm,[215] compared to the 26–30 × 16–19 cm usually seen in the block frames of early Directorate of Ceremonial imprints. Moreover, beginning in the late sixteenth century, not only did the overall quality of the Directorate of Ceremonial's publications decline but also the number of publications decreased.[216] The correlation between the decline in the Directorate of Ceremonial's publishing enterprise and the decline of the Ming imperial court's fortunes is clear.

THE WANLI EMPEROR AND THE DIRECTORATE OF CEREMONIAL PUBLICATIONS

The eunuch Liu Ruoyu blamed the Wanli emperor for the decline of the Directorate of Ceremonial's publishing enterprise. In 1638, when Liu Ruoyu wrote his *Weighted and Unbiased Records*, the Directorate of Ceremonial still had intact woodblocks for 3,188 volumes (*ben* 本), both secular and religious.[217] According to Liu, this equaled only 30–40 percent of what had existed in the early 1570s.[218] In other words, in the early 1570s, the Directorate of Ceremonial's collection of its own publications may have amounted to around 8,000 volumes.

Liu Ruoyu lamented that the drastic decrease in the output of the Directorate of Ceremonial publications resulted from neglect, an implicit criticism of the Wanli emperor.[219] He observed that later in the Wanli reign, little attention was paid to scholarship and cultural matters. The book production efforts of the Directorate of Ceremonial were a shambles. The

---

(1627–44), the 1630 edition of the *Collected Administrative Statutes of the Great Ming* and the 1636 *Chongzhen Treatise on [Astronomy and] Calendrical Science* (*Chongzhen lishu* 崇禎曆書), the first form of the Jesuit astronomical encyclopedia in China. See *MDCZSK*, pp. 69, 71, 72–73; and Franke, "Historical Writing During the Ming," p. 750. Ming emperors' *baoxun* (precious injunctions) were in fact compiled posthumously by court officials when their respective Veritable Records were compiled.

215. See a copy of this edition held at Harvard-Yenching Library, Rare Book T4678 0214.

216. *ZZZ*, 18.2081.

217. Li Zhizhong, *Lidai keshu kaoshu*, p. 228.

218. *ZZZ*, 18.2082. Not included in this list were also handwritten books and non–Directorate of Ceremonial books collected for the emperor over time.

219. Ibid., pp. 2083–84.

eunuchs in charge had neither the knowledge to catalogue the books nor the ability to keep track of them. Even learned eunuchs were lackadaisical; their promotion seldom depended on what they might learn from books. Moreover, since Directorate of Ceremonial publishing was an inner court affair, outer court officials felt it would be improper to overstep their assigned responsibilities and speak to the emperor. As a result, artisans and cooks stole many books and sold them outside the palace. No one dared ask about the provenance of books in gold satin cases with imperial seals. Liu also reported that the space in the inner court compound formerly reserved for sunning the woodblocks was now used for vegetable gardens. Warped by moisture, the carved letters became illegible. Sometimes the letters would be planed off, and the woodblocks reused for other purposes. Worse, some became firewood. Others suffered from rats and worms.[220]

Banished to South China by the Wanli emperor as a result of the power struggles in the Directorate of Ceremonial, Liu Ruoyu was far from an unbiased observer. The decline of imperial publishing had already begun during the reign of Wanli's father, the Longqing emperor. Wanli is commonly criticized as inept and uninterested in government: beginning in the late 1580s, he held no imperial audiences for decades, ignored thousands of memorials, and abandoned altogether the hallowed institution of the thrice-monthly and daily lectures. As Kenneth Swope argues elsewhere in this volume, however, Wanli was keenly interested in such major state affairs as military campaigns and border defense. Rather, it was Wanli's disillusionment with his civil ministers and the bureaucracy as a whole that explains his refusal to hold formal audiences, respond to memorials by civil officials, and listen to lectures by Hanlin scholars about how a ruler should conduct himself. Liu Ruoyu's poignant comment that dust covered the imperial lecture hall[221] is another reminder that the ongoing tensions over who had the right to determine the role, behavior, and patronage of the emperor could sometimes have unexpected consequences. One consequence was the decline of the imperial publishing.

As a result of the Wanli emperor's battles with his civil bureaucracy and his focus on military affairs, inner court book production, inextricably linked to the educational and ideological enterprises described in the preceding pages, languished in neglect. The three depositories—the Depository of Chinese Classics, the Depository of Foreign Sutras, and the De-

---

220. *ZZZ*, 18.2081.
221. Ibid.

pository of Daoist Texts and Scriptures—were now also used to train young girls and eunuch boys to tend temples inside the imperial compound and to perform the religious rituals held in the Forbidden City.[222] From then on, the majority of the finest-quality books, especially the beautifully illustrated ones, would be produced by the many commercial as well as private publishers that dominated publishing in Ming China.[223] The interplay of wider late Ming socioeconomic trends (a flourishing publishing industry, the growth of high-end publishers, and a wealthy consumer market) and court dynamics (tensions over the emperor's role, personal relations, and increasingly rancorous factional politics) had a clear impact on this important feature of court culture, inner court publications.

QING SCHOLARS' VIEWS

Although the Ming author Taiping laoren ranked the Directorate of Ceremonial publications at the very top of his list of the best things of the Ming empire, Qing Confucian scholars criticized the same publications for their textual errors as well as, occasionally, their subject matter. Despite these publications' fine, elaborate designs, Qing book collectors also shunned them. They claimed that many of them had serious textual errors, such as incorrect characters or missing or jumbled passages, apparently the result of careless proofreading and collating before printing.[224] Their complaints have some basis. As Liu Ruoyu pointed out, the recut edition of the *Supplement to the Extended Meanings of the Great Learning (Daxue yanyi bu* 大學衍義補)[225] published by the Directorate of Ceremonial had many textual errors. Liu blamed the eunuchs who supervised the transcribing and carving.[226]

These textual and printing errors also appear, however, in publications by such government offices as the National University in both Nanjing and

---

222. Each year when new eunuchs and young girls were admitted to the inner court, a number of them would be selected and sent to the three depositories, where they were trained for these purposes. They did not have to become full-fledged monks or nuns if they did not wish to do so (*ZZZ*, 16.2035, 2038, 2041).

223. For instance, in the late sixteenth century during the Wanli reign, the Huang family commercial publishing house in Huizhou produced some of the best-quality books, many of them beautifully illustrated dramas or musical plays; see, e.g., Zhou Xinhui, *Mingdai banke tushi*, 4: 250–51.

224. Ye Dehui, *Shulin qinghua*, 5.97.

225. This title was compiled by the Ming Grand Secretary Qiu Jun 丘濬 (1429–95), originally dated 1487.

226. *ZZZ*, 7.1935.

Beijing. During the Ming, the National University produced more books than any other government office, including the Directorate of Ceremonial. Students in the National University played an important role in collating and proofreading its publications. Yet they were often carelessly done, and as a result, sometimes leaves might be missing from a book or might be assembled out of sequence.[227] The Ming scholar Shen Defu 沈德符 (1578–1642) called their wood blocks *zaimu* 災木, "disastrous woodblocks"—woodblocks that caused disasters[228]—because they misled or misinformed students.

Moreover, the characters in the final versions of the Nanjing National University publications were often a mixture of rounded and square forms, and their ink values differ. This resulted from the use of *buban* 補版 (repaired woodblocks). The majority of the woodblocks used for history books published by the National University in Nanjing had previously been used by the Song dynasty National University and the government-sponsored academies of the Yuan dynasty. Many of the carved characters had grown blurred and illegible from repeated printing. The worn portion of the block was carved out, and the missing characters were carved on a new piece of wood, which was then inserted into the sunken space. Books produced by the National University in Nanjing were thus called *da hualian* 大花臉 (big, messy face) editions. The result may be seen in Fig. 3.7, in which the characters in the first few lines differ from the rest in terms of size and style.[229] Moreover, the ink values are inconsistent.

After the Ming capital was moved to Beijing in 1421, the National University there had new woodblocks carved and issued books based on those produced by the National University in Nanjing. Although the characters were generally uniform in size and style, many textual and collating errors remained.[230] In the preface of the 1573 edition of the *Encyclopedia for Beginners* (*Chuxueji* 初學記), the commercial publishing house Chongwentang 崇文堂 boasts of its careful, meticulous proofreading and its correction of all the textual errors found in the edition published by the National University in Beijing.[231]

———

227. Ye Dehui, *Shulin qinghua*, 7.151.

228. Cited in Zhou Xinhui, *Mingdai banke tushi*, 1: 8.

229. This particular book was in fact produced by the Beijing National University. Apparently the blocks were old ones from the Nanjing National University.

230. Zhou Xinhui, *Mingdai banke tushi*, 1: 8.

231. Wei Yinru and Wang Jinyu, *Guji banben jianding congtan*, p. 86.

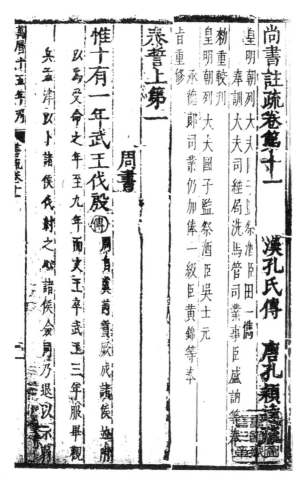

Fig. 3.7 Half of a leaf from the Wu Shiyuan (*js.* 1619) edition of the *Shisanjing zhushu* 十三經注疏 using woodblocks of the 1587 edition of the same title published by the Beijing Guozijian 國子監. After Zhou Xinhui, *Mingdai banke tushi*, 2: 3.

Many commercial publishers, however, committed similar and sometimes more egregious offenses. Concerned with the many errors made in the commentaries of commercial editions of the Four Books and the Five Classics, in 1447 the imperial court commanded that the Directorate of Ceremonial versions of these titles be used as master copies by commercial bookstores for reprinting.[232] Again, in 1523, during the Jiajing era, it was also discovered that the pocket-size editions of the Four Books and the

---

232. Pan Chengbi and Gu Tinglong, *Mingdai banben tulu chubian*, p. 164.

Five Classics published by Fujian commercial bookstores contained serious collating errors. Fearing that these errors would affect beginners and civil service examination participants alike, the office of the Fujian Provincial Surveillance Commission issued a notice requiring that the commercial publishers have these books checked and double-checked and carefully collated in accordance with the government-sanctioned editions. Furthermore, the names of the woodblock carvers were to be added at the end of each book. Publishers and the woodblock carvers who did not follow the regulations would be prosecuted.[233]

Although it is not clear to what extent the laws were enforced, Lucille Chia's study of Jianyang commercial publishers during the Ming indicates that local and regional officials in Fujian were involved in commercial publishing in part to regulate the quality of scholarly publications in Jianyang.[234] In fact, the Jianyang prefectural government confiscated and occasionally destroyed commercial printing blocks.[235] The enforcement of the laws is also seen in the Jiajing-era editions of the Five Classics published by the Jianning prefectural government, which carefully list the names of the block carvers.[236]

These measures attest to the Ming imperial court's periodic efforts to protect the sanctity of its own publications. They also had serious political implications. Since the Four Books and Five Classics formed the major curriculum for all levels of Ming civil service examinations, any errors in the commentary could be seen as contempt of imperial authority and a threat to the officially sanctioned interpretations of the classics, which during the Ming were those of Cheng Yi 程頤 (1033–1107) and Zhu Xi 朱熹 (1130–1200).[237] In this regard, the Directorate of Ceremonial's trusted role in safeguarding orthodoxy illustrates the eunuch agency's political and ideological significance.

So far as subject matter is concerned, the editors of the Siku quanshu 四庫全書 (Comprehensive collection of books under the four classifications), compiled under the auspices of the Qing Qianlong emperor (r. 1736–95), criticized the Directorate of Ceremonial for publishing petty and vul-

---

233. Ye Dehui, *Shulin qinghua*, 7.149.

234. Chia, *Printing for Profit*, p. 175.

235. This is recorded in the 1504 supplement to an earlier Jianyang local history (cited in ibid., p. 179).

236. Ibid., p. 178.

237. Elman, "Changes in Confucian Civil Service Examinations," pp. 114–15.

gar books of no scholarly significance, namely primers, such as *Poems by Child Prodigies* (*Shentongshi* 神童詩) compiled by Wang Zhu 汪洙 (*js.* 1100) and *One Hundred Family Names*.[238] Although lacking scholarly significance, these primers nonetheless were indispensable in the education of child emperors and in the curricula for eunuchs and palace women, whose literacy, as we have seen, had important political consequences. Qing scholars' criticisms of these books therefore missed the point. Besides, not all the publications by government offices were scholarly in nature. As a matter of fact, the late Qing and Republican scholar Ye Dehui 葉德輝 (1864–1927) did not approve of the fact that the Ming Bureau of Surveillance in Beijing published such popular novels as *Popular Explication of the Histories of the Three Kingdoms* and *Stories of the Water Margins* (水滸傳),[239] probably because he saw them as entertainments, not as serious scholarly books.

In the end, however, Qing scholars' criticisms of Directorate of Ceremonial publications were less about their textual errors or frivolous subject matter and more an indication of Confucian scholars' uneasiness that the Directorate of Ceremonial, a eunuch agency, published important textbooks for the civil service examinations, not to mention books for the education of the Son of Heaven. As Julia Murray, Hung-lam Chu, and David Robinson argue elsewhere in this volume, Confucian scholars claimed education, including education of the imperial family, as their unique privilege and responsibility. The Directorate of Ceremonial's inroads into their special preserve were especially galling. In the minds of Confucian scholars, nothing was more inappropriate, or perhaps humiliating, than the Directorate of Ceremonial's usurpation of their responsibilities in these matters. Rather than acknowledging the existence of multiple points of legitimacy, literati officials cast eunuch power as an aberration, berating the court's weakness and impropriety. Ye Dehui expressed these sentiments well: "The reason that the big-character Sutra and Classics Depository editions of the Four Books and the Five Classics have received such severe criticism was not entirely because of the sloppy collating. The Ming government's laxity in principle may be seen in the fact that it entrusted eunuchs with matters related to culture and education."[240]

---

238. Zhou Xinhui, *Mingdai banke tushi*, 1: 6.
239. Zhou Hongzu, *Gujin shuke*, 2.2b.
240. Ye Dehui, *Shulin qinghua*, 5.97–98.

Conclusion

By investigating the Ming imperial court's publication of texts and by delineating the patterns of their production and consumption, I have tried to demonstrate that the Directorate of Ceremonial had a special role and power in the Ming court through its publication of the texts used or written by the imperial family and palace eunuchs' deep involvement in education in the Forbidden City. The emperor's education depended on books published by the Directorate of Ceremonial. Memorials to the emperor passed through this eunuch agency, and his responses to them were often shaped by it, sometimes even written by the eunuchs themselves, acting as the emperor's proxies.

The Directorate of Ceremonial published the books that the emperor used to regulate his family, consorts, ministers, subjects, and surrounding countries. On issues ranging from the education and roles of women, determination of the proper imperial successor, and regulation of all affairs on earth in accordance with Heaven through the official calendar, the Directorate of Ceremonial played a central role through its unique publishing enterprise. The extensive classical educations of elite eunuchs were often vital to their rise to power in the inner court. Their education and duties placed them in competition with the traditional arbiters of power in officialdom, the Confucian literati.

Through the texts published by the Directorate of Ceremonial, one can often trace the dynamic balance of influence between the emperor and his subjects; between the educated elite eunuchs and the scholar-officials; and between the inner court and the outer world. Through artistic styles and materials used over time in Directorate of Ceremonial publications, one can trace the subtle influences—economic, philosophical, social, political, and personal—on the art of books throughout the realm.

Works Cited

Brook, Timothy. "Censorship in Eighteenth-Century China: A View from the Book Trade." *Canadian Journal of History* 23, no. 2 (Aug. 1998): 177–96.

Cai Cheng 蔡澄. *Jichuang conghua* 雞窗叢話. Reprinted—Taibei: Kuangwen shuju, 1969.

CGZS, see Sakai Tadao, *Zōho Chūgoku zensho no kenkyū*

Chan Hok-lam 陳學霖. "The Chien-wen, Yung-lo, Hung-hsi, and Hsüan-te Reigns, 1399–1435." In *CHC*, 7: 182–304.

———. "Ming chu Chaoxian ruchao huangguan juyu—Hai Shou shiji tansuo" 明初朝鮮入朝官官舉隅—海壽事蹟探索. *Gugong xueshu jikan* 16, no. 4 (1999): 57–93.

CHC, see Mote and Twitchett, *Cambridge History of China*

Chen Shiqi 陳詩啓. *Mingdai guanshougongye de yanjiu* 明代官手工業的研究. Wuhan: Hubei renmin chubanshe, 1958.

Cihai 辭海. Taibei: Zhonghua shuju, 1975.

Chia, Lucille. *Printing for Profit: The Commercial Publishers of Jianyang, Fujian (11th to 17th Centuries).* Cambridge: Harvard University Asia Center, 2002.

Connery, Leigh Christopher. *The Empire of the Text: Writing and Authority in Early Imperial China.* New York: Rowman & Littlefield, 1998.

Dardess, John W. *Blood and History in China: The Donglin Faction and Its Repression, 1620–1627.* Honolulu: University of Hawai'i Press, 2002.

de Bary, Wm. Theodore, and John W. Chaffee, eds. *Neo-Confucian Education: The Formative Stage.* Berkeley: University of California Press, 1989.

DMHD, see Shen Shixing et al., *Da Ming huidian*

Edgren, Sören, ed. *Chinese Rare Books in American Collections.* New York: China House Gallery and China Institute in America, 1985.

Elman, Benjamin A. "Changes in Confucian Civil Service Examinations from the Ming to the Qing Dynasty." In *Education and Society in Late Imperial China, 1600–1900,* ed. idem and Alexander Woodside. Berkeley: University of California Press, 1994, pp. 109–49.

Elman, Benjamin A., and Alexander Woodside, eds. *Education and Society in Late Imperial China, 1600–1900.* Berkeley: University of California Press, 1994.

Empress Dowager Zhangshengciren 章聖慈仁皇太后 (d. 1538). *Nüxun* 女訓. 1530 inner court ed. Copy at Harvard-Yenching Library (Cambridge, MA), Rare Book T1682 0182.

Empress Renxiao wenhuanghou 仁孝文皇后 (1362–1407). *Neixun* 內訓. 1530 inner court ed. Copy at Harvard-Yenching Library (Cambridge, MA), Rare Book T1682 0182.

Empress Sohye wanghu Han ssi 昭惠王后韓氏 (1437–1504). *Naehun* 內訓. Reprinted with annotations by Yi Min-su 李民樹. Seoul: Iisin sojok chu'lp'ansa, 1992.

Fisher, Carney T. *The Chosen One: Succession and Adoption in the Court of Ming Shizong.* Boston: Allen & Unwin, 1990.

Franke, Wolfgang. "Historical Writing During the Ming." In *CHC*, 7: 726–82.

Fu An 扶安 (1454–1525), comp. *Zizhi tongjian gangmu jishuo* 資治通鑑綱目集説. Shanxi, 1529? Copy held at Harvard-Yenching Library (Cambridge, MA), Rare Book T2512 2523.5.

Geiss, James. "The Chia-ching Reign, 1522–1566." In *CHC*, 7: 440–510.

———. "Peking Under the Ming, 1368–1644." Ph.D. diss., Princeton University, 1979.

Gu Yingtai 谷應泰 (1620–1690). *Mingshi jishi benmo* 明史紀事本末. Reprinted—Shanghai: Shanghai guji chubanshe, 1994.

Guy, R. Kent. *The Emperor's Four Treasuries: Scholars and the State in the Late Ch'ien-lung Era.* Cambridge: Council on East Asian Studies, Harvard University, 1987.

Haboush, JaHyun Kim. "Filial Emotions and Filial Values." *Harvard Journal of Asiatic Studies* 55, no. 1 (1995): 129–77.

Handlin, Joanna. "Lü Kun's New Audience: The Influence of Women's Literacy on 16th Century Thought." In *Women in Chinese Society*, ed. Margery Wolf and Roxane Witke. Stanford: Stanford University Press, 1975, pp. 1–38.

He Weizhi 何偉幟. *Mingchu de huanguan zhenghzhi* 明初的宦官政治. Jiulong: Wenxing tushu, 2000.

Hsieh Bao Hua 謝寶華. "From Charwoman to Empress Dowager: Serving-women in the Ming Palace." *Ming Studies* 42 (1999): 26–80.

Huang, Ray. "The Lung-ch'ing and Wan-li Reigns, 1567–1620." In *CHC*, 7: 511–84.

———. *1587, A Year of No Significance: The Ming Dynasty in Decline.* New Haven: Yale University Press, 1981.

———. *Taxation and Government Finance in Sixteenth-Century Ming China.* New York: Cambridge University Press, 1974.

Huang Zhangjian 黃彰健. "Lun *Zuxun lu* suoji Mingchu huanguan zhidu" 論祖訓錄所記明初宦官制度. In idem, *Ming Qing shi yanjiu conggao* 明清史研究叢稿. Taibei: Taiwan Shangwu yinshuguan, 1977, pp. 1–30.

Hucker, Charles O. *A Dictionary of Official Titles in Imperial China.* Stanford: Stanford University Press, 1985.

———. "The Tung-lin Movement of the Late Ming Period." In *Chinese Thought and Institutions*, ed. John K. Fairbank. Chicago: University of Chicago Press, 1957.

Jang, Scarlett. "Issues of Public Service in the Themes of Chinese Court Painting." Ph.D. diss., University of California at Berkeley, 1989.

———. "Form, Content, and Audience: A Common Theme in Painting and Woodblock-Printed Books of the Ming Dynasty." *Ars Orientalis* 27 (1997): 1–26.

Jiang Shunyuan 姜舜源. "Ming Qing gongting Chaoxian cainü yanjiu" 明清宮廷朝鮮采女研究. *Gugong bowuyuan yuankan* 4 (1997): 79–89.

Jiang Yonglin, trans. *The Great Ming Code: Da Ming Lü* 大明律. Seattle: University of Washington Press, 2005.

JSBM, see Gu Yingtai, *Mingshi jishi benmo*

Ko, Dorothy. *Teachers of the Inner Chambers: Women and Culture in Seventeenth-Century China.* Stanford: Stanford University Press, 1994.

Ku Chieh-kang 顧頡剛 and L. Carrington Goodrich. "A Study of Literary Persecution During the Ming." *Harvard Journal of Asiatic Studies* 3, no. 3/4 (Dec. 1938): 254–311.

Langlois, John, Jr. "The Hung-wu Reign, 1368–1398." In *CHC*, 7: 107–81.

Langlois, John, Jr., and J. P. Morgan. "Ming Law." In *CHC*, 8: 172–213.

Li Jinhua 李晉華. *Mingdai chizhuanshu kao fu yinde* 明代敕撰書考附引得. 1932. Reprinted—Taipei: Chengwen, 1966.

Li Zhizhong 李致忠. *Gushu banbenxue gailun* 古書版本學概論. Beijing: Wenxian shumu chubanshe, 1990.

———. *Lidai keshu kaoshu* 歷代刻書考述. Chengdu: Bashu shushe, 1989.

————. *Zhongguo gudai shuji shi* 中國古代書籍史. Beijing: Wenwu chubanshe, 1985.

Li Xü 李詡 (1505–93). *Jiean laoren manbi* 戒庵老人漫筆. Reprinted—Beijing: Xinhua shudian, 1982.

Liu Dajie 劉大杰. *Zhongguo wenxue fada shi* 中國文學發達史. Taibei: Zhonghua shuju, 1973.

Liu Ruoyu 劉若愚 (1584–1642). *Zhuo zhong zhi* 酌中志. Siku jinshu 四庫禁書 ed. Reprinted—Beijing: Jinghua chubanshe, 2001, vol. 3.

Lo Jung-pang. "Ming Policy Formulation and Decision-making on Issues Respecting Peace and War." In *Chinese Government in Ming Times: Seven Studies*, ed. Charles O. Hucker. New York: Columbia University Press, 1969, pp. 41–72.

Lü Kun 呂坤 (1536–1618). *Guifan tushuo* 閨範圖説. Photoreprint of the 1620 edition published in Xin'an, Anhui province. N.p.: Jiangning Wei shi, 1927.

Lu Rong 陸容 (1436–1494). *Shuyuan zaji* 菽園雜記. Reprinted—Taibei: Guangwen shuju, 1970.

Luo Shubao 羅樹寶. *Zhongguo gudai yinshua shi* 中國古代印刷史. Beijing: Yinshua gongye chubanshe, 1993.

Mammitzsch, Ulrich. "Wei Chung-hsien (1568–1627): A Reappraisal of the Eunuch and the Factional Strife at the Late Ming Court." Ph.D. diss., University of Hawai'i, 1968.

Mao Chunxiang 毛春翔. *Gushu banben changtan* 古書版本常談. Shanghai: Zhonghua shuju, 1962.

MDCZSK, see Li Jinhua, *Mingdai chizhuanshu kao fu yinde*

Miao Di 苗棣. *Wei Zhongxian zhuanquan yanjiu* 魏忠賢專權研究. Beijing: Zhongguo shehui kexue chubanshe, 1994.

Ming neiting guizhi kao 明内廷規制考. 17th century? Reprinted—Beijing: Zhonghua shuju, 1985.

Mote, Frederick W., and Denis Twitchett, eds. *The Cambridge History of China*, vol. 7, *The Ming Dynasty, 1368–1644, Part I*. Cambridge: Cambridge University Press, 1988.

MS, see Zhang Tingyu et al., *Mingshi*

Ono Kazuko 小野和子. *Minki tōsha kō: Tōrin to Fukusha* 明季党社考: 東林と復社. Kyoto: Dōhōsha shuppan, 1996.

Ouyang Chen 歐陽琛. "Ming neifu neishutang kaolüe—jian lun Ming Silijian he neige gongli chaozheng" 明内府内書堂考略—兼論明司禮監和内閣共理朝政. *Jiangxi shifan daxue xuebao* 2 (1990): 56–61.

Pan Chengbi 潘承弼 and Gu Tinglong 顧廷龍. *Mingdai banben tulu chubian* 明代版本圖錄初編. Taibei: Wenhai chubanshe, 1971.

Qu Yihua 屈義華 and Xun Changrong 荀昌榮. *Zhongguo shuwenhua* 中國書文化. Changsha: Hunan daxue chubanshe, 2002.

Raphals, Lisa. *Sharing the Light: Representations of Women and Virtues in Early China*. Albany: State University of New York Press, 1998.

Sakai Tadao 酒井忠夫. *Zōho Chūgoku zensho no kenkyū* 増補中国善書の研究. Tokyo: Kokusho kankōkai, 1999.

Shen Defu 沈德符 (1577–1642). *Wanli yehuo bian* 萬歷野獲編. Reprinted—Beijing: Zhonghua shuju, 1959.

Shen Shixing 申時行 (1535–1614) et al., comps. *Da Ming huidian* 大明會典. Xuxiu siku quanshu 續修四庫全書, vol. 792. Reprinted—Shanghai: Gudian wenxue chubanshe, 1995–99.

Soullière, Ellen Felicia. "Palace Women in the Ming Dynasty: 1368–1644 (China)." Ph.D. diss., Princeton University, 1987.

Sun Chengze 孫承澤 (1592–1676). *Chunming mengyu lu* 春明夢餘錄. Reprinted—Beijing: Guji chubanshe, 1992.

Taiping laoren 太平老人 (active 1621–44). *Xiuzhong jin* 袖中錦. Congshu jicheng chubian 叢書集成初編, vol. 87. Reprinted—Taibei: Xinwenfeng chubanshe, 1985.

Tsai, Shih-shan Henry. *Perpetual Happiness: The Ming Emperor Yongle.* Seattle: University of Washington Press, 2001.

———. *The Eunuchs in the Ming Dynasty.* Albany: State University of New York Press, 1996.

Twitchett, Denis, and Tilemann Grimm, "The Cheng-t'ung, Ching-t'ai, and T'ien-shun Reigns, 1436–1464." In *CHC*, 7: 305–42.

Wang Chunyu 王春瑜 and Du Wanyan 杜婉言. *Mingchao huanguan* 明朝宦官. Beijing: Zijincheng chubanshe, 1989.

Wei Yinru 魏隱儒. *Zhongguo guji yinshua shi* 中國古籍印刷史. Beijing: Yinshua gongye chubanshe, 1988.

Wei Yinru 魏隱儒 and Wang Jinyu 王金雨. *Guji banben jianding congtan* 古籍版本鑒定叢談. Beijing: Yinshua gongye chubanshe, 1984.

Wen Gongyi 溫功義. *Mingdai de huanguan he gongting* 明代的宦官和宮廷. Chongqing: Chongqing chubanshe, 1989.

Wu, K. T. "Ming Printing and Printers." *Harvard Journal of Asiatic Studies* 7, no. 3 (1943): 203–60.

Wu, Silas. "Transmission of Ming Memorials." *T'oung Pao* 54 (1968): 275–87.

Wu Yingji 吳應箕 (1594–1645). *Donglin shilüe* 東林史略. Reprinted—Shanghai: Shanghai guji chubanshe, 1995–99.

Wulun tushuo 五倫圖説. Preface by Wan Guoqin 萬國欽 (*jinshi* 1584). Reprinted—Haihoushi: Hainan chubanshe, 2001.

Xie Mincong 謝敏聰. *Ming Qing Beijing de chengyuan yu gongque zhi yanjiu* 明清北京的城垣與宮闕之研究. Taibei: Xuesheng shuju, 1980.

Xu Daling 許大齡 and Wang Tianyou 王天有. *Mingchao shiliudi* 明朝十六帝. Beijing: Zijincheng chubanshe, 1991.

Xu Pingfang 徐苹芳, comp. *Ming Qing Beijingcheng tu* 明清北京城圖. Beijing: Ditu chubanshe, 1986.

Xu Yikui 徐一夔 (14th c.) et al., comps. *Da Ming jili* 大明集禮. 1530 Sijian ed. Copy at Harvard-Yenching Library (Cambridge, MA), Rare Book T4678 2914.

Yang Yiqing 楊一清 (1454–1530) et al., comps. *Minglun dadian* 明倫大典. 1528 inner court ed. Copy at Harvard-Yenching (Cambridge, MA), Rare Book T4686 4213.

YCHP, see Zhu Guozhen, *Yongchuang xiaopin*

Ye Dehui 葉德輝 (1863–1927). *Shulin qinghua* 書林清話. Reprinted—Changsha: Yuelu chubanshe, 1999.

YHB, see Shen Defu, *Wanli yehuo bian*

Zhang Lian 張璉. "Mingdai zhuanzhi wenhua zhengce xia de tushu chuban qingxing" 明代專制文化政策下的圖書出版情行. *Hanxue yanjiu* 10, no. 2 (Dec. 1992): 355–69.

———. "Song Ming zhengfu zhi yuwai cishu yu shujin tanyan—yi Han (Gaoli, Chaoxian) Ri erguo weili" 宋明政府之域外賜書與書禁探研—以韓 (高麗, 朝鮮) 日二

國爲例. In *Disanjie Zhongguo yuwai hanji guoji xueshu huiyi lunwenji* 第三屆中國域外漢籍國際學術會議論文集. Taibei: Lianhebao jijinhui guoxue wenxianguan, 1990, pp. 145–60.

Zhang Shudong 張樹棟 et al., eds. *Zhongguo yinshua tongshi* 中國印刷通史. Beijing: Yinshua gongye chubanshe, 1999.

Zhang Tingyu 張廷玉 (1672–1755) et al., eds. *Mingshi* 明史. Reprinted—Taibei: Guofang yanjiuyuan, 1962.

Zhang Zhian 張治安. *Mingdai zhengzhi yanjiu* 明代政治研究. Taibei: Lianjing chuban, 1992.

Zhao Qian 趙前. *Mingben* 明本. In *Zhongguo banben wenhua congshu* 中國版本文化叢書, ed. Ren Jiyu 任繼愈. Nanjing: Jiangsu guji chubanshe, 2003.

Zhou Hongzu 周弘祖 (*jinshi* 1559). *Gujin shuke* 古今書刻. Reprinted—Changsha: Guangutang of the Ye Family, 1906.

Zhou Xinhui 周心慧, ed. *Mingdai banke tushi* 明代版刻圖釋. Beijing: Xueyuan chubanshe, 1998.

———. *Zhongguo gudai banke banhuashi lunji* 中國古代版刻版畫史論集. Beijing: Xueyuan chubanshe, 1998.

———. *Zhongguo gudai fojiao banhua ji* 中國古代佛教版畫集. Beijing: Xueyuan chubanshe, 1998.

Zhu Guozhen 朱國禎 (1557–1632). *Yongchuang xiaopin* 湧幢小品. Reprinted—Shanghai: Zhonghua shuju, 1959.

Zhu Xie 朱偰 (1907–?). *Ming Qing liangdai gongyuan jianzhi kao* 明清兩代宮苑建置考. Shanghai: Shangwu shuju, 1947.

Zhu Youyan 朱佑杬 (d. 1519). *Enji shiji* 恩紀詩集. Gugong zhenben congkan ed. Reprinted—Haikoushi: Hainan chubanshe, 2000, vol. 531.

———. *Hanchuntang gao* 含春堂稿. Gugong zhenben congkan ed. Reprinted—Haikoushi: Hainan chubanshe, vol. 531.

Zhu Zhanji 朱瞻基 (Xuande emperor, 1398–1435). *Wulun shu* 五倫書. 1447 inner court ed. Copy at Harvard-Yenching Library (Cambridge, MA), Rare Book T1667 6630.

ZZZ, see Liu Ruoyu, *Zhuozhong zhi*

FOUR

The Jiajing Emperor's Interaction with His Lecturers

Hung-lam Chu

In an imperial court that operated mainly through ceremonial protocol and written communication, as the Ming court did, one institution allowed the emperor and his learned officials to have direct intellectual and social contact: the thrice-monthly classics-mat lectures and the daily lectures on the classics and histories. Patterns of interaction were fluid, because both the lecturers and the emperor assumed dual roles. The emperor was the ruler. The lecturers might consider him their student as well, and he in turn might see them not only as his teachers but also as his servitors. Furthermore, according to classical precepts, he was the teacher of all his subjects. How each person understood his role and determined which facet of his role was paramount in a given situation affected both the course and the result of the interaction. Personality and atmosphere dictated different styles of expression at the court. Moreover, despite their common educational and career backgrounds, the interactions among lecturers were complicated by personal connections and differences in rank. In the case of court lectures, cooperation and struggle between the emperor and his lecturers and among the lecturers themselves often resulted in tense relations, mainly because the stakes were so high—who was to define the proper moral and social standards for the ruler and the ruled.

This chapter examines the inherent tensions in the triangular relationship of the emperor, the lecturer, and the lecturer's supervisor, the grand secretary, as well as the political maneuvers that inadvertently changed the culture of the court during the late Ming period. It focuses on the interaction of the Jiajing emperor (r. 1521–66) and his learned elite courtiers as seen in their classics-mat and daily lectures on Confucian classics and histories. The chapter begins with a brief description of the lectures during the first sixteen years of the Jiajing emperor's reign drawn from court chronicles and more detailed accounts by the participants. It then traces the shifting relations between the emperor and his lecturers as revealed through such issues as the proper observance of the death anniversaries of imperial ancestors and other sensitive subjects, lecturers' styles and skills, and the mutual responses of the emperor and lecturers. Finally, it shows the limits of the institution in educating and guiding the emperor along the paths advocated by the Confucian scholar-official.

Other issues are important for a fuller understanding of the Ming lecture system. The protocol of a typical lecture, lecture essays as a genre of writing, contending books on the imperial reading list, the lecturers' backgrounds, and the political thinking of eminent lecturers all deserve closer attention. This chapter touches on them only in passing; fuller treatment must await separate studies.

The Institution of Classics-Mat Lectures in the Ming

The first Chinese emperor to study the Confucian classics seriously was Emperor Xuandi 宣帝 (r. 73–49 BCE) of the Western Han dynasty, who convened the famous colloquium on the Five Classics in the Stone Ditch Pavilion (Shiquge 石渠閣). Institutionalized sessions in the palace to read the classics began in the reign of Tang Emperor Xuanzong 玄宗 (r. 712–55) when learned officials were appointed attendant academicians.[1] The term "classics-mat" (*jingyan* 經筵) was adopted in Northern Song times for the regular lectures or colloquia attended by the emperor and his courtiers. Academicians from the prestigious Hanlin Academy were appointed attendant readers and expositors. Granted the title *shuoshu* (説書, lit. "expounding the book"), junior lecturers staffed the sessions. The basic organization and format devised in the Song were retained, with some modifications, in later times. The idea behind the institution proved to be so attractive that the practice was continued in all later dynasties, including the Yuan when the lectures were given in Mongol or Uighur rather than in Chinese.[2]

---

1. For accounts of imperial lectures and colloquia in Han and Tang times, see Wang Yinglin, *Yuhai*, 26.549–51.

2. For accounts of the institution in Song and Yuan times, see Zhu Ruixi, "Songchao jingyan zhidu"; and Zhang Fan, "Yuandai jingyan shulun."

In the Ming, imperial lectures began with the founding Hongwu emperor, and many of his discussions on classical exegesis and historical lessons survive to the present.[3] The study sessions became formalized, in the institutions of the large classics-mat lecture and the small daily lecture (*rijiang* 日講), only when the Zhengtong emperor began his reign in 1436, at the age of nine *sui*. From then on, the lectures were held in the Literary Splendor Palace (Wenhuadian 文華殿) in the southeast quarter of the Forbidden City, immediately after the morning court audiences.[4]

Classics-mat lectures were major gatherings, and attendance by the senior officials in both the civil and the military echelons of the central government was obligatory. The grand secretaries, ennobled officers, the heads of the Six Ministries, censors in chief, the minister of the Court of Judicial Review, the commissioner of the Office of Transmission, senior academicians of the Hanlin Academy, and the pair of investigating censors and the pair of supervising secretaries serving as prefects for the occasion attended the emperor with the added generic title of "classics-mat officials" (*jingyanguan* 經筵官). The lecturers were invariably chosen from among the grand secretaries, Hanlin officials, and the chancellor of the National University.

The event cannot quite be understood as a colloquium during the Ming. In Song times, the emperor himself engaged in a discussion with the lecturer, and interested participants could query one another.[5] Most of the time in the Ming, the emperor listened from his seat, while the lecturer stood before him and delivered a monologue. The daily lectures could be somewhat more relaxed, since normally only a pair of lecturers under the supervision of a grand secretary attended the emperor. In both the classics-mat and the daily lectures, the lecturers on duty submitted the text of their talk to the palace office managing the event a day before the occasion.

By the early sixteenth century, classics-mat lectures were normally held on the second day of each ten-day cycle during the second, third, and fourth months (the spring series), and the eighth, ninth, and tenth months

---

3. For a recent study on this topic, see Zhu Honglin (Hung-lam Chu), "Ming Taizu de jingshi jianglun qingxing."

4. For the general protocols of the Ming institution of the imperial lecture and major events in its history to the late sixteenth century, see Liao Daonan, *Diange cilin ji*, 15.1a–18b; and Yu Ruji, *Libu zhigao*, 14.1a–4b. These sources inform the description in the following paragraphs.

5. See Zhu Ruixi, "Songchao jingyan zhidu," pp. 240–43.

(the fall series) of the year. During these months, daily lectures were given on the remaining days.[6] Except when he had to fulfill more important state functions or familial obligations, the emperor, according to the class schedule drawn up by the grand secretariat and approved by the emperor, was to appear at all lectures unless he was sick or the weather was too inclement. Theoretically, nine large lectures were held each season; in practice they were often suspended. High-ranking members of the court and mid-ranking officials from the literary, censorial, and supervisory bodies, however, were zealous in urging new emperors to attend these study sessions in order to advance their learning and to become familiar with their advisors. The ultimate goal was the perfection of their virtue and enhancement of the welfare of the state. Most Ming emperors, however, remained enthusiastic only during the first few years of their reigns. The Jiajing emperor, a cousin of the heirless Zhengde emperor (r. 1506–21) called to the throne from his princedom in Huguang province, was no exception to this rule, although he did not cease attending lectures until his sixteenth year on the throne.

In the following, I first briefly chronicle the Jiajing court's lectures, using the reign's Veritable Records as the major source.[7] Memorials and personal writings of the lecturers and their supervisors, as well as comments by later Ming writers, are then used to illuminate the more intimate interactions of the parties involved.[8]

---

6. Liao Daonan, *Diange cilin ji*, 15.4a–6a. To make the distinction, some Ming institutional historians, like Liao Daonan, also called the larger lectures "monthly lectures" (*yuejiang* 月講).

7. The *Ming Shizong shilu* 明世宗實錄, hereafter cited as *MSZSL*, is cited according to the following convention: in a citation such as *MSZSL* 3.115–16/Zhengde 16/6/xinsi or *MSZSL* 12.427/Jiajing 1/3/wuwu = *MSZSL* A.B/C/D/E, A = *juan* number in *MSZSL*, B = page number(s) in the reprint edition, C = year under the Zhengde or Jiajing reign titles, D = month of the year (a + before the number indicates an intercalary month), and E = day in the 60-day cycle.

8. For a study of lectures during the Hongzhi reign (1488–1505), discussed in terms of imperial education, which also includes contemporary opinions that reflect early Ming ideas and ideals of the institution and assessments of its implementation, see Mano Senryū, "Mindai no shinkō ni tsuite." For descriptions of the format of the Wanli emperor's lectures and comments on the imperial commitment to the institution as a state function, see Ray Huang, *1587*, pp. 10–12, 42–48.

The Study Sessions of the Jiajing Emperor

The Jiajing emperor's first study session was held about two months after he ascended the throne on May 27, 1521. As proposed by the chief grand secretary, Yang Tinghe 楊廷和 (1459–1529), once every three or five days, the grand secretaries and selected Hanlin officials would present to the emperor oral expositions of the Ming founder's admonitions to his successors, the *Ancestral Instructions* (*Zuxun* 祖訓), in plain language in the Informal Hall (Biandian 便殿). Called "straightforward elucidations" (*zhijie* 直解) in their written form, these expositions were afterward submitted in clearly written memorandums (*jietie* 揭帖). The early harmony between emperor and officials[9] ended a few months later when Yang Tinghe and his colleagues refused the emperor's proposal to elevate the titles of his deceased father and his mother, who was still alive.[10]

This refusal sparked the so-called Great Rites Controversy (*Dali yi* 大禮議), a protracted struggle between the Jiajing emperor and the majority of civil officials. The central issue was whether a prince inherited the throne because of his blood or because of dynastic need. Also in dispute was whether a prince could posthumously be installed as a full-fledged emperor in the imperial ritual hierarchy when his son became an emperor.[11] This set of controversies would deeply influence the classics-mat lectures of the Jiajing emperor, the political atmosphere of his reign, and bureaucratic ethics and styles during the rest of the Ming dynasty.[12]

The first classics-mat lecture was convened in the eighth month (September 2, 1521) as scheduled.[13] The State Duke of Ding 定國公, Xu Guangzuo 徐光祚 (d. 1527), and Grand Secretary Yang Tinghe were appointed co-administrators of the lectures; the other three grand secretaries were associate administrators. The staff included sixteen lecturers.[14]

The grand inaugural lecture was delivered by the second grand secretary, Jiang Mian 蔣冕 (1463–1533), since Yang Tinghe was on leave because

---

9. *MSZSL* 3.115–16/Zhengde 16/6/xinsi.

10. *MSZSL* 4.181/Zhengde 16/7/jiazi.

11. On the nature and significance of this controversy, see Fisher, *The Chosen One*. For a different view of the controversy, see Hung-lam Chu, Review of *The Chosen One*.

12. For a recent study on the impact of the Great Rites Controversy on bureaucratic ethics in the Jiajing reign, see Hu Jixun 胡吉勛, "*Dali yi* yu Mingting renshi bianju."

13. *MSZSL* 4.186/Zhengde 16/7/dingmao.

14. For the various appointments and participants in this occasion, see *MSZSL* 4.194–97/Zhengde 16/7/renshen; and Jiang Mian, *Xianggao ji*, 23.11b–12a.

of an eye disease. Jiang Mian noted that the emperor was so pleased with the lectures that he showered the lecturers with gifts and feasted the participants after the event. Jiang, too, was pleased that the assembled officials wore pale green robes instead of red ones to show their respect to the deceased Zhengde emperor, and especially so when, subsequently, the emperor "attended the daily lectures uninterruptedly. Even on rainy days, [he attended] his exposition and reading sessions, until he called for a halt to them at the end of the year."[15]

The emperor, however, declined the grand secretaries' request for more lecture sessions at the conclusion of the year. The emperor was displeased at their repeated refusals to elevate the status of his deceased father and his soon-to-arrive mother.[16] Obviously, the early promise of the lectures fell under the shadow of the unfolding ritual disputes between the emperor and his officials.

The first year of the Jiajing era (1522) in fact saw only one classics-mat lecture.[17] Failing to move the emperor, Yang Tinghe and his colleagues could only urge him to accept their straightforward elucidations and to study privately and practice calligraphy with the aid of selected eunuchs from the Directorate of Ceremonial (Silijian 司禮監). Specifically, the grand secretaries proposed, these eunuchs would accompany the emperor to his study after court audiences. They and the emperor together would read aloud at least ten times the text of the book assigned at a given session. The eunuchs were also to ensure that the emperor thoroughly understood the words he had read. The lecturers, meanwhile, stood ready to answer whatever questions the emperor might have about his reading.[18]

During the following two years, only one large lecture was held.[19] No other scheduled lectures were conducted, even after Yang Tinghe retired in the spring of the third year (1524)[20] and after the emperor's parents were elevated as "Emperor and Empress Dowager Who Bore the Present Emperor" (*bensheng* 本生).[21] However, to judge from an imperial order to sus-

---

15. Jiang Mian, *Xianggao ji*, 23.11b–12a.
16. *MSZSL* 7.281/Zhengde 16/10/guimao.
17. *MSZSL* 13.465/Jiajing 1/4/wuxu.
18. *MSZSL* 15.489/Jiajing 1/6/dingchou.
19. *MSZSL* 24.694/Jiajing 2/3/guihai.
20. *MSZSL* 36.899/Jiajing 3/2/bingwu.
21. *MSZSL* 38.964–5/Jiajing 3/4/guichou.

pend the lectures and from a censor's response that "the suspension is too early,"[22] the daily lectures were still being held.

In the meantime, tension between the emperor and his few supporters from the junior ranks on the one hand and the multitude of courtiers on the other increased as the emperor slighted the beloved Hongzhi emperor (r. 1488–1505; and formally Jiajing's adoptive father) and his surviving empress. The outcome was bloodshed. On August 19, 1524, a week after a mass protest to the throne in front of the Left Concord Gate, more than 220 officials, who had been detained and awaited punishment, were further interrogated and variously sentenced to exile after torture, suspension of salaries, or a beating with a pole in the open court. Sixteen lower-ranked officials died on the spot.[23]

The triumphant emperor also began to change the format of his study sessions; Hanlin officials could no longer monopolize the delivery of lectures. Zhan Ruoshui 湛若水 (1466–1560) informs us that the emperor decreed in the seventh month of the fourth year (July 1525) that civil officials could present plainly worded elucidation of the classics and the histories to the throne. As a result, Zhan wrote his voluminous work of statecraft learning, *Sage Learning Thoroughly Understood by the Investigation of Things* (*Shengxue gewutong* 聖學格物通).[24] Now especially interested in the *Book of Documents*, the emperor later that year ordered the grand secretaries to annotate three chapters from the classic, using as their model the founding emperor's annotation of the "Great Plan" ("Hongfan" 洪範) chapter. These chapters in question—"Counsels of Gao Yao" ("Gaoyaomo" 皋陶謨), "Instructions of Yi" ("Yixun" 伊訓), and "Against Luxurious Ease" ("Wuyi" 無逸)—are considered rich in the principles of governance. The resultant compilation was entitled *The Three Essentials of the Book of Documents* (*Shujing sanyao* 書經三要).[25]

In the second half of the fifth year (1526), the lectures briefly resumed. The emperor did not appear at court most of the time. More than 800 officials even missed the court gathering one morning in the tenth month when a classics-mat lecture was supposed to be held.[26] More regular lectures, on the "Great Plan" chapter of the *Book of Documents*, were held only in the following year (1527). Lecturer Gu Dingchen's 顧鼎臣 (1473–1540)

---

22. *MSZSL* 38.970/Jiajing 3/4/guichou.

23. *MSZSL* 41.1080/Jiajing 3/7/guiwei.

24. See Zhu Honglin (Hung-lam Chu), "Mingru Zhan Ruoshui."

25. *MSZSL* 58.1394–95/Jiajing 4/12/wushen.

26. *MSZSL* 69.1579/Jiajing 5/10/renshen.

original expositions had captured the emperor's attention.[27] Hanlin Compiler Liao Daonan's 廖道南 (*js.* 1521, d. 1547) elucidation of the "nine standards" of the Great Plan also proved stimulating.[28]

Most noteworthy were the lectures on Zhen Dexiu's 眞德秀 (1178–1235) *Extended Meaning of the Great Learning* (*Daxue yanyi* 大學衍義), the great statecraft classic in the Neo-Confucian tradition, which contains both the maxims of the Classics and the main lessons of the great historical compilation *Comprehensive Mirror* (*Zizhi tongjian* 資治通鑑) by Sima Guang 司馬光 (1019–86). Beginning in the fifth month, both straightforward elucidations and oral expositions were presented regularly on the third and eighth days of the ten-day cycle by six additionally appointed daily lecturers and six lecturers from the Hanlin ranks specifically appointed for the task.[29] The regular daily lectures also grew more frequent. In the tenth month, five lecturers were promoted to senior positions in the Hanlin Academy for their diligent service.[30] In contrast, the emperor reprimanded daily lecturer Dong Qi 董玘 (1483–1546) for improper movements during an exposition and reading session.[31] The emperor also demoted lecturer Wang Tian 汪佃 (1474–1540) to the provinces for a slow and unsatisfactory presentation.

The same year (1527) witnessed an unprecedented shake-up of the Hanlin. It ended the Grand Secretariat's long-standing role as the institutional mentor, and de facto director, of the Hanlin Academy. Only officials of solid learning, good writing skills, and fine conduct were to stay. Many of the new lecturers who filled the twenty-two vacancies had supported the imperial position in the Great Rites Controversy.[32]

The eventful sixth year ended with the emperor emerging as an accomplished Neo-Confucian author. He wrote a "Maxim of Seriousness and Oneness" ("Jingyi zhen" 敬一箴) and annotated both the "Maxim of the Mind" ("Xin zhen" 心箴) by the Song scholar Fan Jun 范浚 (fl. 1130s–40s) and the "Four Maxims [of Seeing, Hearing, Speaking, and Acting]" ("[Shi-ting-yan-dong] Si zhen" [視聽言動]四箴) by the Neo-Confucian master Cheng Yi 程頤 (1033–1107). These works were glossed primarily by Zhang

---

27. *MSZSL* 75.1682/Jiajing 6/4/wuchen.

28. *MSZSL* 76.1690–3/Jiajing 6/5/xinsi, 104.2460–1/Jiajing 8/8/bingxu.

29. *MSZSL* 76.1695–7/Jiajing 6/5/yiyou; for details, see Yang Yiqing, *Chenhanlu* 宸翰錄 4 (first printed in mid- or late Jiajing period), in *Yang Yiqing ji*, pp. 815–17.

30. *MSZSL* 81.1801/Jiajing 6/10/wuwu.

31. *MSZSL* 81.1811/Jiajing 6/10/yichou.

32. *MSZSL* 81.1813–15/Jiajing 6/10/bingyin.

Cong 張璁 (1475–1539), the new dominant grand secretary. The emperor's handwritten copies of the texts were soon copied and carved on stone steles erected in the two Hanlin academies and the two national universities in Beijing and Nanjing, and in all government schools throughout the empire.[33]

The emperor's interest in the lectures revived in the seventh year of his reign (1528). He attended three classics-mat lectures in the spring series.[34] He devoted all the fall daily lectures to the "Great Plan" chapter of the *Documents*, which was expounded solely by Gu Dingchen.[35] A poem by Gu reveals that evening sessions were also held.[36] That enthusiasm probably reflected the state of his emotional life. The Empress Chen, who died in the tenth month and was given the uncomplimentary posthumous title of Regretful Intelligence (Daoling 悼靈), was denied a last visit from her father on her deathbed.[37] The emperor even rejected the lecturers' requests that they be allowed to wear light-colored gowns to express their grief.[38]

During the sole classics-mat lecture recorded in the eighth year (1529), lecturer Lu Shen 陸深 (1477–1544) protested to Jiajing that when Grand Secretary Gui E 桂萼 (*js.* 1511, d. 1531) had edited Lu's essay, he had distorted its meaning.[39] Lu petitioned that such editing be prohibited. Furious, the emperor lambasted Lu as prone to exaggeration, deceit, maliciousness, and self-indulgence for making such a solicitation and demoted him to a minor post in Fujian.[40]

In the next year (1530), the emperor became increasingly engaged but watchful during the daily lectures and over the occasional lecture essays. He disapproved of lecturers who skipped certain texts in order to avoid sensitive subjects.[41] He ordered each of the grand secretaries and lecturers to present an exposition of one chapter of a classic.[42] He summoned Vice Minister Xia Yan 夏言 (1482–1548) to expound the *Extended Meaning*.[43]

---

33. *MSZSL* 82.1843/Jiajing 6/11/jiawu; Zhang Cong, *Yudui lu*, 2.18b–20a.

34. *MSZSL* 84.1893/Jiajing 7/1/xinsi, 85.1919/Jiajing 7/2/dingwei, 86.1947–49/Jiajing 7/3/jiashen.

35. Gu Dingchen, *Gu Wenkang gong xugao*, 2.1a–2b.

36. Ibid., 6.6a–b.

37. *MSZSL* 92.2126–27/Jiajing 7/9/xinmao, 93.2137–43/Jiajing 7/10/dingwei.

38. *MSZSL* 94.2194/Jiajing 7/+10/xinmao.

39. *MSZSL* 99.2333/Jiajing 8/3/wuxu.

40. *MSZSL* 99.2335–36/Jiajing 8/3/guimao.

41. Zhang Cong, *Yudui lu*, 12.16a–17b.

42. *MSZSL* 120.2868–69/Jiajing 9/12/dingchou.

43. Xia Yan, *Guizhou xiansheng zouyi*, 7.4b–5b.

Most tellingly, on New Year's Day of the tenth year (January 18, 1531), he forwarded to Zhang Cong abstracts of lectures by Gui E and the other lecturers during the preceding year. Zhang was instructed to read them carefully and confidentially and to submit an evaluation. Zhang reported back that same day.[44]

A new ceremony introduced early in the tenth year suggests the importance the emperor placed on the lectures. A rite of paying homage to the "former sages and teacher"—that is, the Duke of Zhou and all the sage-kings from Fu Xi to King Wu of Zhou, and Confucius—was ordered to be held on the first day of the spring and the fall series of the classics-mat lectures.[45] The unexpected absence of three lecturers two months later, however, again suggests a continuous suspension of lectures—in all likelihood due to the emperor's health.[46] But evidence also suggests that lectures resumed in the fall series.[47] Special lectures on the "The Seven Month" ("Qi-yue" 七月) poem from the *Book of Poetry* and the "Against Luxurious Ease" chapter from the *Book of Documents*—classic examples extolling imperial concern for agriculture and personal diligence—were also delivered in the newly constructed Against Luxurious Ease Hall (Wuyidian 無逸殿) in the West Park (Xiyuan 西苑).[48]

Anxious for an heir, however, the emperor turned to Daoist practices. On December 31, 1531 (eleventh month of the tenth year), a *jiao* 醮 ceremony was held in the Respectful and Peaceful Hall (Qin'andian 欽安殿) for the purpose of gaining an heir. Minister of Rites Xia Yan was appointed commissioner of the ceremony, and Vice Ministers Zhan Ruoshui and Gu Dingchen served as the guiding officials who received the offering-prayer (*yingci [qingci] daoyinguan* 迎詞【青詞】導引官). In rotation, the five highest-ranking military and civil officials daily offered incense and conducted appropriate rites. On the first and the last day of the ceremony,

---

44. Zhang Cong, *Yudui lu*, 26.1a–3b.

45. *MSZSL* 121.2904–5/Jiajing 10/1/renzi.

46. *MSZSL* 123.2955/Jiajing 10/3/yiwei.

47. See *MSZSL* 129.3066/Jiajing 10/8/guiwei for the emperor's rejection of a lecturer's request for leave to visit his ancestors' graveyards, citing his involvement in the daily lectures; and *MSZSL* 132.3132/Jiajing 10/11/xinwei for Minister of Rites Xia Yan's disapproval of a suggestion that the emperor visit the National University and listen to lectures there delivered before the beginning of the spring and fall series of lectures. He noted that doing so might be too much for the emperor, since he was "continuing with his classics-mat and daily lectures."

48. *MSZSL* 129.3080–81/Jiajing 10/8/dingwei, 130.3092–93/Jiajing 10/9/renshen.

the emperor himself conducted the rituals.[49] A month later (January 12, 1532), Gu Dingchen presented seven "Walking in the Void" prayers (*buxuci* 步虛詞) for the ceremony to maximize its effect. The emperor praised his loyalty and affection, and kept copies of Gu's prayers in the palace as a sign of his appreciation.[50]

In the eleventh year of Jiajing's reign (1532), lectures were still occasionally held.[51] Confucian-minded lecturers, however, now entered a new era in which they had to surrender even the rhetoric of shaping the imperial personality. With the veteran lecturer Gu Dingchen leading the change, classics-mat lecture essays were soon superseded by Daoist offering-prayers (*qingci* 青詞) as a way of interesting the emperor or procuring his favor.

During the twelfth year (1533), only one classics-mat lecture is recorded for the spring series and one for the fall series.[52] The fall one seems to have been a celebration to mark the birth of the first imperial son.[53] Lingering antagonism among the lecturing staff, however, marred a summer lecture on the *Extended Meaning*. Gu Dingchen could not attend because of illness. Two of his colleagues declined Grand Secretary Zhang Cong's request to serve as his substitute. The emperor disciplined the two by replacing them with new lecturers.[54]

No lecture was recorded in the thirteenth year (1534). The emperor was ill in the spring,[55] and his sixty-day absence from the court initiated a lingering, bureaucratic malaise. One day in the eighth month (October 4, 1534), 184 civil and military officials failed to appear at the morning court audience.[56] Only one classics-mat lecture was held in the fourteenth year (1535), in the third month.[57]

---

49. *MSZSL* 132.3134–35/Jiajing 10/11/guiyou.

50. *MSZSL* 133.3147–48/Jiajing 10/12/yiyou.

51. See *MSZSL* 137.3231/Jiajing 11/4/guimao for two censors alleged to have mishandled their business because of a classics-mat lecture; and *MSZSL* 142.3303–5/Jiajing 11/9/dingsi for the emperor asking the grand secretaries what Wu Hui 吳惠 and Guo Weifan 郭維藩 had meant in their lectures. The lectures had suggested, respectively, restraining "unnecessary expenditures and constructions" and ending "malpractice but showing magnanimity."

52. *MSZSL* 148.3411/Jiajing 12/3/yisi.

53. *MSZSL* 153.3472/Jiajing 12/8/jichou.

54. *MSZSL* 152.3455–56/Jiajing 12/7/yisi.

55. *MSZSL* 160.3576/Jiajing 13/+2/dingsi.

56. *MSZSL* 166.3656/Jiajing 13/8/xinyou.

57. *MSZSL* 173.3753/Jiajing 14/3/renxu.

The last classics-mat lecture of the Jiajing reign found in the Veritable Records was held on the eleventh day of the third month of the fifteenth year (April 1, 1536).[58] A few months later, when an official petitioned the throne to collect books for the palace library and for the emperor to attend lectures during his free time, Jiajing responded, "Books may be stacked up like pillars, but if one does not read them seriously, their accumulation is just for vain glory. In addition, if officials do not correctly nourish their minds, it would be useless even if they are called [to lecture]."[59] He would have occasion to appoint another lecturer as a substitute for one on leave, but that was merely to fill the roster.[60] The last memorial calling for classics-mat lectures came a year later, in the seventh month of the sixteenth year (1537). The emperor struggled for a pretext for his inactivity: "I have not lightly abandoned the classics-mat lectures. It was because of the renovation of the Literary Splendor Palace that the spring lecture series was suspended this year. Shen Han 沈瀚 [*js.* 1535; the memorializing supervising secretary] should be open and honest in what he has to say but should not express himself in the way he does. For in doing so, he is only inviting fame for himself by going against the monarch."[61] No one would subsequently challenge the emperor to resume his study of the classics and histories.

Meanwhile, beginning from the fall of 1536, when the first imperial daughter was born,[62] the Jiajing emperor emerged at once as a devoted filial descendent and a fertile father, apparently on the advice and prescriptions of his Daoist advisors. For two years, he made five visits to his ancestors' mausoleums and begot six princes and one more princess. Now quite busy as a father devoted to the Daoist rituals, he observed more *jiao* ceremonies and read more *qingci* prayers.[63]

A review of the sixteen years of the Jiajing court's lecture activities makes it apparent that the lectures were not purely educational, not merely learning sessions devoted to the classics and histories. Although in accordance with institutional requirements but in effect much conditioned by

---

58. *MSZSL* 185.3913/Jiajing 15/3/bingyin. This is corroborated by a late Ming historian who noted that "only since the sixteenth year of Jiajing was the emperor rarely to be seen in the lectures" (Huang Jingfang, *Guoshi weiyi*, p. 187).

59. *MSZSL* 189.3996/Jiajing 15/7/gengchen.

60. *MSZSL* 190.4007/Jiajing 15/8/gengzi.

61. *MSZSL* 202.4242/Jiajing 16/7/dinghai.

62. *MSZSL* 190.4006/Jiajing 15/8/wuxu.

63. For these events, see *MSZSL* 191.4038/Jiajing 15/9/gengwu to 216.4409/Jiajing 17/9/xinwei.

the political situation, the performance of all those involved in the lectures revealed tensions in the ethics of government and differences in the implementation of dynastic rites. The Confucian scholar-officials grew disillusioned with the ideal of molding the Jiajing emperor into a sympathetic monarch through their elucidation of the classics and the sages. Why the emperor proved reluctant to learn from them becomes apparent upon closer examination of their interactions.

Observing Death Anniversary Rites and Dealing with Sensitive Subjects

Two events concerning observance of the death anniversaries of the imperial ancestors might have subtly affected the psyches of the Jiajing emperor and his lecturers. Both happened in the first year of the Jiajing reign. The first was triggered by Lü Nan 呂柟 (1479–1542), a well-known Confucian scholar and moralist of the time.[64] After expounding the Be Respectful Morning and Night (Suyeweiyin 夙夜惟寅) section of the "Canon of Shun" ("Shundian" 舜典) chapter of the *Book of Documents* in a classics-mat lecture, Lü made the unconventional move of memorializing the throne in person. The day happened to be the anniversary of the death of the founding emperor's mother. Feeling it relevant to the classical lesson he had just expounded, Lü asked the emperor to observe this anniversary and to "brighten his filial piety by accepting remonstrance" and to wear the *shenfu* (襂服), a kind of unadorned dress for the observance of that rite. He also requested the emperor to cancel the routine banquet for the participating officials that day.[65] The emperor interrupted Lü by saying "I know" and then left. Lü was obliged to submit a memorial asking punishment for his breach of the rule that the lecturer presented nothing other than his exposition. He was pardoned.[66]

The other event took place a month later. On a scheduled classics-mat day, the lecture was canceled to observe the anniversary of the death of the Hongxi emperor, the fourth monarch of the dynasty. Earlier, Supervising Secretary An Pan 安磐 (*js.* 1505) and others had memorialized on the difficulties this coincidence presented. If the attending officials were to dress in red and to have the banquet afterward as protocol required, they would

---

64. Lü Nan, *Jingyezi neipian*, p. 328, biographic accounts of Lü Nan.
65. Ibid., p. 328.
66. *MSZSL* 13.465/Jiajing 1/4/wuxu.

demonstrate a lack of filial piety. If, however, the lecture were canceled, it would mean abandoning learning. They suggested moving the lecture to the previous day as the correct course of action.[67]

The emperor asked the Ministry of Rites to deliberate the suggestion. The ministry's reply was based on the authority of the *Classic of Rites* regarding death anniversaries: "When the Hongzhi emperor was on the throne, the classics-mat lecture was conducted on the anniversary of the Chenghua emperor's death. He wore a green flower-patterned robe and bestowed the after-lecture banquet. We suggest this practice be followed."[68] The emperor settled the divergent opinions by canceling the lecture in a solemn but grand show of filial piety—sending sacrificial offerings to the mausoleum of Hongxi.

These two events show what was considered appropriate in offering advice to the emperor. As the emperor saw it, Lü Nan was at fault; his petition was more show than substance. If he had truly been serious about the emperor's ritual obligations, he should have urged him earlier in a memorial, not broken the rule against pronouncing it in the presence of all the court dignitaries. Lü, for his part, was proposing ritual remedies for the emperor. The emperor seems to have understood Lü's intention at least; he subsequently pardoned Lü's breach of etiquette. But he still had not grasped the nuances of Lü's thought. In asking the emperor to observe the death anniversary of his ancestress, Lü was reminding him not to forget her descendants, especially, of course, the Hongzhi emperor, who was now the emperor's adoptive father.

This idea was also embedded in the Ministry of Rites' deliberation of An Pan's suggestion. An Pan's suggestion both to arouse the emperor's sense of filial piety and to keep his learning session at the same time made good sense. By sending An's memorial for ministerial deliberation, the emperor was signaling his inclination to approve it. The response of the Ministry of Rites, headed by Yang Tinghe's staunchest ally, Mao Cheng 毛澄 (1461–1523), was the problem. One eminent historian of the dynasty, Zhu Guozhen 朱國禎 (1557–1632), perceptively observed, "The discussants argued for such trivialities to the effect that the great rite [of holding the lecture] was abandoned; as for the Hongzhi emperor, he truly was the sage ruler of ten thousand generations."[69] The Ministry of Rites, in its inflexible

67. *MSZSL* 14.475/Jiajing 1/5/dingsi.
68. Zhu Guozhen, *Yongchuang xiaopin*, p. 31.
69. Ibid.

counter-suggestion, was not so much trying to maintain its authority in matters within its jurisdiction or merely trying to avoid possible inconveniences resulting from schedule changes. Rather, it was attempting to instill in the emperor a sense of respect for the late Hongzhi emperor by recommending that his practice be emulated. Aware of his courtiers' intention, the emperor's reaction was equally subtle: he would be even more filial to his ancestors but would not follow Hongzhi's example.

As the observance of death anniversaries became a standard reason for suspending the classics-mat lecture, the emperor also became more mindful of expressions his lecturers considered taboo. For a time, he appears to have been broadminded. In the fourth year of his reign (1525), Supervising Secretary Zheng Yipeng 鄭一鵬 (js. 1521) memorialized that since history was a mirror for the emperor, the lecturers should not lecture, as they had been, only on ordered times but not chaotic times, on cases of successes but not cases of failures. The emperor agreed that in their lecture essays and oral expositions the lecturers not avoid anything they considered a sensitive subject.[70]

A Wanli period (1573–1620) historian also informs us that the emperor could be rather understanding. One day in the fall of the sixth year of his reign, before he reprimanded the daily lecturer Dong Qi for his bad manners,[71] the emperor noticed that in that day's lecture on the *Analects*, the entry about Zengzi 曾子 (one of Confucius' leading disciples) on his deathbed had not been expounded. Presumably the lecturer had skipped it because he considered it a taboo for an auspicious occasion like the lecture. The emperor, however, told his attendants that since life and death were natural to mankind, mention of death should not be avoided. The emperor ordered both a written presentation and an oral exposition of this entry. The same historian agreed with the lecturer's judgment, but also praised the emperor's decision as "excelling the ordinary view of the world."[72]

"The Metal-Bound Coffer" ("Jinteng" 金滕) chapter of the *Book of Documents* was also skipped in the lectures of the eighth year. The emperor confided to Zhang Cong that he believed the reason for the omission was that this chapter dealt at length with King Wu's illness. The emperor insisted, however, that it be elucidated. Zhang Cong was instructed to ask

---

70. Chen Zilong and Xu Fuyuan, eds., [*Huang*] *Ming jingshi wenbian*, 3.2188, memorial by Zheng Yipeng.
71. *MSZSL* 81.1811/Jiajing 6/10/yichou.
72. Deng Shilong, *Guochao diangu*, 35.637–8.

the lecturers to compose and present the missing lecture essays.[73] To borrow another Wanli period historian's praise for the imperial reaction in this case, the emperor appears as "*this* understanding and broadminded."[74]

The same historian immediately added, however: "This would happen only during his early years on the throne. In his later years, even sickness and illness of the officials themselves were not to be mentioned because even these words had become taboos, much less an inauspicious word like death."[75] True, but the point is that this change occurred only toward the very end of his reign. An observation by the late Ming historian Huang Jingfang 黄景昉 (1596–1662) further suggests that the emperor was once rather openminded about the texts the lecturers expounded.

During the last years of the Jiajing reign, the emperor sought long life and revered Daoism. He thought many things violated taboo. This was rather unlike his early years on the throne. Liao Daonan had the occasion to lecture on the section "Gaozong of Yin in Mourning" ("Gaozong liang'an" 高宗諒闇) [of the *Book of Documents*]. For not following Grand Secretary Zhang Cong's instruction for avoiding the taboo, he was impeached by Zhang. The responding decree nonetheless said, "Life and death are the normal way of mankind; to offer advice is the responsibility of the lecturers. Have Liao Daonan present his lecture as usual." The emperor also commanded, "Formerly Xu Jin 徐縉 [*js.* 1505] omitted the section 'Mengjingzi 孟敬子 asking about illness' in the *Analects*. That was not appropriate." How enlightening and penetrating was the imperial opinion. It exceeded all expectations.[76]

The change in the emperor's attitude and the consequent circumspection of the lecturers were tied to the Great Rites Controversy. Many things might be misconstrued as an allusion to it. The coordinating and supervising grand secretaries favored a prudent silence. The emperor's failure to discourage his lecturers from subscribing to such taboos, on the other hand, shows the resilience of a cultural tradition in addition to the precariousness of the time. The lecturers were playing their proper role as servitors. Since a servitor should always respect his monarch, expressions that might invoke ominous associations had to be avoided. It was incumbent on the monarch to exercise discretion in his reactions to these sensitive questions. Broadmindedness might encourage him to be accommodating, but his officials would not ignore the taboo unless they were so instructed.

---

73. Zhang Cong, *Yudui lu*, 12.16a–17b.

74. Xu Xuemo, *Shimiao zhiyulu*, 5.2a.

75. Ibid., 5.2a.

76. Huang Jingfang, *Guoshi weiyi*, p. 187.

The Sensitive Emperor and
His Insensitive Lecturers

The emperor's sensitivity to the implications of the lecturers' words and gestures is amply demonstrated in the repeated requests that he treat the lecturers kindly. In a memorial not included in the Veritable Records, Yang Tinghe revealed that the imperial presence had awed and terrified the lecturer Zhao Yong 趙永 (*js.* 1502). In the eighth month of 1522, Zhao, a first-time temporary lecturer, was ordered to lecture in the rear hall of the Literary Splendor Palace on short notice. He arrived in great haste without an opportunity to prepare properly. Immediately after he performed the kowtow ceremony, he was ushered to the lectern facing the imperial seat. He was too frightened to make himself fluent. Eventually his exposition was discontinued to bring an end to the awkward situation. The emperor later dispatched a senior eunuch to console Zhao. The grand secretaries acknowledged the imperial grace the following day by sending the memorial noted above.[77]

As chancellor of the National University, Zhao Yong had lectured in public with success when the emperor visited the university earlier in the year.[78] This time, in contrast, the awesome aura of the emperor in the lecture room shattered his self-confidence. The emperor, however, was not ungracious in the end.

The emperor's demands on the lecturers' deportment increased as his readings in classical exegeses and the dynasty's governmental statutes progressed.[79] In the tenth month of 1527, he ordered the Grand Secretariat to inform the veteran lecturer Dong Qi that his movements during an exposition and reading session had been inappropriate. When the frightened Dong rectified himself and memorialized his gratitude, the emperor then replied:

Your job is that of exposition and reading, and your position is that of a great minister. How could you lose the integrity of being respectful and modest? I cannot bear reprimanding you in words. So I especially ordered the Grand Secretariat to

---

77. Yang Tinghe, *Yang Wenzhong sanlu,* 2.17a–18a.

78. *MSZSL* 12.425/Jiajing 1/3/jiayin.

79. For instances of the emperor's recent enthusiasm for reading classical writings and asking questions based on them, see *MSZSL* 76.1695–7/Jiajing 6/5/yiyou, 76.1699/Jiajing 6/5/xinmao, 77.120–21/Jiajing 6/6/guihai, and 81.1795–6/Jiajing 6/10/yiyou.

inform you. You should respectfully appreciate my intention and strive to do your job well to satisfy the demands of your appointment.[80]

The nature of Dong's offense is unclear. A Wanli period observer put the affair this way: "During classics-mat lectures, a lecturer's appearance and deportment and his language could make manifest his virtue. . . . Emperor Shizong's warning to Dong Qi was effective. Dong quickly reformed himself and was then known for his respect and circumspection. It could be said that the emperor and servitors of those times complemented one another."[81] The last sentence is intriguing. Does it mean the servitors deliberately misbehaved in order to allow the emperor to display his sagacity?

Probably not: the next day Hanlin Reader-in-Waiting Wang Tian was dismissed from his lectureship and sent away from the court for being "slow and unversed in his presentation" on the "nine standards" of the "Great Plan" chapter. The emperor in fact took it upon himself to do the expounding. He told the grand secretaries that "when an emperor is able to exhaust what ethical principles demand of him as one who stands above all, and when the people below are thus transformed and when ethical order is made clear and the way of humanity made perfect, fortune will come by itself." His Majesty simply did not see "teachers" in his lecturers.[82]

Shortly thereafter the shake-up of the Hanlin establishment began. According to a late Ming reckoning, the housecleaning entailed sixteen dismissals and affected more than 70 percent of all positions in the academy.[83] Both Hanlin scholarship and lecturing skills were called into question. Thereafter, more Hanlin officials put the knowledge they had gained from experience in other offices at the disposal of the emperor. Gui

---

80. *MSZSL* 81.1811/Jiajing 6/10/yichou.

81. Deng Shilong, *Guochao diangu*, 35.637–38.

82. The Great Rites Controversy probably figured in the charges against Wang Tian. Wang was the brother of Wang Jun 汪俊 (*js.* 1493), the minister of rites who in 1524 led 250 court officials in memorializing against an early step the Jiajing emperor took to distance himself from the late Hongzhi emperor and to elevate the status of his own deceased father. The same year, Wang Tian and another of his brothers, Wang Wei 汪偉 (*js.* 1496), a vice minister of personnel, also separately joined in memorials that objected to other facets of the issue. For details of the Wang Tian incident, see Hu Jixun, "*Dali yi yu Mingting renshi bianju*," pp. 445–52.

83. *MSZSL* 81.1813–15/Jiajing 6/10/bingyin; Jiao Hong, *Yutang congyu*, p. 278.

E, for instance, may be considered representative in offering to the throne works of a more practical nature.[84]

Yet, not all lecturers proved to be well trained for the job. In the eighth year of the Jiajing era (1529), lecturer Sheng Duanming 盛端明 (1470–1550) was impeached by an attending supervising secretary for his rushed delivery (*ciqi pocu* 詞氣迫促) of a classics-mat exposition of the *Mencius*. The emperor replied that "lecturing officials must be carefully chosen; those like Sheng Duanming surely are not helpful." Sheng was then transferred to Nanjing.[85] The new Hanlin leadership did not significantly improve the manner or skill of the lecturers.

Proper outward appearance and serious inner cultivation were essential for successful lecturers. Ray Huang describes a later paragon of a lecturer, Zhang Juzheng 張居正 (1525–82), as "always well-groomed, [his] mind was just as sharp and meticulous as his clothing and manners."[86] Those qualities were as true of the successful lecturers half a century earlier. During the Zhengde and the early Jiajing reigns, Yang Tinghe had also been impeccably groomed. In the seventh year of Jiajing (1528), when he was a classics-mat lecturer, Lu Shen wrote about the lecturers' seriousness in preparing their person and mind for their job as follows:

Whenever a lecturer was about to deliver his lecture, he perfumed his cloth, hat, belt, and boots. When he went home after the event, these articles would be stored in a particular case to show that he dared not slight them. Before the day of presentation, he would fast and bathe, and rehearse his lecture in the hope that he could move the emperor when he lectured. This single thought of sincerity could not be easily expressed in words.[87]

The understanding that proper appearance and manners were closely tied to respect and reverence is clear in the case of Senior Compiler He Tang's 何瑭 (1474–1543) lecture to the Zhengde emperor. He Tang was dismissed from the court for what happened during a classics-mat lecture he delivered in 1513. According to the Veritable Records of the Zhengde era:

He Tang was uncultivated in his appearance and manner; his clothes were threadbare, and his face was dirty. Now at his first presentation, he read in a crippled and

---

84. For some of the works presented by Gui E, see *MSZSL* 83.1872/Jiajing 6/12/dingsi, 102.2400/Jiajing 8/6/wuchen, and 120.2873/Jiajing 9/12/renwu.

85. *MSZSL* 100.2361/Jiajing 8/4/dingmao.

86. Ray Huang, *1587*, p. 10.

87. Zhu Guozhen, *Yongchuang xiaopin*, p. 31.

dry tone, so raggedy that he was almost unable to finish his lecture. All the attending great ministers were taken by surprise. The emperor was furious when the lecture was over. He dispatched eunuchs to inform the Grand Secretariat that he intended to beat He Tang in the court. Grand Secretaries Yang Tinghe and others came to He's rescue in roundabout ways. A decree was then issued to categorically reprimand his disrespectful manner and to send him away for an appointment in the provinces.[88]

The point noted in the *Veritable Records* was that the occasion itself demanded elegant attire and a fluent and clear presentation. These were expressions of serious commitment to the lectures, and hence respect for the emperor and the audience at large.[89]

Another incident, however, shows the Jiajing emperor's sensitivity to the language of his lecturers. A memorial by Minister of Personnel Fang Xianfu 方獻夫 (*js.* 1505, d. 1544) in the ninth month of the eighth year (1529) revealed that Advisor to the Heir Apparent Lun Yixun 倫以訓 (b. 1498, *js.* 1517), Fang's fellow Guangdong native, had lectured on a passage from the *Book of Documents*. In his exposition, Lun made the statement that "posterity's learning of the mind-and-heart is not clear." The emperor told Fang that Lun's "exposition is not sound," and asked Fang for an elucidation.

Fang came to Lun's defense most tactfully, relating his impression of Lun's exposition and his own understanding of the issue Lun raised.

Lun Yixun said, "Posterity's learning of the mind-and-heart is not clear. The good mind-and-heart is, rather, understood in terms of mercy and compassion" (*cibei lianmin* 慈悲憐憫). At that time I also felt that his exposition was lacking clarity. Probably in saying this, he was referring to Buddhist learning, which takes quietude and the void as the heart of the method of cultivation and takes mercy and compassion as the good fruit [of practicing the teaching], but does not understand that in the kingly way [i.e., in Confucianism] benevolence and righteousness go hand in hand. It was simply that his words failed to focus on the main points and were not clear.

Fang then went on to offer his elucidation of the essence of the learning of mind-and-heart, drawn entirely from the theories of Neo-Confucian masters, ranging from Zhou Dunyi 周敦頤 (1017–73) and the Cheng brothers

---

88. *Ming Wuzong shilu*, 99.2067/Zhengde 8/4/gengshen.

89. A modern annotator of He Tang's works has argued that He angered the emperor, or rather the grand secretaries, for not heeding the grand secretaries' advice for modifying his lecture essay, which contained remonstrance of the emperor. For this, he was reprimanded and dismissed from office. See He Tang, *He Tang ji*, p. 449.

to their Southern Song intellectual heirs. He contrasted them with Buddhist doctrines.[90]

From another memorial Fang Xianfu submitted later, it is clear that the emperor had forwarded Fang's response to the Grand Secretariat for another explanation. The emperor ordered the grand secretaries to discuss the errors in the Buddhist doctrine of mercy, the distinction between good mind-and-heart and good nature, and the effort to exert to the utmost one's mind-and-heart and one's nature.[91] Fang said since the emperor's points were clear and the Grand Secretariat's detailed answer was also clear, he would not dwell on the question further but would discuss the new issue the emperor had raised with him: the effort to establish the original moral and intellectual foundation of the imperial person.[92]

Why was the emperor so suspicious of and unsatisfied with Lun Yixun's exposition? Lun's exposition might have been understood as disapproval of the emperor's actions in the great ritual disputes or as critical of the emperor's general attitude toward the highest level of the bureaucracy. The emperor had recently been lauded for his accomplishments in the learning of the mind-and-heart. Now, according to Lun, mercy and compassion were not part of that learning. Lun seemed to be suggesting that the emperor lacked these qualities, and that it was acceptable for him to lack them. The emperor thus could view this exposition as ridiculing him.

The Successful Lecturer—Gu Dingchen

The contrasting example of a successful lecturer is Gu Dingchen, who was among the first group of lecturers appointed to the initial classics-mat and daily lectures of the Jiajing emperor in the summer of 1521. By the time

---

90. Fang Xianfu, *Xiqiao yigao*, 3.3b–6b. It is not clear whether Lun had a southern accent that gave rise to the emperor's misunderstanding and criticism and commission. Fang Xianfu, however, spoke the same dialect as Lun did. Facility in Mandarin was as necessary as mastery of the classics for success. We know that two years prior to this, the eminent fellow Guangdong native of Lun and Fang, Huo Tao 霍韜, had declined an appointment to the lectureship, because he was afraid that his southern accent might give rise to misunderstanding (*MSZSL* 78.1738–39/Jiajing 6/7/jichou).

91. At this time, the Grand Secretariat was staffed only by Zhai Luan 翟鑾 (1477–1546) and possibly the newly recalled Zhang Cong. Yang Yiqing retired in the ninth month of the year. Gui E was dismissed in the eighth month. That perhaps was another reason, even the main reason, for asking Fang Xianfu, who was not a grand secretary but nonetheless counted as a confidant of the emperor.

92. Fang Xianfu, *Xiqiao yigao*, 3.6b–7b.

the emperor ended his study sessions fifteen years later, Gu was a minister of rites (rank 2a) and a concurrent Hanlin academician (5a), exclusively in charge of the instruction of a new class of Hanlin bachelors—the "teacher" of potential future ministers and even grand secretaries.[93] Three years later (1538), he was appointed a grand secretary. Since he had been the *optimus*—the first-place graduate of the palace examination—of the class of 1505, he thus achieved all that a Confucian literatus could hope for as an official.[94]

Little is known about Gu's early career as a lecturer, but he must have been competent and well received. In the sixth year (1527), after Gu recovered from a long period of illness, Grand Secretary Yang Yiqing 楊一清 (1454–1530) was happy to request his return to the classics-mat and daily lectures. The emperor's loyal supporters, Zhang Cong and Gui E, were appointed at the same time.[95] Gu soon stimulated the emperor to a new level of interest in classical exegesis when he expounded on the "Great Plan" chapter of the *Book of Documents*, in which he ventured an interpretation different from that of the standard commentary by the Song Confucian scholar Cai Chen 蔡沉 (1167–1230), an important disciple of Zhu Xi 朱熹 (1130–1200). The emperor was so struck with Gu's originality that he confidentially asked both Gui E and Yang Yiqing for an assessment. The replies by Gui E and Yang Yiqing reveal the emperor's motives and the exegetical differences at issue.[96]

Gui's reply was drafted by his confidant and ghostwriter, the eminent Confucian scholar Wei Xiao 魏校 (1483–1543).[97] It includes the imperial inquiry, which suggests that the emperor had first asked help from Gui E

---

93. *MSZSL* 173.3754–56/Jiajing 14/3/dingmao, 174.3786–87/Jiajing 14/4/wushen.

94. Jiao Hong, *Guochao xianzhenglu*, 16.41; Gu's epitaph was written by Yan Song 嚴嵩 (1480–1565).

95. *MSZSL* 75.1677/Jiajing 6/4/jiayin.

96. *MSZSL* 75.1682/Jiajing 6/4/wuchen. For the imperial inquiry to Gui E and Gui's reply, see Wei Xiao, *Zhuangqu yishu*, 2.14a–17a.

97. This relation has eluded modern scholars. When, however, the works of Gui and Wei are compared against their respective careers, it is plain. In one Ming edition of Wei Xiao's collection, *Zhuangqu xiansheng yishu* 莊渠先生遺書, collated and published by one of his eminent disciples, the famous writer Gui Youguang 歸有光 (1507–71), there are notes under the titles of replies to the emperor's questions stating that the replies were composed for Gui E. Wei's improvement of Gui's memorials was also no secret among Ming writers. It, for example, is mentioned in Huang Jingfang, *Guoshi weiyi*, p. 157. Note that Wei Xiao is misromanized Wei Chiao (Wei Jiao) in Goodrich and Fang, eds., *Dictionary of Ming Biography*, pp. 204, 990, 1625.

and then confirmed his own understanding with Yang Yiqing. It also reveals the sensitive and careful emperor's initial inclination toward Gu Dingchen's interpretation and his uneasiness about the traditional exegesis. Gui, slightly modifying the words of Wei Xiao, offered an interpretation in support of Cai Chen. It is unclear whether Gui was trying to forestall Gu's rise. But his answer was perhaps why the emperor solicited a second opinion from Yang Yiqing.[98]

Yang Yiqing's reply makes clear that Gu Dingchen offered an unconventional elucidation by altering the order of two key words—and concepts—in a line of the "Great Plan" chapter. But Gu felt unsure about the implications of this rereading, because then the meaning and moral of the classical text would differ from the traditional understanding. He resolved to leave the validity of his interpretation for the emperor to decide himself. Gu's unassuming attitude worked: it drove the emperor to compose a response, which upheld the standard interpretation, from which we know he was then under the influence of Gui E. But he was not certain about his own understanding and asked for Yang Yiqing's judgment. He was modest enough to instruct Yang that "if my answer is acceptable, then you improve its wording. If not, then do nothing about it." Yang, after a careful, and seemingly convincing, analysis, upheld the classic interpretation, hence concurring with the emperor's understanding.

In the middle of his reply, where his own analysis of the classical exegesis began, the well-rounded Yang Yiqing stressed that Cai Chen's interpretation was based on the interpretation passed down by classical experts of the Han and the Tang. In his conclusion, Yang emphasized that the crux of the issue—the word order—had been confirmed by Confucian masters of Han and Tang times as well as by Neo-Confucian masters of the Song. The founding Ming emperor, too, based himself on the old text when he annotated the "Great Plan" chapter. When the Yongle emperor exalted the *Six Classics* and the *Four Books* and had the *Great Compendia* of them distributed to the government schools over the empire, the exegesis for the *Book of Documents* adopted was also that by Cai Chen. Since no one had doubted it in the past, there was no reason to doubt it now. Thus, Yang was sure Gu's exegesis was no good. But Gu's effort to get at the truth when he had doubts was proper to the discussion of learning. Implicitly, therefore, Gu should not be reprimanded even if the result of his inquiry was unsound.

---

98. Wei Xiao, *Zhuangqu yishu*, 2.814a–17a; see also Gui E, *Wenxiang gong zouyi*, 5.18a–20a.

The emperor received Yang's reply with approval, and Gu stayed on as a lecturer.[99]

Obviously, it was Gu Dingchen's stimulating thinking and apparently unpretentious attitude that brought him so much regard from the emperor, who was eager to learn and to show what he knew. A month later, Gu was appointed one of eight special lecturers to expound the *Extended Meaning of the Great Learning* in the summer months and beyond.[100] Soon after the shake-up of the Hanlin Academy in the same month, he lectured on the "Maxim of the Mind" by Fan Jun of the Song, prompting the emperor to annotate the text. The emperor subsequently also annotated the "Four Maxims [of Seeing, Hearing, Speaking, and Acting]" by Cheng Yi and his own "Maxim of Seriousness and Oneness." Gu was thus the inadvertent architect of the many pavilions that housed the steles inscribed with imperial words and brushwork in the Hanlin academies and national universities and government schools throughout the empire.[101]

In the eighth month of the following year (1528), Gu was appointed the sole daily expositor to lecture on the "Great Plan" chapter, which the emperor said was the great norm and great model for rulership. For three months, he lectured "unceasingly through summer and winter." The emperor was so solicitous about Gu's health as to order the grand secretaries to delete a few sentences from the long text to ease Gu's job. He wanted Gu to compose his straightforward elucidation more carefully and elaborately to better aid his governing.[102] Gu noted in a poem that the emperor ordered him to give his best in the lectures to match the imperial intention to seek learning and governance. The end of the poem suggests their harmony: "I thereby pledge my little effort to repay Your graceful treatment, without daring to say that our relationship is as congenial as the fish and the water."[103] Indeed, the emperor also commended Gu for having "finished the exposition of the entire chapter, in detail and with all his heart."[104] Gu occasionally had to lecture even in the evening.[105] He was rewarded with promotion to

---

99. Yang Yiqing, *Miyulu* 密諭錄 1, in *Yang Yiqing ji*, pp. 918–29.

100. *MSZSL* 76.1695–97/Jiajing 6/5/yiyou.

101. Jiao Hong, *Guochao xianzhenglu*, 16.41; see also Huang Jingfang, *Guoshi weiyi*, p. 165.

102. Gu Dingchen, *Gu Wenkang gong xugao*, 2.1a–2b.

103. Gu Dingchen, *Gu Wenkang gong shigao*, 5.13a–b.

104. Gu Dingchen, *Gu Wenkang gong xugao*, 2.1a–2b.

105. Ibid., 6.6a–b, for the poem; 2.3a–36a, for the entire text of his lecture notes and essays on the "Hongfan" chapter.

supervisor of the Household of the Heir Apparent (rank 3a). Later, on Gu's request, the emperor also bestowed imperial pronouncements to commend his grandparents, parents, and himself.[106]

Gu's fish-and-water interaction with the emperor was again apparent when late in the ninth year of Jiajing (1530), the emperor initiated the rite of sacrificing to the "former sages and teacher [Confucius]." He was among the three grand secretaries and seven lecturers especially summoned to pay homage and obeisance to them in the Literary Splendor Palace. Each of the favored officials was commanded to present an exposition of a passage from a classic. Gu wrote on one from the first chapter of the *Doctrine of the Mean.*[107]

Despite the emperor's occasional suspicions, Gu maintained the imperial trust. Early in the tenth year, we find the emperor confiding to Zhang Cong that Gu's lecture essays submitted in the year past contained "words of hidden disloyalty."[108] Fortunately for Gu, nothing worse ensued. Some time later, Gu also survived a false accusation (the details of which are unknown) by his fellow lecturer Dong Qi.[109] Gu's failure to appear at a daily lecture suddenly attended by the emperor after a long suspension was pardoned.[110]

Gu cemented the imperial favor by presenting to the throne the aforementioned "Walking in the Void" prayers—seven in total—as an aid to the Daoist ritual for the birth of an imperial son. The emperor praised Gu's loyalty and affection and kept his offering prayers in the palace.[111] Gu again escaped severe discipline when he was sick and failed to present a lecture one day in the twelfth year. Both Grand Secretary Zhang Cong and the emperor were much angered by the refusal of two other lecturers to serve as ad hoc substitutes.[112] In the third month of the fourteenth year (1535), with the approval of Grand Secretaries Zhang Cong and Li Shi 李時 (1471–1538), Gu was given the unprecedented appointment of sole instructor of the next class of Hanlin bachelors.[113] As noted above, little more than three years later, he would be appointed grand secretary.

Late in 1540, after having composed many more *qingci* prayers for the emperor, Gu died in office. For this, he has been mocked in history as the

---

106. Gu Dingchen, *Gu Wenkang gong shucao*, 1.12a–14a.
107. Ibid., 1.16a–18a.
108. Zhang Cong, *Yudui lu*, 26.3a–5a.
109. *MSZSL* 121.2903/Jiajing 10/1/bingwu.
110. *MSZSL* 123.2955/Jiajing 10/3/yiwei.
111. *MSZSL* 133.3147–48/Jiajing 10/12/yiyou.
112. *MSZSL* 152.3455–56/Jiajing 12/7/yisi.
113. *MSZSL* 173.3754–56/Jiajing 14/3/dingmao.

"grand councilor of *qingci* prayers," excelling in nothing but pleasing the emperor with non-Confucian literature. His influence was such that for the remainder of the Jiajing reign, Hanlin scholar-officials rather then Daoist priests composed the *qingci* prayers.[114]

In a more positive light, posterity remembered Gu for his harmonious relations with the emperor, an interaction characterized as being like "salt and sour plum," one complementing the other and resulting in a state of mutual respect.[115] Versatile both as a classical student and as a writer, he put to good use a flexible mind and an unpretentious if sometimes diffident attitude. He was no blind follower of traditional commentaries, but neither was he a vocal anti-traditionalist. He was not afraid to make his own point known, even to the emperor, yet he did not insist on the validity of his originality. Thus he impressed the emperor with his earnestness and his honesty.

But he could not have been a dull lecturer to be able to finish his discussions of the long and difficult "Great Plan" chapter in the first place. We have no direct information on how Gu lectured. The erudite Jiao Hong 焦竑 (1541–1620) in the Wanli period related the following anecdote about him as a lecturer. Gu was lecturing on the passage on Xianqiu Meng 咸丘蒙 in the *Mencius*. When he came to the line "Yao died," the attending officials were all frightened, looking at each other with surprise [for the topic was considered proscribed in the classics-mat lectures]. Gu then continued slowly, saying, "Yao was then one hundred and twenty years old." On that note the officials regained their poise.[116] Such were the art and the craft of a masterful lecturer, combining suspense with a witty punch line. This story may suggest more about the late Ming image of a successful lecturer, but it is probably not far off the mark as far as Gu's pleasing qualities as the emperor's regular lecturer are concerned.

Lu Shen's Grievances Against the Grand Secretariat

The case of Lu Shen further shows the complexity of interaction with the emperor and lecturers. The immediate issue was whether it was appropriate for the grand secretaries to edit and modify the lecturers' essays. In the

---

114. Tan Qian, *Guoque*, 55.3456.

115. Gu Dingchen, *Gu Wenkang gong wencao*, undated preface by Jiang Dejing 蔣德璟 (*js.* 1622, d. 1646). This term was first used in "The Charge to Yue" ("Yueming" 說命) chapter of the *Documents* to denote the job of a prime minister, which is to govern the state effectively, much as the functions of salt and sour plum are to flavor thick soup.

116. Jiao Hong, *Yutang congyu*, p. 32.

fall of the seventh year (1528), Lu was appointed classics-mat lecturer as chancellor of the National University. According to his biography, his elucidation was earnest and honest, and the emperor listened to him with favor. Soon, he was given a copy of the *Canon for the Clarification of Human Relations* (*Minglun dadian* 明倫大典), the "white paper" of the history of the Great Rites Controversy, an imperial gesture that marked him as a loyal senior official.[117] But, as noted above, he violated classics-mat etiquette and was dismissed after a stern reprimand.[118] Lu's memorial inveighing against the editorial efforts of the grand secretaries is worth quoting at length, because it reveals much about the incident itself, the daily practices of the institution of the classics-mat lectures, and the aspirations of the lecturers.

The matter of the classics-mat lectures is of great consequence [to governance]. Its foremost task is to help nourish the emperor's virtue, which also does much to spur the [lecturing] officials' integrity. Why? When the emperor is sitting in front of a lecturer, his awesome appearance only a few feet away, the latter respectfully bows and then rises to elucidate the classics, talking about filial piety and loyalty, about benevolence and righteousness, about honesty and shame, about propriety and modesty. If he, reflecting on his own behavior, should find a lack of any of these virtues and yet does not feel shame in his face, who of the listeners would believe his words? Hence he, the lecturer, must enhance his effort to inculcate and embody these virtues before he can move the emperor and have him sincerely believe in what he has heard. This is why the lecture essay must come from the very hand of the lecturer himself. The essay is not merely for the convenience of reading and oral presentation.

However, lecture essays need to be worded in a warm and mild tone to fit the style of informing an emperor. This could seldom be achieved without the help of the [experienced] grand secretaries. That is why they have to be sent to the Grand Secretariat for modification. The real intention here is to get rid of any appearance of shallowness and vulgarity, and thus to nourish the emperor's intention of growing close to his Confucian officials. It is not merely for the refinement of the writing itself.

I have already considered the matter thoroughly. I dare not disregard the established practice and lightly act on what I believe. But if I lecture in this way [reading only the modified lecture essay], I am not sincere. What good is this for Your sagely learning? When I memorialized You in person, I said much of the good sense of my lecture essay was not presented, the essay's coverage was rather broad, and that it did not confine itself to the matter of literary expressions. Now, reading

---

117. Jiao Hong, *Guochao xianzhenglu*, 18.42; Lu Shen's epitaph was written by Xu Zan 許讚 (1473–1548).

118. *MSZSL* 99.2333/Jiajing 8/3/wuxu, 99.2335–36/Jiajing 8/3/guimao.

Your instruction [that I should speak what I have to say], my fear increases even more. It appears that in my haste, my foolish opinions did not reach You after all.

Moreover, now that the grand secretaries are in charge of everything and, according to the established practice, they are given concurrent directorship of the lectures, as they are all furthermore experienced in the study of literature, it is reasonable that when they modify the lecture essays they impart refined ideas to them. But this is only a minor point. If the lecture essays completely reflect the ideas of the Grand Secretariat, and the lecturers only read them out aloud, it would simply be incommensurate with the very intention [of the lecture institution], and thus far from the way of reciprocating sincere expressions between the emperor and the lecturer. This is why I present my forthright admonition.

I hope You realize my humble sincerity and specifically tell the Grand Secretariat to simply graciously allow us lecturers to present our opinions in the lecture essays. By way of this, the grand secretaries can also measure the level of our accomplishment. As for the discussion of ideas imbedded in the essays and the refinement of their literary expressions, they may do all they can and not merely read them.

I wish to ask that [in the lecture essays] apart from offering annotation and elucidation of the classical texts, all major government issues of the empire be allowed to be presented in analogy to the classics, one by one or in categories. In this way, whatever is not completely implemented by the ministerial offices, whatever the supervising secretaries and investigating censors know but dare not speak out, whatever the various provincial authorities are charged with but could not accomplish, can all be heard by Your Majesty in due course. In this way, the imperial position will daily grow more exalted, Your sagely learning will daily deepen, and we Your officials will further improve ourselves.[119]

The last paragraph was the cause of Lu Shen's dismissal. Given that the young emperor was prone to dominate the court, and the Grand Secretariat was working to control information and to influence policy, Lu's memorial inevitably raised a set of issues that could hardly be settled to the satisfaction of all concerned. Lu's contemporaries would have easily grasped the implications of his request. His sponsor, Grand Secretary Yang Yiqing, was losing the imperial ear and Zhang Cong, Yang's competitor, had recently been joined by Gui E in the Grand Secretariat. For Yang to regain the initiative, Zhang and Gui would have to be confronted and their domination undermined. Gui E was in actuality eliciting imperial support to expel Lu from the court when he memorialized in his own defense that Lu submit his original essay to justify his claim.[120]

---

119. Chen Zilong and Xu Fuyuan, eds., [*Huang*] *Ming jingshi wenbian*, 2.1552; Lu Shen, *Xingyuan ji*, 2.1a–3a.

120. He Liangju, *Siyouzhai congshuo*, pp. 147–48.

Theoretically speaking, if Lu prevailed, the Grand Secretariat's power and influence would be much reduced. If the lecturers were able to advise the emperor freely and converse with him in the lectures, the grand secretaries would be weakened in their monitoring and coordinating of the most critical state affairs. As the institutional administrators of the classics-mat and daily lectures, they would also more easily be exposed to the unpleasant consequences of unanticipated blunders by the lecturers.

The last point was indeed raised by Xu Xuemo 徐學謨 (1522–93), a perceptive ex-minister and unofficial historian of the Jiajing reign. As Xu saw it, "the established practice of the previous reigns" (*leichao taoshu* 累朝套數) was for the lecturer to submit his draft essay "ten days before the lecture to the Grand Secretariat for revision, and expound the revised essay when the day came." Xu thought Lu right in requesting an end to this practice in favor of the lecturers' presenting their independently written essays unaltered. But problems remained. "Suppose the lecture essays are not revised by the grand secretaries, and there comes a frantic youth who indulges himself in wild talk while great civil and military ministers are standing at the side of the emperor. What if the emperor could not bear listening? That is why lecture essays have to be previewed as a precaution."[121] For the grand secretaries and the lecturers not to reach some prior understanding about what the emperor was to hear was imprudent, to say the least.

Xu did not advocate heavy editing by the grand secretaries. With excessive rewriting, "the lecturers are unable to convey their thoughts regarding correcting the emperor." A late Ming commentator also said that modification of lecture essays was a common problem. Words of remonstrance would be considered taboo and thus avoided.[122] True enough. But there was no lack of ambitious officials who, given the avenue, would ignore any taboo in pursuit of personal advantage, often under the pretense of loyalty and uprightness.

A case in point is Hu Shining 胡世寧 (1469–1530), no "frantic youth" but a seasoned senior bureaucrat, who submitted unsolicited lecture essays to lodge charges against other senior courtiers. In the winter of the fourth year (early 1526), as vice minister of war, Hu submitted a memorial on the emperor's health and learning. In it he also stated, "if the emperor does not maintain proper confidentiality, he will lose his officials." Hu asked the em-

---

121. Xu Xuemo, *Shimiao zhiyulu*, 6.1a–b.
122. Chen Zilong and Xu Fuyuan, eds., [*Huang*] *Ming jingshi wenbian*, 2.1552; Lu Shen, *Xingyuan ji*, 2.1a–3a.

peror not to forward the memorial to the ministries, where it would become public knowledge. For this request, one supervising secretary impeached him as evil and treacherous and for opening an avenue for secret reports.[123] The Veritable Records' short account aimed merely at showing Hu's lack of the ethical integrity demanded of a Confucian scholar-official. The substance of the impeachment, however, is revealed in the memorial itself. The outcome of unedited lecture essays being read in public can be inferred.

The problem with Hu Shining's memorial, titled "Pledging Loyalty and Giving Aid" ("Zhongyishu" 忠益疏),[124] was the three attached lecture essays. Hu wrote that he meant to submit these essays when he was called to the capital. Concerned that this might invite the "world's ridicule and offend the court" but unable to overcome his "utmost and uncontrollable loyalty to and affection for the emperor," he presented them alongside his memorial. He hoped the emperor would read them and keep them for further reference if he found them relevant to the way of government. But if the emperor deemed them irresponsible or disloyal in nature, he hoped the emperor would give him a critical written reply and punish him, which he would willingly accept.

The first of these extraordinarily long "lecture essays" elaborated on the celebrated section of the *Great Learning* that taught that only a benevolent man (ruler) could love the good man (minister) and dislike the bad man (minister) and that a great minister was one who knew how to apply this principle in his unselfish and impartial recommendation of officials to the ruler. The implication was that the present court lacked such great ministers.

The second essay elaborated on a passage of the *Book of Documents* that stated that only the king, not the ministers, could give favor, mete out punishment, and enjoy good food. Hu was actually talking about restoring the power to recommend official appointments to the Ministry of Personnel from the Grand Secretariat. Most specifically, he cited the recent appointment of Grand Secretary Jia Yong 賈詠 (1464–1547) as evidence that the imperial influence was far overshadowed by that of the Grand Secretariat. Despite having lost his initial bid to head the Ministry of Personnel to the emperor's handpicked Xi Shu 席書 (1461–1527), Hu charged, Jia Yong became a grand secretary by the endorsement of the Grand Secretariat, which enjoyed the support of many courtiers. Hu went on to urge the emperor to

---

123. *MSZSL* 59.1404/Jiajing 4/+12/gengchen.

124. For the text of Hu's memorial and accompanying essays, see Hu Shining, *Hu Duanmin gong zouyi*, 5.24b–39a.

be resolute "for the benefit of the dynasty." Hu's actual target was the head grand secretary, Fei Hong 費宏 (1468–1535). His ambition to succeed Fei was not altogether unknown.[125]

The last essay went beyond the pale. Elaborating on the teaching of the *Book of Changes* that both ruler and servitor must observe the greatest confidentiality in handling affairs of mutual interest, Hu in effect asked the emperor to keep the memorialist's advice [and ill reports of others] to himself to prevent open attacks from the courtiers.[126]

It is difficult to imagine what might have happened if a similar essay had been presented in the open classics-mat lecture. Would the implicated officials have had to ask for pardon on the spot? Was the emperor to uphold or dismiss the charges? What if the emperor had no time to reflect and could not answer and hence caused an awkward impasse in the lecture hall or an embarrassingly abrupt end to the solemn but also joyous event? Hu Shining obviously knew that his request for confidentiality from the emperor was extraordinary. Fortunately, he was no lecturer. The Jiajing emperor certainly was also aware of difficulties of this kind when he sided with Grand Secretaries Zhang Cong and Gui E against Lu Shen.

The most nettlesome issue was the degree of revision satisfactory to the grand secretaries or both them and the lecturers. In what spirit should modifications be made and for what reasons? The case of He Tang during the Zhengde reign shows that the grand secretaries did not force a lecturer to modify his lecture essay if he was unwilling. Lu Shen's case also suggests that changes in the final version of the essays needed the common assent of the lecturers and their seniors. Lu Shen made his case precisely because Gui E recklessly edited his essay. What the emperor should or should not be told in the lectures was not simply an academic issue. Unfortunately, we do not have Lu Shen's original essay to see if it might have proven offensive to the emperor or have jeopardized the grand secretaries.

Since an emperor's learning was in the last analysis the learning of ruling and governing, classics-mat lectures theoretically were not confined to textual exposition but, rather, were to bring classical lessons to bear on current government issues and policies. Combining classical elucidation and political discussion, however, might not deliver what the lecturers had hoped for. It is unlikely that the lecturers' knowledge of the operations of the government surpassed that of the grand secretaries. The emperor, too,

---

125. Huang Jingfang, *Guoshi weiyi*, p. 158.
126. Hu Shining, *Hu Duanmin gong zouyi*, 5.24b–39a.

was likely to be uninformed but autocratic if forced to make decisions without prior deliberations with his senior advisors when issues were suddenly raised in the lecture sessions. The emperor could respond well to governmental issues only when he was well versed in the governing codes and administrative statutes of the dynasties and was fairly knowledgeable of affairs of state. That, however, would require another kind of imperial learning, such as that Qiu Jun 丘濬 (1421–95) elaborated in his 1487 statecraft work, *Supplement to the Extended Meaning of the Great Learning (Daxue yanyi bu 大學衍義補)*, which provided a body of organized and fact-oriented knowledge pragmatic enough to diagnose governmental problems and offer remedies.[127]

The Interactions of the Emperor, Grand Secretaries, and Lecturers

The triangular relationship among the Jiajing emperor, his grand secretaries, and his lecturers grew increasingly complicated. Early in his reign, Jiajing heeded the grand secretaries' advice and diligently attended the lectures. Even when he was sufficiently displeased by his antagonists in the ritual disputes to halt the classics-mat lectures and reduce his daily lectures, he did not stop his own reading. His special study of the *Extended Meaning of the Great Learning* was unprecedented for an emperor. He was keenly interested in scholarship and learning, and he no doubt had educated eunuchs to answer his queries.

Most of the time he placed great trust in the senior grand secretary. For example, he accepted the format and personnel proposed by Yang Yiqing for the daily exposition of the *Extended Meaning*, as well as the lecturers recommended by head grand secretaries Yang Tinghe, Fei Hong, Yang Yiqing, and Zhang Cong. In most cases, he also granted their requests to lighten punishments for lecturers who had offended him in some way. He even invited the grand secretaries to excursions, lectures, and banquets in the imperial parks.

Response memorandums by grand secretaries published after they died reveal some of the emperor's concerns in learning. A few examples may suffice. Yang Yiqing's replies show that the emperor read the classics and the laws and statutes of the dynasty closely in order to make decisions and implement policy. For instance, he asked about improving the text of a

---

127. Hung-lam Chu, "Ch'iu Chün's *Ta-hsüeh yen-i pu*."

section of the *Collected Administrative Statutes of the Great Ming* (*Da Ming huidian* 大明會典) on the capping rite.[128] His frequent questions to Fei Hong about poetry and essay composition prompted the jealous Gui E to compose a critical memorial.[129] Gui also opposed trite and convoluted exegesis by lecturers.[130] All the emperor's inquiries to him were about the classics. Gui's replies proved satisfactory; he employed the eminent classical scholar and Neo-Confucian theorist Wei Xiao to draft most of them during the years Wei served at the court.[131] The subjects of Jiajing's questions to Zhang Cong ranged from poetry appreciation to the emperor's annotations of three chapters of the *Book of Documents* to points made in lecture essays.[132] Most important, Zhang Cong was asked to polish the emperor's own annotations of the "Maxim of the Mind" by Fan Jun and the "Four Maxims" by Cheng Yi.[133]

In effect satisfying the Jiajing emperor's desire to reach the classical ideal of embodying the role of a ruler and the role of a teacher in one person, Zhang enjoyed the emperor's trust longer than anyone. Marked by trust and candidness, the relationship between the emperor and Zhang indeed approached the classical ideal that the ruler treat his officials as neighbors treat each other—friendly and close—if not yet as close as the "salt and sour plum" relation that Gu Dingchen's admirer would have us believe existed between Gu and the throne.

A measure of cordiality was maintained even when the emperor's trust in a grand secretary dissipated and another advisor took center stage. Yang Tinghe was verbally abused only long after he returned home, and then posthumously when the final verdict of the Great Rites Controversy was made public. The favorite Zhang Cong suffered three forced retirements, but those were due to Zhang's arrogance and his scheming against his rivals, not because the emperor had an inclination to be impolite to him.

When the emperor disagreed with his senior advisors, he usually showed his displeasure indirectly by denying them audiences, refusing to

---

128. For Yang Yiqing's replies, in which the imperial inquiries were cited, see Yang Yiqing, *Miyulu* 1, in *Yang Yiqing ji*, pp. 918–29.

129. For Gui's memorial, see *MSZSL* 68.1565/Jiajing 5/9/bingwu. For the full text, see Gui E, *Wenxiang gong zouyi*, 1.22a–24b; for Fei's reply, *MSZSL* 69.1573–74/Jiajing 5/10/wuchen.

130. See Wei Xiao, *Zhuangqu yishu*, 2.43a–46a; Gui E, *Wenxiang gong zouyi*, 7.26b–29a.

131. Wei Xiao, *Zhuangqu yishu*, 2.33b–46a; Gui E, *Wenxiang gong zouyi*, 7.17b–29a.

132. Zhang Cong, *Yudui lu*, 12.13a–14a, 14a–15a, 16a–17b.

133. Ibid., 2.18b–21a, 23a–24b.

attend study sessions at which they were present, or punishing a lecturer they had recommended. Generally the grand secretaries responded by trying to maintain their dignity as best they could. Seldom would they initiate changes in the routine of the study sessions or criticize individual lecturers. They made their opinions and ideas known when they were ordered to draft responses to critical memorials.

When the emperor raised questions about the lecturers, the grand secretaries' usual response was first to offer opinions for the emperor's reference. Even the headstrong Zhang Cong and Gui E followed this course. Zhang would not comment categorically on the shortcomings of individual lecturers until the emperor issued a second order for him to do so. Likewise, when accused by Lu Shen of changing the meaning of his lecture essay, Gui asked permission to submit Lu's original to the emperor so that Jiajing could judge for himself.

The grand secretaries prevailed when the emperor consulted them on classical or literary questions by offering learned answers that displayed a ready grasp of the classics. Yang Yiqing was a master of this art. The emperor asked him if Fei Hong's opinion that Ouyang Xiu 歐陽修 (1007–72) not be honored in the Confucian temple was right, since he had found in Ouyang's exegesis of "The Successful Completion of the War" ("Wucheng" 武成) chapter in the *Documents* reasons to justify his elevation of his deceased father during the ritual disputes. Yang honestly and calmly answered that since only a single piece of Ouyang's exegetical works on the subject could be found, he could not be considered a candidate for such an honor, which was reserved exclusively for recognized, esteemed classical scholars alone.[134] Xu Xuemo judged Yang's answer a model reply by an official to an emperor.[135]

Much of the Jiajing emperor's interaction with his grand secretaries in the study sessions also bore on the debates and disputes surrounding the rites to elevate his own parents. Relations peaked after Yang Tinghe's staunch supporters and identifiable sympathizers in the court were cashiered. But the emperor's good mood was soon dissipated by the struggles among the grand secretaries and among their protégés. When the emperor's interest in literature deepened, Fei Hong and Yang Yiqing polished his compositions. Gui E and Huo Tao 霍韜 (1487–1540), who were not grand secretaries but were close associates of Zhang Cong, memorialized

---

134. Yang Yiqing, *Miyulu*, in *Yang Yiqing ji*, 1.927–28.
135. Xu Xuemo, *Shimiao zhiyulu*, 4.5a–b.

the emperor advising him to end his literary exercises and censured Fei and Yang for engaging the emperor in poetry composition. Their criticisms were motivated by jealousy of potential rivals for the emperor's favor and a desire to encourage the emperor to pursue more philosophical and seemingly more pragmatic studies.

Their protests ironically undermined their influence on the emperor. When the imperial interest in literature declined, the emperor became more ideological and religious. After the emperor shifted his favor decisively to Daoism, his formal study of Confucian classics and histories ceased.

The Jiajing emperor's interactions with the lecturers were relatively simple. He was seldom in direct contact with them. When it became necessary to commend or reprimand them, the emperor normally referred the matter to the grand secretaries. He also sought the grand secretaries' counsel when he was not sure about a lecturer's point. Otherwise, the interactions took place through official documents—rescripts and memorials.

During the lectures, the emperor was sensitive to what he heard and saw. He showed disapproval of circuitous criticisms given by Wu Hui 吳惠 (*js.* 1511) and Guo Weifan 郭維藩 (1475–1537). When they presented substantial evidence of the malpractices they had hinted at in their lectures, however, the emperor did not fault their precise but critical memorials. The point to be noted here is that prudent lecturers might act in concert, but they had to begin with hints and suggestions and dwell on principles until they were commanded to be concrete and specific.

The emperor's reaction was harsher when a lecturer was arrogant, as in the case of Dong Qi. His ire was roused, too, when the lecturer was ill prepared, as Wang Tian's case illustrates. One reason for his impatience was his own strong educational background. Unlike most of his predecessors, he had received a good education as a prince in the province. As Yang Yiqing remarked to reaffirm the imperial commitment to the lectures, "Royal tutors and reader-companions were ordered to read and expound the classics and histories to You. No things for pleasure were allowed in Your presence, no mean persons were allowed by Your side."[136] Jiajing's solid intellectual foundation made simple and routine elucidation by the lecturers unappealing.

The lecturers' tendency to be pedantic also bored the emperor. Hu Shining accurately described the situation: "Your Majesty has reached a stage of sagacious comprehension. . . . [The lecturers] should not read and

136. Yang Yiqing, *Miyulu*, in *Yang Yiqing ji*, 18.694–96.

expound [the classics] line by line and chapter by chapter, which wastes much time and squanders one's mind and labors." Hu wanted the lecturers to discuss personnel matters and the handling of state affairs.[137] Yang Yi-qing also pointed out the lecturers' regrettable practices: "They would choose to expound delightful expressions from the [assigned] books [but] not expressions they felt to be slightly suspicious or taboo. . . . [Or] they would present flattery at the end of the lecture to make the emperor feel self-important."[138] The lecturers' preferences were inspired more by a desire for self-protection than by an effort to promote imperial arrogance. In the end, however, they also lost the emperor's interest.

Many lecturers and potential lecturers sought the emperor's attention by presenting unsolicited writings under the pretext of displaying loyalty and affection. The results were mixed. Hanlin Compiler Sun Cheng'en 孫承恩 (1481–1561), who lectured on the *Extended Meaning*,[139] earned imperial praise when he presented his rhymed writings and memorials urging the emperor to devote himself to learning and personal cultivation.[140] Liao Daonan, as mentioned above, gained imperial approval when he presented his unsolicited elucidation of the "Great Plan" chapter of the *Documents*.[141] Often lecturers presented congratulatory writings en masse to the throne for the celebration of auspicious events or natural phenomena. These likewise met with approval. In contrast, the emperor coldly rebuffed Zhan Ruoshui and told him that he could better achieve his aims by not bothering the emperor with memorials urging serious learning and courtesy to the ministers.[142]

The emperor became furious when the lecturer's comments implied criticism of the emperor's position in the Great Rites Controversy—the singular event that haunted his psyche as well as the atmosphere of the lectures. Even writings of dubious relevance could provoke criticisms of officials who had once opposed his position. For instance, when he read Zhu Xi's "Inscription for the Hall to Brighten Ethical Relationships of the Youxi County School in Nanjian Subprefecture" ("Nanjian zhou Youxi xianxue Mingluntang ming" 南劍州尤溪縣學明倫堂銘), he charged his adversaries with the following: Qiao Yu 喬宇 (1457–1524) did not listen to

---

137. Hu Shining, *Hu Duanmin gong zouyi*, 8.35a–43a.

138. Yang Yiqing, *Miyulu*, in *Yang Yiqing ji*, 18.694–96.

139. Jiao Hong, *Guochao xianzhenglu*, 18.24; Sun's epitaph was written by Xu Jie 徐階 (1503–83).

140. *MSZSL* 2.88/Zhengde 16/5/gengshen, 5.223/Zhengde 16/8/yiwei.

141. *MSZSL* 76.1690–93/Jiajing 6/5/xinsi.

142. *MSZSL* 133.3150/Jiajing 10/12/wuzi.

his teacher Yang Yiqing; Gui Hua 桂華 (*juren* 1513) was on poor terms with his brother Gui E; Zhan Ruoshui kept his distance from his friend Fang Xianfu.[143] The second person in each pair supported Jiajing in the Great Rites Controversy.

The case of Hanlin Compiler and potential lecturer Yang Ming 楊名 (1505–59) shows how far the Jiajing emperor could go when provoked. Yang criticized Minister of Personnel Wang Hong 汪鋐 (*js.* 1502, d. 1536) and Marquis of Wuding Guo Xun 武定侯郭勛 (d. 1541) as bad ministers. He also criticized the emperor for patronizing Daoist priests inside the palace. The infuriated emperor shot back that Yang was "fishing for reputation and marketing uprightness" (*guming maizhi* 沽名賣直), drawing wrong analogies, and attempting to avenge the losers in the ritual controversy. Yang was imprisoned for interrogation and torture. The incident grew more serious when Wang Hong countered that Yang Ming was attempting to rehabilitate the disgraced former grand secretary Yang Tinghe, his fellow native and close neighbor, by forming alliances with other officials. Wang added that Yang was encouraged to be so deceptive and daring because the grand secretaries were enforcing conformity and consolidating their power by forming cliques. The emperor ordered an investigation of those behind Yang Ming, which implicated Hanlin officials Cheng Wende 程文德 (1497–1559) and Huang Zongming 黃宗明 (*js.* 1514, d. 1536). They were demoted to the provinces, and Yang Ming was exiled.[144]

The emperor's rage and scorn for the lecturers were often well founded. In addition to an occasional lack of preparation and unapproved leaves of absence, some of the longtime daily lecturers exhibited a lack of personal integrity and official ethics. Despite the lecturers' various shortcomings, the emperor stopped the supervising secretaries and investigating censors from following the practice of enumerating lecturers' failings in their lectures.[145] The seasonal gifts to the lecturers continued, and their deceased parents were always given exceptional honors—posthumous titles, government funds for the construction of graveyards, and sacrificial offerings from imperial envoys—"in consideration of their [sons'] service in the reading and exposition sessions." For the same reason, lecturers received good appointments in the higher levels of the central government. Even imprudent and corrupt lecturers were punished relatively lightly. When the

---

143. *MSZSL* 73.1653–54/Jiajing 6/2/jiaxu.

144. *MSZSL* 143.3326–31/Jiajing 11/10/jiashen.

145. *MSZSL* 73.1644/Jiajing 6/2/renzi.

veteran lecturer Dong Qi was found guilty of making unsubstantiated accusations against his fellow lecturers and of delaying the observation of his mourning obligations in anticipation of a favorable appointment, he was permanently dismissed from officialdom. However, he was spared an exhaustive investigation and allowed to continue to wear official attire.[146] When Xu Jin, another veteran, was impeached, interrogated, and found guilty of bribery, the emperor only deprived him of his official status.[147]

All in all, the interactions of the emperor and his lecturers were cordial, formal, and serious. The emperor was never easygoing but seldom overly harsh. Occasionally, he surprised the lecturers by calling an unscheduled session or by meeting in an unfamiliar location. The lecturers were also respectful, particularly following a reprimand for lack of proper manners. Few lecturers were able to gain the favor and regard the Jiajing emperor showed Gu Dingchen. The secret of Gu's success was his modest but honest expression of his own understanding of the classical texts he was expounding. One can only wonder why so few of his colleagues studied his example.

The relationship between the grand secretaries and the lecturers was more ambiguous. The grand secretaries were unanimous in urging the emperor to study and to grant frequent audiences to senior officials. Their institutional roles, however, differed. The grand secretaries' duty was to nominate and evaluate lecturers, and they did promote their own candidates. Even Gui E, who was critical of the lecture tradition, promoted his scholarly advisor and ghostwriter Wei Xiao to a position that qualified him to be appointed a classics-mat lecturer.[148] But since all the grand secretaries before Zhang Cong and Gui E began their careers as Hanlin officials, they shared a general understanding with the lecturers regarding the appropriate content and delivery of the lectures. Harmony and cooperation were made possible by the fact that there was a kind of teacher-disciple relationship between them. The result of this relationship was reciprocal: the grand secretaries were willing to help the junior lecturers they introduced to overcome their initial difficulties, but they also counted on the latter's support when they confronted the emperor. Thus, most lecturers were protégés of the grand secretaries.

---

146. *MSZSL* 121.2903/Jiajing 10/1/bingxu.

147. *MSZSL* 127.3024–26/Jiajing 10/+6/gengyin.

148. For Gui's recommendation of Wei, see Gui E, *Wenxiang gong zouyi*, 6.23a–24a; for Wei's promotion to chancellor of the National University, see *MSZSL* 99.2352/Jiajing 8/3/renxu.

That relationship, however, began to change following the departure of Yang Yiqing, the last of the statesmen who had began their career in the Hanlin Academy and matured during the Hongzhi reign. Zhang Cong and Gui E adopted a markedly different style in handling relations with lecturers. When Zhang felt that classics-mat lecturer Wei Xiao was threatening to engage the scholarly attention of the emperor, he did not hesitate to promote Wei to a high-ranking office, the officials of which nonetheless were disqualified from serving as lecturers.[149] The unprecedented shakeup of the Hanlin Academy in 1527 testifies to the threat the emperor's confidants perceived in the close alliance of the Grand Secretariat and the Hanlin Academy. The bloody group protest in 1524 against the emperor's resolute elevation of his parents, on the other hand, was proof of the success of the more traditional relationship between the grand secretaries and the lecturers. Lu Shen's later protests against Gui E were a counter-example in two senses—a show of support for Yang Yiqing's more amiable relations with the lecturers and criticism of Gui E's adversarial style of relations. If it had been Yang Yiqing who modified Lu Shen's essay, one wonders whether Lu would have protested.

Despite the domination of Zhang Cong and Gui E, some continuity with the old style of relations survived. It was the rivalries among the lecturers themselves and their sponsors that encouraged the emperor's arbitrary behavior and eventually led to his loss of respect for the institution altogether. When the grand secretaries and the lecturers held the same views or stood on the same ground, even a headstrong emperor could be guided to a compromise. For instance, the Jiajing emperor accepted the same traditional exegesis advocated by both Yang Yiqing and Gui E at the expense of a new interpretation by Gu Dingchen, to which he was initially inclined.

However, it was also Gui E who demanded that each day one lecturer be called to lecture without a supervising grand secretary being present so that advice could be given free from intimidation and possible retaliation.[150] This mistrust of, or challenge to, higher authority weakened the strength of the institution in the long run. The days when Lü Nan and Lu Shen courageously voiced their opinions to the face of the emperor came to an end when the lecturers, and eventually their mentoring and supervis-

---

149. Huang Jingfang, *Guoshi weiyi*, p. 157.
150. Gui E, *Wenxiang gong zouyi*, 2.1a–2b; see *MSZSL* 76.1695–97/Jiajing 6/5/yiyou for the date.

ing grand secretaries, became adept at and willing to present Daoist *qingci* prayers. No longer could they aspire to the mantle of imperial "teacher"; their new function was to cater to the emperor's wishes. Their ability to claim the moral high ground and serve as a wise counselor or a critic was vanquished by their desire to please the emperor and advance their own careers.

Conclusion

The Jiajing emperor obviously took the lectures seriously. Ever sensitive to his lecturers and their lecture essays, he was also dissatisfied with certain conventions of the system and traditional interpretation of the classics. His moods, however, were much conditioned by the lingering ritual disputes over the clan and dynastic status of his parents.

As David Robinson argues in Chapter 8 in this volume on the imperial family and the Mongol legacy, the Jiajing emperor's status as an outsider— a prince from the provinces—deeply influenced his perception and reception of court culture. Unfamiliar with the style the prestigious Hanlin academicians adopted in the lectures, he deeply distrusted the courtiers in ascendance during the early years of his reign, who extolled the harmony of civil officials under the leadership of the Grand Secretariat in negotiation or confrontation with the throne.[151] His confidants, who eventually came to dominate the Grand Secretariat and the Hanlin Academy, had not begun their civil service careers in the Hanlin. Their antagonism against the establishment led to hostility toward the lectures and lecturers as traditionally constituted. Tension developed among all those involved in the institution. In good times, cordiality and mutual respect prevailed; in bad times, the emperor suspended both lectures and court audiences, and the grand secretaries chastised disrespectful lecturers.

Most fundamentally, these tensions betrayed the emperor's sense of frustration. From his lecturers, he demanded a seriousness that was to be manifested in their manner and preparation. If the student should be respectful to his teachers, so his servitors (the teachers) should also be respectful to their monarch (the student). The problem lay in the priority to be given these conflicting roles. Timely emphasis of their political, social, and ethical roles proved difficult for both the Jiajing emperor and his lecturers.

———

151. For this point as it relates to the preceding Zhengde emperor, see Hung-lam Chu, Review of *The Chosen One*, esp. p. 275.

The nature of the court vastly complicated the question of what role was to be adopted at what time. Culture may be understood as expressions that a large group of people deeply believe in and unconsciously act out. The court was burdened because its actions had far-reaching repercussions. It was not merely the center of government. It was also the source of civilization. The scholarship it promoted, the ways of learning it practiced, the morals it exalted, the ethics it professed, eventually influenced the rest of the empire. The behavior of the emperor and his officials was emulated by aspirants to court life and high culture. Whether the emperor indeed behaved as a respectful student of his courtiers had a great impact on the aspirations and morals of officials and the populace at large.

The problem was who was to dictate what expressions and styles were correct and worthy for the court to exemplify. The grand secretaries and the lecturers cherished their job in the belief that an emperor's classical and historical learning was an inseparable part of statecraft. An emperor who could learn from what they taught would tend to share their political culture and thus be more inclined to respect the institutions and administrative mechanisms through which government functioned and operated. Accordingly, they saw themselves both as teachers and as advisors to the emperor. Their ideal demanded the monarch to learn from them before he ruled them.

The Jiajing emperor did not entertain this idea for long. Competing attractions vied for his body and his spirit, his emotions and his intellect. In fact, he learned quickly to turn himself into the ruler and teacher of all. Early in his reign, the format and the substance of the lecture were defined for him by Grand Secretary Yang Tinghe, who also urged him to study the founding emperor's *Ancestral Instructions* in hopes that he would become a strong ruler. In the end, he not only specifically studied the *Extended Meaning*, a text the dynastic founder exalted, but also emulated the founder in annotating classical works of statecraft value and authoring maxims in the tradition of Neo-Confucian philosophy. In doing so, he showed himself not only a worthy filial descendant but also an embodiment of the classical ideal of combining the roles of ruler and teacher in one person. The function of the lecture now changed from instruction of the emperor to observation and evaluation of the lecturer. As the lecturer's dual roles of teacher and servitor shrank to the latter, halfhearted and perfunctory performances became the rule. The serious lecturer found no genuine satisfaction in what had become a hollow performance. The nature of the lecture changed when ambitious courtiers used it for career advancement and power.

Equally observable in the court lectures throughout these years were imperial comments on such values as filial piety, loyalty, affection, sincerity, respectfulness, and seriousness. "Loyalty and affection," that is, an official's loyalty to and affection for his emperor, were especially emphasized. But the understanding of these terms changed over the years. The argument between lecturer Lu Shen and Grand Secretary Gui E over the control or promotion of the kind of information and knowledge deemed important for the emperor to receive in the classics-mat lecture was also a matter of showing loyalty and affection. Both Lu Shen's demand for consistency in style and substance in the presentation of lectures—sincere, earnest, and relevant to current issues—as a proper way of informing an emperor and the monitoring grand secretary's stress on smooth and direct elucidation of classical precepts were inspired by the ideal of loyalty and affection. Their divergent stations led them to stress different facets of the same goal.

It remained for the emperor to endow the sense of "loyalty and affection" with a new form and substance. The emperor was fond of using the phrase "loyalty and affection" to praise officials whose deeds he appreciated. Both good-willed and self-serving memorialists invoked the same phrase. Only the lecturers seldom belabored the point. They considered their very job an unmistakable manifestation of their loyalty and affection. What could be more loyal and loving than educating the imperial person in the sages' wisdom and virtues they extolled? They defined loyal as faithful. Faithfulness to the lecture institution and earnestness in their lectures were expressions of supreme loyalty.

The Jiajing emperor, however, favored a more personal expression of the same value, as evinced in his use of the same phrase to praise Gu Dingchen's composition and presentation of Daoist *qingci* prayers for the imperial cause. Although neither the first nor the only Ming monarch with this preference, he was the most successful. For a long time to come, the loyalty and affection of his courtiers would be transformed from respect for dynastic statutes and institutions to a sycophancy symbolized by leading courtiers' expertise and enthusiasm in the composition of *qingci* prayers. Daoist priests, alchemists, and whoever satisfied his personal whims and lusts were loyal and loving to him, and by extension to the state and the dynasty.

In so doing, the Jiajing emperor fostered a political culture that eventually saw civil courtiers degenerate into imperial sycophants. In the process, the courtiers forfeited their political significance in relentless struggles for power and wealth under an autocracy that appeared dictatorial but was in fact subject to many competing influences. This drastic change in court culture did not go unnoticed. As a late Ming comment on Hu Shining's lecture–cum–confiding report writings noted: "One wonders if it was not the customs of his times that caused him to behave thus, evidence that even the worthies were not exempted [from selfish considerations]."[152]

---

152. Huang Jingfang, *Guoshi weiyi*, p. 158.

Works Cited

Chen Zilong 陳子龍 and Xu Fuyuan 徐孚遠, eds. [*Huang*] *Ming jingshi wenbian* [皇]明經世文編. 1638. Reprinted—Beijing: Zhonghua shuju, 1962.

Chu, Hung-lam (Zhu Honglin) 朱鴻林. "Ch'iu Chün's *Ta-hsüeh yen-i pu* and Its Influence in the Sixteenth and Seventeenth Centuries." *Ming Studies* 22 (Fall 1986): 1–32.

———. "Mingru Zhan Ruoshui zhuan dixue yongshu *Shengxue gewutong* de zhengzhi beijing yu neirong tese" 明儒湛若水撰帝學用書《聖學格物通》的政治背景與內容特色. *Zhongyang yanjiuyuan, Lishi yuyan yanjiusuo jikan* 中央研究院歷史語言研究所集刊 62, no. 3 (1993): 495–530.

———. "Ming Taizu de jingshi jianglun qingxing" 明太祖的經史講論情形. *Zhongguo wenhua yanjiusuo xuebao* 中國文化研究所學報 45 (2005): 141–72.

———. Review of *The Chosen One: Succession and Adoption in the Court of Ming Shizong* by Carney T. Fisher. *Harvard Journal of Asiatic Studies* 54, no. 1 (July 1994): 266–77.

Deng Shilong 鄧士龍. *Guochao diangu* 國朝典故. Late Wanli period. Reprinted—Beijing: Beijing daxue chubanshe, 1993.

Fang Xianfu 方獻夫. *Xiqiao yigao* 西樵遺稿. 1696. Reprinted in Siku quanshu cunmu congshu—jibu 四庫全書存目叢書集部. Tainan: Zhuangyan wenhua shiye, 1997.

Fisher, Carney T. *The Chosen One: Succession and Adoption in the Court of Ming Shizong.* Sidney: Allen and Unwin, 1990.

Goodrich, L. Carrington, and Chaoying Fang, eds. *Dictionary of Ming Biography, 1368–1644.* New York: Columbia University Press, 1976.

Gu Dingchen 顧鼎臣. *Gu Wenkang gong shigao* 顧文康公詩稿. 1639. Reprinted in Siku quanshu cunmu congshu—jibu 四庫全書存目叢書集部. Tainan: Zhuangyan wenhua shiye, 1997.

———. *Gu Wenkang gong shucao* 顧文康公疏草. 1620. Reprinted in Siku quanshu cunmu congshu—jibu 四庫全書存目叢書集部. Tainan: Zhuangyan wenhua shiye, 1997.

———. *Gu Wenkang gong wencao* 顧文康公文草. 1638. Reprinted in Siku quanshu cunmu congshu—jibu 四庫全書存目叢書集部. Tainan: Zhuangyan wenhua shiye, 1997.

———. *Gu Wenkang gong xugao* 顧文康公續稿. 1643. Reprinted in Siku jinhuishu congkan—jibu 四庫禁燬書叢刊集部. Beijing: Beijing chubanshe, 2000.

Gui E 桂萼. *Wenxiang gong zouyi* 文襄公奏議. 1544. Reprinted in Siku quanshu cunmu congshu—shibu 四庫全書存目叢書史部. Tainan: Zhuangyan wenhua shiye, 1996.

He Liangjun 何良俊 (1506–73). *Siyouzhai congshuo* 四友齋叢説. 1579. Reprinted—Beijing: Zhonghua shuju, 1959.

He Tang 何瑭. *He Tang ji* 何瑭集. First printed in 1554 and 1576 under other titles. Reprinted—Zhengzhou: Zhongzhou guji chubanshe, 1999.

Hu Jixun 胡吉勛. "*Dali yi* yu Mingting renshi bianju ji zhengzhi lunli zhuanxiang yanjiu" "大禮議"與明廷人事變局及政治倫理轉向研究. Ph.D. diss., The Chinese University of Hong Kong, 2005.

Hu Shining 胡世寧. *Hu Duanmin gong zouyi* 胡端敏公奏議. Preface 1540. Reprinted in Yingyin Wenyuange Siku quanshu 景印文淵閣四庫全書. Taibei: Shangwu yinshuguan, 1983.

Huang Jingfang 黃景昉. *Guoshi weiyi* 國史唯疑. 1644. Reprinted—Shanghai: Shanghai guji chubanshe, 2002.

Huang, Ray. *1587, A Year of No Significance*. New Haven: Yale University Press, 1981.

Jiang Mian 蔣冕. *Xianggao ji* 湘皋集. 1554. Reprinted in Siku quanshu cunmu congshu—jibu 四庫全書存目叢書集部. Tainan: Zhuangyan wenhua shiye, 1997.

Jiao Hong 焦竑. *Guochao xianzhenglu* 國朝獻徵錄. 1616. Reprinted—Taibei: Xuesheng shuju, 1965.

———. *Yutang congyu* 玉堂叢語. 1618. Reprinted—Beijing: Zhonghua shuju, 1981.

Liao Daonan 廖道南. *Diange cilin ji* 殿閣詞林記. 1545. Hubei xianzheng yishu 湖北先正遺書 ed.

Lü Nan 呂柟. *Jingyezi neipian* 涇野子內篇. Preface 1533. Reprinted—Beijing: Zhonghua shuju, 1992.

Lu Shen 陸深. [*Lu Wenyu gong*] *Xingyuan ji* [陸文裕公] 行遠集. 1722. Reprinted in Siku quanshu cunmu congshu—jibu 四庫全書存目叢書集部. Tainan: Zhuangyan wenhua shiye, 1997.

Mano Senryū 間野潛龍. "Mindai no shinkō ni tsuite" 明代の進講について. *Toyama daigaku bungakka kiyō* 富山大学文学科紀要 2 (1975): 1–15.

Ming Shizong shilu 明世宗實錄. 1577. Reprinted—Taibei: Zhongyang yanjiuyuan, Lishi yuyan yanjiusuo, 1965.

Ming Wuzong shilu 明武宗實錄. 1525. Reprinted—Taibei: Zhongyang yanjiuyuan, Lishi yuyan yanjiusuo, 1964.

MSZSL, see *Ming Shizong shilu*

Tan Qian 談遷. *Guoque* 國榷. Preface 1654. Reprinted—Beijing: Guji chubanshe, 1958.

Wang Yinglin 王應麟 (1223–96). *Yuhai* 玉海. 1337. Reprinted—Taibei: Huawen shuju, 1964.

Wei Xiao 魏校. *Zhuangqu yishu* 莊渠遺書. Preface 1561. Reprinted in Yingyin Wenyuange Siku quanshu 景印文淵閣四庫全書. Taibei: Shangwu yinshuguan, 1983.

Xia Yan 夏言. *Guizhou xiansheng zouyi* 桂州先生奏議. Reprint of undated late Ming original. In Siku quanshu cunmu congshu—shibu 四庫全書存目叢書史部. Tainan: Zhuangyan wenhua shiye, 1996.

Xu Xuemo 徐學謨. *Shimiao zhiyulu* 世廟識餘錄. Wanli period block-cut edition. Reprinted—Taibei: Guofeng chubanshe, 1965.

Yang Tinghe 楊廷和. *Yang Wenzhong sanlu* 楊文忠三錄. First printed in Wanli period. Reprinted in Yingyin Wenyuange Siku quanshu 景印文淵閣四庫全書. Taibei: Shangwu yinshuguan, 1983.

Yang Yiqing 楊一清. *Yang Yiqing ji* 楊一清集. Beijing: Zhonghua shuju, 2001.

Yu Ruji 俞汝楫. *Libu zhigao* 禮部志稿. 1620. Reprinted in Yingyin Wenguange Siku quanshu 景印文淵閣四庫全書. Taibei: Shangwu yinshuguan, 1983.

Zhang Cong 張璁. *Yudui lu* 諭對錄. 1609. Reprinted in Siku quanshu cunmu congshu—shibu 四庫全書存目叢書史部. Tainan: Zhuangyan wenhua shiye, 1996.

Zhang Fan 張帆. "Yuandai jingyan shulun" 元代經筵述論. In *Yuanshi luncong* 元史論叢, no. 5. Beijing: Zhongguo shehui kexue chubanshe, 1993, pp. 136–59.

Zhu Guozhen 朱國禎. *Yongchuang xiaopin* 湧幢小品. 1622. Reprinted—Beijing: Wenhua yishu chubanshe, 1998.

Zhu Ruixi 朱瑞熙. "Songchao jingyan zhidu" 宋朝經筵制度. In *Dier jie Songshi xueshu yantaohui lunwenji* 第二屆宋史學術研討會論文集, ed. Dier jie Song shi xueshu yantaohui, Mishuchu 第二屆宋史學術研討會秘書處. Taibei: Zhongguo wenhua daxue, Shixue yanjiusuo and Shixuexi, 1996, pp. 229–64.

FIVE

Didactic Picturebooks for Late Ming Emperors and Princes

Julia K. Murray

This chapter examines Ming officials' use of pictures as a means of encouraging a young emperor or heir apparent to develop into an ideal Confucian sage ruler. It focuses on four illustrated anthologies of historical exemplars, all of which were devised as supplements to the normal princely curriculum of the *Four Books* and *Five Classics*. Created over a 100-year period, from 1495 to about 1595, these compendia took the form of albums of paintings matched with punctuated and annotated texts. Three were sponsored by officials whose duties included lecturing to the emperor or crown prince, and one was submitted by a minister at the Nanjing court. Chronologically and in certain other respects, the four compilations fall into two pairs. The earlier two, submitted in 1495 and 1539, respectively, bore the same title, *Shenggong tu* 聖功圖 (Pictures of sagely accomplishment).[1] Intended for instructing very young crown princes, both were rejected by the reigning emperor and neither has survived, except through descriptions in documentary accounts. By contrast, numerous woodblock-printed editions reproduced and perpetuated the two later collections, *Dijian tushuo* 帝鑑圖說 (The emperor's mirror, illustrated and discussed; submitted to the throne in 1573) and *Yangzheng tujie* 養正圖解 (Cultivating rectitude, illustrated and explained; 1597). Even though the handpainted originals are not

---

1. Submission memorials for both are recorded in *Xiaozong shilu* in *Ming shilu* (hereafter cited as *XZSL*), 105.2b–3a (pp. 1914–15); and *Shizong shilu* in *Ming shilu* (hereafter cited as *SZSL*), 226.6a–b (pp. 4703–4), respectively.

extant, the printed versions gained wide circulation and found diverse functions outside the palace.[2]

Although enhancements to imperial education were not unknown in earlier periods, the resort to pictures reflects a sixteenth-century interest in visuality as an expedient means of stimulating innate moral potential.[3] As suggested by explicit words in their titles like *tushuo* 圖説 and *tujie* 圖解, which were particularly in vogue in the late sixteenth century, pictorial and verbal exposition played equally important roles in such compilations. To use a term found in Western scholarship on children's literature, these works could be called "picturebooks."[4] In both *Dijian tushuo* and *Yangzheng tujie*, and at least one of the two *Shenggong tu*, the illustrations preceded the accompanying textual explanations, to pique the interest of their young target audience. This sequence reverses the priority usually given to writing over pictorial images and marks the intended viewer as less literate.[5] As the sponsors of all four compilations asserted, illustrated stories made abstract concepts easier to understand. In traditional writings, reliance on visual aids was usually associated with "stupid men and women" (*yufu yufu* 愚夫 愚婦) and with the very young. However, in the sixteenth century, some moralists also considered pictures useful for awakening the moral heart-mind (*liang zhi* 良知) or nature (*liang xin* 良心).[6]

In addition to placing the four illustrated anthologies in a longer tradition of didactic literature produced at court, this chapter also examines the differences in their initial reception and subsequent fates. The trajectories

———

2. I analyze the origins and development of *Dijian tushuo*, and its numerous editions in China and Japan, in "From Textbook to Testimonial"; I examine prefaces and other ancillary writings that reposition it for different intended audiences in "Changing the Frame." I similarly investigate the creation and various editions of *Yangzheng tujie* in "Squaring Connoisseurship with History." I discuss the significance of the woodblock medium for both in "Didactic Illustrations in Printed Books."

3. For relevant discussions, see Clunas, *Pictures and Visuality in Early Modern China*; and Handlin, *Action in Late Ming Thought*.

4. See Nikolajeva and Scott, *How Picturebooks Work*, introduction.

5. For example, Zheng Qiao 鄭樵 (1104–62) wrote: "Pictures are very summary, and writing is very extensive. With pictures one seeks what is easy; with writing, one seeks what is difficult. When scholars of antiquity went about learning, they had to set up the picture on their left and the writing on their right" (*Tongzhi, juan* 72, *tupu* 圖譜 1, p. 837, upper). His statement is repeated by Wang Yinglin, *Yuhai*, 56.31b (p. 1072).

6. This view was based on ideas associated with Wang Yangming 王陽明 (1472–1529; *js*. 1499) and particularly his Taizhou-school follower Geng Dingxiang 耿定向 (1524–96, *js*. 1556), whom the compilers of *Dijian tushuo* and *Yangzheng tujie* considered a mentor; see below.

of the four compilations shed light on the political and cultural environments of the middle to late Ming court, including its interactions with various external constituencies and its responses to the great expansion of publishing in the late sixteenth century.

Background

During the Ming period, the preparation of heirs to the throne was a critical problem. Because the Hongwu emperor had abolished the post of prime minister in 1380, the official bureaucracy had no chief executive to coordinate the routine administration of the empire. In order to function well, Ming governance required a well-educated and hard-working emperor, one able and willing to participate actively in daily bureaucratic affairs, in addition to maintaining an extensive schedule of ceremonial rituals. If an emperor chose not to devote much attention to the minutiae of governing, edicts and responses to memorials still had to go out in his name, forcing the bureaucracy to rely on eunuchs who could handle matters. To ensure his dynasty's longevity, the Hongwu emperor had taken great care with the preparation of his heir and had provided a thorough education to all his many sons.

Confucian ideology also defined the emperor as the pivotal figure in a cosmological system that connected heaven and earth. The ideal Son of Heaven was a ruler who cultivated his character into harmony with the workings of heavenly principle (*tian li* 天理) so that he could order the world. During the Song dynasty, Confucian scholars gave formal lectures and conducted study sessions to assist the emperor or the designated heir apparent in his pursuit of learning and cultivation of virtue. The lectures typically linked the rectification of the ruler's heart-mind with his study of historical role models.[7] The Hongwu emperor found such ideas congenial and utilized them in establishing his dynasty. Displaying his moral authority to shape the realm, he promulgated didactic tracts to various groups, a legitimizing strategy also followed by his son, the usurping Yongle emperor.[8] The latter also prescribed orthodox learning more comprehensively by publishing official editions of the *Four Books* and *Five Classics* with the commentaries of Zhu Xi 朱熹 (1130–1200), in part to demonstrate himself

---

7. De Bary, *Neo-Confucian Orthodoxy and the Learning of the Mind-and-Heart*, pp. 29–30; see also Elman, *A Cultural History of Civil Examinations in Late Imperial China*, pp. 68–69, 101.

8. See Scarlett Jang's chapter in this volume, pp. 116–85, for a list of some of the titles.

worthy of the throne that he had seized from his young nephew, the Jianwen emperor.

As the founder of the Ming dynasty, the Hongwu emperor had the energy and ambition equal to the enormous burdens of imperial-Confucian rulership, as did the Yongle emperor. However, most subsequent Ming emperors showed less inclination to work so hard, perhaps because they gained the throne by routine succession and did not have to prove their legitimacy. In order to influence later emperors to perform according to Confucian ideals, civil officials developed the court lecture system into a regular institution, as described in Hung-lam Chu's chapter in this volume. Nonetheless, they could do little if the ruler chose instead to devote his attention to interests that reflected a different conception of his imperial role, such as waging war, going on hunting expeditions, patronizing religious cults, acquiring women, or consuming luxury goods.[9] Nor could civil officials keep him away from the eunuchs and palace women who had access to him in the private reaches of the inner palace. One strategy to circumvent their influence was to inculcate Confucian moral values as early as possible. Showing the heir apparent attractive, didactic pictures before he was old enough to begin formal instruction might potentially shape his thoughts and behavior in the desired way.

The use of pictures as models or warnings was an ancient tradition, going back at least to the celebrated murals of the second century BCE in the Lingguangdian 靈光殿 palace of the Western Han prince of Lu 魯.[10] A more recent and relevant precedent was Song Emperor Renzong's (r. 1022–63) *Guanwen jiangu tu* 觀文見古圖 (Pictures of contemplating texts and using the past as a mirror), a work containing 120 annotated paintings of the admirable or despicable deeds of ancient rulers, from the Yellow Emperor to Tang Emperor Taizong (r. 626–49).[11] Renzong had court artists illus-

---

9. See David Robinson's chapter in this volume, pp. 365–421.

10. See relevant discussion in Wu, *The Wu Liang Shrine*, chap. 5. For the text of the *Lingguangdian fu* 靈光殿賦 (Rhapsody on the Hall of Numinous Light), see Xiao Tong, *Wen xuan*, 2: 262–77.

11. Wang Yinglin, *Yuhai*, 56.22b–23a (p. 1068). Wang Mingqing (*Huizhu lu, houlu, juan* 1, p. 53) gives a somewhat different account, crediting Empress Dowager Liu 劉太后 (970–1033) with ordering the compilation *for* the young Renzong. The work is listed as *Renzong Guanwen jiangu tu* 仁宗觀文見古圖 (Renzong's *Pictures of Contemplating Texts and Using the Past as a Mirror*) in *Songshi*, 203.5103. It left the palace during the Jin 金 invasions of 1126–27 but was recovered and presented to Song Gaozong (r. 1127–62) in 1135. I have found no further mention of it after the Southern Song period.

trate these events and wrote summaries of them and a record of the project himself. Completed in 1041, the work filled twelve handscrolls. Renzong showed them to his high ministers on several occasions in the early 1040s, perhaps to help impress his authority on them in a period of political ferment. He also had the set carved for reproduction as a woodblock-printed edition to bestow on his courtiers. In 1090, Lecturer-in-Waiting Fan Zuyu 范祖禹 (1041–98, *js.* 1063) urged the thirteen-year-old Emperor Zhezong (r. 1085–1100) to view the pictures, so that he would recognize virtuous and evil conduct and understand the difficulty of the ruler's enterprise.[12]

Besides being useful for educating a child-emperor, visual aids might also be efficacious for instructing an imperial pupil who was not Chinese. In 1282, the Chinese official Wang Yun 王惲 (1227–1304) submitted an illustrated compendium called *Chenghua shilüe* 承華事略 (Summary of the actions of a crown prince) for the use of Zhenjin 真金 (1243–86), the son and heir apparent of Yuan Shizu (Khubilai; r. 1260–94).[13] To teach the Mongol scion about Chinese ways of statecraft and Confucian values of conduct, the work introduced exemplary crown princes from the Shang through the Tang periods. Grouped into twenty thematic sections containing one to five examples each, the pictures were followed by short quotations from a classical or historical source.[14] At the end of each section, Wang summarized the main points, sometimes making them more relevant by connecting them to specific concerns of Zhenjin or his father. Eventually, the compendium was translated into Mongolian.

Ming Imperial Precedents

The Ming court produced a large number of didactic works published by the Directorate of Ceremonial (Silijian 司禮監), discussed in this volume by Scarlett Jang. These publications often seem calculated as much to help

---

12. Wang Yishan, *Jiacun leigao*, 20.5a–b.

13. For further discussion, see my *Mirror of Morality*, pp. 87–88; see also Franke, "Wang Yun." Zhenjin was named heir in 1275 but died before his father and never ruled; Wang submitted *Chenghua shilüe* in the twelfth month of Zhiyuan 18 (January 1282). The work was reconstructed and printed at the late Qing court as *Qinding Yuan Wang Yun Chenghua shilüe butu* 欽定元王惲承華事略補圖; for sample illustrations, see *Qingdai gongting banhua*, pp. 199–207.

14. The twenty thematic sections are listed by name in Wang's biography; see *Yuanshi*, 167.3934. According to Franke ("Wang Yun," esp. p. 170), twenty-six examples came from dynastic histories, nine came from the Confucian classics, and five from other Han or Tang works.

legitimize the ruler's exercise of power as to instruct their intended readers. Mostly not illustrated, such compilations used positive and negative
examples from earlier history to reinforce moralistic prescriptions.[15] Even
before founding the dynasty, the Hongwu emperor had actively promoted
this mode of indoctrination in the region under his control. In 1366,
he commanded Xiong Ding 熊鼎 (1322–76) and Zhu Mengyan 朱夢炎
(d. 1378) to compile a didactic text for the sons of his supporters and told
them:

Even the sons and younger brothers of officials and nobles who read many books
cannot understand their profound meanings. It is better to collect real accounts of
loyal goodness or traitorous evil in antiquity and explain them directly in common
language to make it easy to understand for those who look; so that in other days,
when the learning they have indulged in produces no results, they will nonetheless
know the deeds of the ancients and can advise and explain.[16]

The Hongwu emperor also ordered the palace tutors to teach his sons
stories about exemplary rulers and ministers, to show them illustrations of
paragons of filial piety, and to use pictures of agricultural livelihood to
make them appreciate the hardships of the common people.[17] One of the
compilations distributed to the princes was *Zhaojian lu* 昭鑒錄 (Bright mirror records; 1373), which contained stories about 144 Han, Tang, and Song
princes, divided into three groups: eighty-one belonged to "the good, to
serve as models" (*shan ke wei fa* 善可爲法); four were "first bad, later
good" (*xian e hou shan* 先惡後善); and fifty-nine were "the bad, to serve as
warnings" (*e ke wei jie* 惡可爲戒).[18] The intermediate category disappeared
in subsequent works, such as *Chujun zhaojian lu* 儲君昭鑒錄 (Bright mirror
records for the crown prince),[19] leaving the clear-cut dichotomy between
positive and negative role models later seen in *Dijian tushuo*. Moreover, the

---

15. For brief descriptions of specific works, see Sakai, *Chūgoku zensho no kenkyū*,
pp. 8–30.

16. Ibid., p. 31; see also *Taizu shilu* in *Ming shilu*, 21.7b (p. 0308).

17. The Hongwu emperor's well-known attention to his sons' education, likened to
the Duke of Zhou's 周公 instruction of King Cheng 周成王 of the Zhou dynasty, is
invoked in the prefaces to *Shenggong tu* and *Yangzheng tujie*, discussed below.

18. Sakai, *Chūgoku zensho no kenkyū*, pp. 9–10. The chief compilers were Tao Kai 陶凱
(*juren* 1347) and Zhang Chou 張籌 (fl. 14th c.); Song Lian 宋濂 (1310–81) contributed a
preface. Only fragments of the work survived by the late Ming.

19. No longer extant and its date of compilation unknown, *Chujun zhaojian lu* was intended specifically for the heir apparent, with sixty stories about good crown princes of
earlier times and twenty about bad ones; see ibid., p. 16.

Hongwu emperor promulgated several sets of imperial instructions to various groups, often combining moralistic generalities with specific examples.[20]

Equally energetic, the Yongle emperor was more systematic in preparing and issuing didactic compendia to establish standards of orthodox morality.[21] Eager to legitimize his usurpation, he published the tracts to prove himself an exemplary ruler. He compiled some of these works himself, such as *Shengxue xinfa* 聖學心法 (The heart-mind method in the sages' learning), published by the eunuch-run Directorate of Ceremonial in 1409.[22] The book generally followed the format of Zhen Dexiu's 眞德秀 (1178–1235) *Daxue yanyi* 大學演義 (Extended meanings of the *Great Learning*), with quotes from the classics and Neo-Confucian philosophers, but the Yongle emperor added moralizing comments of his own to many of the sections. The work explained the Way of the Ruler for his successors' benefit, with a concluding section that clarified expectations for ministers. For a younger or less erudite audience, the Yongle emperor published *Xiaoshun shishi* 孝順事實 (Stories of the filial and obedient) in 1420, which contained accounts of 207 exemplary individuals who had performed filial deeds.[23] Drawn from various historical sources, the stories covered a broad chronological and social range, from the emperors Yu and Shun in remote antiquity to officials and commoners (including women) of the Southern Song and Yuan periods. A four-character title and punctuation were added to the main text of each selection, and a discussion and two poems by the emperor were appended to it. The emperor's preface affirms that he

---

20. De Bary, *Neo-Confucian Orthodoxy and the Learning of the Heart-and-Mind*, p. 158; also Sakai, *Chūgoku zensho no kenkyū*, pp. 12–16, 34–38.

21. Even more renowned than the titles I discuss are the great compilations made by court scholars at the Yongle emperor's command, such as *Wujing Sishu Xingli daquan* 五經四書性理大全 (Great compendia on the *Five Classics*, *Four Books*, and human nature and principle; completed in 1415), and *Yongle dadian* 永樂大典 (Great literary repository of the Yongle reign), completed in 1408 and now surviving only in fragments. For further discussion, see Tsai, *Perpetual Happiness*, chap. 7; and Elman, *A Cultural History of Civil Examinations in Late Imperial China*, pp. 97–116 *passim*.

22. Mote and Twitchett, *Cambridge History of China* (hereafter cited as *CHC*), 7: 218–19; also de Bary, *Neo-Confucian Orthodoxy and the Learning of the Heart-and-Mind*, pp. 158–63. For a punctuated transcription of the emperor's lengthy preface, see *Guoli zhongyang tushuguan xuba jilu, zibu*, 1: 111–17.

23. An example of the original palace edition can be found in the National Library, Taibei (Rare Book 05562); two others are in Princeton's East Asian Library (TB117/662 and TB117/3717). An edition in the National Library, Beijing, has been reproduced in *Beijing tushuguan guji zhenben congkan*, vol. 14. For a punctuated transcription of the Yongle emperor's preface, see *Guoli zhongyang tushuguan xuba jilu, zibu*, 1: 117–18.

compiled the book so that people would grasp the fundamental importance of the principle of filiality. Acknowledging that his collection was not
the final word on the subject, he expressed the hope that his more learned
successors would gather additional examples and publish a supplementary
volume. According to the eighteenth-century *Official History of the Ming Dynasty*, *Xiaoshun shishi* was one of the texts to be chanted by uncapped boys
in the imperial clan school (*zong xue* 宗學).[24]

    In 1426, shortly after coming to the throne, the Xuande emperor had
the Directorate of Ceremonial publish a pair of hortatory works containing
chronologically organized stories of positive and negative exemplars from
antiquity through the Yuan dynasty. One was addressed to high officials,
and the other to relatives of empresses and consorts.[25] His preface to the
former, *Lidai chen jian* 歷代臣鑑 (The mirror of ministers throughout the
ages), emphasized that wise and virtuous advisors were essential for the
Son of Heaven to fulfill his awesome responsibilities.[26] By presenting historical models, the Xuande emperor hoped to encourage contemporary officials to serve conscientiously. Each story was followed by an explanatory
discussion, with printed punctuation. The other work, *Waiqi shijian* 外戚
事鑑 (The mirror of the deeds of imperial affines), contained illustrations
in addition to stories and explanations.[27] The emperor's preface indicates
that the work was intended to caution the family members of imperial
women against using their palace connections to interfere in governmental
affairs. The inclusion of pictures in this work, unlike other didactic compilations by Ming emperors, suggests that the women themselves were also
supposed to view it.

    The mid-fifteenth-century Jingtai emperor issued *Lidai jun jian* 歷代
君鑑 (The mirror of rulers throughout the ages), again divided into posi-

---

24. *Mingshi* (hereafter cited as *MS*), 69.1689.

25. Sakai, *Chūgoku zensho no kenkyū*, pp. 21–22.

26. An example of the original palace edition can be found in the National Library,
Taibei (Rare Book 02418); the Princeton East Asian Library has three examples (TC-
328/1241b, /711b, and /2061). For a punctuated transcription of the Xuande emperor's
preface, see *Guoli zhongyang tushuguan xuba jilu, shibu*, 2: 38–39.

27. The Xuande emperor's preface is transcribed in *Xuande shilu* in *Ming shilu*, 16.7b–
8b (pp. 0432–34); and the Directorate of Ceremony's publication of the work is noted
in Liu Ruoyu, *Zhuo zhong zhi* (hereafter cited as *ZZZ*), 18.160. Sakai (*Chūgoku zensho no
kenkyū*, pp. 21–22) describes a manuscript version with colorful and finely painted illustrations in the Tōyō bunko, which he judged to be close to the original printed edition,
which apparently does not survive.

tive and cautionary sections, whose examples ranged from high antiquity to the end of the Yuan dynasty.[28] His preface asserts that he had compiled the examples for his own edification as well as for future rulers, and suggests that he would show the book to court officials so they would know how to encourage and assist him properly. The publication appeared in 1453, just after he had named his own infant son as heir apparent and removed the son of the temporarily deposed Zhengtong emperor. This timing suggests that the Jingtai emperor intended his reflections on the Way of the Ruler to enhance his moral authority, thus strengthening his political legitimacy as he shifted the imperial succession to his own line.

The Four Picturebooks

The Ming imperial publications described above were published at the emperor's behest. Disseminated down the social hierarchy, some of them also circulated outside the palace, and multiple copies have survived. By contrast, the handpainted picturebooks that officials created to present to the throne represent attempts to project influence upward and, in one case, from outside Beijing altogether.[29] However, neither the emperor nor the majority of officials condoned the submission of educational materials on individual initiative. Factional rivalries may have fueled most of the opposition, but some submissions genuinely violated accepted protocols. Despite all the rhetoric about a minister's duty to advise and correct his ruler, it took a suspension of the normal balance of power for a late Ming official to succeed in getting an emperor to accept a pious compendium of illustrated role models that was blatantly intended to improve him or his heir. Indeed, three of the four works discussed below were not put to their intended use, and two soon disappeared without a trace. The other two picturebooks survived because they were launched into circulation outside the palace, where their format, contents, and courtly associations made them appealing to a booming market in woodblock-printed illustrated books.

---

28. An example of the original palace edition can be found in the National Library, Taibei (Rare Book 03091). For a punctuated transcription of the Jingtai emperor's preface, see *Guoli zhongyang tushuguan xuba jilu, shibu*, 3: 3.

    29. See discussion of the 1495 *Shenggong tu* below.

THE TWO *SHENGGONG TU*

In 1495, Zheng Ji 鄭紀 (1439–1508, *js.* 1460), chief minister in the Nanjing Court of Imperial Sacrifice, presented an album entitled *Shenggong tu* for use by the future Zhengde emperor, a child of four at the time.[30] The album contained 100 illustrated stories about exemplary crown princes from the predynastic Zhou period to the Ming dynasty. Accompanied by brief explanatory texts, the pictures were painted in the lavish "gold and green" style characteristic of court productions, particularly Buddhist paintings.[31] As in Wang Yun's *Chenghua shilüe*, the illustrations were organized thematically, according to stages in the life of a crown prince: birth and infancy, boyhood and schooling, and capping and enthronement.

In his memorial explaining why he had submitted the album, Zheng argued that dynastic longevity depended on the proper preparation of imperial successors, as shown by the Zhou dynasty's survival for some 870 years, in contrast to the shorter tenure enjoyed by the houses of Han, Tang, and Song.[32] The Hongwu and Yongle emperors had established even better procedures than the Zhou's, surrounding heirs to the Ming throne with famous scholars and talented statesmen. At present, however, palace attendants (eunuchs) were allowing the heir simply to enjoy himself. Without upright officials teaching him to restrain his desires, he would become depraved, and after he reached the age of ten, even a great advisor would be unable to change his character. Although the prince was old enough to begin formal instruction, Zheng worried that the *Five Classics* and *Four Books* would be difficult for a child to understand; so he had made pictures of exemplary stories that would be much easier to grasp and pleasurable to view. By internalizing "excellent words and meritorious deeds, ancient and modern" (*gujin zhi jiayan shanxing* 古今之嘉言善行) the prince would nourish his innate sagely merit and build a good foundation for more advanced studies.

---

30. Shen Defu, *Wanli yehuo bian* (hereafter cited as *YHB*), 4.102.

31. For roughly contemporaneous paintings in the "green and gold" 金碧 style by court artists, see the 84-leaf album depicting events in the Buddha's life, done ca. 1483 for the Chongshansi 崇善寺, a Buddhist monastery in Taiyuan 太原 patronized by the Prince of Jin 晉王; reproduced in *Taiyuan Chongshansi wenwu tulu*. The color scheme is reminiscent of Buddhist paintings from Eastern Tibet, another manifestation of the court's continued interest in Tibetan Buddhism discussed by David Robinson and Dora Ching elsewhere in this volume. See, e.g., Ching's Fig. 7.7.

32. For an excerpt from Zheng Ji's memorial, see *XZSL*, 105.2b–3a (pp. 1914–15); for the full text, see Zheng's collectanea, *Dongyuan wenji*, 3.8b–13a.

In Zheng's foreword to the album, which he wrote in the form of a memorial addressed directly to the crown prince himself, he explained the picturebook's purpose again.[33] He stressed that although the heir's virtuous nature was inborn, active effort was required to cultivate his moral heart-mind (*liang xin*). While he was young, he would enjoy looking at the pictures and would find them easy to understand. Also, his tutors could point to specific pictures when they explained the cardinal virtues, so that he could strive to imitate their exemplars. In conclusion, Zheng asserted that when the One Man is perfectly good (*yi ren yuan liang* 一人元良), then the myriad realms will be upright.

Despite the lofty premises on which the album was based, Zheng Ji's official duties did not involve him in the heir's education, and the unsolicited submission was highly irregular. Accordingly, Zheng's contemporaries did not support his attempt to inaugurate the crown prince's moral indoctrination from afar, and they did not give credence to Zheng's rationale for presenting the work. Indeed, they suspected that he had orchestrated it in hopes of being promoted to a position in the Beijing court, because the sumptuous production seemed to pander to palace tastes.[34] In the end, the Hongzhi emperor simply ignored the submission, and the album disappeared.[35] Coincidentally or not, the Zhengde emperor later became notorious for conduct particularly at odds with the ideals of the Confucian sage-ruler, as David Robinson describes elsewhere in this volume.

Some 45 years later, in 1539, the imperial tutors Huo Tao 霍韜 (1487–1540, *js.* 1514) and Zou Shouyi 鄒守益 (1491–1562, *js.* 1526) prepared a second album entitled *Shenggong tu*.[36] A much smaller compilation, it had just

---

33. Zheng Ji, *Dongyuan wenji*, 1.13a–16a.

34. *XZSL*, 105.3a (p. 1915). Hung-lam Chu notes that it was not uncommon for lecturers and potential lecturers to seek the emperor's attention by submitting unsolicited writings; see his chapter in this volume, pp. 186–230.

35. The only indication that Zheng's *Shenggong tu* may have survived for a while is a listing in Huang Yuji (1629–91), *Qianqingtang shumu*, p. 314; it is not clear whether the reference is to the painted album or an otherwise unknown printed replica.

36. For brief biographies of Huo and Zou, see *Dictionary of Ming Biography* (hereafter cited as *DMB*), pp. 681–82, 1310; and *Mingren zhuanji ziliao suoyin* (hereafter cited as *MRZJ*), pp. 864, 741–42. As Hung-lam Chu notes, Huo had gained favor and career advancement during the Great Rites Controversy 大禮議, because he had supported the Jiajing emperor's desire to recognize his own parents rather than be ritually adopted as the son of the Hongzhi emperor. Zou had been on the other side, which insisted that succession required adoption; for details of the conflict, see Fisher, *The Chosen*

thirteen illustrations, including three dealing with the Ming.[37] The first three introduced the exemplary Zhou King Wen 周文王 as heir apparent, who inquired after his parents three times a day, made sure that their food was the right temperature, and showed respect for his elders while receiving instruction. In other scenes, Zhou scions observed the labors of farmers and silkmakers in order to appreciate the suffering of ordinary people and learn to curb their own extravagances. Two compositions illustrated annual rituals in the Western Park (Xiyuan 西苑) by which the Ming court honored agriculture and sericulture, and one depicted courtiers frugally planting vegetables in a vacant lot.[38] Several of the accompanying texts likened Ming emperors to ancient paragons and compared the dynasty to the Zhou.

Huo and Zou submitted the picture album to the Jiajing emperor in hopes that he would order palace attendants to show it to Zhu Zaihuo 朱載壑 (1536–49), the three-year-old heir apparent. As their accompanying memorial explained, the prince would cultivate an upright character if he saw pictures of moral exemplars and heard about them every day, even though he was still too young to leave the women's apartments and be taught with texts written in the literary language.[39] Besides briefly identifying each of the thirteen pictures, the memorial also clearly stated the precepts they embodied. However, the Jiajing emperor considered the explanations accompanying the pictures slanderous. In fact, some of the appended texts contain startlingly direct criticisms of the Ming court's extravagance, coupled with repeated admonitions to return to the frugality and discipline established by the Hongwu emperor. Fortunately for Huo and Zou, the Jiajing emperor did not punish them, but he did discard their album.[40]

One. It is not clear how the two men subsequently became allies, although both were followers of Wang Yangming.

37. *SZSL*, 226.6a–b (pp. 4703–4); also *YHB*, 4.102. The work is described, with all the relevant texts, in Huo Tao's collected works, *Weiya wenji*, 4.62b–78a.

38. The Hongwu emperor had established rites honoring agriculture, but the sericulture ritual was inaugurated only in 1530, under the Jiajing emperor. The rites were meant to remind the Ming court of the hardship suffered by farmers and silk workers to produce the goods it consumed. In their commentaries to these illustrations, Huo and Zou vividly describe the misery that labor levies and tax quotas inflicted on the common people; see Huo Tao, *Weiya wenji*, 4.66a–78a.

39. For the memorial and the emperor's response, see Huo Tao, *Weiya wenji*, 4.62b–65b.

40. Shen Defu 沈德符 (*YHB*, 4.102) suggests that Huo and Zou expected to be rewarded with promotions. However, their stringent criticisms of the court's extravagance suggest more complicated motivations.

DIJIAN TUSHUO

In the summer of 1572, a rare conjunction of circumstances finally enabled a Ming official to impose a didactic picturebook on the emperor.[41] The sudden death of the 35-year-old Longqing emperor brought an earnest young boy to the throne as the Wanli emperor, and the domineering Zhang Juzheng 張居正 (1525–82, *js.* 1547) became senior grand secretary.[42] Not quite nine years old and clearly intelligent, the Wanli emperor's formal education had begun after becoming heir apparent in 1568. Initially aspiring to be a conscientious ruler, he readily accepted instruction. To help him grasp the principles of "order and chaos, flourishing and destruction" (*zhi luan xing wang* 治亂興亡) and inspire him to develop into an outstanding ruler, Zhang gave him a picturebook, *Dijian tushuo*. Colorfully illustrated and extensively annotated, its stories centered on specific actions by earlier emperors, some of whom were paragons to emulate, while others were examples to avoid.[43]

At Zhang's instigation, Grand Secretary Lü Tiaoyang 呂調陽 (1516–80, *js.* 1550), Hanlin Academician Ma Ziqiang 馬自強 (1513–78, *js.* 1553), and several unnamed lecturers had selected the accounts from historical sources and turned them into memorable and easily digested lessons. Each story was given a four-character title and an illustration, probably painted by palace artisans. The names of the protagonists were written next to the figures, who inhabited panoramic compositions that depicted the palace and surrounding landscape. The accompanying text was punctuated and followed by a discursive section, labeled *jie* 解 (explanation). Written in indented columns to set it off from the main account, it used simplified classical language and sometimes vernacular expressions to explain proper names and difficult terms and to draw the lessons to be learned.

The completed work was an album containing 117 stories in two volumes.[44] The first, entitled *Shengzhe fanggui* 聖哲芳規 (Honorable patterns

---

41. The following discussion is drawn from my more detailed studies of *Dijian tushuo* and its editions: "From Textbook to Testimonial" and "Changing the Frame."

42. For Zhang Juzheng's life and career, see *DMB*, pp. 53–61; *MS*, 213.5643–52; and *Zhang Juzheng ji, juan* 47. For his relationship with the young Wanli emperor, see Ray Huang, *1587*, chap. 1.

43. Zhang characterized them as *shan ke wei fa* 善可為法 and *e ke wei jie* 惡可為戒, respectively, using the same terms as the Hongwu emperor's compendia; see above.

44. Although the original album with painted pictures does not survive, subsequent printed versions make it possible to reconstruct many of its features; see my "From Textbook to Testimonial," esp. pp. 68–74.

of the sagely and wise), presented eighty-one positive examples in chronological order, ranging from Sage Emperor Yao of hoary antiquity to the
comparatively recent Song Emperor Zhezong. The other volume, *Kuangyu
fuche* 狂愚覆轍 (Destructive tracks of the uninhibited and stupid), contained thirty-six cautionary examples to avoid, from Taikang 太康 in the
Xia dynasty to Song Emperor Huizong (r. 1100–1125).[45] Both divisions concluded with a moralizing statement that Zhang Juzheng composed to
summarize and clarify the main points.

Zhang formally submitted *Dijian tushuo* with a memorial dated Longqing
6/12/18 (January 21, 1573).[46] Eyewitnesses claimed that when Zhang presented the work to the young emperor, the latter rose from his throne to
receive the album and started looking through it, pointing to various pages
and asking questions.[47] His official response to the memorial accompanying the compendium reaffirmed this enthusiastic reaction: "We have
looked at Our ministers' memorial and regard it as loyal, loving, and very
sincere. When We imitate the ancients, the [models of] governance in the
pictures will be profoundly useful. We welcome the picture album (*tu ce*
圖冊) and will keep it to look at."[48] Without help, the emperor was able to
read more than one-third of the characters used in the text of the *Dijian tushuo*.[49] Initially, he kept the album to the right of his seat in the lecture hall,
an indication of its importance to him. In the following days and months,
Zhang based lessons on the stories several times, sometimes relating them
to contemporary situations.[50] For example, on Wanli 1/3/4 (April 5, 1573),

---

45. As Zhang Juzheng explained in his memorial (see next note), these numbers
were not random; eighty-one (nine nines) was very *yang* 陽 and thus appropriate for
positive models, and thirty-six (six sixes) was very *yin* 陰 and fitting for negative ones.

46. Cosigned by Lü Tiaoyang, the memorial is reproduced at the front of many early
printed editions of *Dijian tushuo* and is included in Zhang Juzheng's collected writings,
compiled by his sons; for a punctuated and annotated transcription, see *Zhang Juzheng ji*,
3.103–7.

47. The young emperor's reaction is vividly described in *Shenzong shilu* in *Ming shilu*
(hereafter cited as *HZSL*), 8.7b–8a (pp. 0290–91). Independent accounts by Lu Shusheng
陸樹聲 (1509–1605, *js.* 1541) and Wang Zongmu 王宗沐 (1523–91, *js.* 1544) appear in their
1573-dated prefaces to printed editions of *Dijian tushuo* and are reproduced in their respective collected works, *Lu Wending gong ji*, 9.1a–3a; and *Jingsuo Wang xiansheng wenji*, 5.42b–45a.

48. The Wanli emperor's response, which may have been composed by his advisors,
is included in the front matter of most printed editions of *Dijian tushuo*, after the text of
the memorial itself; it is also transcribed in *HZSL*, 8.7b–8a (pp. 0290–91).

49. *HZSL*, 8.7b (p. 0290).

50. See *Wanli qiju zhu*, 1: 59–61, 109–12. The latest date on which *Dijian tushuo* is mentioned is Wanli 1/10/8 (Nov. 2, 1573).

he used a story about Han Emperor Wendi (r. 180–157 BCE) testing his border garrison at Xiliu 細柳 to discuss the necessity of maintaining proper
defensive procedures even in times of relative peace, as at present.[51] Court
records indicate that even after the lecture was over, the Wanli emperor
tried to continue the discussion with his attendants, but they were unable
to answer his questions. Thinking things through on his own, he is reported to have said:

"Teacher's [Zhang Juzheng's] meaning must be to say that for governance, one
must surely use civil [means] but also military [means]. . . . Although Teacher
Zhang is a civil official himself, he does not conceal the shortcomings [of civil
means]. On behalf of the court, he wants to protect field commanders and repair
and arrange armaments and military provisions. Truly this can be called public loyalty and devotion to the country." For a long time he sighed in admiration.[52]

As Kenneth Swope demonstrates in his chapter in this volume, Zhang's
lessons about the interplay of the military and civil components of governance made a profound impression on the Wanli emperor.

In addition to using the painted *Dijian tushuo* album to indoctrinate the
emperor, Zhang also circulated a small, woodblock-printed version of the
work among capital officials to remind them of their responsibility for establishing an ideal social and political order (Fig. 5.1).[53] Carved from a set
of duplicate pictures and texts that Zhang had retained after submitting the
painted album, the blocks may have been prepared and printed by palace
artisans under the aegis of Feng Bao 馮保 (fl. 1530–83), the powerful
eunuch director of the Directorate of Ceremonial, with whom Zhang had
developed a mutually beneficial working relationship.[54] The reason for dis-
tributing the book is explained in an afterword that Zhang solicited from
Wang Xilie 王希烈 (*js.* 1553), a Hanlin academician and vice minister of
personnel, temporarily in charge of the Household of the Heir Apparent:

---

51. *Wanli qiju zhu*, 1: 59–60. The Han Wendi story is the twenty-third in the "good"
section of *Dijian tushuo*.

52. Ibid., 1: 60–61.

53. Many examples survive today; I have personally examined those in the National
Library, Taibei (Rare Book no. 05239), the National Library, Beijing (Rare Book
no. 17486), and Princeton University's East Asia Library (Rare Book TB–367/609). A
1575 reprint edition is reproduced in *Beijing tushuguan guji zhenben congkan*, vol. 14.

54. The edition itself bears no evidence of Feng's direct involvement. A later
eunuch, Liu Ruoyu 劉若愚 (1584–ca. 1642), explicitly claims that Feng published *Dijian
tushuo* for Zhang; see ZZZ, 5.1a–b. Feng's relationship with Zhang Juzheng is detailed in
Ray Huang, *1587*, chap. 1.

Fig. 5.1 *Dijian tushuo* 帝鑑圖説 (The emperor's mirror, illustrated and discussed), Zhang Juzheng's 張居正 edition of 1573. Illustration of exemplary story no. 2, "Admonition Drum and Criticism Board" ("Jian gu bang mu" 諫鼓謗木). In the original, the left half of the picture would have been overleaf from the right half and would have been visible only after turning the page. The two parts of the image have been digitally manipulated here to splice them together. Woodblock-printed book, 4a–b. Block frame H: ca. 20 cm. Princeton University, East Asian Library (Rare Book TB367/609)

"If everyone takes up his duty, then the ruler will be able to be a sage, and governance will be able to flourish; and we can look forward to peace in the near future. This is why my lord [Zhang] also had [the compilation] carved and disseminated."[55]

By circulating the didactic compendium, Zhang was also putting himself in the position of earlier emperors, described above, who displayed or bestowed such works in order to enhance their political power and exert moral influence over their officials. His distribution of *Dijian tushuo* may have been part of a strategy to discourage factional challenges by project-

---

55. Wang Xilie's preface is included in most editions of *Dijian tushuo*; for a punctuated transcription, see *Guoli zhongyang tushuguan shanben xuba jilu, shibu*, 4: 399–400.

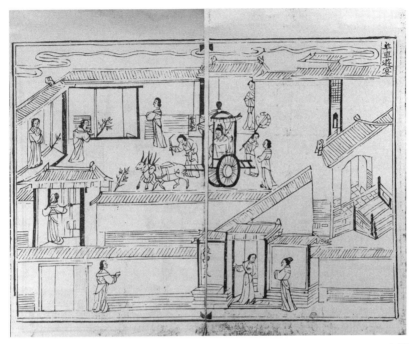

Fig. 5.2   *Dijian tushuo* 帝鑑圖說 (The emperor's mirror, illustrated and discussed), Hu Xian's 胡賢 edition of 1573. Illustration of cautionary story no. 19 (overall no. 100), "Traveling and Feasting by Goat Carriage" ("Yang che you yan" 羊車遊宴). In the original, the left half of the picture would have been overleaf from the right half and would have been visible only after turning the page. The two parts of the image have been digitally manipulated here to splice them together. Woodblock-printed book, *hou* 後 48a–b. Block frame H: ca. 20.6 cm. National Central Library, Taibei (Rare Book 05241).

ing strong moral authority from the center. For nearly a decade, Zhang's firm control over both the Wanli emperor and the central government resulted in a period of relative peace and stability.

In the 1570s, *Dijian tushuo* was republished several times by commercial publishers, as well as by individual officials.[56] The profusion of editions attests to considerable interest outside the palace. The combination of pictures and annotated stories, which had made it accessible to a child-emperor, also appealed more widely to people of modest literacy. For the reading public, *Dijian tushuo* offered a digest of political and cultural history, parts of which may have been as entertaining as contemporary works of

---

56. For details concerning these editions and the circumstances of their publication, see my "From Textbook to Testimonial," pp. 74–82; and "Changing the Frame," pp. 26–38.

illustrated fiction. In particular, the stories in the *Kuangyu fuche* section vividly described how "depraved" emperors gratified their hedonistic desires, patronized Buddhism or Daoism, and indulged aspirations that deviated from Confucian norms (Fig. 5.2).[57] Moreover, the pictures were lively and varied, bringing the exotic world of the palace to life.

After Zhang's death in 1582, posthumous accusations of corruption and malfeasance led the Wanli emperor to repudiate his late mentor and punish him and his family.[58] Disillusioned with the ideal of being a sage ruler and resentful that Zhang had duped him into striving for it, the young man became increasingly erratic in performing his imperial duties. His officials disgusted him with their factional infighting and annoyed him with their incessant memorials. After a son was born in 1586 to his favorite consort, Lady Zheng 鄭貴妃 (ca. 1568–1630), he became exasperated by their persistent efforts to persuade him to designate his eldest son, Zhu Changluo 朱常洛 (1582–1620; Taichang emperor, r. 1620) as his successor. Eventually, he stopped attending court lectures, gave up holding audiences for outer court officials, and rarely met even with the grand secretaries to deal with urgent matters. As Kenneth Swope describes, the Wanli emperor remained engaged only with military affairs, where he found the bureaucracy less constraining.

YANGZHENG TUJIE

A generation after Zhang submitted *Dijian tushuo*, Hanlin Senior Compiler Jiao Hong 焦竑 (1541–1620, *js.* 1589) created *Yangzheng tujie* to broaden Zhu Changluo's educational curriculum.[59] Although the prince had not been

---

57. As David Robinson observed at the conference, such pursuits were elements of a more activist kind of "imperial emperorship" (*huangdi* 皇帝), even if at odds with Confucian "kingship" (*wang* 王).

58. Among the many treatments of the turbulent period, particularly useful are Ray Huang, *1587*, *CHC*, 7: 528–56; and *DMB*, esp. pp. 208–11, 324–37.

59. I treat the creation and editions of *Yangzheng tujie* in more detail in "Squaring Connoisseurship with History"; and relationships between printed versions and painted handscrolls of excerpts in "Didactic Illustrations in Printed Books," pp. 427–33, and *Mirror of Morality*, pp. 102–5. Shen Defu (*YHB*, 25.636) dates the compilation of *Yangzheng tujie* to 1595–96. This is consistent with Zhu Shilu's 祝世錄 (1539–1610, *js.* 1589) preface (see below), which refers to 228 annual sacrifices during the Ming. Seventeenth-century accounts differ on details concerning the production and circulation of *Yangzheng tujie*; see also *YHB*, 4.102–3; Zhu Guozhen, *Yongchuang xiaopin* (hereafter cited as *YCXP*), 10.216; and *MS*, 288.7393. For modern discussions, see Yü, "The Intel-

formally named heir apparent, the Wanli emperor grudgingly allowed him to begin his formal studies in 1594. As one of six Hanlin officials appointed to instruct him, Jiao Hong considered the traditional lecture format and orthodox curriculum too restrictive for molding a future ruler.[60] In addition, during his first year of tutoring, he found that the prince was having trouble comprehending the *Four Books* and *Five Classics*. To stimulate him and encourage him to participate in discussion, Jiao compiled sixty stories about exemplary men of earlier times and had them illustrated.[61]

Smaller than *Dijian tushuo*, *Yangzheng tujie* was similar in its format and general conception. Each account began with a picture, labeled with a four-character title. The accompanying story consisted of a punctuated excerpt from a historical source and a more colloquial explanation indented from the primary text. However, like the two *Shenggong tu*, *Yangzheng tujie* treated only positive models, rather than including cautionary tales. Its protagonists included rulers, princes, and wise advisors from the predynastic Zhou period through the early Northern Song dynasty. In contrast to all three earlier picturebooks, *Yangzheng tujie*'s illustrations were not designed by anonymous palace artisans but by Ding Yunpeng 丁雲鵬 (1547–1628), a painter and print designer who associated with members of the Jiangnan scholar-elite.[62] Depicting large figures close up and without labels, Ding created illustrations that are quite different from the panoramic compositions of *Dijian tushuo*.

---

lectual World of Chiao Hung Revisited," p. 28; and Ch'ien, *Chiao Hung and the Restructuring of Neo-Confucianism*, pp. 51–52.

60. Such views apparently were typical of literati associated with the Taizhou school, which favored a pragmatic approach to learning and self-cultivation; see Handlin, *Action in Late Ming Thought*, esp. pp. 16, 74, 148; see also Ch'ien, *Chiao Hung and the Restructuring of Neo-Confucianism*, esp. pp. 50–52.

61. In my more detailed account in "Squaring Connoisseurship with History," I explain how my reconstruction of the creation of *Yangzheng tujie* differs from those of writers who rely on erroneous bibliographic entries dating the work to 1593 or 1594, or who assume that the Wanli emperor ordered Jiao to compile the work.

62. Ding Yunpeng's participation in *Yangzheng tujie* is mentioned both in Zhu Shilu's preface to the work (discussed below) and in *YHB*, 25.636. An educated artist from Huizhou, Ding was active in Nanjing and Songjiang 松江 in the 1590s and associated with up-and-coming literati, including Jiao's examination classmate Dong Qichang 董其昌 (1555–1636, *js.* 1589); see Oertling, "Ting Yun-p'eng," pp. 12–32 *passim*. The logistics of Jiao Hong's commission are unclear. Oertling (p. 72) suggests that the two worked together on *Yangzheng tujie* in Nanjing, based on the incorrect assumption that the compilation was made in 1593–94.

Because Zhu Changluo was already in his early teens and beyond the normal age for the elementary curriculum (*xiaoxue*) 小學,[63] it was not appropriate for him to use a picturebook in his formal studies. Accordingly, Jiao suggested that the prince could peruse *Yangzheng tujie* during his hours of leisure, after his lectures were over for the day. In his preface, Jiao was careful to justify the work by invoking the Hongwu emperor's example of educating his sons in a broad way that fostered character formation as well as classical learning:

Widely [the Hongwu emperor] gathered aged and great gentlemen to attend the Heir Apparent and the other princes; and he ordered the officials, when they had leisure from lecturing on the classics, to tell them stories about enlightened rulers and good prime ministers, filial sons and loyal ministers, as well as the vagaries of current government and examples of sufferings among the people. He also ordered them to paint pictures of the difficulties and misfortunes of the agricultural enterprise, and pictures of filial conduct in antiquity, and submit them. Thus, the teachings they presented could be called complete from root to tip. . . . Respectfully following the Ancestor's [the Hongwu emperor's] instructions, I have selected ancient speeches and actions that can provide exhortation and admonition, and composed them into picture-explanations, whose name is *Cultivating Rectitude, Illustrated and Explained.*[64]

Without consulting the other lecturers, Jiao prepared to submit the compilation for the Wanli emperor's approval in order to use it to supplement Zhu Changluo's curriculum. When the lead tutor, Guo Zhengyu 郭正域 (1554–1612; *js.* 1583), found out, he chastised Jiao for presuming that his work could be taught on equal terms with the classics.[65] Jiao then ostensibly abandoned the idea, but his son took the album to Nanjing and had it handsomely published there (Fig. 5.3). The artistic quality of the edi-

---

63. In an earlier memorial urging the Wanli emperor to establish his heir, Jiao Hong (*Jiaoshi Danyuan ji*, 3.4b [p. 184]) asserted that a boy should begin his elementary education at eight *sui*, while his character was still malleable.

64. For Jiao's preface to *Yangzheng tujie*, reproduced in all editions of the book as well as in his collected writings, see ibid., 15.1a–2a (pp. 541–43). For a punctuated transcription, see *Guoli zhongyang tushuguan xuba jilu, zibu*, 1: 197. Ch'ien (*Chiao Hung and the Restructuring of Neo-Confucianism*, pp. 26–27) notes that late Ming syncretic thinkers (including Jiao Hong and Zhu Shilu) invoked the Hongwu emperor also to validate their use of Buddhist and Daoist concepts in explicating Confucian ideas.

65. *YCXP*, 10.216. Guo Zhengyu also accused Jiao of making more senior scholars appear unlearned, a reasonable worry, given that Jiao had been the *optimus* of the 1589 *jinshi* examination and was renowned for his erudition.

Fig. 5.3 *Yangzheng tujie* 養正圖解 (Cultivating rectitude, illustrated and explained), ca. 1595, with pictures designed by Ding Yunpeng 丁雲鵬 and carved by Huang Qi 黃奇. Illustration of story no. 3, "Giving Aid to Destitute People" ("Zhen dai pin min" 振貸貧民). Woodblock-printed book, 5a. Block frame H: ca. 23.5 cm. National Library of China, Taibei (Rare Book 05654).

tion suggests an expensive production. Not only did it contain illustrations designed by a noted artist, the blocks were carved by Huang Qi 黃奇 (b. 1568), a master craftsman from Huizhou 徽州, who preserved the calligraphic nuances of the brush-written text. A preface by Jiao Hong's examination classmate and Nanjing official, Zhu Shilu 祝世錄 (1539–1610, *js.* 1589),[66] made a point of naming everyone involved in the production, suggesting that he thought their eminence enhanced the work.[67]

---

66. At the time, Zhu was a supervising secretary in the Nanjing Office of Scrutiny for Personnel. Like Jiao Hong, he was a disciple of Geng Dingxiang, a Taizhou-school

Zhu Shilu's preface also delicately linked the book's pedagogical project to the contentious issue of the Wanli emperor's delay in designating his heir apparent. Diplomatically speculating that the emperor must be anxious to have his son properly educated before naming him crown prince, Zhu asserted that these priorities conformed to those of high antiquity, whereas the conscientious officials who were pressing for investiture were merely following more recent precedents:

In the early Zhou system, when the heir (*tai zi* 太子) was first born, his name was determined, and then this was made known in the southern suburb [sacrifice to Heaven and Earth]. . . . When somewhat grown, he entered the imperial university (*taixue* 太學), where he was taught the way of cultivating his body and governing all under Heaven, and they didn't bother [yet] with his investiture. So down through the Three Ages, ruler education was urgent and investiture was leisurely, and the heir would wait until he was grown [to be named crown prince]. But after the Three Ages, investiture was stressed and ruler education was leisurely, and the eldest son was treasured as crown prince and as the ruler's assistant. How could he put his head down to attend to the business of [learning] the *Odes*, *Documents*, string music, and chanting, if they were matters for his leisure time? In this regard, a short while ago the officials sincerely considered investiture as a responsibility, but the emperor was determined to decide on his own, and he said it was fitting [to pursue] ruler education earlier. Profound indeed is the emperor's propriety![68]

Zhu Shilu also reiterated the educational premises of *Yangzheng tujie*, affirming that pictures of concrete events made abstract principles easier to

---

follower of the philosopher Wang Yangming and patron of Zhang Juzheng; see *MRZJ*, p. 406; and *DMB*, pp. 718–21. Zhu's preface to *Yangzheng tujie* is reproduced in all editions of the book; for a punctuated transcription, see *Guoli zhongyang tushuguan xuba jilu, zibu*, 1: 197–98.

67. Besides naming Ding Yunpeng and Huang Qi, Zhu credited the calligraphy to Wu Jixu 吳繼序 (fl. Wanli era), who is identified as a native of Shexian 歙縣 in Zhou Wu, *Huipai banhua shi lunji*, p. 55, notes for pl. 23. Huang Qi (or Deqi 德奇) is listed in the twenty-sixth generation of the Huang genealogy, as carver of three works; see ibid., p. 40. Zhu Shilu also noted that the costs of block-carving were underwritten by Wu Huairang 吳懷讓 (fl. Wanli era), whose style-name is given as Shaoyi 少逸 in Du Xinfu, *Mingdai banke zonglu*, 2.42b. On the significance of the late Ming emergence of "name" craftsmen from previously anonymous traditions, see Clunas, *Art in China*, chap. 5.

68. From Zhu Shilu's preface to *Yangzheng tujie*; see note 66. The subtle admonition implicit in his carefully worded comments suggests that he expected that the emperor might eventually see them.

understand and that illustrations of the words and deeds from the past could serve as admonitions:

In general, lectures and readings just analyze principle (*li* 理), whereas both pictures and explanations demonstrate events. The functioning of principle is abstract, and the abstract is obscure and concisely spoken of, and it does not necessarily indicate what it refers to. Events refer to reality, and the observation of reality is easy; accordingly it is more useful for illuminating principle. Therefore, [Jiao] selected discussions of events from ancient times that provide admonitions and warnings, [had them] painted in pictures, and wrote explanations, to offer up. . . . Truly, when the imperial eldest son opens the pictures, his eyes will be pleased, and when he savors the explanations, his heart-mind will be respectful.[69]

After *Yangzheng tujie* was published in Nanjing, copies of the book were sent to Jiao Hong in Beijing. According to Zhu Guozhen 朱國楨 (1557–1632), when the eunuch Chen Ju 陳矩 (1539–1608) came to visit Jiao, he saw them lying on a table and took some to show to the Wanli emperor.[70] When Jiao's colleagues and the grand secretaries found out, they were furious and suspected Jiao of being devious. In October 1597, Jiao officially submitted the work, with a memorial describing it as an enhancement to ruler education, summarizing the arguments he had already made in his preface:

In 1594, when the eldest imperial son left the women's quarters, I was favored with the job of advising and lecturing [to him]. It has already been four years since then, but his academic preparation is deficient, with nothing to supplement and benefit [his curriculum]. Now, the eldest imperial son's intellectual capacity is more abundant every day, and he is increasing in age. To know more about the words and deeds of former times would be appropriate and timely. But every day, his lectures and readings are limited to two books, the *Shangshu* 尚書 (*Book of Documents*) and

---

69. Ibid. The last part of this passage suggests that Zhu expected the work to reach Zhu Changluo.

70. *YCXP*, 10.216. Shen Defu (*YHB*, 25.636) says that Chen *bought* the books. One of Chen's duties was to collect books for the Eastern Depot (Dongchang 東廠), which makes his action more understandable; see *DMB*, p. 151. Liu Ruoyu (*ZZZ*, 1.1) claims that the Wanli emperor was very interested in all kinds of books, including illustrated ones, and sent eunuchs out to buy them. Jiao Hong probably knew that the emperor liked books and fine productions and may indeed have intended the printed *Yangzheng tujie* to reach him by this indirect route. Two copies of *Yangzheng tujie*, now in the Palace Museum library, were previously kept in the palace halls Zhaorendian 昭仁殿 and Dunbendian Halls 敦本殿, respectively; see Li Jinhua, *Mingdai chizhuanshu kao fu yinde*, p. 69.

Lunyu 論語 (*Analects* of Confucius). Although Heaven has conferred abundant intelligence on him, what he observes and remembers still is not very broad.[71]

Jiao's memorial then turned to Ming precedents for supplementing
princely education. Unlike the general discussion of this issue in his preface
to *Yangzheng tujie*, his memorial specified what other works the Hongwu
emperor's sons had studied, including Sima Guang's 司馬光 (1019–86,
js. 1038) widely influential eleventh-century historical compendium, *Zizhi
tongjian* 資治通鑑 (Comprehensive mirror for aid in governance), and
Zhen Dexiu's thirteenth-century work on statecraft in the Neo-Confucian
tradition, *Extended Meaning of the Great Learning*, and Jiao listed the many
kinds of instructive stories they had been told. As the immediate model for
his own compilation of pictures and texts, he brought up more recent
works:

Then the former ministers Zheng Ji, Zou Shouyi, and Huo Tao also jointly created
Shenggong tu to offer at court.[72] These contained nothing that did not comply with
canonical institutions and uphold the primal good, and they were calculated to
perpetuate the ancestral altars for a long time. Recently grand secretary so-and-so
[the then-unmentionable Zhang Juzheng] presented *Jiangjie tongjian* 講解通鑑
(Lectures explaining the *Comprehensive Mirror*)[73] and respectfully awaited Your decree. His action does not allow any other interpretation. Your servant [Jiao Hong]
is stupid and does not rely on himself but follows accomplished predecessors. Like
[these] previous compilers, I have selected and transcribed stories from books that
are relevant as models and warnings and added instructive explanations and illustrated them in pictures.[74]

---

71. From Jiao Hong's memorial, dated Wanli 25/9/8 (Oct. 18, 1597); reproduced in
some editions of *Yangzheng tujie* and in *Jiaoshi Danyuan ji*, 3.6a–7a (pp. 187–89). Jiao's
submission of two copies (*er bu* 二部) of *Yangzheng tujie* and the emperor's response are
recorded on the *wuxu* (10th) day of the ninth month (Oct. 20, 1597) in *HZSL*, 314.4
(p. 5871). There is no entry in *Wanli qiju zhu*.

72. Shen Defu (*YHB*, 4.103) expresses amazement that the erudite Jiao seemed not
to realize that the two rejected *Shenggong tu* were inauspicious precedents.

73. Liu Ruoyu (*ZZZ*, 5.1a) lists a primer of this title published by the Directorate of
Ceremonial under the eunuch Feng Bao, who worked closely with Zhang Juzheng.
Zhang is credited with several works of the "straightforward explanation" (*zhijie* 直解)
type, which he may have used in lectures, and for which the blocks were kept in the
Secretariat; see *Zhang Jiangling yanjiu*, pp. 157–58. Titles include *Sishu zhijie* 四書直解
(Straightforward explanation of the *Four Books*), and *Shujing zhijie* 書經直解 (Straight-
forward explanation of the *Book of Documents*).

74. From Jiao's memorial; see note 71.

Jiao did not mention *Dijian tushuo*, the most direct and obvious precedent, probably to avoid reminding the Wanli emperor of Zhang Juzheng's efforts to indoctrinate him.

At the end of his memorial, Jiao requested that the emperor order his son to examine *Yangzheng tujie* during his ample hours of leisure, after his daily lessons were over. Although the emperor accepted the book and gave it to his son, he would not allow the boy to start studying it, lest it jeopardize his health.[75] As it turned out, Jiao never had a chance to find out whether the emperor would relent. Shortly after submitting *Yangzheng tujie*, Jiao was accused of improprieties in supervising the civil examinations for Shuntian prefecture, and his enemies engineered his demotion to a minor post in faraway Fujian.[76] In 1599, he resigned and returned to private life in Nanjing; he was no longer at court when Zhu Changluo finally was invested as crown prince in 1601.[77]

From Instruction to Appreciation

Even though *Yangzheng tujie* was not adopted for princely education, it circulated outside the palace as a woodblock-printed book, like *Dijian tushuo*. Unlike printed editions of the earlier picturebook, whose artistic quality was unremarkable, *Yangzheng tujie* entered at the high end of the late Ming book market. Some two decades later, Shen Defu 沈德符 (1578–1642) recalled: "The pear and jujube [hardwood blocks] carved by Huizhou men were of exquisite workmanship; and the pictorial images, which also came from the hand of a famous Xin'an master, Ding Nanyu [Ding Yunpeng], were even more flying and moving, as if alive. The capital treasured it as a rare and precious commodity."[78] The durable woodblocks evidently stayed in Nanjing and continued to be used for printing additional copies.[79] Some

———

75. The Wanli emperor's response is recorded at the end of Jiao's memorial in some editions of *Yangzheng tujie*; e.g., one in the National Library, Taibei (Rare Book 05656); for an abbreviated transcription, see *HZSL* (see note 71).

76. Some candidates were said to have used certain Daoist words as a code to enable Jiao to identify their examinations and judge them favorably; see Elman, *The Cultural History of Civil Examinations in Late Imperial China*, p. 203.

77. *YHB*, 25.637; also Ch'ien, *Chiao Hung and the Restructuring of Neo-Confucianism*, p. 59 and sources cited in his note 155.

78. *YHB*, 25.636.

79. There is a great deal of confusion about the various editions and reprints of *Yangzheng tujie*, and many errors in published scholarship; for detailed discussion, see my "Squaring Connoisseurship with History."

included a table of contents, which may indicate a broadening of the intended readership. A table of contents made it easier for readers to get an overview of the book and select specific stories. The table of contents first appears in versions that also include Jiao's 1597 memorial and probably were printed only slightly later.[80]

A second edition of *Yangzheng tujie*, which features slightly embellished versions of the illustrations, divided the sixty stories into two *juan*, each with its own table of contents.[81] The pictures differ mostly in very minor details, such as grander screens and carriages, and slight changes in facial expressions and postures, but the aesthetic ambiance is distinctly heightened. Instead of didactic cartouches directly superimposed on the pictures, inside the frames, the scene titles are placed outside the lower left margins, and the accompanying texts are carved in the elegant "printed" style (*jiang ti* 匠體) frequently seen in sixteenth-century publications.[82] These subtle variations reconfigured this edition more explicitly for the late Ming book market. It was soon appropriated by a Huizhou commercial publisher, Wang Yunpeng 汪雲鵬 (fl. Wanli era), who reissued it under his own imprint, Wanhuxuan 玩虎軒 (Playing with the tiger studio; Fig. 5.4).[83] Following a convention used in illustrated editions of dramas, another genre in which

---

80. In one group (e.g., Rare Book 05656 in the National Library, Taibei), a table of contents separately carved by Dai Weixiao has been added to what otherwise is a printing from the original blocks. Another group (e.g., British Museum OA 1992.1–7) represents a new carving of the entire compendium, which is now divided into two *juan*, and each *juan* has a table of contents.

81. An example of this edition was submitted by Ruan Yuan 阮元 (1764–1849, *js.* 1715) to the Qing palace in 1807 as part of the Wanwei biecang 宛委別藏 collection, of which hand-copies were made shortly afterward and individual titles published in the 1930s and 1980s. I have examined a hand-copy of *Yangzheng tujie* (inexplicably attributed to the Guangxu era, 1874–1908) in the National Palace Museum Library, which seems identical to the hand-copy of the Wanwei biecang example as published by Jiangsu Guji chubanshe in 1988. The original book probably is in the Palace Museum, Beijing.

82. For detailed discussion of printed versus calligraphic style, see Heijdra, "A Tale of Two Aesthetics."

83. In his signature, Wang Yunpeng identified himself only as a student in the national university (*guozi sheng* 國子生), but other sources indicate that he was a commercial publisher from Huizhou; see Carlitz, "The Social Uses of Female Virtue," p. 137; and Chia, "Of Three Mountains Street," p. 126. Given his surname and Huizhou origins, Wang Yunpeng may have been related to Ding Yunpeng's mother and to Wang Daokun 汪道昆 (1525–93, *js.* 1543), a noted literary figure and publisher.

Fig. 5.4 *Yangzheng tujie* 養正圖解 (Cultivating rectitude, illustrated and explained), ca. 1600, Wang Yunpeng's 汪雲鵬 Wanhuxuan 玩虎軒 edition, with pictures designed by Ding Yunpeng 丁雲鵬 and carved by Huang Lin 黃鏻. Illustration of story no. 3, "Giving Aid to Destitute People" ("Zhen dai pin min" 振貸貧民). Woodblock-printed book, 5a. Block frame H: ca. 22.4 cm. British Museum (OA 1992.1–7).

he was active, Wang added his Wanhuxuan logo to each page.[84] To make room for it, however, he deleted the scene titles, thus rendering the tables of contents ineffective. In further adapting *Yangzheng tujie* for an audience of book lovers, Wang also rearranged the framing texts to emphasize the work's courtly origins and its production by famous artists, changes that

---

84. Wang's publications include editions of *Pipa ji* 琵琶記 (The story of the lute) and *Bei Xixiang ji* 北西廂記 (Northern story of the Western Wing). For seven books that Wang published under the Wanhuxuan imprint, see Du Xinfu, *Mingdai banke zonglu*, 3.4; also Zhou Wu, *Huipai banhua shilun ji*, pp. 29, 55–56, and pls. 7–9, figs. 23–29.

downplayed Jiao Hong's didactic intentions. Jiao's 1597 memorial and the Wanli emperor's response now appear at the beginning, along with Wang's self-aggrandizing note, "respectfully transcribed by the National University student (*guozi sheng* 國子生), servitor (*chen* 臣) Wang Yunpeng."[85] The placement of Zhu Shilu's preface immediately after Wang's note and right before the first table of contents foregrounds the names of the people responsible for the book's creation.[86] Wang moved Jiao Hong's original preface, with its long-winded discussion of pedagogical issues, to the end of the book, where it might easily be overlooked.

A tendency to merge the didactic into the artistic is also found in the only edition of *Dijian tushuo* to appear in the later years of the Wanli reign. Although Zhang Juzheng was in posthumous disgrace and all but unmentionable, a printed edition of *Dijian tushuo* remained in the palace library, where it was seen in 1604 by Jin Lian 金濂 (fl. Wanli era), a minor official in the Central Drafting Office.[87] Jin published a new edition based on Zhang's but reconceptualized the pictures to inspire aesthetic pleasure as well as moral cultivation (Fig. 5.5). Rather than copying Zhang's anonymously designed and repetitious compositions, Jin commissioned new pictures from the Huang family workshop.[88] Not only did the replacements display more variety and imagination, they seemed less didactic because the name labels were omitted and the scene titles moved to an inconspicuous position outside the frame. In addition, the two halves of the new pictures

---

85. This position could be purchased in the late Ming period.

86. Some of the credit details are different, however. Neither Wu Jixu nor Wu Huairang is mentioned, and the block-carver is identified as Huang Lin 黃鏻, not Huang Qi. Huang Lin (1565–after 1617; *zi* Ruoyu 若愚) is listed in the twenty-fifth generation of the Huang genealogy and cut blocks for other Wanhuxuan editions, such as *Bei xixiang ji* and *Chengshi moyuan* 程氏墨苑 (Mr. Cheng's ink garden; 1606); see Zhou Wu, *Huipai banhua shi lunji*, pp. 29, 31, 39, and pls. 7–9, figs. 23, 26–27.

87. Information about Jin Lian (dates unrecorded) comes only from the prefaces to his edition of *Dijian tushuo*. He was a native of Xin'an 新安 (probably the one in Anhui), with the style-name Zijun 子濬 and the prestige title "Gentleman-for-summoning"; for further discussion of his sketchy biography, see my "From Textbook to Testimonial," note 68.

88. The signatures of Huang Jun 黃鋑 (1553–1620) and his son Huang Yingxiao 黃應孝 (1582–1662) appear on the work. Zhou Wu (*Huipai banhua shi lunji*, pp. 39, 42) notes them in the twenty-fifth and twenty-sixth generations of the Huang genealogy, respectively, and identifies other publications they carved. I have examined Jin Lian's edition in the National Library, Beijing (Rare Book 14125) and the British Library (OR 74 d.45).

Fig. 5.5   *Dijian tushuo* 帝鑑圖説 (The emperor's mirror, illustrated and discussed), Jin Lian's 金濂 edition of 1604, with pictures carved by Huang Jun 黃鋑 and Huang Yingxiao 黃應孝. Illustration of exemplary story no. 31, "Nighttime Lectures on the Classics" ("Ye fen jiang jing" 夜分講經). Woodblock-printed book, vol. 2 [*ren ji* 壬集], 31b–32a. Block frame H: ca. 21.3 cm. British Library (OR 74 d.45).

were carved on separate blocks and became facing pages when printed and bound, whereas Zhang's illustrations were divided in half by the page folds.[89] Thus, Jin Lian's edition displayed an entire composition all at once, perhaps encouraging viewers to linger and savor it; Zhang's required them to turn the page to see the second half of the picture, an action that brought the accompanying text into view.

Even though Jin Lian's edition was aesthetically more satisfying, it was not just a collection of appealing pictures. Although omitting Zhang Ju-zheng's memorial and the earlier prefaces, the edition includes the moralistic stories and their explanations, as well as Zhang's unsigned commentaries at the end of the exemplary and cautionary sections. Moreover, in his preface, Jin Lian focused on the utility of *Dijian tushuo* as a guide for emperor and

89. For a well-illustrated discussion of relationships between the block-printed sheet and the book's binding, see Helliwell, "The Repair and Binding of Old Chinese Books."

commoner alike in cultivating virtue. The other preface, by the eminent Li Weizhen 李維楨 (1547–1626, js. 1568), affirmed the value of portraying exemplars and cautionary models for moral cultivation, which Li implied was sorely lacking in this chaotic era of bad governance.[90] Commending Jin Lian for rescuing *Dijian tushuo* from obscurity in the palace library, Li suggested that its dissemination would give *haoshizhe* 好事者 (aficionados) substantive information about the past to discuss.[91] Li's forthright criticisms, considered together with the outstanding quality of the edition, suggest that despite Jin's inclusive rhetoric, the book was intended for a limited audience of highly educated and morally engaged men who had been unable to realize their aspirations in government service.[92] Moreover, the facts that this edition of *Dijian tushuo* was never republished and is rare today suggest that copies were produced for a small and select circle.

After Zhang Juzheng was posthumously restored to his ranks and honors by the Tianqi emperor in the fifth lunar month of 1622, imperial tutors lost no time in petitioning for permission to use *Dijian tushuo* in their lectures to him.[93] The rather simpleminded youth liked the book so much that in the eighth month, he had it recarved and reprinted, minus the prefaces that had framed the 1573 edition with lofty moral sentiments.[94] Even though Zhang was no longer in disgrace, his name does not appear

---

90. Li Weizhen's preface is reprinted in his collected works, *Dabishanfang ji*, 8.6a. He had been close to Zhang Juzheng, assisting him in compiling the Veritable Records of the Longqing emperor; see his biography in *MS*, 288.7385. By 1604, some thirty years of subsequent promotion and demotion in provincial posts had demoralized him into early retirement in Nanjing, where he associated with Jiao Hong and Ding Yunpeng, among others.

91. The connotations of the term *haoshizhe*, literally, "those who like things," range from mildly positive (aficionado) to rather negative (busybody); see Clunas, *Superfluous Things*, pp. 86–87. In late Ming book culture, *haoshizhe* were the people who had the cultivation and leisure to involve themselves in both production and connoisseurship of woodblock-printed books.

92. For other fine woodblock-printed books that appealed to this group, see Hegel, *Reading Illustrated Fiction in Late Imperial China*; Jang, "Form, Content, and Audience"; and Chu-tsing Li and Watt, *The Chinese Scholar's Studio*.

93. *Xizong shilu* in *Ming shilu* (hereafter cited as *IZSL*), 23.12a (p. 1145), 25.3b (p. 1242).

94. I have examined a copy in the Beijing University Library Rare Book collection (■ 910.5/1171). Technical details show that it was not based directly on Zhang Juzheng's edition but on the Nanjing bookseller Hu Xian's 胡賢 slightly altered recut version published a few months later (cf. Fig. 5.2), an edition that also made its way to Japan; see my "From Textbook to Testimonial," pp. 75, 86.

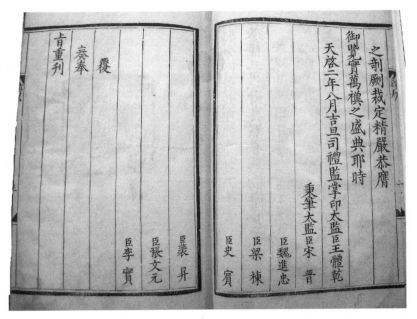

Fig. 5.6   *Dijian tushuo* 帝鑑圖説 (The emperor's mirror, illustrated and discussed), Directorate of Ceremonial (Silijian 司禮監) edition of 1622. End of preface, with eunuch signatures. Woodblock-printed book, preface, 2b–3a. Block frame H: ca. 19.5 cm. Beijing University Library (Rare Book, 910.5/1171).

anywhere in the book. Instead, a single preface briefly summarizes the book's contents and instructional purpose. It is signed by eight eunuchs in the Directorate of Ceremonial, one of whom was the increasingly powerful and villainous Wei Zhongxian 魏忠賢 (1568–1627; Fig. 5.6).[95] The following year, the Tianqi emperor refused a request to add *Comprehensive Mirror for Aid in Governance* to his lecture curriculum, on the grounds that the lectures on *Dijian tushuo* already provided him with a complete treatment of the principles of governance.[96]

Conclusion

Prior to the "long" sixteenth century, officials presented picturebooks for imperial instruction on just two occasions, both of which differ from the four Ming cases analyzed here. As noted above, in the eleventh century

95. Signing his earlier name, Wei Jinzhong 魏進忠, Wei Zhongxian was only the third signatory and apparently not the most important one at the time.

96. Dardess, *Blood and History in China*, p. 37; see also *IZSL*, 30.6a (p. 1505).

Fan Zuyu showed Song Emperor Zhezong a work originally promulgated by an imperial forebear; and in the thirteenth century, Wang Yun prepared a compilation for the heir of a non-Chinese emperor, who was then actively adopting certain Chinese institutions to rule China more effectively. Although similar in format, the four picturebooks submitted by Ming civil officials on their own initiative represent a new phenomenon, which emerged when officials' increasing frustration with later Ming emperors was combined with new, pragmatic methods of self-cultivation promoted by the Taizhou-school 泰州派 followers of Wang Yangming 王陽明. The resort to pictures and stories to awaken a young emperor's or heir apparent's innate moral sense is a classic example of the practical approaches explored by Taizhou thinkers for developing character as a sound basis for proper action. The officials who prepared the two *Shenggong tu* were direct followers of Wang Yangming, and Zhang Juzheng and Jiao Hong were clients of his disciple Geng Dingxiang 耿定向 (1524–96, *js.* 1556).

By the late sixteenth century, the use of stories and pictures to promote character development was much in vogue. Representational images were widely circulated to teach and improve various kinds of people, especially members of the lower classes, women, and children. In 1587 the censor Zhong Huamin 鍾化民 (1537–97, *js.* 1580) created *Shengyu tujie* 聖諭圖解 (*The Sacred Edict*, illustrated and explained), a version of the Hongwu emperor's *Six Injunctions* with pictures and vernacular explanations, and had the work carved onto a stone tablet (Fig. 5.7).[97] His inscription suggests that rubbings were issued to every county and district, which were to recarve and reprint them, so that 1,000 copies could be distributed annually to township elders (*xiangqi* 鄉耆) and security-group heads (*baozhang* 保長) to read to the common people at the twice-monthly convocations. For women, Lü Kun 呂坤 (1536–1618, *js.* 1574) published *Guifan tushuo* 閨範圖説 (Stories of model women for the inner chambers, illustrated and discussed) in 1590, reworking the stories in Liu Xiang's 劉向 (ca. 79–6 BCE) *Lienü zhuan* 列女傳 (Biographies of exemplary women) into a form more readily understood and enjoyed by Ming audiences.[98] It proved to be very

<hr />

97. Zhong Huamin's stele is now in the Forest of Steles 碑林 museum in Xi'an. Sakai's extensive discussion (*Chūgoku zensho no kenkyū*, pp. 34–57) of the various iterations of the founding emperor's *Six Injunctions* in sixteenth-century community compacts (*xiangyue* 鄉約) and family instructions (*jiaxun* 家訓) does not mention Zhong's illustrated version.

98. See Handlin, *Action in Late Ming Thought*, pp. 143–44, 147–48.

Fig. 5.7   Zhong Huamin 鍾化民, *Shengyu tujie* 聖諭圖解 (*The Sacred Edict*, illustrated and explained), 1587. Rubbing of a stone tablet. 158 × 80 cm. Field Museum, Chicago (acc. no. 245254).

popular and went through multiple editions. According to Zhu Guozhen, Jiao Hong visited Lü in Shanxi and brought copies of *Guifan tushuo* back to Beijing, where it came into the hands of Lady Zheng, who republished it in 1595.[99] Lü's compilation may well have been another inspiration for Jiao Hong; moreover, the submission of *Yangzheng tujie* to the emperor similarly addressed palace interest in the publishing trends of the outside world.

The failure of the two *Shenggong tu* and *Yangzheng tujie* to be adopted for instructing the emperor's eldest son clearly shows that Ming rulers did not grant officials the right to initiate efforts to indoctrinate their heirs. The exceptional success of *Dijian tushuo* is explained by the temporary reversal in the balance of power occasioned by Zhang Juzheng's tutelage of the Wanli emperor, a regency in all but name. The two earlier picturebooks simply disappeared after being rejected, but the subsequent boom in publishing enabled the two later works to survive and proliferate as woodblock-printed books, reaching varied audiences. The circulation of both *Dijian tushuo* and *Yangzheng tujie* outside the palace led to their appropriation for other purposes, as commercial publishers, government officials, and private individuals issued reprints and new editions. Thus, works that had been initially conceived as textbooks to educate the ruler became objects of delectation for connoisseurs, tokens of authority for officials, sources of cultural knowledge or entertainment for the reading public, and much else.[100] No matter how unrealistically the pictures portrayed life at court, they offered outsiders voyeuristic access to it, and the pleasure of looking was legitimized by the premise that contemplating exemplars was morally efficacious. In the late Ming period, pleasure and propriety made an appealing combination.

---

99. *YCXP*, 10.216–17. Subsequently, Lü was accused of supporting her son to be named crown prince, rather than Zhu Changluo; see Handlin, *Action in Late Ming Thought*, p. 110; *ZZZ*, 1.1–5; and *DMB*, p. 210. Jang explores the possibility that Lady Zheng was using the publication in a bid to be named empress; see her chapter in this volume, pp. 116–85.

100. For details of these and other uses of *Dijian tushuo*, see my articles "Changing the Frame" and "From Textbook to Testimonial"; for *Yangzheng tujie*, see my "Squaring Connoisseurship with History."

Works Cited

Beijing tushuguan guji zhenben congkan 北京圖書館古籍珍本叢刊, vol. 14. Beijing: Shumu wenxian chubanshe, 1988.

Carlitz, Katherine. "The Social Uses of Female Virtue in Late Ming Editions of *Lienü zhuan.*" *Late Imperial China* 12, no. 2 (1991): 117–48.

CHC, see Mote and Twitchett, *Cambridge History of China*

Chia, Lucille. "Of Three Mountains Street: The Commercial Publishers of Ming Nanjing." In *Printing and Book Culture in Late Imperial China,* ed. Cynthia J. Brokaw and Kai-wing Chow. Berkeley: University of California Press, 2005, pp. 107–51.

Ch'ien, Edward. *Chiao Hung and the Restructuring of Neo-Confucianism in the Late Ming.* New York: Columbia University Press, 1986.

Clunas, Craig. *Art in China.* Oxford: Oxford University Press, 1997.

———. *Pictures and Visuality in Early Modern China.* London: Reaktion Books, 1997.

———. *Superfluous Things: Material Culture and Social Status in Early Modern China.* Cambridge, Eng.: Polity Press, 1991.

Dardess, John W. *Blood and History in China: The Donglin Faction and Its Repression, 1620–1627.* Honolulu: University of Hawai'i Press, 2002.

de Bary, W. T. *Neo-Confucian Orthodoxy and the Learning of the Mind-and-Heart.* New York: Columbia University Press, 1981.

DMB, see Goodrich and Fang, *Dictionary of Ming Biography*

Du Xinfu 杜信孚. *Mingdai banke zonglu* 明代版刻綜錄. Yangzhou: Jiangsu Guangling guji keyinshe, 1983.

Elman, Benjamin A. *A Cultural History of Civil Examinations in Late Imperial China.* Berkeley: University of California Press, 2000.

Fisher, Carney T. *The Chosen One: Succession and Adoption in the Court of Ming Shizong.* Sydney: Allen & Unwin, 1990.

Franke, Herbert. "Wang Yun (1227–1304): A Transmitter of Chinese Values." In *Yuan Thought: Chinese Thought and Religion Under the Mongols,* ed. Hok-lam Chan and Wm. Theodore de Bary. New York: Columbia University Press, 1982, pp. 153–96.

Goodrich, L. Carrington, and Chaoying Fang, eds. *Dictionary of Ming Biography.* New York: Columbia University Press, 1976.

Guoli zhongyang tushuguan shanben xuba jilu, shibu 國立中央圖書館善本序跋集錄, 史部. Taibei: National Central Library, 1993.

Guoli zhongyang tushuguan shanben xuba jilu, zibu 國立中央圖書館善本序跋集錄, 子部. Taibei: National Central Library, 1993.

Handlin, Joanna F. *Action in Late Ming Thought: The Reorientation of Lü Kun and Other Scholar-Officials.* Berkeley: University of California Press, 1983.

Hegel, Robert E. *Reading Illustrated Fiction in Late Imperial China.* Stanford: Stanford University Press, 1998.

Heijdra, Martin J. "A Tale of Two Aesthetics: Typography Versus Calligraphy in the Pre-modern Chinese Book." In *The Art of the Book in China,* ed. Ming Wilson and Stacey Pierson. Colloquies on Art & Archaeology in Asia, no. 23. London: Percival David Foundation of Chinese Art, 2006, pp. 15–27.

Helliwell, David. "The Repair and Binding of Old Chinese Books." *East Asian Library Journal* 8, no. 1 (Spring 1998): 27–150.

Huang, Ray. *1587, A Year of No Significance: The Ming Dynasty in Decline*. New Haven: Yale University Press, 1981.

Huang Yuji 黃虞稷 (1629–91). *Qianqingtang shumu* 千頃堂書目. Reprinted—Shanghai: Guji chubanshe, 2001.

Huo Tao 霍韜 (1487–1540). *Weiya wenji* 渭厓文集. Prefaces dated 1552 and 1576. *Hishi* reproduction of copy in Naikaku bunko, Tokyo.

HZSL, Shenzong shilu in *Ming shilu* (q.v.)

IZSL, Xizong shilu in *Ming shilu* (q.v.)

Jang, Scarlett R. "Form, Content, and Audience: A Common Theme in Painting and Woodblock-Printed Books of the Ming Dynasty." *Ars Orientalis* 27 (1997): 1–26.

Jiao Hong 焦竑 (1541–1620). *Jiaoshi Danyuan ji* 焦氏澹園集. 1606. Reprinted in Mingdai lunzhu congkan 明代論著叢刊, series 3. Taibei: Weiwen tushu, 1977.

Li, Chu-tsing, and James C. Y. Watt. *The Chinese Scholar's Studio: Artistic Life in the Late Ming Period*. New York: Thames and Hudson, 1987.

Li Jinhua 李晉華. *Mingdai chizhuanshu kao fu yinde* 明代勅撰書考附引得. Harvard-Yenching Institute Sinological Index Series no. 3. Beiping: Yanjing daxue tushuguan, 1932; reprinted—Taibei: Chinese Materials and Research Aids Service Center, 1966.

Li Weizhen 李維楨 (1547–1626). *Dabishanfang ji* 大泌山方集. N.p., n.d.

Liu Ruoyu 劉若愚 (1584–ca. 1642). *Zhuo zhong zhi* 酌中志. Ca. 1641. Included in Haishan xianguan congshu 海山仙館叢書, ed. Pan Shicheng 潘仕成. Qing, Daoguang era. Reprinted in Baibu congshu jicheng 百部叢書集成, vol. 12, pts. 1–4. Taibei: Yiwen yinshuguan, 1967.

Lu Shusheng 陸樹聲 (1509–1605). *Lu Wendinggong ji* 陸文定公集. N.p., 1616.

Mingren zhuanji ziliao suoyin 明人傳記資料索引. Comp. National Central Library. Taibei: National Central Library, 1965.

Mingshi 明史 (1739). Comp. Zhang Tingyu 張廷玉 et al. Punctuated and annotated ed. Beijing: Zhonghua shuju, 1974.

Ming shilu 明實錄. Reproduction of MS in the Zhongyang yanjiuyuan 中央研究院, Shixue yuyan yanjiusuo 史學語言研究所. Taibei: Shiyusuo, 1961–66.

Mote, F. W., and Denis Twitchett, eds. *The Cambridge History of China*, vol. 7, *The Ming Dynasty, 1368–1644, Part I*. Cambridge: Cambridge University Press, 1988.

MRZJ, see *Mingren zhuanji ziliao suoyin*

MS, see *Mingshi*

Murray, Julia K. "Changing the Frame: Prefaces and Colophons in the Chinese Illustrated Book, *Dijian tushuo*." *East Asian Library Journal* 12, no. 1 (Spring 2006): 20–67.

———. "Didactic Illustrations in Printed Books." In *Printing and Book Culture in Late Imperial China*, ed. Cynthia J. Brokaw and Kai-wing Chow. Berkeley: University of California Press, 2005, pp. 417–450.

———. "From Textbook to Testimonial: The *Di jian tu shuo / Teikan zusetsu* (The Emperor's Mirror, An Illustrated Discussion) in China and Japan." *Ars Orientalis* 31 (2001): 65–101.

———. *Mirror of Morality: Chinese Narrative Illustration and Confucian Ideology*. Honolulu: University of Hawai'i Press, 2007.

————. "Squaring Connoisseurship with History: Jiao Hong's *Yangzheng tujie*." In *The Art of the Book in China,* ed. Ming Wilson and Stacey Pierson. Colloquies on Art & Archaeology in Asia, no. 23. London: Percival David Foundation of Chinese Art, 2006, pp. 139–57.

Nikolajeva, Maria, and Carole Scott. *How Picturebooks Work.* New York: Garland Publishers, 2001.

Oertling, Sewall J., II. "Ting Yun-p'eng: A Chinese Artist of the Late Ming Dynasty." Ph.D. diss., University of Michigan, 1980.

Qinding Yuan Wang Yun Chenghua shilüe butu 欽定元王惲承華事略補圖—see Wang Yun

Qingdai gongting banhua 清代宮廷版畫. Comp. Weng Lianxi 翁連奚. Beijing: Wenwu chubanshe, 2001.

Sakai Tadao 酒井忠夫. *Chūgoku zensho no kenkyū* 中國善書の研究. Tokyo: Kōbundō, 1960.

Shen Defu 沈德符 (1578–1642). *Wanli yehuo bian* 萬曆野獲編. 1619. Punctuated ed. Beijing: Zhonghua shuju, 1959.

Songshi 宋史 (1345). Comp. Toqto 脫脫 et al. Punctuated and annotated ed. Beijing: Zhonghua shuju, 1977.

SZSL, Shizong shilu, in *Ming shilu* (q.v.)

Taiyuan Chongshansi wenwu tulu 太原崇善寺文物圖錄. Ed. Zhang Jizhong 張紀仲 and An Ji 安笈. Taiyuan: Shanxi renmin chubanshe, 1987.

Tsai, Henry Shih-shan. *Perpetual Happiness: The Ming Emperor Yongle.* Seattle: University of Washington Press, 2001.

Wang Mingqing 王明清 (1127–after 1214). *Huizhu lu, houlu* 揮麈錄, 後錄. 1194. Reprinted—Shanghai: Zhonghua shuju, 1961.

Wang Yinglin 王應麟 (1223–96). *Yuhai* 玉海. Reprint of 1883 Zhejiang shuju ed. Shanghai: Jiangsu guji chubanshe and Shanghai shudian, 1987.

Wang Yishan 王義山. *Jiacun leigao* 稼村類藁. Ca. 1260–64. In Siku quanshu zhenben, chuji 四庫全書珍本, 初集, vol. 336. Reprinted—Taibei: Shangwu yinshuguan, 1970.

Wang Yun 王惲 (1227–1304). *Chenghua shilüe* 承華事略. 1282. Reconstructed edition entitled *Qinding Yuan Wang Yun Chenghua shilüe butu* 欽定元王惲承華事略補圖. Beijing: Qing palace, 1896. Lithographic reproduction—Shanghai: Saoye shanfang, 1898.

Wang Zongmu 王宗沐 (1523–91). *Jingsuo Wang xiansheng wenji* 敬所王先生文集. N.p., 1574.

Wanli qiju zhu 萬曆起居注, vol. 1. Beijing: Beijing daxue chubanshe, 1988.

Wu Hung. *The Wu Liang Shrine: The Ideology of Early Chinese Pictorial Art.* Stanford: Stanford University Press, 1989.

Xiao Tong. *Wen xuan, or, Selections of Refined Literature,* vol. 1. Trans. and annot. David R. Knechtges. Princeton: Princeton University Press, 1982.

XZSL, Xiaozong shilu, in *Ming shilu* (q.v.)

YCXP, see Zhu Guozhen, *Yongchuang xiaopin*

YHB, see Shen Defu, *Wanli yehuo bian*

Yü, Ying-shih. "The Intellectual World of Chiao Hung Revisited: A Review Article." *Ming Studies* 25 (Spring 1988): 24–66.

Yuanshi 元史 (1370). Comp. Song Lian 宋濂. Punctuated and annotated ed. Beijing: Zhonghua shuju, 1976.

Zhang Jiangling yanjiu 張江陵研究. Comp. Zhou Rongjing 周榮靜. Taibei: Wenjin chubanshe, 1975.

Zhang Juzheng ji 張居正集. Zhang Shunhui 張舜徽, chief compiler and editor. Wuhan: Jing Chu shu she, 1987.

Zheng Ji 鄭紀 (1439–1508). *Dongyuan wenji* 東園文集. In Siku quanshu zhenben, san ji 四庫全書珍本, 三集, vol. 310: *jibu* 集部 6, *bieji lei* 別集類 5 (Ming). Taibei: Shangwu yinshuguan, 1972.

Zheng Qiao 鄭樵 (1104–62). *Tong zhi* 通志. In Guoxue jiben congshu 國學基本叢書, vol. 3. Taibei: Xinxing shuju, 1963.

Zhou Wu 周蕪. *Huipai banhua shilun ji* 徽派版畫史論集. Hefei: Anhui renmin chubanshe, 1983.

Zhu Guozhen 朱國楨 (1557–1632). *Yongchuang xiaopin* 湧幢小品. Punctuated ed. Beijing: Zhonghua shuju, 1959.

ZZZ, see Liu Ruoyu, *Zhuo zhong zhi*

SIX

Imperial Agency in Ming Music Culture

Joseph S. C. Lam

Emperors shaped not only empires but also music cultures.[1] Whether this traditional Chinese view reflects a past reality, an intellectual-political agenda, or a mixture of fact and fiction, it is historically significant as a native interpretation and historiographically stimulating as a perspective. As described in Chinese dynastic histories and other records of imperial activities, emperors had an undeniable presence in traditional Chinese music culture, playing roles that no historical narrative can ignore.[2] Emperors, however, did not shape music cultures by themselves. They made music with many of their subjects—imperial clansmen, palace ladies, eunuchs, scholar-officials, court musicians, and commoners. All were agents who directly or indirectly shaped Chinese music culture. How these agents operated individually and collectively is, however, a fundamental, and as yet unresolved, question in Chinese music history. Until it is answered, the significance of music in Chinese history and culture cannot be critically discussed.

Traditional and socialist histories of Chinese music and music culture have presented conflicting views, begging questions not only of historical

---

1. This view permeates music histories written during the imperial period. For a representative statement, one that shows a Qing assessment of Ming court music, see Zhang Tingyu et al., eds., *Mingshi* (hereafter cited as *MS*), 61.1499–50. For a broad social and political analysis of Chinese emperorship and its impact on Chinese music, see Xu Lianda and Zhu Ziyan, *Zhongguo huangdi zhidu*, pp. 541–57.

2. Two Chinese emperors whose musical legacies are historically much discussed are Xuanzong 玄宗 (r. 712–56) of the Tang and Huizong 徽宗 (r. 1101–25) of the Northern Song. For a discussion of Tang court music, see Kishibe Shigeo, *Tōdai ongaku no rekishiteki kenkyū*. For a discussion of Huizong's music legacy, see Lam, "Huizong's *Dashengyue*"; and idem, "Huizong's Ritual and Musical Insignia."

facts but also of historiographic issues of paradigms, perspectives, interpretations, and narrative strategies.[3] During the past fifty or so years, musicologists in Mainland China have effectively promoted socialist narratives
at the expense of traditional ones. These scholars have argued that commoners were the primary agents in the historical development of Chinese
music culture, and that since the Southern Song, vernacular musics constituted the mainstream of Chinese musical expression and development.[4]
Supported by a wealth of musical, historical, and ethnographic evidence,
this socialist argument is musicologically insightful and persuasive. It is also
political and tendentious, because it ignores unambiguous evidence that
highlights the musical agency of elites. For example, by marginalizing the
role of elite music patrons and connoisseurs and emphasizing the role of
commoner musicians who composed and performed, socialist musicologists can conveniently relegate the elite to secondary status. Few could argue that in traditional China, musical commoners outnumbered their elite
counterparts. However, is the answer to the question of agency in music to
be based on numbers of musicians and differences in musical structures
and styles?

---

3. Learning from early twentieth-century Western musicology, socialist Chinese music historiography of the 1950s through the 1990s emphasized technical data about historical music compositions, structures, and styles, biographies of composers, and sociopolitical dynamics in music developments that spanned two or more reigns or even
dynasties. Traditional Chinese music historiography considered these topics secondary
to chronologies of court music activities, theories of tuning and temperament, biographical sketches of musical emperors and scholar-officials, and moralistic-political assessments of musical developments. For a discussion of the relationships between socialist and traditional Chinese music historiographies, see Lam, "Chinese Music
Scholarship." Since the 1990s, Chinese music historiography has been changing rapidly,
and its perspectives and methodologies have become more flexible and diverse, incorporating ideas and techniques from current Western musicology and ethnomusicology.
Chinese music historiography, however, has yet to bridge the gap between traditional
and socialist practices. Answers are not to be found in Western musicology and ethnomusicology; the first is tailored to the examination of Western art music and its issues,
whereas ethnomusicology essentially limits its purview to contemporary genres and
phenomena at the expense of historical ones. Uncritical introduction of Western musicological arguments creates unnecessary difficulties for Chinese music historians. For
example, some scholars consider early Chinese music history "mute" (*yaba yinyueshi*
啞吧音樂史) and unknowable, because it cannot be studied with "authentic" and "intelligible" notated sources.

4. For two representative statements of the socialist argument, see Yang Yinliu,
Zhongguo gudai yinyue shigao, 1: 401–4, and 417–18; and Huang Xiangpeng, "Yayue bushi
Zhongguo yinyue chuantong di zhuliu."

Constructing a more realistic understanding of Chinese musical agency, one that balances traditional and socialist views, requires answers to many musicological questions. What roles did emperors and scholar-officials play in the development of traditional Chinese music culture? Was the imperial court a nexus of musical developments? Were Chinese elites and commoners musically different? Did they interact with one another musically? If they did, how and where did the interactions take place? And did their interactions generate sonic phenomena that complemented in one way or another the intellectual, visual, and material dimensions of traditional Chinese culture and society?

To attempt to answer these questions, this chapter examines the ways in which Ming emperors made music inside and outside their courts. Accepting as a historiographic premise the traditional view that emperors shaped Chinese music culture directly and indirectly, this chapter, nevertheless, nuances this view with the argument that imperial agency operated in conjunction with, and in reaction to, that of the other agents. In other words, both emperors and their subjects, be they palace eunuchs, court officials, or commoner musicians, contributed to the development of Chinese music culture by performing in particular musical, biographical, historical, and social moments and sites and, in the process, generating interactive and transformative changes in both court and non-court musics. Rather than being exclusive or competing musical agents, Chinese emperors and their subjects were dynamic partners in musical and cultural change. Singularly and collectively, they propelled the development of Chinese music as the sonic dimension of Chinese culture and society. No single element among these partners can be simplistically categorized as greater or lesser agents. None of their musics is culturally and socially more significant than others.

A focus on Ming emperors, their musics, and music activities is convenient and meaningful. There is a wealth of textual descriptions and notated sources on Ming court and non-court musics, a richness that is not available for studies of Chinese music and music cultures of the Yuan or earlier times.[5] These data not only demonstrate Ming music culture as a diverse and complex phenomenon but also reveal fascinating details about individual music participants and their interactions. As a result, the evidence

———

5. See *Zhongguo yinyue shupuzhi*, pp. 1–50. The bulk of preserved notated sources of historical Chinese music comes from the late Ming or even later. For recent summaries of Ming music culture, see Feng Wenci, "Xiqu yishu di you yige huangjin shidai," and "Pinzhong fansheng di yinyue yishu."

underscores the Ming emperors as a distinctive group of musical agents, whose activities and influences constitute a yardstick for assessing the agency of Ming elites and commoners.

The data also reveal the Ming court as a contested site of music making,[6] where diverse musical agents performing in institutionally defined roles competed, generating actions and results that helped Ming musics and music culture evolve. As such, the Ming court constitutes an analytical frame of reference with which the many variables and results of musical agency can be systematically coordinated and discussed. Some of these operational variables are the personhood, rulership, and musicality of individual emperors; the motives, conditions, and venues for their music activities; and the reactions from their subjects. The many results include, for example, the musics being created, performed, negotiated, and transmitted from one generation to the next, and the chain of changes in repertories, styles, and performance practices, musical meanings, and aesthetics that unfolded over the course of Ming history.

As the nexus of an empire, the Ming court was a privileged and documented music site. The musics practiced and negotiated there drew national attention, and musical theories, aesthetics, and documents related to the court stimulated agents operating inside and outside the court. Zhang Juzheng's 張居正 (1525–82) *The Emperor's Mirror, An Illustrated Discussion* (*Dijian tushuo* 帝鑒圖説), a document that Julia K. Murray analyzes in her chapter in this volume, for example, includes the story of Chen Houzhu 陳後主 (r. 583–89), a warning to rulers against indulging in licentious music.[7] In short, the Ming court conveniently serves as a beacon to chart the broad musical, historical, and cultural sea that Ming musicians, elite or commoner, navigated.

To chart this sea, a broad approach to music is needed. Music cannot be narrowly defined and examined as a performance/composition/expression of sounds and tones, a conventional understanding that works against historicizing our understanding of traditional Chinese music and music culture.[8] Music needs to be approached as a mode of human discourse that

—·—

6. See David Robinson's discussion of the Ming court in Chapter 1 of this volume, pp. 21–60.

7. See Julia Murray's chapter in this volume, pp. 231–68; and Chen Shenxi and Jia Naiqian, *Dijian tushuo*, pp. 394–97.

8. Current and global music scholarship no longer rigidly defines and studies music in terms of compositions, composers, repertories, tonal structures, styles, and notation. Nevertheless, such concepts still dominate the average music audience's understanding

takes place in specific times and places, and for specific agendas. For the purposes of this discussion, this music discourse will be termed "musiking"; and to engage in such a discourse will be termed "to musik."[9] When people "musik," they manipulate sonic and non-sonic objects in particularized sites that prompt those present to negotiate their agendas subjectively and strategically. For example, when the Ming founder and his court manipulated music to help legitimize the new Ming empire, the emperor and his official-scholars musiked with state sacrificial songs, traditions of court music, and Confucian aesthetics. When performed at imperial altars and temples, the music generated a biographically, intellectually, temporally, and physically particularized context that prompted all present to respond positively or negatively to the founder's emperorship and the new empire.[10]

The Ming Court's Relation to Music Culture and Subcultures

Audiences had to respond because the Ming founder's musiking was a discourse of the realities that they were experiencing. As manifestations of those realities, Ming music culture unfolded as a complex of distinctive but closely interrelated subcultures—namely, the court (*gongting* 宮廷), literati (*wenren* 文人), religious (*simiao* 寺廟), and commoner (*minjian* 民間) music subcultures.[11] Each subculture was distinctive insofar as it manifested itself

---

and discussion of music throughout the westernized world. The concepts are rooted in traditional Western music theories and practices and, as such, can generate unnecessary difficulties for historical studies of Chinese music and music culture. Discussion of Ming musics, for example, can hardly proceed if one demands, as evidence, authenticated notated sources and verifiable provenance of the music being discussed. Much of Ming musics is not supported by such "hard" evidence: as they were sonically experienced by Ming people, Ming musics have vanished. However, as cultural and historical expressions or manifestations, Ming musics can still be meaningfully examined in the present, because there is a wealth of verbal and notated data that broadly tells what the musics, their contexts, and meanings were.

9. My theory of "musiking / to musik" is inspired by Christopher Small's *Musicking*. As defined and applied here, my "musiking / to musik" represents my attempt to develop a theoretical framework to analyze and discuss historical Chinese music and culture. A full version of this theory will be comprehensively presented in a monograph being developed. For a published discussion and application of the theory, see Lam, "Music and Male Bonding in Ming China," esp. pp. 74–83.

10. See Lam, *State Sacrifices and Music in Ming China*, pp. 37–53.

11. Chinese music scholars have proposed various schemes to dissect traditional Chinese music culture. The scheme presented here is a current solution. For a brief

through particular sets of patrons, musicians, institutions, repertories, musical instruments, aesthetics, transmission processes, performance practices, venues, and other historically, culturally, and physically defined elements. None of the subcultures, however, can be exclusively and rigidly defined. Given the trafficking among agents, musical thoughts, practices, and products traveled beyond their own subcultures.

As a result, the subcultures shared many common elements, none of which, however, can by itself meaningfully and comprehensively identity a particular music subculture. For example, as musically dominant as Ming emperors were, neither their imperial presence nor privileged musiking defined, by itself, the Ming court music subculture. Each of the four subcultures mentioned above can further be divided according to musical functions, practices, identities, and other parameters. The literati's musiking, for instance, generated music centers in Beijing, Nanjing, Suzhou, and other cities where significant numbers of scholar-officials and elite artists visited or lived.[12] Commoners produced many localized music communities marked by geographical, linguistic, lineage, and other boundaries.[13] Each of the centers and communities can be examined as a subculture or sub-subculture.

As distinctive but interrelated phenomena within a complex music culture, the subcultures developed along their own trajectories. The Ming court music subculture unfolded during the successive reigns of different emperors. Institutionally, it operated through the State Sacrificial Music Office (Shenyue guan 神樂觀) and other court establishments and was sonically manifested through performances of genres monopolized by the court—state sacrificial music (*yayue* 雅樂, *dayue* 大樂), state banquet music (*yanyue* 燕樂 / 宴樂), and state processional music.[14] The performances

———

statement, see the preface (*xuyan* 序言) by Jiang Jing and Qian Rong, in Jiang Jing et al., *Zhongguo yinyue wenhua daguan*, p. 6. For a general discussion of various issues that help define Chinese music culture and history, see Huang Xiangpeng, "Lun Zhongguo gudai yinyue di chuancheng guanxi."

12. For a discussion of such cities as *qin* music centers, see Xu Jian, *Qinshi chubian*, pp. 122–50.

13. This is best reflected by the ongoing gigantic project (1979 to present) of publishing all Chinese folk music that musicologists have collected and notated since the 1950s. Each of the many published and individually titled volumes presents the musics according to not only genre classifications but also particular geographical, linguistic, ethnic, cultural, and political boundaries. For an English introduction to the project, see Jones, "Reading Between the Lines."

14. I use the term "state processional music" to refer to musics that accompany imperial processions and travels. In traditional Chinese music documents, such musics are

were grand because they involved hundreds of professionally trained musician-dancers performing at palace halls, imperial altars, temples, and thoroughfares throughout the capital and its suburbs. The performances were sonically communicative because they projected the Confucian aesthetics of practicing music as a means of self-cultivation and governance, an ideology transmitted via written, oral, musical, and other forms of communication.[15]

The Ming court music subculture, however, involved more than genres specific to the court. In fact, it shared many types of music practiced by literati, clergymen, and commoners, which include, for example, *qin* music, operas, Buddhist chants, Daoist hymns, popular songs, and other vernacular and ethnic genres from all parts of Ming China. Ming court music subculture interacted with the other subcultures continuously and from an advantaged position. Commanding political, social, and artistic prestige, it appropriated musics and musicians from the other music subcultures as often and as much as needed. At the same time, its practices and products were valorized as sophisticated and desirable, something that Ming people often tried to emulate directly or indirectly. No other Ming music subculture operated with such privileges so comprehensively and continuously.

In comparison, other Ming music subcultures were at once more expansive and less institutionalized; each was distinctive in some way. The literati music subculture was marked by its socially privileged practitioners who intellectually explicated the Confucian ideology of music; publicly engaged with *qin* music, poetic songs (*shiyue* 詩樂), and other elitist genres; and privately enjoyed a variety of vernacular entertainment musics performed by professional musicians, many of whom were public courtesans, household servants and maids, and itinerant performers. Ming religious music subculture was characterized by sacred hymns and chants, which Buddhist monks, Daoist priests, and laymen performed on ritual occasions and at sacred sites and private homes. Ming commoners' music subculture featured a large variety of folk and popular songs that commoners sang in their daily lives and for a variety of musical and non-musical reasons.

———

either labeled with specific terms like "drum and wind music" (*guchui* 鼓吹) and "introit" (*daoyin* 導引) or indirectly described with lists of musical instruments employed in imperial regalia (*lubu* 鹵簿). Processional music was almost not considered music (*yue* 樂).

15. For further information on the Confucian ideology and practice of music, see Lam, "Musical Confucianism"; and idem, "The Presence and Absence of Female Musicians and Music in China."

To navigate among these music subcultures, Ming people conceptually compartmentalized them into distinct units, a fact vividly attested by the way they wrote about music. Most preserved Ming music sources are exclusive reports on specific subcultures, describing musical instruments, repertories, genres, music theories, aesthetics, people, social classes, geographical locales, and other particularized concerns. For example, the *Collected Rites of the Great Ming Dynasty* (*Da Ming jili* 大明集禮), the *Veritable Records of the Ming Dynasty* (*Ming shilu* 明實錄), the *Collected Administrative Statutes of the Great Ming Dynasty* (*Da Ming huidian* 大明會典),[16] and the *Official History of the Ming Dynasty* (*Mingshi* 明史) chronicle details of genres monopolized by the court; the documents seldom mention other Ming musics.

Ming scholar-officials' learned treatises are similarly focused. Comprehensive studies, such as Huang Zuo's 黃佐 (1490–1566) *Music Classics* (*Yuedian* 樂典) and Zhu Zaiyu's 朱載堉 (1536–1611) *Collected Works on Music History and Theory* (*Yuelü quanshu* 樂律全書) concentrate on comments in the Confucian classics about music, the history of music, musical instruments, and technical-theoretical topics like tuning, temperament, and cosmological coordination among sonic and non-sonic elements. Treatises on the *qin*, such as Zhu Houjue's 朱厚爝 (fl. 1530–40s) *Classical and Civilizing Qin Music* (*Fengxuan xuanpin* 風宣玄品),[17] contain *qin* compositions and discussions of performance skills, histories, theories, music notation, and texts, as well as illustrations. Librettos and song registers (*qupu* 曲譜, *gongpu* 宮譜) of operas, such as Zhu Quan's 朱權 (1378–1448) *Song Register of Supreme Harmony and Proper Tones* (*Taihe zhengyinpu* 太和正音譜) document musical modes, tune titles, poetic rhyme schemes, and other musical and literary concerns. Obliquely, the literati's writings allude to religious musics, notated sources of which were usually guarded by religious establishments or communities.[18]

Descriptions of commoner musicians and musics are relatively rare. Much that has been preserved involves occasional poems and essays by male elites, writings that casually described the musical skills and charm of commoner musicians, especially female ones. Shen Defu's 沈德符 (1578–

---

16. Xu Yikui et al., *Ming jili*; *Ming shilu*; Shen Shixing et al., *Da Ming huidian* (hereafter *DMHD*).

17. See note 44 below for an explanation of the term "civilizing."

18. See *Zhongguo yinyue shupuzhi*, pp. 45–46. Most of the currently known notated sources of Buddhist and Daoist musics were discovered or collected by Mainland Chinese scholars in the past fifty or so years.

1642) informative *Miscellaneous Notes from the Wanli Period* (*Wanli yehuo bian* 萬曆野獲編) is an exception. Historical records on commoners' musical activities tend to portray them as local phenomena, a fact that twentieth-century ethnographic reports corroborate. For example, Xi'an Drum Music (*Xi'an guyue* 西安鼓樂), a traditional genre of wind and drum music with verifiable roots in Ming and Qing musics,[19] largely developed in Xi'an and its suburbs. Most paintings and other material products represent specific music genres and practices, attesting to the ways Ming people musiked in specific music subcultures and with particularized strategies.[20]

A Founder's Musiking

Ming people musiked strategically because they negotiated their music realities and agendas at biographically, historically, culturally, socially, and politically particularized moments. Even emperors, who were nominally free to musik whenever and however they desired, had to coordinate their musiking with court politics, institutions, and traditions. In fact, any perusal of Chinese court music history reveals that the more the emperors' musiking creatively and strategically tapped into the forces of music agents, ideologies, court institutions, and cultural traditions, the more powerful their agency became. A case in point is the musiking of the Hongwu emperor, founder of the Ming empire, who played a direct role in shaping the institutional foundation of Ming court music.

To provide for the various musical needs of his new empire and to manage the multitude of musicians employed at court, Hongwu, with the help of his scholar-officials and music officers, nominally continued court music traditions by setting up four court music offices:[21] the State Sacrificial Music Office, the Entertainment Music Office (Jiaofang 教坊), the Eunuch Music Office (Zhonggusi 鐘鼓司), and the Palace Women Music Office (Siyue 司樂), all of which operated as hierarchical troupes of officials, musicians, and dancers.[22] The State Sacrificial Music Office, a subsidiary of the Ministry of Rites, was responsible for state sacrificial music, the music played during state sacrifices at the imperial altars and temples.

---

19. For a brief summary of ethnographic data about the genre, see Jiang Jing et al., *Zhongguo yinyue wenhua daguan*, pp. 403–4.

20. See Han Bing et al., *Zhongguo yinyue wenwu daxi*.

21. For a brief and chronological survey of Chinese court music institutions, see Li Jian, *Lidai yueguan zhidu shixi*.

22. *DMHD*, 109.569–71, 226.1110–13; *MS*, 74.1817–18, 1825, 1827.

The office was administered by a director (*tidian* 提點), two vice directors (*zhiguan* 知觀), and a body of composer-supervisors (*xielü lang* 協律郎) and musician-dancers (*yuewusheng* 樂舞生). The Entertainment Music Office, also a subsidiary of the Ministry of Rites, furnished state banquet music for state functions. Its staff included a director (*fengluan* 奉鑾), two music supervisors (*siyue* 司樂), two dance supervisors (*siwu* 司舞), and a body of registered musician-dancers (*yuewusheng* 樂舞生, *yuegong* 樂工, *yuehu* 樂戶). The Eunuch Music Office, administered by one director (*sizheng* 司正) and two vice directors (*sifu* 司副), took care of the ritual, processional, and entertainment music needs inside the palace.[23] The Palace Women's Music Office, a palace institution, served the music needs of the empresses and other palace women. It was administered by four music supervisors (*siyue* 司樂), four vice supervisors (*dianyue* 典樂), four music controllers (*zhangyue* 掌樂), and two female scribes (*nüshi* 女史).

In addition to these court music offices, which formed the institutional core of the Ming court music subculture, other court offices and personnel were also involved.[24] The Ministry of Works (Gongbu 工部), for example, was responsible for the manufacture of a large quantity and variety of musical instruments needed by various Ming court musicians. Some members of the Brocade Guard (Jinyiwei 錦衣衛) and other military-police units doubled as performers of processional music that escorted imperial travelers outside the palace, complementing their official duties of providing security for the emperors and other court dignitaries.

Hongwu's involvement in the development of Ming court music institutions was personal, direct, and continuous.[25] As soon as he proclaimed himself King of Wu in 1365, Hongwu appointed a music manager to address the musical needs of his emerging court. In the summer of 1367, as preparations for the formal establishment of the Ming empire were under way, he personally reviewed the current state of court music by inspecting musical instruments and discussing theories with his scholar-officials. During that review, Hongwu struck a tone on the stone-chimes set there, and asked Zhu Sheng 朱昇 (1299–1371), one of two scholar-officials overseeing the event, to name the musical tone. The scholar, who was known to be learned in music, misidentified it and would have been punished but for

---

23. For a historical discussion of the Eunuch Music Office, see Xu Zifang, *Ming zajushi*, pp. 47–51.

24. *DMHD*, 182.922, 183.931–32, 184.932–33, 185.936, 185.938, and 189.950–62.

25. *MS*, 61.1499–508; Lam, *State Sacrifices and Music in Ming China*, pp. 37–53.

the learned explanation offered by Xiong Ding 熊鼎, the court diarist recording the review.[26] Zhu Sheng's mistake was grave because errors could lead to disastrous results. Mistuning of the musical instruments or misuse of the pitches could jeopardize the efficacy of the music for the new empire—only music featuring theoretically and performatively accurate tones would coordinate human and cosmic forces so that the empire would operate harmoniously. Two months later, Taizu appointed Leng Qian 冷謙 (ca. 1310–ca. 1371),[27] a purported Daoist music master from Hangzhou, to create new tunes for the state sacrifices. In 1369, Taizu ordered Xu Yikui 徐一夔 (1318–1400) and other scholar-officials to compile a ritual and music reference book. The following year, they completed the *Collected Rites of the Great Ming Dynasty* in 50 fascicles; it preserves notated music and summarizes contemporary music theories and practices, and coincidentally demonstrates the continuity between the music of the Yuan and that of the early Ming.[28] Among the notated music preserved in the document is a set of five tunes from Yuan China, musical works that attest not only to Ming memories of Yuan music but also to the negotiation of Han and non-Han elements by Ming emperors and scholar-officials.[29]

Although significant, the scholar-officials' musiking with words and historical examples is clearly subordinate to that of Hongwu. The founder forcefully musiked from his privileged position. As the *Official History of the Ming Dynasty* notes, he was dissatisfied with the court musics created in the first three years of his empire, finding them improper and deficient in one way or another.[30] In 1371, he ordered a revision of the *Imperial Homecoming Songs* (*Huiliange* 回鑾歌), state processional music that accompanied the emperor's return to the palace from trips outside; he demanded lyrics that were more elegant in literary terms and more suitable for singing. Late in the 1370s, Hongwu revised the state sacrifices and had new ritual songs composed. In the process, he personally wrote twenty ritual lyrics, eight of

---

26. *MS*, 61.1500.

27. Goodrich and Fang, *Dictionary of Ming Biography* (hereafter cited as *DMB*), s.v. "Leng Ch'ien."

28. Xu Yikui et al., *Ming jili*. For a bibliographic discussion of the court manual, see Lam, *State Sacrifices and Music in Ming China*, pp. 123–24.

29. Xu Yikui et al., *Ming jili* 53a.26a–37b. For a musicological description of the tunes, see Lam, "'There Is No Music in Chinese Music History.'" Elsewhere in this volume, Dora Ching (pp. 321–64) and David Robinson (pp. 365–421) discuss the Ming court's political and cultural engagement with non-Han elements.

30. *MS*, 61.1507–8.

which subsequently became texts sung at the combined state sacrifice to Heaven and Earth that premiered in 1379.[31] Eventually, as imperial audiences, state banquets, and other court functions were ritually codified, Ming court musics became institutionalized, thanks to Hongwu's direct supervision. A hands-on imperial music agent, he exercised his imperial authority to shape what music was acceptable in his court.

Hongwu's agency was effective because he relied on and promoted the Confucian ideology of employing music as a means of governance and self-cultivation. This intellectual and strategic musiking was not accidental; it resulted from not only political and administrative needs of the time but also Hongwu's cultural and ethnic concerns. As Dora C. Y. Ching and David Robinson show elsewhere in this volume,[32] Hong found the Mongol/Yuan legacies both a political resource and a challenge. On one hand, he might valorize his own emperorship by appropriating the Mongol rulers' unprecedented grandeur and strength. On the other hand, he felt a need to authenticate his political and cultural authority by projecting his Han identity and by eradicating Mongol influences, at least nominally. Thus, in his musiking of state sacrificial music, he manipulated selected Confucian truths and Han historical memories. Extolling Shao 韶, Wu 武, and other musical works that ancient and meritorious Han rulers had allegedly created and used to help build harmonious societies, Hongwu commanded that the state sacrificial music of his court emulate historical examples.

Hongwu's implementation of Confucian ideology and court music traditions was, needless to say, neither literal nor orthodox. He did not hesitate to assert his personal views and needs: witness his introduction of Daoist elements into the Ming court music subculture.[33] When he established the State Sacrificial Music Office in 1379, he entrusted its operation to Daoist monk-officials, an action that effectively secured for Daoists an institutionalized role in the development of Ming state sacrificial music. Since the monk-officials had the authority to recruit and train disciples / musician-dancers, they had ample opportunities to assert their Daoist or Daoist-related music aesthetics and practices.[34] Traditionally, the Court of State Sacrifices (Taichangsi 太常寺), a subsidiary of the Ministry of Rites

---

31. *MS*, 62.1521, 1523–24.

32. See the chapters by Dora Ching (pp. 321–64) and David Robertson (pp. 365–421) in this volume.

33. Taizu favored Zhiyi 正一 Daoism; see *Zhonghua wenhua shi: Mingdai*, pp. 588–90.

34. For a genealogy of the Daoist monk-officials and their music students, see *Taichang xukao* 7.51b–97a.

controlled by Confucian scholar-officials, had been responsible for state sacrificial music.

To tap the religious force of Daoism, Hongwu promoted it through active participation in Daoist ritual and musical activities. In 1374, he wrote the preface for a book of Daoist lyrics, *Daoist Ritual Songs* (*Daojiao keyi yuezhang* 道教科儀樂章).[35] In 1382, he authored a set of lyrics for the rite entitled Imperial Daoist Inauguration Ritual (*Da Ming xuanjiao licheng zhaijiaoyi* 大明玄教立成齋醮儀). Hongwu's participation clearly gave Daoist ritual and music an imperial gloss and a historically significant promotion. Hongwu was not the first Chinese emperor to welcome Daoists into his court, but he was the first one to formally entrust to them the operation of state sacrificial music.[36] It was an imperial act that secured a Daoist presence in what was nominally a Confucian tradition of music.

In addition to musiking for the Ming empire, Hongwu also musiked for his personal pleasure, patronizing various genres of entertainment and vernacular musics, filling the early Ming palace with musics and musicians, and raising musical princes.[37] As a matter of fact, Hongwu's active patronage of operatic music helped create the Official String Accompanied Arias (*Xiansuo guandiao* 弦索官調), an act that foreshadowed the ways Ming elite promoted operatic musics in later periods of the dynasty. Commenting on the artistic merits of Gao Ming's 高明 (ca. 1301–ca. 1371) *The Lute* (*Pipa ji* 琵琶記),[38] an opera featuring southern arias (*nanqu* 南曲), Hongwu said: "The *Five Classics* and the *Four Books* are basics like cloth, silk, beans, and nuts; every home has them. Gao Ming's *The Lute* is like delicacies from mountains and seas; noble and rich families cannot do without it."[39] To share his enjoyment of music with his imperial sons and ennobled official-scholars, or to divert their attention from court affairs, he ordered that librettos and other written materials of operas and songs be bestowed on the princely establishments (*wangfu* 王府), thus contributing to their rise as regional centers for Ming music development (see below).

As Hongwu became familiar with the music of *The Lute*, he grew dissatisfied that the arias had no string accompaniment. In his role as music critic, he lamented that in employing the southern style of music, Gao had

---

35. Pu Hengqiang, *Daojiao yu Zhongguo chuantong yinyue*, p. 291.

36. The most famous Chinese emperor who actively engaged with Daoism and music is Huizong of the Northern Song; see Lam, "Huizong's *Dashengyue*."

37. Zhu Quan, *Gongci qishi shou*.

38. For an English translation of the work, see Mulligan, *The Lute*.

39. Xu Wei, *Nanci xulu*, pp. 239–41.

used good materials inappropriately, a misstep comparable to using brocade to make shoes. Responding to the emperor's criticism of the music,
Liu Gao 劉杲, a section leader (sechang 色長) in the Entertainment Music
Office, created new arrangements, in which both the northern melodies
(beiqu 北曲) of Yuan drama and the southern arias (nanqu 南曲) of southern operas (nanxi 南戲) could be accompanied on the pipa and other string
instruments. Developed as court entertainment music and historically
known as Official String Accompanied Arias, Liu's arrangements were musically soft, slow, and rhapsodic. They reflected court and elite preferences,
but never blossomed into a major genre of Ming operatic music.[40]

In 1393, to promote leisure and socializing activities among his scholar-
officials, Hongwu had fifteen wine parlors (jiulou 酒樓) built in the capital;
five of them featured women singers.[41] To support the scholar-officials'
musiking in those entertainment establishments, he provided them with
funds. Hongwu was, however, less benevolent to his commoner subjects;
he did not tolerate their musical abuses. As an emperor who manipulated
ritual and music as a means of governance, he wanted to stop licentious
musics and improper performances from undermining morals and social
roles. In 1369, he forbade soldiers from singing like entertainers.[42] In 1397,
he prohibited actors from impersonating emperors and empresses because
their performances misrepresented imperial personae. Hongwu wished to
maintain strict control over the imperial image, a point that Dora Ching
makes in her analysis of imperial portraiture in this volume.

If this summary of Hongwu's music actions show how a powerful emperor musiked to shape early Ming music culture according to his imperial
agenda, it also underscores how imperial agency operated in collaboration
with many other music agents and under many constraints. It was a process that, on one hand, rendered the Ming court music subculture distinctive and, on the other hand, made it closely related to the other music subcultures of the empire. When emperors and scholar-officials ideologically
and artistically developed court musics as expressions of their political
identities and power, they generated musics stylistically distinct from those
expressions of the commoners. As a result, the gap between court and
other music subcultures grew ever wider. When emperors and other palace

---

40. Feng Wenci, "Xiqu yishu di you yige huangjin shidai," p. 668.
41. Shen Defu, Wanli yehuo bian (hereafter cited as YHB), 3.899; Li Guoxiang and
Yang Chang, Ming shilu leizuan, p. 1482.
42. Wang Liqi, Yuan Ming Qing sandai jinhui xiaoshuo xiqu shiliao, pp. 12–13.

inhabitants pursued contemporary musics, especially the entertainment genres fashionable among commoners, however, musical bridges connecting the court with the rest of the empire were built.

To further understand this operation of imperial agency in Hongwu's case, it is crucial to note how specific combinations of players, times, and places affected its processes and results. As the founder of the Ming empire, Hongwu was *relatively but never absolutely* free to musik in ways he desired. Exercising his imperial power and authority, he could direct his music officials to create new music and institutions for his new empire. He could order his officials to selectively continue or adjust musical institutions and legacies by arguing that all new dynasties created their own court music by, on one hand, emulating meritorious historical examples and by, on the other hand, expressing feelings and needs specific to their empire. Indeed, he used these arguments to revise early Ming court music.

His arguments were persuasive because they evoked a logic difficult to challenge in imperial China. Corrupted musics caused empires to topple, and the collapse of former empires showed that their musics were not "perfect." Had they employed "perfect" musics, they would still be thriving. Convenient as this argument was, it was not one that Hongwu's imperial descendants, or any emperor who did not found a dynasty, could easily use. For succeeding emperors, their imperial ancestors' musical legacies were sacrosanct and could be changed only with great determination and effort, and only after the "mistakes" of lowly music workers (*yuegong*) had been identified and the need for revision established. No emperor who projected himself as a filial Son of Heaven would casually change an ancestral legacy, an act that conservative court officials would promptly construe as a disrespectful affront to the ancestors' virtuous and meritorious governance.

In other words, unencumbered by any ancestral musical heritage, Hongwu could musik much more freely than his descendants—the eleventh Ming emperor, Jiajing, faced enormous challenges when he revised court ritual and music in the 1530s and 1540s (see below). This does not mean, however, that Hongwu could musik with no constraints. Indeed, upon close scrutiny, it is clear that Hongwu essentially abided by court music institutions and traditions that had been culturally and historically transmitted by his scholar-officials from earlier courts to his own.

Despite his force as an imperial music agent, Hongwu could not ignore his scholar-officials and their prescriptions for court musics. Rather than resist the prescriptions comprehensively documented and continuously implemented by historical courts, Hongwu found it far more advantageous to strategically manipulate the prescriptions, which could be creatively implemented by his court music officers and performers. Hongwu chose to do so because he realized that the prescriptions were deeply rooted in the Confucian, cosmological, and political thoughts of imperial China. As described in Confucian classics, emperors were supposed to implement ritual and music as a means of governance and self-cultivation, an ideology that Chinese rulers found instrumental in propping up their own authority and in sustaining traditional morality and social structure.

The *Record of Music* (*Yueji* 樂記),[43] a seminal document in Chinese music history, for example, declares that as a natural phenomenon of the cosmos and as genuine expressions of and communications between human heart-minds (*xin* 心), music is expressive and efficacious. Civilized/civilizing music (*yayue* 雅樂) nurtures people's virtues and guides them to live properly,[44] whereas "vulgar" and "licentious sounds" (*yinsheng* 淫聲, *chiyue* 侈樂) encourage personal indulgence and cause social disorder that topples dynasties. Thus, to build and operate orderly empires, emperors should promote civilized music and suppress vulgar sounds. It was a prescription that Chinese emperors had nominally followed since the early Han dynasty when Confucianism became state orthodoxy.

Since that time, Chinese emperors and courts ostentatiously performed state and ritual genres of court music to demonstrate their power and to civilize their subjects. To ensure results, they strove to implement classical theories in their court music, idealistically believing that it would activate harmonious correspondences among musical, human, and cosmic elements. This is why their court music featured what they claimed to be the theoretically accurate and orderly use of pitches and other musical elements. The *gong* 宮 (*do*) of the five tones (*wuyin* 五音) used in a civilized piece of court music, for example, was theoretically the most important

---

43. "Yueji," in Qian Bocheng, *Baihua shisan jing, fu yuanwen*, 1: 1262–68. *Yueji*, a Han dynasty compilation of Confucian descriptions about music, is also chapter 19 of *Liji* 禮記.

44. To underscore the Confucian ideology of music and its social and political ramifications, the term *yayue*, when used in a general sense, will be translated as "civilized music" or "civilizing music." When *yayue* is used to denote specific genres of court music, it will be translated as "state sacrificial music," "state banquet music," and so forth. Conventional translations of the term as "proper music" or "elegant music" do not clearly register its political and social implications.

sound, one that ruled the other tones the way an emperor controlled his subjects.[45]

Hongwu also understood that the prescriptions could be comprehensively implemented only through the scholar-officials, the guardians of the Confucian ideology. Thus he promptly entrusted the task of creating authentic and efficacious court musics to Tao An 陶安 (1312–68) and other learned Confucian experts at his court.[46] In response to the emperor's command, they produced music by emulating, or claiming to have emulated, not only ancient musics that the classics valorized but also those that legitimate courts had practiced in the past.

In other words, Hongwu's imperial music agency set in motion a dynamic chain of actions and reactions that propelled a diversity of agents to musik their parts in the contexts of a new empire, a process that can be summarized as follows. Acting as the Son of Heaven and exercising his moral and political authority, Hongwu ordered the creation of civilized music for his court as a means of governance and self-cultivation. Performing their duties as servants/advisors to the emperors, Tao An and other scholar-officials of his court researched, debated, formulated, and proposed recommendations to Hongwu. Once Hongwu and the scholar-officials agreed/compromised on their solutions, they directed court officers to compose the music required. Once approved by the authorities, the newly composed music became works that court musician-dancers meticulously performed as imperial expressions and faithfully maintained as ancestral legacies for posterity.

In composing the music, the music officers worked with established court aesthetics, genres, and contextually particularized needs. Ming state sacrificial songs were, for example, composed as syllabic tunes and sung solemnly to realize the supposed features of ancient music (see Fig. 6.1). In composing music for specific court rituals and functions, the music officers considered many ritual and non-sonic concerns. The number of songs and dances performed in any individual state sacrifice was, for example, dictated not by imperial wish or the expressive impulses of individual agents but by the identities of the deities being honored and by the hierarchical ranks that the court had assigned them.

---

45. For further details on Ming music theory, see Lam, *State Sacrifices and Music in Ming China*, pp. 75–97.

46. *MS*, 47.1223–24, 61.1499. See *DMB*, s.v. "T'ao An."

眇 眇 微 躬 何 敢 請 于 九 重 以 煩 帝 聽

帝 心 矜 憐 有 感 而 通 既 俯 臨 于 几 筵

神 繽 紛 而 景 從 臣 雖 愚 蒙 鼓 舞 懽 容

乃 子 孫 之 親 祖 宗 酌 清 酒 兮 在 鐙 仰 至 德 兮 玄 功

Fig. 6.1   First offering of wine for the state sacrifice to Heaven. 1370. From Lam, *State Sacrifices and Music in Ming China*, p. 134.

The more highly ranked the deity, the grander the ritual music was. The state sacrifice honoring Heaven, the grandest among state rituals, for example, involved nine ceremonial stages and thus nine ritual songs. In contrast, the state sacrifice honoring Confucius, usually a middle-rank ceremonial, had only seven stages and six songs (two of the ritual stages shared the same ritual tune). Neither a deity like Heaven nor a deified person like an imperial ancestor, Confucius was merely a sage and did not rank in the highest stratum of Ming cosmology.

The same considerations also applied to the composition of state banquet music. As Robinson notes in Chapter 1 to this volume, court banquets were both celebration and ceremony, occasions to regulate individuals and the social order. Thus, their music programs were ritualized and codified. During Hongwu's reign, the most elaborate state banquet unfolded as a series of nine formalized sections of instrumental music, dances, and theatrical performances.[47] Each began with ritual songs featuring precomposed lyrics and standardized tunes.[48] Only after the singing of the ritual songs were theatrical and improvised shows (*baixi* 百戲) performed.

---

47. *MS*, 61.1052–55.
48. *MS*, 63.1559–78.

In designing the performance details of court music, the music officers followed prescriptions about the use of musical instruments, which were not only specific tools for making music but also embodiments of music and cosmological theories, court institutions, and history. As described in Ming court documents, the music for each particular state sacrifice and banquet was performed with its own designated orchestra of a specific grouping and arrangement of musical instruments, designed to communicate a wealth of social and cultural meanings. For instance, the orchestra for the state sacrifice to Heaven, a grand ceremonial, featured one wooden crate (*zhu* 柷), one wooden tiger (*yu* 敔), two barrel drums (*pofu* 搏拊), two large suspended drums (*yinggu* 應鼓, *jiangu* 建鼓), ten *qin*, four 25-stringed zithers (*se* 瑟), twelve vertical flutes (*xiao* 簫), twelve mouth organs (*sheng* 笙), twelve *di* flutes (笛), four ocarinas (*xun* 塤), four *chi* flutes (篪), four panpipes (*paixiao* 排簫), two sets of bell chimes (*bianzhong* 編鐘), two sets of stone-chimes (*bianqing* 編磬), and twelve singers.[49] In contrast, the orchestra used in the state sacrifice honoring Confucius consisted of one wooden crate, one wooden tiger, four barrel drums, one large drum (*dagu*), ten *qin*, four 25-stringed zithers, eight vertical flutes, eight mouth organs, four *di* flutes, four ocarinas, four *chi* flutes, one set of bell chimes, one set of stone-chimes, and ten singers (see Fig. 6.2).[50]

The same principle of hierarchy guided the composition and physical display of the orchestras at state banquets and in imperial processions.[51] Two Ming court paintings, *The Emperor's Procession to the Imperial Tombs* (*Chujingtu* 出警圖) and *The Emperor's Return to the Capital* (*Rubitu* 入蹕圖), provide rare visual glimpses of the elaborate musical entourages that surrounded Ming emperors and evoke how the musicians employed selected musical instruments to rhythmically and loudly announce the imperial presence to all within hearing range.[52] The first painting shows the imperial entourage traveling on boats (Fig. 6.3). Performing on two of the boats are eunuchs. Their musical instruments include single nippled gongs

---

49. *DMHD*, 183.931–32; *MS*, 61.1505–6. The number of instruments in each of the orchestras fluctuated over the course of the dynasty.

50. *MS*, 61.1505.

51. For detailed listings of the instruments, see *DMHD*, 105.569–71.

52. Wu Zhao, *Zhuixun xiqu di yinyue zongji*, pp. 306–9. Original paintings held in National Palace Museum, Taibei. For a detailed discussion of the paintings as representations of Jiajing's travel, see Na and Kohler, *The Emperor's Procession*. See also Fong, "Imperial Portraiture of the Ming Dynasty."

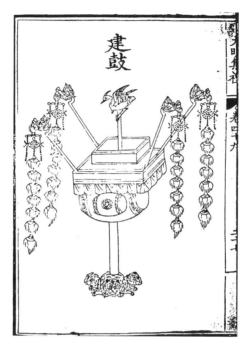

Fig. 6.2   A large suspended drum for performance during imperial state sacrifices. 1370. From Xu
Yikui et al., *Da Ming jili*, 49.27a.

suspended on frames, big barrel drums, cymbals, flutes, gong-chimes
(*yunluo* 雲鑼), small handheld drums, flutes, hour-glass drums, and
wooden clappers.[53] The second painting features a troupe of eunuchs riding horses and playing drum and wind instruments. Their cymbals, single
gongs, nippled gongs, flutes, trumpets, wooden clappers, and barrel drums
sharply contrast with the instruments used to perform state sacrificial music (Fig. 6.4). If the paintings evoke the music of Ming state processional
music, their depiction of eunuchs attests to the central roles they played in
Ming court music (see "Eunuchs and Music" below).[54]

---

53. The painting gives information that is more detailed but also different from that
in the *DMHD*'s (140.723–25) lists of musical instruments prescribed for imperial tours.

54. Whether the paintings accurately and specifically depict mid-Ming imperial processional music cannot be settled until other paintings of the same subject matter are
examined. Accepting the thesis that the emperor depicted in the paintings was indeed
Jiajing (see note 52), I would argue that the paintings give realistic information about
musicians and musical instruments in Jiajing's tours. Unless painters have direct and
personal experiences with the music activities that they depict, they do not always present musical details realistically. Iconographic sources that refer to music and music

(*top*) Fig. 6.3   Palace eunuch musicians performing on imperial barges. From Wu Zhao, *Zhuixun xiqu di yinyue zongji*, pp. 308–9. (*bottom*) Fig. 6.4   Palace eunuch musicians performing on horses. From Na and Kohler, *The Emperor's Procession*, fig. 37.

activities in abstract and generalized forms always include ambiguous, if not ludicrous, features, such as an impractical way of holding a musical instrument. The paintings in question show the musicians holding and playing musical instruments with gestures that are visually and musically credible.

Among all court genres, entertainment music performed in private quarters inside the palace was least constrained by ritual, contextual, sonic, and non-sonic considerations. As Hongwu's engagement with the Official String Accompanied Arias illustrates, such private entertainment musics could be created or adjusted according to imperial and personal preferences. Nevertheless, even such musics and musiking could not operate with total aesthetic and artistic freedom. As soon as court censors found the emperors' pri-vate musiking excessive, vulgar, or anomalous by Confucian standards, they would criticize, as we will see in the discussion below of Zhengde's musiking.

The Yongle Emperor and the Ming Princes

To evade the criticisms of censors, most Ming emperors kept their private music activities inside their palaces. In fact, only four of Hongwu's successors, the Yongle, Hongzhi, Zhengde, and Jiajing emperors, left relatively clear records of their musiking, revealing how their agency conformed to or resisted court traditions and institutions.

Yongle (r. 1403–24), the third Ming emperor, was a strong ruler who usurped the throne from Huidi (r. 1398–1402), the second Ming emperor, and changed the course of the Ming dynasty. Yongle also appears to have been a musical emperor: he favored a Korean concubine who was a skilled flautist. As a music agent, Yongle greatly affected Ming music culture and subcultures by following the course his father, the Hongwu emperor, had set and by implementing measures that generated immediate as well as long-term music results. This musiking was deliberate. Although playing the role of a filial son, Yongle, nevertheless, brought to the Ming throne a vision of governance different from his father's. As Robinson demonstrates in Chapter 8 in this volume, Yongle ignored his father's repeated injunctions against foreign entanglements, against granting eunuchs a place in imperial government, and against excessive imperial expenditure.

In 1420, Yongle moved the Ming capital from Nanjing to Beijing, an action that not only necessitated revisions in state banquet music but also led to the recruitment of many court musician-dancers from the vicinity of Beijing.[55] How these musicians-dancers affected Ming court musics remains to be analyzed, but it is reasonable to presume that over the years they would have introduced regional characteristics into the music they

---

55. See *Taichang xukao*, 7.51b–97a.

performed.[56] Another action of Yongle's that had far-reaching effects was his entrusting to eunuchs official and unofficial tasks inside and outside the court. As eunuchs' presence and power grew, they gradually took over the duties of the women palace musicians and came to dominate music making inside the Ming palace.[57]

As Yongle built his new capital, he also manipulated religious forces to advance his imperial vision and political agendas.[58] Thus, he promoted Daoist and Buddhist music inside and outside the palace, ordering the compilation and publication of ritual liturgies and anthologies of ritual lyrics. One such compilation is the *Ming Daoist Songs* (*Da Ming xuanjiao yue-zhang* 大明玄教樂章), which is now included in the *Daoist Canon* (*Daozang* 道藏) and preserves in traditional Chinese notation (*gongche pu* 工尺譜) the melodies for twelve Daoist ritual songs.[59] An analogous anthology of Buddhist ritual lyrics is the *Efficacious Songs* (*Ganying gequ* 感應歌曲) of 1419.[60] Both documents attest to the interactions among court, religious, and vernacular songs of the time. In addition to the ritual titles of the song lyrics preserved, such as "Welcome the Deities" ("Ying shen" 迎神), the documents list the vernacular names of pre-existing tunes (*qupai* 曲牌), such as "Every Step Higher" ("Bubugao" 步步高), to which the ritual lyrics were sung.

Historically and musically, the most significant action in Yongle's promotion of Daoism was, however, his support for the Daoist shrine at Wudang Mountain 武當山 in Hubei province. By providing continuous court support and by assigning eunuchs to supervise its operation, he elevated the shrine into an imperial and influential center of Daoism where court and non-court music subcultures intersected. By sending Daoist monks from all over the empire to the shrine, he created a site where Daoist music agents and styles from diverse geographical locales converged.[61] Even

---

56. Chinese musicologists have extensively discussed the distinctive regional characteristics of Chinese music. The characteristics can also be readily experienced through recorded examples of traditional Chinese music.

57. For an overview of Ming eunuchs, see Tsai, *The Eunuchs in the Ming Dynasty*. See also Scarlet Jang's discussion of Ming eunuchs and court arts in her chapter in this volume (pp. 116–85).

58. For Yongle's manipulation of religious and political forces, see the chapters by Dora Ching (pp. 321–64) and David Robinson (pp. 365–421) in this volume.

59. *Daozang*, 616.1–6.

60. *Ganying gequ*, rare book in the collection of Hong Kong University Library.

61. Pu Hengqiang, "Mingdai Wudangshan daojiao yinyue kaolüe."

today, Wudangshan Daoist music features a mix of native and imported styles and contrasting sounds.[62]

Yongle's manipulations of intellectual traditions to advance his emperorship also had an impact on the long-term development of Ming literati music subculture. By promoting Zhu Xi 朱熹 (1130–1200) and his Neo-Confucianism, he helped shape ideological and aesthetic foundations of music among the literati. With the publication and distribution of canonic texts such as the *Great Compendium on the Five Classics* (*Wujing daquan* 五經大全) and the *Great Compendium on Human Nature* (*Xingli daquan* 性理大全), the emperor created an environment in which teachers and students implemented Confucian/Neo-Confucian aesthetics of music by singing civilized music such as poetic songs and discussing music theories developed by Song and earlier scholar-official-theorists. The Twelve Ritual Songs (*Fengya shier shipu* 風雅十二詩譜) that Zhu Xi preserved in his *General Survey of Ritual* (*Yili jingchuan tongjie* 儀禮經傳通解) became, for example, the earliest available and notated exemplars of ancient music that Ming literati strove to reconstruct.[63] Similarly, Cai Yuanding's 蔡元定 (1135–98) influential music theories, which he postulated in his *New Treatise of Music Theory* (*Lülü xinshu* 律呂新書) and which received favorable comments from Zhu Xi, became canonized explanations of music that Ming theorists examined, critiqued, and even refuted.[64]

The canonizing of Cai's music theories was, needless to say, an indirect result of Yongle's control of cultural matters. As such, it parallels another indirect but perhaps more significant facet of Yongle's music agency. To forestall political threats from imperial clansmen living in princely establishments outside the capital, Yongle forbade them to engage in the civil or military affairs of the empire in any official capacity.[65] In so doing, Yongle fostered a group of educated, salaried, and privileged men who lived in palatial mansions and could afford to devote their time and energy to the arts. Should these men actively musik, they became privileged music agents, and their princely establishments, sites of musical creation and changes. Thus, when Zhu Quan, a brother and erstwhile supporter of Yongle, was sent away from the capital, the nexus of state politics, to take

---

62. Shi Xinmin, "Lun dangdai Wudang daoyue zhi tezheng."

63. For a musicological discussion and transcription of the Twelve Ritual Songs, see Pian, *Song Music Sources and Their Interpretations*, pp. 154–73.

64. For a musicological discussion of the treatise, see ibid., pp. 7–8; and Lam, *State Sacrifices and Music in Ming China*, pp. 76, 95–96.

65. Hucker, "Ming Government," p. 26.

residence in his princely establishment in Nanchang 南昌, Jiangxi, he turned his attention to music and other studies, securing for himself a permanent place in Ming music history. Zhu Quan's pursuit of music, however, began before his arrival at Nanchang in 1403. In 1398, Zhu Quan published his *Song Register of Supreme Harmony and Proper Tones*, the earliest known song register of Yuan drama and northern arias, preserving not only historical and biographical notes about the genre but also prescriptions on the modal and rhyme schemes of 335 northern arias.

Read as a Ming prince's views on the music culture at the turn of the fifteenth century, Zhu's preface for the document attests to the political and social ramifications of imperial musiking.[66] Having lived in a peaceful world for thirty-some years, Zhu wrote, Ming people sang and danced to express themselves and to laud the government; their harmonious arias and charming tones appealed even to non-Han peoples. If Zhu extolled imperial influence on commoners' musiking, however, he did not allude to imperial censorship—for example, in 1411, Yongle banned all theatrical performances not sanctioned by the court.[67]

In 1425, Zhu completed his musical magnum opus, *Fantastic and Secret Notation of Qin Music* (*Shenqi mipu* 神奇密譜), the earliest known and verifiable anthology of *qin* music in tablature notation (*jianzipu* 減字譜).[68] In his preface to the anthology,[69] Zhu declared that sixteen among the sixty-four compositions preserved in the anthology represented authentic music from Tang, Song, and earlier times, a claim that twentieth-century analyses generally corroborate.[70] Zhu also stated that he had spent twelve years compiling the document, during the process of which he had studied and performed all of the preserved pieces.

This statement not only marks a Ming prince's individual and active agency in the development and transmission of Chinese music repertories and traditions but also highlights the ways Ming princely establishments promoted music interactions and developments. Zhu's princely position allowed him to pursue his music interests over a long period of time, bringing master musicians, sophisticated performances, and precious musi-

---

66. Zhu Quan, *Taihe zhengyinpu*, p. 11.

67. Wang Liqi, *Yuan Ming Qing sandai jinhui xiaoshuo xiqu shiliao*, p. 14.

68. Zhu Quan, *Shenqi mipu*.

69. Goormaghtigh and Yung, "Preface of *Shenqi mipu*."

70. For a persuasive demonstration of the pre-Ming genesis of the *qin* works, see Wang Di, *Qinqu* Guanglingsan *chutan*.

cal knowledge and resources to his princely court. Zhu Quan's music agency was not an isolated case. One early Ming librettist was Zhu Youdun 朱有燉 (1379–1439), also a Ming prince. His thirty-two music dramas were noted for their innovations and were once popular.[71]

The Zhengde Emperor: A Challenge to Orthodoxy

After Yongle, the next Ming emperor who musically impacted Ming music culture in substantive ways was Zhengde (r. 1506–21), who changed entertainment musics throughout the empire.[72] Ming scholar-officials and traditional historians criticized Zhengde's unusual, even bizarre, behavior and strove to restrain it.[73] As Robinson argues in Chapter 8 in this book, Zhengde generated controversy because his ideas about the proper role of the emperor clashed with those of civil bureaucracy. Music was one manifestation of the deep tension that ran through much of court life and court culture during the Ming period.

In the summer of 1508, Zhengde ordered court officials to provide entertainment music for state functions so that foreign dignitaries could witness the empire's greatness. Demanding immediate results, he supplemented his officials' proposal to train young but unskilled musicians by ordering that talented performers from all over the empire be promptly brought to the court. As a result, all kinds of musicians and musics gathered in the capital, a situation that promoted musical competition and exchange. Later Zhengde built the Leopard Quarter 豹房, his primary residence and command center for the remainder of his reign. To the Leopard Quarter, he summoned more musician-dancers, including twelve Uighur women.[74] Zhengde enjoyed non-Han musics, a taste that reflected his curiosity about foreign lands, peoples, and cultures: allegedly Zhengde favored Lady Ma for her mastery of Central Asian music (huyue 胡樂).[75]

---

71. *DMB*, s.v. "Chu Yu-tun." For a discussion of Zhu's dramas, see Xu Zifang, *Ming zajushi*, pp. 114–40.

72. For an official description of Zhengde's musiking, see *MS*, 61.1509. For Zhengde's biography, see Mao Qiling, *Wuzong waiji*; and Li Xun, *Zhengde huangdi dazhuan*.

73. *MS*, 16.213.

74. For an argument that the Leopard Quarter was also an alternative site of Zhengde's imperial government, see Geiss, "The Leopard Quarter During the Cheng-te reign."

75. See David Robinson's discussion of Zhengde in his chapter in this volume, pp. 365–421. Ming music sources include a fair number of cryptic references to non-Han musicians and musics. Their impact on Ming musics and music culture has yet to be musicologically investigated.

Zhengde's taste and musiking, however, challenged Confucian music aesthetics and practices.

As Robinson notes elsewhere in this volume, Zhengde took long trips outside the capital. Along the way, he summoned local musicians to perform for him and added those he fancied to his personal troupes. In the winter of 1517, for example, he commanded theatrical performances at Xuanfu 宣府, a critical military garrison northwest of the capital. In 1518, he visited Taiyuan 太原 and ordered many female musicians to entertain himself. There he became intimate with Madame Liu 劉, who followed Zhengde in his subsequent trips, leaving behind her husband, a musician in the Jin 晉 princely establishment. In 1520, Zhengde traveled to the south, staying at the home of Yang Yiqing 楊一清 (1454–1530), a noted Ming scholar-official, whose family music troupe entertained the emperor with lavish performances of music and drama.

By prompting musicians to perform together and by collecting musicians, female and male, for his court, Zhengde promoted the traffic in musicians and musics. From the home of Yang Yiqing, for example, he took a boy singer to the north, who spent several years in the imperial court, during which he acquired new musical experiences and skills.[76] What he did after he left Zhengde's court remains to be investigated, but it is reasonable to presume that he would show repertories and performance practices he had learned to his fellow musicians. This process of musical transmission through individual agents is also attested in Dun Ren's 頓仁 case. A southern singer, Dun joined the emperor's entourage and traveled north to the capital.[77] After learning the art of northern arias (*beiqu* 北曲) in the capital, Dun returned to the south and taught He Liangjun 何良俊 (1506–73), the famed Ming scholar and music patron. He and Dun collaborated to revive interest in northern arias, a genre that by the early sixteenth century was no longer popular in the south.

Being constantly surrounded by music and musicians, Zhengde probably acquired some musical skills himself. He reportedly created a repertory of ensemble music known as Music from Pacified Borders (*Jingbian yue* 靖邊樂), which was performed with mouth organ, flutes, drums, and other melody and percussion instruments and featured loud and crisp sounds and bouncy rhythms. The genre further developed in Nanjing, the southern capital of the Ming, where entertainment musics

---

76. *YHB*, *buyi* 3.891.
77. He Liangjun, "Qulun," pp. 3, 11.

flourished.[78] A derivative of Zhengde's alleged creation evolved into the Ten Brocade Ensemble Music (*Shiyangjin* 十樣錦), which thrived in the Jiangnan area during the Wanli period.[79]

Zhengde's travels drew court, literati, and commoner music subcultures closer by creating moving sites of his imperial presence, where command performances of diverse musics took place. On these occasions musicians learned from one another in ways that could not easily be duplicated elsewhere. Although the geographical ranges of Ming musics overlapped, each had its own performance occasions and venues, a fact that is not only clearly described by Ming documents but also evocatively represented by the painting *Going Upriver at the Qing Ming Festival* (*Qingming shanghetu* 清明上河圖). Although the identity of the painter of the work is contested,[80] it depicts daily life in Suzhou, revealing clearly defined sites and audiences for songs, dances, operas, narrative singing, and instrumental music played with strings, pipes, drums, and gongs.[81] To observe more than one genre of music closely and critically, it is clear, musicians usually had to travel from site to site. By participating in Zhengde's command performances, however, musicians could witness a diversity of musics in one site. Furthermore, they could hear different musics performed by the most skilled musicians of the time—emperors demanded only the best of what was available.[82]

---

78. Xiu Jun and Jian Jin, *Zhongguo yueji shi*, 302–33.

79. *YHB*, 25.650; Li Xu, *Jiean laoren manbi*, 1.12.

80. Wu Zhao, *Zhuixun shiqu di yinyue zongji*, 322–31. Wu Zhao attributed the painting to Shen Zhou 沈周 (1427–1509), with no substantiation. Julia Murray and other American art historians have communicated their skepticism to me. On the assumption that the painting reflects traditional understanding of Ming music culture, it is heuristically discussed here as an artistic and visual representation of the fact that Ming music venues were musically, socially, and physically defined. See also Ina Asim's discussion and digital presentation of musical instruments and sites in her *Colorful Lanterns at Shangyuan*, pp. 42, 45, 50, 53, and CD; the anonymous painting she discusses presents musical scenes of a lantern festival held in mid- to late Ming Nanjing.

81. Feng Wenci, "Xiqu yishu di you yige huangjin shidai," pp. 670–71: and idem, "Pinzhong fansheng di yinyue yishu," pp. 708–9.

82. This historical interpretation of Zhengde's command performances is based on my fieldwork experiences of musical festivals in contemporary China and the United States. During those public, artificially programmed events, musicians are exposed to a diversity of musics that they would not regularly experience. Such exposure always stimulates musicians to create and change. Zhengde's agency generated such "music festivals" and sites of musical learning in the places he visited.

The Jiajing Emperor: Music and Power

Zhengde's atypical musiking was not continued by Jiajing (r. 1522–66), his successor, and the eleventh Ming emperor. Exploiting the Confucian ideology of music and its role in state sacrificial music to advance his personal identity and imperial agenda, Jiajing transformed Ming music culture with an intense and individualized force, one that was totally different from that of Zhengde. Born an imperial prince in a distant province, Jiajing came to the Ming throne when Zhengde, his cousin, died without an heir. Jiajing accepted the throne but rejected the idea that he would act as the adopted son of the deceased Zhengde.

Traveling to the capital to ascend to the throne, in 1521, he refused to enter the city until he was welcomed with imperial ceremonies, rituals that confirmed his status as emperor, not as heir apparent. Then, Jiajing ordered performances of imperial ritual and music to honor his biological parents. Eventually, his father, who was born and died a prince, was posthumously elevated as the Xingxian emperor. As Hung-lam Chu and Scarlett Jang discuss elsewhere in this volume, the political and intellectual struggles of the Great Rites Controversy had far-reaching consequences and posed great moral and political challenges for scholar-officials.[83]

The stakes were high. On August 14, 1524, a group of more than two hundred scholar-officials protested against the emperor's action by demonstrating outside the palace gate; the protest was brutally crushed, and at least sixteen demonstrators were flogged so severely that they died.[84] Punishing his opponents ruthlessly and rewarding his supporters generously, Jiajing emerged as the victor; the effects of his victory echoed broadly throughout the empire.

This was the context behind Jiajing's launching of a comprehensive ritual and musical reform in the 1530s–40s, a musiking that represented not only a complex negotiation among personal, political, and ideological conflicts but also a performance of emperorship. Jiajing and his supporters claimed that the reform was needed to rejuvenate (*zhongxing* 中興) the empire. To launch the reform, Jiajing ordered his court scholar-officials to debate ritual and musical matters; when they identified the need for

---

83. For discussion of the struggle, see Fisher, *The Chosen One*. See also Hung-lam Chu's portrayal (pp. 186–230) of Jiajing as a strong-willed emperor who was also very sensitive to ritual and cultural matters.

84. See Fisher, *The Chosen One*, pp. 90–97. See also Tan Qian, *Guoque*, 53.3305–6.

Fig. 6.5   First offering of wine for the state sacrifice to Heaven. 1530. From Lam, *State Sacrifices and Music in Ming China*, p. 142.

additional music experts,[85] Jiajing summoned music masters like Zhang E 張鶚 (fl. 1530–36) and Li Wencha 李文察 (fl. 1535–40s) to his court. Then he had new state sacrificial music composed, featuring distinctive musical modes and melodic structures (Fig. 6.5).[86] To supplement the changes in state sacrificial music, Jiajing had programs of banquet music revised, arrangements of musical instruments in imperial orchestras and bands adjusted, numerous musical instruments manufactured, and thousands of musician-dancers recruited to his court.

A dazzling musical and political development, Jiajing's music reform left deep marks on Ming music culture in general, particularly on the development of music theory in the literati music subculture. To serve Jiajing's musiking emperorship and to advance their own interpretations, and perhaps careers, scholar-officials energetically theorized about music, generating a wave of music theory writings during and after Jiajing's reign. These treatises include, for example, Zhang Yu's 張敔 *Detailed Explanations of Civilized Music* (*Yayue fawei* 雅樂發微), presented to the court in 1538; Li Wencha's six music treatises of the 1530s and 1540s; and Liu Lian's 劉廉 (fl. 1540–50s) *Original Meaning of the Classic of Music* (*Yuejing yuanyi* 樂經元義) of 1550.[87]

Many direct and indirect references to Jiajing's musiking appear in these publications. Zhang Yu, for example, wrote that he presented his treatise to the court as an aid for Jiajing's ritual and musical guide for common-

85. For more details about Jiajing's music reform and personal involvement, see Lam, *State Sacrifices and Music in Ming Music*, pp. 55–74, 99–120.

86. For technical and structural features of the tunes, see ibid., pp. 129–54.

87. See Li Wencha, *Lishi yueshu*. For a discussion of the pseudo-ritual tunes composed by Li and Liu, see Lam, *State Sacrifices and Music in Ming China*, 153–54.

ers.[88] Recommending Zhang's treatise to the court, Fei Cai 費寀 (1483–1549) declared that its insightful theories would help the court's pursuit of civilized music.[89] Li Wencha wrote and presented his treatises to Jiajing as specific proposals to serve the emperor's ritual and musical needs, a fact that Li's memorials explicitly stated.[90] His writing and presentation of the *Tunes for the Heir Apparent* (*Qinggong yuediao* 青宮樂調) in 1545 was a musik-ing response to court concerns about educating Jiajing's three growing sons, all born in the late 1530s.[91] In the 1596 preface to his *Essentials of Music Theory* (*Lülü jingyi* 律呂精義), Zhu Zaiyu declared that the blossoming of music scholarship in his time began with Jiajing's revision of court music and promotion of scholarship.[92]

Before the full impact of his music reform became clear, however, Jiajing had turned his attention to Daoism. Beginning in the late 1540s, he began to mount elaborate Daoist rituals inside the palace, the musical details and influence of which have yet to be identified and studied. As Jiajing retreated into his Daoist world, his musiking became less noticeable and less documented, even though music was an integral part of the emperor's Daoist rituals.[93] Jiajing had, by that time, directly and indirectly shepherded Ming music culture to an intensified round of development. Stimulated by the emperor's interest in musical matters, blessed by the relative peace of his reign, and supported by the thriving trade in printed books and other cultural and material products, all Ming music subcultures were given a chance to develop along their own courses.

Advances in *qin* and operatic musics in the literati's music subculture were particularly spectacular. In 1539, Zhu Houjue of the Hui princely establishment 徽藩 produced the *Classical and Civilizing Qin Music*, an anthology of *qin* music, history, and theory, and 154 annotated pictograms of performance techniques (Fig. 6.6). The earliest known examples of their kind, the pictograms were a new method of explaining complex *qin* performance techniques through textual and visual representations. The work represented a significant change: the complex performance techniques not only indicate advances in *qin* composition and techniques but also suggest an

---

88. Zhang Yu, "Jin Yayue fawei biao" 進雅樂發微表, in idem, *Yayue fawei*, pp. 196–97.

89. Fei Cai, "Yayue fawei tici" 雅樂發微題辭, in Zhang Yu, *Yayue fawei*, p. 198.

90. Li Wencha, "Jian jinbiao" 前進表, in idem, *Lishi yueshu*, pp. 1–2.

91. See Li Wencha, "*Huang Ming Qinggong yuediao* xu" 皇明青宮樂調序, in idem, *Li-shi yueshu*, p. 271.

92. Zhu Zaiyu, "*Lülü jingyi* xu" 律呂精義序, in idem, *Yuelü quanshu*, p. 148.

93. See Wang Shizhen 王世貞, *Xicheng gongci 12 shou*.

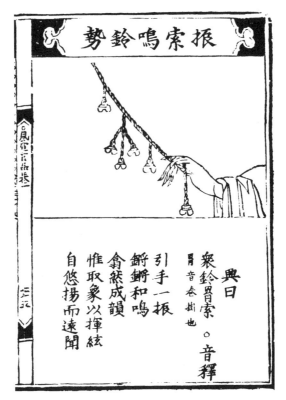

Fig. 6.6 Playing harmonics like pulling a string of bells. From Zhou Houjue, *Fengxuan xuan-pin*, 1.75a.

increased number of literati *qin* players, amateur musicians who needed explicit guides. That a nobleman produced the anthology in a princely establishment is also noteworthy; it reaffirms the leadership roles princely agents and courts played in the growth of Ming music.

The development of opera music during Jiajing's time was equally spectacular. This is attested by Jiang Xiao's 蔣孝 *Register of Southern Arias in Nine Modes* (*Nan jiugong pu* 南九宮譜) of 1525,[94] a song register that attempts to prescribe modes and other musical features of contemporary southern arias. By the latter years of Jiajing's reign, the four major styles of Ming operatic music, Yiyang 弋陽, Haiyan 海鹽, Yuyao 餘姚, and Kunshan 昆山,

---

94. Jiang's register is no longer extant. A facsimile printing of Shen Jing's 沈璟 (1533–1610) revision of Jiang's register is preserved in Ju Tongsheng's *Nanci xinpu*.

dominated Ming theaters.[95] Kunshan-style operatic music, which first emerged as a local genre in that county in Jiangsu province, eventually became the literati's operatic music *par excellence.*

The Wanli Emperor: A Generous Patron

Jiajing's music agency was complex: it began with the emperor's active and direct involvement but ended with his retreat into Daoist musiking, which nevertheless created conditions for other agents to develop Ming music cultures. This indirect but empowering force of imperial music agency underscores Wanli's musiking.[96] Emperor for forty-eight years (1573–1620), Wanli did not force any musical reforms, large or small, but he was a generous patron of operas. To honor and entertain his two imperial dowagers and to project himself as a filial son, Wanli founded a special troupe of 200-plus eunuch-actor-musicians to perform in the Qianqing Palace 乾清宮 and present traditional court operas as well as new ones sung in the fashionable Yiyang and Kun styles. For his own entertainment at the Yuxi Palace 玉熙殿, Wanli maintained another troupe of more than 300 eunuch performers.[97] This imperial patronage and large performance force obviously allowed the operas performed inside the Ming court to be elaborate and helped develop a court and operatic tradition dominated by palace eunuchs, agents who promoted operatic interactions between court and other music subcultures (see "Eunuchs and Music" below).

Wanli's music agency is historically attested by the blossoming of Ming music subcultures during his long reign and by his reception of two different musical gifts to his court. In 1606, Zhu Zaiyu, a Ming nobleman, pre-

---

95. Lu Rong, *Shuyuan zaji*, p. 10. See also Ye Sheng, *Shuidong riji*, p. 214; and Feng Wenci, *Lüxue xinshuo*, pp. 668–69.

96. Wanli's biography parallels and reflects many late Ming developments. These include, for example, Wanli's indulgent lifestyle, which he shared with many late Ming elites; his transformation from an active to an inactive emperor, a process that cannot be separated from the accelerating decline of the late Ming court; and the contradictions in Wanli's personhood and emperorship, which echoed the internal conflicts of late Ming society. For a biographical description that highlights the relationships between Wanli's life events and late Ming history, see Lin Jinshu, *Wanli di*. See also Kenneth Swope's discussion of Wanli's reign in this volume, pp. 61–115; the emperor's active and passive involvements with affairs of the empire echo well with his musiking. If Wanli actively engaged with secular operas, he obviously ignored civilized musics of the court.

97. Liu Ruoru, *Minggong shi*, p. 41.

sented to Wanli a copy of his music encyclopedia, *Collected Works on Music History and Theory*, a monumental collection of theoretical treatises, music histories, and notated scores of court and experimental musics. Learning directly from his father, Zhu Houwan 朱厚烷 (1518–91), and indirectly from music treatises by a number of music scholar-official-theorists, Zhu was able to author a gigantic work that summarized contemporary Ming music knowledge and practices. In addition, he also formally presented what is arguably the world's earliest theory of equal temperament in the *New Theory of Tuning and Temperament* (*Lüxue xinshuo* 律學新説, 1584) volume of the collection.[98]

Read as a whole, Zhu's music encyclopedia is, nevertheless, more retrospective than forward-looking, more theoretical than practical. As such, it underscores the ways in which imperial and princely music agents operated and influenced Ming music culture and subcultures. Wanli's court did not take Zhu Zaiyu's music theories seriously, but it did acknowledge the theorist's music offering to the empire and sent his documents to the imperial library. To honor his scholarly achievement and filial integrity—Zhu gave up the princely title that he should have inherited from his father to a cousin who schemed to snatch the privilege—Zhu was allowed to keep his title as the heir apparent (*shizi* 世子) of a princely establishment. This imperial acceptance of Zhu obviously helped secure a place for his encyclopedia in court and elite discussion of music theory. Zhu's status as a princely heir apparent and his ability to print his encyclopedia in his establishment also promoted its transmission.

The reception of Zhu's encyclopedia contrasts revealingly with that of another musical gift to the court, one that is equally significant in Chinese music history. In 1601, the Italian Jesuit Matteo Ricci (1552–1610) arrived in Beijing and introduced to the Ming court not only Christianity but also European music and musical instruments.[99] Ricci's musical gift did not, however, seem to have impressed Wanli personally, even though he sent eunuchs to learn to play a Western keyboard instrument. The inherent conservatism in Ming court music and traditional Chinese music theory did not allow Wanli and his court officials to appreciate the different nature of

---

98. See Feng Wenci, *Lüxue xinshuo*. For a concise explanation of Zhu's theory and its significance in world music history, see Needham, *Science & Civilization in China*, 4, 1: 220–28. See also *DMB*, s.v. "Chu Tsai-yü."

99. Tao Yabing, *Ming Qing jian di Zhongxi yinyue jiaoliu*, preface pp. 1–11, text pp. 7–26. See also Lindorff, "Missionaries, Keyboards and Musical Exchange in the Ming and Qing Courts," p. 405.

Western and Christian music and the challenge it subsequently brought to China. Without imperial or princely backing and intellectual appeal, Western music and musical instruments evoked only passing curiosity among Ming literati and commoners.

Ming literati and commoners of Wanli's time, however, were very curious about music, and they actively musiked with operas, especially Kun operas. If they were stimulated by operatic practices inside the court, they manipulated the resources available to them to develop their own operatic expressions. In fact, by the late Wanli period, literati patrons and connoisseurs had, with their distinctive aesthetics and sophisticated sensibilities, transformed Kun music into a most sophisticated art, one that the court noticed and appropriated as a court entertainment. Kun music is distinguished by its florid melodies, a stylistic feature first developed by Wei Liangfu 魏良輔 (1522–72), a musician and a medical doctor, but made popular by Liang Chenyu 梁辰魚 (ca. 1510–ca. 1582), an eccentric literatus and playwright, and performances of his *Washing Silk* (*Wanshaji* 浣紗記).[100] Reflecting the elite's tastes and their command of material and human resources, Kun opera performances are noted for their artistic coordination among melodies, literary lyrics, costume, and singer-actors' bodily movements / dance choreography.[101]

Also reflective of elite tastes and the significant overlap between the court and literati music subcultures is the late Ming production of new *qin* repertories, styles, and documents. Eloquent evidence of such an overlap is Yan Cheng's 嚴澂 (1547–1625) *Pine and Breeze Pavilion Qin Music Collection* (*Songfengge qinpu* 松風閣琴譜) of 1614. It promoted the Yushan 虞山 School repertory and its aesthetic of performing *qin* music as clear, subtle, simple, and nostalgic (*qing, wei, dan, yuan* 清微淡遠) tones. Representing a new musical and aesthetic frontier that Yan and his eunuch *qin* collaborators explored, the collection revealingly contrasts with Jiang Keqian's 蔣克謙 *Comprehensive Collection of Qin Documents* (*Qinshu daquan* 琴書大全) of 1590. Essentially an anthology of pre-existing *qin* music writings, Jiang's document affirms the court and intellectual roots of late Ming *qin* music. A descendent of the same family as Jiajing's mother, Jiang Keqian claimed that he published his anthology to realize his ancestors' goals. Devoted to

---

100. Lu Eting, *Kunju yanchu shigao*, pp. 14–37. See also *DMB*, s.v. "Liang ch'en-yü" and "Wei Liang-fu."

101. See Wei Liangfu, *Qulü*, pp. 67–111. See also Chen Duo and Ye Changhai, *Wang Jide qulü*.

qin music, Jiang claimed, they copied precious and historical sources of *qin* music from archives in the court but had not had the opportunity to publish their collected materials.[102]

Musiking Court Officials, Eunuchs, and Commoners

Not all Ming emperors were as active in musiking as Hongwu, Yongle, Zhengde, Jiajing, and Wanli. The musiking of the fifteenth-century emperors Xuande, Chenghua, and Hongzhi, for instance, allowed their subordinates to take active roles in developing the court music subculture and relating it to Ming society at large. Despite the centrality of Ming emperors in their courts, they did not, and could not, take active roles in all cultural and expressive activities. Some emperors deferred to scholar-officials in musiking of court ritual music, submitting to the latter's public and political agendas, while keeping their private and entertainment musiking behind palace walls.

Witness the case of Xuande (r. 1426–35), the fifth Ming emperor. The eldest son of Hongxi, and nurtured by Yongle, his grandfather, Xuande grew up an imperial heir, living a luxurious and cultured life. A poet, a painter, and a patron of the arts, he mostly musiked in banquets, festivals, and trips outside the palace to seek aesthetic and personal enjoyment; he hardly needed to manipulate court ritual and music to assert his imperial identity. To indulge his musiking needs, Xuande's court employed numerous entertainers; after his death, more than 3,800 were released from court service.[103]

Acting as a benevolent emperor, he encouraged his officials and commoners to enjoy life: in 1427, he formalized the ten-day celebration of the Lantern Festival, a practice that began during Yongle's time.[104] In 1428, Xuande granted the princes the privilege of keeping musician-dancers for sacrificial music, an imperial action that contributed to the princely courts' role as regional music centers.[105] The emperor's largess stimulated music activities among both elites and commoners, and this in turn elicited negative criticism from conservative scholar-officials who found such musiking excessive and undesirable.

---

102. See Jiang Keqian, "*Qinshu daquan* xu."
103. *YHB*, 1.14.
104. *YHB*, *buyi* 3.898.
105. *MS*, 172.4583.

In the middle of Xuande's reign, Censor Gu Zuo 顧佐 (d. 1446) requested the emperor to stop officials' drinking and musiking in the official wine parlors.[106] As a result, the entertainment establishments that Hongwu had established soon ceased to be musically and socially relevant, a critical development in Ming music culture. The ban did not stop Ming scholar-officials' musiking; it only prompted them to move their music activities inside courtesans' studios and private homes, sites that favored intimate musiking practices and vernacular genres. As an imperial agent of change, Xuande did not musik strategically. He submitted to the censor's forceful and conservative demand, one that asserted Confucian values and accidentally forced the Ming elite and commoners to musik with one another, in private venues, satisfying their personal desires, and generating individualized music genres, performances, and styles, which blossomed in the late Ming.

Chenghua (r. 1465–87), the eighth Ming emperor, also played second fiddle to scholar-officials' forceful musiking with court institutions and official policies. When Chenghua ascended the throne, the dynasty's century-old music system needed updating. To document state sacrificial music of the time and to use the information as a reference for subsequent ritual-musical actions during the early 1470s, scholar-officials of the Court of State Sacrifices compiled the *General Record of the Court of State Sacrifices* (*Taichang zonglan* 太常總覽).[107] The work did not lead to specific musical reforms, but its compilation attested to the scholar-officials' bureaucratic management of court ritual and music: as soon as they identified a "problem," they memorialized the emperor and demanded correction. In 1475, Zhou Hongmu 周洪模 (1419–91) requested that the empire honor Confucius with the most exalted form of court ritual and music, the one reserved for honoring imperial ancestors, as well as Heaven and other deities of the highest rank.[108] Zhou's request bore fruit the following year: the number of dancers in the ceremonial for Confucius was raised from thirty-six to sixty-four—the use of sixty-four dancers in state sacrifices was an imperial monopoly and thus an indicator of imperial status.

The specificity of Zhou's request and the result that followed attested to the limited range in which emperors and scholar-officials musiked with one

---

106. *YHB, buyi* 3.900–901.

107. *Taichang zonglan.*

108. *Xianzong chunhuangdi shilu,* 155.9b–11b. See also Goodrich and Fang, *Dictionary of Ming Biography,* s.v. "Chou Hung-mu."

another. Because of such a limit, however, every change in detail, no matter how localized and limited, was significant as a negotiated expression of values, ritual protocol, and court politics. Thus, when Zhou successfully negotiated an increase in the number of dancers for the ceremonial for Confucius, he actively performed as a musiking agent, even though he was not able to persuade the emperor to grant everything he demanded.

The ninth Ming emperor, Hongzhi (r. 1488–1505), enjoys a historical reputation for being musically sophisticated, but his music agency only highlighted scholar-officials' control of court musiking. In 1495, Hongzhi's request that court musicians compose songs for Daoist rituals performed inside the court was promptly blocked by senior official Xu Pu 徐溥 (1428–99), who argued that the emperor and his court musicians should not engage in such improper and undesirable music.[109] Since Daoist ritual and music had always been practiced inside the palace,[110] and since Xu's action did not stop Daoist musiking inside the Ming court, it served only to underscore how a Confucian scholar-official could check an emperor's musiking by evoking the force of Confucian aesthetics and court traditions.

In 1502, court entertainers used vulgar words during a theatrical presentation that concluded Hongzhi's performance at the agricultural ritual (gengjili 耕籍禮).[111] Censor Ma Wensheng 馬文昇 (1420–1510) scolded the entertainers and had them removed from the ritual venue. Ma's musiking and censoring action was categorically Confucian and active. In fact, such actions prompted Ming emperors to serve as successful and meritorious rulers. It should be noted that Chinese emperors, especially those who inherited the throne from their fathers, were expected to pay attention to the matters of state and ritual music, ordering revisions when needed. Ritual and music reforms constituted a sanctioned means for restorative (zhong-xing 中興) emperors to revive declining empires. Sometime during his reign, Hongzhi and his court officials attempted to revise court ritual and music, but the results of this endeavor are now unknown.

In 1641, the last Ming emperor, Chongzhen (r. 1628–44), attempted to reform state sacrificial music, an imperial action that neither changed Ming music culture nor revived his failing empire, which ended three years later. Chongzhen's music agency is now more remembered for his musiking

---

109. *Xiaozong shilu*, in *Ming shilu*, 107.1b–3a.
110. See *YHB*, 27.683–88. See also *Daojiao shi ziliao*, 363–68.
111. *MS*, 61.1508.

with Imperial Concubine Tian (Tian Guifei 田貴妃), his favorite consort and a master *qin* performer, who had learned to play the instrument from a concubine of her father, who had once been a courtesan in
Yangzhou.[112]

Chongzhen's musiking with Tian Guifei and the Yangzhou connection
of her *qin* music underscores the fact that Ming emperors did not musik by
themselves. They always musiked with those around them, allowing the latter to bring diverse musics into the court. As Tian Guifei's case attests, palace women, who were drafted as wives and servants into the court, always
connected the Ming court with the Ming musical world at large. However,
palace women were not the only agents trafficking music between the emperors and their subjects.[113] Once absorbed into the court, palace women
could not freely and regularly move in and out of the institution.

Eunuchs and Music

As several authors have shown elsewhere in this volume, palace eunuchs
played an essential role as agents of transmission, facilitating the flow of
tastes, information, and personnel in and out of the court.[114] Their activities created many opportunities for music exchanges. Musiking with emperors, scholar-officials, and commoners, palace eunuchs had plenty of occasions and reasons to exercise their agency.

Palace eunuchs, for example, played the *qin* to musik as artistic, intellectual, and gendered equals to scholar-officials. The Ming palace eunuchs' *qin*
tradition started early in the dynasty. One mid-fifteenth-century emperor
once summoned to court a commoner *qin* master, who not only entertained the emperor but also taught *qin* music to palace eunuchs. One student was Dai Yi 戴義 (fl. 1500–1510s), who subsequently became a *qin* master performer and teacher himself.[115] Among Dai's eunuch students was
Wang Xian 王獻 (1485–1561), who in 1546 compiled the *Parasol Tree Mound
Anthology of Qin Music* (*Wugang qin pu* 梧岡琴譜). A representative collection of the historically significant Xu School (Xumen 徐門) of *qin* music, it

---

112. *MS*, 114.3545. See also Wang Yuchang, "Chongzhen gongci 186 shou," pp. 78–
79.

113. Very little is currently known about female musicians inside the Ming court, a
topic that I will explore in a future publication.

114. See the chapters by Scarlett Jang (pp. 116–85) and David Robinson (pp. 365–421)
for their discussions of eunuch's operations inside and outside the court.

115. Xu Jian, *Qinshi chubian*, p. 124; Wang Xian, *Wugang qin pu*, 1: 441.

attests to the palace eunuchs' command of the instrument and its artistic tradition. Two late Ming palace eunuchs collaborated with Yan Cheng, the *qin* master discussed above. Fourteen out of the twenty-seven *qin* compositions presented in his *Pine and Breeze Pavilion Qin Music Collection* are taken from an earlier anthology, the *Qin Music Collection from the Basin of Stored Spring* (*Cangchunwu qinpu* 藏春塢琴譜), which Yan compiled with the two eunuch *qin* musicians.[116]

If Ming palace eunuchs' involvement with *qin* music aligned them with elite tastes and identities, their engagement in processional, religious, and operatic music allowed them to musik with a wide variety of commoners and thus connect Ming music subcultures. As shown in the massive scroll paintings *The Emperor's Procession to the Imperial Tombs* and *The Emperor's Return to the Capital*, palace eunuchs performed processional music alongside court and military musicians. Such imperial processional music probably impressed Ming commoners and stimulated music exchanges. One sixteenth-century source reported that wealthy commoners had begun to emulate the elite by employing drum and wind processional music to escort their travels.[117] Even rural people hired drum and wind ensembles to help celebrate their personal festivities, generating a sonic breaking down of the social hierarchies of his time, the observer lamented.[118] Such a view is elitist, but it underscores the fact that by the sixteenth century, drum and wind processional music, which was once a monopoly of the court, had become an integral part of Ming music culture, a result of active music trafficking by diverse agents.

Ming palace eunuchs' personal interests contributed to the exchange of musical styles between the court and the world outside. Concerned with their afterlife, eunuchs built many Buddhist temples inside and outside the capital, sites where clergymen and commoners performed many rituals and ritual music.[119] In 1443, Wang Zhen 王振 (d. 1449), one of the most influential eunuchs in Ming China, built a family temple in the capital, the Bao'en zhihuasi 報恩智化寺, which subsequently became the home of a Ming Buddhist music tradition that has survived to the

---

116. Yan Cheng et al., *Cangchunwu qinqu*. See also Zhang Huaying, "Yushan qinpai yanji," pp. 14–15; and Zhu Xi, "Chongping Yan Tianchi."

117. Chen Hongmo, *Zhishi yuwen*, pp. 53–54.

118. Wang Qi, *Yufu zaji*, p. 41.

119. Chen Yunü, *Mingdai ershisi yamen huanguan yu Beijing fojiao*, pp. 95–97. For a historical analysis of Ming eunuchs' involvement in Buddhism and the construction of temples, see Naquin, *Peking*, pp. 161–67, 179–86.

present.[120] The temple and its music are reminders of Ming palace eunuchs' agency in blurring boundaries among court, religious, and commoner musics. As realistically evoked by the historical novel of *The Plum in the Golden Vase* (*Jinpingmei* 金瓶梅),[121] Ming eunuchs had many social interactions with commoners, who sang many religious chants and hymns in not only temples but also private residences.[122]

With their extensive social interactions with Ming commoners, eunuchs observed and learned from the latter's fashionable musics, appropriating what they found entertaining for themselves and for their emperors. Eunuchs performed the most popular form of musical entertainment in late Ming China, namely, opera/theater, inside the court. An informative source on Ming court culture used by both Jang and Robinson, the painting *Emperor Chenghua's Pleasures* (*Xianzong xingle tu* 憲宗行樂圖) portrays a scene with opera/theater (Fig. 6.7).[123] The painting depicts the court musicians as either men or young boys, confirming the tradition of eunuchs as court music/operatic performers, a tradition that supported the blossoming of operatic performances inside Wanli's court. By featuring musical instruments commonly used all over China—*pipa*, gong, small cymbals, wood clappers, hour-glass drum, flat drum, shawn (*touguan* 頭管), bowed zither (*zhazheng* 軋箏), and mouth organ—the picture demonstrates that the operatic tradition of the Ming eunuchs and their emperors had commoner roots. The painting's visual reference to Zhong Kui 鐘馗, a popular figure on Chinese stage, underscores that operas inside and outside the court shared some thematic commonalities.[124]

---

120. For a historical sketch of the music tradition and its notated sources, see Yuan Jingfang, *Zhongguo Hanchuan fojiao yinyue wenhua*, pp. 212, 221. For a biography of Wang Chen, see *DMB*, s.v. "Wang Chen."

121. Tian Qing, "Cong *Jinpingmei* kan Mingdai fojiao yinyue." See also Wei-hua Zhang, "Music in Ming Daily Life."

122. There are many references to performances of religious music in Ming Beijing in Liu Tong and Yu Yizheng, *Dijing jingwu lüe*. Palace poems often allude to performances of Buddhist and Daoist musics in the Ming court. See, e.g., Zhang Yuankai, *Xiyuan gongci 24 shou*, pp. 15–16; and Wang Yuchang, "Chongzhen gongci 186 shou," pp. 88, 98, 100.

123. Wu Zhao, *Zhuixun shiqu di yinyue zongji*, pp. 310–17. Original painting held in National Museum of Chinese History, Beijing.

124. For a sample of dramatic themes in early Ming expressive culture, see Feng Wenci, "Pinzhong fansheng di yinyue yishu," pp. 700–701. See also Zhu Yixuan, *Ming Chenghua shuochang cihua congkan*.

Fig. 6.7   Theatrical performance inside the palace. From Wu Zhao, *Zhuixun xiqu di yinyue zongji*, p. 315.

The painting does not show Chenghua performing, but musical emperors definitely sang and danced. For instance, the early seventeen-century Tianqi emperor (r. 1621–27) performed his favorite operatic scenes with eunuch companions. An avid opera fan, Tianqi particularly enjoyed comical shows and dramatic enactment of the military maneuvers of Yue Fei 岳飛 (1103–42), the martyred Southern Song general.[125] A meticulous amateur performer, Tianqi once wore winter clothes in a summer performance enacting a story set on a snowy night. In developing his operatic knowledge and performance skills, Tianqi probably learned much from his eunuch playmates, fellow performers, and music masters.

Ming palace eunuchs' involvement with operatic musics was not merely an official duty to entertain the emperor; it also reflected the entertainment culture of the time. By the late sixteenth century, operas were performed so commonly that some local officials found them a social threat.[126] In 1592,

125. *Ming gongci*, pp. 60, 289–90.
126. Zhang Han, *Songchuang mengyu*, p. 139.

the government in Fujian banned a local performance as licentious, because it featured thirty musician-actors parading in excessively ornate costumes.[127] Such censorship was futile, however, because opera was an integral part of late Ming commoners' life, which created an insatiable demand for that communal form of musiking. In cities like Hangzhou, thousands participated in opera productions to earn their living,[128] just like hundreds of palace eunuch actors/musicians performed operas to entertain Wanli and the empress dowagers.

Dominating the late Ming entertainment industry, these operatic professionals did not, however, represent all Ming musicians. Many others would musik as professional or amateur performers of a variety of vernacular genres. Professional musicians, like Li Jinlou 李近樓 (?–1588) and Tang Yingzeng 湯應曾 (1590s–1620s), would perform *pipa* and other instrumental music, such as the *Shifangu* 十番鼓, for their patrons and audiences. The singing of folk and popular songs constituted a core of musiking in urbanized locales. Tunes like "Dazaogan" 打棗干 and "Guazhi'er" 掛枝兒 were sung by everyone, regardless of their profession, age, gender, and social status.[129]

This vibrant music subculture of Ming commoners interacted with the court and literati subcultures. Through agents of musical transmission, such as Ming palace eunuchs and palace women, the subcultures influenced one another, generating interconnections and forming a complex of distinctive but closely interrelated units. The subcultures did not blend into a singular phenomenon, however: different Ming people, be they emperors, eunuchs, scholar-officials, clergymen, or commoners, musiked from different and unequal sociocultural positions, negotiating personalized agendas in specific sites and times.

Reflecting commoners' realities, vernacular theater, for instance, portrayed unfaithful husbands, cruel stepmothers, and other social concerns of the time. Similarly, "The Crescent Moon Shining over the Counties" ("Yuezi wanwan zhao jizhou" 月子彎彎照幾州), a folksong widely sung in the Wu area, questioned the widening gaps between have and have-nots living in that culturally and economically prosperous area. Although musically simple, the song nevertheless conveyed a serious musiking agenda.[130]

———

127. Wang Liqi, *Yuan Ming Qing sandai jinhui xiaoshuo xiqu shiliao*, p. 93.

128. Zhang Han, *Songchuang mengyu*, p. 139.

129. *YHB*, 25.647. No authentic scores of the songs are currently known. For their lyrics, see Feng Menglong, *Guazhi'er*.

130. For a notated score of the song as sung in 1951, see Feng Wenci, "Pinzhong fansheng di yinyue yishu," p. 699.

Concluding Remarks: Musiking Roles
and Interacting Subcultures

Viewed comprehensively, Ming music culture appears to be a theater with many actors and subplots. Rather than ranking one group of actors above the others or pitting one line of development against another, it is historiographically more constructive to analyze how the theater worked as a whole and how individual actors performed. Narratives about Chinese music, musicians, and music culture will only become more informative as our understanding of Chinese music agents deepens. In this sense, Ming imperial music agency provides a most revealing lesson.

Ming emperors musiked inside and outside their palaces with scholar-officials, palace women, eunuchs, clergymen, and court musicians. Actively or passively, Ming emperors contributed to the development of Ming music culture and subcultures. As traditional histories declared, emperors shaped not only empires but also music cultures. This declaration is, however, a generalization that needs factual and theoretical clarification and elaboration.

As Sons of Heaven, Chinese emperors constituted the raison d'être for state sacrificial music, state banquet music, and state processional music, genres that tenaciously operated according to historical norms and court institutions. As political administrators who oversaw the bureaucracy and resources of the empire and as cultural-moral leaders, they shaped the conditions under which their subjects were to musik throughout the empire. As patrons and consumers, they provided opportunities and venues for other music agents to musik, exchanging music ideas, repertories, styles, and genres within and beyond the court. As individuals at the apex of the Ming world, they musiked according to their personal needs and situations, generating models of music expressions and activities that Ming people valorized and attempted to emulate. The nature and the impact of the models, needless to say, varied tremendously. Hongwu's musiking, for example, was strikingly different from that of Zhengde.

Chinese emperors' musiking always prompted other music agents to play their parts. Catering to their emperors' music needs and actions, Ming scholar-officials played the roles of music teachers, collaborators, critics, and censors. They taught princes and emperors Confucian theories and practices of employing music as a means of governance and self-cultivation; they supervised court musicians in implementing Confucian aesthetics and prescriptions. Some scholar-officials even criticized emperors' private musiking, attempting to banish what they deemed licentious and vulgar sounds from court, if not the empire. Others put up with, or even encouraged, their emperors to musik indulgently.

In their own homes, scholar-officials, however, musiked as literati, idealizing aesthetic sophistication and musical erudition. Some Ming literati practiced *qin* music as an elitist genre, creating exquisite compositions, and producing erudite anthologies of notated *qin* music, theories, histories, and performance instructions. Other literati engaged with operas and various multimedia performance arts. If they artistically pursued beautiful tunes and literary lyrics and if they self-indulgently maintained family troupes of female performers, they did so according to ideals they cherished and with resources they commanded. In this sense, and as far as entertainment musics were concerned, many Ming princes and scholar-officials, especially those who held great power and wealth, musiked almost like their emperors.

Many music performers, patrons, and audience members in the Ming court music subculture were palace women, musiking according to their institutionalized positions and personal needs. All low-ranking palace women musicians were servants whose duty was to entertain their superiors musically. All high-ranking court ladies, such as Empress Dowager Li, Wanli's mother, commanded personal but elaborate performances of entertainment music inside their private quarters and grand processional music escorts when they traveled. Religious palace women sang Buddhist and Daoist chants. As performers and audience members, palace women engaged with most kinds of court and non-court musics, facilitating music interactions and connections. A case in point is Chongzhen's Imperial Concubine Tian, whose performance of *qin* music pleased the emperor. Her exquisite music, nevertheless, had commoner roots. The only genre in which Ming palace women did not participate was state sacrificial music, which emperors, scholar-officials, and male musician-dancers monopolized.[131]

Like palace women, Ming eunuchs played significant roles in providing entertainment musics inside the Ming palace and in the trafficking of musics among Ming music subcultures. Their music agency was shaped and propelled by many forces. If the eunuchs entered the palace as children, they had ample opportunities to learn all kinds of court entertainment musics and

---

131. The only exception was the Ming palace ladies' participation in Jiajing's sericultural ceremonial, which was officiated over by the empress. See Lam, "Ritual and Musical Politics in the Court of Ming Shizong."

become skilled performers needed for various palace functions. Those who entered the palace as adults brought with them memories and practices from beyond the court. Those who rose to the top of the eunuch hierarchy easily moved between the court and the non-court world. With the power and privileges they had acquired, they could show, on one hand, court music practices to society at large and introduce, on the other hand, the latest fashions in vernacular musics to the palace. Many powerful eunuchs were master musicians, sophisticated connoisseurs, and generous patrons, and some of whom left distinctive stamps on Ming music subcultures.

Eunuch musicians were particularly well situated to promote vernacular musics and stylistic changes inside the palace. As servants who had constant contact with their masters, the eunuchs had a vested interest in knowing the emperors' desires. Armed with insiders' knowledge, they made effective performers/entertainers. If they did not possess the necessary music skills, they could identify and draft those commoner musicians who did. Ming eunuchs were motivated to help Ming emperors musik. By delivering what the emperors desired, the eunuchs could advance their own careers and personal interests.[132]

Thus it is no accident that the eunuchs' performances closely followed popular and vernacular trends. The operas Wanli enjoyed, for example, featured contemporary Yiyang and Kun arias. Since eunuchs had access to palace resources, their entertainment performances for the emperors showcased imperial grandeur and theatrical fancy: witness the water-puppet shows of the Monkey King (*Xiyouji* 西游記), which palace eunuchs staged for Tianqi.[133] Judged by Confucian standards, these shows were elaborate if not vulgar. They flourished because they occurred inside private quarters of the palace, where court censors seldom trod. They could hardly criticize what they could not witness.

Eunuch musicians, however, did not replace the many court musicians whom the court drafted to perform state and ritual musics. In fact, court musicians constituted the largest group of professional musicians who created and performed music for all kinds of public functions in the Ming court. Despite such roles, most court musicians were mere servants whose individual impact on the music they performed was extremely limited. As the case of Liu Gao who served the Ming founder shows, however, occa-

132. For more historical accounts of Ming eunuchs, their institutions, and politics, see Wen Gongyi, *Mingdai de huanguan he gongting*; and Wei Jianlin, *Mingdai huanguan zhengzhi*.
133. Liu Ruoru, *Minggong shi*, p. 40.

sionally lowly court musicians did rise to powerful positions from which they could assert their individual agency to generate changes in Ming music.

Among all the agents who contributed to the development of Ming music culture and subcultures, the roles of clergymen are least clear. The indispensability of their ritual and music expertise is, however, irrefutable. During private worship and engagement with religious forces, Ming court and non-court people often sang Buddhist chants, Daoist hymns, or other religious tunes. However, as individuals and laymen, they could not furnish the music for formal religious ceremonies, especially those involving a multitude of believers and held in sacred and public temples and shrines. Such rituals required the guidance or service of ordained clergymen.

Viewed from the perspectives of agency, roles, musical and contextual constraints, and music culture and subcultures, Ming emperors were influential and distinctive music agents. Their operations ranged from those that promoted the status quo by following established ideology and norms to those that forced changes with individualized musiking. As Ming emperors prompted their subjects to musik, a powerful and large troop of music agents emerged, propelling extensive chains of actions and reactions that resulted in the trafficking of musics from one subculture to another, stimulating interactions and changes. The traditional Chinese view of imperial music agency has highlighted but failed to specify this complex and dynamic phenomenon. Historians need to examine Ming music agents' diverse musiking as a creative and purposeful discourse, one that renders music an integral dimension of Ming history and culture.

Works Cited

Asim, Ina. *Colorful Lanterns at Shangyuan*. N.p., 2006.

CHC, see Twitchett and Mote, *Cambridge History of China*

Chen Duo 陳多 and Ye Changhai 葉長海, eds. *Wang Jide qulü* 王驥德曲律. Changsha: Hunan renmin chubanshe, 1983.

Chen Hongmo 陳洪謨. *Zhishi yuwen* 治世餘聞. 1521. Reprinted—Beijing: Zhonghua, 1985.

Chen Shenxi 陳生璽 and Jia Naiqian 賈乃謙, eds. *Dijian tushuo* 帝鑒圖說. Zhengzhou: Zhongzhou guji chubanshe, 1996.

Chen Yunü 陳玉女. *Mingdai ershisi yamen huanguan yu Beijing fojiao* 明代二十四衙門宦官與北京佛教. Taibei: Ruwen chubanshe, 2001.

Daojiao shi ziliao 道教史資料. Shanghai: Guji chubanshe, 1991.

Daozang 道藏. 1436–49 ed. Reprinted—Taibei: Taiwan Yiwen shuju, 1962.

DMB, see Goodrich and Fang, *Dictionary of Ming Biography*

DMHD, see Shen Shixing et al., *Da Ming huidian*

Feng Menglong 馮夢龍. *Guazhi'er* 掛枝兒. Ca. 1640s. Reprinted in *Ming Qing min'ge shidiaoji* 明清民歌時調集. Shanghai: Guji chubanshe, 1987, 1: 1–244.

Feng Wenci 馮文慈, ed. *Lüxue xinshuo* 律學新說. Beijing: Xinhua shudian, 1986.

———. "Xiqu yishu di you yige huangjin shidai" 戲曲藝術的又一個黃金時代 and "Pinzhong fansheng de yinyue yishu" 品種繁盛的音樂藝術. In *Zhonghua wenmingshi*, 8: 667–721.

Fisher, Carney T. *The Chosen One: Succession and Adoption in the Court of Ming Shizong*. Sydney: Allen & Allen, 1990.

Fong, Wen C. "Imperial Portraiture of the Ming Dynasty." In idem and James C. Y. Watt, *Possessing the Past: Treasures from the National Museum*. New York: Metropolitan Museum of Art; Taibei: National Palace Museum, 1996, pp. 327–34.

Geiss, James. "The Leopard Quarter During the Cheng-te Reign." *Ming Studies* 24 (1987): 1–38.

Goodrich, L. Carrington, and Chaoying Fang, eds. *Dictionary of Ming Biography*. New York: Columbia University Press, 1976.

Goormaghtigh, Georges, and Bell Yung. "Preface of *Shenqi mipu*: Translation with Commentary." *ACMR Reports, Journal of the Association for Chinese Music Research* 10, no. 1 (1997): 1–13.

Han Bing 韓冰 et al., eds. *Zhongguo yinyue wenwu daxi: Beijing juan* 中國音樂文物大系北京卷. Zhengzhou: Daxiang chubanshe, 1996.

He Liangjun 何良俊. "Qulun" 曲論. 1579. Reprinted in *Zhongguo gudian xiqu lunzhu jicheng* 中國古典戲曲論著集成. Beijing: Zhongguo xiju chubanshe, 1959, 4: 1–15.

Huang Xiangpeng 黃翔鵬. "Lun Zhongguo gudai yinyue di chuancheng guanxi— yinyue shilun zhi yi" 論中國古代音樂的傳承關係—音樂史論之一. In idem, *Chuantong shi yitiao heliu* 傳統是一條河流. Beijing: Renmin yinyue chubanshe, 1990, pp. 105–43.

———. "Yayue bushi Zhongguo yinyue chuantong di zhuliu" 雅樂不是中國音樂傳統的主流. In idem, *Chuantong shi yitiao heliu* (see preceding entry), 35–38.

Huang Zuo 黃佐. *Yuedian* 樂典. Preface dated 1544. Reprinted in Xuxiu Siku quanshu 續修四庫全書. Shanghai: Guji chubanshe, 1995, vol. 113, part 6.

Hucker, Charles O. "Ming Government." In *CHC*, 8: 9–105.

Jiang Jing 蔣菁, Guan Jianhua 管建華, and Qian Rong 錢茸, eds. *Zhongguo yinyue wenhua daguan* 中國音樂文化大觀. Beijing: Beijing daxue chubanshe, 2001.

Jiang Keqian 蔣克謙. "*Qinshu daquan* xu" 琴書大全序. In *Qinshu daquan* 琴書大全. 1590. Reprinted in *Qinqu jicheng* 琴曲集成. Beijing: Zhonghua shuju, 1980, 5: 3–5.

Jones, Stephen. "Reading Between the Lines: Reflections on the Massive Anthology of Folk Music of the Chinese Peoples." *Ethnomusicology* 47, no. 3 (2003): 287–337.

Ju Tongsheng 鞠通生. *Nanci xinpu* 南詞新譜. Beijing: Xinhua shudian, 1985.

Kishibe Shigeo 岸辺成雄. *Tōdai ongaku no rekishiteki kenkyū* 唐代音楽の歴史的研究. Tokyo: University of Tokyo Press, 1960, 1961. 2 vols.

Lam, Joseph S. C. "Chinese Music Scholarship: From Yang Yinliu's *A Draft History of Ancient Chinese Music* to Confucian Classics." *ACMR Reports, Journal of the Association for Chinese Music Research* 8, no. 2 (1995): 1–45.

———. "Huizong's *Dashengyue*, a Musical Performance of Emperorship." In *Emperor Huizong and Late Northern Song China: The Politics of Culture and the Culture of Politics*, ed. Patricia Buckley Ebrey and Maggie Bickford. Cambridge: Harvard University Asia Center, 2006, pp. 395–452.

———. "Huizong's Ritual and Musical Insignia." *Journal of Ritual Studies* 19, no. 1 (2005): 1–18.

———. "Musical Confucianism: The Case of *Jikong yuewu*." In *On Sacred Grounds: Culture, Society, Politics, and the Formation of the Cult of Confucius*, ed. Thomas Wilson. Cambridge: Harvard University Asia Center, 2002, pp. 134–72.

———. "Music and Male Bonding in Ming China." *Nan Nü* 9 (2007): 70–110.

———. "The Presence and Absence of Female Musicians and Music in China." In *Women and Confucian Cultures in Premodern China, Korea, and Japan*, ed. Dorothy Ko, JaHyun Kim Haboush, and Joan R. Piggott. Berkeley: University of California Press, 2003, pp. 97–120.

———. "Ritual and Musical Politics in the Court of Ming Shizong." In *Harmony and Counterpoint: Ritual Music in Chinese Context*, ed. Bell Yung, Evelyn S. Rawski, and Rubie S. Watson. Stanford: Stanford University Press, 1996, pp. 35–53.

———. *State Sacrifices and Music in Ming China: Orthodoxy, Creativity, and Expressiveness.* Albany: State University of New York Press, 1998.

———. "'There Is No Music in Chinese Music History': Five Tunes of Court Music from the Yuan Dynasty (A.D. 1271–1368)." *Journal of the Royal Musical Association* 119 (1994): 165–88.

Li Guoxiang 李國祥 and Yang Chang 楊昶, eds. *Ming shilu leizuan: gongting shiliao juan* 明實錄類纂: 宮廷史料卷. Wuhan: Wuhan chubanshe, 1992.

Li Jian 李健. *Lidai yueguan zhidu shixi* 歷代樂官制度試析. Hong Kong: Shijie tushu gongsi, 1975.

Li Wencha 李文察. *Lishi yueshu* 李氏樂書. Preface dated 1545. Reprinted in Xuxiu Siku quanshu 續修四庫全書. Shanghai: Guji chubanshe, 1995, vol. 114, part 1.

Li Xu 李詡. *Jiean laoren manbi* 戒庵老人漫筆. 1597. Reprinted—Beijing: Zhonghua shuju, 1982.

Li Xun 李洵. *Zhengde huangdi dazhuan* 正德皇帝大傳. Shenyang: Liaoning jiaoyu chubanshe, 1993.

Lin Jinshu 林金樹. *Wanli di* 萬歷帝. Changchun: Jilin wenshi chubanshe, 1996.

Lindroff, Joyce. "Missionaries, Keyboards and Musical Exchange in the Ming and Qing Courts." *Early Music* 32, no. 3 (2004): 403–14.

Liu Tong 劉侗 and Yu Yizheng 于奕正. *Dijing jingwu lüe* 帝京景物略. 1635. Reprinted—Shanghai: Gudian wenxue chubanshe, 1957.

Liu Lian 劉廉. *Yuejing yuanyi* 樂經元義. Preface dated 1550. Reprinted in Xuxiu Siku quanshu 續修四庫全書. Shanghai: Guji chubanshe, 1995, vol. 113, part 7.

Liu Ruoru 劉若愚. *Minggong shi* 明宮史. Ca. 1640. Reprinted in idem, *Minggong shi,* and Gao Shiqi 高士奇, *Jin ao tuishi biji* 金鰲退食筆記. Beijing: Xinhua shuju, 1980.

Lu Eting 陸萼庭. *Kunju yanchu shigao* 崑劇演出史稿. Shanghai: Xinhua shuju, 1980.

Lu Rong 陸容. *Shuyuan zaji* 菽園雜記. 1494. Reprinted—Beijing: Zhonghua shuju, 1985.

Mao Qiling 毛奇齡. *Wuzong waiji* 武宗外紀. Early Qing. Reprinted in *Gongwei yishi* 宮闈遺事, ed. Xu Fuchu 徐復初. Shanghai: Qizhi shuju, 1936, pp. 125–45.

Ming gongci 明宮詞. Beijing: Xinhua shudian, 1987.

Ming shilu 明實錄. Taibei: Academia Sinica, 1962–67.

Mulligan, Jean, trans. *The Lute: Kao Ming's P'i-p'a chi*. New York: Columbia University Press, 1980.

Na Chih-liang and William Kohler. *The Emperor's Procession: Two Scrolls of the Ming Dynasty*. Taibei: National Palace Museum, 1970.

Naquin, Susan. *Peking: Temples and City Life, 1400–1900*. Berkeley: University of California Press, 2000.

Needham, Joseph. *Science & Civilisation in China*, vol. 4, *Physics and Physical Technology*, pt. 1, *Physics*. Cambridge: Cambridge University Press, 1962.

Pian, Rulan Chao. *Song Music Sources and Their Interpretations*. Cambridge: Harvard University Press, 1967. Reprinted—Hong Kong: Chinese University Press, 2003.

Pu Hengqiang 浦亨強. *Daojiao yu Zhongguo chuantong yinyue* 道教與中國傳統音樂. Taibei: Wenjin, 1993.

———. "Mingdai Wudangshan daojiao yinyue kaolüe" 明代武當山道教音樂考略. In *1991 nian Xianggang dierjie daojiao keyi yinyue yantaohui lunwenji* 1991 年香港第二屆道教科儀音樂研討會論文集. Beijing: Xinhua shuju, 1991, pp. 42–57.

Qian Bocheng 錢伯城, ed. *Baihua shisan jing, fu yuanwen* 白話十三經附原文. Beijing: Guoji wenhua chubanshe, 1996.

Shen Defu 沈德符. *Wanli yehuo bian* 萬曆野獲編. 1619. Reprinted—Beijing: Zhonghua shuju, 1957; 2d ed., 1997.

Shen Shixing 申時行 et al., eds. *Da Ming huidian* 大明會典. 1587. Reprinted—Beijing: Zhonghua, 1989.

Shi Xinmin 史新民. "Lun dangdai Wudang daoyue zhi tezheng" 論當代武當道樂之特徵. In *1991 nian Xianggang dierjie daojiao keyi yinyue yantaohui lunwenji* 年香港第二屆道教科儀音樂研討會論文集. Beijing: Xinhua shuju, 1991, pp. 140–44.

Small, Christopher. *Musicking: The Meanings of Performing and Listening*. Hanover, NH: Wesleyan University Press, 1998.

Taichang xukao 太常續考. Ca. 1640. Reprinted in Yingyin Wenyuange Siku quanshu 影印文淵閣司庫全書, no. 599. Taibei: Shangwu yinshuguan, 1983.

Taichang zonglan 太常總覽. 1470s. National Library of Peiping, Rare Books Collection Microfilm, no. 964.

Tan Qian 談遷. *Guoque* 國榷. 1958. Reprinted—Beijing: Zhonghua shuju, 1988.

Tao Yabing 陶亞兵. *Ming Qing jian di Zhongxi yinyue jiaoliu* 明清間的中西音樂交流. Beijing: Dongfang chubanshe, 2001.

Tian Qing 田青. "Cong *Jinpingmei* kan Mingdai fojiao yinyue" 從金瓶梅看明代佛教音樂. *Zhongguo yinyuexue* 1992, no. 2: 276–83.

Tsai, Shih-shan Henry. *The Eunuchs in the Ming Dynasty.* Albany: SUNY, 1996.

Twitchett, Denis, and Frederick W. Mote, eds. *The Cambridge History of China*, vol. 8, *The Ming Dynasty, 1368–1644, Part II.* Cambridge: Cambridge University Press, 1998.

Wang Di 王迪. *Qinqu* Guanglingsan *chutan* 琴曲《廣陵散》初探. Beijing: Zhongguo yishu yanjiuyuan, Yinyue yanjiusuo, 1984.

Wang Liqi 王利器. *Yuan Ming Qing sandai jinhui xiaoshuo xiqu shiliao* 元明清三代禁毀小說戲曲史料. Shanghai: Guji chubanshe, 1981.

Wang Qi 王錡. *Yufu zaji* 寓圃雜記. Preface dated 1500. Reprinted—Beijing: Zhonghua, 1997.

Wang Shizhen 王世貞. *Xicheng gongci 12 shou*, 西城宮詞 12 首. Reprinted in *Ming gongci* 明宮詞. Beijing: Xinhua shudian, 1987, pp. 13–14.

Wang Xian 王獻, *Wugang qin pu* 梧岡琴譜. Preface dated 1546. Reprinted in *Qinqu jicheng* 琴曲集成. Beijing: Zhonghua shuju, 1980, 1: 373–441.

Wang Yuchang 王譽昌. "Chongzhen gongci 186 shou" 崇禎宮詞 186 首. Reprinted in *Ming gongci* 明宮詞. Beijing: Xinhua shudian, 1987, pp. 72–112.

Wei Jianlin 衛建林. *Mingdai huanguan zhengzhi* 明代宦官政治. Taiyuan: Xinhua shuju, 1991.

Wei Liangfu 魏良輔. *Qulü* 曲律. 16th c. Reprinted in *Xiqu yanchang lunzhu jishi* 戲曲演唱論著輯釋, ed. Zhou Yibai 周貽白. Beijing: Zhongguo xiju chubanshe, 1962, pp. 67–111.

Wen Gongyi 溫功義. *Mingdai de huanguan he gongting* 明代的宦官和宮廷. Chongqing: Xinhua shuju, 2000.

Wu Zhao 吳釗. *Zhuixun shiqu di yinyue zongji: tushuo Zhongguo yinyueshi* 追尋逝去的音樂縱跡: 圖說中國音樂史. Beijing: Dongfang, 1999.

Xianzong chunhuangdi shilu 憲宗純皇帝實錄. 1491. Reprinted in *Ming shilu.*

Xiu Jun 修君 and Jian Jin 鑑今. *Zhongguo yueji shi* 中國樂妓史. Beijing: Zhongguo wenlian, 2003.

Xu Jian 許建. *Qinshi chubian* 琴史初編. Beijing: Renmin yinyue, 1982.

Xu Lianda 徐連達 and Zhu Ziyan 朱子彥. *Zhongguo huangdi zhidu* 中國皇帝制度. N.p.: Guangdong jiaoyu chubanshe, 1996.

Xu Wei 徐渭. *Nanci xulu* 南詞續錄. Late 16th c. Reprinted in *Zhongguo gudian xiqu lunzhu jicheng* 中國古典戲曲論著集成. Beijing: Zhongguo xiju chubanshe, 1959, 3: 239–41.

Xu Yikui 徐一夔 et al. *Da Ming jili* 大明集禮. 1370; 2d ed., 1530. Siku quanshu ed.

Xu Zifang 徐子方. *Ming zajushi* 明雜劇史. Beijing: Zhonghua shuju, 2003.

Yan Cheng 嚴澂. *Songfengge qinpu* 松風閣琴譜. 1614. Reprinted in *Qinshi, wai shizhong* 琴史, 外十種. Shanghai: Guji chubanshe, 1991, pp. 71–138.

Yan Cheng 嚴澂, Hao Ning 郝寧, and Wang Dingan 王定安. *Cangchunwu qinqu* 藏春塢琴曲. Reprinted in *Qinqu jicheng* 琴曲集成. Beijing: Zhonghua shuju, 1980, 6: 285–452.

Yang Yinliu 楊蔭瀏. *Zhongguo gudai yinyue shigao* 中國古代音樂史稿. Beijing: Renmin yinyue chubanshe, 1981.

Ye Sheng 葉盛. *Shuidong riji* 水東日記. Between 1465 and 1472. Reprinted—Beijing: Zhonghua, 1997.

YHB, see Shen Defu, *Wanli yehuo bian*

Yuan Jingfang 袁靜芳. *Zhongguo Hanchuan fojiao yinyue wenhua* 中國漢傳佛教音樂文化. Beijing: Zhongyang minzu daxue chubanshe, 2003.

Zhang Han 張瀚. *Songchuang mengyu* 松窗夢語. 1593. Reprinted in *Zhishi yuwen* 治世餘聞, *Jishi jiwen* 繼世紀聞, *Songchuang mengyu*. Beijing: Zhonghua shuju, 1985.

Zhang Huaying 章華英. "Yushan qinpai yanji" 虞山琴派研究. M.A. thesis, Zhongguo yishu yanjiuyuan, 2002.

Zhang Tingyu 張廷玉 et al., eds. *Mingshi* 明史. 1736. Reprinted—Beijing: Zhonghua shuju, 1974.

Zhang, Wei-hua. "Music in Ming Daily Life, as Portrayed in the Narrative *Jin Ping Mei*." *Asian Music* 23, no. 2 (1992): 105–34.

Zhang Yu 張敔. *Yayue fawei* 雅樂發微. Preface dated 1538. Reprinted in Siku quanshu, vol. 113, part 4.

Zhang Yuankai 張元凱. *Xiyuan gongci 24 shou* 西苑宮詞 24 首. 1550s. Reprinted in *Ming gongci* 明宮詞. Beijing: Xinhua shudian, 1987, pp. 15–16.

Zhongguo yinyue shupuzhi 中國音樂書譜誌. Beijing: Renmin yinyue chubanshe, 1984.

Zhonghua wenming shi, vol. 8, *Mingdai* 中華文明史：明代. Shijiazhuang: Hebei jiaoyu chubanshe, 1994.

Zhu Houjue 朱厚爝. *Fengxuan xuanpin* 風宣玄品. 1539. Reprinted in *Qinqu jicheng* 琴曲集成. Beijing: Zhonghua shuju, 1980, 2: 1–380.

Zhu Quan 朱權. *Gongci qishi shou* 宮詞七十首. Preface dated 1408. Reprinted in *Ming gongci* 明宮詞. Beijing: Xinhua shudian, 1987, pp. 1–5.

———. *Shenqi mipu* 神奇密譜. 1425. Reprinted in 琴曲集成. Beijing: Zhonghua shuju, 1980, 1: 95–169.

———. *Taihe zhengyinpu* 太和正音譜. Preface dated 1398. Reprinted in *Zhongguo gudian xiqu lunzhu jicheng* 中國古典戲曲論著集成. Beijing: Zhongguo xiju chubanshe, 1959, pp. 11–231.

Zhu Xi 朱晞. "Chongping Yan tianchi" 重評嚴天池. *Zhongyang yinyue xueyuan xuebao* 中央音樂學院學報 3 (2003): 46–52.

Zhu Yixuan 朱一玄, ed. *Ming Chenghua shuochang cihua congkan* 明成化説唱詞話叢刊. Zhengzhou: Zhongzhou guji chubanshe, 1997.

Zhu Zaiyu 朱載堉. *Yuelü quanshu* 樂律全書. 1584–1606. Reprinted in *Beijing tushuguan guji zhenben congkan* 北京圖書館古籍珍本叢刊. Beijing: Shumu wenxian chubanshe, n.d., vol. 4.

SEVEN

Tibetan Buddhism and the Creation of the Ming Imperial Image

Dora C. Y. Ching

In a little over a century, between the reigns of the first and ninth emperors, the Hongwu emperor (r. 1368–98, Fig. 7.1) and the Hongzhi emperor (r. 1488–1505, Fig. 7.2), the Ming imperial image changed dramatically. At the beginning of the Ming dynasty, the Hongwu emperor was portrayed in a naturalistic pose that emphasized three-dimensionality.[1] Seated on a gold-leaf-covered chair in a nearly frontal position, he faces slightly to the viewer's left. His right hand rests on his knee, and his left hand grasps the curled end of the arm rest. His countenance is stern, and his piercing eyes are framed by bushy eyebrows. He wears "ordinary attire" (*changfu* 常服) suitable for normal ordinary occasions at court: a black silk gauze cap and a simple yellow robe decorated only with a few dragon medallions. The setting, composed of a chair and a carpet against an unpainted background, is minimal.

In the late fifteenth century, the Hongzhi emperor, by contrast, was depicted in a striking pose of rigid frontality. The emperor is centered within

———

I thank David Robinson for inviting me to participate in the first workshop sponsored by the James P. Geiss Foundation and express my gratitude to him for his patience and insightful comments. I have benefited greatly from his suggestions as well as those of Anne Reinhardt, Frances Yuan, and Christine Tan.

1. Also extant in the National Palace Museum are the so-called ugly portraits of the Hongwu emperor, which are not generally considered officially sanctioned portraits; see So Yü–ming, "Authenticity of the Portraiture of the Ming T'ai–tsu"; see also Dora C. Y. Ching, "Visual Images of Zhu Yuanzhang."

a monumental composition, seated on a richly decorated throne, and framed by a screen of elaborately painted dragons. He stares directly outward, nearly expressionless, and clasps his hands within his sleeves. His body dissolves beneath robes decorated with cosmological symbols of rulership. Six dragon medallions are visible on the skirt of his robe, one containing a frontal dragon is emblazoned on his chest, and two more grace his shoulders along with discs symbolizing the sun and the moon. Pairs of bronze sacrificial cups, waterweed, grains of millet, flames, sacrificial axes, and the *fu* 黻 symbol, denoting the right to punish, adorn the skirt.[2] Four pheasants embellish the sleeves. The symmetry and clarity of the symbols and the framework surrounding the Hongzhi emperor create a portrait that downplays his individuality and broadcasts his role as ruler of the Ming empire. Nearly every succeeding emperor through the end of the dynasty is portrayed in this arresting manner. Although they are differentiated from one another through their distinctive faces, the primary features of these images—frontality, symmetry, and symbolic imagery—eclipse their individuality and transform the portraits into icons of rulership.

This shift in the visual structure of painted imperial portraits represents a dramatic departure from the more traditional formula for imperial portraiture prevalent during the early Ming. The change culminated with the portrait of the Hongzhi emperor and continued to have lasting influence on all later imperial portraits. The differences between the early and the mid- to late Ming portraits are easily discernable, and scholars of Chinese figure painting generally agree that formal portraiture evolved from a profile to a three-quarter and finally to a frontal orientation. Interpretations of this transformation have ranged from straightforward observations of the phenomenon to hypotheses that attribute the change to the art of physiognomy (*xiangshu* 相術) to arguments that suggest a mid- to late Ming need to portray individuals in a more godlike manner.[3]

———

2. Zhou Xibao, *Zhongguo gudai fushi shi*, pp. 378–448. See also Shen Shixing et al., *Da Ming huidian* (hereafter cited as *DMHD*), 60.365–83. See also Cammann, *China's Dragon Robes*, pp. 85–94.

3. For a sampling of scholars who have charted the development of portraiture and noticed this change, see Seckel, "The Rise of Portraiture in Chinese Art." See also Wai-kam Ho, "Developments of Chinese Portrait Painting." Shan Guoqiang has also written a number of short articles in which he, too, remarks on this general evolution; see, e.g., "Xiaoxiang hua leixing chuyi." For the relationship between the orientation of the portrait subject and physiognomy, see Siggstedt, "Forms of Fate." Li Guoan directly addresses the change from a three-quarter to a frontal orientation in "Mingmo xiaoxiang hua," pp. 119–57. It should be noted also that there are instances in Chinese art

What during the reigns of the early Ming emperors might have triggered the change toward a more imposing, iconic depiction of the emperor? It is tempting to attribute the frontality and symmetry of the mid- to late Ming imperial portraits to differences between the earthy, active personalities of the early Ming emperors and the more effete, almost absent emperors who succeeded them. Similarly, the changes in the visual structure of the imperial portraits could be explained as mirroring the increasing absolutism of imperial power. The reasons behind the shift, however, are far more complex and closely tied to a variety of processes within the court. This chapter argues that imperial artistic agency, a shift in the rituals used to establish dynastic authority, and personal faith all contributed to the transformation. The complex relationships Ming emperors developed and fostered at court with artists and artisans, officials, and especially Tibetan Buddhist hierarchs also helped shape the new imperial icon. Although Tibetan influence in Chinese imperial portraiture has been noted in brief by Wen Fong,[4] this chapter presents an in-depth study of the relationship of Tibetan Buddhist hierarchs in Ming China to artistic production and establishes the links between Tibetan Buddhism and the creation of a Ming imperial icon. The evolution of the imperial image into an icon of rulership is further revelatory of the many interactions at the Ming court concerning issues of artistic tastes, ritual protocol, and legitimacy.

The changing image of the emperor demonstrates that imperial imagery and rule were far from stagnant through the late fifteenth century. Following the codification of the new imperial image during the Hongzhi reign, subsequent Ming emperors could then utilize the new imperial portrait formula and its symbolism to pursue their own personal interests regardless of religious beliefs. The import of the new image is most telling in the case of the Jiajing emperor (r. 1522–66). He was neither a patron of Tibetan Buddhism nor an adherent of court practices, but, as discussed below, he used the imperial image to further his own agendas in direct conflict to those of the court bureaucracy. In the early to mid-Ming, imperial portraits

———

where images are portrayed frontally, such as in religious paintings of Buddhas, as well as secular figure paintings in tombs or in narrative, didactic handscrolls such as the *Classic of Filial Piety*, attributed to Li Gonglin 李公麟 (ca. 1041–1106). Never before had formal imperial portraiture, however, utilized such an option.

4. For a cursory description of the development of imperial portraiture with the suggestion that artistic exchange with Tibet contributed to the reformulation of the imperial portrait, see Fong, "Imperial Portraiture in the Song, Yuan, and Ming Periods." He later briefly revisited this same issue in Fong and Watt, *Possessing the Past*, pp. 327–33.

visually reflected certain emperors' religious convictions and functioned as physical signs of imperial agency. After the Hongzhi reign, imperial portraits not only symbolized emperorship but also took on more politicized roles that highlighted long-standing issues at the Ming court such as tensions over the personal identity of the emperor versus his role as ruler of the empire. At face value, Ming imperial portraits are representations of emperors and the office of emperorship; they can also be viewed, however, as the material embodiment of contacts among various constituencies at the Ming court and as physical objects used to fulfill political objectives of emperors.

Portraits as Possessions of the Court

As objects produced and used at imperial courts, portraits of emperors and empresses were valued as proof of political authority and remained important possessions for later rulers. Since the Song period (960–1279), imperial portraits have played an often hidden but significant role in the legitimation of a new dynasty. Possession of the portraits and art collections of past dynasties counted as an outward sign of having inherited the mandate of Heaven. Starting with the Song, each successive dynasty made a practice of confiscating the art collections of the previous dynasty. For instance, the Jin (1115–1234) appropriated the collections of the Northern Song in 1127 and moved them to Beijing.[5] The Southern Song (1127–1279), intent on reclaiming the Song political heritage, ransomed back many of the art objects taken by the Jin. The rulers of the Yuan dynasty (1279–1368), in turn, appropriated the collection of the Southern Song dynasty. The Mongol rulers prized the imperial portraits for their artistic qualities but perhaps even more for their power as records of dynastic legitimacy.[6] Utilizing what had become a standard method for establishing legitimacy, the Hongwu emperor took over the Yuan imperial art collection and with it the collection of imperial portraits. The portraits were hard-won political capital and were therefore guarded as possessions of the court.

When the Qing dynasty (1644–1911) overthrew the Ming, the collection of imperial portraits passed into the possession of the new rulers. Ruling emperors attached great importance to possessing and maintaining the imperial portrait collection. They made cataloguing the collection a high pri-

---

5. Cui Wenyin, *Jingkang bai shi jian zheng*, pp. 74–78.
6. Anning Jing, "The Portraits of Khubilai Khan and Chabi."

ority. In 1749, the Qianlong emperor (r. 1736–95) ordered the portraits of past emperors, empresses, and officials to be consolidated and stored in the Hall of Southern Fragrance (Nanxundian 南薰殿) in the western part of the Forbidden City.[7] The Storage Office (Guangchu si 廣儲司) of the Imperial Household Department (Neiwufu 内務府) was put in charge of the collection. Other portraits of sages and meritorious officials previously housed in the Imperial Tea Storehouse (Chaku chu 茶庫儲) were also moved to the Nanxundian at this time. The Qianlong emperor further ordered that the portraits of past emperors and empresses be remounted.[8] To commemorate this event, he wrote the "Record of Portraits Stored in the Nanxundian" ("Nanxundian feng cang tuxiang ji" 南薰殿奉藏圖像記) as well as a poem. Two inventories were made: the "Catalogue of Portraits Venerably Stored in the Nanxundian" ("Nanxundian zuncang tuxiang mu" 南薰殿尊藏圖像目) and the "Catalogue of Portraits from the Imperial Tea Storehouse" ("Chaku chu cang tuxiang mu" 茶庫儲藏圖像目). Both inventories are cursory, recording only titles, media, and measurements of the paintings. Prior to this, the Qianlong emperor had also commissioned an ambitious catalogue called the *Treasured Boxes of the Stony Moat [Catalogue of Painting and Calligraphy in the Qianlong Imperial Collection]* (*Shiqu baoji* 石渠寶笈), which was completed in 1745.

The Jiaqing emperor (r. 1796–1820), successor to the Qianlong emperor, expressed a similar interest in the imperial portrait collection. In 1815, he commissioned Hu Jing 胡敬, an official in his court, to compile a catalogue of works in the imperial collection acquired since the Qianlong emperor's 1749 catalogue and its 1793 sequel (*Shiqu baoji xu bian* 石渠寶笈續編). Hu Jing compiled the third in the series, *Shiqu baoji san bian* 石渠寶笈三編, which contains a section called "Nanxundian tuxiang kao" 南薰殿圖像考 (Study of portraits from the Nanxundian). Although part of the *Shiqu baoji san bian*, the "Nanxundian tuxiang kao" is often treated as a separate work of two *juan*, preface dated 1815. In this work, Hu Jing combined previous inventories, added more detailed measurements and information on materials, and included descriptions and references to relevant historical texts. The first *juan* discusses the hanging scrolls, and the second lists the albums and handscrolls. Hu recorded one hundred hanging scrolls,

----

7. Chen Kangqi, *Langqian jiwen*, 12.545–56. See also Hu Jing, "Nanxundian tuxiang kao," pp. 1–3.

8. (*Qinding*) *Da Qing huidian*, 90.819–20. The *Qing huidian* also includes an inventory of the portraits.

seventeen albums, and three handscrolls.[9] Of these, seventy-nine hanging
scrolls, fifteen albums, and three handscrolls were portraits of emperors
and empresses. This inventory matches almost exactly that in another imperially sponsored work, the *Qing huidian* 清會典, with the exceptions of a
hanging scroll portrait of Yao Guangxiao 姚廣孝 (Monk Daoyan 道衍)
recorded by Hu and an album entitled *Lidai wuchen xiang* 歷代武臣像,
which seems to correspond to the album entitled *Lidai gongchen xiang* 歷代
功臣像 in the *Qing huidian*.[10]

This pattern of appropriating the imperial art collections continued into
the twentieth century. The Chinese Nationalist government (Guomindang)
similarly claimed ownership of the Qing imperial collection. Although the
Nationalists never ruled from the Forbidden City, they valued its treasures
and treated the artwork as their cultural inheritance. As they were losing
the civil war to the Communists, they transferred as much of the collection
as they could to Taiwan in the 1940s. Eventually these works became the
foundation for the National Palace Museum in Taipei, Taiwan.[11] The majority of the imperial portraits recorded in the "Nanxundian tuxiang kao"
survive today primarily in this collection. Although nearly all the Song,
Yuan, and Ming emperors and empresses are represented, the collection
provides only a partial view of imperial portraiture in China. Of the seventy-
nine hanging scrolls, fifteen albums, and three handscrolls listed by Hu
Jing, twelve hanging scrolls, three albums, and one handscroll are missing.
Some of these are in mainland Chinese collections; others are lost. The
Qing dynasty catalogues may not have included all extant works, for there
may have been other portraits that escaped cataloguing. Furthermore, the
National Palace Museum portrait collection contains only painted portraits
even though numerous records throughout the Song and Yuan indicate
that emperors and empresses were portrayed in sculptures[12] and woven
tapestries[13] as well. Notably absent are the Qing imperial portraits. As ritual
objects still in use when the Qing dynasty fell, they had not yet entered the
imperial collection as "art objects." Today, most of these remain in

———

9. Hu Jing, "Nanxundian tuxiang kao."

10. (*Qinding*) *Da Qing huidian*, 90.819–20.

11. Chang Lin-sheng, "The National Palace Museum," pp. 24–25.

12. See Ebrey, "Portrait Sculptures in Imperial Ancestral Rites in Song China"; and
idem, "The Ritual Context of Sung Imperial Portraiture."

13. See Anning Jing, "The Portraits of Khubilai Khan and Chabi," p. 74. See also
Yuandai huasu ji, p. 13.

mainland Chinese collections.[14] Despite such lacunae, the National Palace Museum collection provides a solid core of visual images—in fact, the majority of extant images available for the study of Ming imperial portraiture.[15] The transformation visible in this lineup of portraits of Ming emperors poses the question of why such changes occurred at the Ming court.

———

14. During the Qing period, the Qing imperial portraits were kept in the Hall of Imperial Longevity (Shouhuangdian 壽皇殿) and functioned as ritual objects; see Yu Minzhong, *Rixia jiuwen kao*, 1: 259–61.

15. The corpus of Ming works includes both hanging scroll and album-leaf portraits of each of the Ming emperors except Jianwen, Jingtai, and Chongzhen; hanging scroll portraits of Empress Ma (1332–82) and Prince Xian of Xing (the natural father of Jiajing); album-leaf portraits of all the empresses; and several handscrolls belonging to the categories of processions—*xingle tu* 行樂圖 or the "pleasures" of the emperor—which depict various emperors at leisure activities. For a discussion of the Nanxundian collection, see Jiang Fucong, "Guoli gugong bowuyuan"; and Li Lincan, "Gugong bowuyuan de tuxianghua." For a complete listing of the portraits in the National Palace Museum, see *Gugong shuhua lu*, vol. 3, 7.1–96. A small number of *xingle*-type scrolls of Ming emperors are also extant in mainland Chinese collections. These include a hanging scroll titled *Xuanzong's Pleasures* 宣宗行樂圖 painted by Shang Xi 商喜 (ink and colors on paper, 211.0 × 353.0 cm); another hanging scroll, *Xuanzong's Hunt* 宣宗打獵圖 (ink and colors on silk, 29.5 × 34.6); and a handscroll *Xianzong's Pleasures* 憲宗行樂圖 (catalogued as *Xuanzong's Pleasures* 宣宗行樂圖; ink and colors on silk, 36.4 × 688.5), all in the Palace Museum, Beijing. The Chinese Historical Museum in Beijing has two works featuring emperors: a handscroll *Xianzong's Pleasures in the Lantern Festival* 憲宗元宵行樂圖 (ink and colors on silk, 37.0 × 624.0 cm) and a small hanging scroll *Xianzong with Birds* 憲宗調禽圖 (ink and colors on silk, 67.0 × 52.8 cm). Certain emperors, such as Hongwu and Xuande, are also represented by more than one large-scale portrait. Extant in the National Palace Museum in Taipei are a total of twelve portraits of Hongwu: the hanging-scroll and album-leaf portraits mentioned in this note as well as eleven other "grotesque" or "ugly" portraits. Various scholars have written about the dating and authenticity of Hongwu's portraits. See, e.g., So Yü-ming (Suo Yuming), "Ming Taizu huaxiang zhenweibian"; and idem, "Ming Taizu huaxiangkao." Although the authenticity of the Hongwu portrait in Fig. 7.1 and its designation as the officially sanctioned one has not always been accepted, strong internal visual evidence, conventions in imperial portraiture, and corroborative material in the textual record contribute to this interpretation. Discrepancies between the various inventories and catalogues written when the collection in the Nanxundian was formed reveal that the "grotesque" portraits were not recorded in the imperial collection until Hu Jing's catalogue of 1815 ("Nanxundian tuxiang kao"). In an inventory undertaken in 1744 by the Imperial Household Department, only two portraits of Hongwu were listed and neither of them was described as "grotesque" or "ugly." Instead, such portraits must have become popular much after Hongwu's lifetime in the late Ming and early Qing. Cheng-hua Wang also agrees with this interpretation; see her "Material Culture and Emperorship," pp. 157–59. See also Dora C. Y. Ching, "Visual Images of Zhu Yuanzhang."

Portraits as Expressions of Imperial Taste

The early Ming emperors exercised their personal tastes on artistic projects at court through sponsorship of artists and artisans and interactions with them. Certain emperors played a significant role in sponsoring artistic activity, whereas others had only a more limited involvement. Cognizant of the importance of portraiture, the Hongwu emperor played an active role in the creation of his portrait image. Having inherited a gallery of portraits of past emperors and empresses from previous imperial collections, he had numerous examples to serve as models. He also had the legacy of Yuan artistic traditions. The Yuan dynasty left a deep imprint on the early Ming emperors through various institutions and inherited cultural objects, and the overthrow of the dynasty did not result in the wholesale abandonment of the traditions of the Mongol rulers. Central Asian and Mongol designs were prevalent on the artistic horizon during the first reign of the dynasty, and apprentices and craftsmen, many of them trained under the Yuan and conscripted into the new dynasty's service, embraced such designs and techniques.[16]

The development of imperial portraiture can be traced through comparisons of the Hongwu emperor's portrait and Song and Yuan models. Hongwu's portrait reveals a blend of the tastes of the early Ming emperors and the artistic abilities of early Ming professional painters, who created a new imperial idiom from existing Song and Yuan portrait styles. Stylistically his portrait (see Fig. 7.1) bears some similarity to Song dynasty portraits such as that of Song Taizu (r. 960–76; Fig. 7.3). Both emperors are depicted seated in a chair in a more or less three-quarter pose wearing "ordinary attire," clothing less formal than ceremonial attire (*lifu* 禮服 or *mianfu* 冕服). At the same time, certain features in the Hongwu emperor's portrait, however, show more affinity with Yuan imperial portraiture. The nearly frontal orientation of the Hongwu emperor is reminiscent of the stance in the half-portrait of Khubilai Khan (1215–94; Fig. 7.4). In this bust-length portrait, Khubilai is depicted facing slightly toward the viewer's right, just shy of a frontal position. Like Khubilai, the Hongwu emperor also faces almost completely frontally. This new stance possibly derives from the portraits of the Yuan emperors and represents a fundamental

---

16. For a discussion of artisans and craftsmen in the Yuan period, see Allsen, *Commodity and Exchange in the Mongol Empire*, esp. pp. 27–45. See also Matsuda Kōichi, "Mongoru teikoku ni okeru kōshō no kakuho to kanri no shosō."

change in the traditional portrait formula. The Hongwu emperor's heirs, however, while clearly still modeling their portraits on his, switched back to the three-quarter pose of the Song model. Only a number of decades later, after a fuller integration of different visual sensibilities at court, as seen in the portrait of the Hongzhi emperor (see Fig. 7.2) did true frontality occur.

On the level of painting technique, the method of depicting facial features in the Hongwu emperor's portrait resembles that in Yuan imperial portraits. His face has substantial areas of thick color shading painted in a planar manner, akin more to the treatment of facial features in Khubilai Khan's portrait (see Fig. 7.4) than to that in Song Taizu's. Song Taizu's face, on the other hand, is built up mainly through line and only a modicum of ink wash (see Fig. 7.3). The Yuan artist Wang Yi 王繹 had described such a painting method in his "Secrets of Portrait Painting" ("Xiexiang mijue" 寫像秘訣); he emphasized that each facial element is connected and grows naturally into the next.[17] The Hongwu emperor's portrait incorporated this painterly technique, as did the portraits of his successors. In addition to the portrayal of faces, other stylistic features relate to the Yuan mural painting tradition. For instance, the eye-catching gold leaf on the chair and the dramatic color contrasts are illusionistic devices often used in temple painting to make images readable from a distance.[18]

Originating with the official portrait of the Hongwu emperor, elaborate carpets became a permanent component in the portrait formula. The carpet in this portrait is a brilliant display of design, color, and texture. Deep blue, rich red, green, white, gold, yellow, and black are painted into a complex geometric pattern suggesting an intricate woven textile. Pointillism or stippling was used to create the illusion of a textured surface. The design is unusual for an indigenous Chinese carpet and points to a non–Han Chinese origin. The geometric patterning of the square panels filled with a floral, star-like design woven into the center strip derives from Central Asian sources. The "foreign" elements in this carpet should not be surprising, as Thomas Allsen has demonstrated through his study of the exchange of textiles and the movement of artisans throughout the Mongol empire in

---

17. See Franke, "Two Yüan Treatises on the Technique of Portrait Painting"; and Wang Yi, "Xiexiang mijue," 11.163.

18. See, e.g., the painting technique of the figures and thrones in the Daoist wall paintings of the Yonglegong 永樂宮. Gold was often used to highlight important figures to make them more visible from a distance; see Jin Weinuo, *Yonglegong bihua quanji.*

various regions between Persia and China.[19] The innovation of the carpet in the Hongwu emperor's portrait dramatically changed the look of imperial portraits, but the type of carpet as part of a range of textiles was already firmly embedded in the visual culture of the period.[20] The carpet distinguishes Hongwu's portrait from portraits of past emperors, helps to place the portrait at the beginning of the Ming period, and establishes a new convention in portraiture of the Ming dynasty. It also provided another "surface" for the display of designs that take on symbolic meanings in the ensuing reigns.

The Hongwu emperor's involvement in the making of his portraits consisted primarily of commissioning and evaluating portraits throughout his life.[21] Artists were called to court to paint imperial portraits, and some were rewarded for such services. Chen Yu 陳遇, for example, who had various official appointments that culminated in a post as a minister, painted a portrait of the Hongwu emperor that gained high praise.[22] His younger brother, Chen Yuan 陳遠, was awarded a job as a "painter-in-waiting" (daizhao 待詔) in the Hall of Literary Profundity (Wenyuange 文淵閣) because his portrait of the emperor was accepted and highly appreciated.[23] Shen Xiyuan 沈希遠 gained employment as a Secretariat drafter (Zhongshu sheren 中書舍人) for his painting of the Hongwu emperor.[24] Such textual evidence suggests that Hongwu controlled the "look" of his portrait by exercising the power of approval or rejection. A century later, Lu Rong 陸容 (1436–94),[25] a government official in the Bureau of Operations in the Ministry of War, recorded an anecdote about Hongwu's involvement in the making of his portraits:

Ming Taizu [the Hongwu emperor] once gathered craftsmen painters to paint his portraits, but all the portraits were deemed unsuitable. Some who had "brush idea" and painted truthful likenesses mistakenly thought that their works would be re-

19. Allsen, *Commodity and Exchange in the Mongol Empire*, pp. 27–45, 71.

20. Ibid. Allsen stresses the close tie between imperial patronage and textile production. Such a relationship and the skills of the artisans would have persisted into the early Ming.

21. For a discussion of Hongwu's attitudes toward artists, see Jang, "Issues of Public Service," pp. 96–101.

22. Xu Qin, "Ming hua lu," p. 1124.

23. Ibid.

24. Ibid.

25. Original name Xu Rong, *js.* 1466, from Kunshan, Jiangsu. See *Mingren zhuanji ziliao suoyin*, p. 567.

warded. However, when they presented their portraits to the emperor, the reaction was the same. One painter understood the emperor's intention, and to his portrait added a "majestic aura" that went beyond physical likeness. When the emperor saw it, he was extremely pleased and ordered that many copies be made and bestowed on all the princes.[26]

Although the Hongwu emperor may not have controlled the actual process of making his portrait, his clearly expressed likes and dislikes contributed to the shaping of the imperial image.

The Hongwu emperor's portrait set the "look" of early Ming imperial portraits, and the portraits of his successors, the Yongle emperor (r. 1403–24; Fig. 7.5), the Hongxi emperor (r. 1425), and the Xuande emperor (r. 1426–35; Fig. 7.6), adhere to this basic paradigm. They relate stylistically to the Ming founder's portrait, even though they reverted to a three-quarter pose. As in the Hongwu emperor's portrait, each of these emperors wears "ordinary" attire. The handling of their facial features, particularly in the case of the Yongle and Xuande emperors, mirrors the techniques in the Hongwu emperor's portrait. Multiple portraits of Yongle were also painted, as evidenced by the existence of another portrait in the Potala Palace in Lhasa that corresponds to the one in the National Palace Museum, Taipei.[27] Because of the brevity of the Hongxi emperor's reign, it is likely that his portrait was painted during the Xuande emperor's reign. Xuande similarly had more than one portrait, since several are extant in the National Palace Museum collection. All these portraits were painted during the lifetime or shortly after the death of each emperor.

Both Yongle and Xuande became involved with artists and artisans, but to different degrees. The Yongle emperor, for instance, judged portraits of his likeness presented to him, much as his father, the Hongwu emperor, had. He reportedly reacted favorably to a portrait painted by Chen Hui

---

26. Lu Rong, *Shuyuan zaji*, 14.170. From the historical record, we know that many portraits of Hongwu were painted, but it remains a vexing question as to how these portraits as well as others were used. Anecdotes about "false" portraits of Hongwu produced to mislead people about his physical traits so that he could roam about the country without being recognized also exist. See, e.g., Tan Qian, "Yixiang." For uses of Ming imperial portraits, see the next section, "Portraits as Objects of Court Rituals."

27. See Ou Chaogui, "Budalagong cang Ming Chengzu Zhu Di huaxiang." There is also a third portrait of the Yongle emperor (Chengzu) in which he is depicted at the feet of his guru Helima in an eighteenth-century *thangka*. Despite the lapse in time, the image of Yongle matches his fifteenth-century portrait. See Berger, "Preserving the Nation," pp. 107–8. See also idem, "Miracles in Nanjing," pp. 150–51.

陳撝.[28] Modern scholars have shown that the Yongle emperor also took an interest in viewing the imperial painting collection and in commissioning bird-and-flower, Buddhist, and other such decorative and religious works. Both professional and literati artists worked at court and were associated primarily with several halls, the Wuyingdian 武英殿, the Renzhidian 仁智殿, and the Wenhuadian 文華殿; others were employed as drafters in the Secretariat. High-ranking artists, often with a scholarly background, gained prominence through support from officials at court, especially the powerful grand secretaries Yang Shiqi 楊士奇 (1365–1440), Yang Rong 楊榮 (1371–1440), and Huang Huai 黃淮 (1367–1449).[29] Specific references to the Yongle emperor's dealings with artists or the mechanisms of court workshop production, however, are scattered and scant.

By contrast, the Xuande emperor, an accomplished painter and calligrapher himself, fostered close relationships with artists. Although he probably was involved with the production of the portrait for his father, the Hongxi emperor, who reigned for less than a month, as well as his own, the historical record is silent on his interactions with portrait artists. Instead, references to his artistic activities as a painter and his sponsorship of artists at court abound. For instance, the Xuande emperor occasionally honored artists by bestowing his works on them. He also awarded special ranks to artists he particularly favored, such as Xie Huan 謝環 (ca. 1360s–after 1452), who first became a court painter under the Yongle emperor, then became one of the most influential painters during the Xuande emperor's reign, and finally painted under the Zhengtong/ Tianshun emperor (r. 1436–49, 1457–64).[30] Such personal interactions through the bestowal of gifts, titles, and positions at court characterize the Xuande emperor's relationship with artists, in which he actively directed the artistic tastes and the fortunes of individual artists. By extension, Xuande most likely also expressed his personal preferences concerning his own portraits. Through their varying involvement with artists

---

28. Xu Qin, *Ming hua lu*, p. 1124.

29. See Hou-mei Sung Ishida, "Early Ming Painters in Nanking," pp. 74–80. See also Jang, "Issues of Public Service," pp. 101–38; and Mu Yiqin, "Mingdai de gongting huihua."

30. See Hou-mei Sung, "From the Min-Che Tradition to the Che School," pp. 1–4. See also Cheng-hua Wang, "Material Culture and Emperorship," pp. 325–41. In fact, shortly after Xuande's death, during the reign of Zhengtong, Xie Huan painted the *Literary Gathering in the Apricot Garden* 杏園雅集圖 in 1437; this painting presented a cavalcade of all the important officials in the garden of the Grand Secretary Yang Rong.

at court, the Hongwu, Yongle, and Xuande emperors conveyed their tastes and contributed to the development of imperial portraiture in the early Ming.

Portraits as Objects of Court Rituals

For the Ming emperors, imperial portraits served as ritual objects for ancestor worship and as strategic tokens in political jockeying. The proper use of portraits was an ongoing topic of discussion and debate between emperors and court officials. Officials generally relied on historical precedents to advocate specific uses for them, but certain emperors introduced changes that fundamentally altered the role of imperial portraits at court.

Early during his reign, the Hongwu emperor established the ritual space and ceremonies for the worship of Ming ancestors using imperial portraits. Because he considered the Seasonal Sacrifices at the Ancestral Temple (Taimiao 太廟) inadequate for paying due respect to his ancestors, he requested an additional venue where he could make daily sacrifices. In response, Minister of Rites Tao Kai 陶凱 (*juren* 1347) reviewed Song dynasty precedents and suggested the construction of a hall for ancestor worship.[31] In "Imperial Order to Build the Hall of Ancestor Worship," dated 1371, Tao Kai described the Hongwu emperor's desire to make twice daily offerings in addition to the regular seasonal offerings. He cited specific Song precedents and offered the solution of building a special hall in the Inner Court east of the Hall of Imperial Tranquility (Qianqinggong 乾清宮). Using the Song rituals as a model, Tao Kai stated that

in the Song dynasty, the Grand Temple (Taimiao) received five Seasonal Offerings each year, but in the palaces [i.e., the Inner Court], it had the Pavilion of Ancestor Worship and Heavenly Emblems (Fengxian tianzhangge 奉先天章閣) and the Hall of Filial Longing for the Imperial Forebears (Qinxian xiaosidian 欽先孝思殿) to house the imperial portraiture. The Song emperor burned incense there every day. On seasonal festivals, the first and fifteenth days of a month, the birthdays of emperors and empresses, offerings were made.

The recommendation for Hongwu was therefore to

build the Hall of Ancestor Worship (Fengxiandian) . . . to house the imperial portraiture. In the hall, incense should be burned every day, and fresh foods in season

---

31. For a full discussion of the use of imperial portraits in the Song dynasty, see Ebrey, "Portrait Sculptures in Imperial Ancestral Rites in Song China"; and idem, "The Ritual Context of Sung Imperial Portraiture."

should be presented on the first and fifteenth of every month. The offerings should be made during seasonal festivals and on the birthday (of every emperor and empress). The offerings should be of daily dishes and performed according to the rites used for family members.[32]

For the Hongwu emperor, imperial portraits were private, familial ritual objects revered and worshipped outside the purview of court officials, and the minister of rites was in complete agreement. In the Fengxiandian, imperial portraits were usually shrouded with silk embroidered with gold thread. On special days, the portraits were uncovered, and ritual implements and offerings were placed on tables.[33] Imperial portraits also received the respects and bows of the heir apparent and his new bride as the final ritual in the wedding ceremony.[34] In this venue, the portraits were objects of rituals distinctly familial and private.

Unlike his father, the Yongle emperor used imperial portraits in new ways; he included them in ceremonies well beyond the realm of family rituals during his reign. Most unusual was his decision to perform the ritual of Presenting a Posthumous Honorific Title (*zunshiyi* 尊諡儀) to his father, the Hongwu emperor, and Empress Ma, directly in front of their portraits. This ritual was normally performed in front of spirit tablets carved with the names of the deceased. The Hongwu emperor had conferred posthumous honorific titles on his father and mother in the first year of his reign using tablets and seals made of jade.[35] By contrast, the Yongle emperor performed the elaborate ceremony in the Grand Temple where he presented the posthumous title plaques and seals to the portraits of the Hongwu emperor and Empress Ma. This ceremony took place in the sixth month of the first year of Yongle's reign and involved a host of officials both as participants and as observers.[36] The portraits had emerged from the private space of the Fengxiandian and entered the public sphere of officials and politics.

This break in tradition, remarkable though it was, did not result in a new trend because succeeding emperors made different choices about using imperial portraits. The Yongle emperor's successor, the Hongxi

---

32. *Ming Taizu shilu*, 59.3a–b. Translation by Cheng-hua Wang; see Wang, "Material Culture and Emperorship," pp. 82–83, for the complete translation of this passage.

33. *Ming Xuanzong shilu*, 14.7a–b.

34. *Ming Taizu shilu*, 224.7b–8a; *DMHD*, 68.25–26, 609.18–20.

35. *Mingshi* (hereafter cited as *MS*), 51.1325

36. Ibid., pp. 1325–28.

emperor, reverted back to using spirit tablets for this ceremony; Yongle's spirit tablet and not his portrait received his posthumous honorific title. The Xuande emperor, Yongle's grandson, on the other hand, presented the posthumous honorific title to his father's portrait. Instead of holding this ceremony at the Grand Temple, however, Xuande performed it at the Renzhidian.[37] In turn, Xuande's son, the Zhengtong emperor, similarly followed his father's ritual protocol and performed the ceremony of Presenting a Posthumous Honorific Title in front of Xuande's portrait.[38] Imperial portraits were thus used in non-familial ceremonies witnessed by officials, even if only sporadically.

For the Seasonal Offerings at the Grand Temple, which occurred five times a year (in the first month of each season and on New Year's Eve), imperial portraits as opposed to spirit tablets were once again the objects of worship. In the Xuande period, for example, the portraits were moved from the Fengxiandian to the Grand Temple and hung in generational order for each seasonal offering. The portrait of the Hongwu emperor's great-great grandfather occupied the central position facing south. Flanking him on either side were ancestors of the second and fourth generations and Yongle on the right, and ancestors of the third generation, Hongwu, and Hongxi on the left. Such ceremonies were witnessed and performed by musicians, officials, and censors, all of whom had the opportunity to see the portraits.[39] As the imperial portraits took on these more visible roles in court ritual during the Yongle, Xuande, and Zhengtong reigns, they became more elaborate and began to evolve into icons of rulership.

Portraits as Manifestations of Religious Interaction

Tibetan Buddhism figured notably at the Ming court, and a majority of Ming emperors from Hongwu to Zhengde (r. 1506–21) both held personal religious convictions and recognized the potential political advantages of supporting such beliefs. Both Satō Hisashi and Otosaka Tomoko have documented the extensive interaction among Tibetan hierarchs and Ming emperors from the late fourteenth through the early sixteenth century. Satō outlined the transition from the Yuan and Ming dynasties and traced the lineages of the major sects of Tibetan Buddhism through the Ming

---

37. *Ming Xuanzong shilu*, 2.12a–13b.
38. *Ming Yingzong shilu*, 1.12a–13b.
39. *DMHD*, 86.14–24.

period.[40] He also described and analyzed the relationships that favored Tibetan hierarchs enjoyed at the Ming court.[41] Otosaka similarly investigated the numerous instances of interaction between Tibetan hierarchs and Ming emperors in the first half of the dynasty. Tibetans of various sects frequented the Ming capital and gained much influence with a series of Ming emperors; they performed special initiation rites, and numerous temples were constructed or supported by imperial decree.[42] Imperial patronage brought Tibetan Buddhists considerable privileges as well as tangible gifts at the Ming court.

The Ming emperors' deep and sustained interest in Tibetan Buddhism contributed to the transformation of the imperial portrait during the first half of the dynasty. Regardless of the degree of their involvement in the production of art, the Ming emperors' long-term relationship with Tibetan clerics created an environment conducive for artistic exchange. The imperial portraits, as well as other artistic objects produced at court as gifts or for the court's own use, reveal cross-influences and the sharing of new visual material primarily Tibetan Buddhist in nature. Few art historians have remarked on the Tibetan connections,[43] and Wang Cheng-hua has discounted Tibetan artistic influence, dismissing it as "exotic." She considers the sudden change in the imperial portrait format not so much a natural, linear stylistic evolution attributable to Tibetan influence but a result of conscious choices made by the early Ming emperors.[44] This chapter has analyzed the role played by emperors in creating their portraits and establishing new rituals involving portraits and thus supports Wang's argument that emperors made deliberate choices. In addition, however, the following discussion attempts to deepen this understanding by examining the instances in which interactions between emperors and Tibetan hierarchs contributed to visual changes in imperial portraiture and to a new conceptual understanding of rulership. The frequent contacts among early Ming

---

40. Satō Hisashi, "Genmatsu Minsho no Chibetto jōsei." For an in-depth study of one particular sect, the lineage of the Hbri gun pa in Tibet, see also idem, "Mindai Chibetto no Rigonpa-ha no keitō ni tsuite."

41. Satō Hisashi, "Mintei ni okeru Ramakyō sūhai ni tsuite." On the eight Tibetan priest-kings, see idem, "Mindai Chibetto no hachi daikyōō ni tsuite."

42. Otosaka Tomoko, "Kaette kita shokumokujin"; see also idem, "Tabi suru Peruden tashi."

43. See, e.g., Wen Fong's preliminary remarks in his "Imperial Portraiture in the Song, Yuan, and Ming Periods"; and Fong and Watt, *Possessing the Past,* pp. 327–33.

44. See Cheng-hua Wang, "Material Culture and Emperorship," pp. 205–11.

emperors and Tibetan hierarchs and the production of imperially sponsored Tibetan-style objects suggest serious and sustained exchanges that resulted in both artistic and even perhaps theological/political cross-borrowings. The evolution was by no means a natural, linear progression; rather, it was a complex mix of artistic elements that occurred gradually during the fifteenth century.

THE YONGLE EMPEROR AND TIBETAN HIERARCHS

The Hongwu emperor fostered some contact with Tibetan Buddhist clerics,[45] but it was his son Yongle who intensified efforts to forge deep and long-lasting relationships. Although Yongle's rulership was grounded in Confucian principles, his religious convictions enabled him to capitalize on political benefits from missions to and from Tibet and the performance of Tibetan Buddhist ceremonies. His interest in Tibetan Buddhism provided an early impetus for changes in the visual structure of the imperial image.

Having usurped the throne from his nephew, the Jianwen emperor (r. 1399–1402), Yongle engaged in many activities to legitimize his claim to the throne.[46] One key method entailed gaining the support of Tibetan clerics in order to become a *cakravartin*, a consecrated Buddhist ruler, who wielded both political and religious authority.[47] Although there are no overt references to his political agenda in Chinese sources, his sense of history and his political aspirations are quite explicit in Tibetan sources. He recognized the strategic political value in the priest-patron relationship that

---

45. See Chen Gaohua, "Zhu Yuanzhang de fojiao zhengce."

46. To gain legitimacy, Yongle pursued a policy of supporting Confucian orthodoxy. He ascribed to the philosophy of Zhu Xi 朱熹 (1130–1200), "the learning of the heart-mind," and adopted the Song Confucian scholar's method of classical exegesis as the model for the civil service examinations. He also sponsored several works on Confucian orthodoxy and published his own work, the *Sheng xue xin fa* 聖學心法 (The heart-mind method in the sage's learning), in 1409 with the assistance of Hanlin scholars. In 1414, he commissioned compilations on the Five Classics and the Four Books called *Wujing Sishu daquan* 五經四書大全 (Great compendia on the Five Classics and the Four Books). The commission was fulfilled in 1415, and an additional compendium, *Xingli daquan* 性理大全 (Great compendium on human nature), was presented in 1417. Another project he commissioned was the *Yongle dadian* 永樂大典 (Great literary repository of the Yongle reign), a compilation begun in 1403 and completed in 1407 of an enormous number of literary sources. See Hok-lam Chan, "The Chien-wen, Yung-lo, Hung-hsi, and Hsüan-te reigns," esp. pp. 200–201.

47. For the concept of the *cakravartin*, see Forte, *Political Propaganda and Ideology in China*.

the Yuan emperor Khubilai had established with Phakpa ('Phags pa), the chief hierarch of the Sakya (Sa skya) order, and he aspired to create a similar relationship.[48] For Yongle, ties to Tibetan clerics were advantageous not only because they affirmed his sincere religious beliefs but also because they could be used to buttress his legitimacy.

Yongle's activities vis-à-vis Tibetan Buddhist hierarchs can be reconstructed from a substantial body of records of imperial missions sent to Tibet. These missions both confirm his deep interest in Tibetan Buddhism and illustrate his strategy of legitimizing his rule through all possible methods. In one of his first contacts, he invited to court an eminent Tibetan hierarch who was known to perform miraculous feats—the Fifth Karmapa (Karma pa), Dezhin Shegpa (1384–1415), known in Chinese as Helima 哈立麻.[49] In 1403, Yongle sent a mission headed by a eunuch to Tibet to invite Helima to court to perform funerary rituals for his parents, the Hongwu emperor and Empress Ma.[50] Yongle's interest in meeting the Fifth Karmapa may indeed have been motivated by sincere religious beliefs, but an invitation to perform funerary rituals also served to demonstrate his filial piety and his claim to the throne. Helima accepted the invitation and arrived in the capital, Nanjing, three years later in 1407.[51] To prepare for his arrival, Yongle constructed a Karmapa monastery within the palace and a separate monastery, the Linggu Monastery (Linggu si 靈谷寺) outside the palace compound.[52] When Helima arrived, Yongle held elaborate celebrations and showered the hierarch and his entourage with gifts. In return, Helima conducted the funerary rites requested by Yongle at the Linggu Monastery.[53]

---

48. Sperling, "Early Ming Policy Toward Tibet," pp. 89–91.

49. For his biography, see Goodrich and Fang, *Dictionary of Ming Biography*, 2: 481–83; see also Fang Jianchang, "Xizang Rulai dabao fawang kao."

50. For a record of the eunuch's journey and activities in Tibet, see *MS*, 304.7768. It should be noted here that Yongle claimed that he was the son of the Hongwu emperor and his primary consort, Empress Ma, although Empress Ma was most certainly not his natural mother. In order to claim legitimacy, however, he had to assert that Empress Ma was indeed his mother. See Wu Han, "Ming Chengzu shengmu kao"; and Li Jinhua, "Ming Chengzu shengmu wenti huizheng."

51. For a discussion of the period between the Yongle emperor's issuance of the invitation and Helima's arrival in Nanjing, see Sperling, "Early Ming's Policy Toward Tibet," pp. 79–80.

52. Ibid., pp. 86–88.

53. *Linggu chan lin zhi*, 11.1b–3a. The rites were performed on the fifth day of the second month of the fifth year of the Yongle period (Mar. 14, 1407).

Fig. 7.1 Artist(s) unknown, *Portrait of Zhu Yuanzhang*, the Hongwu emperor (r. 1368–98). Hanging scroll, ink and colors on silk, 270.0 × 163.6 cm. National Palace Museum, Taipei, Taiwan, Republic of China.

Fig. 7.2 Artist(s) unknown, *Portrait of Zhu Youtang*, the Hongzhi emperor (r. 1488–1505). Hanging scroll, ink and colors on silk, 209.8 × 115.0 cm. National Palace Museum, Taipei, Taiwan, Republic of China.

(*top*) Fig. 7.3   Artist(s) unknown, *Portrait of Song Taizu* (r. 960–76). Hanging scroll, ink and colors on silk, 191.0 × 169.7 cm. National Palace Museum, Taipei, Taiwan, Republic of China.

(*bottom*) Fig. 7.4   Artist(s) unknown, *Portrait of Khubilai Khan* (Yuan Shizu). Album leaf, ink and colors on silk, 59.4 × 47.0 cm. National Palace Museum, Taipei, Taiwan, Republic of China.

Fig. 7.5 Artist(s) unknown, *Portrait of Zhu Di*, the Yongle emperor (r. 1403–24). Hanging scroll, ink and colors on silk, 220.0 × 150.0 cm. National Palace Museum, Taipei, Taiwan, Republic of China.

Fig. 7.6 Artist(s) unknown, *Portrait of Zhu Zhanji*, the Xuande emperor (r. 1426–35). Hanging scroll, ink and colors on silk, 210.0 × 171.8 cm. National Palace Museum, Taipei, Taiwan, Republic of China.

Fig. 7.7 Artist(s) unknown, *Luohan* (possibly Ajita), Yongle period. Hanging scroll mounted as framed panel; ink, pigments, and gold on silk, 77 × 50 cm. Robert Rosenkranz Collection.

(*left*) Fig. 7.8   Artist(s) unknown, *Portrait of Sakya Yeshe*, the Great Compassionate Dharma King. Silk embroidery, 76.0 × 65.0 cm, Tibet Museum, Lhasa. From *Wenwu* 1985, no. 9, colorplate.

(*right*) Fig. 7.9   Artist(s) unknown, *Portrait of Sakya Yeshe*, the Great Compassionate Dharma King. Silk tapestry, 108.5 × 63.0 cm, Norbulingka Palace Collection. From *Bao zang*, p. 55.

Fig. 7.10   Artist(s) unknown, *Portrait of Zhu Qizhen*, the Zhengtong (r. 1436–49) and Tianshun emperor (r. 1457–64). Hanging scroll, ink and colors on silk, 208.3 × 154.5 cm. National Palace Museum, Taipei, Taiwan, Republic of China.

Helima's religious activities at the Linggu Monastery are commemorated in a long handscroll entitled *Miracles of the Mass of Universal Salvation Conducted by the Fifth Karmapa for the Yongle Emperor* (*Rulai dabao fawang wei Ming Taizu ji huanghou jian pu du da zhai chang shoujuan hua* 如來大寶法王爲明太祖及皇后建普渡大齋長手卷畫), or more commonly known as *Miracles in Nanjing*. Commissioned by Yongle, this scroll records through text and images the miraculous events that occurred during the rituals. The inscription in Chinese at the beginning of the scroll documents Yongle's invitation to Helima, the Tathagata Great Treasure Prince of the Dharma, his wish for the Buddhist funerary rituals for his parents, and the date. Inscriptions presumably of similar content in four other languages, including Tibetan, Mongolian, and Persian, follow the Chinese inscription.[54]

The scroll, produced by court artists, includes a total of forty-nine images, each preceded by inscriptions in five languages. A picture commemorates each day of the rituals performed from the fifth through the eighteenth day of the second lunar month, and some of the rituals that took place on days in the third lunar month. Many of the pictures show Helima's residence, the location where sutras were chanted, and pagodas. Swirling clouds and five-colored beams radiate throughout the pictures, suggesting auspicious, miraculous events and manifestations. Many people at court witnessed and recorded the miracles that occurred as Helima and his entourage of monks performed rituals. "Propitious clouds, heavenly flowers, sweet dew . . . white elephants, white cranes . . . were seen."[55] Even Hanlin officials such as the scholar Hu Guang 胡廣 (1370–1418) composed poems on the auspicious sights.[56]

On the same day that Helima carried out rituals for the deceased emperor and empress, he also began a series of twelve initiations for Yongle and his principal consort, Empress Xu. Specially constructed mystical

---

54. This scroll was formerly in Tsurphu Monastery and now in the collection of the Norbulingkha. Handscroll, ink and colors on silk, 66.0 × 4968.0 cm. For an excellent complete reproduction, see *Bao Zang*, 3: 94–137. For a detailed analysis of this scroll, see Berger, "Miracles in Nanjing." Various scholars have identified the five languages differently. The general consensus is that four of the languages are Chinese, Tibetan, Mongolian, and Persian. The fifth language, however, has not been securely identified. Martin Heijdra of Princeton University, however, has suggested that it is "Baiyi," which is related to old Burmese, and is conducting further research. Various scholars have also suggested Baiyi or old Burmese, but such claims have yet to be substantiated.

55. *MS*, 304.7768–69.

56. Ibid. The title of Hu Guang's poem is "Sheng xiao rui ying ge" 聖孝瑞應歌. See also *MS*, 147.4124–25 for Hu Guang's biography.

mandalas served as the focal points for each initiation rite.[57] Although Chinese-language sources, such as the *Official History of the Ming Dynasty*, do not mention the esoteric rites, nor are these initiation ceremonies depicted in the painted scroll, this period of religious instruction is well documented in Tibetan religious texts.[58] As Patricia Berger has pointed out, the

> Linggu Monastery miracles were distributed in an orchestrated crescendo to honor the Karmapa and his ritual actions, the sacredness of the monastery itself embodied in the relics in its pagoda, the imperial ancestors whose remains were entombed nearby, and, last but not least, Zhu Di, the Karmapa's patron and disciple. The purpose of the miracles was twofold: to establish the primacy of the Karmapa and proclaim simultaneously that the emperor and his parents were doubly legitimate as virtuous monarchs recognized by a Confucian Heaven and the chakravartin rulers whose rule foretold a new Buddhist epoch.[59]

Throughout Helima's stay in the capital, Yongle presented numerous gifts to him. Upon the Tibetan hierarch's arrival in Nanjing, he received "an offering of tea, a wheel of gold, and a white conch shell."[60] According to entries in the *Ming shilu* 明實錄, Yongle gave gifts of gold, silver, paper money, silk, and ritual implements to the Tibetan lama and his entourage on several different occasions.[61] Such gifts and the many days Yongle spent in religious instruction underline his deep esteem for Helima and his faith in Buddhism.

In an act carrying much political significance, Yongle bestowed on Helima a lengthy title whose shortened form was *dabao fawang* 大寶法王,

---

57. The mandalas were Jinasāgara (Tib. Rgyal-ba rgya-mtsho), Kīla (Tib. Phur-pa), Guhyasamāja (Tib. Gsang-'dus), Mitra (Tib. Mi-tra), Vajradhātu (Tib. Rdor-dbyings), Dharmadhātu-vagīsvara (Tib. Chos-dbyings gsimg-dbang), Hevajra (Tib. Dgyes-rdor), Bhattārikā (Tib. Rje-btsun-ma), Sarvavid (Tib. Kun-rig), Bhaisyajaguru (Tib. Sman-bla), Tārā-vidhi (Tib. Sgrol-chog), and Mahākarunika-dhārani-sādhanā (Tib. Thugs-rje chen-po'i gzungs-sgrub). The list is from Dpa'-bo Gtsup-lag 'phreng-ba, *Chos-'byung mkhas-pa'i dga'-ston*, p. 521, as cited in Sperling, "Early Ming Policy Toward Tibet," p. 115n33.

58. See Sperling, "Early Ming Policy Toward Tibet," pp. 83, 116n36. *MS*, 331.8573, provides the official Chinese historical version of the events at the Linggu Monastery.

59. Berger, "Miracles in Nanjing," p. 159.

60. Sperling, "Early Ming Policy Toward Tibet," p. 86. Sperling cites Tibetan sources for this information (Dpa'-bo, p. 519).

61. See Sperling, "Early Ming Policy Toward Tibet," p. 87. Entries in the *Ming shilu* that mention gifts include those for Feb. 2 and 26, 1407; Mar. 14, 1407; Apr. 10, 1407; Aug. 24, 1407; Dec. 5, 1407; and May 17, 1408.

Great and Precious Dharma King.[62] By awarding rank and title to Tibetan hierarchs, Chinese emperors placed themselves in a higher position. By accepting religious instruction, they conversely acknowledged religious indebtedness. This combination of political and religious interconnectedness fulfilled the notion of the priest-patron relationship and fed into the idea of the *cakravartin*, the consecrated Buddhist ruler. Yongle must have been aware of the past usage of the title *dabao fawang*, which the Yuan emperor Khubilai had bestowed on Phakpa, the chief hierarch of the Sakya. Khubilai used this title to establish a priest-patron relationship with Phakpa, who represented secular and religious authority in Tibet.[63] As the passage from his biography shows, Helima was aware of the Mongol precedent and Yongle's bid to emulate it:

> Generally, although the emperor, as a result of his pondering, intended to subjugate the administration of Tibet militarily, as in the Mongol era, and to suppress the country by means of a unitary government of priest and patron like that of the Sa[-skay-pa] and the Mongols, because the precious *dharmasvāmin* [Tib. chos-rje; i.e., the Karma-pa] taught in accordance with the dharma, he [i.e., the Karma-pa] was unhappy with Chinese military action. Finally the emperor petitioned [the Karma-pa, saying:] "Since there exist various different religious traditions in the land of Tibet, they will quarrel. Because the *dharmasvāmin* will not be pleased if actual troops are sent, I will send a number of horsemen to escort and convey the titles of Gser-thog left behind in Ho-chou [Tib. Ga-chu]. . . . All religious traditions will gather around your sect. Because the people of Eastern Tibet [Tib. Mdokhams], Rab-sgang, and Central Tibet yearly perform great religious activities [in Lhasa], I request that you grant this." However [the Karma-pa] said, "One religious tradition alone cannot tame the sentient beings. The Buddha's mercy will be imbued in accordance with each individual's devotion. If each one acts in accordance with the religious character of his own sect, it will be sufficient," and he did not grant [the emperor's request].[64]

---

62. The full title is *Wanxing juzu shifang zuisheng yuanjue miaozhihui shanpuying youguo yanjiao rulai dabao fawang Xitian dashan zizai fo* 萬行具足十方最勝圓覺妙智慧善普應佑國演教如來大寶法王西天大善自在佛, *MS*, 331.8573. The title can be translated as "Great goodness of the western heaven, self-abiding Buddha (who is) fully perfected in the ten thousand actions, most victorious in the ten directions, completely enlightened, wonderfully wise, excellently all-responsive, and (who) aids the nation and expounds the doctrine"; see Berger, "Miracles in Nanjing," p. 149; and Sperling, "Early Ming Policy Toward Tibet," pp. 122–23n73.

63. *Yuan shi, juan* 202. See also *MS*, 331.8571.

64. As quoted and translated by Sperling, "Early Ming Policy Toward Tibet," pp. 89–90.

Like Phakpa in the Yuan dynasty, Helima preached the multiplicity of Buddhist sects, but unlike Phakpa he declined to enter into a relationship with the Ming emperor.[65] In order for the priest-patron relationship to have succeeded, the Fifth Karmapa would have had to have subjugated all other Buddhist sects in Tibet. Because Helima refused to do this, Yongle was unable to form an institutional relationship with him. Yongle, however, did grant him complete authority over all Buddhists in China.[66] Despite this political disappointment, however, he continued to enjoy a close relationship with the Fifth Karmapa.[67]

Yongle continued sending missions to the Fifth Karmapa even after the hierarch returned to Tibet in 1408.[68] One letter written in 1413 is a testament to the intertwining of his religious and political interests. He writes of his visions—in particular one in which the Buddha appeared to him bearing the thirty-two marks of a *cakravartin*; Yongle believed this apparition to be a sign that he himself was one.[69] The concept of the consecrated Buddhist ruler—a *cakravartin*—was a powerful tool in political legitimation. Not only would he be secular head of the Ming empire, but he would also be the supreme theocratic monarch. This was by no means the first time that a Chinese emperor claimed to be a *cakravartin*,[70] but Yongle's aspirations set the foundation for a reformulation of the image of the emperor and a new conception of Chinese emperorship.

During and following his interaction with Helima, Yongle sponsored other missions to Tibet and issued formal invitations to a number of Buddhist clerics of various sects. Most generous in his bestowal of titles and gifts, he honored seven other hierarchs.[71] His relationship with two of the seven—Kunga Taishi (Kun-dga' bkra-shis) of the Sakya order, the *dacheng*

---

65. Sperling, "Early Ming Policy Toward Tibet," pp. 91–96.

66. Richardson, "The Karma-pa Sect," p. 1.

67. The Fifth Karmapa was even able to influence the Yongle emperor in his treatment of both Buddhist and Daoist monks, in securing a decree mitigating some harsh early Ming regulations governing these groups. See Sperling, "Early Ming Policy in Tibet," pp. 68–73. For further information on Yongle and Helima, see Shiga Takayoshi, "Min no Seiso to Chibetto."

68. Sperling, "Early Ming Policy in Tibet," pp. 97–99.

69. Xizang zizhiqu wenwu guanli weiyuanhui, "Mingchao huangdi ci gei Xizang Chubusi Gama huofo de liang jian zhao shu," pp. 43–44.

70. See, e.g., Forte, *Political Propaganda and Ideology in China*.

71. For the names and titles of the seven hierarchs, see Sperling, "Early Ming Policy Toward Tibet," pp. 136–37. These seven hierarchs are discussed in *MS*, 331.8575–85; see also Satō, "Mindai Chibetto no hachi daikyōō ni tsuite."

fawang 大乘法王 (Great Vehicle Dharma King), and Sakya Yeshe of the Gelugpa order, the *daci fawang* 大慈法王 (Great Compassionate Dharma King)—are particularly important, because they reveal his political and religious aspirations.

In his invitation to Kunga Taishi, Yongle referred to himself as the "*balacakravartin*, the great Da-Ming emperor."[72] In his letters to the Tibetan lama, the Chinese ruler clearly represented himself not only as the Son of Heaven in Confucian terms but also as an enlightened, consecrated Buddhist sovereign. With these two "powers," he could claim a much larger mandate that encompassed legalistic power as well as mystical, religious power. The basis for his claim to be a *cakravartin* had its foundation in the initiation and consecration rituals performed by the Fifth Karmapa on his behalf at the Linggu Monastery. As a hierarch of the Sakya order, Kunga Taishi would have understood this, since it was reminiscent of the relationship between his sect and the Mongol emperors of the Yuan dynasty.

Kunga Taishi accepted Yongle's invitation and arrived at the Ming court in 1413.[73] Although his activities at the Ming court appear to be mainly religious, they had political ramifications. He instructed Yongle on Mahākāla and Hevajra, two politically charged deities. Both Mahākāla and Hevajra are "important tutelary deities to the Sakya, and initiation rites involving them were central to consecrations which Phakpa bestowed on Khubilai, making him a cakravartin."[74] Based on historical precedent, such consecrations would endow Yongle with similar status. Furthermore, the initiation with a mandala of Hevajra was also the final rite to complete the consecrations that the Fifth Karmapa had performed for him in 1407. After Helima declined to enter into the priest-patron relationship, Yongle may well have been casting about for another hierarch to fulfill his desires. He would have known that Mahākāla and Hevajra were key deities to the Sakya order, and that in all likelihood Kunga Taishi would perform rites involving these two deities.

In 1410 Yongle also invited Tsongkhapa (1357–1419), the founder of the Gelugpa order. Tsongkhapa declined to journey to the Ming court, plead-

———

72. Sperling, "Early Ming Policy Toward Tibet," p. 140. For a definition of *balacakravartin*, translated by Sperling as "a ruler whose wheels of power roll everywhere without obstruction," see ibid., p. 174.

73. *MS*, 331.8575–76.

74. Sperling, "Early Ming Policy Toward Tibet," p. 142. For a discussion and examples of images of Mahākāla and Hevajra in the Ming palace and imperially sponsored temples in the capital, see Chapter 8 by David Robinson in this volume, pp. 365–421.

ing poor health and apprehension about the rigorous travel conditions. Upon receiving the second invitation in 1413, Tsongkhapa sent his disciple, Sakya Yeshe (Shijia yeshi 釋迦也失, 1355–1435), to represent him at the Ming court. Although Sakya Yeshe had not officially been invited by Yongle, as Tsongkhapa's emissary he was received with great ceremony.[75] During his stay at the Ming court, he performed numerous rites that took place over several months for Yongle. Mandalas associated with Tantric deities composed the major subject matter of the rites. As with the rites performed by the Fifth Karmapa, Yongle experienced apparitions and auspicious visions.[76] In appreciation for the religious instruction, in 1415 he granted Sakya Yeshe the title *Miaojue yuantong huici puying fuguo xianjiao guanding hongshan xitian fozi da guoshi* 妙覺圓通慧慈普應輔國顯教灌頂弘善西天佛子大國師 (Anointed son of the Buddha of the western heavens who spreads goodness, and great dynastic preceptor [who is] wonderfully enlightened, universally penetrating, wise and compassionate, all responsive, [and who] supports the nation and reveals the doctrine).[77] As spiritual advisor to Yongle, Sakya Yeshe had close contact with him, particularly when performing ceremonies for the emperor's longevity.[78] He even traveled to Mount Wutai, where he performed various religious ceremonies.[79] When Sakya Yeshe departed the Ming capital to return to Tibet, Yongle bestowed many gifts on him, including some scriptures from the Buddhist canon printed in Beijing in 1410, a gift that he had also given to Kunga Taishi.

The Yongle emperor's involvement with Tibetan Buddhist hierarchs had other far-reaching effects. The traffic between Tibetan hierarchs and the Ming court was not restricted to visits and letters carried by emissaries; vast quantities of precious objects and religious images were exchanged in the form of gifts. Such gifts introduced new artistic styles to the Chinese court, styles that were quickly mastered and absorbed into the repertoire of

---

75. *MS*, 331.8577. See also Sperling, "Early Ming Policy Toward Tibet," pp. 147–48, 184–85.

76. Sperling, "Early Ming Policy Toward Tibet," p. 149.

77. Ibid., p. 187*n*73; *MS*, 331.8577. Sakya Yeshe's title reflects a slightly lesser degree of honor than the exalted titles of the Fifth Karmapa and Kunga Taishi, and perhaps even that which Tsongkhapa would have received had he come. Such a difference is attributable to Yongle's sense of protocol; since Sakya Yeshe had not been personally invited to court but came in Tsongkhapa's stead, he received a lower-level title.

78. Sperling, "Early Ming Policy Toward Tibet," p. 151. Sakya Yeshe performed the initiations of Amitāyus for the Yongle emperor's longevity.

79. Ibid., p. 152. Most of the sources Sperling cites are Tibetan.

artists and craftsman at court. Heather Karmay has remarked on the fact that "the Yongle period saw the sudden appearance of a richly mature, full blown Tibetan style, showing a definite move towards the later period of Tibetan art."[80] Tibetan lamas first brought gifts to the Ming court, but Ming artists, who may have been Chinese, Tibetan, Nepalese, or Mongolian, quickly became adept at copying and even introducing technological improvements on the Tibetan models.[81] For example, Ming Tibetan-style bronzes bearing the Yongle reign mark reached an apogee of artistic refinement in the hands of court bronze casters.[82] These lavish objects were created at court as gifts for visiting Tibetan hierarchs as well as ritual objects reserved for the court's own use. The high quality of works such as bronzes represents a tangible expression of the Yongle emperor's support and interest in Tibetan Buddhism. Recently, Marsha Haufler and Patricia Berger have established without question the imperial patronage of Buddhist art and the artistic activity surrounding it. Both have discussed the various types of objects flowing in and out of the Ming court,[83] such as gilt bronzes, a rich assortment of textiles including robes, woven and embroidered *thangka*s, and religious paintings among others.[84] A set of painted portraits of Tibetan deities and monks demonstrates the high level of artistry involved in the production of religious paintings and underscores the interactions among emperors, Tibetan hierarchs, and artists (Fig. 7.7).[85] These bronzes and the portraits, all in Tibetan styles, were produced not in Tibet but at the Ming court.

The exchange of motifs and styles between Tibet and the court manifested itself first in small details in imperial portraiture. In Yongle's portrait (see Fig. 7.5), certain elements reveal their Buddhist origins. For example, encoded into the background design of the carpet between the medallions

———

80. Karmay, *Early Sino-Tibetan Art*, p. 73. The search for correct terminology for Tibetan-style art produced at the Ming court has resulted in terms such as Sino-Tibetan and Tibeto-Chinese. Patricia Berger addresses this issue in *Empire of Emptiness*, p. 7.

81. Karmay, *Early Sino-Tibetan Art*, pp. 72–83.

82. Ibid.

83. See Weidner, "Buddhist Pictorial Art in the Ming Dynasty"; and Berger, "Preserving the Nation." See also Weidner, "Imperial Engagements with Buddhist Art and Architecture"; and Berger, "Miracles at Nanjing."

84. See "Dazhaosi cang Yongle nianjian wenwu"; Wen Zhu, "Xizang difang Mingfeng bawang de youguan wenwu," pp. 89–90; and Simcox, "Early Chinese Embroideries."

85. See Watt and Leidy, *Defining Yongle*, for an overview of art of all media (ceramic, bronze, lacquer, textiles, painting, etc.) produced at the Ming court during the Yongle reign.

of dragons are some of the eight auspicious Tibetan Buddhist symbols: the measuring unit, one of the seven precious jewels, elephant tusks, the three-eyed jewel, and the queen's earrings. The subtle introduction of these elements into Yongle's portrait suggests a level of understanding and familiarity with Tibetan Buddhist motifs both on an imperial level and on the level of artistic production. Yongle's preoccupation with this religion set the stage for the dramatic change in the visual structure of imperial portraits several decades after his reign.

THE XUANDE EMPEROR AND SAKYA YESHE

The Xuande emperor shared his grandfather's religious interest and, like him, invited Tibetan hierarchs to perform a range of religious rituals at court. Gifts were exchanged, and court artists and craftsmen honed their skills in producing works with once-foreign Tibetan Buddhist motifs. Objects made for court consumption and gift giving characteristically do not bear the name of their makers; the Yongle bronzes, for example, have a Yongle reign mark but do not record the names of the casters. Craftsmen specializing in other media such as textiles similarly remain unidentified, as do painters of imperial portraits, who traditionally never signed imperial portraits. Such artworks, including the Yongle bronzes in Tibetan style and the portraits of Tibetan hierarchs painted at the Ming court, clearly demonstrate the artists' ability to produce high-quality Tibetan-like objects.

During the Xuande period, artists experimented with Sino-Tibetan portrait styles, although the imperial portrait formula remained essentially unchanged. Two works produced for Sakya Yeshe, one of Xuande's favored Tibetan hierarchs, serve as intermediaries between the traditional imperial portrait type and the emerging imperial icon. In 1434, Xuande invited Sakya Yeshe, a Tibetan hierarch of the Gelugpa order who had already visited during the Yongle period, to the Ming court. As mentioned, on his previous visit, Sakya Yeshe came in Tsongkhapa's stead and received the title of *fozi da guoshi* (Anointed Son of the Buddha, Great Dynastic Preceptor) from Yongle; this time he was invited in his own right, honored with an elevated title, and became known as *daci fawang* (Great Benevolent Dharma King), the shortened version of the title Xuande bestowed on him.[86] Sakya Yeshe performed various rituals and remained at the Ming court for a year.

———

86. *MS*, 331.8577.

The timing of Sakya Yeshe's visit to the Ming capital in 1434, the conferral of his title in the same year, his departure from the capital, and his death en route to Tibet in 1435 provide a series of events that can be used to date two important cultural objects produced at the Ming court: a silk embroidery and a silk tapestry depicting Sakya Yeshe. Because both works contain his new title, they can be dated to 1434 or 1435.

These pivotal works contributed to the Ming invention of a new iconic imperial image, and they reveal how court artists portrayed an individual who possessed both secular and religious power. They arrived at two artistic solutions: a portrait of a Buddhist hierarch and a Tibetan Buddhist religious icon. A comparison between these two images highlights the differences in conception between a portrait and an icon, a distinction that court portraitists later conflated in the painting of imperial portraits.

The silk embroidery, now in the collection of the Committee for Cultural Artifacts of the Tibetan Autonomous Region, is a traditional Tibetan-style portrait-icon of Sakya Yeshe, emphasizing his role as a Tibetan lama (Fig. 7.8).[87] The religious aspects of the Tibetan hierarch are highlighted: placed in the center of the composition, Sakya Yeshe sits in the cross-legged position of meditation on an elaborate pedestal-throne, framed by a mandorla composed of various Buddhist deities and creatures. The frontality of his position and the framing of his entire body create the impression that he is an immutable icon.[88] He wears an elaborate monk's pointed cap decorated with jewels and an orange-yellow robe. A halo behind his head accentuates his divine status. He is flanked by two important Buddhist symbols, the *vajra* bell and the *vajra* thunderbolt, and two inscriptions embroidered in gold against the deep blue background. The inscription in Chinese on the right reads *zhishan daci fawang da yuantong fo* 至善大慈法王大圓通佛 (Perfectly excellent Great Compassionate Dharma King), a shortened version of his title. On the left is an inscription in Tibetan. Two

---

87. *Portrait of Daci fawang* 明代刺繡大慈法王像 (Sakya Yeshe), silk embroidery, 76.0 × 65.0 cm. See Xizang zizhiqu wenwu guanli weiyuanhui (Committee for Cultural Artifacts of the Tibetan Autonomous Region), *Wenwu* 1985, no. 9: color plate.

88. For a discussion of frontality and icons, see Wu Hung, "What Is Bianxiang?" Specifically, Wu Hung defines iconic depiction as "a symmetrical composition centered on an icon—a Buddha or a bodhisattva . . . in an iconic scene, the central icon, portrayed frontally as a solemn image of majesty, ignores the surrounding crowds and stares at the viewer outside the picture. The composition is thus not self-contained; although the icon exists in the pictorial context within the composition, its significance relies on the presence of the viewer or worshipper outside it" (ibid., pp. 129–30).

elephants with elaborate trappings support the mandorla, which is composed of lions, dragons, and Buddhist figures amid ornamental flowers. The pedestal-throne has a top tier decorated with stylized lotus leaves on three highly ornamental platforms. In the upper corners of the embroidery are two figures set within roundels embedded in the colorful cloud scrolls: a green Tara and a white Tara. A border of Sanskrit vowels frames the entire composition. The composition was first established through an outline embroidered in gold thread. Other colors, including large sections of gold, were then added. Great care was also taken in embroidering the Chinese characters and Tibetan script. Such an artistic object required the expensive materials and highly skilled craftsmanship available in the imperial workshops, and this silk embroidery provides a material record of the artistic expertise at Xuande's court.

Although this embroidery can be considered as a portrait of Sakya Yeshe, it functions more as an icon. As a leader of a specific lineage who relied on mystical means of reaching enlightenment, Sakya Yeshe held both religious and secular power. Buddhist followers would have respected the Tibetan hierarch's proximity to the Buddha, and depictions of him therefore emphasized more iconic aspects. Similar to images of Buddhas, the Tibetan hierarch's facial features are simplified and generic, almost otherworldly. In the embroidery, Sakya Yeshe's religious office takes precedence over his personal individuality.

By contrast, the other depiction of Sakya Yeshe presents a completely different image of the Tibetan hierarch (Fig. 7.9).[89] Instead of resembling a religious icon, the tapestry image portrays Sakya Yeshe as a distinct person with recognizable facial features: a more secular, individualized portrait. Many of the elements in the tapestry correspond to comparable ones in the embroidery, but the dissimilarities indicate a different goal for the portrait. Sakya Yeshe, seated in the same cross-legged fashion as in the embroidery, still commands the central focus of the portrait. As in the religious icon, he stares out frontally, yet this frontal disposition does not diminish the impression of his individuality. Instead of appearing in the timeless manner of a Buddha, Sakya Yeshe looks like a wise, old cleric who shows the telltale signs of aging with wrinkles and a slight puffiness around his eyes. He makes the same hand gesture as in the embroidery, and a halo denoting his

------

89. *Portrait of Daci fawang* 明代大慈法王緙絲唐卡 (Sakya Yeshe), silk tapestry, 108.5 × 63.0 cm, Sera Monastery, illustrated in Norbulingka Palace Collection, p. 1; also illustrated in *Bao Zang*, 3: 150–51.

divine status also surrounds his head, but his attire differs significantly from the monk's robe and cap used in the embroidery. He wears instead a five-petaled Buddhist crown featuring a depiction of a Buddha on each petal. Although his inner garment resembles the robe in the embroidery, his outer robe is a yellow ceremonial garment decorated with dragons, reminiscent of more secular ceremonial robes.[90] Objects denoting the Tibetan hierarch's status are placed on the table behind the dragon throne: the *vajra* thunderbolt and bell, an incense burner, and sutras. On the right, an inscription woven in gold denotes Sakya Yeshe's bestowed title in Chinese,[91] and an inscription in Tibetan is further to the right. On the left, a large official seal that the Xuande emperor gave Sakya Yeshe is also woven into the tapestry. A jeweled canopy with energetically scrolling clouds serves to frame the Tibetan hierarch and accentuate the centrality of his image.

Together the embroidery and the tapestry suggest that Ming court artists distinguished between religious icons and portraits of individuals, albeit individuals who wielded considerable power. Both images include religious elements, but the tapestry combines secular and religious symbols, reflecting perhaps a Chinese notion of a secularized portrait of a Tibetan hierarch. Elements from the Tibetan Buddhist iconic depiction of Sakya Yeshe have also been incorporated into a Chinese-style portrait scheme, mixing Tibetan Buddhist religious iconic imagery with the traditions of indigenous Chinese portraiture. For example, Sakya Yeshe's throne is remarkably similar to the dragon throne in Yongle's portrait (see Figs. 7.5, 9). As in Yongle's portrait, the highly ornamented throne has dragon heads on the chair back and arms that spew sumptuous jewels. Although this type of throne may be indebted in some ways to thrones of Buddhist deities, the artisans at court would have known them as imperial thrones used in imperial portraits. The inclusion of such a throne in Sakya Yeshe's portrait suggests that he may have been considered a political ruler in his own right and therefore appropriately seated on a dragon throne. The carpet also recalls designs found in the carpets in Yongle's and Xuande's portraits. Decorated with lotus flowers and a border at the edges, it resembles the motif of dragon roundels spaced evenly over a ground design of flowers and Buddhist symbols in the imperial portraits.

---

90. Formal portraiture for Buddhist leaders such as head abbots was well developed as early as the Song period. See, e.g., the portrait of Wuzhun shifan 無準師範, dated 1238, in which he is depicted seated in a chair wearing formal robes and carrying the attributes that signify his religious authority.

91. The text of the Chinese inscription matches Sakya Yeshe's title as recorded in *MS*, 331.8577.

Even the handling of the carpet, which is laid out flat on the pictorial surface like wallpaper with little regard for spatial recession, is similar to those in the early Ming imperial portraits.

The tapestry emphasizes the secular aspects of the Tibetan hierarch's position while using religious elements, whereas the embroidered image is wholly religious. The existence of these two images—a more individualized, secular-like portrait and a religious icon—suggests that the Ming court artists were aware of the Tibetan hierarch's role as both a near-divine religious figure and as a charismatic theocratic ruler. The tapestry of Sakya Yeshe as "Dharma King" prefigures changes in the structure of imperial portraits. It shows how court artisans developed a portrait image that incorporated religious symbols in a more politicized setting. Many religious symbols appear in the portrait, but the overall effect is one of a powerful being—a consciously political portrait.

Both Xuande and Sakya Yeshe passed away in 1435, but their interactions had an immediate effect on the artistic production of portraits in the following reigns. Whereas Xuande's portrait (see Fig. 7.6) had been modeled directly on that of his grandfather, Yongle, those of his successors show clear signs of influence from the tapestry portrait of Sakya Yeshe. In Sakya Yeshe's portrait, the dragon throne was pivoted to provide a frontal setting for the Tibetan hierarch, in accordance with the frontal nature of religious icons and other Tibetan lama portraits.[92] This new formula became the model for imperial portraits. Although the portraits of Sakya Yeshe are textiles and the imperial portraits are paintings, and the method of production would necessarily have been different, the overall design and conception of the portraits are comparable despite the differences in medium.

THE HONGZHI EMPEROR AND THE IMPERIAL ICON

In visual terms, the distance between the tapestry portrait of Sakya Yeshe and those of Xuande's immediate successor, the Zhengtong emperor (see Figs. 7.9, 10), and in turn his successor, the Chenghua emperor (r. 1465–87), is minimal. Zhengtong is firmly seated in a frontal position and stares straight out of the picture. The portraitist reoriented the emperor's body and the dragon throne so that every element was parallel to the picture plane. Although Zhengtong is frontal, his arms are not arranged symmetrically; he is still depicted with his left hand grasping his belt and his right

---

92. For various comparative materials, see *Xizang wenwu jingcui.*

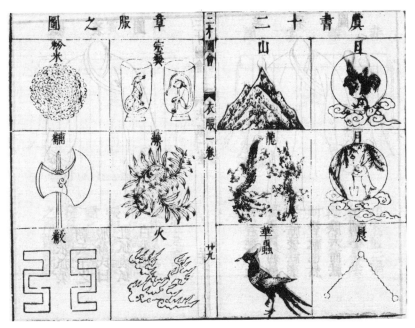

Fig. 7.11   Diagram of symbols of sovereignty from *Sancai tuhui* 三才圖會.

hand resting on his knee. The Chenghua emperor's portrait similarly follows this formula.

This shift toward frontality inspired by Tibetan icons coincided with several other changes: a change in imperial attire and a general tendency in early to mid-Ming painting toward flatness and surface decoration.[93] The early Ming emperors from Hongwu to Xuande wore "ordinary attire," a lesser level of formality than "ceremonial attire."[94] Zhengtong, however, is depicted wearing a robe that incorporates the cosmological symbols of rulership—the sun, the moon, the constellation of the Big Dipper, a mountain, dragons, colorful pheasants, and pairs of bronze sacrificial cups, waterweed, grains of millet, flames, sacrificial axe, and the *fu* symbol (see Figs. 7.10, 11). Chenghua is portrayed in exactly the same manner.[95]

———

93. For an overview of Ming court painting, see Barnhart et al., *Painters of the Great Ming*.

94. *DMHD*, 60.19. See also Zhou Xibao, *Zhongguo gudai fushi shi*, p. 398.

95. Chenghua's portrait is so close to that of Zhengtong that it is possible that the artists simply copied Zhengtong's portrait and introduced slight changes in the background. The carpet in Chenghua's portrait is quite different from that in Zhengtong's. One may conjecture that the body was painted following the model of Zhengtong, and

Although few references document Zhengtong's and Chenghua's in-volvement with the production of their portraits, the textual record reveals that both emperors continued to cultivate relationships with Tibetan Bud-dhists.[96] For example, Zhengtong had contact with the Tibetan monks at the Honghua Temple 弘化寺 in Qinghai, where Sakya Yeshe died on his return to Tibet. Monks from this temple petitioned the court for preferen-tial treatment, since the temple was the burial ground of Sakya Yeshe, the Dharma King. In response, the Ming court granted farmlands and varying degrees of economic assistance. Sakya Yeshe's disciples also sent tribute missions to the Ming court every several years during Zhengtong's reign, which demonstrated their continuous contact with his court.[97] Honghua Temple furthermore served as a military outpost that was able to repulse attacks from Mongols and put down local rebellions during the reigns of Chenghua and Hongzhi.[98] The Ming court's support of the Honghua Temple was thus both politically and religiously motivated and serves as just one example of continued interactions with Tibetan Buddhists.

In the capital, imperial sponsorship of Buddhist temples and temple decoration similarly flourished. The Fahai Monastery 法海寺 is a prime example of collaborative efforts by Ming court painters. Sponsored by the eunuchs at court and supported by Zhengtong, the monastery was con-structed between 1439 and 1443 under the direction of the Works Project Office (Yingshansuo 營繕所) of the Ministry of Works (Gongbu 工部). Two court painters, Wan Fuqing 宛福清 and Wang Shu 王恕, were as-sisted by fifteen low-ranking court painters to paint the huge Buddhist mu-rals.[99] Fahai Monastery represents only one of many projects sponsored by the court. The pool of court artists must have been varied and large enough to support so much religious and secular artistic activity. Such art-ists may also have been involved with the making of the imperial portraits.

As Tibetan hierarchs continued to frequent the Ming court, the formula for the imperial portrait incorporated elements from Tibetan art until the new paradigm for imperial portraiture emerged fully developed during the Hongzhi period (see Fig. 7.2). Unlike the portraits of his immediate prede-

---

Chenghua's face was added in. The striking resemblance also suggests Chenghua's por-trait was based heavily on Zhengtong's.

96. Sātō, "Mintei ni okeru Ramakyō sūhai ni tsuite."
97. Otosaka Tomoko, "A Study of the Hong Hua Si Temple," pp. 72–74.
98. Ibid., pp. 75–76.
99. Li Song, "Beijing Fahai si"; Yang Boxian, *Beijing Fahaisi*, p. 52.

cessors, which were frontal but not symmetrical, Hongzhi's portrait is completely symmetrical. His hands are clasped in front of his body and hidden within his sleeves. Pheasants arranged on his sleeves line up in a row, a pair on one sleeve directly facing a pair on the other. In addition to the symmetrical rendering of the body and the decoration, the entire portrait has become flatter, as though the three-dimensional body has flattened out and disappeared beneath the dragon robe. The skirt of the robe has been spread out so that the dragon medallions on the sides show more clearly. Vestiges of lines once indicative of clothing folds that followed the contour of the knees now appear flat and decorative, no longer serving to create shape and volume. The Hongzhi emperor looks almost lost amid the sea of symbols—the brilliant color of the robe and symbols, the lavishly decorated dragon throne surrounded by a screen of swirling dragons, and the carpet create a much greater visual impact than the Hongzhi emperor's face. Most noticeable about the portrait is the imperial setting: the dragon robe and the throne. The office takes precedence over the individual, almost eclipsing him. The imperial portrait was transformed into an icon of rulership, and the individual's identity played a diminished role.

Subsequent Ming imperial portraits are oriented so that the emperor faces directly out of the picture with perfect symmetry. The portraits were no longer merely familial ancestors, as were those of the early Ming dynasty; rather, they were distant, imposing, quasi-religious, political icons. This change in visual structure coincided with the influx of Tibetan Buddhist artistic motifs and the evolving function of the portraits. The increased flatness of the portraits furthermore echoed a general trend in Ming court painting, which tended toward more surface abstraction. Although pre-Ming emperors had fostered relationships with Tibetan Buddhists and also presumably had access to Tibetan objects, it was only during the fifteenth century that Tibetan modes of representation were incorporated into the imperial portrait formula, helping to shape Chinese imperial portraiture. Although it is unclear exactly what visual impact the resulting image had on those who had access to the portraits—the emperors themselves, civil and military officials, foreign emissaries—and this remains a topic for further inquiry, it is clear that the change in the imperial image occurred after decades of interaction among artists, Tibetan hierarchs, officials, and emperors at the Ming court.

Portraits as Political Objects

After the transformation of the imperial portrait into an icon of rulership, the portrait became a visual representation of the power and authority of emperorship. The emperor as an individual was almost less important than his role as holder of the office of rulership, with his body garbed in a garment encoded with the emblems symbolic of that office. The Jiajing emperor (r. 1522–66), however, utilized the imperial portrait formula in the Great Rites Controversy to show that he would not be molded into a figurehead emperor. In the process, he manipulated the imperial image to suit his needs, using it for political purposes in the imperial succession crisis.

When the Zhengde emperor died with neither an heir nor a designated heir, a succession crisis threatened to undermine the stability of the Ming court. To avert dynastic instability and to circumvent coups by the Zhengde emperor's favorites, Grand Secretary Yang Tinghe 楊廷和 (1459–1529)[100] chose a cousin of the Zhengde emperor (a nephew of the Hongzhi emperor) to accede to the throne. This cousin, who represented a cadet branch of the dynastic family, would reign as the Jiajing emperor.[101] Yang Tinghe orchestrated Jiajing's rise to emperorship. Prior to the Zhengde emperor's death, Yang issued instructions to make it possible to summon the future Jiajing emperor to court, who at the time was in mourning for his father. Citing the *Ancestral Injunctions*, Yang convinced the eunuchs of the Directorate of Ceremonial that Jiajing was the legitimate heir, although in reality he stretched the meaning of the injunctions so that Jiajing could be placed on the throne.[102] When the Zhengde emperor died, at Yang's request the Directorate of Ceremonial issued an official succession edict stating that Jiajing should "come to the capital to succeed to the imperial throne."[103] With no more instructions or stipulations other than simply to appear at court, Jiajing journeyed from his residence in Anlu in Huguang province (modern Zhongxiang county, Hubei province) to Beijing.

Absent in the cursory edict was an explanation of how Jiajing should treat his natural parents and what sort of sacrificial ceremonies he should

---

100. For Yang Tinghe's biography, see Goodrich and Fang, *Dictionary of Ming Biography*, 2: 1542–46.

101. For Jiajing's biography, see ibid., 1: 315–21.

102. Geiss, "The Chia-ching Reign," 7: 442 and note 3. The description of the Great Rites Controversy is a summary of Geiss's detailed treatment.

103. Translation quoted in ibid. The original text of the edict can be found in *Ming shilu, Wuzong shilu*, p. 3681.

perform for the Hongzhi and Zhengde emperors, his uncle and cousin, respectively. Yang Tinghe probably assumed that Jiajing would consider himself the adopted son of the Hongzhi emperor in order to continue the legitimate line of succession, and the officials had offered the throne to Jiajing without explicitly stipulating that he honor the Hongzhi emperor as his imperial father. Jiajing and his own advisors, however, had no such idea, and he refused to be the obedient stand-in as a brother to the Zhengde emperor and a "son" to the Hongzhi emperor. Instead, from the beginning he asserted his independence and exerted his imperial power over the bureaucracy.

What ensued was an extended controversy that took place over two periods, from 1521 to 1524 and then from 1524 to 1545, over the proper imperial rituals for honoring the Jiajing emperor's natural parents. From the beginning of his reign, the Jiajing emperor challenged the recommendations for titles, ceremonies, and rituals for his natural parents submitted by officials of the Ministry of Rites. Adopting an intransigent attitude, he refused to accept the officials' recommendations. Grand Secretary Yang Tinghe, on the other hand, took every opportunity to force his will on the Jiajing emperor. Although he had little success in swaying the emperor, he used the rites controversy to strengthen his own power base at court, causing the removal from office of all officials who expressed dissenting views. For several years, however, the emperor and the grand secretary were at a stalemate. In 1524, however, the Jiajing emperor finally impressed his will on Yang Tinghe and the bureaucracy, ending the debate about his parents' titles.[104]

The emperor's triumph over the bureaucracy in the ritual controversy took physical form in two ways. Although he had established his parents' titles, the Jiajing emperor wished to secure more imperial recognition for them. From 1524 to 1545, he schemed to build a temple in the Ancestral Temple complex (Taimiao) in Beijing to house his father's spirit tablet. During this period, he relentlessly pursued his goal.[105] In 1524, he first broached the subject of building a temple for his father to officials of the Ministry of Rites. Although they were against the idea, they compromised and suggested that a separate temple in honor of the Jiajing emperor's

---

104. For a detailed examination of the entire controversy, see Geiss, "The Chiaching Reign," pp. 442–50.

105. Ibid., pp. 457–61. The following summarizes Geiss's research on the Ancestral Temple and Jiajing.

father be constructed near the Ancestral Temple complex. At first this satisfied the Jiajing emperor, but later he wanted his father's tablet to be placed within the Ancestral Temple complex itself. In the following years, the Jiajing emperor pressured officials, making incremental changes in performing rituals so that he could elevate the status of his father. For instance, he insisted on changing the entrance to his father's temple so that he could enter it directly from the Ancestral Temple complex. He also held sacrifices for his father on the same day as those performed at the Ancestral Temple complex.[106] In 1538 he furthermore revived an ancient ritual that allowed his deceased father to participate posthumously, thereby placing his father into the imperial lineage.[107]

During this same period, the Ancestral Temple complex underwent construction. When the Ancestral Temple complex in Nanjing burned down in 1534, officials decided to rebuild the complex in Beijing. The architectural layout consisted of a central temple for the founding emperor (the Hongwu emperor) and his ancestors, and smaller temples for each of the other emperors, for a total of nine temples. The temple for the Jiajing emperor's father, built previously, was not incorporated into this scheme but remained situated alongside the new temples. The complex was completed in December 1536. In April 1541, the nine newly constructed temples of the Ancestral Temple caught fire during a storm and burned down. The only remaining temple left standing was the one that had been dedicated to the Jiajing emperor's father.

The Jiajing emperor capitalized on this convenient destruction; in December 1543 he ordered the building of a new complex that would accommodate all the spirit tablets in one temple. Upon completion of the construction in July 1545, the Jiajing emperor had all the spirit tablets, including that of his father, placed within the temple. They were arranged so that the founding emperor's tablet stood in the center, facing south. All the other tablets were arranged to the left and right of the central tablet, but facing east and west. The Jiajing emperor in effect inserted his father's spirit tablet into the imperial lineage and even ranked his father above his immediate predecessor, the Zhengde emperor.

Visual signs of the Jiajing emperor's success in according imperial honors posthumously to his father did not cease with the rearrangement of the spirit tablets in the new Ancestral Temple complex. He commissioned an

106. Geiss, "The Chia-ching Reign," p. 457.
107. Ibid., p. 459.

imperial portrait of his father, Prince Xian of Xing 興獻王. In this portrait, now in the collection of the National Palace Museum, Taipei, Prince Xian is depicted wearing the imperial dragon robe and seated on a dragon throne. He stares impassively straight out of the picture plane and is seated in a completely frontal and symmetrical position. His hands, hidden in his sleeves, are clasped in front of his chest, and his feet rest on a footstool. He is in the exact same pose as the Hongzhi (see Fig. 7.2) and Zhengde emperors. He does not have a dragon screen behind his throne as in the portrait of the Hongzhi emperor, but this absence does not indicate lesser status since the Zhengde emperor also did not have a dragon screen behind his throne. Prince Xian is clearly depicted in the guise of an emperor. The dragon robe and the setting are the visual signs that symbolize emperorship, and the pictorial and symbolic formula of this portrait unambiguously proclaims this exalted position. Prince Xian died in 1519 at the age of 43, and it is likely that this portrait was painted posthumously at the order of the Jiajing emperor.

Although it would have been standard practice to commission ancestral portraits for one's parents, portraying someone as an emperor with all the symbols of rulership was an unusual and bold move on the part of the Jiajing emperor. An imperial portrait functioned as an exalted ritual object, and the iconic portrait of a person wearing the yellow dragon robe adorned with the symbols of rulership was reserved solely for emperors. Only the emperor had the privilege to wear such a robe; robes for the princes and other members of the imperial family were distinguished by differences in color and symbols.[108]

For the Jiajing emperor, the commissioning of an imperial portrait for his natural father was a symbolic act elevating his father to the position of emperor. The portrait is visual proof of his determination to exert his desires over the arguments of the bureaucracy. From the perspective of the officials, however, it must have seemed revolutionary that a prince was depicted in full imperial raiment in an imperial portrait, a format previously always reserved for an emperor. Never before had there been such an example, and in the remaining decades of the Ming dynasty this never happened again. Through the construction of a new temple complex and the painting of an imperial portrait, the Jiajing emperor in effect invented a position for his father both physically in the ancestral complex and symbolically in the imperial portrait. In this way, the imperial portrait as an icon of

---

108. Zhou Xibao, *Zhongguo gudai fushi shi*, pp. 378–413.

rulership was manipulated as an object in the Jiajing emperor's plan to elevate his natural parents to the status of emperor and empress despite the vociferous and protracted objections of the court bureaucracy.

Conclusion

The Ming imperial image symbolizes a nexus of interactions at the Ming court. At the beginning of the dynasty, possession of past imperial portraits and the production of new imperial portraits served to legitimize the new dynasty. The early Ming emperors, in particular those from Hongwu through Xuande, asserted their individual agency by approving or rejecting their portraits as well as by awarding ranks and emolument to favored artists. Their tastes and agendas influenced the type and look of art at the capital and contributed to the emergence of a new imperial image. The manner in which the emperors used imperial portraits fueled debates with officials about protocol and court ritual. The shift from using imperial portraits in familial rituals in the Fengxiandian to occasional appearances in more public ceremonies in the Grand Temple is underscored by the subtle changes in the visual structure of imperial portraits.

The indebtedness of the new iconic imperial image to Tibetan Buddhism furthermore reveals both the sincere and deep interest the Ming emperors had in the foreign religion and their ability to capitalize on religious convictions to political advantage. Many of the emperors from the first half of the Ming dynasty cultivated ties with Tibetan hierarchs through the performance of Tibetan rituals and the exchange of gifts. During their reigns, Tibetan artistic elements crucial to the development of the new imperial portrait formula circulated at court and contributed to the change in imperial portraiture evident in the portrait of the Zhengtong emperor and fully formed in the portrait of the Hongzhi emperor. The shaping of the imperial image through the fifteenth century thus occurred gradually through interactions among emperors, artists, Tibetan lamas, and officials at the Ming court. Once the new image emerged, emperors such as Jiajing took advantage of its new significance and impact, using it in turn as a symbolic object in his own political struggles with court officials.

Works Cited

Allsen, Thomas T. *Commodity and Exchange in the Mongol Empire: A Cultural History of Islamic Textiles*. Cambridge Studies in Islamic Civilization. New York: Cambridge University Press, 1997.

Bao Zang: Zhongguo Xizang lishi wenwu 寶藏: 中國西藏歷史文物, di 1 ban, vol. 3, *Yuanchao shiqi, Mingchao shiqi* 元朝時期明朝時期. Beijing: Zhaohua chubanshe, 2000.

Barnhart, Richard M., et al. *Painters of the Great Ming: The Imperial Court and the Zhe School*. Dallas: Dallas Museum of Art, 1993.

Berger, Patricia Ann. *Empire of Emptiness: Buddhist Art and Political Authority in Qing China*. Honolulu: University of Hawai'i Press, 2003.

————. "Miracles in Nanjing: An Imperial Record of the Fifth Karmapa's Visit to the Chinese Capital." In *Cultural Intersections in Later Chinese Buddhism*, ed. Marsha Smith Weidner. Honolulu: University of Hawai'i Press, 2001, pp. 145–69.

————. "Preserving the Nation: The Political Uses of Tantric Art in China." In *Latter Days of the Law: Images of Chinese Buddhism, 850–1850*, ed. Marsha Smith Weidner. Lawrence: Spencer Museum of Art, University of Kansas, 1994, pp. 89–124.

Cammann, Schuyler V. R. *China's Dragon Robes*. New York: Ronald Press, 1952.

Chan, Hok-lam. "The Chien-wen, Yung-lo, Hung-hsi, and Hsüan-te Reigns, 1399–1434." In *CHC*, 7: 182–304.

Chang Lin-sheng. "The National Palace Museum: History of the Collection." In *Possessing the Past: Treasures from the National Palace Museum, Taibei*, ed. Wen C. Fong and James C. Y. Watt. New York: The Metropolitan Museum of Art, 1996, pp. 3–25.

CHC, see Mote and Twitchett, *Cambridge History of China*

Chen Gaohua 陳高華. "Zhu Yuanzhang de fojiao zhengce" 朱元璋的佛教政策. *Mingshi yanjiu* 明史研究 1 (1991): 110–18.

Chen Kangqi 陳康祺 (b. 1840). *Langqian jiwen, chu bi, er bi, san bi* 郎潛紀聞, 初筆, 二筆, 三筆. Preface dated 1881. Reprinted—Beijing: Zhonghua shuju, 1984.

Ching, Dora C. Y. "Visual Images of Zhu Yuanzhang." In *Long Live the Emperor: Uses of the Ming Founder Across Six Centuries of East Asian History*, ed. Sarah Schneewind. Ming Studies Research Series 4. Minneapolis: Society for Ming Studies, 2008, pp. 170–209.

Cui Wenyin 崔文印, Que'an 確庵 and Nai'an 耐庵, eds. *Jingkang bai shi jian zheng* 靖康稗史箋證. Beijing: Zhonghua shuju, 1988.

(Qinding) Da Qing huidian (欽定)大清會典. Reprinted—Beijing: Zhonghua shuju, 1991.

"Dazhaosi cang Yongle nianjian wenwu" 大照寺藏永樂年間文物. *Wenwu* 1985, no. 11: 66–71.

DMHD, see Shen Shixing et al., *Da Ming huidian*

Dpa'-bo Gtsup-lag 'phreng-ba. *Chos-'byung mkhas-pa'i dga'-ston*. New Delhi: International Academy of Indian Culture, 1982.

Ebrey, Patricia. "Portrait Sculptures in Imperial Ancestral Rites in Song China." *T'oung Pao* 83, no. 1–3 (1997): 42–92.

————. "The Ritual Context of Sung Imperial Portraiture." In *Arts of the Sung and Yüan: Ritual, Ethnicity, and Style in Painting*, ed. Cary Y. Liu and Dora C. Y. Ching. Princeton: The Art Museum, Princeton University, 1999, pp. 68–93.

Fang Jianchang 房建昌. "Xizang rulai dabao fawang kao" 西藏如來大寶法王考. *Zhongyang minzu xueyuan xuebao* 中央民族學院學報 5 (1991): 52–56.

Fong, Wen C. "Imperial Portraiture in the Song, Yuan, and Ming Periods." *Ars Orientalis* 25 (1995): 47–60.

Fong, Wen C., and James C. Y. Watt, eds. *Possessing the Past: Treasures from the National Palace Museum.* New York: The Metropolitan Museum of Art, 1996.

Forte, Antonino. *Political Propaganda and Ideology in China at the End of the Seventh Century.* Napoli: Istituto universitario orientale, Seminario di studi asiatici, 1976.

Franke, Herbert. "Two Yüan Treatises on the Technique of Portrait Painting." *Oriental Art* 3, no. 1 (1950): 27–32.

Fu Shen 傅申. *Yuandai huang shi shuhua shoucang shilüe* 元代皇室書畫收藏史略. Taibei: Guoli gugong bowuyuan, 1981.

Garrett, Valery M. *Chinese Clothing: An Illustrated Guide.* Hong Kong and New York: Oxford University Press, 1994.

Ge Yinliang 葛寅亮. "Jinling fanchazhi" 金陵梵刹志. In *Zhongguo fosi zhi* 中國佛寺志, 5: 1068–69. Reprinted—Taibei: Mingwen chubanshe, 1980.

Geiss, James. "The Chia-ching Reign, 1522–1566." In *CHC*, 7: 440–510.

Goodrich, L. Carrington, and Zhaoying Fang, eds. *Dictionary of Ming Biography, 1368–1644.* New York: Columbia University Press, 1976.

Gugong shuhua lu 故宮書畫錄. 4 vols. Taibei: Guoli gugong bowuyuan, 1956.

Ho, Wai-kam. "Developments of Chinese Portrait Painting as Seen from the Face-Orientation of the Subjects." In *Portraiture: International Symposium on Art Historical Studies 1987.* Kyoto: Kyoto University, 1990, pp. 131–36.

Hu Jing 胡敬 (1769–1845). "Nanxundian tuxiang kao" 南薰殿圖像考. Preface dated 1815. In *Hu Shi shuhuakao sanzhong* 胡氏書畫考三種. Facsimile reprint. Taibei: Hanhua chuban, 1971.

Huang Zhangjian 黃彰建, ed. *Mingdai lüli huibian* 明代律例彙編. Taibei: Zhongyang yanjiuyuan, Lishi yuyan yanjiusuo, 1994.

Ishida, Hou-mei Sung. "Early Ming Painters in Nanking and the Formation of the Wu School." *Ars Orientalis* 17 (1987): 73–115.

Jang, Scarlett Ju-yu. "Issues of Public Service in the Themes of Chinese Court Painting." Ph.D. diss., University of California at Berkeley, 1989.

Jiang Fucong (Chiang Fu-ts'ung) 蔣復璁. "Guoli gugong bowuyuan cang Qing Nanxundian tuxiangkao" 國立故宮博物院藏清南薰殿圖像考. *Gugong jikan* 故宮季刊 8, no. 4 (Summer 1974): 1–16.

Jin Weinuo 金維諾, ed. *Yonglegong bihua quanji* 永樂宮壁畫全集. Tianjin: Tianjin renmin meishu chubanshe, 1997.

Jing, Anning. "The Portraits of Khubilai Khan and Chabi by Anige (1245–1306), a Nepali Artist at the Yuan Court." *Artibus Asiae* 54, no. 1/2 (1994): 40–86.

Karmay, Heather. *Early Sino-Tibetan Art.* Warminster, Eng.: Aris and Phillips, 1975.

Li Guoan 李國安. "Mingmo xiaoxiang hua zhuangzuo de liangge shehuixing tezheng" 明末肖像畫裝作的兩個社會性特徵. *Yishu xue* 藝術學 6 (1991): 119–57.

Li Jinhua 李晉華. "Ming Chengzu shengmu wenti huizheng" 明成祖生母問題彙證. *Zhongyang yanjiuyuan, Lishi yuyan yanjiusuo jikan* 中央研究院歷史語言研究所集刊 6, no. 1 (Mar. 1936): 55–77.

Li Lincan (Li Lin-ts'an) 李霖燦. "Gugong bowuyuan de tuxianghua" 故宮博物院的圖像畫. *Gugong jikan* 故宮季刊 5, no. 1 (Fall 1970): 51–61.

Li Song 李松. "Beijing Fahai si" 北京法海寺. In *Zhongguo fojiao sita shi zhi* 中國佛教寺塔史志. Xiandai fojiao xueshu congkan 現代佛教學術叢刊. Taibei: Dasheng wenhua chubanshe, 1978, pp. 188–201.

Linggu chan lin zhi 靈古禪林志. Jiangsu: Jiangsu guangling guji keyinshe, 1988.

Liu Ruoyu 劉若愚 (1584–ca. 1642). *Zhuo zhong zhi* 酌中志. Ca. 1638. In Haishanxian guan congshu 海山仙館叢書. Taibei: Yiwen yinshuguan, 1967.

Lu Rong 陸容. *Shuyuan zaji* 菽園雜記. 1494. Beijing: Zhonghua shuju, 1985.

Matsuda Kōichi 松田孝一. "Mongoru teikoku ni okeru kōshō no kakuho to kanri no shosō" モンゴル帝国における工匠の確保と管理の諸相. In idem, *Hikokutō shiryō no sōgōteki bunseki ni yoru Mongoru teikoku Genchō no seiji keizai shisutemu no kisoteki kenkyū* 碑刻等史料の総合的分析によるモンゴル帝国・元朝の政治・経済システムの基礎的研究. Hirakata: Matsuda Kōichi (personal papers), 2002.

Mingren zhuanji ziliao suoyin 明人傳記資料索引. Ed. National Central Library 國立中央圖書館編. Taibei: Wenshizhe chubanshe, 1965, 1978.

Mingshi 明史. Ed. and comp. Zhang Tingyu 張廷玉 et al. Reprinted—Beijing: Zhonghua shuju, 1995.

Ming shilu 明實錄. Taibei: Zhongyang yanjiuyuan, Lishi yuyan yanjiusuo, 1966.

Mote, Frederick W., and Denis Twitchett, eds. *The Cambridge History of China*, vol. 7, *The Ming Dynasty, 1368–1644, Part I.* Cambridge: Cambridge University Press, 1988.

MS, see *Mingshi*

Mu Yiqin 穆益勤. "Mingdai de gongting huihua" 明代的宮廷繪畫. *Wenwu* 1981, no. 7: 70–75.

Otosaka Tomoko 乙坂智子. "Kaette kita shokumokujin—Mindai kōtei kenryoku to Pekin Juntenfu no Chibetto bukkyō" 歸ってきた色目人—明代皇帝權力と北京順天府のチベット佛教. *Yokohama shiritsu daigaku ronsō* 横浜市立大学論叢 51, no. 102 (2000): 247–82.

———. "A Study of Hong-Hua-Si Temple Regarding the Relationship Between the Dge-Lugs-Pa and the Ming Dynasty." In *Memoirs of the Research Department of the Toyo Bunko*, ed. Shiba Yoshinobu. Tokyo: Tōyō bunko, 1994, pp. 69–101.

———. "Tabi suru Peruden tashi—Mindai shinkō seisō yūrekitan" 旅するペルデンタシ—明代進貢西僧遊歷譚. In *Chūka sekai no rekishiteki tenkai* 中華世界の歷史的展開, ed. Noguchi Tetsurō Sensei koki kinen ronshū kankō iinkai 野口鐵郎先生古稀記念論集刊行委員会編. Tokyo: Kyūko shoin, 2002, pp. 267–87.

Ou Chaogui 歐朝貴. "Budalagong cang Ming Chengzu Zhu Di huaxiang" 布達拉宮藏明成祖朱棣畫像. *Wenwu* 1985, no. 10: 65.

Richardson, Hugh. "The Karma-Pa Sect (Part 2)." *Journal of the Royal Asiatic Society of Great Britain and Ireland*, Apr. 1959: 1–19.

Satō Hisashi 佐藤長. "Genmatsu Minsho no Chibetto jōsei" 元末明初のチベット状勢. In *Mindai Man-Mō shi kenkyū* 明代満蒙史研究, ed. Tamura Jitsuzō 田村實造. Kyoto: Kyōto daigaku, Bungakubu, 1963, pp. 485–585.

———. "Mindai Chibetto no hachi daikyōō ni tsuite" 明代チベットの八大教王について. 3 pts. *Tōyōshi kenkyū* 東京史研究 21, no. 2 (Sept. 1962): 51–70; 22, no. 2 (Oct. 1963): 79–101; 22, no. 4 (Mar. 1964): 74–89.

———. "Mindai Chibetto no Rigonpa-ha no keitō ni tsuite" 明代チベットのリゴンパ派の系統について. *Tōyō gakuhō* 東洋学報 45, no. 4 (Mar. 1963): 1–19.

————. "Mintei ni okeru Ramakyō sūhai ni tsuite" 明廷におけるラマ教崇拝に
ついて. In *Chūsei Chibetto shi kenkyū* 中世チベット史研究, ed. idem. Kyoto: Dōhōsha, 1986, pp. 287–320.

Seckel, Dietrich. "The Rise of Portraiture in Chinese Art." *Artibus Asiae* 53, no. 1/2
(1993): 7–26.

Sera Thekchen Ling (Sela dacheng zhou). Beijing: Minzu chubanshe, 1995.

Shan Guoqiang 單國強. "Xiaoxiang hua leixing chuyi" 肖像畫類型芻議. *Gugong jikan*
故宮季刊, no. 50 (Apr. 1990): 11–23.

Shen Shixing 申時行 et al., eds. and comps. *Da Ming huidian* 大明會典. 1587 Wanli ed.
Beijing: Zhonghua shuju, 1989.

Shiga Takayoshi 滋智高義. "Min no Seiso to Chibetto" 明の成祖と西藏. *Ōtani shigaku* 大谷史学 8 (1961): 44–57.

Shiqu baoji 石渠寶笈. Preface dated 1745. Ed. and comp. Zhang Zhao 張照 (1691–1745)
et al. Facsimile reprint. Taibei: Guoli gugong bowuyuan, 1971.

Shiqu baoji sanbian 石渠寶笈三編. Ed. and comp. Ying He 英和 (1771–1839), Hu Jing
胡敬, et al. Facsimile reprint. Taibei: Guoli gugong bowuyuan, 1971.

Shiqu baoji xubian 石渠寶笈續編. Preface dated 1793. Ed. and comp. Wang Jie 王杰
(1725–1805) et al. Facsimile reprint. Taibei: Guoli gugong bowuyuan, 1971.

Siggstedt, Mette. "Forms of Fate: An Investigation of the Relationship Between Formal
Portraiture, Especially Ancestral Portraits, and Physiognomy (*Xiangshu*) in China."
In *International Colloquium on Chinese Art History, 1991, Proceedings, Paintings and Calligra-
phy, Part 2*. Taibei: Guoli gugong bowuyuan, 1992, pp. 713–49.

Simcox, Jacqueline. "Early Chinese Embroideries." *Hali*, no. 43 (Jan. 1989): 26.

Sperling, Elliott. "Early Ming Policy Toward Tibet: An Examination of the Proposition
That the Early Ming Emperors Adopted a 'Divide and Rule' Policy Toward Tibet."
Ph.D. diss., Indiana University, 1983.

Stuart, Jan, and Evelyn Sakakida Rawski. *Worshiping the Ancestors: Chinese Commemorative
Portraits*. Washington, DC: Freer Gallery of Art and Arthur M. Sackler Gallery,
Smithsonian Institution; Stanford: Stanford University Press, 2001.

Sung, Hou-mei. "From the Min-Che Tradition to the Che School, Part II, Precursors of
the Che School: Hsieh Huan and Tai Chin." *Gugong jikan* 故宮季刊 7, no. 1 (Autumn 1989): 1–15.

Suo Yuming (So Yü-ming) 索予明. "Authenticity of the Portraiture of the Ming T'ai-
Tsu." *National Palace Museum Bulletin* 3, no. 5 (1968): 3–7.

————. "Ming Taizu huaxiang kao" 明太祖畫像考. *Gugong jikan* 故宮季刊 7, no. 3
(Spring 1973): 61–75.

————. "Ming Taizu huaxiang zhenweibian" 明太祖畫像眞偽辨. *Dalu zazhi* 大陸雜
誌 38, no. 6 (Mar. 1969): 203–6.

————. "A Study of the Portraits of the Ming Emperor T'ai-Tsu." *National Palace Museum Quarterly* 7, no. 3 (Spring 1973): 61–75.

Tan Qian 談遷 (1594–1657). "Beiyou lu" 北游錄. In *Guoque; fu, Beiyou lu* 國榷; 附, 北游
錄. Taibei: Dingwen shuju, 1978.

————. "Yixiang" 疑像. Preface by Gao Hongtu 高弘圖, dated 1644, but text completed after 1644. In *Biji xiaoshuo daguan* 筆記小説大觀. Taibei: Xinxing shuju, 1962,
2.1606b.

Wang, Cheng-hua. "Material Culture and Emperorship: The Shaping of Imperial Roles at the Court of Xuanzong (r. 1426–35)." Ph.D. diss., Yale University, 1998.

Wang Shidian 王士點 (14th c.). *Mishujianzhi* 秘書監志. In Wenyuange Siku quanshu, vol. 596, 5.11–12, p. 801.

Wang Yi 王繹. "Xiexiang mijue" 寫像秘訣. In *Chuo geng lu* 輟耕錄, ed. Tao Zongyi 陶宗儀 (14th c.). Beijing: Zhonghua shuju, 1959, 11.163.

Watt, James C. Y., and Denise Patry Leidy. *Defining Yongle: Imperial Art in Early Fifteenth Century China*. New York: The Metropolitan Museum of Art; New Haven: Yale University Press, 2005.

Weidner, Marsha Smith. "Buddhist Pictorial Art in the Ming Dynasty (1368–1644): Patronage, Regionalism, and Interactions." In *Latter Days of the Law: Images of Chinese Buddhism 850–1850*, ed. Marsha Smith Weidner. Lawrence: Spencer Museum of Art, University of Kansas; Honolulu: University of Hawai'i Press, 1994, pp. 51–87.

————. "Imperial Engagements with Buddhist Art and Architecture: Ming Variations on an Old Theme." In idem, *Cultural Intersections in Later Chinese Buddhism*. Honolulu: University of Hawai'i Press, 2001, pp. 117–44.

————. "Painting and Patronage at the Mongol Court of China, 1260–1368." Ph.D. diss., University of California at Berkeley, 1982.

Weidner, Marsha Smith, ed. *Latter Days of the Law: Images of Chinese Buddhism, 850–1850*. 1st ed. Lawrence: Spencer Museum of Art, University of Kansas; Honolulu: University of Hawai'i Press, 1994.

Wen Zhu 文竹. "Xizang difang Ming feng bawang de youguan wenwu" 西藏地方明封八王的有關文物. *Wenwu*, 1985, no. 9: 78, 89–94.

Wu Han 吳晗. "Ming Chengzu shengmu kao" 明成祖生母考. *Qinghua xuebao* 清華學報 10, no. 3 (1935): 631–46.

Wu Hung. "What Is Bianxiang?—On the Relationship Between Dunhuang Art and Dunhuang Literature." *Harvard Journal of Asiatic Studies* 42, no. 1 (June 1992): 111–92.

Wylie, Turrell V. "Lama Tribute in the Ming Dynasty." In *Tibetan Studies in Honour of Hugh Richardson*, ed. Michael Aris and Aung San Suu Kyi. Warminster, Eng.: Aris and Phillips, 1980, pp. 335–40.

Xizang wenwu jingcui 西藏文物精粹. Di 1 ban. Ed. Xizang zizhiqu wenwu guanli weiyuan hui 西藏自治區文物管理委員會. Beijing: Gugong bowuyuan Zijincheng chubanshe, 1992.

Xizang zizhiqu wenwu guanli weiyuanhui 西藏自治區文物管理委員會. "Mingchao huangdi ci gei Xizang Chubusi Gama huofo de liang jian zhao shu" 明朝皇帝賜給西藏楚布寺噶瑪活佛的兩件詔書. *Wenwu* 1981, no. 11: 42–44.

Xu Mengxin 徐夢莘 (1124–1205). *Sanchao Bei meng huibian* 三朝北盟彙編. In Wenyuange Siku quanshu, vol. 350. Taibei: Taiwan shangwu yinshuguan, 1983–86, *juan* 97.6–14, pp. 750–54.

Xu Qin 徐沁. *Ming hua lu* 明畫錄. In *Huashi congshu* 畫史叢書, comp. Yu Haiyan 于海晏. Taibei: Wenshizhe chubanshe, 1974.

Yang Boxian 楊博賢, ed. *Beijing Fahaisi* 北京法海寺. Beijing: Huatian lüyou guoji guanggao gongsi, 1994.

Yu Minzhong 于敏中. (*Qinding*) *Rixia jiuwenkao* (欽定)日下舊聞考. Beijing: Guji chubanshe, 1981.
Yuandai huasu ji 元代畫塑記. Beijing: Renmin meishu chubanshe, 1964.
Zhou Xibao 周錫保. *Zhongguo gudai fushi shi* 中國古代服飾史. Di 1 ban. Beijing: Zhongguo xiju chubanshe and Xinhua shudian, Beijing faxingsuo, 1984.

EIGHT

The Ming Court and the Legacy of the Yuan Mongols

David M. Robinson

When the Mongol empire collapsed in the fourteenth century after roughly 150 years of hegemony in Eurasia (circa 1200–1350), it bequeathed a complex legacy of political institutions, global trade networks, and notions of rulership. The way each of its successor polities dealt with this legacy reveals much about the particular polity and about Eurasia as a whole. This chapter examines how the Ming imperial family dealt with the Mongol Yuan legacy.

The Mongols created the greatest land empire known to Asia. Although established at a steep price in death and destruction, each of the *ulus*es, or khanates, that constituted the greater empire eventually wrung acknowledgment from local peoples that it was a legitimate dynasty or polity.

The present chapter adumbrates points that are developed and documented in greater detail in a full-length study tentatively entitled *The Ming Court in Eurasia*. I am grateful to Fuma Susumu and Sugiyama Masaaki of Kyoto University for the opportunity to present a version of this essay at the International Order and Exchange in East Asia, Second International Symposium. In addition to acknowledging my great debt for the many fruitful observations offered by the participants of the Ming Court Culture conference, I would also like to thank the following people for reading and commenting on earlier versions of this essay: Thomas Allsen, Christopher Atwood, Craig Clunas, Johan Elverskog, Shen Weirong, Gray Tuttle, and the two anonymous readers for the press. Their suggestions, corrections, and bibliographic help have saved me from many embarrassing mistakes. The credit for all remaining gaffs and blunders is entirely my own.

Scholars debate the overall impact of Mongol rule on the living conditions of people throughout Eurasia. None, however, contests that the Mongol courts of Dadu, Shangdu, Sultaniyya, and Saray were renowned throughout the world as centers of wealth, learning, power, religion, and lavish spectacle.[1] The Mongols established standards by which future rulers in Eurasia would measure themselves. This was especially true during the turbulent decades following the collapse of the Mongol empire. Whatever other indigenous traditions rulers exploited for legitimacy and power, the Mongols and their legacy represented a critical source of political capital for ambitious dynasties across Eurasia. No one who aspired to power at home or on the greater stage of Eurasia could ignore that repository of imperial glory.

During the latter half of the fourteenth century, perhaps the most influential Mongol successor in Eurasia was Temür (d. 1405; better known in the West as Tamerlane), who confronted the limitations and advantages of the Mongol legacy as he strove to conquer Central Asia and much of the Middle East. As Beatrice Forbes Manz has observed, "The achievements of the Chinggisid dynasty had given it a unique charisma, and according to the traditions of the Mongol empire accepted throughout Temür's dominions, only Chinghis Qan's descendents could adopt the title of Qan and aspire to sovereign power." Temür then "adopted the pose of the Chinggisid line, installing a puppet khan and ruling in his name. He further acquired the title of royal son-in-law, *güregen*, by virtue of his marriage to a princess of the Chinggisid line."[2] As Manz points out elsewhere, by representing himself as a defender of the rights of the Mongol ruling houses, Temür thus lay "claim potentially to the whole of the former Mongol empire.[3]

The early Ottoman and Rus empires also sought to gain legitimacy and charisma from association with the Mongol empire. Charles Halperin has noted that although Muscovy's variety of Christian rhetoric did not allow open acknowledgment of the legitimacy of infidel Mongol rule, the court nevertheless "foster[ed] its image as the successor state to the Golden

---

1. For descriptions of culture at the Ilkhanate courts, see Komaroff and Carboni, *The Legacy of Genghis Khan*. For the Mongol capitals during the Yuan, see Ye Xinmin, *Yuan Shangdu yanjiu*; Shi Weimin, *Dushizhong de youmumin*; and Chen Gaohua, *Yuan Dadu*. On Sarai, see Halperin, *Russia and the Golden Horde*, p. 123.

2. Manz, *Rise and Rule of Tamerlane*, p. 14.

3. Manz, "Temür and the Problem of a Conqueror's Legacy," p. 25.

Horde and . . . remain[ed] sensitive to steppe traditions of rule."[4] Michael Khodarkovsky similarly argues, "Throughout the sixteenth century, the assumption that Moscow was one of the successors of the Golden Horde served both to justify its expansion southward and eastward and to legitimate its conquests. . . . Moscow derived its legitimacy simultaneously from . . . the Christian tradition of Byzantium and the secular tradition of the Golden Horde."[5] According to Manz, "Even regions which had not been within the Mongol empire were engaged with the Mongol legacy. The Dehli Sultans, the Ottomans, the Mamluks, and the Turkmen dynasties of western Iran were conscious of their origins in the steppe and formulated their genealogical and political claims with an eye to Mongol traditions."[6]

How did the fledging Ming dynasty view the Mongols' powerful legacy? An oft-repeated passage that appeared with slight variation in many Ming- and Qing-period documents would suggest a clear rejection of the Mongols. "The Grand Progenitor [the Hongwu emperor] drove off the barbarian caitiffs and restored the Central Florescence."[7] Indeed, in scores of edicts and laws, the Ming founder stressed his commitment to purifying the realm of the Mongols' polluting influence.[8] His subjects were no longer to speak Mongolian, wear Mongolian hats or gowns, follow Mongol marriage or burial practices, or play Mongolian tunes.[9] The founder declared his intention to

---

4. Halperin, *Russia and the Golden Horde*, pp. 100–102; quotation appears on p. 100. Halperin further observes, "Through the seventeenth century Moscow continued to play upon its tentative status as the Horde's successor in dealing with Inner Asian peoples, and, less often, European powers" (p. 102). See also Ostrowski, *Muscovy and the Mongols*, pp. 177–88.

5. M. Khodarkovsky, *Russia's Steppe Frontier: The Making of a Colonial Empire, 1500– 1800* (Bloomington: Indiana University Press, 2002), p. 222; cited in Gammer, "Russia and the Eurasian Steppe Nomads," p. 492.

6. Manz ("Temür and the Problem of a Conqueror's Legacy," p. 22) continues, "The influence of the steppe in the Middle East was not limited to the abstract. Miniatures and album illustrations show nomads living in the felt yurts of the steppe and wearing a wide variety of clothing and headgear. Along with the turban and the robe, we find feathers, felt, and skins."

7. For an early articulation, see *Taizu shilu* (hereafter cited as *TZSL*), 26.10b.

8. Farmer, *Zhu Yuanzhang and Early Ming Legislation*; Gao Shouxian, "Hongwu shiqi de shehui jiaoyu yu yifeng yisu." As Gao (p. 90) notes, Zhu Yuanzhang blamed many abuses, not just deviations from Chinese ideals, on the Yuan.

9. For reference to the Yuan's "complete abolition of ancient music" and the "mutual distortion of the sounds of the barbarian caitiff and the pure music [of the Central Plains]," see *TZSL*, 66.6a. For early Ming prohibitions against various Mongol customs,

restore the past glories of true Chinese custom and the political institutions of the Han (206 BCE–220 CE) and Tang (618–907). In an apparent rejection of the Mongols' renowned expansionism and active encouragement of foreign trade, Hongwu explicitly instructed his descendents to restrict incursions into neighboring states and limited private trade and contact.

As many studies have shown, this strand of rhetoric and policy did not comprehend the full complexity of the early Ming court's attitudes toward the Yuan legacy.[10] With often only minor changes, Hongwu adopted major aspects of the Yuan institutional apparatus, including the hereditary garrison system and the hereditary occupation system in general.[11] He attempted to absorb areas conquered by the Mongols but not previously under Chinese control, such as Yunnan, Liaodong, and even parts of Mongolia.[12] In many edicts, he fully acknowledged the legitimacy of the Great Yuan *ulus*.[13] He recruited Mongol military personnel into his government and armies and sought to continue Yuan practices that brought Korean women and eunuchs into the imperial household. Thus, the Ming dynasty was in many ways a true successor to the Great Yuan *ulus*.[14] In addition to using Confucian, Buddhist, Daoist, and other native traditions, Hongwu wished to exploit the powerful Yuan legacy to legitimate his rule within Ming territories and throughout Eurasia.

---

see Serruys, "Remains of Mongol Customs," pp. 148–90; and Gao Shouxian, "Hongwu shiqi de shehui jiaoyu yu yifeng yisu," pp. 89–90.

10. For concise analysis, see Miyazaki Ichisada, "Kōbu kara Eiraku e," pp. 19–20. As Wu Han noted more than half a century ago, not until the very end of his rise to power as a rebel did Zhu Yuanzhang attempt to discredit Mongol rule on the basis of "the Sinic-barbarian divide," a rhetorical strain that would appear more frequently after he became emperor; see Wu Han, *Zhu Yuanzhang zhuan*, pp. 94–99; and idem, *Mingshi jianshu*, pp. 22–24.

11. Serruys, "Remains of Mongol Customs," pp. 143–48. On the Mongol origins of the Ming hereditary military household system, see Taylor, "Yuan Origins of the Wei-so System." Serruys also notes the continued existence of the Mongol Hanlin Academy and the Muslim Bureau of Astronomy.

12. Okada Hidehiro ("China as a Successor State to the Mongols," p. 264) makes this point explicitly. For an overview of Ming military campaigns against the Mongols in the years immediately following the dynasty's establishment, see Dreyer, "Military Origins of Ming China," 7: 98–103. See also Langlois, "The Hung-wu Reign."

13. Langlois, "Introduction," pp. 14–15; Dardess, "Ming T'ai-tsu on the Yuan." On the lack of enmity toward the Mongol regime in the collected works of leading early Ming ministers, see Qian Mu, "Du Mingchu kaiguo zhuchen shiwen ji."

14. For a cogent summary of Yuan influence on Zhu Yuanzhang and his policies, see Danjō Hiroshi, "Shoki Min teikoku taiseiron."

This acute consciousness of the Yuan legacy owed much to the fact that the Great Yuan *ulus* did not simply disappear in 1368. A powerful threat to the fledgling Ming dynasty, it controlled an enormous expanse of territory north and west of China and maintained diplomatic relations with polities from the Korean Koryŏ dynasty to Tamerlane's regime in Central Asia. Japanese scholar Sugiyama Masaaki has provocatively termed the relationship between the Yuan and Ming the "northern and southern dynasties" to highlight the military, political, and ideological competition between the two polities.[15]

The Ming founder's son and third ruler, Yongle (r. 1403–24), identified even more closely with the Mongol legacy. In his classic essay "From Hongwu to Yongle," the eminent Japanese scholar Miyazaki Ichisada argued that Yongle conceived of himself as a "successor to Khubilai," who envisioned "a China not only of the Chinese but a China as the center of an East Asian community . . . in other words, [as] the revival of the Yuan empire."[16] Edward Dreyer has commented that "Yongle attempted to live up to both the Chinese and the Mongol versions of the imperial

---

15. Sugiyama Masaaki, *Mongoru teikoku no kōbō*, 2: 223–24. Sugiyama provides a thought-provoking map of the "northern and southern dynasties" on p. 224. Debates at the Koryŏ court over ties with the Ming and Yuan illustrate the Yuan's continuing political prestige in East Asia. For recent scholarship, see Kim Tangtaek, "Koryŏ Uwang wŏnnyŏn 1375 nyŏn Wŏnkwa ŭi oegyo kwan'gye chaegae"; and To Hyŏnjŏl, "Koryŏ malgi sadaebu ŭi taeoegwan." When viewed in the greater context of Eurasia, it is difficult to accept without qualification Henry Tsai's (*Perpetual Happiness*, p. 149) statement that "after Toyon Temur, the last Yuan emperor, fled Beijing in 1368, the Mongol khan was considered to have lost his mandate to rule." The Yuan court continued to use the dynastic title of Great Yuan until at least 1388. As late as the mid-fifteenth century, the Oirat leader Esen evoked the Yuan legacy, calling himself Khan of the Great Yuan; see Cai Meibiao, "Mingdai Menggu yu Da Yuan guohao," pp. 47–49. Cai argues that the Yuan legacy was so firmly impressed in the minds of Ming officials that Chinese interpreters' mistranslation of Dayan Khan (1464–1532) as Khan of the Great Yuan (Ch. Da Yuan han 大元汗) was widely accepted. Dayan Khan's name was Batu Möngke. Roy Andrew Miller (Goodrich and Fang, *Dictionary of Ming Biography*, pp. 17–20), in contrast, writes that "his royal style, Dayan-qayan, is a loanword version of the Chinese *ta-yüan* 大元." In either case, memories of the Mongol empire remained powerful.

16. Miyazaki Ichisada, "Kōbu kara Eiraku e," pp. 19–20. Terada Takanobu, too, paints Yongle as "a successor to Khubilai," who strove to "succeed to and reproduce the scale of the Yuan dynasty that had unified rule over Mongolia and China"; see Otagi Matsuo and Terada Takanobu, *Mongoru to Dai Min teikoku*, pp. 314–15. Morris Rossabi ("The Ming and Inner Asia," 8: 229) also notes similarities between Yongle's policies and those of "Yuan dynasty models."

ideal."[17] Most discussions of Yongle's links with the Yuan have focused on the emperor's intense interest in foreign relations and an expansionistic military. This chapter examines the Ming imperial family's relation to the legacy of Khubilai as *khaghan*, khan of khans.

The Ming emperor's identity as *khaghan* has been obscured in large part because of the nature of the documentary record available to us today, much of which was compiled by a civil bureaucracy whose interests, views, and self-perceptions often diverged significantly from those of the imperial family. To offset these biases, a variety of both documentary and non-documentary sources has proven useful. The following sections explore the imperial family's associations with the Great Yuan *ulus* through its patronage of Tibetan Buddhism, court portraiture, Korean palace women and eunuchs within the Forbidden City, Mongol military personnel in the capital, funerary figurines from princely tombs, and porcelains with foreign inscriptions. The chapter concludes with a brief reconsideration of the early sixteenth-century emperor Zhengde (r. 1506–21) as a universal ruler and suggests that his death without an heir in 1521 (which brought a cousin raised far from the capital to the throne) weakened the Zhu imperial family's links with Khubilai and the Mongols and marked an important shift in the orientation of the Ming court.

A few final prefatory remarks. First, not all instances of continuity between the Yuan and the Ming courts represent efforts by the Zhu family to foster an association with Khubilai and his descendents. The retention of certain practices and institutions sometimes occurred by default: an acceptance, on occasion unexamined, of existing systems. In other cases, Hongwu and his successors felt it their right to succeed to the Mongols' position and status in East Asia. Second, as many fine studies have demonstrated, the Ming emperors drew on the state religion as well as Confucian, Buddhist, Daoist, and other native traditions in their efforts to secure legitimacy, power, and personal fulfillment. The particular features of Ming

---

17. Dreyer, *Early Ming China: A Political History*, pp. 173–74. Dreyer (pp. 173–74) further observes, "Yongle's reign recalls Khubilai's in its outstanding events: the conquest of the south, the establishment of the capital at Peking, the opening of relations with Japan, an ultimately abortive attempt to conquer Vietnam, and naval expeditions to Southeast Asian and the Indian Ocean." For Dreyer, the Mongol and Chinese ideals led to "hopeless contradictions" and "two different sets of institutions," which often were at loggerheads (p. 174)—the civil bureaucracy and an establishment of eunuchs and military officers. As will become clear below, the fault line was as much the authority of the imperial family versus that of its various competitors as civil versus military.

Fig. 8.1 Shang Xi 商喜. *The Xuande Emperor's Pleasures* 宣宗行樂圖. Fifteenth century, ink and color on silk, 221 × 353 cm. Palace Museum, Beijing.

Fig. 8.2 Anonymous. *The Xuande Emperor Hunting with Bow.* 宣宗射獵圖. Fifteenth century, ink and color on silk, 29.5 × 34.6 cm. Palace Museum, Beijing.

Fig. 8.3 Anonymous. *The Xuande Emperor on a Riding Excursion* 獵騎圖. Fifteenth century. Formerly attributed to thirteenth century, ink and color on silk, 39.4 × 60.1 cm. National Palace Museum, Taipei, Taiwan, Republic of China.

Fig. 8.4 Anonymous. Formerly attributed to Liu Guandao 劉貫道. *Khubilai on the Hunt* 元世祖
出獵圖. Fifteenth century. Formerly attributed to thirteenth century, ink and color on silk,
hanging scroll, 182.9 × 104.1 cm. National Palace Museum, Taipei, Taiwan, Republic of China.

Fig. 8.5   Anonymous. *Traveling Rider* 遊騎圖. Yuan dynasty. 178.8 × 121 cm. National Palace Museum, Taipei, Taiwan, Republic of China.

Fig. 8.6 Attributed to Zhou Quan 周全. *Hunting Pheasants with Bow* 射雉圖. Late fifteenth or early sixteenth century, hanging scroll, ink and color on silk, 137 × 117 cm. National Palace Museum, Taipei, Taiwan, Republic of China.

Fig. 8.7 Anonymous. Polo Scene. *The Chenghua Emperor's Pleasures*. Alternately titled *The Xuande Emperor's Pleasures*. Fifteenth century, scroll, 37 × 624 cm. Palace Museum, Beijing.

Fig. 8.8 Anonymous. *Emperor's Return to the Capital* 入蹕圖. Sixteenth century, scroll, 92.1 × 3000;6 cm. Portion. National Palace Museum, Taipei, Taiwan, Republic of China.

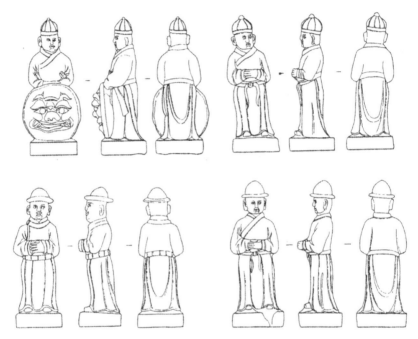

Fig. 8.9 Honor guard figurines from Shu Xiwang Prince's tomb. Fifteenth century. Chengdu Municipal Institute of Relics Preservation and Archeology.

court culture examined in this chapter were chosen because they illustrate the sustained influence of the Mongols, not because they represent the entirety of imperial court culture. The association with Khubilai and the Mongol empire was but one facet among many other, more familiar aspects of Ming imperial identity. Finally, as the chapters in this volume demonstrate, the tone and dynamics of each reign varied considerably. There was no monolithic Ming imperial style. Even during the first half of the dynasty, the importance and understanding of the Mongol legacy varied according to the particular circumstances of individual emperors, court dynamics, and developments on the steppe.[18]

Tibetan Buddhism at the Ming Court

Lavish patronage of Tibetan Buddhism formed an important facet of the Ming imperial family's identity as successors to the Mongol *khaghan*s. Hand in hand with the extension of Mongol influence into the kingdoms of Xixia and Tibet during the thirteenth century went the growing presence of Tibetan Buddhism in the Mongol court of Dadu and from there into other parts of the Mongol imperium.[19] The Tibetan polymath 'Phags pa (1235–80) created an identification between Chinggis (and Khubilai) and the *cakravartin*, the universal wheel-turning king.[20] 'Phags pa also proved critical in introducing Tibetan Buddhist court rituals to the Mongols. Following his lead, on the fifteenth day of the second month, Dadu saw lavish processions to exorcise demons and other forms of pollution. Rituals and parades also marked the first and sixth lunar months. As Morris Rossabi has noted, "For the 'Phags pa lama, these ceremonies were meant to compete with or offer an alternative to the Confucian court ceremonies; for Khubilai, they complemented but did not supplant the Confucian rituals."[21] We glean some sense of Yuan largesse from the amount of food allotted for Buddhist

---

18. These questions are considered more fully in my *The Ming Court in Eurasia*.

19. On the impact of the Xixia on the Mongols' contact with Tibetan Buddhism, see Xiong Wenbin, *Yuandai Zang Han yishu jiaoliu*, pp. 27–30. On the impact of Tibetan Buddhism on contemporaneous Japan, see Sugiyama Masaaki, *Dai Mongoru no jidai*, p. 273. On the brief Mongol patronage of Tibetan Buddhism in Persia, see Morgan, *The Mongols*, p. 58. On evidence of Tibetan Buddhism in Koryŏ, see Chŏn Chongsŏk, "Kōrai bukkyō to Gendai ramakyō to no kankei." See also Sørensen, "Lamaism in Korea During the Late Koryŏ Dynasty."

20. Franke, "From Tribal Chieftain to Universal Emperor and God," pp. 54–69; Ishihama Yumiko, *Chibetto bukkyō sekai no rekishiteki kenkyū*, pp. 1–44.

21. Rossabi, *Khubilai Khan*, p. 145.

activities within the Imperial Palace for the single year of 1317: 439,500 *jin* (one *jin* was equivalent to slightly more than one pound) of flour, 79,000 *jin* of oil, 21,870 *jin* of butter, and 27,300 *jin* of honey.[22] The presence of Tibetan Buddhist monks at the Yuan court was sufficiently prominent that even West European observers noticed; Marco Polo's *Travels* mentions the monks' ability to perform such miracles as controlling the weather and levitating objects.[23]

Born and raised in southern central China and eager to establish proper credentials as a Confucian ruler, the first Ming emperor nevertheless saw Tibetan Buddhist clerics as religiously efficacious and diplomatically useful. Although more familiar and more concerned with homegrown varieties of Buddhism,[24] Hongwu evinced interest in ceremonies and rites conducted by leading Tibetan clerics. At the same time, the Ming founder drew on Tibetan Buddhist clerics, cultural artifacts, and sutras in an effort to establish Ming influence in Tibet.[25] He invested various Tibetan clerics with official titles, granted them imperial audiences, and provided access to the Chinese economy in exchange for nominal acknowledgment of the Ming's privileged diplomatic position within Asia. Here the Ming founder was likely attempting to follow Yuan policies in his relations with Tibet.[26]

Yongle's motives for his lavish patronage of Tibetan monks were perhaps even more complex. There is no reason to doubt his sincere faith in Tibetan Buddhism or his veneration of Tibetan Buddhist hierarchs. At one level, Yongle, like the Ming founder, saw support for Tibetan Buddhism as a useful medium for pursuing political and economic relations with Tibet.[27] Tibetan envoys regularly traveled to the Ming capitals, sojourned in the

---

22. Qiu Shusen, *Yuanchao jianshi*, p. 457.

23. See Otosaka Tomoko, "Make Boluo zhuzuozhong suo miaoshu de Zangchuan fojiao."

24. Chen Gaohua, "Zhu Yuanzhang de fojiao zhengce"; Yang Qiqiao, *Ming Qing shi jueao*, pp. 5–21.

25. Much early scholarship downplays Zhu Yuanzhang's religious engagement with Tibetan Buddhism. See, e.g., Suzuki Masashi, "Mindai teishitsu zaisei to bukkyō," p. 1336; and Ryūchi Kiyoshi, "Mindai Pekin ni okeru ramakyōdan," p. 67. Shiga Takayoshi ("Min no Seiso to Chibetto") also consistently stresses political motives over religious faith in his discussion of Hongwu and Yongle.

26. The policies were clearly not identical. Neither were the relations that obtained between the Ming and Yuan thrones with the Tibetan region. For brief comments on some of the major differences, see Wylie, "Lama Tribute in the Ming Dynasty," pp. 335–40.

27. Sperling, "Early Ming Policy Toward Tibet," pp. 155–243.

government-run hostel for the dynasty's foreign guests, and received imperial support and gifts during their stay. Yongle also periodically dispatched
Tibetans staying in Beijing as his envoys to their native lands. For the next
century, Ming emperors would continue all these practices.

Yongle also cultivated ties with Tibetan Buddhism as a way to establish
a direct association between himself and Khubilai. Both were men who
founded new polities, and both chose Beijing as the site of their new regimes. As a young prince, Yongle made extensive use of the former palaces
of the Great Yuan *ulus*, palaces constructed by Khubilai little more than a
century before as a way to link the steppe with the sown.[28] Once emperor,
Yongle would establish his capital on nearly exactly the same site as the
former Yuan Dadu. During his decades in Beijing, Yongle came into regular contact with many who had served at the Yuan court or in Mongol armies. Yongle was not, as is often argued, chosen to garrison the former
Yuan capital because he enjoyed the special favor of his father.[29] However,
the physical space and the continuity in personnel between his princely
establishment and the Dadu palaces exercised a profound influence on
Yongle's ambitions and attitudes. Contemporary Ming and Chosŏn observers regularly linked the prince's ambitions with his investiture in the
former Yuan capital.[30]

In 1407, Yongle invited the Fifth Karma pa, De bzhin gshegs pa (often
referred to as Helima or Halima 哈立麻 in Chinese sources), to Nanjing to
officiate over a large-scale ceremony of universal salvation in the memory
of his father, the Ming founder, and his putative mother, Empress Ma.[31]
The Karma pa had been reincarnated in the same Kagyu order that had enjoyed close ties to successive Mongol courts during the Yuan period.
Yongle commissioned a lavish fifty-meter-long silk handscroll in forty-nine
separate sections that represented in vivid detail the many miraculous
manifestations associated with the Fifth Karma pa's visit.[32] Art historian
Patricia Berger has argued that Yongle lavished such resources on inviting
the Karma pa and creating a pictorial and pentaglottal account to provide
"spiritual verification of his very muddy claims to the throne he had

---

28. Aramiya Manabu, "Minsho no En'ōfu o meguru shomondai," pp. 83, 88–92.

29. Ibid., pp. 87–88.

30. Ibid., pp. 81–83.

31. Sperling, "Early Ming Policy Toward Tibet," pp. 74–99. For a biography of the
Fifth Karma pa, see Fang Jianchang, "Xizang Rulai dabao fawang kao."

32. Berger, "Miracles in Nanjing," pp. 145, 149.

usurped in 1401 from his nephew, the ill-fated Zhu Yunwen."[33] Rumors swirled that Yongle was the product of a liaison between his father and a Korean or Mongol consort. Even more scandalous for some was the tale that he was actually the son of the last Yuan emperor to rule the Central Plains. Thus, argues Berger, Yongle felt it imperative to demonstrate his filial piety through a massive public mass for universal salvation.

When viewed from a wider Eurasian perspective, a number of additional questions arise. Why did Yongle appeal to the Fifth Karma pa rather than to an eminent Chinese Buddhist cleric?[34] During the early years of his reign, Hongwu had also commissioned large-scale Buddhist services in Nanjing. In 1372 as many as a thousand monks participated in a two-week series of ceremonies: the founder personally attended the opening and closing events.[35] Hongwu clearly wished to use Buddhism for his own purposes. He, however, felt content with Chinese monks. Moreover, why did his son Yongle order textual descriptions to accompany the painting in Chinese, Persian, Tibetan, Mongolian, and an as yet unidentified language?[36] Yongle was apparently invoking the Mongol Yuan legacy and speaking to a larger audience beyond the Ming state. During Yongle's reign, echoes of this legacy were still audible. In a 1420 report of a trip to Yongle's court in Beijing, a Timurid envoy referred to Yongle as the Dayming khan (the khan of the Great Ming) and called Beijing the Khan balïq, the "Khan's City," a Turkic designation for Beijing during the Mongol period that also appears in Rashid al-Din's early fourteenth-century *Compendium of Chronicles*.[37]

---

33. Ibid., p. 149.

34. Yang Qiqiao (*Ming Qingshi jueao*, p. 31) suggests that Yongle's patronage of Tibetan Buddhism followed Yuan precedents. He further holds that Yongle was motivated by the desire to bolster his position in the western border regions where Tibetan Buddhism enjoyed extensive support and by the emperor's sincere faith in Tibetan Buddhism.

35. Chen Gaohua, "Zhu Yuanzhang de fojiao zhengce," p. 112.

36. Berger ("Miracles in Nanjing," p. 162) concludes that these inscriptions "serve an orderly, bureaucratic, and thoroughly Chinese purpose—the sustenance and legitimation of imperial power." Scholars have suggested the fifth language may be Sanskrit, Uighur, Chagatai, or, most recently, Burmese. For a brief overview and a translation of the first few lines of the Mongolian text, see Matsukawa Takeshi, "Chibetto jichiku hakubutsukan zō gogengo gappeki."

37. Ghiyathuddin Naqqash, "Report to Mirza Baysunghur," pp. 287, 291; Rashid al-Din, *Compendium of Chronicles*, pp. 440–41, 444–45.

Yongle's invocation of Khubilai's legacy, in this case by serving as a generous patron of Tibetan Buddhism, was part of his efforts to bolster his position as a legitimate ruler who would usher in dynastic unity and strength. Tibetan annals note far more explicitly than do the Chinese records the parallels between the policies proposed by Yongle and those of Khubilai khan. Yongle offered the Fifth Karma pa a relation similar to that obtaining between Khubilai and 'Phags pa—extensive administrative and religious authority within Tibet for the cleric in exchange for acknowledgment of Ming paramountcy. Although the Fifth Karma pa declined Yongle's offer, the historical precedent was clear to both the Tibetans and the Ming court.[38] Similarly, during at least one state banquet, Yongle yielded to the Fifth Karmapa a seat superior to his own—evoking the religious student-teacher relationship between Khubilai and 'Phags pa.[39]

The Mongols, and later the Qing, routinely issued multilingual proclamations to enhance their image as universal rulers. Yongle was trying to establish a similar reputation. In Tibetan versions of his invitation to a leading Tibetan cleric, Kun dga' bkra shis, Yongle referred to himself as "the *balacakravartin*, the Great Ming emperor." As Elliott Sperling has noted, this would suggest that the emperor was laying claim to being a consecrated Buddhist sovereign, a fully justifiable claim given his religious initiation by the Fifth Karma pa.[40] Emperor as universal ruler through Tibetan initiation was a familiar practice to the contemporary Tibetan political and religious audience. One suspects that the image was equally recognizable to Mongols, Uighurs, and others of the day. Especially noteworthy is the fact that Yongle received from Kun dga' bkra shis religious instruction involving Mahākāla and Hevajra, important tutelary deities of the Sa skya and central to the consecrations that had transformed Khubilai into a *cakravartin*.[41]

Yongle's acts were open to different interpretations in different quarters. Yet the grandeur of Yongle's vision of rulership must have been clear

---

38. Sperling, "Early Ming Policy Toward Tibet," pp. 89–94.

39. Fang Jianchang, "Xizang Rulai dabao fawang kao," p. 53.

40. Sperling, "Early Ming Policy Toward Tibet," p. 140; He Xiaorong, "Mingdai huangdi chongfeng Zangchuan fojiao qianxi," p. 121. According to the account in Kun dga' bsod nams grags pa rgyal mtshan's *Sa skya'i gdun rabs* (composed in 1629), Yongle requested to be initiated into various esoteric rites, including those of Hevajra. For a Chinese translation, see Chen Yingqing et al., *Sajia shixishi*, p. 225.

41. Franke, "From Tribal Chieftain to Universal Emperor and God," pp. 59–60; Sperling, "Early Ming Policy Toward Tibet," p. 142.

to members of the Ming court. It neither stopped at the borders of Ming territory nor was limited to a Ming audience.[42] He actively sought distinguished Tibetan clerics to conduct religious ceremonies for his parents, himself, and his dynasty within the imperial palace and imperially constructed temples in the capitals. He posed as a successor to Khubilai and the Yuan emperors through his dual patron and disciple relationships with leading Tibetan monks. Finally, he performed this role on an international stage. In addition to the multilingual account of the Karma pa's visit noted above, in 1407 Yongle also promulgated an edict protecting Muslim clerics within his empire written in classical Chinese, Persian, and Mongolian.[43] In 1431, the Ming court produced a "collection of *dhāraṇī* in Sanskrit, Chinese, Tibetan, and Mongolian."[44] More famously, stele accounts commemorating Ming expansion under Yongle (such as expeditions to Southeast Asia, the African coast, and the Amur River) were written in Chinese, Persian, Tamil, Jurchen, Mongolian, and Tibetan.[45]

During his reign, Yongle persuaded his courtiers to share his vision: most at the time acknowledged "the blinding light of vajra energy emanating from the vicinity of the Karma pa, the emperor, and his parents' relics; visits from supernatural Buddhist sages, ecumenically minded, gilt Daoist immortals, and the bodhisattva Manjushri himself."[46] His descendents encountered more difficulties selling this image of emperor as *khaghan*.

Most scholarship on Tibetan Buddhism and the Ming dynasty has focused on the first and third Ming emperors. However, as Dora Ching discusses elsewhere in this volume, imperial patronage of Tibetan Buddhism

---

42. Berger ("Miracles in Nanjing," p. 153) notes that the visions contained in the handscroll of the Fifth Karma pa's visit to Nanjing probably evoked associations with Mount Wutai, a sacred Buddhist mountain that was rich in associations to the steppe, imperial power, and the Buddhist deity Mañjuśrī. She refers to David Farquhar's article "Emperor as Bodhisattva," which discusses the links among the multilingual inscriptions of Juyong Pass, Mongol (and later Qing) emperors, and Mañjuśrī. She speculates that Yongle was attempting to cast the Ming founder in the role of a *cakravartin* (p. 159). She does not, however, consider the possibility that this figured in Yongle's efforts to forge a new identity for Ming rulers as *khaghan*.

43. See the imperial edict cited in Li Yihua, "Liangjian Zhengde chao Alabowen Bosiwen ciqi," p. 51*n*1.

44. Serruys, "Early Lamaism in Mongolia," p. 187.

45. Su Bai, "Lasa Budalagong zhuyao diantang he kuzang de bufen Mingdai wenshu," p. 46*n*2; Tsai, *Perpetual Happiness*, p. 158; Dreyer, *Zheng He*, p. 71.

46. Berger, "Miracles in Nanjing," p. 161.

continued well into the sixteenth century.[47] As Otosaka Tomoko has argued, as a counterweight to the growing power of the civil bureaucracy,
Tibetan Buddhism became tightly linked to the emperor's authority.[48] One
tangible sign of this support was that throughout the fifteenth century Tibetan monks were housed at the three principal lamaseries in Beijing—Da
longshan huguo Temple 大隆善護國寺, Nengren Temple 能仁寺, and
Da Cien Temple 大慈恩寺.[49] Their numbers ranged between one and two
thousand from the 1420s through the 1440s. Civil officials often railed
against the impropriety of using imperial funds to finance this "alien creed"
and repeatedly demanded that the ranks of the Tibetan monks be reduced
or eliminated altogether. Despite these protests, all the temples enjoyed financial support from the emperor and the imperial family.

Imperial patronage of Tibetan Buddhism was often tied directly to the
emperor's personal concerns. For instance, over the objections of his ministers, on the second day of the eleventh lunar month of 1472, the Chenghua emperor ordered the composition of a commemorative stele account
of the renovation of Longshan Temple (a fact omitted in the *Veritable Records* of his reign). This date was the emperor's birthday. Otosaka's argument that the stele account was part of the emperor's birthday celebrations
suggests that Tibetan Buddhism formed an important part of the emperor's personal sphere.[50] In 1505, Tibetan monks conducted purification
rites in the Hall of Imperial Tranquility 乾清宮 after the Hongzhi emperor's death.[51] As we shall see below, his son, the early sixteenth-century
emperor, Zhengde, took even more interest in Tibetan Buddhism.

Criticisms of state support for Tibetan monks often focused on what
civil officials viewed as the disruption of proper social and political hierarchies. First, the officials decried the fact that Tibetan monks enjoyed unfettered access to the politically and ritually exclusive space of the Forbidden

---

47. Yang, *Ming Qingshi jueao*, pp. 46, 57–58, 60–61, 66; He Xiaorong, "Mingdai
huangdi chongfeng Zangchuan fojiao qianxi."
48. Otosaka Tomoko, "Kaette kita shokumokujin."
49. Suzuki Masashi, "Mindai teishitsu zaisei to bukkyō," pp. 1339–46; Ryūchi Kiyoshi, "Mindai Pekin ni okeru ramakyōdan," pp. 70–71; Satō Hisashi, "Mintei ni okeru
ramakyō sūhai ni tsuite," pp. 293–98. Da longshan huguo si was popularly known as
Chongguo si 崇國寺; see Jiang Yikui, *Chang'an kehua, juan* 1, "Huangdu zaji" 皇都雜記,
p. 20.
50. Otosaka Tomoko, "Kaette kita shokumokujin," p. 256–57.
51. Ryūchi Kiyoshi, "Mindai Pekin ni okeru ramakyōdan," p. 73.

City. In 1465, shortly after Chenghua came to power one minister invoked the Ming founder's instructions and then objected:

Recently, I have heard that Tibetan monks have entered the Forbidden City to chant sutras. They do not leave until dawn. There have also been cases in which silver vessels have been delivered to temples and lamaseries without the official approval of an imperial edict. I humbly request a clear prohibition [of such practices] in order to restrict access to the palace.[52]

Several officials protested that the emperor granted Tibetan monks social privileges that exceeded even those allowed imperial princes. For instance, in 1473 one supervising secretary complained of a Tibetan monk much favored by Chenghua: "When he sets out [into the city], he rides in a palanquin whose top is constructed of coir palm [*Trachycarpus exscelsa* 棕轎].[53] Those who walk at the head of his procession use the imperial regalia 金吾仗.[54] His emolument surpasses that of princes of the blood."[55]

In addition to whatever ideological issues may have been in play, Ming bureaucrats deeply resented how, through imperial favor, Tibetan monks disrupted what they viewed as proper social hierarchy in the capital. The official quoted above objected to the Tibetan's violation of correct sumptuary practice in his use of modes of transportation and public display reserved for the imperial family, or at least imperial officials. What made the Tibetan monks' presence particularly galling was the public nature of the imperial patronage they enjoyed. Anyone in the streets of the capital could see their power and prestige manifested in their honor guards and carriages, all key social and political markers to which the emperor, his officials, and the savvy population of Beijing were keenly attuned.

---

52. Shen Defu, *Wanli yehuo bian* (hereafter cited as *YHB*), *juan* 27, 3: 683, cited in Satō Hisashi, "Mintei ni okeru ramakyō sūhai ni tsuite," p. 299. The minister was Li Xian 李賢 (1408–67).

53. The original text uses a different character for *zong*, see *Hanyu dacidian*, 4: 1190–91. As early as the first year of his reign, Yongle complained that an imperial in-law had violated sumptuary law and used a *zongjiao*, as though he were no different from the princes of the blood. See Yu Ruji, *Libu zhigao* (hereafter cited as *LBZG*), 2.6a–b.

54. The *Hanyu dacidian* does not list a *Jinwu zhang*. *Jinwu* refers to the imperial honor guard. The *Jinwu niao* was a staff with a carved bird at its head (*Hanyu dacidian*, 11: 1148). The point is that his use of symbols was not commensurate with his rank.

55. *Xianzong shilu* 憲宗實錄, 58.4b, quoted in Satō, "Mintei ni okeru ramakyō sūhai ni tsuite," p. 299. Wang Shizhen 王世貞 further added that personnel from the Brocade Guard walked in front and in back of the palanquin; "All who saw it assumed it was a prince of the blood"; see "Ci shang shi yi zhang" 賜尚師儀仗, in Wang Shizhen, *Yanshantang bieji*, 11.211.

Another dimension of the contested status of Tibetan monks in Beijing involved titles granted by the throne. Our guide to the Ming court, Shen Defu 沈德符 (1578–1642), observed, "During Chenghua's reign, Buddhist and Taoist [monks] were favored by the emperor. For instance, [Chenghua] granted to one Tibetan monk an investiture title of more than thirty characters. This likely follows the old practices of the former Yuan dynasty. It also follows the Yongle reign precedent of Halima."[56] Here we see in the eyes of one well-informed observer the nexus of connections among the Ming imperial family, Tibetan Buddhism, and the Great Yuan *ulus*. Shen drew these links in several other instances.[57]

Another reflection of ties between the imperial family and Tibetan Buddhism may be seen in the production of porcelains. The Ming court ordered imperial kilns to make high-quality porcelains inscribed with Tibetan script or bearing strong influences of Tibetan Buddhism in terms of style and use. Scholars have speculated that these porcelains were produced as gifts for high-ranking clerics, to accommodate them during their sojourns in the Ming capitals, and for use in Tibetan rituals for the imperial family.[58]

Shen provides another example of how closely Tibetan Buddhism, the imperial family, and the Yuan were linked in the minds of contemporary observers.

I have seen the Joyous Buddhas within the Imperial Palace. It is said that they were presented by a foreign country. Others say that they were left by the former Yuan dynasty. Each Buddha wears a red jade pendant. The Buddhas embrace each other. Their reproductive organs fit together. They move by a hinge. I have seen them in several places. The palace eunuchs say that each time a ruler is to marry, they always show him to this hall [containing these statues]. After prostrating himself in

56. Shen Defu, "Shi dao zhenren fenghao zhi yi" 釋道眞人封號之異, in *YHB, juan* 27, 3: 696.

57. When confronted with unfamiliar practices, Shen often attributed them to the Yuan. For instance, he noted when imperial princes were born, a youth was selected as a ritual substitute, his head was shaven, and he became a Buddhist monk. Shen writes, "I do not know whence such a practice originated. I suspect that it follows a remnant practice of the former Yuan dynasty" (ibid., 3: 686).

58. Zhao Hong, "Gugong bowuyuan cang Ming Qing shiqi Zang, Meng su ciqi"; Hu Zhaojing, "Sajia si cang Ming Xuande yuyao qinghua wucaiwan," p. 73. *Thangka*, bronze statues, and even a portrait of the Yongle emperor are also held to have been sent as gifts to prominent Tibetan clerics; see Xizang wenguanhui, Wenwu puchadui, "Dazhao si cang Yongle nianjian wenwu," pp. 69, 71; and Xizang wenguanhui, "Budalalong cang Ming Chengzu Zhu Di huaxiang."

worship before the statues, he is instructed to caress their private parts in order to silently comprehend the way of sexual congress. Later [the ruler and wife] marry. This instruction was in consideration of the emperor's naïveté in this matter [i.e., sexual intercourse]. Now periodically those who sell curios have [similar statues]. They are exquisitely crafted, not local products. Their price is beyond calculation. However, they are much smaller than those within the Imperial Palace. Imperially sponsored temples within the capital also have such Buddhist [figures], which have been granted by the throne. Monks are generally unwilling to show them to people lightly.[59]

Elsewhere Shen notes that the Da Cien Temple, an imperially patronized temple closely associated with Tibetan Buddhism, continued to house a Joyous Buddhas statue until the mid-sixteenth century.[60] Shen's sketch of the Joyous Buddhas aptly describes the genre of statues within the Tibetan Buddhist tradition that represent the underlying unity of the cosmos that may be glimpsed through Tantric sexual meditations.

The impact of Tibetan Buddhism on the Ming court was not limited to emperors and their relations with officialdom. Writing late in the fifteenth century, Lu Rong 陸容 recounts an example of the small ways in which Tibetan Buddhist practices shaped religious and material culture within the Imperial City. Charged with rewarding troops for their efforts in the northwestern province of Ningxia, Lu made his way to one of the warehouses in the Imperial City to secure winter clothing for the soldiers. He noticed a eunuch holding a set of prayer beads whose color was like ivory, only darker and richer. The eunuch informed him that after the pivotal battle of Baigou River 白溝河 against troops loyal to the Jianwen emperor in the spring of 1400, the corpses of fallen soldiers blanketed the field.[61] Moved, Yongle ordered that their skulls be collected and formed into prayer beads. The beads were then given to palace eunuchs who were to pray for the transmigration of the deceased. Especially large skulls were used as vessels for pure water to offer the Buddha. They were named Bowls of Heavenly Grace. Lu attributed these practices to "Tibetan teach-

---

59. Shen Defu, "Wanju chunhua" 玩具春畫, in *YHB, juan* 27, 3: 659. I thank Chu Hung-lam for improving the accuracy of this translation. Craig Clunas has also drawn attention to this passage, noting correctly that Shen failed to grasp the religious significance of the statue; see Clunas, *Pictures and Visuality in Early Modern China*, p. 151.

60. Shen Defu, "Jingshi diwang miao" 京師帝王廟, "Liechao" 列朝, in *YHB, juan* 1, 1: 2.

61. For a description of the battle between the forces of Yongle and loyalist troops under Li Jinglong 李景隆, see Zhao Zhongchen, *Ming Chengzu zhuan*, pp. 116–21.

ings."[62] One presumes that Lu deemed the incident sufficiently interesting to include in his writings. Perhaps most literati were not familiar with such customs within the imperial city.

During the latter half of the fifteenth century, a variation of the practice apparently flourished outside the walls of the imperial palace. One group of enterprising soldiers from the environs of Beijing carried on a brisk trade in Buddhist rosaries made from human cranial bones. Working with Tibetan monks in the capital, the soldiers exhumed corpses in the area, strung the bones together, and sold them in the markets of Beijing, claiming that they had been made in Tibet. The soldiers presented some of these prayer beads to palace eunuchs, calling them the "miraculous method of transmigration." The eunuchs rewarded them handsomely.[63]

Especially noteworthy here is that this same passage notes explicitly that the soldiers also produced *kapāla* (Ch. *gebala wan* 葛巴剌碗). *Kapāla* is the skull cup (an emblem of compassion) held in the right hand of Mahākāla, the tutelary deity closely associated with the Sa skya sect.[64] In his left hand, Mahākāla grasps a flaying knife (or chopper), which indicates the severing of delusions. Several examples of finely crafted statues of Mahākāla dating from the fifteenth century and inscribed with Yongle reign dates have survived in collections in Tibet and China. A small intricately wrought gold statue of Mahākāla was recently excavated from the tomb of an imperial Ming prince who died in the mid-fifteenth century.[65]

Although the scale and composition of the market for these beads and *kapāla* are unclear, this anecdote and Shen Defu's comments on the sale of Tantric artifacts by curio dealers suggest that over time, Tibetan Buddhism, if only as fashion, had expanded beyond the walls of the Forbidden City.[66] The anecdote also serves as a reminder of the critical role that palace eunuchs played in the maintenance of court customs.

———

62. Lu Rong, *Shuyuan zaji*, 1.3.

63. Zhu Guozhen, *Yongchuang xiaopin*, 32.774–75.

64. Franke, "From Tribal Chieftain to Universal Emperor and God," pp. 59–60. Other Tibetan deities are also represented holding the *kapāla* and chopper. For Ming-period examples of Yamantaka-Vajrabhairava rendered in silk embroidery and gilt bronze, see Leidy, "Buddhist Art," plates 26 and 35.

65. Hubeisheng wenwu kaogu yanjiusuo et al., "Hubei Zhongxiang Mingdai Liang-zhuang wang mu fajue jianbao," pp. 16–17. See plate 33 (p. 17) for illustration.

66. An early seventeenth-century guide to the sites and wares of Beijing notes that prayer beads made of cranial bones were available for sale at the City God Market in the capital; see Liu Tong and Yu Yizheng, *Dijing jingwuliie* (hereafter cited as *DJJW*), *juan* 4, "Chenghuang miao shi" 城隍廟市, p. 166.

During the fifteenth century, Ming imperial patronage of Tibetan Buddhism took many forms: the throne provided financial support for thousands of Tibetan monks within the capital; it commissioned the construction of temples strongly associated with Tibetan clerics; and it granted impressive titles, seals, and sumptuary privileges to favored monks. In exchange, Tibetan monks performed religious ceremonies for the imperial family designed to ensure good health, ritual purity, spiritual growth, and peace within the realm. By serving as patrons of Tibetan Buddhism, the Ming imperial family gained a valuable counterweight to the civil bureaucracy. Emperors from Yongle to Zhengde enjoyed access to spiritual, political, and cultural resources largely unavailable to the Chinese bureaucracy. Finally, until the first quarter of the sixteenth century, Ming emperors distinguished themselves from their subjects through the consistent support of religious practices and personages that remained exotic and strange in the eyes of most Chinese. In all these ways, the Ming imperial family followed in the footsteps of Khubilai.

Foreign Personnel Within the Imperial Palaces

Past scholarship has documented in some detail the Ming dynasty's demands for Korean virgins and eunuchs.[67] Until recently, however, few have posed the basic question why the Ming made such demands.[68] The demand for Korean palace personnel—women and eunuchs—constitutes another continuity between the Ming imperial family and its Mongol Yuan predecessors.

Beginning during the reign of Khubilai khan, thousands of Korean women, often from elite families, were presented to the Mongol court.[69] Most of these women served in menial positions within the imperial pal-

---

67. Wang Chongwu, "Ming Chengzu Chaoxian xuanfei kao," pp. 165–76.

68. The most notable exception is Xi Lei's recent monograph, *Yuandai Gaoli gongnü zhidu yanjiu*. She argues (p. 274) that "after succeeding to the Yuan, in order to demonstrate the legality and legitimacy of its own feudal dynasty, the Ming dynasty went to great efforts to continue the Yuan's various special prerogatives." Hok-lam Chan ("Mingchu Chaoxian 'ruchao' huanguan juyu," p. 66) notes in passing that Yongle's request for Korean women "was a return to Mongol Yuan practice." He speculates that perhaps this was related to Yongle's Mongolian blood.

69. For an early and somewhat nationalistic perspective on Korean tribute women to the Yuan court, see Yu Hong'yŏl, "Koryŏ ŭi Wŏn e tae han kong'yŏ." A postscript note indicates that an earlier version of this article was first published in 1937. The most thorough study in any language is now Xi Lei's *Yuandai Gaoli gongnü zhidu yanjiu*.

ace, but some were given to leading Yuan ministers as consorts. In fact, by the mid-fourteenth century, the giving and receiving of Korean women among Yuan elites had grown fashionable in Dadu.[70] A few even gained the affections of Mongol emperors. For instance, in 1282, Palace Woman Yi 李宮人, a Korean woman of good family and considerable skills with the *pipa* (a Chinese lute) entered the Yuan palace and quickly won the favor of Khubilai. Early in the fourteenth century, Lady Kim, known to posterity as Dharmashiri 達麻實里, became the first Korean woman invested as a secondary Yuan empress (皇后). Finally, the most influential Korean woman in Yuan history was Empress Ki 奇皇后 (fl. 1340–68), who, during the mid-fourteenth century, became a full empress and bore the Shundi emperor the heir apparent Ayushiridara.[71]

Ming forces seized many of the Korean palace women and consorts abandoned during the Yuan court's flight from Dadu. The Ming founder, Hongwu, counted Korean women captured from the former Yuan palace among his consorts.[72] Yongle, who identified so closely with the Yuan legacy (especially that of Khubilai), was the first Ming emperor to demand women directly from Korea for his harem. Following Yuan practice, Yongle bestowed positions within the Ming government on the fathers and brothers of several of his Korean consorts. The Xuande emperor would continue to request Korean women for the palace.[73]

---

70. Quan Heng and Ren Chongyue, *Gengshen waishi jianzheng*, p. 96.

71. Xi Lei, "Yuanchao gongtingzhong de Gaoli nüxing," pp. 208–12; Yi Yongbŏm, "Ki hwanghu ŭi ch'aeknip kwa Wŏndae ŭi Chajŏngwŏn"; Min Hyŏn'gu, "Koryŏ Kongmin wang ŭi chŭkwi paegyŏng," pp. 803–4. For fuller discussion of Empress Ki and relations between the Yuan and Koryŏ courts, see Robinson, *Empire's Twilight*.

72. For an anecdote related to what Hongwu perceived as the dangerous connections between Koryŏ women (who had formerly been consorts to Yuan elites) who resided within his palace and foreign diplomacy, see Shen Defu, "Gaoli nü jianyi" 高麗女見疑 in "Gong wei" 宮闈, in *YHB, juan* 3, 1: 74–75. Korean court annals note that in 1368 Ming troops captured a twelve-year-old Korean girl who had just recently arrived in the Yuan; she became a palace woman under the Ming, favored by Hongwu (*Koryŏ sa*, 44.653, 恭愍王二十二年七月甲辰).

73. Shen Defu, "Diwang qu waiguo nü" 帝王娶外國女, in *YHB, juan* 3, 1: 74. Shen notes explicitly that this custom "followed Yuan practice." Wang Shizhen ("Zhongguo yiguan huju" 中國夷官互居, in *Yanshantang bieji*, 18.336) notes an additional four Korean women who gained various ranks within the Ming palace (three of them during Yongle's reign) and whose fathers were then granted honorary posts within the Chinese bureaucracy although they continued to reside in Korea. Shen Defu remarked on the unusually prestigious posts granted to these men; see "Yongle jian hougong fu enze" 永樂間後宮父恩澤, *YHB, juan* 5, 1: 184. See also Jiang Shunyuan, "Ming Qing gong-

Even more strikingly, Korean records reveal that almost immediately on taking the throne, Yongle proposed a marriage alliance with the royal Yi family of the fledgling Chosŏn dynasty. This overture too closely resembles the relation between the ruling families of the Yuan and Koryŏ dynasties to be dismissed as accidental. During the reign of Khubilai, Mongolian princesses began to marry Koryŏ kings. Yongle's offer rankled the Chosŏn king; such marriage alliances had compromised royal autonomy during the preceding century. The Chosŏn king immediately married several daughters to political supporters within Korea.[74] Ming demand for Korean women reached its height under Yongle; the practice seems to have ceased in the 1430s with the death of Xuande (who, among other things, appreciated how Korean women prepared soybean curd, *doufu*).[75]

In the early sixteenth century, however, we read of a Muslim confidant in Zhengde's Leopard Quarter, an alternative site of imperial residence and government where civil ministers seldom trod, praising the superior beauty of "Koryŏ women" to the emperor.[76] Korean records reveal that by the first lunar month of 1521, tales reached the Chosŏn court that Zhengde planned to request Korean women for his palace. A Korean eunuch at the Ming court confirmed the rumor. He informed a Chosŏn official that "the emperor was investigating Xuande period precedents" and that "[the official] was afraid that he would procure women in Korea." Further inquiry revealed that another Korean eunuch had informed Zhengde that there was an overabundance of women in Chosŏn and had praised their beauty and culinary skills.

Zhengde dispatched two Korean eunuchs to Chosŏn to invest the Korean heir apparent and to acquire several dozen women with cooking skills

——

ting Chaoxian 'cai nü' yanjiu," pp. 86–87. In contrast, Ellen Soullière ("Imperial Marriages of the Ming Dynasty," p. 33) maintains that they were given residences in Nanjing. Jiang notes that in total nearly two hundred Korean women were incorporated into the Ming palace as consorts, attendants, entertainers, and cooks.

74. *Chosŏn Taejong sillok* 朝鮮太宗實錄, *kwŏn* 6, 三年九月辛卯, 十二月辛卯, cited in Pak Wŏnho, "Ming 'Jingnan zhi yi' yu Chaoxian," p. 242. For discussions of the marriage ties between the ruling houses of the Yuan and the Koryŏ, see Xiao Qiqing, "Yuan-Li guanxizhong de wangshi huanghun yu qiangquan zhengzhi." See also Morihira Masahiko, "Fuma Kōrai kokuō no seiritsu"; and idem, "Genchō keshike seido to Kōrai ōke."

75. Clark, "The Ming Connection," pp. 86–87; idem, "Sino-Korean Tributary Relations Under the Ming," 8: 291–93. See also Soullière, "Palace Women in the Ming Dynasty," pp. 269–71.

76. Shen Defu, "Diwang qu waiguo nü" 帝王娶外國女, in *YHB*, *juan* 3, 1: 74.

and young girls. Shortly thereafter, Zhengde died, and his successor, Jiajing, rescinded the order. After some initial hesitation, the Chosŏn court decided that approximately fifteen women might be sent back with the Korear-born Ming eunuchs. The new Ming emperor protested that this "was not necessary"; it is unclear whether the women traveled to China in the end.[77]

Chosŏn women were incorporated into the traditions of the Ming imperial family. These traditions linked Zhengde, Xuande, Yongle, and ultimately Khubilai khan. Like so many other practices at the Ming court, the use of Korean women as palace personnel was not constant but reflected the individual interests and agendas of individual emperors and their courts. Even as we can perceive the personal stamp of individual rulers, however, we can see that the importance of eunuchs in Ming diplomacy and imperial family life proved more enduring.

Incessant demands for Korean eunuchs began during the Ming founder's reign. As Hok-lam Chan has noted, the first Korean-born eunuchs were used as Ming envoys to the Koryŏ dynasty.[78] Here again we see the strong influence of the Yuan, which systematically used Korean eunuchs as envoys to the Koryŏ court.[79] As had been the case during the Yuan, Korean eunuchs at the Ming court parlayed their privileged access to the imperial family and influential ministers into prestige and power for themselves and their relatives in Korea.[80] Further, as also had been true during the Mongol period, Korean monarchs attempted to use the Korean eunuchs at the Chinese court to their own advantage throughout most of the Ming period.[81]

The Ming imperial family incorporated foreign men and women into the private sphere of the Forbidden City. Like the Mongol Yuan court, during the first half of the dynasty, the Ming imperial household establishment was international in its composition and interests. Yongle and some of his successors patterned their expectations and behavior on the

---

77. Jiang Shunyuan, "Ming Qing gongting Chaoxian 'cai nü' yanjiu," pp. 82–83. Details related to Korean eunuchs and women are seldom available in Chinese court annals. Jiang draws extensively on materials from the *Koryŏsa* and *Chosŏn sillok*. This incident is also mentioned in Yu Hong'yŏl, "Koryŏ ŭi Wŏn e tae han kong'yŏ," p. 45.

78. Hok-lam Chan, "Mingchu Chaoxian 'ruchao' huanguan juyu." On Ming envoy missions to Seoul led by Korean-born eunuchs, see Tsai, *The Eunuchs in the Ming Dynasty*, pp. 135–40.

79. For recent scholarship, see Chang Tong'ik, *Koryŏ hugi oegyosa yŏn'gu*, pp. 178–85.

80. For a detailed case study drawn from the early Ming, see Hok-lam Chan, "Mingchu Chaoxian 'ruchao' huanguan juyu."

81. For an early sixteenth-century example, see Robinson, "Korean Lobbying at the Ming Court."

precedents of Khubilai and his descendents. The following section demonstrates that several fifteenth- and sixteenth-century Chinese rulers fashioned a visual image modeled closely on the Mongol *khaghan*.

In the Image of the khaghan

As Wang Cheng-hua, Dora Ching, and others have shown, imperial portraiture can tell us much about the Ming court and the imperial family.[82] Perhaps the variety of imperial portraiture most familiar to us is the formal seated portraits of the emperors held in the Palace Museum collection in Taibei.[83] Although the character of these carefully crafted images changed significantly during the first half of the dynasty, the seated portraits depicted the emperor on his throne within the palace dressed in silken robes embroidered with an expanding number of symbols of rulership (see Figs. 7.1 and 7.10). This style of portraiture, which often rendered the subject in an idealized fashion, projected an image of the Ming emperor firmly rooted in Chinese traditions of political and cultural symbolism. However, as Dora Ching's chapter in this volume demonstrates, even this relatively staid form of imperial portraiture owed much to Tibetan styles and concerns.[84]

Less thoroughly investigated varieties of imperial portraiture like paintings in the "pleasures of the emperor" (*xingle tu* 行樂圖) genre reveal a different face of the Ming emperors. Such scholars as Shan Guoqiang characterize the "pleasures of the emperor" paintings as more realistically rendered, historically accurate, and dynamic than the seated formal portraits. This genre, nevertheless, also sought to convey certain visions of the court and the realm. In Richard Barnhart's analysis of Xuande and his court, he notes the cultivated and civil side of the ruler and his reign. Discussing Shang Xi's 商喜 *The Xuande Emperor's Pleasures* (*Xuanzong xingle tu* 宣宗行樂圖),[85] Barnhart stresses the auspicious items found in the work.[86] Wang Cheng-hua remarks that the work portrays a "world enjoying beauti-

---

82. Wang Cheng-hua, "Material Culture and Emperorship." See also Dora Ching's discussion of imperial portraiture in this volume, pp. 321–64.

83. The collection, entitled *Mingdai diwang xiang* 明代帝王像, contains twenty-seven works. See Shan Guoqiang, "Ming Qing gongting xiaoxianghua," p. 417.

84. See also Fong, "Imperial Portraiture of the Ming Dynasty," pp. 329–32.

85. The painting, done on paper, measures 211 × 353 cm and is held at the Palace Museum, Beijing. See Yang Xin, *Gugong bowuyuan cang Ming Qing huihua*, p. 134.

86. Barnhart, "Emperor Xuanzong and the Painting Masters," in idem, *Painters of the Great Ming*, p. 57.

ful weather and a harmonious atmosphere as if the empire under Zhu Zhanji (Xuande)'s reign were such a world."[87]

The Xuande Emperor's Pleasures depicts an outdoor scene full of action and motion (see Fig. 8.1). Court elites are mounted on lively horses; the emperor and his close attendants, arrayed in Mongolian riding tunics and hunting caps, and bows and arrows are on display. The contrast with more familiar formal, seated, indoor court portraiture is striking. The central figure of the painting is the Xuande emperor, mounted on a spirited steed, leading an outing in the imperial menagerie. The emperor wears a Mongolian cap called a *zhanli* 氈笠 (笠子帽), a felt hat with a broad rim—useful for shielding the eyes during the hunt. He wears a sleeveless, body-hugging riding tunic. The outfit closely resembles the Yuan period *bijia* 比甲 tunic.[88] Several of the riders who follow immediately behind him have also donned felt caps and narrow-sleeved robes. One carries a quiver full of arrows on his back, and the other two seem to be holding horns or pennants. In the background, one can make out several pairs of deer, pheasants, ducks, rabbits, and storks—as Barnhart notes, all auspicious animals firmly rooted in Chinese symbolism and aesthetics. In the foreground, nearly two dozen riders, each with a youthful attendant on foot, are grouped in two lines. These riders, probably eunuchs, are dressed in gorgeous gowns with fitted sleeves but wear Chinese-style hats.

Such scholars as Mu Yiqin have noted the extensive Mongol influence on clothing reflected in this painting.[89] Mu appears to assume that the Ming emperors unconsciously continued Mongol styles in clothing.

---

87. Wang Cheng-hua, "Material Culture and Emperorship," p. 241.

88. Entry by Shan Guoqiang in Yang Xin, *Gugong bowuyuan cang Ming Qing huihua*, p. 124.

89. Mu Yiqin, "Mingdai gongting huihua," pp. 40–41. In his discussion of the *Xuanzong xingle tu, Xuanzong she lie tu,* and *Shezhi tu*, Barnhart notes the vivid, lively style of the paintings and their considerable historical value for reflecting reality. He does not consider the significance of portraits of Ming emperors rendered in the likeness of Mongol khans. He does note, however, the importance of horse paintings at the early Ming courts that most scholarship has overlooked (*Painters of the Great Ming*, p. 123). Shan Guoqiang, too, omits the connection to the Mongols; see his "Mingdai gongting huihua," p. 275. In an earlier article, Shan Guoqiang ("Mingdai gongting huihua gaishu," pt. 1, p. 10) did remark that Xuande was dressed "entirely in northern barbarian garb." He does not draw any connection to the Mongols. In regard to Zhou Quan's *Pheasant Hunting* and the anonymous *Xuanzong Hunting with Bow*, Shan ("Mingdai gongting huihua gaishu," pt. 1, p. 11) notes that the paintings reflect Xuande's deep concern with military matters.

However, Barnhart, Wang, and Ching have drawn attention to the carefully crafted political elements of imperial painting—the auspicious animals, the temperate weather, the conspicuous wealth revealed in the rich gowns. As a culturally and politically significant marker, clothing was not rendered without thought. Why, we must ask, did the emperor commission a portrait of himself arrayed in unmistakably Mongolian garb?

The composition of the painting suggests the many layers of the early emperors' identity. Is it accidental that at the center of the work is the emperor in his role as *khaghan*, hunting, riding, and dressed in Mongol clothing? In an implicit contrast, arrayed in a secondary position around the Son of Heaven are his silk-begowned eunuch officials, portrayed in lovingly rich detail and color. Clearly the handsomely attired officials constitute an important facet of Xuande's identity. If, however, on the basis of this work one were to hazard a guess about what sort of self-image Xuande harbored, one would have to conclude that the emperor felt completely at ease with the martial, equestrian, and steppe dimensions of his identity as ruler. At the very least, he wished to project ease with such an image.

Several scholars have argued that the setting for the painting is the Southern Lakes of the imperial city, where the imperial families from the Yuan, Ming, and Qing dynasties honed their martial skills through royal hunts.[90] Wang Cheng-hua, in contrast, holds that the scene depicted is the Island of Beautiful Stones 瓊華島 in the Western Park.[91] On the island, the Great Yuan *ulus* had maintained an imperial zoo, which may have survived into the Ming period. The early Ming emperors Yongle and Xuande were keenly aware of the links between the family enterprise and its predecessor, the Yuan. On one occasion in 1432, Xuande pointed out that the Mongols had once held all the lands visible from a hill on the island before losing them through mismanagement of the empire. Xuande closely associated this theme with Yongle, who had lectured him on the topic more than once.[92] Perhaps more important than the specific setting of *The Xuande Emperor's Pleasures* is the powerful image of a Chinese emperor on horseback armed with bow and arrow, clothed in Mongolian garb—not an indoor setting within the walls of the imperial palace sitting on a throne wearing a Chinese gown.

---

90. Shan Guoqiang, "Mingdai gongting huihua gaishu," pt. 1, p. 10; Mu Yiqin, "Mingdai gongting huihua," pp. 41–42.
91. Wang Cheng-hua, "Material Culture and Emperorship," pp. 233–38.
92. Ibid., pp. 236–37.

The anonymous *Emperor Xuande Hunting with Bow* (*Xuanzong she lie tu* 宣宗射獵圖), too, reveals an image of the emperor indistinguishable from that of a Mongolian *khaghan* on the hunt (see Fig. 8.2). Centered in the foreground, a dark-faced and bearded Xuande holds aloft his first prize, a young deer, two legs grasped in each of his hands. At the same time, he keenly tracks a second deer bolting in flight through the open field. Next to the emperor, his horse grazes peacefully. Xuande wears Mongolian riding gear with tight-fitting sleeves and a Mongolian felt hat. Slung around his waist are a Mongolian compound bow and a quiver of arrows.[93] Although some debate surrounds the exact setting of the painting, the relatively generic quality of the outdoor scene—sparsely inhabited and wild—may represent an effort to claim all such places as the emperor's proper domain. His activities and sphere of authority were not bound by specific place or even time.

Equally striking are richly detailed court portraits of Xuande dressed in Mongol garb on a riding excursion (see Fig. 8.3).[94] The detailed rendering of the expensive fur saddle-blanket closely resembles that in *The Xuande Emperor Hunting with Bow*; it also calls to mind the famous portrait of Khubilai on the hunt (Fig. 8.4). Equally noteworthy is the distinctive "girdle with a pouch" 繫腰合鉢, a detail so prominent in Yuan-period paintings of Mongol and Central Asian figures as to constitute a visual synecdoche (Fig. 8.5).[95] Both Zhou Quan's 周全 *Hunting Pheasants with Bow* (*Shezhi tu* 射雉圖; Fig. 8.6) and Shang Xi's *Xuande Emperor's Pleasures* include this distinctive cultural icon. The pouch's connection with steppe peoples would not have been lost on audiences at the Ming court. Government regulations prescribed the pouch as part of the garb for performers playing the role of Northern Barbarians in the Dance of Pacification of the Barbarians of the Four Directions (*Fu an siyi zhi wu* 撫安四夷之舞), which was performed at banquets and state rituals in the imperial palace.[96]

---

93. Reproduction in Gugong bowuyuan, *Mingdai gongting yu Zhepai huihua xuanji*, p. 53.

94. Barnhart ("The Foundation of Ming Painting," p. 123) attributes the painting to an anonymous Ming painter at Xuande's court.

95. For comments on the pouch, see Serruys, "Remains of Mongol Customs," pp. 159–60n71. For examples of the pouch in Yuan-period paintings, see the four anonymous works, *Youqi tu* 遊騎圖, *Hua hanyuan lieqi* 畫寒原獵騎, *Baixiang yanqing* 百祥衍慶, and *Sanyang kaitai tu* 三陽開泰圖, in *Gugong shuhuatulu*, 5: 191, 251, 263, and 373, respectively.

96. See Xu Yikui, *Da Ming jili*, 57A.6a–b; Yu Ruji, "Yanli" 宴禮 under "Yizhisi zhizhang" 儀制司職掌, in *LBZG*, 21.17a.

Within the walls of the Ming imperial palace too, equestrian skills and prowess with the bow and arrow figured prominently throughout the first half of the Ming. One scene from the long scroll painting *The Chenghua Emperor's Pleasures Within the Palace* (*Ming Xianzong gongzhong xingle tu* 明憲宗宮中行樂圖) depicts a group of six riders exhibiting their equestrian skills for an appreciative Chenghua, who is wearing a Mongolian felt cap (Fig. 8.7).[97] Within the painting itself is a self-standing screen decorated with a number of panels depicting riders playing a version of polo (*jiqiu* 擊球). This suggests that polo was more than an imperial entertainment; paintings of polo were appreciated as decorative art at the court.[98] Another section of *Chenghua's Pleasures Within the Palace* shows an archery contest; men with Mongolian compound bows vie for the favor of an august Chenghua, again wearing a Mongolian hat.

Even when the site of riding and archery contests was contained within the bounded space of the imperial palace, these portraits of the Ming emperors evoked the Mongol Yuan legacy. Each year on the fifth day of the fifth lunar month and the ninth day of the ninth lunar month, the Mongol court in Dadu had sponsored polo competitions within the imperial palace.[99] Scattered entries in the *Veritable Records* from Yongle's reign note that on the fifth day of the fifth month, the Duanwu Festival 端午節, the emperor also viewed "polo (*jiqiu*) and willow archery contests 射柳" in the Eastern Garden of the Imperial Palace. Permission to attend these events was a mark of imperial favor. Ranking military and civil officials, members of the merit aristocracy, visiting foreign dignitaries, and "esteemed elders of the capital" were among those who watched the competitions. On this occasion, the court distributed gifts of cash to the emperor's esteemed guests.[100] A description of one such event in 1413 makes clear that court elites participated in both competitions. These mounted archery contests for military officers continued in the palace at least through the Xuande reign.[101]

---

97. Here I follow Wang Cheng-hua's ("Material Culture and Emperorship," pp. 223–25) redating and renaming of the *Xuanzong xingle tu* to *Xianzong xingle tu* and the Chenghua reign.

98. Reproduction in Gugong bowuyuan, *Mingdai gongting yu Zhepai huihua*, p. 51. On the uses of paintings within the imperial palace, see Barnhart, "Function, Subject, and Symbol," esp. pp. 90–91.

99. Chen Gaohua, "Song Yuan he Mingchu de maqiu," pp. 180–81; Shi Weimin, *Yuandai shehui shenghuoshi*, p. 363–65; Ma Jige, "*Xuanzong xingle tu* tu," p. 35.

100. *Taizong shilu* (hereafter cited as *TSL*), 164.1a, 176.1a.

101. Lu Rong, *Shuyuan zaji*, 1.1.

Yongle explicitly commented on the cosmopolitan nature of the celebrations. Happy with his grandson's skill with the bow, Yongle exclaimed:

Today, the people of China and the foreign countries are all assembled together. We will provide a phrase. You should think of a matching verse. "The wind and clouds bring together the jade and silk of all countries." The son of the heir apparent kowtowed and responded, "The sun and moon brighten the unified rivers and mountains [of the empire]."[102]

Flushed with pleasure, the emperor distributed horses, silk textiles, and "foreign cloth" among his guests. Civil officials composed commemorative poems. The court hosted a banquet for lower-ranking officials; it also handed out gifts of cash.[103] The presence of foreign envoys, the poetic references to foreign tribute, and theme of unification under the Ming imperial family makes clear that these polo and archery contests were not mere divertissements for early Ming emperors. They were also important political (both international and domestic) occasions.[104]

Zhou Quan's undated *Hunting Pheasants with Bow* further suggests the importance of hunting, horses, and archery for mid-Ming emperors (Fig. 8.6).[105] This work features a group of three men and their horses on a

---

102. *TSL*, 140.1b–2a. "Jade and silk" refer to the tribute items that foreign envoys presented to the court. "Sun and moon bright" involves a simple play on words. The character for "*ming*," or "bright," was composed of two elements: sun and moon. Ming was also the name of the dynasty. I thank Chu Hung-lam for improving the translation of this couplet.

103. *TSL*, 140.2a.

104. As late as the Wanli reign, Shen Defu ("Duanyang" 端陽 under "Liechao," in *YHB, juan* 2, 1: 67) commented on the popularity of riding and archery contests during the Duanwu festivities, especially among military men. He observed, "Within the imperial palace, in addition to dragon boats, [the court] maintains [such] past practices [as] willow archery contests. It is called *zoupiaoqi* 走驃騎 (galloping). In general, this follows the practices of the Jin and Yuan dynasties." Imperial gifts were bestowed on senior officials at this time. According to Shen, the contests involved as many as 3,000 skilled riders and reward money totaling more than 20,000 taels of gold. In a separate note, Shen remarked that in recent days, the practice had declined somewhat ("Xuanzong ji she" 宣宗繫射 under "Liechao," *YHB bu yi, juan* 1, 3: 790–91).

105. Done in colors on silk, the painting measures 137.6 cm in length and 117.2 cm in width. Like many court painters in fifteenth-century China, Zhou held the post of regional military commissioner within the Brocade Guard (as the colophon on the painting indicates). Little information regarding Zhou has survived, but he left a reputation for skill in rendering horses. A Zhou Quan was adopted by the eunuch Jin Ying 金英 (1426–50) and held a post in the Brocade Guard until his death in August 1487; see Mu Yiqin, *Mingdai yuanti Zhepai shiliao*, pp. 35, 238. See Hok-lam Chan's biography of Jin

pheasant hunt. In the background are steep outcroppings of rock, a few gnarled pines, and a flowing river that leads to a small waterfall and ends in a pond. Mounted on his steed, the central figure scans the sky for prey and reaches back with his right hand for an arrow that an attendant on foot holds ready. The riders wear silk robes with narrow, fitted sleeves. On their heads are conical Mongolian hats with brims, presumably to protect their eyes against the sun's glare during the hunt.[106] Hung from their waists are "girdles with pouches." Wang Cheng-hua has suggested that the central figure may be either Hongzhi or Zhengde.[107] The repeated visual references to Ming emperors on the hunt call to mind the Mongols' well-known interest in imperial hunting, which served simultaneously as military training, grand spectacle, and opportunity to strengthen personal bonds of loyalty.[108]

The *Emperor's Pleasures* and other court portraits that show Ming emperors on the hunt, riding excursions, bearing arms, and dressed in Mongolian garb remind us of the wisdom of Richard Barnhart's observation apropos newly rediscovered paintings: "We are constantly reminded of how cruelly arbitrary history is, and of the destruction that victors can do to those they defeat—as the scholars ultimately defeated the professionals in Chinese critical and art historical thought—and of the constant need to reexamine the intellectual and cultural biases of historians."[109] Paintings like Zhou Quan's *Hunting Pheasants with Bow* and the anonymous *Xuande Hunting with Bow* confront us with portraits of Ming emperors in the conscious pose of *khaghan*s. The garb, the setting, and the activities evoke the Yuan Mongols. These surviving works may represent only a portion of a far larger number of court portraits lost over time. These portraits do not conform to the most commonly held images of the Ming emperors. In fact, they are so at

———

Ying in Goodrich and Fang, *Dictionary of Ming Biography*, p. 247. The painting is held in the Palace Museum, Taiwan. A second work by Zhou Quan, *Lions* 獅子圖, is apparently held in the Tokyo Museum (Mu Yiqin, *Mingdai yuanti Zhepai shiliao*, p. 238).

106. For a color reproduction, see *Gugong shuhuatulu*, 9: 43.

107. Wang Cheng-hua, "Material Culture and Emperorship," p. 265.

108. For brief comments on Mongol hunts during the Yuan, see Shi Weimin, *Yuandai shehui shenghuoshi*, pp. 362–63. For a wide-ranging discussion of the hunt, see Allsen, *The Royal Hunt in Eurasian History*.

109. See Barnhart, "Emperor Xuanzong and the Painting Masters," in idem, ed., *Painters of the Great Ming*, p. 68. In *Superfluous Things*, Craig Clunas has similarly warned against blithely assuming that aesthetics of later periods and of certain groups can be accurately applied to all periods.

odds with expectations that Qing archivists miscatalogued at least two as Yuan works.[110]

As Dora Ching discusses in detail elsewhere in this volume, over the course of the fifteenth century, imperial portraiture changed from active and personal renderings of emperors to more formalized and circumscribed poses. Even within the *xingle tu* genre, by the late fifteenth century, Chenghua sits tranquilly on a throne as his eunuchs engage in archery and riding within the confines of the imperial palace.[111] One is tempted to describe these activities as increasingly vestigial remnants of a once-vigorous association with the *khaghan*. Such a generalization must, however, remain provisional. Zhou Quan's *Hunting Pheasants with Bow* dates from the late fifteenth or early sixteenth century. If we accept Wang Cheng-hua's argument that it is a portrait of Hongzhi or Zhengde, it represents a vision of the Chinese Son of Heaven as *khaghan* midway through the dynasty. There may have been other such works, especially given what we know of rulers like Zhengde. The evidence indicates that during the first half of the dynasty many Ming emperors retained an association with the Mongol legacy and sought to portray themselves in the image of the *khaghan* through these imperial portraits.

Mongol Military Personnel

Befitting a regime that drew heavily from both steppe tradition and Chinese institutional models, the Yuan Palace Guard comprised two major elements. The first and more important, the *keshig*, evolved directly from steppe practices whereby ambitious tribal leaders assembled bands of followers or companions who owed personal loyalty to their leader rather than to a clan or tribe. These men served not only as their leader's personal bodyguard but also as household staff and government advisors. Chinggis khan owed much of his initial success to his band, and by 1206 he had expanded its ranks to include approximately 10,000 men. Although the *keshig*'s scope of duties and power diminished somewhat as Khubilai introduced more Chinese institutions into his government, the *keshig*

---

110. One wonders if the misidentification was intentional. Qing officials were not encouraged to acknowledge this steppe element of Ming imperial identity, which would have undermined the Qing's claims about its unique qualifications for imperial rule.

111. For another imperial portrait of the Chenghua emperor with a Mongolian cap and his eunuch attendants with waist pouches, see the anonymous, *Emperor Xianzong with Birds*, reproduced in *A Journey into China's Antiquity*, 4: 100, plate 94.

continued to play several key roles in the Yuan empire. The *keshig* symbolized the imperial Mongol family's power, facilitated relations with other aristocratic steppe families, and figured in the maintenance of Mongol identity.

As a military institution, the *keshig* represented the khan's personal forces, which answered not to the Bureau of Military Affairs but to the emperor directly. Drawn largely from the empire's elite families, the *keshig* was dominated first and foremost by Mongols and Central Asians: Jurchens, Koreans, and Chinese members were a distant second. They enjoyed privileged political, economic, and social status within the Yuan.[112] Incorporating potential political rivals into the imperial bodyguard was a central pillar in the Yuan's strategies to forge a more unified pan-empire elite.[113]

The Ming founder continued many important Yuan military institutions, including the hereditary military household system. He also actively recruited former Yuan military personnel, both Mongols and Chinese, into the ranks of the Ming army. Henry Serruys has shown that Mongols were regularly appointed to posts within the elite Brocade Guard (Jinyiwei 錦衣衛) in Nanjing.[114] As Thomas Allsen has noted, the Brocade Guard "is certainly a direct inheritance of the Yuan, which as Marco Polo testifies, dressed its *keshig* in sumptuous clothes."[115] In 1374, the Ming founder ordered outriders in his imperial guard to wear Mongolian *jisün* tunics.[116] When Yongle relocated the capital to the north, most of those Mongols also moved to Beijing. The Ming court incorporated large numbers of recent immigrant Mongol families into elite capital units through the first half of the fifteenth century and on a more limited basis early into the sixteenth century.[117] Late in the sixteenth century, military appointment

---

112. Xiao Qiqing, "Yuandai de suwei zhidu," pp. 71–72.

113. Morihira Masahiko, "Genchō keshike seido to Kōrai ōke." The *keshig* left its mark in the Koryŏ and Chosŏn dynasties in the formation of domestic political alliances. For King Kongmin's use of ties forged during his decade-long tenure in Toghōn Temür's *keshig* in Dadu, see Kim Tangt'aek, "Koryŏ Kongmin wang ch'o ŭi muchang seryŏk," pp. 28–37. For King Ch'unghye's emulation of the *keshig* on his return to Koryŏ, see Kim Tangt'aek, *Wŏn kansŏpha ŭi Koryŏ chŏngch'isa*, p. 109.

114. Serruys, "Foreigners in the Metropolitan Police."

115. Allsen, *Commodity and Exchange in the Mongol Empire*, p. 95.

116. "Yu fu zhi" 輿服志, in Zhang Tingyu et al., *Ming shi* (hereafter cited as *MS*), 67.1648. For further discussion of the *jisün* at the Ming court, see Robinson, *The Ming Court in Eurasia*.

117. Serruys, "Foreigners in the Metropolitan Police."

books indicate that officers of Mongol descent still constituted approximately one-third of the Brocade Guard officer corps and similarly high percentages in at least two other important units in or near the capital.[118]

The Ming court's motivations for incorporating Mongol personnel into imperial military units were multifaceted. The fledgling Ming dynasty strove to increase its military advantage vis-à-vis the Yuan by bolstering its ranks with experienced cavalry fighters. The Ming court was also competing for political legitimacy on the larger Eurasian stage. Winning adherents among Mongols through promises of munificent treatment was a way to undermine support for the Yuan and dash whatever hopes it may have had for unification of the steppe.

The means through which the Ming court attempted to bolster military support and political legitimacy among Mongols, Jurchens, and others owed much to Yuan practices. Under the Great Yuan *ulus*, the *keshig* served simultaneously as a potent military force, a personal entourage of the *khaghan*, and as a way to forge personal loyalty and a sense of elite cohesiveness within the empire. One of the striking elements of the *keshig* was its cosmopolitan composition. Mongols, Jurchens, Koreans, Uighurs, Tibetans, and Kipchaks served. The Ming Brocade Guard and other elite capital garrisons certainly differed from the *keshig* in important ways. However, certain similarities deserve mention.

First, as noted above, men of Mongol and Jurchen descent constituted a surprising percentage of the Brocade Guard until nearly the end of the dynasty. Early in the sixteenth century, newly arrived Mongols and Jurchens, albeit on a modest scale, were still being incorporated into the emperor's personal bodyguard. Second, as an institution, the capital units under the Ming, like their counterparts during the Yuan, were more closely aligned with the emperor and his interests than with the civil bureaucracy. It is no accident that officials frequently criticized the practice of appointing high-ranking palace eunuchs, who served the emperor, to command key units. Third, one can discern elements of the Brocade Guard as a personal entourage. For instance, many court painters were granted posts within the Brocade Guard. Usually seen as sinecures, these appointments may have resulted from an understanding of the elite capital units as a personal or private entourage, just as the Mongols had viewed the *keshig*.

---

118. Robinson, "Images of Subject Mongols Under the Ming Dynasty," pp. 85–92. Further research has shown me that I overstated the reliability of these military appointment books.

However thoroughly integrated into Chinese administrative systems the Mongols may have been, their foreignness was not obscured. In fact, bodyguard units adopted elements of Mongol clothing. The majority of figures in the late-sixteenth-century *Emperor's Departure from the Capital* and *Emperor's Return to the Capital* scrolls show the imperial honor guard in Mongolian hats and riding tunics (see Fig. 8.8).[119] Like Tibetan Buddhism, foreign military personnel in the capital provided a visible link to the Great Yuan *ulus* and offered sources of support and legitimacy to the Ming imperial family beyond the control of the civil bureaucracy. The next section examines the use of Mongol personnel and clothing in figurines of honor guards interred within princely tombs.

Funerary Figurines

Long used as a lens on material culture during the Ming, funerary art provides another avenue for reconstructing lost elements of Ming court culture.[120] The tombs of Ming princes were meant to replicate the pomp and grandeur of their temporal courts. For instance, located in two small side chambers and a slightly larger posterior chamber of Prince Duanyi's 端懿 王 1495 tomb were clay models of three houses, seventeen pieces of furniture (including an ornate bed, a large wardrobe, and several varieties of chairs), and three incense burners. Also interred with the prince's corpse were sacrificial vessels, a wooden seal, two pieces of jade jewelry, his funerary inscription, and thirty-five strings of copper coins. Arrayed in three rows on the right and left sides of the large rectangular anterior chamber were seventy-nine clay figurines representing the princely honor guard: eunuch attendants dressed in silk gowns; men at arms holding spears, swords, or lances; musicians playing flutes or gongs; cavalry outriders; and grooms with their mounts.[121] Such documentary sources as the *Collected Administrative Statutes of the Great Ming Dynasty* (*Da Ming huidian* 大明會典)

———

119. For discussion of the painting, see Na and Kohler, *The Emperor's Procession*. For a preliminary description and effort to identify various weapons, musical instruments, and palanquins in the scrolls, see Lin Lina, "Mingren *Chujing rubi tu* zhi zonghe yanjiu."

120. For a recent overview of early (to the Tang period) funerary figures, see Bower, "From Court to Caravan." Scholarship on funerary figures strongly emphasizes Tang and pre-Tang periods. The materials from the Yuan and Ming periods are often covered in a cursory fashion or dismissed as aesthetically inferior. See Till and Swart, *Images from the Tomb*, p. 26; and Paludan, *Chinese Tomb Figures*, pp. 57–59.

121. Xi'anshi wenwu baohu kaogusuo, "Xi'an nanjiao Huang Ming zongshi," pp. 29–30, 34.

prescribe personal retinues for imperial princes that indeed included eunuchs, musicians, attendants, and military outriders. The tomb complexes of more eminent imperial clansmen were even larger and more lavishly appointed.

This attention to detail was critical to the efficacy of the tomb and its contents. Jessica Rawson has argued in regard to funerary figures, "If an image was convincing, that is, if it had the correct features, then these features gave the image the powers of thing or person depicted."[122] Particularly relevant here are Marc Abramson's observations about foreigners and mortuary art. He notes that "Tang families commissioned tomb figurines and murals with representations of barbarians in large part because of the particular potencies associated with the human 'originals' of these representations."[123] These qualities included "supernatural potency," "barbarian skills," and "martial virtues."[124] Thus, the large number of funerary figures dressed in Mongolian garb excavated from Ming princely tombs raises intriguing questions about Ming court culture and the Yuan legacy. Since mortuary art from the Ming period has never been considered before in this light, a brief review of the evidence follows below.[125]

Mongolian garb includes distinctive hats and robes. Glazed pottery pieces depicting a mounted honor guard excavated in Jianwangjing 簡王井 in Chang'an 長安 county, Shaanxi province, reveal that many men wore several varieties of Mongolian and Yuan period hats. Several standing figures from the same site also wear Mongolian-style conical

---

122. Rawson, "The Power of Images," p. 126.

123. Abramson, "Deep Eyes and High Noses," p. 120.

124. Ibid., pp. 142–43.

125. A more thorough treatment with greater attention to variation according to region, period, and individuals may be found in *The Ming Court in Eurasia*. For useful introductory comments on funerary figurines in Ming royal tombs, see Liu Yi, *Mingdai diwang lingmu zhidu yanjiu*, pp. 426–36. Many of the tombs excavated thus far were long ago plundered, usually more than once. For instance, the only thing left in the mid-sixteenth-century tomb of Zhu Bingmao, a descendent of the Prince Qin line in Xi'an, was the funerary inscription. See Sun Gang, "Ming zongshi Zhu Bingmao muzhikao," p. 67. The tomb of one grandson of Zhu Yuanzhang, enfeoffed in Chengdu, has also been plundered. However, more than 500 ceramic funerary figures have survived. Whether figures in Mongol garb number among these pieces is unclear. They are mentioned in the brief notes by Chen Jiang 陳江 and Hu Weimin 胡衛民 on the funerary figures; see Cao Zhezhi and Sun Binggen, *Zhongguo gudai yong*, pp. 432–39. Some of the figures are now held in the Sichuan Provincial Museum; the rest are in the Archeology Institute of the Chinese Academy of Social Sciences in Beijing.

hats.[126] Pottery figurines of the honor guard excavated from the tomb of one of the Shu Princes 蜀王 located east of Chengdu and dating from the first third of the fifteenth century provide further evidence that Mongolian caps and gowns were standard garb at the courts of the imperial Ming family (Fig. 8.9). Those men wore narrow-sleeved robes that buttoned on the right rather than on the left, as was more typical of Chinese preferences.[127] We may tentatively add to our list a wooden figurine wearing a gown buttoned on the right and what may be a Mongolian cap found in the mid-fifteenth-century tomb of Zhu Quan 朱權 (1378–1448; sixteenth son of Hongwu), Prince Liaojian 遼簡王 in Jiangling 江陵 county, Jingzhou 荆州, Hubei province.[128] Military figures dressed in Mongolian hats and riding tunics have been found in Prince Duanyi's late fifteenth-century tomb in a southern suburb of Xi'an.[129]

Funerary statues of men in Mongolian garb have been found in the tombs of imperial clansmen from the sixteenth century. Among the 110 clay figures of the honor guard found in the 1530 tomb of one Yi Prince 益王, Zhu Youbin 朱祐檳 (Nancheng county 南城縣, Jiangxi province), are ten musicians on horseback wearing "pointed round hats" 尖頂 圓帽, perhaps an indication of a sartorial connection to the Mongols.[130] The 1557 tomb of a later Yi Prince, Zhu Houye 朱厚燁, also contains several porcelain funerary figures from an honor guard with high pointed hats.[131]

Mongolian garb is found in nearly all extant examples of honor guards interred in tombs, including at least one example from the tomb of an in-

———

126. Photographs of the honor guard are reproduced in Cooke, *Imperial China*, pp. 165–66. More than 300 well-preserved funerary statues are held at the Shaanxi Provincial History Museum.

127. Chengdushi wenwu kaogu yanjiusuo, "Chengdu Mingdai Shu Xi wang ling fajue jianbao," pp. 47–50.

128. See the line drawing and brief description in Jingzhou diqu bowuguan and Jianglingxian wenwuju, "Jiangling Balingshan Mingdai Liao Jian wang mu fajue jianbao," pp. 708–9.

129. For black-and-white photographs and textual descriptions, see Xi'anshi wenwu baohu kaogusuo, "Xi'an nanjiao Huang Ming zongshi," pp. 32–35, 37–38.

130. See Jiangxisheng bowuguan, "Jiangxi Nancheng Ming Yiwang Zhu Youbin mu fajue baogao," p. 39.

131. The tomb contained 202 porcelain funerary figures. Three standing musicians and two figures mounted on horseback can be seen in the black-and-white photographs accompanying the archeological report; see Jiangxisheng wenwu guanli weiyuanhui, "Jiangxi Nancheng Ming Yizhuangwang mu chutu wenwu."

fluential eunuch. The tomb of Wu Jing 吳經 (d. 1533), located near Nan-jing, includes an honor guard of more than 120 funerary figures. As was true in the case of princely honor guards, Wu Jing's honor guard includes several figures, both mounted and on foot, that feature Mongolian hats and riding tunics buttoned on the right.[132]

Much more consideration is needed of the variety of ways Yuan Mongol influences manifested themselves. For instance, even a cursory examination reveals that some funerary figures in Mongolian garb have a markedly martial bearing, whereas others were entertainers. The use of Mongolian tunics and caps likely became customary over time. An honor guard rider or musician may have donned Mongolian garb not because it was Mongolian but because it had become the standard expected uniform. How conscious people were of the provenance or significance of the clothing requires further research.

These caveats aside, what significance can be drawn from the tomb figurines? First, the appearance of Mongolian caps and tunics among members of the princely honor guards closely resembles the imperial honor guard as depicted in the sixteenth-century *Emperor's Departure from the Capital* and *Emperor's Return to the Capital* scrolls. Both the funerary figurines and the scrolls reveal a variety of men—musicians, cavalry troops, and foot soldiers—with Mongolian garb. Second, the figures suggest some degree of consistency in court ritual protocol in the capital and the provinces. Third, the funerary figures in steppe gear illustrate once again the close tie between imperial power and the Mongols. If Ming emperors maintained large contingents of Mongols in the elite military units of the capital as a sign of personal power and their unique ability to transcend the Central Plains, Mongolian dress in princely honor guards may have served a similar function in the provinces (albeit on a more modest scale).

The Ming imperial family and its local scions systematically differentiated themselves from the rest of the population.[133] Control over foreign

---

132. For black-and-white photographs and brief textual descriptions, see Gu Su-ning's 顧蘇寧 notes in Cao Zhezhi and Sun Binggen, *Zhongguo gudai yong*, pp. 442–59. Cao notes the Yuan origins of some of the hats, but does not comment on the Mongolian riding tunics. Nor does he consider the significance of an honor guard garbed in Mongolian clothes. The specific references to Mongolian caps and gowns appear on pp. 444–45, 447–49, 454–55. The figures are now held in the Nanjing Municipal Museum.

133. The Ming court paid close attention to the details of the size, structure, and decoration of the physical plant of princely estates in an attempt to allow them suffi-

peoples was one way they made manifest their special status. Several court dances performed at banquets in the imperial palace featured men dressed in steppe, Central Asian, or Korean costume.[134] The dances were one facet of a larger ritual program intended to exalt the Ming court's position through the incorporation and subordination of neighboring peoples.

A Universal Ming Emperor?

The concept of universal rulership under the Mongols and Manchus has long formed a central element in understanding imperial rule during these "conquest dynasties." As foreign rulers who sought to legitimize their reign in the eyes of several constituencies, the Yuan and Qing emperors adopted a variety of identities—Buddhist deity, Islamic patron, Confucian sage, steppe warrior, and even European monarch.[135] Less carefully examined have been the identities adopted by Ming emperors, presumably because they did not answer to such a wide array of subject populations. The most developed studies devoted to Ming rulership have explored the often-acrimonious conflicts between the emperor and his civil bureaucracy over the Son of Heaven's proper role.

At the risk of oversimplification, by no later than the mid-fifteenth century, the civil bureaucracy had made major inroads in defining the emperor's job. He was to be a Confucian sage, to cultivate his morality assiduously and safely within the confines of the Forbidden City, to solicit humbly the opinions of his high officials, to accept their criticisms with gratitude, and to devote himself to important ritual matters. This particular vision of imperial rule left little room for many of the activities that emperors of previous dynasties or even of the early Ming would have taken for granted. These included the emperor's persona as warrior and military strategist, active formulator of government policy, traveling lord inspecting his domains, vigorous huntsman, or ruler over peoples beyond the Central Plains.

Ming emperors and their intimates bitterly contested this narrowing of the ruler's identity. As noted above, mid-fifteenth-century emperors

---

cient grandeur without exceeding their proper status; see Ruo Ya, "Mingdai zhuwangfu guizhi shulüe."

134. See Yu Ruji, "Yanli" 宴禮 under "Yizhisi zhizhang" 儀制司職掌, in *LBZG*, 21.16b–17b, 26a; Shen Shixing et al., *Da Ming huidian*, 73.14a–b.

135. For a discussion of universal rulership during the Yuan, see Franke, "From Tribal Chieftain to Universal Emperor and God." For the Qing case, see Crossley, *A Translucent Mirror*, and Berger, *Empire of Emptiness*.

continued to support Tibetan Buddhist monks despite the opposition of their civil bureaucracies. Mid- and late Ming emperors, too, fought against this vision, with increasingly deleterious consequences for the dynasty.[136] A full treatment of this complex question far exceeds the scope of this chapter. Here, I offer a preliminary reconsideration of Zhengde as a universal ruler in light of the Ming imperial family's continuing engagement with the Yuan legacy.

From the very first days of his reign, Zhengde's efforts to reclaim a more martial and cosmopolitan identity as emperor provoked sharp criticism. As James Geiss has shown, he spent tens of thousands of taels of silver constructing and appointing his Leopard Quarter outside the imperial palace.[137] These living arrangements, and Zhengde's later decision to build a tent city in Xuanfu, north of Beijing, are strongly reminiscent of the Mongol emperors, who also inhabited two worlds through residence in both Chinese-style palaces and steppe-style *ger*. He staffed the Leopard Quarter, the real site of policy formulation during his reign, with many of the people his civil officials found most offensive. Not only did palace eunuchs accompany Zhengde in his varied pursuits, Tibetan Buddhist monks, Central Asian singers and dancers, Jurchen and Mongol (both first-generation and descendents of earlier immigrants) bodyguards, Muslim clerics, and Chinese military men were all frequent guests at the Leopard Quarter.[138] Zhengde frequently visited the official lodgings of foreign envoys in Beijing, spending time with the heads of Mongol and Muslim missions, trying on their clothes, and sampling Muslim cuisine.[139]

Zhengde showed a keen interest in foreign lands and cultures. In the first year of his reign, he informed the Ministry of Rites, "Henceforth when various foreign (barbarian) tribute envoys come to the capital, the food and drink at banquets should be plentiful and clean. Food supplied by the postal stations along their route [to and from the capital] will be according to regulation. [It] should be supplemented to demonstrate Our intention of cherishing those from afar."[140] He possessed at least elementary Tibetan- and Mongolian-language skills. Chinese and Korean sources

---

136. In *1587, A Year of No Significance*, Ray Huang offers a subtle evocation of Wanli's efforts to pursue interests deemed inappropriate to his exalted position.

137. Geiss, "The Leopard Quarter During the Cheng-te Reign."

138. Ibid.; Li Xun, *Zhengde huangdi dazhuan*, pp. 70–94.

139. *Chungjong taewang sillok* 中宗大王實錄, 十四年九月乙巳, in Wu Han, *Chaoxian Lichao shilu zhong de Zhongguo ziliao*, 3: 929.

140. *LBZG*, 6.26a–b.

indicate (with derision) that he often spoke Mongolian with his Mongolian companions and that he wore Mongolian riding garb, including a close-fitting gown with narrow sleeves, boots, and a Mongolian cap. Chinese and Korean sources also indicate that Zhengde observed Muslim dietary restrictions at least some of the time and allowed the Muslims around him to follow these prescriptions more scrupulously.[141] The emperor shared his bed with Central Asian women. Shen Defu notes in his miscellany that the emperor "selected the daughters of Central Asian dukes and marquises and Tatar officers for the imperial harem."[142]

Information contained in the *Veritable Records of the Chosŏn Dynasty* indicates the cosmopolitan nature of Zhengde's entourage. One Korean observed in 1520: "Whenever the emperor ventures out on excursions, he selects two or three envoys each from the kingdoms of the Mongols, Muslims, Portuguese, Champa, and Lama 剌麻 [Tibetans?] to include in his entourage. Sometimes he studies their language; sometimes he views their skills."[143]

These were activities that violated the sensibilities of the majority of the civil bureaucracy. Late in his reign, Zhengde went so far as to prohibit the slaughter of swine, an order that flew in the face of the dietary habits of most of his subjects, especially those of the Jiangnan region. James Geiss has argued that his actions should be understood in view of Zhengde's interest in improving relations with China's Islamic neighbors to the west.[144]

---

141. Robinson, "Disturbing Images," p. 108.

142. Shen Defu, "Diwang qu waiguo nü," in *YHB, juan* 3, 1: 74.

143. *Chungjong taewang sillok* 中宗大王實錄十五年十二月戊戌; cited in Zheng Kecheng, "*Chosŏn Yicho sillok* zhong zhi Ming Wuzong," p. 153. The claims regarding the Portuguese ring true. Although Korean observers stressed the alien nature of Portuguese clothing and outlandish eating manners, they noted that the accommodations for the Portuguese envoys "were no different from those for other kingdoms." Zhengde spent most of 1520 in Nanjing; the Portuguese arrived there in the fifth month of the same year; see *Chungjong taewang sillok* 中宗十大王實錄五年十二月戊戌 in Wu Han, *Chaoxian Li shilu zhong de Zhongguo ziliao*, 3: 933. For Chinese evidence of Zhengde's interaction with the Portuguese and their interpreter and guide, a Chinese Muslim merchant named Hōja Asan, see Qiu Shusen, "Ming Wuzong yu Mingdai Huihuiren."

144. Geiss, "The Cheng-te Emperor's Injunction Against the Slaughter of Swine." In "Ming Wuzong yu Mingdai Huihuiren," Qiu Shusen also contextualizes Zhengde's action in terms of relations with Central Asian rulers. See also Toh Hoong Teik, "Sahkyh 'Alam." In contrast, Li Xun ("Ming Wuzong yu zhujin") has argued that Zhengde's prohibition was the act of a beleaguered ruler desperate for a measure of solace and control.

Perhaps most intriguing, however, is Zhengde's adoption of multiple personas. During his reign, Zhengde adopted a Mongolian name (Khubilai 忽必例) that unambiguously evoked Khubilai khan's legacy; a Buddhist title, Dabao fawang 大寶法王, granted to 'Phags pa; a Persian title, 沙吉敖爛, Sahkyh 'Alam, for a Muslim king; and high-ranking title in the Ming military, Weiwu dajiangjun taishi zhenguo gong 威武大將軍太師鎮國公.[145] Again, none of this endeared Zhengde to his Chinese civil officials. They instead remonstrated heatedly that he had failed to fulfill his obligations as a Chinese Son of Heaven and that he made a mockery of his position. After Zhengde's death, editors of his reign's Veritable Records repaid his intransigence with an unflattering, even ridiculous, portrait of his reign.[146] The resultant documentary record almost completely obscures Zhengde's efforts to forge, or perhaps more accurately revive, an imperial identity as universal ruler. Below, I sketch only one facet of this identity—Zhengde's involvement with Tibetan Buddhism.[147]

Shen Defu, the author of a well-informed late Ming miscellany, notes that "Zhengde was enormously fond of Buddhist doctrine. He arrayed himself among the Tibetan monks, chanting [in a manner] indistinguishable from them. He went so far as to use the title Daqing Dharma King 大慶法王. [Zhengde] smelted an official seal of [precious] metal that he granted [to this fictitious personage] as a patent." Zhengde also used 1,300 taels of gold to gild Buddhist statues.[148] During his reign, Zhengde ordered the construction of Wanshou Temple 萬壽寺 within the precincts of the Forbidden City, "where the emperor personally chanted [sutras] with the

---

145. The titles are given in Tan Qian, *Guo que*, 49.3077, cited in Satō Hisashi, "Min no Busō no 'katsubutsu' geisei ni tsuite," p. 276. Information on the emperor's titles is not included in the *Wuzong shilu* entry for this date (121.3b–4a). A slightly different version of this passage may be found in Huang Jingfang 黃景昉, *Guo shi wei yi* 國史唯疑, *juan* 5 (Xuxiu siku quanshu, 432: 83), cited in Zheng Kecheng, "*Chosŏn Yicho sillok* zhong zhi Ming Wuzong," p. 151. The translations here follow Toh Hoong Teik, "Sahkyh 'Alam," pp. 6–8. Zhengde also adopted the Tibetan name Rin chen dpal ldan, or "Glorious Gem" (Toh, p. 7).

146. For discussion, see Robinson, *Bandits, Eunuchs, and the Son of Heaven*, pp. 117–19.

147. In addition to the essays by Geiss and Toh noted above, Ma Mingdao 馬明道 has also explored Zhengde's engagement with Islam. Ma argues that the Leopard Quarter was actually a mosque. See Ma Mingdao, *Mingchao huangjia xinyangkao chugao*, pp. 69–76.

148. Shen Defu, "Shi jiao sheng shuai" 釋教盛衰, in *YHB*, *juan* 27, 3: 679. Ming- and Qing-period authors seem to have used the titles *Daqing fawang* and *Dabao fawang* interchangeably.

Tibetan monks."[149] In 1512, the year that one of the dynasty's largest rebellions was quelled, Zhengde arranged for such Tibetan monks as Daqing Dharma King 大慶法王 Rin chen dpal ldan 領占班丹 and Dajue Dharma King 大覺法王 Bkra shis bzan po 著藏肖卜, to reside in the Da long-shan huguo 大隆善護國寺 Temple, which was significantly expanded at this time.[150] As noted above, the temple complex had enjoyed Ming imperial patronage for more than a century by this time.[151] The same year, two imperially commissioned steles written in Tibetan (梵字) were erected near the relics (*sheli* 舍利; Skt. śarīra) pagodas.[152] The Ming court also commissioned the production of Tibetan *thangka*s during Zhengde's reign.[153]

Much of the emperor's personal interest in Tibetan Buddhism was firmly rooted in long-standing customs of the Ming court. Perhaps wishing to squelch the young emperor's interest in activities inappropriate to his office, immediately upon Zhengde's accession to the throne, the minister of rites submitted a memorial protesting religious activities within the Forbidden City:

I have recently learned that the Daoist Perfected One 真人 Chen Yingxun 陳應循, the Tibetan Dynastic Preceptor 西番國師 Nor bu rgyal mtshan 那卜堅參, and others each lead their disciples, gaining praise for their exorcisms [purification rituals]. On several occasions, they have entered the Hall of Imperial Tranquility. In front of the tablets honoring the dead, they [behave] without a shred of decorum. There is no one in the capital that is not astounded.[154]

——

149. Shen Defu, "Zhushang chong yijiao" 主上崇異教, in *YHB, juan* 27, 3: 683.

150. Reconstruction of the Tibetan names based on Satō Hisashi, "Mintei ni okeru ramakyō sūhai," p. 292.

151. "Chongguo si" 崇國寺, *DJJW*, 1.33; Yu Minzhong et al., "Chengshi" 城市 under "Neicheng xi cheng si" 内城西城四, in *Qinding rixia jiuwen kao*, 54.843.

152. "Chongguo si," *DJJW*, 1.33; Yu Minzhong et al., "Chengshi" under "Neicheng xicheng si," in *Qinding rixia jiuwen*, 54.843. The account in *DDJW* explicitly comments on the foreign nature of the Tibetan inscriptions, which the authors could not read.

153. Kidd, "Tibetan Painting in China." Kidd discusses *thangka*s with Chinese inscriptions from the years 1477, 1478, 1479, and 1513. The inscription from the 1513 *thangka* appears to link it to the Huguo si.

154. *Wuzong shilu* 武宗實錄, 1.17a–b; Shen Defu, "Zhushang chong yijiao" 主上崇異教, in *YHB, juan* 27, 3: 683. The minister of rites requested that these men's titles be revoked, the gifts, seals, and title patents 誥命 granted by the throne be seized, and that they be driven from the court. The emperor agreed to revoke the title of one or two men and reclaimed their gifts. He also forbid, upon penalty of severe punishment, the practice of gaining access to the Forbidden City through personal connections. Al-

The minister's complaints about Tibetan monks' unfettered access to imperial space at the turn of the sixteenth century are entirely consistent with what we have seen of officialdom's objections during the fifteenth century. His claims that people in the capital were astonished at the alleged impropriety of Tibetan monks within the imperial palace, however, ring hollow. The population of the capital was well aware of the close ties between Tibetan Buddhism and the imperial family. Like Ming emperors before him, Zhengde continued to send bilingual letters of patent to leading Tibetan clerics.[155] Patronage of Tibetan Buddhism was a defining element of imperial identity during the first half of the Ming dynasty.[156]

To return to Zhengde's personal interest in what officials of the day declared "heterodox doctrines," I would suggest that he intended to construct a portfolio of identities in harmony more with his vision of imperial rule rather than with the models advanced by the civil bureaucracy.

Evidence from blue-and-white porcelains poses intriguing questions about Zhengde's aspirations as universal ruler. Although research related to the aesthetics and technical details of production of Ming porcelains has advanced to a high level in recent decades, many questions relating to the social, cultural, and political history of porcelains remain unclear. Among them is that throughout the fifteenth and sixteenth centuries, imperial kilns produced Chinese blue-and-white porcelains bearing Sanskrit and Tibetan inscriptions.[157] These porcelains offer further evidence of the imperial family's continuing engagement with Tibetan Buddhism. Specimens have

———

though Shen Defu writes with apparent approval of the emperor's strict observation of the *Ancestral Injunctions*, we know from later developments that during the Zhengde reign, such prohibitions were not observed with any great punctiliousness. The minister was not alone in his protests. In September 1505, another official called for razing temples and monasteries in and around the capital, driving off the Dharma King Tibetan monks, and halting imperial patronage for "useless ceremonies" (*Wuzong shilu*, 4.16a). The reconstruction of the Tibetan monk's name comes from Satō Hisashi, "Mintei ni okeru ramakyō sūhai," p. 292.

155. For two bilingual examples dating from 1507 and 1515 held in the Potola Temple, see Su Bai, "Lasa Budalagong zhuyao diantang he kuzang de bufen Mingdai wenshu," p. 44.

156. For further details of Zhengde's interest in Tibetan Buddhism, see Nan Bingwen, *Fojiao mimi zongjiao yu Mingdai shehui*, pp. 64–69.

157. For an argument that dates the establishment of the Ming imperial kilns to the Xuande reign, see Wang Guangyao, "Mingdai yuqichang de jianli." Zhengde-period imperial porcelains with Arabic, Persian, and Sanskrit inscriptions also survive. I thank Jan Stuart of the Freer Museum, Washington, DC, for generously providing me with information regarding a Zhengde blue-and-white porcelain with an Arabic inscription.

surfaced in the former Qing imperial collections, in various temples in Tibet, and in temples in Beijing. Zhengde seems to have commissioned porcelains bearing an especially wide variety of foreign inscriptions.

Based on dating inscriptions, shape, and painting styles, Lü Chenglong has recently argued that several blue-and-white porcelains with 'Phags pa script inscriptions formerly attributed to the late Yuan period were actually produced during the Zhengde period by imperial kilns located in Jingdezhen in emulation of Yuan pieces.[158] Named after its developer, 'Phags pa, the eponymous script was designated one of the official writing systems of the Great Yuan *ulus,* which used it extensively but never exclusively in administrative documents and seals. Lü's explanations for why imperial kilns might have produced such imitations include efforts "to satisfy the Zhengde emperor's worshipful attitude toward the Yuan period Dynastic Preceptor 'Phags pa or to provide for use by national preceptors and Living Buddhas within the Leopard Quarter, or possibly as rewards to Mongolian and Tibetan lamas."[159]

A more likely interpretation is that Zhengde was attempting to establish a series of flattering historical connections that linked himself to Khubilai khan. James Geiss has demonstrated that Zhengde attempted to revive the martial traditions of the early Ming rulers. In fact, one might easily extend these early Ming traditions back to the Mongols. As we have seen above, court paintings from the first half of the Ming dynasty reveal extensive Mongolian influences in terms of martial activities, hunting on horseback, archery, and clothing. That Zhengde would attempt to portray himself as a direct descendent of Yongle, and ultimately of Khubilai, is thus not unexpected.

Zhengde's posturing was also diplomatically astute. Although the 'Phags pa script did not gain wide acceptance during the Yuan period, it was inextricably tied to Khubilai and his famed Tibetan monk and advisor 'Phags pa. Thus even if the Tibetan religious leaders to whom Zhengde presented

---

158. Lü Chenglong, "Guanyu Basibazi kuan qinghua ciqi niandai zhi wojian." Lü's work builds upon the observations of Ge Shike, "Yetan Basibawen kuan qinghua ciqi de niandai." On the debate whether porcelains with the Zhizheng reign title were produced during the late Yuan or the mid-Ming, see Cao Ganyuan, "'Zhizheng nianzhi' kuan caiciwan yu Jiajing honglü caici"; Zhang Ying, "Cong 'Zhizheng nianzhi' kuan caiciwan de faxian"; idem, "Dui 'Yetan Basibawen kuan qinghua ciqi de niandai' yiwen de shangque." See also Liu Zhenhua, "Jingdezhen Longzhuge cang qinghua ciwan Basibazi kuan kaochaji."

159. Lü Chenglong, "Guanyu Basibazi kuan qinghua ciqi niandai zhi wojian," p. 79.

these porcelains could not read the 'Phags pa inscriptions, they could readily understand the message. Through the distribution of these imperially
manufactured gifts, the current leader of the Ming dynasty was adopting
the role of a later-day Khubilai. The not-so-subtle inference was that these
contemporary Tibetan leaders were then later-day versions of 'Phags pa.[160]
It was a set of references flattering to both sides, and it owed nothing to
Zhengde's Chinese bureaucracy. If anything, it suggested a time when Chinese officials were marginalized, when much of the most critical functions
of government had been turned over to such non-Chinese groups as Per-
sians, Arabs, Uighurs, Mongols, Khitans, and other Central Asians.[161]

Concluding Remarks

We are in the midst of an important re-evaluation of the Ming court. In an
examination of the interplay of Buddhist art and architecture with Ming
imperial modes, Marsha Weidner Haufler has noted the "exhilarating expansion of geographic and cultural horizons imposed by traditional, lite-
rati-centered accounts of Ming art" to be gained by considering the wider
scope of participants (including women, ethnic minorities, and eunuchs in
the capital and the provinces) involved in such dynamics.[162] Recent studies
by such scholars as Kenneth Hammond, Richard Barnhart, and others also
amply demonstrate the value of decentering literati writings and trying to
repopulate the Ming court in its full complexity and diversity. This re-
evaluation of court dynamics is one element of a larger project, a reconceptualization of Ming history, indeed Chinese history as a whole, that attempts to put in more realistic perspective the roles, tastes, and views of
the literati.

---

160. In 1578, the powerful Mongol leader Altan Khan and Bsod nams rgya mtsho,
the head of the 'Bras spuns monastery in Lhasa, announced precisely this kind of relation. Altan Khan was named the reincarnation of Khubilai, and the Tibetan teacher the
reincarnation of 'Phags pa. For a biographical note on Altan Khan by Henry Serruys
that refers to this relation, see Goodrich and Fang, *Dictionary of Ming Biography*, pp. 6–9.
For extended discussion of these historical allusions and the place of the Ming court in
the revival of Lamaism on the steppe, see Serruys, "Early Lamaism in Mongolia."

161. Other blue-and-white porcelains produced in imperial kilns during the Zhengde
period feature Sanskrit, Persian, and Arabic inscriptions. See Geng Baochang, *Qinghua
youlihong*, color plates, 53, 56, 66, and 77–79 (on pp. 58, 61, 71, 83–85, respectively); Li Yihua, "Liangjian Zhengde chao Alabowen Bosiwen ciqi," p. 50; and Zhao Hong, "Ming
Zhengde qinghua ciqi ji youguan wenti," p. 30.

162. Weidner, "Imperial Engagement with Buddhist Art and Architecture," p. 139.

Ming literati wrote about elements of court life that interested them or flattered them or enhanced their role. Minimized or completely omitted were groups, ethos, practices, and objects that did not harmonize with literati tastes and perspectives. The resultant documentary record is often deeply flawed and misleading. This preliminary account of the Ming imperial family's engagement with the Mongol Yuan legacy has drawn on a variety of evidence: scattered casual observations by literati; evidence in government regulations that took for granted the presence of foreign and military personnel at the Ming court; and finally, materials not subject to the literati's brush. This last category includes pictorial representations of court activities that preserve elements bowdlerized from other accounts; funerary art buried in princely tombs that strongly suggests continuing concern with the Yuan legacy in clothing and material culture; and porcelains produced at imperial kilns.

During the first half of the Ming dynasty, the imperial family's identity was deeply influenced by the Mongol legacy. Even as Hongwu publicly strove to distinguish his new, pure-Chinese regime from what he described as the pernicious influences of the Mongols, he maintained many institutional practices from the Yuan period. The imperial family's links with the Mongols emerged with special clarity during the reign of his son, Yongle. In the public sphere, especially in the arenas of foreign policy, the military, and overseas trade, Yongle implemented a number of policies that bore more than a superficial resemblance to those of the Mongols.

In areas more narrowly related to the imperial family, Ming rulers preserved links to the Mongol legacy. During the fifteenth century, emperors periodically commissioned court painters to portray them in clothing styles and activities indistinguishable from those of steppe *khaghan*. Throughout the first half of the dynasty, Ming emperors included Mongol hats and riding tunics in their wardrobes. The large, finely detailed *Emperor's Procession* scrolls from the late sixteenth century include Mongol personnel or Chinese personnel dressed in Mongol clothing. Funerary figurines of men garbed in Mongolian dress have been found in the tombs of many Ming imperial princes from the fifteenth and sixteenth centuries. Princely courts often replicated on a more modest scale the trappings of the imperial court in Beijing—bodyguards, legal privileges, impressive architecture, and incorporation into imperial sacrifices. All these features defined them as imperial relatives and distinguished them from the rest of the population. One facet of this greater Ming court was a lasting association with the Great Yuan *ulus*.

Another important element of Ming imperial engagement with the Yuan court included the patronage of Tibetan Buddhism. Under the Yuan, Tibetan Buddhist monks such as 'Phags pa enjoyed the generous patronage of the imperial family and considerable renown within capital society. If anything, the association between the imperial family and Tibetan Buddhism grew more exclusive during the first half of the Ming dynasty. Susan Naquin has noted that Tibetan Buddhism did not have a wide popular base of support among the broader population of Ming Beijing.[163] Tibetan monks, however, conducted court rituals, enjoyed privileged status, and gained access to the jealously guarded, private world of the emperors. Temples linked to Tibetan Buddhism through patronage, architectural style, or religious personnel dotted the Forbidden City, the capital, and surrounding counties.

Acknowledgment of the Ming imperial family's ongoing engagement with the Yuan legacy forces reconsideration of the tenth Ming emperor, Zhengde. Conventional wisdom portrays Zhengde as a bizarre aberration whose idiosyncratic interest in Mongols, Tibetan Buddhism, Central Asia, and Islam won him a deserved reputation for the absurd. There is no denying Zhengde's personal excess. However, when considered in terms of the ruling Zhu lineage's extensive engagement with the Yuan, many elements of his behavior seem far less eccentric. Zhengde's death in 1521 marked the end of an age.

Zhengde's death without an heir led to the enthronement of his cousin, Jiajing, who had been raised in distant Anlu, Huguang. Many fine studies have examined the wide-ranging and intensely personal debates over the proper ritual treatment due the new emperor's parents that unfolded during Jiajing's reign.[164] This transition represented not only a shift in political power but also in the identity of the imperial family. Raised far

---

163. Naquin, *Peking*, p. 150. This point should not be overstated. Tantric statues were sold in upscale markets in Beijing. Jiajing was deeply worried that "the ignorant" in the city would rush to acquire the Tibetan relics if they were simply buried. He ordered them desecrated, and the ashes scattered. All told, 169 gold and silver statues and 13,000 *jin* of various bone relics were ordered destroyed. See *Shizong shilu*, 187.4b–5a 嘉靖十五年五月乙丑; Shen Defu, "Fei Fo shi" 廢佛氏 under "Shi dao" 釋道, *YHB bu yi, juan* 4, 3: 916. For a broad discussion of images of Tibetan Buddhism in Ming society, see Shen Weirong, "'Kaijū en-i' gensetsu ni okeru Mindai Chūgoku to Chibetto no seiji bunka kankei," pp. 264–310. See also He Xiaorong, "Mingdai huangdi chongfeng Zangchuan fojiao qianxi," pp. 136–37, for scattered references to the impact of Tibetan Buddhism in Beijing, Nanjing, and Mount Wutai.

164. Geiss, "The Chia-ching Reign"; Fisher, *The Chosen One*.

outside the walls of the Forbidden City and the center of Ming court culture, Jiajing's upbringing did not feature so prominently the trappings of
the Mongol legacy. Perhaps princely courts distant from Beijing were more
inclined to partake of new fashions and tastes, to shed their identification
with the Great Yuan *ulus* more rapidly than the imperial court in the Forbidden City.

For instance, Jiajing severely curtailed imperial patronage of Tibetan
Buddhism.[165] Shen Defu notes:

> In general [the emperor] was happy [only with] the complete elimination of what-
> soever pertained to the Buddhist faith. For instance, under previous reigns, Da
> Cien Temple was the most flourishing of Buddhist temples. During the reigns of
> Chenghua, Hongzhi, and Zhengde, the dharma king, the dynastic preceptor, [and
> others] who resided here [numbered] ten thousand men. All of them depended on
> imperial patronage. During the early Jiajing period, all were removed. [The court]
> drove the Tibetan *sangha* to other places. In the twenty-second year [of the Jiajing
> reign, 1543], [the emperor] ordered the temple razed. Not even a scrap of wood or
> piece of tile remained.[166]

Shen here emphasizes a clear break not only from Zhengde but also from
more long-standing family traditions. Some high officials attacked the Tantric statue of the Joyous Buddhas housed in the Da Cien Temple as "an
ugly custom of the former Yuan dynasty that should be destroyed and discarded." Jiajing fully concurred, calling it a "licentious statue of the barbarian demons."[167]

----

165. Turrell Wylie ("Lama Tribute in the Ming Dynasty," p. 338) has framed the
question differently, stressing the fact that Tibetan monks stopped coming to the Ming
court. He speculates that the return of the Mongols to the Kokonor region rendered
Ming imperial patronage superfluous.

166. Shen's comments appear in a discussion of Jiajing's passion for Daoism. See
Shen Defu, "Ci baiguan shi" 賜百官食 under "Liechao" 列朝, in *YHB, juan* 1, 1: 5. See
also *Shizong shilu* 世宗實錄, 272.5a. See also Tan Qian, *Guo que*, 58.3642. Citing the *Qinding rixia jiuwen kao*, Naquin (*Peking*, p. 150*n*75) dates the destruction of this temple to
1535.

167. Shen Defu, "Jingshi diwang miao" 京師帝王廟 under "Liechao," in *YHB, juan*
1, 1: 2; Sun Chengze, "Diwang miao" 帝王廟, in *Tianfu guangji*, 9.87. Jiajing failed to
sever the Ming court's ties to Tibetan Buddhism. As noted above, the Ming court enjoyed an international reputation as a center for Tibetan Buddhism. When in the 1570s
and 1580s, Mongols wanted to secure copies of Tibetan scriptures or to learn painting
techniques in the Tibetan tradition, they turned to the Ming court. The Ming court often dispatched Tibetan monks to deliver these items to Mongolian leaders on the
steppe. For more details, see Robinson, *The Ming Court in Eurasia*.

Also suggestive of the emerging new view of the Yuan legacy was an effort to remove Khubilai khan from the legitimate line of dynastic emperors. For instance, Jiajing's reign witnessed the abolition of offerings for Khubilai that had been conducted twice a year by Shuntian prefectural officials.[168] In 1545, after some debate, Jiajing struck Khubilai khan and his five ministers from the list of those who received offerings at the Rulers Temple.[169] Shen Defu offers an explanation of Jiajing's decision: "At the time, [the emperor] detested the caitiff raiders for [their] incursions [into Ming territory]."[170] Perhaps, but the major raids into Beijing's suburbs by the great Mongol leader, Altan Khan (1508–82), were still five years in the future. Jiajing's actions suggest his awareness of the continued association between the Ming imperial family and the great Mongol ruler Khubilai khan. His rejection of that association demonstrates the importance of the Mongol legacy to understanding politics and identity at the Ming court.[171]

---

168. See "Diwang lingqin" 帝王陵寢 under "Cijisi zhizhang" 祠祭司職掌, in *LBZG*, 30.15a; and "Lizhi si jili si" 禮志四吉禮四 under "Jingshi jiumiao" 京師九廟, in *MS*, 50.1306. This passage does not make clear the location of the Temple for the Yuan Founder 元世祖廟.

169. See "Lidai diwang" 歷代帝王 under "Cijisi zhizhang" 祠祭司職掌, in *LBZG*, 29.2b. See *Shizong shilu* 296.2b; "Lizhi si jili si" under "Lidai Diwang lingmiao," in *MS*, *juan* 50; and Sun Chengze, "Diwang miao," in *Tianfu guangji*, 9.88.

170. Shen Defu, "Diwang peiting" 帝王配亭 under "Liechao," in *YHB*, *juan* 1, 1: 3.

171. The decision to eliminate offerings to Khubilai needs to be considered in the context of wider intellectual, political, and foreign-relations developments. See my *The Ming Court in Eurasia*.

DAVID M. ROBINSON

Works Cited

Abramson, Marc. "Deep Eyes and High Noses: Physiognomy and the Depiction of Barbarians in Tang China." In *Political Frontiers, Ethnic Boundaries, and Human Geographies in Chinese History*, ed. Nicola Di Cosmo and Don J. Wyatt. London: Routledge Curzon, 2003, pp. 119–59.

Allsen, Thomas. *Commodity and Exchange in the Mongol Empire*. Cambridge: Cambridge University Press, 1997.

———. *Culture and Conquest in Mongol Eurasia*. Cambridge: Cambridge University Press, 2001.

———. *The Royal Hunt in Eurasian History*. Philadelphia: University of Pennsylvania, 2006.

Aramiya Manabu 新宮学. "Minsho no En'ōfu o meguru shomondai" 明初の燕王府をめぐる諸問題. *Tōyōshi kenkyū* 東洋史研究 60, no. 1 (June 2001): 69–103.

Barnhart, Richard. "The Foundation of Ming Painting." In *Painters of the Great Ming: The Imperial Court and the Zhe School*, ed. idem. Dallas: Dallas Museum of Art, 1993, pp. 21–125.

Barnhart, Richard, ed. *Painters of the Great Ming: The Imperial Court and the Zhe School*. Dallas: Dallas Museum of Art, 1993.

Berger, Patricia. *Empire of Emptiness: Buddhist Art and Political Authority in Qing China*. Honolulu: University of Hawai'i Press, 2003.

———. "Miracles in Nanjing: An Imperial Record of the Fifth Karmapa's Visit to the Chinese Capital." In *Cultural Intersections in Later Chinese Buddhism*, ed. Marsha Weidner. Honolulu: University of Hawai'i Press, 2001, pp. 145–69.

Bower, Virginia. "From Court to Caravan: Chinese Tomb Sculptures from the Collection of Anthony M. Solomon." In *From Court to Caravan: Chinese Tomb Sculptures from the Collection of Anthony M. Solomon*, ed. idem. Cambridge: Harvard University Art Museum; and New Haven: Yale University Press, 2002, pp. 21–70.

Cai Meibiao 蔡美彪. "Mingdai Menggu yu Da Yuan guohao" 明代蒙古與大元國號. *Nankai xuebao* 南開學報 1992, no. 1: 43–51.

Cao Ganyuan 曹淦源. "'Zhizheng nianzhi' kuan caiciwan yu Jiajing honglü caici" 「至正年制」款彩瓷碗與嘉靖紅綠彩瓷. *Wenwu*, 1994, no. 8: 74–86.

Cao Zhezhi 曹者祉 and Sun Binggen 孫秉根, eds. *Zhongguo gudai yong* 中國古代俑. Shanghai: Shanghai wenhua chubanshe, 1996.

Chan, Hok-lam 陳學霖. "Mingchu Chaoxian 'ruchao' huanguan juyu—Hae Su shiji tansuo" 明初朝鮮「入朝」宦官舉隅—海壽事蹟探索. *Gugong xueshu jikan* 故宮學術季刊 16, no. 4 (1999): 57–93.

Chang Tong'ik 張東翼. *Koryŏ hugi oegyosa yŏn'gu* 高麗後期外交史研究. Seoul: Ilchogak, 1994.

CHC, 7, see Mote and Twitchett, *Cambridge History of China*; 8, see Twitchett and Mote, *Cambridge History of China*

Chen Gaohua 陳高華. "Song Yuan he Mingchu de maqiu" 宋元和明初的馬球. *Lishi yanjiu* 歷史研究 1984, no. 4: 177–81.

———. *Yuan Dadu* 元大都. Beijing: Beijing chubanshe, 1982.

————. "Zhu Yuanzhang de fojiao zhengce" 朱元璋的佛教政策. *Mingshi yanjiu* 明史研究 1 (1991): 110–18.

Chen Yingqing 陳英慶 et al. *Sajia shixishi* 薩迦世係史. Xizang renmin chubanshe, 2002.

Chengdushi wenwu kaogu yanjiusuo 成都市文物考古研究所. "Chengdu Mingdai Shu Xi wang ling fajue jianbao" 成都明代蜀僖王陵發掘簡報. *Wenwu* 2002, no 4: 41–54.

Chŏn Chongsŏk 全宗釋. "Kōrai bukkyō to Gendai Ramakyō to no kankei—Ramakyō no eikyō o chūshin ni" 高麗仏教と元代喇嘛教との関係—喇嘛教の影響を中心に. *Indogaku bukkyōgaku kenkyū* 印度学仏教学研究 35, no. 2 (1987): 677–79.

Clark, Donald. "The Ming Connection: Notes on Korea's Experience in the Chinese Tributary System." *Transactions of the Korea Branch of the Royal Asiatic Society* 58 (1983): 77–89.

————. "Sino-Korean Tributary Relations Under the Ming." In *CHC*, 8: 272–300.

Clunas, Craig. *Pictures and Visuality in Early Modern China*. Princeton: Princeton University Press, 1996.

————. *Superfluous Things: Material Culture and Social Status in Early Modern China*. Urbana: University of Illinois Press, 1991.

Cooke, Bill, executive ed. *Imperial China: The Art of the Horse in Chinese History*. Lexington: Kentucky Horse Park, 2000.

Crossley, Pamela. *A Translucent Mirror: History and Identity in Qing Imperial Ideology*. Berkeley: University of California, 1999.

Danjō Hiroshi 檀上寛. "Shoki Min teikoku taiseiron" 初期明帝国体制論. In *Iwanami kōza sekai rekishi* 岩波講座世界歷史, vol. 11, *Chūō yūrashia no tōgō* 中央ユーラシアの統合, ed. Kobayama Kōichi 樺山紘一. Tokyo: Iwanami shoten, 1997, pp. 303–24.

Dardess, John. "Ming T'ai-tsu on the Yuan: An Autocrat's Assessment of the Mongol Dynasty." *Bulletin of Song and Yuan Studies* 14 (1978): 6–11.

DJJW, see Liu Tong and Yu Yicheng, *Dijing jingwulüe*

Dreyer, Edward. *Early Ming China: A Political History, 1355–1435*. Stanford: Stanford University Press, 1982.

————. "Military Origins of Ming China." In *CHC*, 7: 58–106.

————. *Zheng He: China and the Oceans in the Early Ming Dynasty, 1405–1433*. New York: Pearson/Longman, 2007.

Fang Jianchang 房建昌. "Xizang Rulai dabao fawang kao" 西藏如來大寶法王考. *Zhongyang minzu xueyuan xuebao* 中央民族學院學報, 1991, no. 5: 52–56.

Farmer, Edward. *Zhu Yuanzhang and Early Ming Legislation: The Reordering of Chinese Society Following the End of Mongol Rule*. Leiden: E. J. Brill, 1995.

Farquhar, David. "Emperor as Bodhisattva in the Governance of the Ch'ing Empire." *Harvard Journal of Asiatic Studies* 38, no. 1 (1978): 5–35.

Fisher, Carney. *The Chosen One: Succession and Adoption in the Court of Ming Shizong*. Sydney: Allen and Allen, 1990.

Fong, Wen C. "Imperial Portraiture of the Ming Dynasty." In *Possessing the Past: Treasures from the National Palace Museum, Taipei*, ed. Wen C. Fong and James Watt. New York: Metropolitan Museum of Art, 1996, pp. 327–33.

Franke, Herbert. "From Tribal Chieftain to Universal Emperor and God: Legitimation of the Yuan Dynasty." In idem, *China Under Mongol Rule*. Brookfield, VT: Variorum Press, 1994, pt. IV, pp. 3–85.

Gammer, Moshe. "Russia and the Eurasian Steppe Nomads: An Overview." In *Mongols, Turks, and Others*, ed. Reuven Amitai and Michal Biran. Leiden: Brill, 2005, pp. 483–502.

Gao Shouxian 高壽仙. "Hongwu shiqi de shehui jiaoyu yu yifeng yisu" 洪武時期的社會教育與移風易俗. *Mingshi yanjiu* 明史研究 1999, no. 6: 83–93.

Ge Shike 葛師科. "Yetan Basibawen kuan qinghua ciqi de niandai" 也談巴思八文款青花瓷器的年代. *Wenwu* 1997, no. 6: 43–47, 38.

Geiss, James. "The Cheng-te Emperor's Injunction Against the Slaughter of Swine." Unpublished MS.

———. "The Chia-ching Reign, 1522–1566." In *CHC*, 7: 440–510.

———. "The Leopard Quarter During the Cheng-te reign." *Ming Studies* 24 (1987): 1–38.

Geng Baochang 耿寶昌, ed. *Qinghua youlihong* 青花釉里紅. Shanghai: Shanghai kexue jishu chubanshe, 2000.

Goodrich, L. C., and Fang Chao-ying, eds. *Dictionary of Ming Biography*. 2 vols. New York: Columbia University Press, 1976.

Gugong bowuyuan 故宮博物院, comp. *Mingdai gongting yu Zhepai huihua xuanji* 明代宮廷與浙派繪畫選集. Beijing: Wenwu chubanshe, 1983.

Guoli gugong bowuyuan 國立故宮博物院. *Gugong shuhuatulu* 故宮書畫圖錄. Taibei: Gugong bowuyuan, 1989– .

Halperin, Charles. *Russia and the Golden Horde: The Mongol Impact on Medieval Russian History*. Bloomington: Indiana University Press, 1985.

He Xiaorong 何孝榮. "Mingdai huangdi chongfeng Zangchuan fojiao qianxi" 明代皇帝崇奉藏傳佛教淺析. *Zhongguoshi yanjiu* 中國史研究 2005, no. 4: 119–37.

Hu Zhaojing 胡昭靜. "Sajia si cang Ming Xuande yuyao qinghua wucaiwan" 薩迦寺藏明宣德御窯青花五彩碗. *Wenwu* 1985, no. 11: 72–73.

Huang, Ray. *1587, A Year of No Significance*. New Haven: Yale University Press, 1981.

Hubeisheng wenwu kaogu yanjiusuo 湖北省文物考古研究所 et al. "Hubei Zhongxiang Mingdai Liangzhuang wang mu fajue jianbao" 湖北鍾祥明代梁莊王墓發掘簡報. *Wenwu* 2003, no. 5: 4–23.

Ishihama Yumiko 石浜裕美子. *Chibetto bukkyō sekai no rekishiteki kenkyū* チベット仏教世界の歴史的研究. Tokyo: Tōhō shoten, 2001.

Jiang Shunyuan 姜舜源. "Ming Qing gongting Chaoxian 'cai nü' yanjiu" 明清宮廷朝鮮「采女」研究. *Gugong bowuyuan yuankan* 故宮博物院院刊, 1997, no. 4: 79–89.

Jiang Yikui 蔣一葵. *Chang'an kehua* 長安客話. Late 16th c. Beijing: Beijing guji chubanshe, 1994.

Jiangxisheng bowuguan 江西省博物館. "Jiangxi Nancheng Ming Yiwang Zhu Youbin mu fajue baogao" 江西南城明益王朱祐檳墓發掘報告. *Wenwu* 1973, no. 3: 33–45.

Jiangxisheng wenwu guanli weiyuanhui 江西省文物管理委員會. "Jiangxi Nancheng Ming Yizhuangwang mu chutu wenwu" 江西南城明益莊王墓出土文物. *Wenwu* 1959, no. 1: 48–49, 52.

Jingzhou diqu bowuguan 荆州地區博物館 and Jianglingxian wenwuju 江陵縣文物局. "Jiangling Balingshan Mingdai Liao Jian wang mu fajue jianbao" 江陵八嶺山明代 遼簡王墓發掘簡報. *Kaogu* 1995, no. 8: 702–12.

A Journey into China's Antiquity. Beijing: Morning Glory Publishers, 1997.

Kidd, David. "Tibetan Painting in China: New Light on a Puzzling Group of Dated *Tangkas*." *Oriental Art* 21, no. 2 (1975): 56–60.

Kim Tangt'aek 金塘澤. "Koryŏ Kongmin wang ch'o ŭi muchang seryŏk" 高麗恭愍 王初의 武將勢力. *Han'guksa yŏn'gu* 韓國史研究 93 (1996): 27–53.

———. "Koryŏ Uwang wŏnnyŏn 1375 nyŏn Wŏnkwa ŭi oegyo kwan'gye chaegae rŭl tŭllŏ ssan chŏngch'i seryŏk kan ŭi kaldŭng" 高麗禑王元年 1375 年元과의외교 관계再開를들러싼정치세력간의갈등. *Chindan hakpo* 震檀學報 83 (1997): 21–41.

———. *Wŏn kansŏpha ŭi Koryŏ chŏngch'isa* 元干涉下의 高麗政治史. Seoul: Ilchogak, 1998.

Komaroff, Linda, and Stefano Carboni, eds. *The Legacy of Genghis Khan: Courtly Art and Culture in Western Asia, 1256–1353*. New York: Metropolitan Museum of Art; and New Haven: Yale University Press, 2003.

Kun dga' bsod nams grags pa rgyal mts'an. *Sa skya'i gdun rabs*. 1629. Trans. from the Tibetan into Chinese by Chen Yingqing 陳英慶 et al. *Sajia shixishi* 薩迦世係史. Xizang renmin chubanshe, 2002.

Langlois, John. "The Hung-wu Reign, 1368–1398." In *CHC*, 7: 107–81.

———. "Introduction." In *China Under Mongol Rule*, ed. idem. Princeton: Princeton University Press, 1981, pp. 3–21.

LBZG, see Yu Ruji, *Libu zhigao*

Leidy, Denise Patry. "Buddhist Art." In *Defining Yongle: Imperial Art in Early Fifteenth Century China*, ed. James C. Y. Watt and Denise Patry Leidy. New York: Metropolitan Museum of Art, 2005, pp. 60–101.

Li Xun 李洵. "Ming Wuzong yu zhujin" 明武宗與豬禁. *Shixue jikan* 史學集刊 1993, no. 2: 13–17, 48.

———. *Zhengde huangdi dazhuan* 正德皇帝大傳. Shenyang: Liaoning jiaoyu chubanshe, 1993.

Li Yihua 李毅華. "Liangjian Zhengde chao Alabowen Bosiwen ciqi" 兩件正德朝阿拉 伯文波斯文瓷器. *Gugong bowuyuan yuankan* 故宮博物院院刊 1984, no. 3: 49–51.

Lin Lina 林莉娜. "Mingren *Chujing rubi tu* zhi zonghe yanjiu" 明人「出警入蹕圖」之 綜合研究. 2 pts. *Gugong wenwu yuekan* 故宮文物月刊 10, no. 7 (1993): 58–77; no. 8: 34–41.

Liu Tong 劉侗 and Yu Yizheng 于奕正, comps. *Dijing jingwulüe* 帝京景物略. 1635. Reprinted—Beijing: Beijing guji chubanshe, 2001.

Liu Zhenhua 劉振華. "Jingdezhen Longzhuge cang qinghua ciwan Basibazi kuan kaochaji" 景德鎮龍珠閣藏青花瓷碗八思巴字款考察記. *Wenwu* 1996, no. 11: 52–54.

Lu Rong 陸容. *Shuyuan zaji* 菽園雜記. 1494. Reprinted—Beijing: Zhonghua shuju, 1985.

Lü Chenglong 呂成龍. "Guanyu Basibazi kuan qinghua ciqi niandai zhi wojian" 關於 八思巴字款青花瓷器年代之我見. *Wenwu* 2001, no. 8: 77–83.

Ma Jige 馬季戈. "*Xuanzong xingle tu* tu" 《宣宗行樂圖》 圖. *Zijincheng* 紫禁城 1990, no. 3: 34–38.

Ma Mingdao 馬明道. *Mingchao huangjia xinyangkao chugao* 明朝皇家信仰考初稿. Taibei?: Zhongguo Huijiao wenhua jiaoyu jijinhui, n.d.

Manz, Beatrice Forbes. *Rise and Rule of Tamerlane.* Cambridge: Cambridge University Press, 1989.

———. "Temür and the Problem of a Conqueror's Legacy." *Journal of the Royal Asiatic Society* 8, no. 1 (1998): 21–41.

Matsukawa Takeshi 松川節. "Chibetto jichiku hakubutsukan zō gogengo gappeki *Rulai dabao fawang jian pudu dazhao changjuanhua* (1407 nen) no Mongorugo tekisute ni tsuite" チベット自治区博物館蔵五言語合璧『如來大寶法王建普度大齋長卷畫』(一四〇七年) のモンゴル語テキステについて. *Ōtani gakuhō* 大谷学報 82, no. 4 (2004): 1–15.

Min Hyŏn'gu. "Koryŏ Kongmin wang ŭi chŭkwi paegyŏng" 高麗恭愍王의即位背景. In *Han U-gŭn paksa chŏngnyŏn kinyŏm sahak nonch'ong* 韓우근博士停念紀年史學論叢. Seoul: Chisik sanopsa, 1981, pp. 791–808.

Ming shilu 明實錄. 1418–mid-17th c. Facsimile reproduction of the Hongge chaoben held at the Guoli Beiping tushuguan. 133 vols. Taibei: Zhongyang yanjiuyuan, Lishi yuyan yanjiusuo, 1961–66.

Miyazaki Ichisada 宮崎市定. "Kōbu kara Eiraku e—shoki Minchō seiken no seikaku" 洪武から永楽へ——初期明朝政権の性格. *Tōyōshi kenkyū* 東洋史研究 27, no. 4 (1969): 1–23.

Morgan, David. *The Mongols.* Malden: Blackwell, 1998.

Morihira Masahiko 森平雅彦. "Fuma Kōrai kokuō no seiritsu—Genchō in okeru Kōraiō no chi'i ni tsuite no yobiteki kōsatsu" 駙馬高麗国王の成立——元朝における高麗王の地位についての予備的考察. *Tōyō gakuhō* 東洋学報 79, no. 4 (Mar. 1998): 1–30.

———. "Genchō keshike seido to Kōrai ōke—Kōrai-Gen chō kankei ni okeru *turyay* no igi ni kanren shite" 元朝ケシケ制度と高麗王家——高麗元朝関係における禿魯花の意義に関連して. *Shigaku zasshi* 史学雑誌 110, no. 2 (Feb. 2001): 60–89.

Mote, Frederick W., and Denis Twitchett, eds. *The Cambridge History of China*, vol. 7, *The Ming Dynasty, 1368–1644, Part I.* Cambridge: Cambridge University Press, 1988.

MS, see Zhang Tingyu et al., *Ming shi*

Mu Yiqin 穆益勤. "Mingdai gongting huihua—*Xuanzong xingle tu*" 明代宮廷繪畫——《宣宗行樂圖》. *Gugong bowuyuan yuankan* 1983, no. 2: 38–42.

Mu Yiqin 穆益勤, comp. *Mingdai yuanti Zhepai shiliao* 明代院體浙派史料. Shanghai: Shanghai renmin chubanshe, 1985.

Na Chih-liang and William Kohler. *The Emperor's Procession: Two Scrolls of the Ming Dynasty.* Taibei: National Palace Museum, 1970.

Nan Bingwen 南炳文, ed. *Fojiao mimi zongjiao yu Mingdai shehui* 佛教秘密宗教與明代社會. Tianjin: Tianjin guji chubanshe, 2002.

Naqqash, Ghiyathuddin. "Report to Mirza Baysunghur on the Timurid Legation to the Ming Court at Peking." Trans. in W. M. Thackston, *A Century of Princes: Sources of Timurid History and Art.* Cambridge: Aga Khan Program for Islamic Architecture at Harvard University, 1989, pp. 279–97.

Naquin, Susan. *Peking: Temples and City Life, 1400–1900.* Berkeley: University of California Press, 2000.

Okada Hidehiro. "China as a Successor State to the Mongols." In *The Mongol Empire and Its Legacy*, ed. Reuven Amitai-Preiss and David Morgan. Leiden: Brill, 1999, pp. 260–72.

Ostrowski, Donald. *Muscovy and the Mongols: Cross-Cultural Influences on the Steppe Frontier, 1304–1589*. Cambridge: Cambridge University Press, 1998.

Otagi Matsuo 愛宕松男 and Terada Takanobu 寺田隆信. *Mongoru to Dai Min teikoku* モンゴルと大明帝国. Tokyo: Kōdansha, 1998.

Otosaka Tomoko 乙坂智子. "Kaette kita shokumokujin—Mindai kōtei kenryoku to Pekin Juntenfu no Chibetto bukkyō" 帰ってきた色目人—明代皇帝権力と北京順天府のチベット仏教. *Yokohama shiritsu daigaku ronsō* 横浜市立大学論叢 51, no. 1–2 (2000): 247–82.

———. "Make Boluo zhuzuozhong suo miaoshu de Zangchuan fojiao" 馬可波羅著作中所描述的藏傳佛教. *Yuanshi luncong* 元史論叢 8 (2001): 62–69.

Pak Wŏnho 朴元熇. "Ming 'Jingnan zhi yi' yu Chaoxian" 明「靖難之役」與朝鮮. *Mingshi yanjiu* 明史研究 1991, no. 1: 227–47.

Paludan, Ann. *Chinese Tomb Figures*. Hong Kong: Oxford University Press, 1994.

Qiu Shusen 邱樹森. "Ming Wuzong yu Mingdai Huihuiren" 明武宗與明代回回人. *Huizu yanjiu* 回族研究 2004, no. 1: 42–46.

———. *Yuanchao jianshi* 元朝簡史. Fuzhou: Fujian renmin chubanshe, 1989; 2d ed., 1999.

Qian Mu 錢穆. "Du Mingchu kaiguo zhuchen shiwen ji" 讀明初開國諸臣詩文集. *Xinya xuebao* 新亞學報 6, no. 2 (1964): 245–326.

Quan Heng 權衡 and Ren Chongyue 任崇岳. *Gengshen waishi jianzheng* 庚申外史箋證. Zhengzhou: Zhongzhou guji chubanshe, 1991.

Rashid al-Din. *Compendium of Chronicles*. Trans. W. M. Thackston. Cambridge: Harvard University Press, 1999.

Rawson, Jessica. "The Power of Images: The Model Universe of the First Emperor and Its Legacy." *Historical Research* 75, no. 188 (May 2002): 123–54.

Robinson, David. *Bandits, Eunuchs, and the Son of Heaven: Rebellion and the Economy of Violence in Mid-Ming China*. Honolulu: University of Hawai'i Press, 2001.

———. *Empire's Twilight: Northeast Asia and the Fall of the Mongol Empire*. Cambridge: Harvard University Asia Center, forthcoming.

———. "Disturbing Images: Rebellion, Usurpation, and Rulership in Early Sixteenth Century East Asia—Korean Writings on Emperor Wuzong." *Journal of Korean Studies* 9, no. 1 (Fall 2004): 97–127.

———. "Images of Subject Mongols Under the Ming Dynasty." *Late Imperial China* 25, no. 1 (June 2004): 59–123.

———. "Korean Lobbying at the Ming Court: King Chungjong's Usurpation of 1506." *Ming Studies* 41 (Spring 1999): 37–53.

Rossabi, Morris. *Khubilai Khan: His Life and Times*. Berkeley: University of California Press, 1988.

———. "The Ming and Inner Asia." In *CHC*, 8: 221–71.

Ruo Ya 若亞. "Mingdai zhuwangfu guizhi shulüe" 明代諸王府規制述略. *Mingshi yanjiu* 明史研究 1993, no. 3: 135–38.

Ryūchi Kiyoshi 龍池清. "Mindai Pekin ni okeru ramakyōdan" 明代北京に於ける喇嘛教団. *Bukkyō kenkyū* 仏教研究 4–6 (1940): 65–76.

Satō Hisashi 佐藤長. "Min no Busō no 'katsubutsu' geisei ni tsuite" 明の武宗の「活佛」迎請について. In idem, *Chūsei Chibettoshi kenkyū* 中世チベット史研究. Kyoto: Dōhōsha, 1986, pp. 273–86.

———. "Mintei ni okeru ramakyō sūhai ni tsuite" 明廷におけるラマ教崇拝について. In idem, *Chūsei Chibettoshi kenkyū* 中世チベット史研究. Kyoto: Dōhōsha, 1986, pp. 293–98.

Serruys, Henry. "Early Lamaism in Mongolia." *Oriens Extremus* 10 (1963): 181–216.

———. "Foreigners in the Metropolitan Police During the Fifteenth Century." *Oriens Extremus* 8, no. 1 (1961): 59–83.

———. "Remains of Mongol Customs in China During the Early Ming Period." *Monumenta Serica* 16 (1957): 137–90.

Shan Guoqiang 單國強. "Mingdai gongting huihua" 明代宮廷繪畫. In *Mingshi luncong* 明史論叢, ed. Wang Chunyu 王春瑜. Beijing: Beijing shehui kexue chubanshe, 1997, pp. 265–80.

———. "Mingdai gongting huihua gaishu" 明代宮廷繪畫概述. 2 pts. *Gugong bowuyuan yuankan* 故宮博物院院刊 1992, no. 4: 3–17; 1993, no. 1: 55–63.

———. "Ming Qing gongting xiaoxianghua" 明清宮廷肖像畫. *Ming Qing luncong* 明清論叢 1 (1999): 414–27.

Shen Defu 沈德符. *Wanli yehuo bian* 萬曆野獲編. 1619. Reprinted—Beijing: Zhonghua shuju, 1997.

Shen Shixing 申時行 et al. *Da Ming huidian* 大明會典. 1587. Reprinted—Taibei: Dongnan shubaoshe, 1964.

Shen Weirong 沈衛榮. "'Kaijū en-i' gensetsu ni okeru Mindai Chūgoku to Chibetto no seiji bunka kankei" "懷柔遠夷"言説における明代中国とチベットの政治・文化関係. In *Chūgoku Higashi Ajia gaikō kōryū no kenkyū* 中国東アジア外交交流の研究, ed. Fuma Susumu 夫馬進. Kyoto: Kyōto daigaku shuppansha, 2007, pp. 264–310.

Shi Weimin 史衛民. *Dushizhong de youmumin* 都市中的遊牧民. Changsha: Hunan chubanshe, 1996.

———. *Yuandai shehui shenghuoshi* 元代社會生活史. Beijing: Zhongguo shehui kexue chubanshe, 1996.

Shiga Takayoshi 滋賀高義. "Min no Seiso to Chibetto—Karitsuma no raichō o chūshin to shite" 明の成祖と西蔵——哈立麻の来朝を中心として. *Ōtani shigaku* 大谷史学 8 (1961): 44–57.

Soullière, Ellen. "The Imperial Marriages of the Ming Dynasty." *Papers on Far Eastern History*, no. 37 (1988): 15–42.

———. "Palace Women in the Ming Dynasty: 1368–1644." Ph.D. diss., Princeton University, 1987.

Sørensen, Henrik. "Lamaism in Korea During the Late Koryŏ Dynasty." *Korea Journal* 33, no. 3 (Autumn 1993): 76–81.

Sperling, Elliot. "Early Ming Policy Toward Tibet: An Examination of the Proposition That the Early Ming Emperor Adopted a 'Divide and Rule' Policy Towards Tibet." Ph.D. diss., Indiana University, 1983.

Su Bai 宿白. "Lasa Budalagong zhuyao diantang he kuzang de bufen Mingdai wenshu" 拉薩布達拉宮主要殿堂和庫藏的部分明代文書. *Wenwu* 1993, no. 8: 37–47. Reprinted with corrections in idem, *Zangchuan fojiao siyuan kaogu* 藏傳佛教寺院考古. Beijing: Wenwu chubanshe, 1996, pp. 208–21.

Sugiyama Masaaki 杉山正明. *Dai Mongoru no jidai* 大モンゴルの時代. *Sekai no rekishi* 世界の歷史, vol. 9. Tokyo: Chūō kōronsha, 1997.

———. *Mongoru teikoku no kōbō* モンゴル帝国の興亡. Tokyo: Kōdansha gendai shinsho, 1996.

Sun Chengze 孫承澤. *Tianfu guangji* 天府廣記. 1704. Reprinted—Beijing: Beijing guji chubanshe, 2001, 2d ed.

Sun Gang 孫鋼. "Ming zongshi Zhu Bingmao muzhikao" 明宗室朱秉栟墓志考. *Kaogu yu wenwu* 1995, no. 5: 67–71.

Suzuki Masashi 鈴木正. "Mindai teishitsu zaisei to bukkyō" 明代帝室財政と仏教. 2 pts. *Rekishigaku kenkyū* 歷史學研究 6, no. 11 (1936): 1221–37; 6, no. 12 (1936): 1323–55.

Taylor, Romeyn. "Yuan Origins of the Wei-so System." In *Chinese Government in Ming Times: Seven Studies*, ed. Charles Hucker. New York: Columbia University Press, 1969, pp. 23–40.

Tan Qian 談遷. *Guo que* 國榷. Ca. 1653. Reprinted—Beijing: Zhonghua shuju, 1988. 6 vols.

Till, Barry, and Paula Swart, eds. *Images from the Tomb: Chinese Burial Figurines*. Victoria: Art Gallery of Greater Victoria, 1988.

To Hyŏnjŏl 都賢喆. "Koryŏ malgi sadaebu ŭi taeoegwan—hwa'iron ŭl chungshim ŭro" 高麗末期士大夫 의 對外觀—華夷論을 중심으로. *Chindan hakpo* 86 (1998): 73–99.

Toh Hoong Teik 桌鴻澤. "Sahkyh 'Alam: The Emperor of Early Sixteenth-Century China." *Sino-Platonic Papers* 110 (Oct. 2000): 1–20.

Tsai, Shih-shan Henry. *The Eunuchs in the Ming Dynasty*. Albany: State University of New York Press, 1996.

———. *Perpetual Happiness: The Ming Emperor Yongle*. Seattle: University of Washington Press, 2001.

TSL, or *Taizong shilu*, see under *Ming shilu*

Twitchett, Denis, and Frederick W. Mote, eds. *The Cambridge History of China*, vol. 8, *The Ming Dynasty, 1368–1644, Part II*. Cambridge: Cambridge University Press, 1998.

TZSL, or *Taizu shilu*, see under *Ming shilu*

Wang Cheng-hua 王正華. "Material Culture and Emperorship: The Shaping of Imperial Power at the Court of Xuanzong (r. 1425–1435)." Ph.D. diss., Yale University, 1998.

Wang Chongwu 王崇武. "Ming Chengzu Chaoxian xuanfei kao" 明成祖朝鮮選妃考. *Zhongyang yanjiuyuan, Lishi yuyansuo jikan* 中央研究院歷史語言所集刊 17 (1948): 165–86.

Wang Guangyao 王光堯. "Mingdai yuqichang de jianli" 明代御器廠的建立. *Gugong bowuyuan yuankan* 故宮博物院院刊 2001, no. 2: 78–86.

Wang Shizhen 王世貞. *Yanshantang bieji* 弇山堂別集. 1590. Reprinted—Beijing: Zhonghua shuju, 1985.

Weidner, Marsha. "Imperial Engagement with Buddhist Art and Architecture." In *Cultural Intersections in Later Chinese Buddhism*, ed. idem. Honolulu: University of Hawai'i Press, 2001, pp. 117–44.

Wylie, Turrell. "Lama Tribute in the Ming Dynasty." In *Tibetan Studies in Honour of Hugh Richardson*, ed. Michael Aris et al. Warminster, Eng.: Aris & Phillips, 1980, pp. 335–40.

Wu Han 吳晗. *Chaoxian Lichao shilu zhong de Zhongguo ziliao* 朝鮮李朝實錄中的中國資料. Beijing: Sanlian shudian, 1980.

———. *Mingshi jianshu* 明史簡述. 1980. Reprinted—Beijing: Zhonghua shuju, 2005.

———. *Zhu Yuanzhang zhuan* 朱元璋傳. Shanghai: 1949. Reprinted—Hong Kong: Xianggang zhuanji wenxueshe, n.d.

Xi Lei 喜蕾. "Yuanchao gongtingzhong de Gaoli nüxing" 元朝宮廷中的高麗女性. *Yuanshi luncong* 元史論叢 8 (2001): 208–14.

———. *Yuandai Gaoli gongnü zhidu yanjiu* 元代高麗貢女制度研究. Beijing: Minzu chubanshe, 2003.

Xi'anshi wenwu baohu kaogusuo 西安市文物保護考古所. "Xi'an nanjiao Huang Ming zongshi Qianyang Duanyiwang Zhu Gongcheng mu qingli jianbao" 西安南郊皇明宗室汧陽端懿王朱公鏳墓清理簡報. *Kaogu yu wenwu* 2001, no. 6: 29–45.

Xizang wenguanhui 西藏文管會. "Budalagong cang Ming Chengzu Zhu Di huaxiang" 布達拉宮藏明成祖朱棣畫像. *Wenwu* 1985, no. 11: 65.

Xizang wenguanhui, Wenwu puchadui 西藏文管會文物普查隊. "Dazhao si cang Yongle nianjian wenwu" 大昭寺藏永樂年間文物. *Wenwu* 1985, no. 11: 66–71.

Xiao Qiqing (Hsiao Ch'i-ch'ing) 蕭啓慶. "Yuandai de suwei zhidu" 元代的宿衛制度. *Guoli zhengzhi daxue, Bianzheng yanjiusuo nianbao* 國立政治大學邊政研究所年報 4 (1973): 369–428. Reprinted in idem, *Yuandaishi xintan* 元代史新探. Taibei: Xinwenfeng chuban, 1983, pp. 59–111.

———. "Yuan-Li guanxizhong de wangshi huanghun yu qiangquan zhengzhi" 元麗關係中的王室皇婚與強權政治. In *Zhong Han guanxishi guoji yantaohui lunwenji* 中韓關係史國際研討會論文集. Taibei: n.p., 1983, pp. 103–23. Reprinted in idem, *Yuandaishi xintan* 元代史新探. Taibei: Xinwenfeng chuban, 1983, pp. 231–62.

Xiong Wenbin 熊文彬. *Yuandai Zang Han yishu jiaoliu* 元代藏漢藝術交流. Shijiazhuang: Hebei jiaoyu chubanshe, 2003.

Xu Yikui 徐一夔. *Da Ming jili* 大明集禮. Hongwu period. Revised under Li Shi 李時. 1530. Jiajing Inner Court edition 內府刊本, held at Rare Book Collection, Chinese Academy of Social Sciences, Beijing.

Yang Qiqiao 楊啓樵. *Ming Qing shi jueao* 明清史抉奧. Hong Kong: Guangjiaojing chubanshe, 1984.

Yang Xin 楊新, ed. *Gugong bowuyuan cang Ming Qing huihua* 故宮博物院藏明清繪畫. Beijing: Zijincheng chubanshe, 1994.

Ye Xinmin 葉新民. *Yuan Shangdu yanjiu* 元上都研究. Hohhot: Neimenggu daxue chubanshe, 1998.

YHB, see Shen Defu, *Wanli yehuo bian*

Yi Yongbŏm 李龍範. "Ki hwanghu ŭi ch'aeknip kwa Wŏndae ŭi Chajŏngwŏn" 奇皇后의册立과 元代의 資政院. *Yŏksa hakpo* 歷史學報 17–18 (1962): 465–513.

Yu Hong'yŏl 柳洪烈. "Koryŏ ŭi Wŏn e tae han kongyŏ" 高麗의 元에 對한貢女. *Chindan hakpo* 18 (1957): 27–46.

Yu Minzhong 于敏中 et al., eds. *Qinding rixia jiuwen kao* 欽定日下舊聞考. 1785–87. Reprinted—Beijing: Beijing guji chubanshe, 2001.

Yu Ruji 俞汝楫. *Libu zhigao* 禮部志稿. 1620. Wenyuange Siku quanshu ed. 1773–83. Reprinted—Taibei: Taiwan shangwu yinshuguan, 1983, vols. 597–98.

Zhang Tingyu 張廷玉 et al., eds. *Ming shi* 明史. 1736. Reprinted—Beijing: Zhonghua shuju, 1974.

Zhang Ying 張英. "Cong 'Zhizheng nianzhi' kuan caiciwan de faxian tan 'Da Ming nianzao (zhi)' kuan ciqi de niandai" 從『至正年制』款彩瓷碗的發現談『大明年造(制)』款瓷器的年代. *Wenwu* 1994, no. 2: 62–71.

———. "Dui 'Yetan Basibawen kuan qinghua ciqi de niandai' yiwen de shangque" 對《也談巴思八文款青花瓷器的年代》一文的商榷. *Wenwu* 1998, no. 10: 62–66.

Zhao Hong 趙宏. "Gugong bowuyuan cang Ming Qing shiqi Zang, Meng su ciqi" 故宮博物院藏明清時期藏, 蒙俗瓷器. *Gugong bowuyuan yuankan* 故宮博物院院刊 1994, no. 1: 43–48.

———. "Ming Zhengde qinghua ciqi ji youguan wenti" 明正德青花瓷器及有關問題. *Gugong bowuyuan yuankan* 故宮博物院院刊 1992, no. 2: 26–30, 60.

Zhao Zhongchen 晁中辰. *Ming Chengzu zhuan* 明成祖傳. Beijing: Renmin chubanshe, 1993.

Zheng Kecheng 鄭克晟. "*Chosŏn Yicho sillok* zhong zhi Ming Wuzong" 朝鮮李朝實錄中之明武宗. In idem, *Ming Qingshi tanshi* 明清史探實. Beijing: Zhongguo shehui kexue chubanshe, 2001, pp. 146–56.

Zhu Guozhen 朱國禎 (1558–1632). *Yongchuang xiaopin* 湧幢小品. 1621. Reprinted—Beijing: Wenhua yishu chubanshe, 1998.

Index

Harvard East Asian Monographs
(*out-of-print)

Harvard East Asian Monographs

Harvard East Asian Monographs

Harvard East Asian Monographs